Christ Revealed

A Commentary on Matthew

Kenneth L. Chumbley

DeWard
for your journey

To all who strive to be like Him

CONTENTS

PREFACE

In 1999, I privately published a commentary on the Gospel of Matthew and for some time have felt that a revision was needed. This book is that revision. Little of the original book has survived intact; virtually every sentence has been rewritten.

In this revision:

1. The text used is the NKJV.
2. Scriptural quotes and points of emphasis are indicated by italics rather than quotation marks; only quotes are indicated by quotation marks.
3. *Gospel*, capital "G," refers to Matthew's book (or Mark's, Luke's, or John's); *gospel*, lowercase "g," refers to Christ's message.
4. As much as possible, I've limited my comments to Matthew's narrative and only occasionally give a side glance to a parallel text in another Gospel.
5. The excurses are extended comments on matters I thought interesting.
6. At the end is a select bibliography. The accessibility of knowledge at the present day is such that every author or book I cite that is not mentioned in the bibliography can be easily identified, and often, after doing a simple Internet search, be read online.

For this second edition, I wish to acknowledge the scholarship of Almon Williams, who has been my mentor since my earliest days in college, and my profound debt to Jim McGuiggan, whose insights and memorable comments are profusely scattered throughout this volume.

There is nothing authoritative about what follows. A commentary is merely one's thoughts that are presented for others to consider. A reader may agree, disagree, or (due to poor writing) not understand the thoughts presented. But if the commentator's reasoning is clear, if—in light of the sacred text—it rings true to where a reader can say that he has been helped to see something he hadn't seen before, the commentary has done about all it could ever hope to do.

Tennyson wrote that at King Arthur's court, none was braver than Sir Percivale. And when the search for the Holy Grail was set before the Knights of the Round Table, Percivale was among the first to commit himself to the quest. But not long after leaving Camelot, a troubling thought seized him: Who was *he* that he should search for the Holy Grail?

> **Then every evil word I had spoken once,**
> **And every evil thought I had thought of old,**
> **And every evil deed I ever did,**
> **Awoke and cried, "This Quest is not for thee."**

I share this trepidation. I have no uncommon talent and not a speck of genius. Who am I to think that anyone would be interested in reading anything I have to say on the Gospel of Matthew? Maybe nobody. But, I've written what I've written and am making it available. If anyone is helped in any small way by the thoughts that follow, to God be the glory.

My deepest thanks go to Dan DeGarmo and Nathan Ward of DeWard Publishing for this their willingness to put this work in print.

Memorial Day, 2017
Rantoul, Illinois

AUTHORSHIP

Both external and internal evidence points, with good probability, to Matthew the apostle (9.9, 10.3) as the author of the first Gospel. "There are solid reasons in support of the early church's unanimous ascription of this book to the apostle Mathew, and on close inspection the objections do not appear substantial" (D. A. Carson, *Matthew*, in *The Expositor's Bible Commentary*, vol. 8, Grand Rapids, MI: Zondervan Publishing House, 19).

External

Thiessen says that "The early Church unanimously ascribed this Gospel to the Apostle Matthew" (*Introduction to the New Testament*, 131), which would be strange indeed if Matthew, a relatively obscure member of the apostolic group, didn't write it.

Eusebius (ca. AD 325) quotes Papias (ca. AD 100) as saying, "Matthew composed the Logia in the Hebrew tongue; and each one interpreted them as he was able" (*Historia Ecclesiae* III.xxxix.16; exactly what is meant by "each one interpreted them as he was able" is disputed). Irenaeus, who claimed to have known Polycarp, who was a student of the asserted that "Matthew also issued a written Gospel among the Hebrews in their own dialect" (*Against Heresies* III.i.1). Origen (early third century AD) also identified Matthew as the author of this Gospel (Eusebius, *Historia Ecclesiae*, VI.xxv.4).

Internal

"Until recently, most scholars tacitly assumed that the four gospels first circulated anonymously and that the present titles were first attached to them about A.D. 125" (D. A. Carson, *An Introduction to the New Testament*, 66). In the mid-1980s, however, Martin Hengel argued persuasively that the title in the Gr. manuscripts, *KATA MATTHAION*, was part of the autograph and identified the author of the Gospel from the start. "It is inconceivable," he argues, "that the Gospels could circulate anonymously for up to sixty years, and then in the second century suddenly display unanimous attribution to certain authors. If they had originally been anonymous, then surely there would have been some variation in second-century attributions (as was the case with some of the second-century apocryphal gospels)" (qtd. by Carson, *Introduction*, 66).

Outline

1.1–4.16: Prologue

> 1.1–2.23: Birth and infancy

> 3.1–4.16: Preparation for ministry

4.17–27.66: The Life of Christ

> 4.17–16.12: God Reveals the Christ

>> 4.17–25: The Gospel of the Kingdom: A Synopsis

>> 5.1–9.35: In Word and Work

>>> 5.1–7.29: Through Words

>>> 8.1–9.35: Through Works

>> 9.36–11.1: Through Disciples

>> 11.2–16.20: Reactions to the Revelation

>>> 11.2–15: John the Baptist

>>> 11.16–30: Galilee

>>> 12.1–14: Pharisees

>>> 12.15–21: Withdrawal

>>> 12.22–37: Blasphemy

>>> 12.38–45: Unbelief

>>> 12.46–50: Belief

>>> 13.1–53: Parables

>>> 13:54–58: Nazareth

>>> 14.1–12: Herod Antipas

>>> 14.13–21: Five Thousand

Select Bibliography

Alexander, Joseph Addison. *The Gospel According to Mark*. Grand Rapids: Baker, 1980.

_____. *The Gospel According to Matthew*. Grand Rapids: Baker 1980

Baille, John. *And the Life Everlasting*. New York: Charles Scribner's Sons, 1933

_____. *Christian Devotion*. New York: Charles Scribner's Sons, 1962

Bales, James D. *Christian, Contend for Thy Cause*. Searcy, AR, 1949

_____. *Christ: The Fulfillment of the Law and the Prophets*. Shreveport, LA: Lambert Book House, 1973

_____. *Jesus the Master Respondent*. Shreveport, LA: Lambert Book House, 1970

_____. *The Sower Goes Forth*. Shreveport, LA: Lambert Book House, 1973

_____. *Woe unto You*. Paragould, AR, nd

Barclay, William. *The Gospel According to Matthew*, 2 vols. Philadelphia: The Westminster Press, 1958

_____. *The Beatitudes & The Lord's Prayer for Everyman*. New York: Harper & Row, 1964

Bauer, Arndt, Gingrich. *Greek-English Lexicon of the New Testament*. The University of Chicago Press, 1956

Blocher, Henri. *Songs of the Servant*. London: Inter-Varsity Christian Fellowship, 1975

Blomberg, Craig L. *Matthew*, in *The New American Commentary*. Nashville: Broadman Press, 1992

Boice, James Montgomery. *The Parables of Jesus*. Chicago: Moody Press, 1983

_____. *The Sermon on the Mount*. Grand Rapids: Zondervan, 1972

Boles, H. Leo. *The Gospel According to Matthew*. Nashville: The Gospel Advocate Co., 1961

Boreham, Frank W. *The Octave of Heaven*. Grand Rapids, MI: Baker Book House, 1936

_____. *A Casket of Cameos*. New York: The Abingdon Press, 1924

_____. *The Nest of Spears*. London: The Epworth Press, 1927

Broadus, John A. *Commentary on the Gospel of Matthew*, An American Commentary. Valley Forge, PA: The American Baptist Publication Society, 1886

Bruce, A. B. *The Parabolic Teaching of Christ*. New York: Hodder & Stoughton, 1886

Bruce, F. F. *The Defence of the Gospel*. Grand Rapids, MI: Wm. B. Eerdmans Publishing Co., 1959

_____. *The Gospel of John*. Grand Rapids, MI: Wm. B. Eerdmans Publishing Co., 1983

Carr, A. *The Gospel According to St. Matthew*, Cambridge Greek Testament for Schools & Colleges. Cambridge: The University Press, 1913

Carson, D. A. *Matthew*, The Expositors Bible Commentary. Grand Rapids: Zondervan, 1984

Chilton, David. *The Days of Vengeance*. Ft. Worth, TX: Dominion Press, 1987

Cooper, Thomas, *The Verity of Christ's Resurrection from the Dead*. London: Hodder and Stoughtton, 1875

Culver, Robert Duncan. *The Life of Christ*. Grand Rapids: Baker, 1976

Dictionary of Christ and the Gospels, 2 vols. New York: Charles Scriber's Sons, 1907

Edersheim, Alfred. *The Life and Times of Jesus the Messiah*, 2 vols. New York: Longmans, Green, and Col, 1906

Erdman, Charles R. *The Gospel of Matthew.* Philadelphia: The Westminster Press, 1920

Finegan, Jack. *The Archaeology of the New Testament.* Princeton: Princeton University Press, 1972

Fosdick, Harry E. *Answers to Real Problems.* Eugene, OR: Wipp & Stock, 2008

_____. *The Assurance of Immortality.* New York: Association Press, 1924

_____. *The Man from Nazareth.* New York: Harper and Brothers, 1949

_____. *The Manhood of the Master.* New York: Association Press, 1914

_____. *The Meaning of Faith.* New York: Association Press, 1925

_____. *The Meaning of Prayer.* Philadelphia: American Baptist Publication Soceity, 1915

_____. *The Second Mile.* New York: Association Press, 1915

Foster, R. C. *Gospel Studies*, 3 vols. Cincinnati: The Cincinnati Bible Society, 1970.

_____. *Studies in the Life of Christ.* Grand Rapids: Baker, 1975

Fowler, Harold. *Matthew,* The Bible Study Textbook Series. Joplin, MO: College Press Publishing Co., 1985

France, R. T. *Matthew,* Tyndale New Testament Commentaries. Grand Rapids: Eerdmans, 1995

Gardner, Richard B. *Matthew,* in *Believer's Bible Commenatry.* Scottsdale, PA: Herald Press, 1991

Garland, David E. *Reading Matthew.* New York: Grassland, 1993

Geisler, Norman and Frank Turek, *I Don't Have Enough Faith to Be an Atheist,* Wheaton, IL: Crossway Books, 2004

Gromacki, Robert G. *The Virgin Birth.* Grand Rapids: Baker, 1974

Hankey, W. A. D. *The Lord of All Good Life*. London: Longmans, Green and Co., 1917

Hare, Douglas R. A. *Matthew*. Louisville: John Knox Press, 1993

Harrison, Everett F. *A Short Life of Christ*. Grand Rapids: Eerdmans, 1968

Hendriksen, William. *Exposition of the Gospel of Matthew*. Grand Rapids: Baker, 1992

Hengstenberg, E. W. *Christology of the Old Testament*. Grand Rapids, MI: Kregel Publications, 1970

Hill, David. *The Gospel of Matthew,* in The New Century Bible Commentary. Grand Rapids: Eerdmans, 1990

Hindson, Edward E. *Isaiah's Immanuel*. Phillipsburg, NJ: Presbyterian & Reformed Publishing Co., 1978

Hobbs, Herschel H. *An Exposition of the Four Gospels,* vol. 1. Grand Rapids: Baker, 1996

Hodges, Zane C. *The Greek New Testament According to the Majority Text*. Nashville: Thomas Nelson Publishers, 1982

Jefferson, Charles. *The Character of Jesus*. New York: Grosset & Dunlap, 1936

Johnson, Paul. *A History of Christianity*. New York: Simon & Schuster, 1976

_____. *A History of the Jews*. New York: Harper & Row, 1987

_____. *Jesus, A Biography from a Believer*. New York: Viking Penguin, 2019

Jones, E. Stanley. *The Christ of the Mount*. New York: Abingdon Press, 1931

Josephus, Flavius. *Complete Works*. Grand Rapids, MI: Kregel Publications, 1971

Kidner, Derek. *The Message of Jeremiah*. Downers Grove, IL: Inter-Varsity Press, 1987

Lenski, R. C. H. *St. Matthew's Gospel*. Minneapolis: Augsburg Publishing House, 1964

Luz, Ulrich. *Matthew, A Commentary*, in *Hermeneia–A Critical and Historical Commentary of the Bible*, 3 vols. Minneapolis: Fortress Press, 2007

_____. *Matthew in History*. Minneapolis: Fortress Press, 2007

_____. *Studies in Matthew*. Grand Rapids, MI: Wm. B. Eerdmans Publishing Co., 2005

_____. *The Theology of the Gospel of Matthew*. Cambrdige: Cambridge University Press, 1995

Machen, J. Gresham. *The Virgin Birth of Christ*. Grand Rapids: Baker, 1975

Macknight, James. *A Harmony of the Four Gospels*, 2 vols. Erlanger, KY: Faith & Facts, 1980

McGarvey, J.W. *A Commentary on Matthew and Mark*. Delight, AR: Gospel Light Publishing Co.

McGuiggan, Jim. *Heading Home with God, Reflections on the Book of Exodus*. n.l.: Weaver Publications, 2011

_____. *The Book of Isaiah*. Lubbock, TX: Montex Publishing, 1985

_____. *The Book of 1 Corinthians*. Ft. Worth, TX: Star Publications, 1984

_____. *The God of the Towel*. Lubbock, TX: Montex Publishing, 1984

_____. *Jesus Hero of Thy Soul*. West Monroe, LA: Howard Publishing Co., 1998

_____. *The Reign of God*. Ft. Worth: Star Publications, 1992

_____. *Where the Spirit of the Lord Is...* West Monroe, LA: Howard Publishing Co., 1999

_____. *Zechariah, The Day of Small Things*. Lubbock, TX: Sunset Institute Press, 2016

Mitchel, Stephen. *The Gospel According to Jesus*. New York: HarperCollins Publishers, 1991

_____. *Jesus, What He Really Did and Said*. New York: HarperCollins Publishers, 2002

Montgomery, John W. *Crisis in Lutheran Theology*, 2 vols. Grand Rapids, MI: Baker Book House, 1968

Morgan, G. Campbell. *The Crisis of the Christ*. Old Tappan, NJ: Revell, 1936

_____. *The Gospel According to Matthew*. Old Tappen, NJ: Revell, 1929

_____. *Peter and the Church*. New York: Revell, 1938

Morris, Leon. *The Apostolic Preaching of the Cross*. Grand Rapids: Eerdman, 1992.

_____. *The Cross of Christ*. Grand Rapids: Eerdmans, 1988

_____. *The Gospel According to Matthew*. Grand Rapids: Eerdmans, 1995

Mounce, Robert H. *Matthew,* in New International Biblical Commentary. Peabody, MA: Hendrickson Publishers, 1995

New Bible Dictionary, 2nd ed. Downer's Grove, IL: Intervarsity Press, 1994

Paher, Stanley W. *If Thou Hadst Known*. Las Vegas: Nevada Publications, 1978

Pfeiffer, Charles F. *Baker's Bible Atlas*. Grand Rapids: Baker, 1971

Richardson, Robert. *Memoirs of Alexander Campbell*. Indianapolis: Religious Book Service, nd

Robertson, A. T. *Word Pictures in the New Testament*, 6 vols. Nashville: Broadman Press, 1930

Salmon, George. *The Infallibility of the Church*. London: John Murray, 1890

Sayers, Dorothy. *Letters to a Diminished Church*. Nashville: W Publishing Group, 2004

Smith, B. T. D. *The Gospel According to St. Matthew,* Cambridge Greek Testament. Cambridge: The University Press, 1927

Spurgeon, Charles. *Commentary on Matthew.* http://grace-ebooks.com/library/Charles%20Spurgeon/CHS_Commentary%20on%20Matthew.PDF

Stott, John R. W. *Christian Mission.* Downers Grove, IL: InterVarsity Press, 1975

_____. *The Cross of Christ.* Downers Grove, IL: Intervarsity Press, 1986

_____. *Confess Your Sins.* Waco, TX: Word Books, 1974

_____. *Men Made New.* Grand Rapids, MI: Baker Book House, 1978

_____. *The Message of the Sermon on the Mount.* Leicester, England: Inter-Varsity Press, 1978

Tenney, Merrill C. *The Genius of the Gospels.* Grand Rapids: Eerdmans, 1951

Trueblood, Elton. *Confronting Christ.* Waco, TX: Word, 1960

_____. *The Humor of Christ.* New York: Harper and Row, 1964

_____. *The Lord's Prayers.* New York: Harper and Row, 1965

Turner, David L. *Matthew.* Grand Rapids: Baker Academic, 2008

Vos, Howard F. *Matthew.* Grand Rapids: Zondervan, 1979

Watson, John (Ian MaClaren). *The Life of the Master.* London: Hodder and Stoughton, 1901

_____. *The Mind of the Master.* New York: Dodd, Mead and Company, 1899

_____. *Respectable Sins.* London: Hodder and Stoughton, 1909

Watson, Richard. *An Exposition of the Gospels of St. Matthew and St. Mark,* London: John Mason, 1833

Whiteside, Robertson L. *Bible Studies,* vol. 4. Denton, TX: Miss Inys Whiteside

_____. *Doctrinal Discourses.* Denton, TX: Inys Whiteside, 1955

_____. *Reflections.* Denton, TX: Inys Whiteside, 1965

Wiersbe, Warren W. *Be Courageous.* Wheaton, IL: Victor Books, 1989

_____. *Meet Your King.* Wheaton, IL: Victor Books, 1983

Yancey, Philip. *The Jesus I Never Knew.* Grand Rapids: Zondervan, 1997

_____. *What's So Amazing About Grace.* Grand Rapids: Zondervan, 1997

Young, Edward J. *The Book of Isaiah,* 3 vols. Grand Rapids: Eerdmans, 1974

Versions

King James Version

The American Standard Bible

The Bible, A New Translation. James Moffatt

The New American Standard Bible

New International Version

The New King James Bible

The New Testament, A New Translation. William Barclay

New Testament in the Language of the People. Charles B. Williams

New Testament in the Language of Today. William F. Beck

The New Testament in Modern English. J. B. Phillips

CHAPTER 1

1.1–4.16: Prologue

1.1–2.23: Birth and infancy

Notes

The Christian religion, reduced to its essence, consists of two elements: *divine revelation* and *human response*. *Whoever hears these sayings of Mine* [revelation] *and does them* [response] lives the life that God approves (7.21–23). In the Gospel of Matthew, the singular divine revelation, stated in the center of the book, is that *Jesus is the Christ, the Son of God* (16.18). The proper human response to this revelation can be summarized as *love righteousness*—a life lived loving God and man (5.20. 22.36–40, 25.41–46).[1]

Like any good book, Matthew has three parts—a beginning, a middle, and an end. The first part is the prologue (1.1–4.16) and covers Christ's prepublic life; the middle part (4.17–27.66) records Christ's public ministry; and the last part, the epilogue (28.1–20), deals with His resurrection.

Prologue	Narrative			Epilogue
1.1–4.16	**God reveals the Christ**	**Jesus is the Christ**	**Christ builds the church**	28.1–20
	4.17–16.12	**16.13–16.20**	**16.21–27.66**	

The prologue subdivides into two parts: chs 1–2 deal with Jesus' birth and infancy; chs 3–4 with His preparation for ministry. The middle section also has two parts that are separated by a central text containing Matthew's proposition: in 4.17 to16.12, God reveals His Christ; in 16.21–27.66, Christ builds His church; and the proposition that Jesus is the Christ is in 16.13–

---

[1] "Christianity," wrote William Law, "requires a change of nature, a new life perfectly devoted to God" (*A Practical Treatise upon Christian Perfection*).

20. The epilogue has three parts consisting of the resurrection (28.1–10), a cover-up (28.11–15), and a commission (28.16–20).[2]

The common Jewish understanding of the Messiah's background is summarized in John 7.42: *Has not the Scripture said that the Christ comes from the seed of David and from the town of Bethlehem?* Matthew's prologue confirms both of these criteria: ch 1 connects Christ to David and ch 2 connects Him to Bethlehem. Prominent in the prologue are *fulfillment quotations* that establish Jesus' Messianic authenticity and bring to the fore aspects of the Messiah not so well understood by the Jews (cf. 2.23 with Jn. 7.41,52: *will the Christ come out of Galilee? … no prophet has arisen out of Galilee*). In the prologue, the fulfillment quotations geographically take us from Bethlehem to Egypt to Nazareth/Galilee (1.22, 2.6,15,18,23, 4.15–16). Not to be overlooked is that the OT quotations are *christological*, revealing singular aspects of Christ's character (1.23, 2.6,15).

TITLE, 1.1

1.1 The book of the genealogy of Jesus Christ, the Son of David, the Son of Abraham:

The first verse lacks a verb, which suggests that it is serves as a title or superscription.

The book of the genealogy tells us two things. First, Jesus' story has been preserved in book form, which suggests that this title applies to the entirety of this Gospel and not just to the genealogy or prologue. Second, *geneseōs* (only here and 1.18) has a range of meanings from origin, birth, and genealogy, to being and existence, to kind and family. Its use recalls Genesis 1.1 and John 1.1 and indicates that this is a *book of beginning*— specifically, the *new beginning* (2 Cor. 5.17) made possible by Christ.

Jesus derives from the Lat. form of the Gr. *Iesous*, which is the Hellenized form of the Heb. *Joshua*. It means *Jehovah is salvation*—or simply, *savior*— and is the name given by heaven to He who would *save his people from their sins* (1.21). Curiously, though people in the Gospel refer to Christ by the name *Jesus* (21.11, 26.69), no one ever addresses Him by this name.

Christ derives from *cheir*, the Gr. word for *hand*. Originally, it signified "the rubbing of the hands together in anointing, [but] then it came to mean 'the anointed one'" (Foster I, 12). The Heb. equivalent, *messiah* (Jn.

---

[2] There are exceptions, of course, to this outline; the church is anticipated in the Christ section and Christ is further revealed in the church section.

1.41, 4.25), referred to the custom of using oil to consecrate a person to some special service. In the OT, prophets (1 Kgs. 19.6), priests (Ex. 28.41), and kings (1 Sam. 16.3,13; Judg. 9.8) were anointed (Isa. 45.1). Since *Christ* is used here without the article, it functions, essentially, as a proper name.

By starting with Jesus' descent from *David* and *Abraham*, Matthew introduces an important characteristic of his Gospel. *David* is a thoroughly Jewish character, whose mention recalls the covenant right given to Him and his descendants to rule Israel forever (2.2, 22.42, 27.37; Lk. 1.32–33; 2 Sam. 7.12–16; 1 Chron. 17.11–14; Ps. 89.3–29). The mention of Abraham might seem redundant, since every descendant of David was a descendant of Abraham, but *Abraham* involves a larger dimension than *David*, for to Abraham was given the promise that *in you all the families of the earth shall be blessed* (Gen. 12.3).

Thus, Matthew, in his first verse, introduces a universal outlook analogous to John 3.16 and its declaration that *God so loved the world*. God's saving love, implied by the mention of David and Abraham, thus brackets the First Gospel (see 28.18–19) and finds its culmination in *Jesus*—the One on whom the Davidic and Abrahamic covenants converged. The order of *David* followed by *Abraham* alludes to the fact the salvation that flowed from God's love came to the Jew first, and then also to the Greek (8.1–13; Rom. 1.16).

As will be seen, *son of* can indicate lineal rather than immediate descent.

CHRIST'S HUMANITY, 1.2–17

Notes

Genealogies, which were common in antiquity,[3] were meant to show *relationship*. As anticipated in v 1, the genealogy in vv 2–17 relates Jesus to Abraham through the Davidic dynasty—for the Messiah was to be *born of the seed of David according to the flesh* (Rom. 1.3). One of the first things Jews would have done when one claimed to be the Messiah, would have been to conduct a background check to verify Davidic descent; if this couldn't be verified, the claimant's Messianic pretensions would have been summarily dismissed (Ezra 2.62). Biblical critics like to point out all sorts of problems with Christ's genealogy, but it's noteworthy that Christ's enemies—who jumped at the slightest pretext to discredit Him—never once challenged His Davidic pedigree.

---

[3] Josephus began his autobiography with his genealogy.

There is an untidiness about Christ's genealogy that is deliberate (nothing in Scripture is accidental or coincidental). The genealogy is outlined into three groups of fourteen generations (v 17). This should yield forty-two names, but only forty-one are listed. There are forty-two if *Jechoniah* in v 11 and v 12 refers to two different individuals (1 Chron. 3.15–16), and we reach forty-two if one person should be counted twice (but if so, we're not told who it is). However we try, it's hard to make the numbers add up. But remembering that Matthew was a tax collector who, presumably, was good with numbers, it's unlikely that his 3/14 arrangement resulted from a miscount (v 17).

Another aberration is the genealogy's deviation from the usual format of *X begat Y*. It begins and ends, for instance, with the same three people (David, Abraham, Jesus, vv 1,17); it twice refers to brothers (vv 2,11); it includes women (vv 3,5,6; male-only listings being the rule, 13.55–56); it alludes to family skeletons (vv 3,6; contrast the Romans' *damnatio memoriae*, wherein all references to individuals who had shamed themselves were expunged from genealogical records); it is not exhaustive (ancient genealogies rarely were); and it uses the passive form *of whom was born* to describe Jesus' birth in v 16. Genealogies were sometimes guided by concerns other than precision and completeness, and such is surely the case here. Christ's genealogy reminds us of the instruments (swindlers, the incestuous, Gentiles, prostitutes, adulterers, murderers, idolaters, etc.) God used to bring His Son into the world and of the kind of people His Son came to save.

1.2 Abraham begot Isaac, Isaac begot Jacob, and Jacob begot Judah and his brothers.

Abraham was the father of the Hebrew race with whom God made a covenant promising universal blessing. *Isaac* is noteworthy for three reasons. First, he was the son of Abraham through whom the promise passed (Gen. 26.3–4); second, his birth, like Christ's, was miraculous (Rom. 4.19, Heb. 11.11–12); and third, his offering (Gen. 22) typified Christ's sacrifice (Heb. 11.17). *Jacob*, the younger son of Isaac, was the last person to whom the Abrahamic promise was personally vouched (Gen. 28.13–14). To him were born twelve sons who became the fathers of the twelve tribes of Israel. Of these, *Judah* (the Gr. form is *Judas*) was the one in the Messianic line (Gen. 49.10; Heb. 7.14).

1.3 Judah begot Perez and Zerah by Tamar, Perez begot Hezron, and Hezron begot Ram.

Tamar is the first of four women mentioned. Not only is the inclusion of women extraordinary, but equally surprising is that the great Hebrew mothers—Sarah, Rebekah, and Rachel—are missing. *Tamar* was a skeleton in Israel's closet, for her sons *Perez* and *Zerah* were born of incest, sired by her father-in-law Judah (Gen. 38). Nothing further is known about *Hezron* or *Ram*.

1.4–5 Ram begot Amminadab, Amminadab begot Nahshon, and Nahshon begot Salmon. Salmon begot Boaz by Rahab, Boaz begot Obed by Ruth, Obed begot Jesse,

Rahab was a Canaanite prostitute who was spared during the fall of Jericho for risking her all on the God of Israel (Josh. 2, Heb. 11.31, Jas. 2.25). Only here do we learn that she was an ancestor of David. Of the women in this genealogy, only *Ruth* was free of scandal. Yet, as a Moabitess (Ruth 1.4), she had an ancestry scarred by incest (Gen. 19.30–37), and she belonged to a people excluded from the assembly of the Lord (Deut. 23.3).

1.6 and Jesse begot David the king. David the king begot Solomon by her *who had been the wife* of Uriah.

The men mentioned from *Abraham* to *David* are usually identified as *patriarchs* (Acts 2.29). *David* is a transitional figure, being a patriarch who became a king. Considering all the good things that could have been said about him (Acts 13.22), it's remarkable that Matthew cites his fatal attraction to Bathsheba, *the wife of Uriah* (2 Sam. 11–12).

The inclusion of *Tamar*, *Rahab*, *Ruth*, and *Bathsheba* is meant to say something about Jesus. All were involved in some sort of marital irregularity, and at least three of the four were Gentiles, which picks up the thread introduced by the mention of *Abraham* in v 1. Not only was Jesus the one in whom the Gentiles would trust (12.21), but Gentile blood flowed in His veins. Even more, the mention of these women points to God's love for the outcasts. Jesus "always seemed to be defending the wrong kind of people. Take a quick glance through the Gospels and see for yourself that he was forever speaking on behalf of the 'bad' people and against the 'good' people" (McGuiggan, *The God of the Towel*, 44).

Solomon is mentioned twice more in Matthew, each time as the lesser figure in a contrast (6.29, 12.42).

1.7–11 Solomon begot Rehoboam, Rehoboam begot Abijah, and Abijah begot Asa. Asa begot Jehoshaphat, Jehoshaphat begot Joram, and Joram begot Uzziah. Uzziah begot Jotham, Jotham begot Ahaz, and Ahaz begot Hezekiah. Hezekiah begot Manasseh, Manasseh begot Amon, and Amon begot Josiah. Josiah begot Jeconiah and his brothers about the time they were carried away to Babylon.

Comparing Matthew's genealogy with the records in Kings and Chronicles shows four names missing: between *Joram* and *Uzziah* belong Ahaziah, Joash, and Amaziah (1 Chron. 3.11–12), and Jehoiakim should be inserted between *Josiah* and *Jechoniah* (1 Chron. 3.15).

The period from *Solomon* to *Jechoniah* was one of spiritual and political decline for the Jews, ending with Judah's exile to Babylon. Asa, Jehoshaphat, Uzziah, Jotham, Hezekiah, and Josiah were good men; the rest weren't, with Manasseh being as bad as can be.[4]

Jechoniah (v 11), Judah's last king, is noteworthy for two reasons. First, like *Judah* (1.3), he is mentioned in connection with *his brothers*, which is puzzling since he apparently had no brothers (1 Chron. 3.16, 2 Chron. 36.10); *brothers*, here, may indicate cousins or countrymen (12.46–50). Second, Jeremiah 22.30 says of him, *Write this man down as childless ... for none of his descendants shall prosper, sitting on the throne of David. Write this man childless* doesn't mean he would have no children, for he did have children (1 Chron. 3.17). The curse of childlessness likely meant that no son of his would succeed him on the throne. If this is the right interpretation, it's possible that the Messianic succession shifted at this time from Solomon to Nathan, another son of David (Lk. 3.31).

1.12–15 And after they were brought to Babylon, Jeconiah begot Shealtiel, and Shealtiel begot Zerubbabel. Zerubbabel begot Abiud, Abiud begot Eliakim, and Eliakim begot Azor. Azor begot Zadok, Zadok begot Achim, and Achim begot Eliud. Eliud begot Eleazar, Eleazar begot Matthan, and Matthan begot Jacob.

The final group in the genealogy spans 600 years and includes the period between the Testaments. *Zerubbabel* is the last person in this genealogy

---

[4] Manasseh "could not do enough evil. There seemed to be no end to his barbarous cruelties. His capacity for inventing new forms of evil seemed bottomless. His appetite for the sordid was insatiable. One day he placed his son on the altar in some black and terrible ritual of witchcraft and burned him as an offering (2 Kings 21)" (Eugene H. Peterson, *Run with the Horses*, 60).

who is mentioned in the OT. This doesn't mean, though, that the Jews had no way to corroborate Christ's lineage from *Abiud* to *Jacob*. Jewish ancestral records were carefully kept, as confirmed by Josephus, who refers to public records from which he gathered information about his ancestry.[5] He also describes measures taken by the Jews to safeguard their genealogies, especially priestly ones.[6] If there was any weakness in Christ's pedigree, the public records would have revealed it.

1.16 And Jacob begot Joseph the husband of Mary, of whom was born Jesus who is called Christ.

The final entry is longer than the others and constitutes the most significant break from the *X begot Y* pattern. Matthew doesn't say that Joseph begot Jesus but that Jesus *was born* of Mary. In the phrase *of whom was born, whom* is feminine. Since Gr. pronouns must agree with their antecedent in gender, the reference can be only to Mary; Jesus was Mary's biological son, not Joseph's. The explanation for this is given in vv 18–25.

1.17 So all the generations from Abraham to David *are* fourteen generations, from David until the captivity in Babylon *are* fourteen generations, and from the captivity in Babylon until the Christ *are* fourteen generations.

The threefold division of the genealogy was a natural one, with the period of the patriarchs followed by the period of the kings followed by the period of Gentile rule. More problematic is why Matthew says that *all* the generations in each group equaled fourteen. Since some names in Christ's lineage were omitted, *all* must refer only to the generations Matthew listed. But why fourteen? Is this an arbitrary number or is there something deeper here?[7]

Carr (76) believes the 3/14 arrangement was a numerical acrostic based on the name *David*, "which consists of three Hebrew letters, their total numerical value being fourteen." "In the ancient world letters served not only as the building blocks of words but also as symbols of numbers.[8] Hence any word had a numerical value; and the use of such symbolism is

---

[5] "Thus have I set down the genealogy of my family as I have found in described in the public records" (*Life*, 1).

[6] *Against Apion*, I.7.

[7] "It was customary among Jewish writers to arrange genealogies according to some convenient scheme, possibly for mnemonic reasons" (Carson, 68).

[8] Just as the Roman I = 1, V = 5, X = 10, etc.

known as gematria. In Hebrew, 'David' is *dwd* ... d = 4, w = 6. Therefore, David = dwd = 4 + 6 + 4 = 14."[9] If this is how Matthew arrived at fourteen, it's the only known case of gematria in the NT (except, possibly, for 666, Rev. 13.17–18; Chilton, 344).

A better interpretation involves the number 42 as being symbolic. In Scripture, certain numbers (e.g., 3, 4, 7, 10, 12) have fig-urative meaning, and 42 is such a number. As Chilton notes, Matthew's "list is written to expound the 'forty-two-ness' of the period leading up to Christ's advent" (275). Biblically, the number 42 (3 × 14) symbolized a time of hardship and trouble that culminated in vindication and victory. Remembering that the Jews used 30-day lunar months, 42 is equivalent to 1,260 days, which is equivalent to three and a half years, which is equivalent to *a time and times and half a time* (Dan. 7.25; Jas. 5.17–18; Rev. 11.2,3,9,11, 12.6,14, 13.5). I think it likely that Matthew's 3/14 scheme was meant to tell Jewish readers that the decline and misfortune suffered by the Davidic dynasty and the nation since the time of David was about to change with the advent of the Christ.[10]

But if Jesus wasn't the son of Joseph, how does Matthew's genealogy connect Him to David? The probable answer is that when Joseph—a *son of David* (v 20)—took Mary as his wife, Jesus became his *legal* son (Jn. 6.42) and thereby gave Him a family connection to David. The prestige and privileges accorded adopted sons were well established in the first century—Augustus Caesar was the adopted son of his great-uncle Julius; Tiberius was the adopted son of his stepfather Augustus, etc.

The Davidic covenant, however, called for one who had more than just a legal claim to David's throne: *I will set up your seed after you, who will come from your body* (2 Sam. 7.12)—the Messiah was to be a physical descendant of David (Acts 2.30, 13.23).

Where, then, does the NT establish the biological connection? Most likely in Luke 3.23–38. From Abraham to David there is agreement between Matthew and Luke's genealogies, but after David, the lists diverge and the only names on which they agree are Shealtiel, Zerubbabel, and Joseph. Though any solution must be tentative, the simplest explanation for

---

[9] Carson, 70.

[10] I think this interpretation is supported, for instance, by 2.17–18 and its reference to Jeremiah 31.15. To those weeping inconsolably, the Lord says, "Don't weep" and promises a glorious future (Jer. 31.16–17). Heartbreak superseded by hope is the essence of Biblical forty-twoness.

this discrepancy is that Matthew gives Christ's legal succession through Joseph, and Luke traces His biological succession through Mary. This conclusion seems reasonable given that Matthew gives prominence to Joseph, whereas Luke emphasizes Mary.

Not to be overlooked is the fact that a genealogy is a historical record. Christianity is based on history—on things that occurred. Christ came as the climax of a historical process that identified and interpreted Him. God has revealed Himself in the majesty of the stars and in the terror of the storm, but the clearest revelation of Himself is in the life of an actual person.

CHRIST'S DEITY, 1.18–25

Notes

As crucial as it was to establish Jesus' ancestral connection to David, as 22.43 reveals, there was another relationship between Christ and David that was more important and that relationship is explained in this section.

The topic statement in v 18a picks up the theme from v 1 and continues the thread of v 16. Verse 18b tells us that this paragraph involves Mary's miraculous pregnancy. The dream sequence in vv 20–21 parallels the dream sequence in 2.13–14 in its principal actor (Joseph), vocabulary (the angel of the Lord, appear, in a dream, rising from sleep, take), and fulfillment quotation. The three-fold mention of the birth of a son in vv 21–25 reveals the thrust of the passage.

If we are to know who God is, it's not enough to look at the mountains or stars or the orderly cosmos; to know God, we must look at Jesus, for *God is in eternity what Jesus was in time*. The manner of Christ's birth revealed His deity (Lk. 1.35). In a real sense, He is *the Son of Man* (8.20)— everything essential to authentic humanness can be predicated of Him— but what's more, He is *the Son of God, Immanuel, God with us* (v 23). The central proposition of the Gospel (16.16) is here introduced.

1.18 Now the birth of Jesus Christ was as follows: After His mother Mary was betrothed to Joseph, before they came together, she was found with child of the Holy Spirit.

As noted above, v 18a connects with v 1 and explains how it was that Jesus was born of Mary (v 16). *Birth* translates *gennesis* (a cognate of *geneseō*, v 1) and means *origin* or *coming into being*. Jesus was conceived while Mary was *betrothed* (*mnesteuō*, to give a souvenir, engagement present) to

Joseph. Under Jewish law, betrothal[11] was a binding contract terminated only by death or divorce. "There is little positive information concerning the ceremony of betrothal in New Testament times proper" (*Dictionary of Christ and the Gospels* I, 260), but the following seems likely.

First, betrothal, which roughly corresponded to our custom of engagement, occurred before a couple *came together* (*sunerchomai*, only here in Matt.), which probably refers to the wife's move to the bridegroom's house at the time of the wedding (25.5–6). Second, it normally occurred about a year before the marriage was consummated. Third, it was a legally binding arrangement wherein a gift or money was sometimes given by the groom to the bride or her family. "*Betrothal*, according to contemporary Jewish customs, was actually a formal act of property transfer (often performed in the house of the bride's father) wherein the groom gave his bride money or something else of monetary value and told her that through it she became betrothed to him 'according to the laws of Moses and Israel'" (Cornfeld, 40; cf. Gen. 29.15–20 where Jacob worked seven years for Rachel, and Gen. 34.12 where Shechem offered a dowry for Dinah). Fourth, the espoused were considered husband and wife (vv 19,20,24). Fifth, infidelity during the espousal period was a capital crime (Deut. 22.23–24).

The term *virgin birth* is a misnomer; Jesus' birth was completely natural—it was His conception that was supernatural. When *Mary*, a virgin (Lk. 1.34), *was found with child of the Holy Spirit*, it's not surprising that she didn't tell anyone, for who would have believed her? She left the explaining to God. By the time she returned to Nazareth from a three-month visit to Judea (Lk. 1.39–56), she would have been showing (Gen. 38.24).

1.19 Then Joseph her husband, being a just *man*, and not wanting to make her a public example, was minded to put her away secretly.

Matthew doesn't tell us whether Joseph knew the explanation for Mary's pregnancy. If he did, his subsequent actions might have been prompted by a fear of taking to himself one who had been made sacred by God (this view of Joseph's behavior was common in the early church and in Catholicism[12]). But more likely, Joseph didn't know the cause of Mary's pregnancy, assumed the worst (wouldn't we all?), and decided to privately divorce her. That he was a *just* man can refer either to his decision to

---

[11] The Eng. *betrothed* lit. means, *be truth*.

[12] Luz I, 94, fn 40.

divorce Mary as the law allowed (Deut. 22.22–27) or to the compassion he showed by sparing her the humiliation of a public trial for infidelity (2 Sam. 12.13; cf. Ps. 37.21 where the just man *shows mercy*). Although it's easy to ascribe noble reasons to Joseph, it should be remembered that adultery was difficult to prove because eyewitnesses were needed (Jn. 8.4), which essentially made the death penalty for adultery a moot point (Lev. 20.10; Deut. 22.22; Jn. 8.5).

Public example (*paradeigmatisai,* to show alongside, to expose to infamy) occurs elsewhere only in Colossians 2.15, but an intensive form is used in Hebrews 6.6 to describe apostates who crucify the Son of God afresh and put Him to an *open shame.*

1.20 But while he thought about these things, behold, an angel of the Lord appeared to him in a dream, saying, "Joseph, son of David, do not be afraid to take to you Mary your wife, for that which is conceived in her is of the Holy Spirit.

While Joseph was deciding what to do, an angel appeared to him in a dream,[13] which was often a medium for divine revelation. The angel tells Joseph to wed Mary, explaining that her pregnancy was caused by the Holy Spirit. "We are to think here of God's creative intervention by the Spirit and not of the ... Spirit as Mary's sexual partner" (Luz I, 95).

1.21 And she will bring forth a Son, and you shall call His name JESUS, for He will save His people from their sins."

The high point of the angelic announcement is the mention of the Child's name; He will be called what He is—*call His name Jesus, for He will save His people from their sins.* Mary's child would be known by other names—Christ, Lord, the Word, Son of Man, Son of God—that all testified to His work and character, but the name that rises highest is *Jesus.* Sin is man's greatest problem, and Jesus should be worshipped and adored for doing what none other could do in saving us from sin. What Christ did for the human race makes it entirely fitting that His birth be the event by which history is dated.

1.22 So all this was done that it might be fulfilled which was spoken by the Lord through the prophet, saying:

---

[13] An angel announced the news of John's birth to Zacharias (Lk. 1.11–13) and the news of Jesus' birth to Mary (Lk. 1.31), Joseph (v 20), and the shepherds (Lk. 2.11).

The first fulfillment quotation—Isaiah 7.14—tells us that Christ's birth, *spoken by the Lord*, was prophetically foretold.[14] *Fulfilled* (*pleroō*, to make full, replete), when used in connection with a prophecy, means to perform fully, to accomplish.

1.23 "Behold, the virgin shall be with child, and bear a Son, and they shall call His name Immanuel,' which is translated, "God with us."

The life of Christ was anticipated, being the climax of a divine process. Isaiah 7.14 is referenced only here in the NT, but John tells us that Isaiah *saw his glory and spoke of Him* (Jn. 12.41), including Christ's supernatural conception.

There is no antecedent in the context for the plural pronoun *they*; a possibility is that the reference is to those in the Gospel who encounter Christ and come away believing that He was indeed *God with us*. Jesus' deity echoes on every page of the Gospel (17.17, 18.20, 26.29) and reaches a crescendo in the final verse (28.20).

Excursus on Isaiah 7.14

Despite Matthew's assertion that Isaiah predicted Christ's birth, few topics in Matthew have generated greater discussion. Opinions on Isaiah 7.14 fall into one of three categories: first, that Isaiah 7.14 is nonmessianic and refers only to an event during Isaiah's time; second, that Isaiah 7.14 had a dual fulfillment, referring to an event in Isaiah's day as well as to the birth of Christ; or third, that Isaiah 7.14 is entirely Messianic with no reference to a child in Isaiah's time.

The first of these, the *nonmessianic view*, denies that Isaiah 7.14 is a reference to the conception and birth of Jesus and asserts that Matthew went beyond Isaiah's true meaning. Advocates of this view include antisupernaturalists who object to a virgin birth owing to its physical impossibility,[15] rationalists who "question the authenticity of the birth narratives and the literary and theological integrity of the writers [and who] do not believe that the Bible is the inspired, inerrant Word of God,"[16] and form critics who attribute accounts of Christ's divine conception to the influence of pagan mythology.[17] And there are theologians (who are often a pretentious bunch) who claim to hold this position on exegetical grounds. Their

---

[14] There are forty-two explicit citations of the OT in Matthew, a fourth of which are introduced by the verb *fulfill*.

[15] Smith, 91–92, Gromacki, 173–176.

[16] Gromacki, 167ff.

[17] Smith, 96–99.

argument is threefold. First, considering that the *sign* of 7.14 was meant to ease Judah's fears over a contemporary threat posed by Israel and Syria, the birth of a child centuries later would be meaningless to them. Second, Isaiah 7.15–16 required an immediate fulfillment, because Judah's danger would pass before the promised child was old enough to discern between good and evil (Isa. 7.15). Third, the word Isaiah used for the child's mother (*almah*) doesn't necessarily mean a *virgin* but only a *young woman* of marriageable age. Critics thus contend that Isaiah foretold the birth of a contemporary child, possibly his own son Mahershalalhashbaz (Isa. 8.48), Hezekiah, or some other child, who would be conceived in the normal way and whose arrival would reassure Isaiah's contemporaries of God's help.

The most obvious problem with this view is that it contradicts Matthew. The arguments can be answered, but any nonmessianic theory that originates from an antisupernatural bias is suspect from the outset. If there is a God, a miraculous birth should be no more difficult than a resurrection. In words similar to Acts 26.8, the angel answers Mary's bewilderment about her pregnancy by saying, *with God nothing will be impossible* (Lk. 1.37). The God who created the world from nothing can certainly arrange for a miraculous conception. There's nothing unreasonable in believing that a supernatural being would enter the world in a supernatural way.

The dual-fulfillment view says that Isaiah 7.14 referred to the birth of a child in Isaiah's time but also predicted Christ's birth.[18] Problematic for this view is the full description of the child in Isaiah 7 to 12. Take, for instance, Isaiah 9.6–7: no child born during Isaiah's time was worthy of the names *Wonderful, Counselor, Mighty God, Everlasting Father, Prince of Peace* (Isa. 8.14, 9.1–2, 11.1–10). The context of Isaiah 7.14 seems set against the dual-fulfillment theory.

The single-fulfillment view believes that Isaiah 7.14 is an exclusive reference to the miraculous conception of Jesus.[19] Though not without difficulties, it nevertheless seems the best interpretation. Hendriksen's assertion "that even in the Isaiah context the son's mother is definitely a virgin and that her child is the Messiah" (136) is supported by two consideration. *First, in the OT, almah "is never employed of a married woman*. It seems to be the only word in the [Hebrew] language which unequivocally signifies an unmarried woman" (Young I, 287–288).[20] When we're told that Isaiah sees an *almah*—an unmarried,

---

[18] Hindson (15–16) believes this view was a compromise position that gained credence among conservative scholars in the middle of the nineteenth century to stem rising support for the nonmessianic interpretation of Isaiah 7.14.

[19] "The Messianic interpretation has been the prevailing one in the Christian Church in all ages. It was followed by all the Fathers and other Christian expositors till the middle of the eighteenth century" (Hengstenberg, 156).

[20] Luther's challenge still stands: "If a Jew or Christian can prove to me that in any passage

pregnant woman—one wonders how she became pregnant? There are only two possibilities: either it occurred naturally as the result of immorality (as with *Tamar*, v 3) or supernaturally, as the result of a miracle. If Isaiah's *almah* conceived through fornication, it's difficult to see how that would have been a sign to Ahaz or typified the birth of Christ. There is nothing, however, in the context of Isaiah 7.14 that hints at immorality. As the great Princeton scholar Robert Dick Wilson wrote, "since the presumption in common law was and is, that every *alma* is a virgin and virtuous, until she is proven not to be, we have a right to assume that the *alma* of Isa. vii. 14, and all other *almas* were virgin and virtuous, until and unless it shall be proven that they were not."[21] If the prophet was not speaking of an immoral woman, the inference is that Isaiah 7.14 exclusively predicted Christ's supernatural conception.

Second, there was no child born shortly after Isaiah's oracle that fits the description of the child described in Isaiah 7–12. The evidence points to Isaiah 7.14 exclusively being a prediction of a supernatural birth.

Three objections are typically urged against the exclusively messianic interpretation.

The first asks how a miraculous birth that occurred centuries after the time of Ahaz could be a sign to Ahaz? The answer is that while Isaiah initially addressed Ahaz (Isa. 7.13), he broadened his audience to include the *house of David* (*you* in Isa. 7.14 is plural; 7.2). Ahaz hypocritically declined the chance to ask for a sign (7.10–12); as 2 Kings 16 and 2 Chronicles 28 show, he had no intention of trusting the Lord for deliverance. Any sign, near or distant, would have been as wasted on him as a *sign from heaven* would have been wasted on Christ's enemies (12.38–39).

After Ahaz's refusal, the Lord gave the house of David a sign of His own choosing, a "wonderful event of futurity, the birth of a Divine Redeemer of a virgin."[22] That God would use a distant, future event to encourage His people wasn't unheard of; this very thing is seen in 2.17–18 and its reference to Jeremiah 31.15, where grieving mothers were consoled by a promise of something that would not occur until centuries later. "Jeremiah and Ezekiel consoled the people, when they were carried away into exile, by predicting the future restoration of the theocracy to a far more glorious condition through the Messiah, *whose appearance was nevertheless many centuries distant.*"[23] "Why

---

of Scripture *almah* means a married woman, I will give him 100 florins, although God knows where I might find them" (qtd. by Hendriksen, 137).

[21] *Princeton Theological Review* XXIV, 1926.

[22] Hengstenberg, 152.

[23] Hengstenberg, 157.

does a prophecy have to be relevant to the immediate circumstances of the people of the prophet's day? Who said that it had to? No Scripture says so. In fact, the Scriptures teach that the prophets spoke of things beyond their day as well as within their day. Immediacy should not be confused with relevancy; a prophecy could be relevant in some way to the people of the prophet's day, even though its fulfillment was centuries in the future. For example, since the Messiah was to come of Israel, a prophecy of His coming which was uttered during dark days in Israel's history would furnish them with the assurance that their nation would not perish during those dark days since she would have to continue to exist in order for the Messiah to be born of her number" (Bales, *Of Whom Speaketh the Prophet?* 10–11). Future promises can have present significance. If we can understand how the prophecy of Christ's second coming has relevance now, we should be able to understand how the distant promise of a miraculous birth could have relevance for Isaiah's generation.

A second objection involves Isaiah's use of the present tense. Although some versions translate the verse in the future tense (a virgin *shall* conceive), most scholars agree that the verb should be rendered in the present (*is* with child). If this is correct, wouldn't it require a fulfillment in Isaiah's time? Not necessarily, for future predictions were sometimes put in the present (Isa. 53.3, *is despised*) and the past (Isa. 53.8, *was taken*).

A third question involves Isaiah 7.15–16. Doesn't the prediction that Rezin and Pekah (7.1) will be destroyed before the child of 7.14 reaches the age of moral discernment require at least a partial fulfillment of the prophecy in Isaiah's day? Not if 7.14 exclusively points to a child whose birth was centuries distant. Isaiah might simply be saying that Judah's enemies would be dealt with in less time than it takes for a child to reach the age of accountability. "As Vitringa pointed out: 'the prophet takes the stages of the Messiah's life out of a distant future, to make them the measure of events about to take place in the immediate future.' Since in vision he sees the child as already conceived, it was natural for him to say that from the time of this conception to the time the child grew to the age of accountability would be the time in which the land would be cleared of the kings. Thus, although the actual birth is far off, yet he saw in vision the virgin was then with child, and this time measure—the time it would take the child to be born and grow up—he uses when showing the period within which the land would be cleared of these kings."[24]

I believe that Isaiah predicted—not typically but exclusively—the

---

[24] Bales, *The Biblical Doctrine of Christ*, 27.

miraculous conception of Christ. This is Matthew's interpretation of Isaiah 7.14, and who should know better than one schooled in Messianic prophecy by the Messiah Himself (Lk. 24.44–45)![25]

1.24 Then Joseph, being aroused from sleep, did as the angel of the Lord commanded him and took to him his wife,

Joseph awoke convinced that he had received a divine revelation, and he did as directed. Taking Mary as his wife was a brave act. "It takes little to imagine what it cost him to give the protection of his spotless reputation and his lineage to Mary and her infant Son. One gets a new appreciation of Joseph as a stalwart of the faith—as a devoted servant of God." [26]

1.25 and did not know her till she had brought forth her firstborn Son. And he called His name JESUS.

Joseph and Mary didn't consummate their marriage until after the child's birth. As instructed, the child was given the name that is above every name: JESUS. From here, Matthew will show us how Christ's unusual birth was followed by an unforgettable life that ended in an unwarranted death that was reversed by an unsurpassed event.

Excursus on Mary's Virginity

The Lateran Council's (AD 649) pronouncement on Mary's perpetual virginity is without Scriptural warrant. For an excellent summary of the debate, see Luz I, 98–99. So extraordinary would a perpetual virginity have been that it's hard to imagine that Matthew (or another NT writer) would not have mentioned it. What is especially egregious is that the virgin birth would ever become a basis for elevating and worshipping Mary. "Let us leave this wonderful passage worshipping the Son of God, who condescended to be born the Son of man" (Spurgeon).

---

[25] "The account [of Christ's birth] reads primarily as if designed for a Christian readership, who wanted to know more precisely how Mary's marriage to Joseph related to the miraculous conception of Jesus' (France 76).

[26] Vos, 25.

CHAPTER 2

THE WISE MEN, 2.1–2

Notes

After introducing the wise men (vv 1–2), this chapter divides into two sections that center on Herod (vv 3–9a) and Jesus (vv 9b–12). The comparisons and contrasts between the sections are obvious: the star is mentioned in v 2 and v 9; the alarm of the Jews (v 3) contrasts with the joy of the Gentiles (v 10); Herod's plan (vv 7–9) is thwarted by God's plan (v 12; see 26.1–5). The universal scope of the gospel (1.1) is again on display as Gentiles from the east come to worship Christ, and Christ is taken west to find sanctuary in Egypt (1.1, 8.11).

2.1 Now after Jesus was born in Bethlehem of Judea in the days of Herod the king, behold, wise men from the East came to Jerusalem,

Bethlehem, the city of David (Lk. 2.4), picks up the Davidic thread from ch 1. Late in Mary's pregnancy, she and Joseph travel to Bethlehem (*house of bread*) of Judea (there was also a Bethlehem in Zebulun, Josh. 19.15) to comply with a Roman census (Lk. 2.1–5). There, Jesus was born *in the days of Herod the king.*

Herod the king was the son of Antipater, an Idumean (Edomite) who sided with Rome against the Arabs and Hasmonaeans.[1] In 47 BC, he was appointed procurator of Judea, and in 40 BC, he assigned administration of Galilee to his son Herod. The Roman Senate confirmed this appointment and gave him the title *King of the Jews.* "Herod was both a Jew and an anti-Jew; an upholder and benefactor of Graeco-Roman civilization, and an oriental barbarian capable of unspeakable cruelties. He was a brilliant politician and in some ways a wise and far-seeing statesman, generous, constructive and highly efficient; but also naive, superstitious, grotesquely

---

[1] Most of our information about Herod comes from Josephus, *Ant.* xiv–xviii.

self-indulgent and hovering on the brink of insanity—sometimes over it" (Johnson, 110). Herod "stole along to his throne like a fox, ruled like a tiger, and died like a dog."

Herod's achievements as a builder won him the sobriquet *the Great*. He rebuilt the temple in Jerusalem (24.1), rebuilt Samaria, and was the impetus for other significant works. Everything said about him in this passage—from his suspicion and lying to his murderous rage—accords with what we know about him from extra-Biblical sources.[2] Historians place his death somewhere between March 13 and April 11, 4 BC.

Wise men translates *magi,* which originally referred to a Persian priestly caste skilled in Eastern theology, philosophy, and natural science. Socially, their prestige was high; they were often part of the entourage at royal courts.[3]

2.2 saying, "Where is He who has been born King of the Jews? For we have seen His star in the East and have come to worship Him."

In their only recorded words, the wise men ask where they can find the one born *King of the Jews*, whom they have come to worship. Their belief in the Jewish king derived from the appearance of *His star in the East* (*en te anatole*, in the rising; 4.16).

Matthew doesn't tell us how the wise men came to understand the significance of the star. Some believe the star was a natural phenomenon—comet, planet, supernova, meteor, etc.—and that the wise men connected it with a Jewish king because of their knowledge of OT prophecy (cf. Balaam's prophecy of the star out of Jacob, Num. 24.17).[4] Here are two problems I have with this view. First, the wise men's star was not a naturally occurring phenomenon—no known astronomical data can explain its movement. Owing to earth's rotation, heavenly bodies appear to move from east to

---

[2] Herod was feared and despised for his cruelty. As he grew older, he became insanely paranoid about perceived threats against himself and his position. Within his own family, he had an uncle, a wife, a brother-in-law, and three sons murdered. A pun attributed to Augustus alluded to the Jews' avoidance of pork and noted that "it is better to be Herod's swine [*hus*] than Herod's son [*huios*]!" To spite the Jews for their hatred of him, Herod ordered that at his death the principal men of the nation be murdered so that the populace would have reason to mourn at his death. The order was not carried out.

[3] *Magi* is the Lat. transliteration of the Gr. *magoi*. Herodotus (I.101) says the magi were originally a tribe of the Medes. The LXX uses *magoi* to translate the Heb. *ashshaph* (astrologer) in Dan. 1.20, 22, et al., Philo, a first-century Jewish author, refers to Balaam as a *magos*. *Magic* and *magician* come from this word (Acts 13.6, 8).

[4] J. Gresham Machen, *The Virgin Birth*, 224–225; Ernest L. Martin, *The Birth of Christ Recalculated* 4–25.

west, but the wise men's star moved from north to south until it *stood over where the young child was* (v 9). "The patently miraculous character of the star in the narrative makes it gratuitous to seek a material explanation of it from astronomical science" (Hill, 83). (Interestingly, coins minted by Alexander, the Diaochi,[5] Julius Caesar, Augustus, Alexander Jannaeus, and Herod had a star on them to signify "king.") Second, to argue that the wise men (or anyone) could discern from this star the arrival of a Jewish king based on OT studies is so implausible as to be impossible.

I think a better explanation is that the wise men's knowledge resulted from divine revelation, just as Joseph's understanding of events resulted from divine revelation (1.20–21). God communicated directly with the wise men about their return (v 12); is it farfetched to believe that a communication from Him started them on their journey? If God announced His Son's birth to the Jews (Lk. 2.8–16), why wouldn't He do the same for the Gentiles?

Though God most likely gave the wise men a revelation about Christ's birth, He didn't give them a street address. Thus, they went to Jerusalem, thinking the Jewish capital the best place to look for a Jewish king.

Worship is the proper response to divine revelation. *Proskuneō* (to kiss toward), according to the Greeks, was a form of veneration due the gods. To the Eastern mind, worship befits superior persons, such as kings. The ASV margin defines worship as "an act of reverence whether paid to a creature, or to the Creator," and it is hard to improve on this definition. Matthew speaks of *worship* thirteen times (vv 11; 8.2, 9.18, 14.33, 15.25, 20.20, 26.6–13, 28.9,17).

HEROD, 2.3–12

2.3 When Herod the king heard this, he was troubled, and all Jerusalem with him.

Considering Herod's unpopularity with the Jews, you would think that the birth of a royal child would trigger rejoicing. Jerusalem's dismay probably indicates a fear of what would happen if Herod's paranoia was aroused. "When Herod the Great trembled the whole city shook" (Morris, 37).

2.4 And when he had gathered all the chief priests and scribes of the people together, he inquired of them where the Christ was to be born.

---

[5] The rival generals who fought for control of Alexander's empire after his death.

Herod convenes an ad hoc meeting of the religious leadership to learn the answer to the wise men's question. Portents that the ancients inferred from astral phenomena were nothing to brush off. The wise men asked about the *King of the Jews*, but Herod asks about the *Christ*, which reflected the popular belief that the expected Messiah would function as Israel's king who would free his people from Roman rule.

The *chief priests* (some of whom were former high priests) held most of the important temple offices, and wielded considerable power.[6] The *scribes* (*grammateus, lawyers*, 22.35; Lk. 7.30) were a literary community "who devoted their lives to the exposition and application of the law.... their aim was to spell out in rules and regulations the great principles set forth in the law" (Mounce, 44). Although most of the scribes were Pharisees, they were sometimes linked with the Sadducees (Mk. 11.18,27). The devotion of the wise men stands in striking contrast to the indifference of the Jewish clergy... .

2.5–6 So they said to him, "In Bethlehem of Judea, for thus it is written by the prophet: "But you, Bethlehem, *in* the land of Judah, are not the least among the rulers of Judah; for out of you shall come a Ruler Who will shepherd My people Israel."

The answer to the wise men's question was found in Micah 5.2. *Bethlehem of Judea* is located about six miles southwest of Jerusalem. There are several small changes between the Hebrew text in Micah and Matthew's quotation (e.g., the ancient name *Ephrathah* [Gen. 48.7] is updated to *Judea*); by making these changes, the chief priests and scribes didn't misquote Micah but quoted him in an interpretive way.

Remarkably, no Jew follows up. This could be due to jaded indifference or to the fear that showing interest could be fatal if Herod learned of it. For whatever reason, instead of reacting to news of the Messiah's birth, the religious community became Herod's accomplices. Knowing the Bible doesn't mean you know the Lord.

2.7 Then Herod, when he had secretly called the wise men, determined from them what time the star appeared.

---

[6] Josephus says there were twenty-eight high priests from the time of Herod to the destruction of Jerusalem (*Ant.* xx.10). Matthew mentions the tenth, *Annas,* and the fourteenth, *Caiaphas.*

After answering the wise men's question, Herod learns from them when they first sighted the star.

2.8 And he sent them to Bethlehem and said, "Go and search carefully for the young Child, and when you have found Him, bring back word to me, that I may come and worship Him also."

Search carefully (*akribos*, accurately; only here in Matt.) means "leave no stone unturned." Herod's duplicity surfaces when he acts like he shares the wise men's excitement and devotion. Given his paranoia, it's curious that he didn't send anyone to accompany or shadow the wise men when they left for Bethlehem.

2.9–10 When they heard the king, they departed; and behold, the star which they had seen in the East went before them, till it came and stood over where the young Child was. When they saw the star, they rejoiced with exceedingly great joy.

The first appearance of the star sent the wise men west to Jerusalem; its next appearance sends them south to Bethlehem. Previously, there has been no indication that the star moved, but it moves now, and the wise men see God's hand in this—the *sight filled them with indescribable joy* (JBP). Eventually, the astral GPS stopped over a house (which implies that the star was a low-hanging object) *where the young Child was*.

2.11 And when they had come into the house, they saw the young Child with Mary His mother, and fell down and worshiped Him. And when they had opened their treasures, they presented gifts to Him: gold, frankincense, and myrrh.

In Matthew, *worship* (v 2) is directed almost exclusively to Jesus as the Son of God (8.2; 9.18; 14.33, 15.25). The wise men worship, giving the Child *treasures* (*thesauros*, originally, a place for putting things, for keeping them safe; then, that which was kept safe, the treasure itself) fit for a king: gold, frankincense, and myrrh. *Gold* is a precious metal that has been prized from time immemorial (Gen. 2.11–12); *frankincense* is the fragrant resin of trees that grow in southeast Arabia, India, and Somalia; *myrrh*, prized for its aroma, is the resin of the myrrh tree that grows in Arabia and Ethiopia and was used in embalming (Jn. 19.39). Both frankincense and myrrh were expensive, imported luxury items.

2.12 Then, being divinely warned in a dream that they should not return to Herod, they departed for their own country another way.

God intervenes (26.1–5) to thwart Herod's murderous intent (Ps. 2.2–4). Warned via a dream, the wise men bypass Jerusalem and return home by a different route.

FLIGHT, 2.13–18

Notes

The different attitudes between Herod and the wise men regarding Christ will be seen throughout Matthew. This paragraph has three parts: vv 13–15, 16–18, and 19–23, each of which ends with a fulfillment quotation. The instructions to Joseph in the first and third, and his reaction, are almost identical.

2.13 Now when they had departed, behold, an angel of the Lord appeared to Joseph in a dream, saying, "Arise, take the young Child and His mother, flee to Egypt, and stay there until I bring you word; for Herod will seek the young Child to destroy Him."

Through an angel, God tells Joseph to take Jesus and Mary, flee to Egypt, and remain there until further notice in order to evade the search-and-destroy mission authorized by Herod. Repeatedly, in John's Gospel, the failure of Christ's enemies to arrest Him is explained on the basis that *His hour had not yet come* (e.g., 7.30). As Matthew shows, God unfailingly protected His Son from murderous designs until it was time for His Son to die.

2.14 When he arose, he took the young Child and His mother by night and departed for Egypt,

In Israelite history, *Egypt* was better known as a place of bondage than a place of refuge. It was from Egypt that Moses fled and Israel departed, but now it is the Promised Land that is the place of danger and Egypt that is the place of sanctuary.[7]

Even though it was night, Joseph responds immediately. Depending on the point of entry, the distance from Bethlehem to Egypt was approximately seventy-five miles. Once there, Jesus was safely outside

---

[7] In the OT, there were others who found sanctuary in Egypt: Hadad (1 Kgs. 11.17), Jeroboam (1 Kgs. 11.40), et al.

Herod's jurisdiction. Every Egyptian city of any size had a Jewish colony (it is estimated that over 2 million Jews lived in Alexandria at this time), and the gifts brought by the wise men (v 11) would financially support the family while in exile.

2.15 and was there until the death of Herod, that it might be fulfilled which was spoken by the Lord through the prophet, saying, "Out of Egypt I called My Son."
This is the first of three fulfillment quotations in this chapter. Its placement here is anticipatory, for it refers to Christ's exit from Egypt (v 23) rather than His entrance into Egypt (v 21). The prophecy is Hosea 11.1, and the consensus among commentators is that the prophecy refers to Jesus only typically (McGarvey, 29), whereas others explain Matthew's use of Hosea as an example of *eisegesis*, wherein a NT writer *reads into* the text something that isn't there (Barclay I, 27).

James Smith, though, argues that "all of Hosea 11.1 is personal Messianic prediction" and only implicates the Exodus in a remote, allusive sense (*What the Bible Teaches about the Promised Messiah*, 239). Smith says that Hosea 11.1 is a conclusion to the preceding text rather than an introduction to what follows.[8] In 10.1, God accuses Israel of being an *empty vine* because of her idolatry (vv 5,8), despicable behavior (v 9), and iniquity (v 13). For this, the nation would be punished—a ruthless enemy would spoil her, sparing neither mother nor child (v 14), and her king would be utterly cut off (v 15). In 11.1, God gives His chastened people hope, as often occurs in the prophets (Hos. 3.4–5). "Taken as a genuine prediction, Hosea 11: 1 adds several important points to the Messianic expectation. 1. Messiah would be an Israelite. 2. The Messianic Israel would come into the world as a child. 3. God would have a special loving concern for this Messianic child. 4. Messianic Israel, like the man Israel and the nation Israel, would spend some time in Egypt. 5. Messianic Israel would be the Son of God" (241).

McGarvey and others may be right about the typical nature of Hosea 11.1, but the direct application to Christ is tighter than many realize.

This is the first time in Matthew that Jesus is explicitly identified as God's Son.

---

[8] Note that the subject and object in 11.1 are first-person singular, whereas the subject and object in 11.2–4 are plural and no copula connects them.

2.16 Then Herod, when he saw that he was deceived by the wise men, was exceedingly angry; and he sent forth and put to death all the male children who were in Bethlehem and in all its districts, from two years old and under, according to the time which he had determined from the wise men.

The threat Joseph's family escaped was real. Since Bethlehem is only a couple hours' walk from Jerusalem, Herod probably expected the wise men to return within a day or so. When he realized they weren't coming back, he was *exceedingly angry* (*thumoō*, only here in the NT) and expressed his malice in a command to *put to death* (*anaireō*, only here in Matt.) *all the male children* (the article *tous* is masculine) in and around Bethlehem, two years old or younger. He who could murder three of his own sons didn't hesitate to murder the sons of others.

2.17–18 Then was fulfilled what was spoken by Jeremiah the prophet, saying: "A voice was heard in Ramah, Lamentation, weeping, and great mourning, Rachel weeping for her children, refusing to be comforted, Because they are no more."

The slaughter was foreseen in Jeremiah 31.15.[9] Ramah was where the Judean captives assembled for deportation to Babylon (Jer. 40.1). Jeremiah personifies the mothers of Judah as *Rachel*—Jacob's favorite wife and the idealized mother of Israel—who weeps inconsolably over her children's deaths. Matthew doesn't explain how a good God could allow such an atrocity to happen. But what happened to Bethlehem's sons at the start of this Gospel is a precursor to what happens to God's Son at the end. This Gospel is bracketed by the slaughter of the innocent.

Excursus on Suffering

The greatest obstacle to faith has never been belief's irrationality but life's injustice. There are things in life that are hard to understand *unless* God is, and there are things that are hard to understand *if* God is. Herod's *slaughter of the innocents* (v 16) is an example of the latter.[10]

The ancients were no strangers to the agonies of mind and heart that try to comprehend why God allows certain things to hap-pen. Moses cried, *Lord, why*

---

[9] Jeremiah appears three times in Matthew: here, 16.14, and 27.9.

[10] *Tell me, if there was any sunshine / When this old world of ours was made / Why the architect of all the worlds / Put into ours so much of shade?* Charles F. May.

have You brought trouble on this people? … for since I came to Pharaoh to speak in Your name, he has done evil to this people; neither have You delivered Your people at all (Ex. 5.22–23). Elijah lamented, *O Lord my God, have You also brought tragedy on the widow with whom I lodge, by killing her son?* (1 Kgs. 17.20). And Job moaned, *Although You know that I am not wicked … yet You would destroy me* (Job 10.8).

To those dealing with horrendous, inexplicable evil, it's important to understand that God's comfort most usually comes not in an explanation but in a revelation. In the case of the Bethlehem children, God didn't explain why He allowed the slaughter to happen; instead, He tells us that He allowed the same fate to befall His Son. Dorothy Sayers explained it this way: "For whatever reason God chose to make man as he is—limited and suffering and subject to sorrows and death—he [God] had the honesty and the courage to take His own medicine. Whatever game he is playing with his creation, he has kept His own rules and played fair. He can exact nothing from man that He has not exacted from Himself. He has himself gone through the whole of human experience, from the trivial irritations of family life and the cramping restrictions of hard work and lack of money to the worst horrors of pain and humiliation, defeat, despair, and death. When he was a man, he played the man. He was born in poverty and died in disgrace and thought it well worthwhile" ("The Greatest Drama Ever Staged," *Letters to a Diminished Church*, 2). *In all their affliction He was afflicted* (Isa. 63.9), and having endured hell on earth, the message He sends is *Let not your heart be troubled; you believe in God, believe also in Me* (Jn. 14.1). Believing in Christ and His promise takes the edge off our agony and will leave us still standing after the storm has spent its fury (7.24–27). We don't need to know the explanation so long as we know that there is an explanation. Because of Christ, we measure God's goodness neither by our happiness nor by our hurt but by His victory. Because of Christ, we do not merely hold beliefs about God, we are held by them.

George MacDonald tells of a woman who could not be argued out of her belief that her sailor-boys were in God's care and, thus, perfectly safe. "But," asked an objector, "what would you say if some of your sons were drowned at sea?" "Well, sir," she answered with a sigh, "I trust they are none the less safe for that. It would be a strange thing for an old woman like me to suppose that safety lay in not being drowned. What is the bottom of the sea, sir? The bottom of the sea is the hollow of His hand!"

Possibly the best answer to suffering, the answer to which the Gospel of Matthew turns time and again, is found in these words of Thomas Carlyle: "Man issues from Eternity, is encompassed in Eternity, and again in Eternity disappears.

It is fearful and wonderful. This only we know, that God is above it, that God made it, and that rules it for good."

Our children are safe even if Herod gets at them; we are certain of this because of the Child Herod didn't get.

Excursus on Jeremiah 31.15

Derek Kidner offers this on Jeremiah 31.15. "How did the weeping for the massacre of the innocents (Mt. 2.17–18) 'fulfil' this oracle? It is a question for a commentary on Matthew; but as a tentative reply we may note that in Matthew 2, we are pointed to Jesus as the one upon whom the Old Testament's lines converge: the Christ (Mt. 2.1–6); the true Son, with the true Exodus to accomplish (Mt. 2.15); the greater than Moses (Mt. 2.20 echoing Ex. 4.19); the *nēṣer* ('branch', Is. 11.1) suggested by the name Nazarene (Mt. 2.23); and at Matthew 2.17–18, the one whose disturbing presence brought yet another draught of suffering to tragic people. The mothers of Bethlehem, like Rachel the mother of the Joseph tribes, could only weep; yet our passage tells us that Rachel's tears were not in vain and not for ever (31.16–17). Did the gospel's allusion to it hint at the same long view? 'There is hope for your future,' says the Lord, and your children shall come back' (17)—*these to a better country than they had lost*" (*The Message of Jeremiah*, 108–109, emp. mine).

RETURN, 2.19–23

2.19–21 Now when Herod was dead, behold, an angel of the Lord appeared in a dream to Joseph in Egypt, saying, "Arise, take the young Child and His mother, and go to the land of Israel, for those who sought the young Child's life are dead.' Then he arose, took the young Child and His mother, and came into the land of Israel.

When Herod dies (Josephus gives a gruesome description of his death in *Ant.* xvii.6.5), an angel, in a dream, gives Joseph the green light to return to *the land of Israel* (in Matt., only here and v 21). *Those* may simply be a general plural, used when there is no need to individualize (cf., "They say," when only one person said it), or it may indicate that others had joined Herod in his conspiracy against Israel's Messiah.

2.22 But when he heard that Archelaus was reigning over Judea instead of his father Herod, he was afraid to go there. And being warned by God in a dream, he turned aside into the region of Galilee.

Joseph's fear was justified. *Archelaus* was made ethnarch (ruler of an ethnic group, a governor) and given control of Judea after his father's death. His cruelty nearly equaled his father's—he began his tenure by massacring 3,000 citizens in the Temple precincts. After ten years, Augustus sacked him for mismanagement.

For the fourth time, Joseph receives a revelation via a dream, this one directing him to Galilee where he and Mary had previously lived (Lk. 1.26–27, 2.4).

2.23 And he came and dwelt in a city called Nazareth, that it might be fulfilled which was spoken by the prophets, "He shall be called a Nazarene."

The ending to this chapter parallels the ending to the first: *he called his name Jesus* (1.25) … *He will be called a Nazarene.* This fulfillment quotation is a curiosity for it appears nowhere in the OT. How, then, did Christ's upbringing in Nazareth fulfill that *which was spoken by the prophets*? Matthew doesn't tell us, but he does give a hint by his use of the plural *prophets*, which attributes the quote to the prophets collectively, thereby indicating that he is summarizing a prophetic theme rather than quoting a specific prophecy.

To be called a *Nazarene* in first-century Judea meant that you were from the wrong side of the tracks. "During Jesus' lifetime Nazareth was a small, unfortified rocky village, nestling between two valleys, inhabited by peasants and artisans, eking a meager livelihood out of their olive groves, vineyards and cattle. It possessed no strategic or religious importance and stood far from the busy thoroughfares and Galilean cities" (Cornfeld, 50). The town is never mentioned in the OT or by Josephus; in Judea, it was considered an embarrassment (Jn. 1.46; 7.41–42,52).

"No such passage as Matt. 2.23 occurs in the Old Testament, nor can Matthew refer to any particular text, because he does not refer to any particular prophet; for his phrase is, 'that it might be fulfilled, which was spoken by *the prophets*', in the plural; so that something was thus accomplished in Christ, to which all the prophets gave concurrent testimony. Now it is plain that they all agree that he should be 'despised' as well as 'rejected of men'; that he should be an object of contumely and reproach, and therefore, as Whitby well remarks, 'the angel sent him to this contemptible place, that he might have a name of infamy put upon him.' He shall be called mean and contemptible, as the root of the word signifies, as well as separated. How Nazareth was esteemed, we learn from the words of the mild Nathaniel, — 'Can any good thing come out of Nazareth?' — and the title Nazarene has been by Jews, and other enemies, always given in contempt to our Savior and his disciples" (R. Watson, *Commentary on Matthew*, 42).

In the obscurity of Nazareth, then, the prophetic predictions of a humble, despised background for the Messiah found their fulfillment (Ps. 22.6–8; Isa. 49.7; 53.2–3; Zech. 11.4–14).[11]

Excursus on the Bethlehem Victims

An increase in European travelers to Palestine in the fifteenth century greatly expanded the market for relics (religious souvenirs)—objects thought to be connected, no matter how tenuously, to Jesus. At that time, tradition held that more than 10,000 children[12] had been murdered by Herod at Bethlehem and, as gruesome as it seems, acquiring the corpse of one of these *holy innocents* was a hot item for pilgrims. When the Sultan of Egypt learned of this, he saw a chance to fleece some Europeans. How he did so is recounted by Felix Fabri, a German friar who left an extensive record of his 15th-century journey to Jerusalem, Sinai, and Egypt. Fabri was told by an Arab informant "that Saracens and Mamelukes receive the bodies of still-born children, or of children who have died soon after their birth, slash them with knives, making wounds, then embalm the bodies by pressing balsam, myrrh, and other preservative drugs into the wounds, and sell them to Christian kings, princes, and wealthy people as bodies of the Holy Innocents" (*Evagatorium in Terram Sanctam, Wanderings in the Holy Land*).

Excursus on the Jewish Messianic Prophecies and Julius Caesar

According to English writer Frances Minto Dickinson Elliott in her *Pictures of Old Rome,* the OT predictions of a coming king may have played a role in the death of Julius Caesar. "Doubtless the eastern prophecies of a coming Messiah who was to rule over all nations, backed as they were by the local oracles of the Sibyls, materially affected the imagination of Caesar. These vague floating legends,

---

[11] James 4.5 is another instance of where a scriptural theme is the subject of a prophecy.

[12] *The Anchor Bible* (Vol. 26, 19) estimates that the population of Bethlehem at the time of the slaughter was 300. I was raised in a rural Midwest community of 300. During the time of the baby boomers, I began first grade with about twenty-five other boys (from town and surrounding farms). The 1910 *Catholic Encyclopedia* estimates the number of boys killed in Bethlehem at thirty.

these ancient traditions (the Jewish prophecies especially), pointing to the very time and century, seemed to mark Caesar as the man, at least he might think so. But the coming Messiah was to be a king: the Pythian oracle, the Egyptian priest, the Jewish prophet, all agreed in this." Elliott speculates that Caesar's fascination with these royal predictions led him to seek the title of *king*, even when it was clear to everyone that republican Rome was adamantly opposed to being ruled by a king (186). It was to keep him from becoming a king that he was assassinated.

CHAPTER 3

3.1–4.16: Preparation for ministry

Notes

For four centuries the prophetic voice had been silent, but with John's coming there appeared the promised Elijah (17.10–13; Mal. 4.5) ushering in the day of the Lord.[1] By any valid measure, John the Baptist was a great man. By Christ's own testimony, John was *more than a prophet* (11.9)—miraculously born and *filled with the Holy Spirit from his mother's womb* (Lk. 1.15), he was *sent from God to bear witness of the Light* (Jn. 1.6–7)—God's special instrument sent to do a special work.

The second half of Matthew's prologue runs from 3.1 to 4.16 and consists of three parts. The first (3.1–12) and third (4.12–16) are alike in that both include an OT scripture containing geographical information. The middle part (3.13–4.11) records Christ's baptism and temptation.

This paragraph opens with the appearance of John (vv 1–3), followed by a description of him (v 4), popular reaction to him (vv 5–7a), and the content of his preaching (vv 7b–12), which includes an invective (vv 7b–9b), threatened judgment (vv 9c–12), and a promise (v 11c).

JOHN THE BAPTIST, 3.1–12

3.1 In those days John the Baptist came preaching in the wilderness of Judea,

In those days connects John's appearance to Christ's infancy even though there is a gap of nearly thirty years between chs 2 and 3. *Came* recalls 2.1, where the word is used of the wise men, and it looks ahead to 3.13 where it is used of Christ. Luke 3.1 dates the start of John's ministry in the fifteenth year of Tiberius (AD 28–29).

---

[1] John is mentioned no fewer than ninety times in the NT, more than any other apostle, except for Peter and Paul.

John was called *the Baptist* because baptizing the penitent was part of his ministry. It has long been debated whether his baptism merely symbolized repentance or actually resulted in the forgiveness of sins. According to Luz, "Only in isolated cases did the ancient church attribute to John's baptism the character of an actual baptism of forgiveness" (136). The Council of Trent went so far as to pronounce anathema on the view that John's baptism and Christ's baptism had the same power. Mark 1.4, however, settles the issue by affirming that John's baptism was *for* the remission of sins.

Preaching (*kerussō*, to announce, make known by a herald) fits well with v 3, which describes John as the herald of a king. Ancient kings often had servants precede them to announce their approach (10.23), and John fulfilled that role for Christ.

The wilderness of Judea was a badland region that stretched from the ridge of the Judean hills to the Jordan River (1 Sam. 23.14–25, 24.1). This seems a strange location for John's ministry since preachers normally gravitate to areas where people are abundant. But John was a commanding personality who could not be ignored. And as Matthew shows, the *wilderness of Judea* carried Messianic overtones (v 3, 4.1).

3.2 and saying, "Repent, for the kingdom of heaven is at hand!"

Repent for the kingdom of heaven is at hand was the message of John, Jesus (4.17), and the disciples (10.7). Although John was an OT prophet, he was the transitional prophet chosen to announce the imminence of the kingdom.

Repent (*metanoeō*, after thought) is a difficult word to translate; "we have no one English word that reproduces exactly the meaning and atmosphere of the Greek word" (Robertson, 24). Essentially, repentance means that if men are to change their behavior, they must first change their mind. Repentance is neither penance (religious masochism wherein guilt is absolved through self-punishment) nor sorrow (though sorrow should accompany it, 2 Cor. 7.9) but an inward change that manifests itself outwardly (v 8). It is not only an appeal to God to save from sin but is a commitment to burn the bridges across which sin continually comes.[2]

Only Matthew uses the expression *kingdom of heaven*. *Kingdom* is a contraction of *king's dominion*;[3] *of heaven* indicates its divine nature. The

---

[2] *Ah, for a man to arise in me, / That the man I am may cease to be!* (Tennyson, *Maud*).

[3] At the time of the Norman conquest, England was divided into *earldoms* (i.e., an earl's dominion).

primary meaning of the Gr. word translated *kingdom* (*basileia*) is abstract, referring to a king's rule, authority, or sovereignty; *kingship* gets at the meaning. The secondary meaning is the concrete one and refers to the sphere (geographical territory or people) over which a king rules (4.8).[4] To say that the *kingdom of heaven is at hand* is to say that God is about to reign or rule. But how could John preach this, considering that God has always ruled (1 Chron. 29.11–12; Ps. 10.16)? The answer is that John referred to the rule of God over Israel *as expressed through a son of David* (2 Sam. 7.8–14; Ps. 89; 2 Chron. 13.8; Acts 2.30,32,36). God's covenant with David (1.1) gave to David and his sons the right to rule Israel forever. But the Davidic covenant contained a punitive element (Ps. 89.30–34); if David's sons fell into unbelief, God would punish them, and this God did when He removed David's ungodly descendants from the throne and for six hundred years ruled Israel through Gentiles (Babylonians, Persians, Greeks, Romans).

But the time has come for the kingship to be returned to a Davidic descendant—Jesus Christ (1.1, 28.18; Acts 2.36).[5] *At hand* (*eggizō*, to approach, come near) indicates imminence, just around the corner.

3.3 For this is he who was spoken of by the prophet Isaiah, saying: "The voice of one crying in the wilderness: "Prepare the way of the LORD; Make His paths straight.'

John the Baptist was prophetically anticipated, having been predicted by Isaiah (40.3–5) and Malachi (3.1; 4.5–6). His job was to be a *voice*—a spokesman—*preparing the way of the Lord* by preaching repentance. Before Rome ruled the world, infrastructure (roads, bridges) was scarce; when kings traveled, construction crews went ahead to prepare the way. This could mean leveling a mountain, filling in a valley or swamp, bridging a river, etc. Isaiah's prophecy was to be understood figuratively: John prepared the way for Christ by urging men to deal with their sin through repentance and baptism. *Lord* (*kurios*) originally meant *owner*, but when OT Heb. was translated into Gr., *kurios* was used to render the divine name *Jehovah* and came to be looked upon as a God-title. Its use in Isaiah 40 agrees with 1.23 and the proposition that Jesus is God (16.16).

---

[4] In *The Living Oracles*, a translation of the NT edited by Alexander Campbell, the *kingdom of heaven* is translated as the *reign of heaven*.

[5] In my judgment, the finest study in print on the kingdom is Jim McGuiggan's, *The Reign of Heaven*.

3.4 Now John himself was clothed in camel's hair, with a leather belt around his waist; and his food was locusts and wild honey.

Heaven often scandalizes the correct and conventional, and the shockingly unconventional John the Baptist was a prime example of this divine penchant. John's clothes and diet indicate an austere lifestyle that evoked Elijah (11.14, 17.12; Lk. 1.17; 2 Kgs. 1.8; Zech. 13.4; Mal. 4.5–6), and, as William Ellis noted, "John the Baptist was God's laugh at the rabbis and the Pharisees" (*Billy Sunday, The Man and His Message*, PTL Television Network, 15).

3.5 Then Jerusalem, all Judea, and all the region around the Jordan went out to him

John's preaching had an electrifying effect (11.9). *All* is a synecdoche (wherein a part is put for the whole)—not everyone in Jerusalem and Judea responded favorably to John, but a sizable portion did. *Went out* (*exeporeuetō*) indicates continuous action—a steady stream of people went to hear him. The mention of *Jerusalem* offers a contrast: in 2.3, Jerusalem is uninterested in Jesus, but here, Jerusalem is drawn to John. As v 7 indicates, the common people and the ruling class were divided in their opinion about him.

3.6 and were baptized by him in the Jordan, confessing their sins.

Five things characterized John's baptism. First, it was authorized by God (21.25; Jn. 1.33). Second, it was predicated upon repentance (Mk. 1.4) and was unto repentance (v 11); John baptized only those who admitted the need to change and who committed to change (v 8). Third, it was an immersion in water (v 11). *Baptize* (*baptizō*) means to dip, immerse, plunge, overwhelm. "The Greek word *baptizō* was of very common use, as is seen in every period of Greek literature, and was applied to a great variety of matters, including the most familiar acts of every-day life. It was thus a word which every Greek speaking hearer and reader in apostolic times would at once and clearly understand. It meant what we express by 'immerse' and kindred terms, and no one could then have thought of attributing to it a wholly different sense, such as 'sprinkle,' or 'pour,' without distinct explanation to that effect" (Broadus, 39).[6] Fourth, it was

---

[6] "J. W. Shepherd compiled a book of testimonies on the subject of baptism called *Handbook on Baptism*. On the 'action of baptism' he cites the testimony of 33 lexicographers, 21 encyclopaedias, 26 church historians, 18 church 'fathers' and 63 theologians. They all agree

a provisional measure (Acts 19.1–5; Eph. 4.5). And fifth, it was for the remission of sins (Mk. 1.4).

Confess indicates a public acknowledgment (10.32–33).

3.7 But when he saw many of the Pharisees and Sadducees coming to his baptism, he said to them, "Brood of vipers! Who warned you to flee from the wrath to come?

Some of the worst characters in history, as well as some of the best, have been motivated by religion, and prominent among the worst were the *Pharisees* and *Sadducees.* Although sharply divided doctrinally, they will close ranks to destroy Christ.

The Pharisees—*the strictest sect of our religion* (Acts 26.5)—dominated the synagogues and were the more popular of the two groups. *Pharisee* probably derives from a Heb. word meaning *separated,*[7] which indicated the sect's desire to maintain the integrity of Judaism by avoiding contact with pagan culture. To this end, the Pharisees tried to make God's Law relevant to life in a way that left few areas unregulated. "They drew out corollary rules from major laws, deduced specific regulations from general principles, created detailed precepts applying to endless concrete situations, and so built up their immense and complicated legal system" (Fosdick, *The Man from Nazareth,* 90). Josephus said that they "valued themselves highly upon the exact skill they had in the law of their fathers, and made men believe they were highly favoured by God" (*Ant.* xvii.2.4). Consequently, instead of protecting Judaism, the Pharisees perverted it with their interpretations and traditions.[8] They were characterized by an external obedience that lent itself to legalistic hypocrisy. Sermons have been preached praising the Pharisees' admirable qualities, but this misses the point—it is the corruption of the best that makes for the worst. To borrow a line from Mark Twain, many a Pharisee was "a good man in the worst sense of the word." In Pharisaism, conscientiousness degenerated into fanaticism, sincerity into hypocrisy, and determination into obstinacy until human opinion was held more highly than true

with the definition given above. These sources are all recognized people from many denominations. Included are all the standard reference works" (McGuigan, *The Book of Romans* 190–191).

[7] "We do not know for certain neither what [Pharisee] means nor whether the Pharisees used it to refer to themselves" (Luz III, 142).

[8] Whoever elevates his opinion to a position equal to or superior to the Law of God (15.1–11) is no conservative.

righteousness, and the goodness of God was twisted into something loathsome. Among the evils that "destroy the world," the Mishna lists "the plagues of the Pharisees" (Sotah 3.4).[9]

Less is known about the *Sadducees*, the priestly sect. Their name likely derives from Zadok, high priest during the time of David (2 Sam. 8.17, 15.24). As a class, they were aristocratic, disdained the traditions of the Pharisees, claimed only the five books of Moses as their authority, and were materialists who denied the reality of the resurrection, spirits, and angels (22.23–33; Acts 23.8). As is true of most aristocrats, they maintained their position at the expense of the people, did not share in the struggles of the people, and sometimes defied the will of the people. They had made peace with the Roman eagle, and their concern was to maintain the privileges and revenues granted them by their Imperial overlords.

Why the Pharisees and Sadducees sought out John isn't revealed; they may have been acting in an official capacity to investigate the goings-on in the wilderness. John's question to the *brood of vipers* (12.34, 23.33) is sarcastic and seems to question their sincerity. *Who warned you to flee?* refers to the fact that snakes will leave their dens to escape an approaching fire.

3.8 Therefore bear fruits worthy of repentance,

Judgment was coming and the Jewish establishment needed to repent (Isa. 11.8). *Fruit* refers to the result of human deeds, which is a major theme in this Gospel (7.21–23, 25.31–46). Deeds worthy of repentance are those that reflect a lifestyle that has turned from sin to God.

3.9 and do not think to say to yourselves, "We have Abraham as *our* father.' For I say to you that God is able to raise up children to Abraham from these stones.

Anticipating a counter, John challenges "the popular assumption that descent from Abraham guaranteed one a share in the blessings promised to Abraham" (Gardner, 62; Jn. 8.39). The true children of Abraham are those who share Abraham's faith rather than his blood (Rom. 4.12ff, Gal. 3.7,9).[10]

---

[9] In contrast to the wealthy Sadducees, the Pharisees typically were blue-collar workers who supported themselves by common labor. Hillel was a woodcutter; Shammai was a builder; Saul of Tarsus was a tentmaker.

[10] Those whose faith rests on the fact that they were "raised in the church" are guilty of the

3.10 And even now the ax is laid to the root of the trees. Therefore every tree which does not bear good fruit is cut down and thrown into the fire.
Continuing the metaphor of a fruit tree, John announces that God will cull the unfruitful—impenitent—Jews from His orchard and cast them into the fire of judgment (7.19; Rom. 11.7–24).

3.11 I indeed baptize you with water unto repentance, but He who is coming after me is mightier than I, whose sandals I am not worthy to carry. He will baptize you with the Holy Spirit and fire.
Luke 3.15 says the people were wondering whether John was the Messiah. He answers their musing by contrasting his and the Messiah's baptism and position—he baptized with water unto repentance,[11] but the Messiah would baptize with the Holy Spirit and fire.

Excursus on the Baptism of the Holy Spirit
In the NT, only six passages mention *Holy Spirit baptism*. In the four Gospel references (here, Mk. 1.8; Lk. 3.16; Jn. 1.33) John is the speaker. Jesus refers to it in Acts 1.5, and Peter references it in Acts 11.16. From these texts, two facts should be noted. First, Christ is the One who baptizes with the Holy Spirit. Second, Holy Spirit baptism was a group baptism (in *he will baptize you*, you is pl.).[12] In Acts 1.5, Christ tells the apostles that they would be baptized with the Holy Spirit to equip them as His witnesses under the Great Commission (Acts 1.8; Jn. 14.16–18,26, 15.26, 16.7–8,13–14). In Acts 2.1–4, the apostles were baptized (immersed, overwhelmed) in the Spirit (Lk. 24.47–49), and four things marked the event: first, no human agent administered the baptism—the unseen baptizer was Christ; second, audible and visual phenomena occurred (2.2–3); third, it was a group baptism experienced by all the apostles simultaneously (2.4); and fourth, the apostles miraculously spoke the languages of the nations represented in the audience (2.6–11). In Acts 10, the household of Cornelius was involved in

---

same mistake made by the Jews regarding their descent from Abraham.

[11] *Unto* (*eis*) generally denotes purpose (with a view to), but here it has a causal use. See 12.41 where Jonah's preaching was the cause (*eis*) of Nineveh's repentance. "Did John baptize that they might repent, or because of repentance? If the former, we have no further Scriptural confirmation of it. If the latter, his practice was confirmed and followed by the apostles, and is in full harmony with Christ's demand for inward, genuine righteousness" (Dana and Mantey, 104).

[12] "John speaks as if the Holy Spirit was to be as general under Christ as baptism in water was under his own ministry. But a prediction is best understood in the light of its fulfillment; and it is a fact that the apostles on Pentecost, and the household of Cornelius, are the only persons said in the New Testament to have received his baptism" (McGarvey, 38).

the second, and final, instance of Holy Spirit baptism. Peter summarized the incident this way: as he began to speak to Cornelius and his household, the Holy Spirit fell on his listeners as He had fallen on the apostles in Acts 2. When this happened, he remembered what the Lord said in Acts 1 about the baptism of the Holy Spirit. Peter interpreted the baptism of Cornelius and his family in the Holy Spirit as signifying that Gentiles were worthy to be baptized in water for the remission of sins. So convinced was he of this that he concluded to not baptize Cornelius's household into Christ (because they were Gentiles) would have been to withstand God. As in Acts 2, the baptism in Acts 10 was direct, with no intermediary doing the baptizing (11.17); it was a group experience (l0.44); and those baptized spoke in tongues (l0.46). Unlike Acts 2, there were no visible tongues like fire.

Whereas the apostles' baptism equipped them to preach the gospel, Cornelius's baptism showed that Gentiles should hear and obey the gospel (Acts 10.15). No one was ever commanded to be baptized in the Holy Spirit; it was a promise—fulfilled in Acts 2 and 10—that made possible the fulfillment of the Abrahamic promise of universal blessing (1.1).[13]

What is the baptism with *fire*? Given that a single preposition governs both nouns (*en pneumatic kai puri*), many believe that a single baptism is in view (the *fire* being figuratively understood as referring to the purifying work of the Spirit). It seems to me, however, that John speaks of two separate events. Note that in v 10, *fire* destroys unfruitful trees, and in v 12 it consumes chaff, which suggests judgment (7.19, 13.40,42,50, 18.9). By the baptism of the Spirit, grace flowed that could bring salvation; to resist this grace and remain in sin would invite judgment.

The religious establishment was impressed with John, but John was impressed with the One to come. The difference between the Christ and himself was so stark that he felt unworthy to even carry His sandals—the task of the lowliest slave.

3.12 His winnowing fan *is* in His hand, and He will thoroughly clean out His threshing floor, and gather His wheat into the barn; but He will burn up the chaff with unquenchable fire."

---

[13] "While the baptism in the Spirit, then, was actually confined to these two groups of persons, the benefits resulting from it extended to all. The benefit of this baptism in the house of Cornelius was the admission of all Gentile converts into the church on an equality with the Jews; and the benefit of that on Pentecost was to extend the blessed fruits of plenary inspiration to all disciples, both Jews and Gentiles" (McGarvey, 38).

These words expand the theme of judgment by picturing Christ as a farmer who uses a winnowing fork to toss grain into the air so that the wind can blow away the chaff (husks, straw; a metaphor for that which is worthless). *Thoroughly* (*diakatharizō*, only here in the NT) indicates a complete cleaning of the threshing floor (*halon*, only here and Lk. 3.17). The grain (the penitent) will be gathered into the barn (kingdom), but the chaff (the impenitent) will be burned with *unquenchable fire* (*asbestos*). Judgment is thus found near the beginning and end of this Gospel — John's preaching of judgment (vv 7–11) is enforced by Christ's picture of judgment (25.31–46). If we will not be purified by Christ, we will be purged by Christ (21.44).

JESUS THE CHRIST, 3.13–17

Notes
Matthew uses the same phrase to introduce Jesus that he used to introduce John: *John the Baptist came … Jesus came.*

3.13 Then Jesus came from Galilee to John at the Jordan to be baptized by him.

Then, while John was preaching and baptizing, Jesus (being about thirty years old, Lk. 2.23) came from Galilee (2.23) to be baptized by John (Acts 1.21–22).

3.14 And John *tried to* prevent Him, saying, "I need to be baptized by You, and are You coming to me?"

When John looked at Jesus, he saw no trace of sin, and this caused him to balk at the Lord's request. *Prevent* translates an imperfect tense that indicates continuous action — John repeatedly tried to dissuade Jesus from being baptized. Recognizing the *mightierness* of Jesus (v 11; Matthew doesn't tell us how John knew of Christ's sterling character), John thought it inappropriate that he should baptize Him; if anything, Jesus should baptize him. *The lesser is blessed by the better* (Heb. 7.7).

3.15 But Jesus answered and said to him, "Permit *it to be so* now, for thus it is fitting for us to fulfill all righteousness." Then he allowed Him.

In His first words, Jesus states a major theme of this Gospel, insisting that John, despite his misgivings, baptize Him, for such is necessary to *fulfill all righteousness.* Others came to John confessing sin; Jesus came to fulfill all righteousness.

This phrase occurs nowhere else in the NT. *Fulfill* means to realize, to attain. In the Epistles, *righteousness* often (but not always) refers to what God does when He justifies a sinner (Rom. 1.17). Justification, said David, involves forgiving iniquities, covering sin, not imputing sin (Ps. 32.1–2; Rom. 4.7–8); when God declares one righteous, He ascribes neither the *act of sin* nor the *penalty of sin* to the sinner—it is a restoration of innocence such that the individual is no longer under sin's condemnation (Rom. 8.1).

In Matthew, however, righteousness tends to have a different nuance. The basic meaning of *dikaiosunē* is *conformity to the relevant norm*, and Matthew uses this term as a synonym for *obedience*. In the Epistles, *righteousness* is usually something God does for man, but in Matthew, it is something man does for God. For all practical purposes, *righteousness*, in Matthew, means *obedience* to the will of God (5.20; Jas. 1.20).

Obedience unleashes powerful forces that uphold and sustain God's rule in this world. "The little town on the seven hills," wrote Edith Hamilton, "conquered the other little towns around her, because her citizens could obey orders" (*The Roman Way*, 197). It is through obedient followers that Christ goes out to conquer.

All includes every part of God's will (4.4, *every* word that proceeds from the mouth of God; 28.20, observe *all* things that I have commanded; also 5.17–19). Jesus presented Himself to be baptized because it was God's will that He do so. Why He had to undergo something meant for sinners isn't stated, but the likeliest explanation is that it related to His identification with sinners (Lev. 16.21–22). By His baptism, Christ laid aside His divine dignity and pledged His solidarity with sinners. To save His people (1.21), He had to be *numbered with the transgressors* (Isa. 53.11–12; Heb. 2.11). "Jesus might well have been up there in front standing with John and calling on sinners to repent. Instead he was down there with the sinners, affirming his solidarity with them, making himself one with them in the process of the salvation that he would in due course accomplish" (Morris 65).

The emphasis here is Christ's obedience to God even when, from a human perspective, it was humiliating. Jesus is unique, not just because He is God, but because of His unfailing obedience as a man to the will of God, even when it involved ignominy, suffering, and sorrow. It is Christ's obedience that Satan attacks in the next chapter.

And well may God with the serving-folk
Cast in His dreadful lot;
Is not He too a servant,
And is not he forgot?
G. K. Chesterton
The Ballad of the White Horse, IV.85–88

3.16 When He had been baptized, Jesus came up immediately from the water; and behold, the heavens were opened to Him, and He saw the Spirit of God descending like a dove and alighting upon Him.

The heavens were opened is a formula sometimes used to introduce visions of God (Eze. 1.1; Acts 7.56; Rev. 19.11), but here it describes something empirically visible. Commentators are divided on the manner of the Holy Spirit's descent. Some believe that the Spirit appeared looking like a dove. This seems the case in Luke 3.22, where *like a dove* is an adjectival phrase modifying *bodily form*. But in this text and in John 1.32, *like a dove* is an adverbial phrase modifying *descending*. (Mark's account is ambiguous; *dove* is positioned between the noun *Spirit* and the verb *descending*, 1.10.) The question, then, is whether we allow Luke to explain Matthew, Mark, and John or allow Matthew and John to explain Mark and Luke.

If the Spirit appeared as a bird, this is the only time in Scripture where deity was incarnate in animal form; and if the Spirit looked like a dove, might not some have mistaken Him for a tame bird?[14] I think it more likely that the Spirit appeared in human or angelic form (as God had previously appeared to men, Gen. 18.1–2, 34.28, 48.16), and that His descent resembled the fluttering motion characteristic of doves when they alight (cf. Gen. 1.2 where the Spirit *hovered*, a verb used of birds).

3.17 And suddenly a voice *came* from heaven, saying, "This is My beloved Son, in whom I am well pleased."

After the Spirit's descent, the Father spoke from heaven to declare that He who stooped so low for love's sake was His beloved Son (17.5). This is the first of three times during Christ's life when God audibly spoke from heaven (17.5; Jn. 12.27–30). All Jesus had done to this point was well pleasing to the Father, because He had lived in perfect obedience to His

---

[14] During my childhood, we had a pet crow named Blackie. In time, Blackie flew off. But one day when a flock of crows came over, dad yelled, "Blackie!"—and out from the flock spiraled our crow who landed just a step away from us.

Father's will, which included His baptism. *Son* doesn't describe the *divine nature* of the second person of the Godhead but is a functional term that refers to the role Christ assumed in the redemption of men.

At the start of Christ's public ministry, therefore, His chief quality — which we encounter throughout Matthew — is His absolute obedience to God.[15]

---

[15] Note the witness in the baptismal scene to the triune God.

CHAPTER 4

Notes

After their *baptism* during the Exodus (1 Cor. 10.2), Israel was led by God into the wilderness in order to humble them, test their character, and find out whether or not they would obey His commandments. To this end, God allowed them to go hungry (Ex. 16.1ff; Deut. 8.2–3). "What he wanted was for them to respond nobly, gallantly, but the Wilderness ... became a token of their unbelief. ... Israel's Messiah, Jesus of Nazareth, came to represent Israel (and consequently, humanity at large) and endured a Wilderness experience" (McGuiggan, *Heading Home with* God, 139). I think this is the perspective from which to view the wilderness experience of Jesus. In His temptation (vv 1–11), He did all that Israel was supposed to do and didn't. How Jesus responded in the wilderness was how God wanted Israel to respond. It is how He wants us to respond.

The temptation of Jesus has played a central role in every discussion of the paradox involved in Christ's nature. Was His temptation like ours? Was there a genuine appeal from outside Himself, involving real desire, to which He had the power of yielding or resisting? If the answer is no— if His temptation was like a lighted match falling on ice—then Christ's humanity was different from ours. If He didn't sin because He couldn't sin, the difference between Him and us is not a *superiority* of the same nature, but a genuine *difference* in nature, and He is not bone of our bones or flesh of our flesh. If Christ wasn't like us, His encounters with Satan were sham battles in which the bullets fired at Him were blanks, and the outcome could not have been other than it was.

These lines from Dorothy Sayers incisively frame the issue: "The central dogma of the Incarnation is that by which relevance stands or falls. If Christ were only man, then he is entirely irrelevant to any thought about God; if he is only God, then he is entirely irrelevant to any experience of human life. It is, in the strictest sense, necessary to the salvation of relevance that a man should believe rightly the Incarnation of Our Lord, Jesus Christ. Unless he believes rightly, there is not the faintest reason why he should believe at all" ("Creed or Chaos," *Letters to a Diminished Church*, 54).

Christ's temptation is significant precisely because He ss huiman as are we. Nothing divine or human was foreign to Him. He overcame not because He was invulnerable but because He was strong. His perfection of character came not from His inability to sin but from His determination to conquer. For this reason, the account of His temptation—indeed, the entire Gospel of Matthew—is not simply a *source* for Christ's life but a *resource* for Christ- ians. By seeing how He dealt with temptation, we learn how to deal with temptation.

Theological liberals tend to downplay the deity of Jesus, theological conservatives weaken His humanity. But as the God-man, Jesus istotally unique, and we must take caution not to stress one aspect of His nature over the other. Whenever we attempt to explain a paradox, we invariably end up denying one aspect of it. The nature of Jesus is a paradox, and like all Biblical paradoxes, it is best believed rather than explained.[1]

Excursus on the Wilderness

Walter Brueggemann's book *The Land* offers a remarkable insight into the spiritual significance of the *wilderness*. "The Old Testament," wrote Brueggemann, "was not all about 'deeds,' but was concerned with *place*, specific real estate that was invested with powerful *promises* … Once I had seen that much, then it was a ready development to see the dialectic in Israel's fortunes between landlessness (wilderness, exile) and *landedness*." Figurately, *land* is the place of blessing and the *wilderness* is a reminder of the curse. Thus, it is highly significant that the first thing after Christ's baptism involves an incident in the *wilderness*; He who came to undo sin's curse is driven by the Spirit to an area that symbolized the curse. There, Israel's Messiah succeeds where Israel failed; There, the Christ displays the trust and obedience God sought from the nation. Christ's wilderness victory at the start of His ministry heralded the later victory He would achieve at the end of His ministry, at a desolate place called Golgotha.

---

[1] "Bad religion answers the unanswerable; good religion cherishes the mystery" (Martin Dalby, BBC).

TEMPTATION, 4.1–11

4.1 Then Jesus was led up by the Spirit into the wilderness to be tempted by the devil.

The Spirit who descended on Jesus at the Jordan (3.16) now leads Him into another part of the wilderness *to be tempted of the devil*. *Led up* is a topographical reference that indicates the mountain wilderness west of the Jordan. Satan was the agent of temptation, but the initiative was God's. Christ wasn't cornered by the devil but was deliberately placed in harm's way. The tempter is called the *devil* (*diabolos*, slanderer, accuser), and his approach to Jesus reveals the reason behind his name.

4.2 And when He had fasted forty days and forty nights, afterward He was hungry.

When He had fasted forty days and forty nights contains an insight that can be traced through the Gospel: whenever Satan mounts an attack against Christ, God stacks the deck in the devil's favor.[2] Satan is never bested by Christ because he (Satan) was having a bad day. Even in encounters when it seems hell has won, hell loses; in every combat, Christ shows that He is stronger than the devil (12.29; 1 Jn. 3.8).

Three times Jesus is approached, and each time Satan's strategy is different. The first temptation appeals to the physical; after having gone forty days without eating, Satan sees a target of opportunity in Christ's hunger.

Three other forty-day fasts are mentioned in Scripture: one by Moses atop Sinai (Ex. 34.28; Deut. 9.9,18), one by Elijah on his way to Sinai (1 Kgs. 19.8), and this one by Christ before going to a mountain where He reveals a new covenant (chs 5–7). If the Lord can resist temptation with all odds against Him, it only enhances His value as our example.

4.3 Now when the tempter came to Him, he said, "If You are the Son of God, command that these stones become bread."

The insidiousness of the first temptation was its reasonableness. *If thou be*

---

[2] One of the best examples of this is the contest between Elijah and the prophets of Baal atop Mt. Carmel (1 Kgs. 18). Elijah's challenge that *the God who answers by fire, let Him be God* is acceptable to the Baal prophets because Baal was the god of fire (lighting), and if there's one thing a fire god out to be able to do, it's light a fire. After Baal's failure to do so, Elijah further stacks the deck against Jehovah by ordered that his sacrifice, wood, and altar be drenched with water. But still *the fire of the* LORD FELL AND CONSUMED THE BURNT SACRIFICE, AND THE WOOD AND THE STONES AND THE DUST, AND IT LICKED UP THE WATER THAT WAS IN THE TRENCH.

the Son of God doesn't doubt Jesus' deity (3.17; this wasn't the first time Jesus and Satan had met); the devil knew full well who Christ was.[3] The devil's point is that *because* Jesus is the Son of God, there's no reason for Him to be hungry. Didn't the Baptist say that God could turn stones into bread (3.9)? And wouldn't Jesus later use His divine power to feed thousands (14.15–23, 15.32–38)? If He could this for others, why not for Himself? Why be hungry if you have the ability to fix yourself something to eat?

The reasonableness of the suggestion (fix yourself something to eat),[4] the intensity of the hunger (which can cause a man to sell his birthright, Gen. 25.29–34; Heb. 12.16), and the ease of a solution (changing stones to bread was no harder for Christ than changing water to wine) added up to a potent temptation.

4.4 But He answered and said, "It is written, 'Man shall not live by bread alone, but by every word that proceeds from the mouth of God.'"

Unfortunately for Satan, he was tempting someone who valued a bread greater than physical bread. Physical bread can *sustain* life, but He who identified Himself as *the bread of God* (Jn. 6) was committed to the bread that *gives* life—eternal life. Christ's bread/food was to do the will of God (Jn. 4.34).

Accordingly, Jesus appeals to the word of God, which is where the will of God is found. *It is written* (*gegraptai*) is perfect tense and means, *it is written and stands written* (4.7,10). Christ considered Deuteronomy 8.3 as relevant for Him as it was the day Moses wrote it (if our ability to resist temptation depended on our knowledge of Deuteronomy, how would we do?). Jesus said that He *always did those things that please the Father* (Jn. 8.29), and to find out what pleased God in this situation, He went to His Father's word and found instruction applicable to His situation. Jesus was hungry because God had led Him to a place of hunger (v 1); but believing that God knew what He was doing, and believing that God was a Father who wouldn't mock Him with stones when He needed bread (7.9), and believing that to obey is better than to eat, Christ waited for His Father to meet His needs in the Father's own time. If He used His divine power to relieve His hunger, might He not do the same to escape more desperate

---

[3] The devil's question was a first-class conditional statement, which assumes the truth of the condition stated.

[4] "The more cunningly the sinfulness of a wrong act is disguised, the more easily are we induced to commit it" (McGarvey, 41).

situations that loomed ahead? At the end of the story, Christ will hear the taunt *He saved others; Himself He cannot save* (Mk. 15.31); and though He fed others, Himself He would not feed, but will wait on His Father to deliver Him from hunger … and death.

In life, temptation is the germ, and sin is the disease. Everyone is constantly exposed to germs, but not everyone gets sick, for some have an immune system that is stronger than the germs; a good immune system is worth a case of disinfectant. We sin not because temptation is strong, but because we are weak. To strengthen ourselves to where we can resist, God's word must be in our heart (1 Jn. 2.14; Ps. 119.11).

When dealing with Satan, it's important to have an applicable text. Deuteronomy 8.3 was meant to guide Israel in a wilderness place where food was scarce. Having promised to provide for His people, the Lord wanted to see if Israel would keep faith when they didn't see how He could keep His promise. Israel failed; Jesus didn't.

This first temptation anticipates the cross: led by God into a situation of danger, Jesus held to His Father's will and refused to spare Himself by calling on heavenly deliverance (26.53–54), trusting totally in God (6.13; Jn. 12.27–28).

4.5 Then the devil took Him up into the holy city, set Him on the pinnacle of the temple,

The second temptation shifts from physical to spiritual and from wilderness to *city* (Jerusalem, 27.53; Lk. 4.9), specifically, a *pinnacle of the temple* (*pterugion,* wing, the tip or extremity of anything) from which a fall would be fatal.[5] Whereas the strength of the first temptation was its reasonableness, the strength of the second was its scripturalness.

4.6 and said to Him, "If You are the Son of God, throw Yourself down. For it is written: 'He shall give His angels charge over you,' and, 'In *their* hands they shall bear you up, lest you dash your foot against a stone.'"

Satan turns Christ's weapon against Him. "So, you intend to live by what *is written*? Well, if it's Scripture you want, I'll give you Scripture. *It is written* in Psalm 91.11–12 that God will *give his angels charge concerning you*. If you really believe this, demonstrate it by jumping off the temple." Whereas the first temptation sought to create doubt in God, the second requests

---

[5] Several places fit this description; the southeast corner of Solomon's Porch, for instance, offered a drop of over 500 feet.

a demonstration of faith. When our belief is questioned, we sometimes foolishly leap before we look, and maybe Satan hoped to exploit this human foible. As with the first temptation, this one also anticipates the cross by asking for a demonstration that would undeniably reveal divine power (27.40).

4.7 Jesus said to him, "It is written again, 'You shall not tempt the LORD your God.'"

The second temptation is unique in that it is the only time in the Bible when Satan quotes Scripture. But Christ's, *it is written again*, shows that the devil misused what he quoted. Prefacing Deuteronomy 6.16 with *again*, Jesus stresses the *harmony* of revelation. God's word is not *Yes* and *No* (2 Cor. 1.18), it's only *Yes!* It doesn't contradict itself; it doesn't promote sin. By taking the totality of God's revelation (v 4), Jesus saw as sin what Satan portrayed as trust. In his use of Psalm 91, Satan mishandled Scripture about every way it can be mishandled: by making the figurative literal, the conditional unconditional, and by not taking into account everything the Bible has to say about jumping off a building (Ps. 119.160). A logician would characterize Satan's argument as *the fallacy of the general rule*, wherein a general rule (God's care of the righteous) is applied to a particular case that differs from cases to which the general rule applies—there is a vast difference between accidentally stumbling and deliberately jumping. By mischaracterizing the stumbling in Psalm 91 as jumping, Satan encouraged Christ to *tempt* God under the guise of *trusting* God. Tempting God is an act of unbelief, an act of presumption that expects God to prove Himself after He has already proven Himself (12.38–42; Acts 14.17). If we refuse to trust God after the abundant reasons He has provided for doing so, it's because we are wicked and depraved, not because more proof is needed (16.1–4).[6]

4.8 Again, the devil took Him up on an exceedingly high mountain, and showed Him all the kingdoms of the world and their glory.

Since the curvature of the earth makes it impossible for the eye to view the entire globe, *showed Him all the kingdoms of the world and their glory* may have been accomplished through rhetorical dscription (Gal. 3.1; the

---

[6] "Every false teacher who has divided the Church, has had an 'it is written' on which to hang his doctrine" (Morgan, *The Crises of the Christ*, 182). Just because a sermon contains Scripture doesn't mean it declares truth.

forest is often better seen with the mind than with the eye[7]), geographical synecdoche (Jer. 34.2), or supernatural vision (Lk. 4.5; Eze. 40.2). *Mountain* is a significant term in Matthew (5.1, 17.1, 28.16); used as a figure, it can refer to rule or government (Rev. 8.8). Attempting to destroy Christ's *mountain* (Isa. 2.2–3), Satan sought Christ's worship atop a mountain.

4.9 And he said to Him, "All these things I will give You if You will fall down and worship me."

The subtlety of the previous temptations disappears and—possibly in an act of desperation— the devil offers an undisguised deal. In exchange for a single act of worship, he offers Christ the world, thus placing before Him the path of least resistance. *Fall down* and *worship* are both aorist, indicating a single act of falling and worshipping—which Jesus is asked to do just once. How much misery has this world seen because Satan has convinced people that they could get away with something just once?

4.10 Then Jesus said to him, "Away with you, Satan! For it is written, "You shall worship the LORD your God, and Him only you shall serve."'

"There was no short cut to the kingdom. It could only be won by love that knew no limit" (Donald Hankey, *The Lord of All Good Life*, 26). Christ will not take an evil means to a good end. He will not bow to him for a second, even though it means He must die on a cross. By *Away with you!* (*hupagō*, 8.32), He orders Satan from His presence. This will not be the last time Satan poses these temptations, nor will it be the last time Christ tells Satan to leave (16.22–23).

Deuteronomy 6.13—which summarized the first (and primary) commandment given Israel (Ex. 20.2–3; Deut. 5.7–8)—is the text Christ quotes. On *worship*, see 2.2. *Serve* (*latreuō*; translated *worship* in Acts 24.14; Phil. 3.3) refers to religious or priestly service (Heb. 9.9). Though here it is virtually synonymous with *proskuneō* (2.2, *worship*), it enlarges our understanding of worship by showing that true worship involves more than public ritual on holy days.

---

[7] In crossing the Alps, the morale of Hannibal's army was low due to the mountains and the cold. To encourage his men, Hannibal gave a rousing speech, pointing toward the Lombard plain, assuring his troops of the loot and glory that awaited. "The ability to view the northern Italian plain is one of the many criteria used by scholars to decide which Alpine pass Hannibal actually used, although we cannot be sure whether such a view was literally visible, or conjured in the men's minds by their general's words" (Adrian Goldsworthy, *The Fall of Carthage*, 165).

4.11 Then the devil left Him, and behold, angels came and ministered to Him.

What began with heavenly leading (v 1) ends with heavenly care as angels arrive to serve Christ. The devil leaves to lick his wounds, but he will return again. "One victory never guarantees freedom from further temptation. If anything, each victory we experience only makes Satan try harder" (Wiersbe, 28).

LIGHT, 4.12–16

Notes

Matthew's prologue ends with Jesus returning to Galilee, thus supplying a bookend for what follows: the redemptive work that began in Galilee would end in Galilee (28.16–20). Between vv 11 and 12 is a gap of several months during which most of the events mentioned in John 1.29 to 4.42 occur.

4.12 Now when Jesus heard that John had been put in prison, He departed to Galilee.

Had been put in translates *paradidōmi*, which means to *deliver up*, a term that will be prominent in the passion section of the Gospel. Jesus isn't running scared or attempting to get beyond the reach of Herod Antipas (who imprisoned John and ordered his death, 14.1–12), for Antipas also governed Galilee (2.22). He who had just gone head-to-head with the devil wasn't afraid of a fifth-rate politician. Matthew is simply indicating that Christ began His publicwork about the time John *finished his race* (2 Tim. 4.7).[8]

Judea, Samaria, Perea, Decapolis, and Galilee were the five provinces that occupied the territory of ancient Israel.[9] Galilee was the northernmost, bounded on the east by the Jordan and the Sea of Galilee, on the west by Phoenicia, on the north by Syria, and on the south by Samaria. It was approximately forty-five miles from north to south, twenty-five miles from east to west, and was the most densely populated province in the area.

---

[8] *Galilee* comes from *Galil*, "a circle or circuit, originally confined to a 'circle' of 20 cities given by Solomon to Hiram, 1 Kings ix.11. Cp. Josh. Xx.7 and Josh. Viii.2 (where the Vulgate reads Galilaea Philistim, 'the circle' or 'district' of the Philistines). From this small beginning the name spread to a larger district" (Carr, 107).

[9] *Palestine* was not used as a name for the territory of ancient Israel until the second century AD.

4.13 And leaving Nazareth, He came and dwelt in Capernaum, which is by the sea, in the regions of Zebulun and Naphtali,

Jesus visits His hometown of Nazareth, but after being rejected there (Lk. 4.16–30) goes to Capernaum. *Capernaum* (village of Nahum, mentioned sixteen times in the Gospels) was the commercial capital of Galilee. Located on the northwestern shore of the Sea of Galilee (modern Tell Hum), it straddled the main trade route between Jerusalem and Damascus. It was a fishing port (4.18–22), and, because of its proximity to a political boundary, had a Roman military presence (8.5–8) and customs post (9.9). As the headquarters of Christ's work in the district, it became known as His *own city* (9.1).

4.14–16 that it might be fulfilled which was spoken by Isaiah the prophet, saying: "The land of Zebulun and the land of Naphtali, By the way of the sea, beyond the Jordan, Galilee of the Gentiles: The people who sat in darkness have seen a great light, and upon those who sat in the region and shadow of death Light has dawned."

The quotation from Isaiah 9.1–2 (the seventh prophecy quoted in Matthew) contains five geographical references to the area (*the way of the sea* and *beyond Jordan* should be understood from the Assyrian perspective, from the east side of the Jordan). Situated on Israel's northern boundary, the region had borne the brunt of foreign invasion. Because of its proximity to Gentile territory, Galilee had a large Gentile population and had become an ethnic melting pot. Many Judean Jews were embarrassed by their country cousins in Galilee and referred to the region by the disparaging expression Galilee *of the Gentiles* (Jn. 7.40–42,52). Politically, spiritually, and culturally, the region was stigmatized as being *in the dark*. Isaiah, however, said that those in darkness would see *a great light*—namely, Christ (v 18). Matthew's use of Isaiah 9.1–2 is his counterpart to John's *light shining in the darkness* (Jn. 1.5). Since Jesus came to call sinners to repentance (9.13), what better place to begin than in an area noted for its sinning?[10] Christ shone light (5.16) where light was needed. The implications of *Galilee* remind us that *Jesus came to save His people from their sins* (1.21).

---

[10] Which recalls the line attributed to bank robber Willie Sutton. When asked why he robbed banks, he is reported to have said, "Because that's where the money is."

4.17–27.66: The Life of Christ

    4.17–16.12: God Reveals the Christ

       4.17–25: The Gospel of the Kingdom: A Synopsis

CALLING DISCIPLES, 4.17–22

Notes

The main body of the book now begins by introducing three major elements in Christ's work: His preaching, calling (followers), and healings. It was a day forever noteworthy in the annals of our race when Jesus began preaching the gospel of the kingdom of God.

4.17 From that time Jesus began to preach and to say, "Repent, for the kingdom of heaven is at hand."

From that time signals the start of Christ's public ministry (Acts 10.37). His message repeated John's verbatim. Repentance (see 3.2), and all that it implies, is the indispensable condition for inclusion in God's kingdom.

4.18 And Jesus, walking by the Sea of Galilee, saw two brothers, Simon called Peter, and Andrew his brother, casting a net into the sea; for they were fishermen.

The Sea (lake) *of Galilee* was called *Chinnereth* in the OT (Deut. 3.17; 1 Kgs. 15.20), *Gennesaret* by Luke (5.1), and *Tiberias* by the Romans (Jn. 6.1, 21.1). Located in the upper reaches of the Jordan River system, its surface is 682 feet below sea level. At its longest and broadest it measures twelve miles by nine miles. That Jesus walked by the sea recalls Isaiah's prophecy about *the way of the sea* (v 15).

On the shore, Jesus sees two brothers — *Simon called Peter, and Andrew*[11] — fishing. *Net* (*amphiblēston*, only here in the NT) refers to a circular casting net that could be thrown by a single man, rather than to the large seine net (*sagēnē*) that required two or more boats to deploy (13.47; in v 20, the generic term for net, *diktuon*, is used).

4.19 Then He said to them, "Follow Me, and I will make you fishers of men."

---

[11] We know less about Andrew than we do about the others in this group of four, but this hasn't stopped those who wish to embellish the Biblical record with myth and paganism. November 30 became known as *St. Andrew's Day*, on which he is honored as the protector against gout, anthrax, magic, ghosts, and the like.

In various ways, Christ broke with Jewish custom, and one of the clearest examples of this is seen in those He called to be His disciples. He called laymen, not seminary students. His calling of fishermen was odd, His calling of a tax collector was outrageous (9.9). *Follow* (*akoloutheō*, lit., come behind me) is a key term in Matthew that appears here for the first time and introduces the concept of *discipleship*. Only once does Matthew speak of *apostles* (10.2); elsewhere, his term is *mathētēs*, which means one who *follows*.[12]

In calling men to follow Him, Jesus was calling men to be His *students*. As Matthew will show, Jesus put no real hope in the masses. Although there was always a crowd around Him, the presence of crowds was no indication of deep commitment. As John explained, *many believed in His name when they saw the signs which He did. But Jesus did not commit Himself to them, because He knew all men* (Jn. 2.23–24)—the multitudes believed in Christ, but He didn't believe in them. Instead, Christ put His faith in a small group of true believers who were insignificant by Greek and Roman standards, but who would launch a movement that would long survive Greece and Rome and which continues to this day. "The strategy of Christ," said Trueblood, "was the strategy of dependence upon the hard core" (*Confronting Christ*, 21).[13] "By saturating a little circle of chosen followers with his spirit, he made them capable of carrying on their shoulders a lost race to God" (Jefferson, *The Character of Jesus*, 121).

Jesus invites the brothers not only to follow, but to follow Him in a work similar to their vocation. They would continue to fish, only now, they would fish for men (10.5–16, 13.47–50) through evangelistic activity (10.5ff, 28.18–20).[14] By following Jesus, they would hear His message, see His miracles, witness His example, and thus be readied for their work (28.19).

4.20 They immediately left *their* nets and followed Him.

Immediately indicates a radical break in which the brothers walked away from the life they had known.

---

[12] See, e.g., 6.19–34, 8.18–27, 9.9–13, 10.9–10, 34–37, 19.16–21, 27–30.

[13] This was God's strategy in the story of Gideon (Judg. 4).

[14] "The term 'fishers of men' was not new. For centuries, Greek and Roman philosophers had used it to describe the work of the man who seeks to 'catch' others by teaching and persuasion" (Wiersbe, 30).

4.21 Going on from there, He saw two other brothers, James *the son* **of Zebedee, and John his brother, in the boat with Zebedee their father, mending their nets. He called them,**

Farther down the shore, Jesus comes upon another pair of brothers, *James* and *John*, who sometimes partnered with Peter in fishing (Lk. 5.10). *Mending* translates *katartizō*, which means to put right, put in order, restore, or make complete. It is a significant term in the NT, being used in a moral sense to describe the restoration of a backslider (Gal. 6.1), the maturing of faith (1Thes. 3.10), the perfecting of character (1 Pet. 5.10), etc.

4.22 and immediately they left the boat and their father, and followed Him.

If it was extraordinary for Peter and Andrew to walk away from their work, how much more so was it for James and John to leave their work *and father!* The absolute nature of discipleship is further discussed in 8.21–22, 10.35, and 19.27.

The final words in the calling of the first four disciples parallel each other (*immediately, left, followed Him*) and indicate that unhesitating obedience is to mark those who follow Jesus (3.15). Their call illustrates God's use of the despised things of the world to confound the wise (1 Cor. 1.27–28). When Jesus needed associates, He recruited ordinary blue-collar workers. The kingdom depends not on the brilliant or gifted, but upon those willing to surrender their all and do their utmost to follow the King.

MINISTRY, 4.23–25

Notes

Verses 23–25 serve as the heading for the section that continues to 16.12 — a general statement about Christ's preaching, teaching, and healing — that is followed in chs 5ff with specific examples of each. Verse 23, which is repeated nearly verbatim in 9.35, demarks chs 5 to 9 as a unit. Christ's preaching and teaching occupies chs 5 to 7; His healings and other miracles are featured in chs 8 to 9.

4.23 And Jesus went about all Galilee, teaching in their synagogues, preaching the gospel of the kingdom, and healing all kinds of sickness and all kinds of disease among the people.

Neither the OT, the Apocrypha, nor the NT explains the origin of the synagogue (*sunagōgē,* to gather together). General opinion holds that it came into existence during the Babylonian exile when Jews gathered for prayer and Bible study (Edersheim I, 431–432). Eventually, the place of meeting took on the name used for the act of meeting (cf. our expression, "going to church"). At synagogue services, visitors were sometimes invited to address the audience, and Christ (and later, Paul) used such opportunities to teach (Lk. 4.16–30; Acts 13.14, 14.1, 17.1, etc.).[15]

Teaching (*didaskein,* instruction) and *preaching* (*kērussein*) are virtual synonyms that refer to the verbal communication of the *gospel* (9.35, 11.1). *Gospel* (*euaggelion*) originally described a reward given a bearer of good news (2 Sam. 4.10) but eventually came to signify the good news itself.[16] In 3.2 and 4.17, preaching the gospel involved a call to repent because of the coming kingdom. Chapters 5 to 7 unpack the gospel's content.

Healing all kinds of sickness was part and parcel of the objective proof by which Jesus authenticated His message (11.2–6; Mk. 2.1–12) and revealed His character.

4.24 Then His fame went throughout all Syria; and they brought to Him all sick people who were afflicted with various diseases and torments, and those who were demon-possessed, epileptics, and paralytics; and He healed them.

There was no illness Christ couldn't cure. *All kinds of sickness, all kinds of disease, all sick people* (including those the doctors couldn't heal, Lk. 8.43) were brought to Him, and *He healed them all.* Three terms in this verse will be given greater attention by Matthew: the *demon-possessed* (8.28–34), *epileptics* (17.14–21),[17] and *paralytics* (9.1–8). Since Matthew puts Christ's teaching (chs 5–7) before Christ's healing, the implication is that the teaching isprimary and the healing secondary. But can you imagine the excitement in Syria when the word spread that there was again one in Israel who could cleanse a man of leprosy (2 Kgs. 5)?

---

[15] Possibly the most in-depth study of the synagogue is that by Israel Abrahams, *Studies in Pharisaism and the Gospels* (Cambridge: The University Press), 1917. See especially the first chapter titled "The Freedom of the Synagogue." https://archive.org/stream/cihm_66393#page/n15/mode/2up

[16] The Eng. *gospel* derives from the Anglo-Saxon *godspell,* which means either *God story* or *good story. Spell* is OE meaning to talk, announce, or discourse.

[17] *Epileptics* translates the rare word *selēniazomai,* moon-struck (17.15).

4.25 Great multitudes followed Him—from Galilee, and *from* Decapolis, Jerusalem, Judea, and beyond the Jordan.

"It is important to understand that there were no hospitals or insane asylums in ancient Israel and that the few doctors available were ignorant and expensive. People who got sick … had to be taken care of at home, by their own families. This was a difficult job, especially for poor people, who had enough trouble earning a meager living. Very few people were trained to take care of sick relatives. Sometimes taking care of someone who had become sick or insane was simply too much for a family to deal with, and the patient was forced out of his home and left to wander in the streets like an animal. When Jesus came to a town, and performed healings, without even charging any money, he must have seemed to these people like an angel from heaven. Of *course* he was mobbed!" (Mitchell, *Jesus, What He Really Said and Did*, 28).

Christ's popularity isn't surprising; the same would happen today to anyone who miraculously emptied hospitals. As the Gospels make clear, though, not all *following* rises to the level of discipleship (Lk. 14.26ff; Jn. 6.59ff). At the start of His ministry, many follow, but a winnowing process will separate the grain from the chaff (3.12) until at the end of the story, Christ is left utterly alone (27.44).

The light that dawned in Galilee (v 16) shined far beyond Galilee. From every direction—*Decapolis* (a confederacy of ten Greek cities located southeast of the Sea of Galilee), *Jerusalem, Judea*, and *beyond Jordan* (Perea)—they came.

CHAPTER 5

5.1–9.35: In Word and Work

5.1–7.29: Through Words

PROLOGUE, 5.1–16

Notes

The *Sermon on the Mount* is a representative sermon of what Christ taught when He preached the *gospel of the kingdom* (4.23). The designation *Sermon on the* Mount traces to Augustine; *sayings on the mount* (7.28) is Matthew's characterization. This is the first of five extended discourses found in Matthew (the others are in chs 10, 13, 18, 24–25), each of which ends with the words *when Jesus had finished these sayings*. Structurally, the sermon has a beginning (vv 3–16), a middle (5.17–7.12, with the Lord's Prayer at the center, 6.9–13), and an end (7.13–27). A key theme throughout is *righteousness* (5.6,10,20; 6.1,35)—which refers to "how people who have chosen to place themselves under the reign of God are to live out their lives" (Mounce, 37).

When Christ told His apostles to teach the baptized *to observe all things that I have commanded* (28.19–20), my guess is that they began their instruction with the Sermon on the Mount. There are many reasons why they would have done so, not the least of which is that the Sermon is a treatise on the greatest subject of all, for the Sermon is a lesson on love—not the shallow, selfish, fleeting emotion flaunted in culture, but the unconditional, sacrificial, full-of-mercy love found in heaven. To not see love in every verse of the Sermon is to miss the the meaning of the Sermon.

5.1 And seeing the multitudes, He went up on a mountain, and when He was seated His disciples came to Him.

More than a miracle (4.23,25), the crowds that followed Jesus needed a message.[1] Christ goes up on *a mountain* not to escape the crowd but to find

---

[1] Miracles were acts of God used to confirm the word of God (*Notes* to ch 8; Mk. 16.20,

a pulpit from which to address it. As at Sinai, so here—the appearance of God on a mountain signals a new phase in heaven's dealings with men.

Rabbis *sat* when officially teaching (23.2; Lk. 4.20; the Lat. *cathedra/ cathedral* refer to the *chair* in which a bishop or professor sat while teaching). Around Jesus were gathered two groups: *disciples* (*mathētes*, learner, pupil) and *people* (*laos*, 7.28). A *disciple* is a student who learns certain principles from a teacher and then lives those principles on the basis of the teacher's authority. Christians live as they do based on Christ's teaching and authority (7.29, 11.29; Eph. 4.20). The *people* were those who had not yet made a disciple's commitment to Jesus.

5.2 Then He opened His mouth and taught them, saying:

Opened *his mouth* is more than an elaborate way of saying *He said*; it is an idiomatic formula used in Scripture to introduce a solemn or authoritative pronouncement (Job 3.1, Acts 8.35, 10.34). *Taught* is in the imperfect tense, indicating continuous, repeated action; the Sermon on the Mount is what Christ preached everywhere to everyone.[2]

Beatitudes, 3–12

Notes

The Sermon on the Mount—with its profound exposition of love—is the heart of the gospel. Its opening—known as the *beatitudes*[3] (charmingly called *the heavenly octave* by Boreham)—reveals that Christianity is more than just thinking, doing, or praying (the three ways by which a man cooperates with God); it is more than being diligent at being dutiful. Christianity is, pre-eminently, about *being*, and specifically, about *being that is governed by love.* Nothing we do amounts to anything apart from love (1 Cor. 13.1–3). Nothing done is ever better than the heart from which it comes.

The Sermon's prologue has three parts. The first (vv 3–10) opens and closes with the phrase *kingdom of heaven* (vv 3,10), which connects

---

Heb. 2.1–4).

[2] A comparison of the Gospels reveals that Christ taught the same lessons in different settings and contexts (e.g., Matt. 23.23–35 and Lk. 11.37–42).

[3] *Beatitude* derives from *beatus*, the Latin word for happiness. *Blessed* comes from the OE *blod*, blood. To bless originally referred to that which had been consecrated or sanctified by blood. Because of its similarity to *bliss*, bless eventually assimilated its meaning and came to mean happiness or joy.

it to 4.17,23. This first section lists the qualities of being that make love possible. *Righteousness*, introduced in 3.15, is carried forward by the fourth and eighth beatitudes, and the second half of each beatitudes identifies a constituent element of the Abrahamic blessing (1.1). The second part (vv 11–12) is a postscript to the eighth beatitude, in which Christ shifts from the third to the second person. The third part (vv 13–16) features two metaphors that describe the effect of the character produced by the beatitudes. Verse 16's mention of *good works* transitions from what has preceded to what follows.

"The world has its own idea of blessedness. Blessed is the man who is always right. Blessed is the man who is satisfied with himself. Blessed is the man who is strong. Blessed is the man who rules. Blessed is the man who is rich. Blessed is the man who is popular. Blessed is the man who enjoys life. These are the beatitudes of sight and this present world. It comes with a shock and opens a new realm of thought that not one of these men entered Jesus' mind when he treated of blessedness" (Ian Maclaren).

5.3 "Blessed *are* the poor in spirit, for theirs is the kingdom of heaven.

Ask a man the one thing he wants most in life, and chances are he'll say *happiness*. But though desired and sought, happiness is rarely found, because people look for it in all the wrong places. As Christ teaches, the only way true happiness—blessing—can be had is in *being, character*. Whereas the Ten Commandments was a list of *do's* and *don'ts*, the beatitudes are a list of *is*, making blessing contingent on being. Unless a man's heart is right, he can do all the right things, abstain from all the wrong things, and still be unrighteous and unblessed.

Blessed (*makarios*) is difficult to translate. The idea that best communicates its meaning is *human flourishing*. In Homer's Greek, *makarios* described the happiness of the gods—if anyone was truly happy, surely it was the gods. In the Epistles, Paul applies *makarios* to God (1 Tim. 1.11, 6.15). Cyprus was known as the *Blessed Isle* because of its perfect climate, fertile soil, and abundant resources—Cyprus was self-contained: you didn't have to leave it to be happy. Thus is the kingdom of God; it is a self-contained entity of blessing—you don't have to look outside it to find what you need.

Blessed are the poor. The Greeks had two words for *poor*. *Penes* (penury) referred to one who had nothing extra; he had enough, but with nothing left over (Socrates used this word to describe himself). *Ptochos* (to crouch,

cower) indicated destitution, abject poverty, and is the word used here—
the one who was *penes* didn't have extra, but the one who was *ptochos*
didn't have enough (Isa. 55.1). The beggar Lazarus was *ptochos* (Lk. 16.20),
as was the widow (Mk. 12.42) and the *poor* brother in James 2.2. *Ptochos*
carried a note of shame; the Jews considered wealth a sign of divine favor
and poverty, to them, was evidence of divine displeasure (19.23–26). In
the *Republic*, Plato so disdained the poor (*ptochoi*) that he banned them
from his ideal society. It was utterly startling, therefore, when Christ
pronounced a blessing on those who were everywhere despised.

In spirit identifies the character of the poverty; it is *spiritual poverty*—
humility—that Christ describes. Barclay claims that neither the Romans nor
Greeks had a specific word for *humility*; it was Christ who coined *ptochos* to
express humility. Pride sees itself as rich, loaded with resources (Rev. 3.17),
but humility knows it is destitute, without resources (Lk. 18.10–14).

The *kingdom of heaven*—the rule of God—recalls 3.2 and 4.17 and serves
as a phrase bracketing the beatitudes (v 10). Poverty and persecution have
historically been thought evidence of God's disapproval, but humility,
says Jesus, is blessed by God. Like Alice entering Wonderland, we must
grow small before we can grow large.

5.4 Blessed *are* those who mourn, for they shall be comforted.

The world has no philosophy that comes closed to saying *blessed are those
who mourn*, for the world sees no advantage in sorrow. *Pentheō* is one of
the strongest Gr. words for mourning. It speaks of crying or wailing over
something that is breaking our heart. Mourning is often an emotional
reaction, but the mourning of which Christ speaks goes deeper than our
emotions. Emotions come and go, rise and fall, but being/character is
constant. I think *mourning* should here be understood not as an occasional
emotion but as a constant recognition of our spiritual bankruptcy due to
sin. *Blessed are those who mourn* is a natural sequel to *blessed are the poor in
spirit*; we mourn because we know we are spiritually destitute, with no
one to blame but ourselves. As long as we are humble, aware of our inner
impoverishment, we will mourn over it.

Such mourning, however, is a *good* grief for it brings comfort. *Comfort*
contains the word *fort*, which indicates a place of strength (Fort Apache,
Fort Knox). The paradox is unmistakable: mourning, because of weakness,
yields comfort, indicative of strength. On one level, mourning ceases

when comfort comes, but at the kingdom level, mourning and comfort coexist. Comfort balances mourning, but doesn't end it, for the condition that causes mourning (poor in spirit) doesn't end. But Jesus strengthens the weak. And He does so by forgiveness. Rather than damning us for our sins, He forgives our sins (Ps. 103, 2 Cor. 7.10). Even as we sorrow over our inner depravity, we are comforted in knowing what He does for us.[4] Because of Christ, they who sorrow have reason to sing.

The story of the prodigal son (Lk. 15) illustrates this. A boy spent himself into poverty (15.14) and finally realizes what he has done (15.21). Returning home (but only when he has no other option), and aware that his sins have rendered him unworthy of being his father's son, he asks only to be made a servant. To his surprise, he is given the rich blessings of a son (15.22–23). When mourning does its perfect work, comfort does its perfect work.

Though Christ uses *shall*, He isn't consigning comfort to some pie-in-the-sky future phase of the kingdom. There is, of course, a sense in which God's blessings find their perfection hereafter (v 12), but this doesn't preclude blessing now, as indicated by Christ's use of the present tense in vv 3,10 (for theirs *is* the kingdom).

5.5 Blessed *are* the meek, for they shall inherit the earth.

In contrast to poverty and mourning, *gentleness* (*praus, meekness,* KJV) was a noble ideal to the Greeks. Nowadays, meekness is synonymous with weakness, but in antiquity it was a virtue, combining the paradoxical ideas of softness and strength.[5] It was used of a horse that had been broken and whose power had been harnessed; it described Aristotle's *golden mean*, where all virtues are in balance; and it was used of a king who could have reacted with vengeance toward the conquered, but instead showed kindness ("it is excellent to have a giant's strength; but it is tyrannous to use it like a giant," Shakespeare, *Measure for Measure,* Act II, Scene 2). Meekness is self-discipline, the ability to not respond in kind (vv 10–12,39–42), to remain calm despite provocation — "keeping your head when all about you are losing theirs, and blaming it on you."

The outstanding example of meekness in the OT was Moses (Num.

---

[4] In the Mary Poppins' story, "The Marble Boy," P. L. Travers writes a humorous scene in which a park keeper, falsely accused of stealing a statue, is told, "You might as well confess. ... It won't save you, of course, ... but you'll *feel* so much better!" Sinners aren't comforted by mere confession, but by knowing that God has forgiven their sin.

[5] The Eng. *meek* derives from the Gothic *muka,* soft.

12.3), who led a selfish, spoiled, ungrateful, complaining, and slandering people for forty years. But for one costly exception (Num. 20.12), he kept his poise in the face of constant irritation (cf. David's response to Shimei, 2 Sam. 16.5–10).

The outstanding example of meekness in the NT, of course, is Jesus (11.28–30). Did anyone endure more personal attacks than He? He was slighted for being a Nazarene (2.23), castigated as a bastard (Jn. 8.41), characterized as an agent of the devil (12.24), called a Samaritan, labelled insane (Jn. 8.48), accused of blasphemy, spied upon around the clock—and never once lost control (v 39).

Shall inherit the earth comes from Psalm 37. The phrase is a Hebraism (idiom) that speaks of blessing in contrast to cursing. It the fate of the wicked, who will be cut down and cut off from the goodness and bounty of the land (Ps. 37.2), with that of the meek, who will fully possess and occupy the land, enjoying every blessing God has placed in it (Ps. 84.11). They who best themselves will have the best God gives (19.29).

5.6 Blessed *are* those who hunger and thirst for righteousness, for they shall be filled.

Barclay reminds that it takes more than a dictionary to define a word; once a word is part of our experience, we define it by our experience. *Hunger* doesn't mean to me what it meant to a prisoner in Auschwitz, for there has never been a moment in my life when I didn't have plenty of food and water. But in biblical times, food and water could be hard to come by (4.1–2). *Hunger* and *thirst* here refer to more than a hunger pang or normal thirst—they indicate extreme, intense craving.[6] The hungry and thirsty don't talk about eating and drinking; they eat and drink; people who only talk about eating and drinking aren't really hungry or thirsty. To hunger and thirst after righteousness means that every man can do right if he wants to do right badly enough. Two examples in ch 19 illustrate this: the *rich, young ruler* talked about eating and drinking, but his hunger and thirst for righteousness fell far short of the level indicated by this beatitude; but the disciples, who left all (family, job, etc.) to follow Jesus, possessed kingdom-worthy desire.

As noted previously, each half of the beatitudes (vv 6,10) ends with *righteousness* (3.15). And as vv 20ff show, kingdom righteousness makes

---

[6] Luz notes that in Jewish and Hellenistic texts, hunger and thirst are sometimes used with the meaning *to exert oneself for* (I, 197–198).

demands that can involve discomfort, embarrassment, and suffering for those who follow Christ.

They who desire righteousness—Christ's way of living—will be *filled* (*chortazō*). This word originally referred to the fattening of animals but came to describe the meeting of human need (14.20). God's promises aren't empty platitudes—*He who comes to Me shall never hunger and never thirst* (Jn. 6.35).

5.7 Blessed *are* the merciful, for they shall obtain mercy.

Nemesis, the Gr. goddess of retribution, saw to it that the wicked got what was coming to them, but *mercy* characterizes the God of the Bible—He doesn't give sinners what they deserve (Ps. 103.110; Ez. 9.13). *The* Lord *is longsuffering and abundant in mercy, forgiving iniquity and transgression. ... Pardon the iniquity of this people, I pray, according to the greatness of Your mercy* (Num. 14.18–19). Moses didn't plead for God to show mercy to Israel because Israel deserved it; he pled for God to be merciful because merciful is what God is.

What characterizes God must characterize His people, especially when it comes to mercy. In the judgment scene of 25.34–40, the only thing considered is the quality of one's mercy. Mercy—compassion—is that aspect of love that is unable to walk away from another's hurt (even if self-inflicted, 18.27). We cannot be without it and be right with the God who can forgive anything except an unmerciful heart (Jas. 2.13). Although being merciful doesn't earn mercy, being merciless will cost us mercy. If mercy is to find us, we must find it.

5.8 Blessed *are* the pure in heart, for they shall see God.

One of the major debates Christ had with the Jews was over what made a man clean or unclean before God (15.1–20). Jesus taught that cleanness (purity) is inward, not determined by what goes into a man. What goes into a man is material and temporal; what comes out reveals the spiritual disposition of the true man. The Pharisees believed defilement was due to external considerations, and in this, they were wrong.

In many ways, this is the most daunting of the beatitudes, for we know how bankrupt we are (v 3) and how dirty we are (Zech. 3.3, Jas. 2.21; are we right to think that not even the angels around the throne are pure has God is pure, Job 4.18?). *Pure* had a variety of applications in the first century, being used of unsoiled clothes, unblemished animals, and unalloyed silver and gold (it was even used of proper grammar; a *pure* grammarian wouldn't say *ain't*). The word did have an external application, referring to the ritual purity a priest needed to enter the temple or presence of God (23.25–28).

Christ locates purity inwardly, *in the heart*. His followers are transparent, clean externally (in their doing) because they are clean essentially. A dirty heart is one overtaken by sin (15.19; Jas. 1.21); and the only thing that can remove the stain of sin is the blood of the Lamb (1 Pet., 3.21; Rev. 1.5).

See means to gaze "with wide-open eyes, as at something remarkable" (Strong). The invisible God can be seen (Jn. 1.18, 14.9; 1 Cor. 13.12), but sin dims sight; to clear the eye, we must cleanse the heart.[7]

5.9 Blessed *are* the peacemakers, for they shall be called sons of God.
The wisdom that is from above is first pure, then peaceable (Jas. 3.17).

Seven centuries before Christ, Numa Pompilius, the second king of Rome, built the Temple of Janus to honor the two-faced god who looked to the past and future. Curiously, Pompilius decreed that the doors to the temple be shut during times of peace and opened only during times of war. Over the next 700 years, the doors were shut on just three occasions: during Numa's reign, after the first Punic War, and during the reign of Augustus—which shows that peace is hard to come by.

Biblically, *peace* is more than the absence of war—it includes everything that promotes contentment, goodness, prosperity, and serenity (Ps. 122.6–7). Cold wars may lack the physical devastation of hot wars, but they are wars nevertheless (Jas. 4.1–2). In the kingdom, broken relationships are not to be left broken; breaches are to be repaired. A *peace* that tolerates estrangement—"let sleeping dogs lie"—may be pragmatic for the world, but in the kingdom, such peace is spurious (vv 23–24).

They who are the children of God are the *peacemakers* (*eirenopoios*, only here in the NT; Col. 1.20). It's good to be a peace lover or peacekeeper, but the Prince of Peace pronounces a special blessing on those who *make* peace (5.23–25, 18.15–20). Blessed are they who turn swords into plowshares and replace alienation with reconciliation![8]

---

[7] In both Platonic and Aristotelian philosophy, the true meaning of existence is realized in the vision of God (e.g., *Republic* Bk. VII).

[8] Boreham speaks of three levels of peacemaking. Third-level peacemaking is when an

5.10 Blessed *are* those who are persecuted for righteousness' sake, for theirs is the kingdom of heaven.

There is a difference between the first seven beatitudes and the eighth. Whereas the first seven describe *components* of kingdom character, the eighth addresses the *consequences* of such character.

I've had a hard time relating to this last beatitude, because I've encountered little persecution as a believer. This may be due to compromise on my part (2 Tim. 3.12) or because I have lived among people who basically shared my worldview—or possibly a combination of both. For me, persecution occurred in antiquity or in countries with oppressive governments. Government (even a democratically elected one), designed by God as His minister (Rom. 13.4), can be turned by Satan into his monster (Rev. 13.1).[9] Even on a community or individual scale, a Christian can be attacked for no other reason than that he is a Christian. In the first century, Christian "avoidance of social activities which involved idolatry and the like was misinterpreted as due to 'hatred of the human race'" (F. F. Bruce, *The Defence of the Gospel*, 61), and the same is happening now, as Biblical views on various matters are being labeled *hate crimes*. If this trend continues, persecution will increase, and as in the first century, the day may come when life as we have known it will end (1 Pet. 4.7,12).

Note that this last beatitude repeats the concepts of *righteousness* and *kingdom of heaven* and lends weight to the interpretation that Matthew's *righteousness* primarily refers to obedience (3.15)—to be persecuted for *righteousness' sake* is to suffer for how one thinks and behaves, not for whether one is in an invisible relationship with God.

5.11 "Blessed are you when they revile and persecute you, and say all kinds of evil against you falsely for My sake.

Just as 6.14–15 is an addendum to the Lord's prayer, so vv 11–12 are an addendum to the eighth beatitude (v 10).

Christ uses the second-person plural *you* to drive home the certainty that His disciples *will* suffer persecution. The fulfillment of this is seen in the

outside party intervenes to reconcile estranged parties. Marriage counselors and mediators are in this category. Second-level peacemaking is when we are careful *not to give offense*. First-level peacemaking is when we *abstain from taking offense*. If we give offense to none, even when provoked, and if we take offense from none, even when perturbed, we will be a peacemaker.

[9] Luke and Paul are the chief Biblical expositors of government as a minister; Peter and John have the most to say about government as a monster.

fact that before the end of the first century, the Gr. word for *witness* (*martus, martyr*) came to describe Christians who were physically persecuted for their faith (Acts 22.20), with the scope of persecution ranging from verbal abuse (*revile, oneidizō*, to defame, rail at; slander, *say all kinds of evil against you falsely*)[10] to the sadistic (tying victims in a bag with snakes, tying them in a bag and drowning them at sea, launching them from catapults, tying them to horses to be ripped apart, throwing them to wild animals, setting them on fire, crucifixion, etc.).

5.12 Rejoice and be exceedingly glad, for great *is* your reward in heaven, for so they persecuted the prophets who were before you.

If the prophets were persecuted, why should Christians expect exemption? The blessing of this beatitude isn't because persecution is pleasurable (it isn't) but stems from what *enduring* persecution (Jas. 1.12) can produce— an outcome so wondrous that it should be anticipated with *rejoicing* and *exceeding gladness* (*agalliaō*, to jump for joy, exult). Believers "are not masochists who enjoy being hurt. We are not even Stoics who grit their teeth and endure. We are Christians, who see in our sufferings the outworking of a gracious, divine purpose. We rejoice because of what suffering 'produces'" (Stott, *Men Made New*, 14). In Matthew, *reward* usually refers to something bestowed in the hereafter. For disciples of Christ, a journey that begins in poverty (v 3) ends in paradise. May the greatness of the reward steady us during any momentary, light affliction that comes our way (2 Cor. 4.17; Heb. 11.26).

Thomas Bilney was an eighteenth-century English Catholic layman who obtained a license to preach. In his preaching, though, he criticized various Catholic dogmas, such as the veneration of saints and relics. For this, he was condemned to be burned at the stake. The night before his death, when visited by some friends who came to comfort him, Bilney quoted a passage from Isaiah: *When you pass through the waters, I will be with you; and through the rivers, they shall not overflow you. When you walk through the fire, you shall not be burned, nor shall the flame scorch you.* In this promise, he found the strength to face his death with courage and serenity.[11]

Blessed are the dead who die in the Lord.

---

[10] In Luke 6.22, persecution is defined as hatred, ostracism, destructive criticism, and libel.

[11] What is believed to be Bilney's Bible, with this passage marked, is in the library of Corpus Christi College, University of Cambridge, Cambridge, England.

Metaphors, 5.13–16

Notes

The eight beatitudes are followed by two metaphors. Verse 16, and its mention of *good works,* serves as a title to vv 17–48. *Good works* and *your Father which is in heaven* reappear in 6.1, thus bracketing vv 17–48.

Two significant truths are found in this paragraph. First, Christians are more than mere individuals—they stand for something larger than themselves; they represent Christ and His cause. His honor and reputation are, in a real sense, in their hands. Second, believers are to have a power about them that touches the lives of those around them. This power, as the context makes clear, is *love.* Faith can be caught as well as taught, and nothing encourages belief in Christ more than love shown by Christians. Christian love is the salt and light of this paragraph and constitutes the energy and genius of evangelism.[12]

Implicit in the metaphors is the assumption that Christ's disciples are in contact with the unforgiven. *Salt* in the shaker and *light* that is hid have no power. Christians cannot discharge their responsibility unless they are lovingly engaged in regular, practical ways with the lost.

5.13 "You are the salt of the earth; but if the salt loses its flavor, how shall it be seasoned? It is then good for nothing but to be thrown out and trampled underfoot by men.

This section continues the plural *you* found in vv 11–12—*you,* the persecuted and reviled. That the pronoun appears first in this sentence makes it emphatic: you *and you alone* are the salt of the earth.[13]

Salt has many uses,[14] but Christ cites its seasoning and flavoring ability. Christian righteousness (vv 3–10) introduces a spiritual and moral flavor into the world. The adage *you can lead a horse to water, but you can't make him drink* was amended by one old-timer who said, "True, but you can give 'em salt." Salt creates thirst, and the love a follower of Christ manifests in his life will create a thirst for righteousness (v 6) among the unforgiven. *World* picks up the universal theme in Matthew (1.1, 28.19).

---

[12] Lenin said that he didn't mind a corrupt and sinful priest; such were easily dispensed with. But he hated and feared the saints; the purer the religion, the more dangerous it was.

[13] For other examples of *you* in the first or emphatic position, see 10.30; 13.11,16,18; 15.5,16; 16.15; 23.8–9.

[14] The value placed on salt in ancient times is seen in the word *salary,* which derives from the word salt.

Salt that loses its saltiness (flavor; *moraine,* moronic, foolish; 1 Cor. 1.20) creates a problem, because there is no substitute for salt. Since sodium chloride is a stable compound that rarely breaks down chemically, how does salt lose its flavor? Usually, by contamination with other substances, like dirt; nobody wants to sprinkle salt mixed with dirt on their eggs. Matthew doesn't explain how losing saltiness occurs, but the context in which this statement is found in Luke 14.34 helps. Salt loses its flavor when Christ isn't our priority (14.26), when we do not say "No" to sin (14.27; Tit. 2.12), and when we value stuff more than Christ (14.33; see Matt. 19.21–22). To live in violation of these conditions means we *cannot* be Christ's disciple, and any claim we make to the contrary will be thrown back in our face (Jon. 1.9–10)—*thrown out and trampled underfoot.*

Salt doesn't exist for itself—its purpose is to affect other things. Similarly, Christians exist not for themselves but for those around them. To the degree that we compromise our character, we become ineffective in influencing others for eternity.

5.14 You are the light of the world. A city that is set on a hill cannot be hidden.

Again, *you* is emphatic: you—My disciples, and no one else—*are the light of the world.* Light enables sight by making things bright, visible. Just as cities situated on hills can be seen from a distance, so love righteousness in a Christian shines brightly in a sin-darkened world (Phil. 2.15).

5.15 Nor do they light a lamp and put it under a basket, but on a lampstand, and it gives light to all *who are* in the house.

What use is light you can't see? Why light an oil *lamp* if you're going to cover it with a *basket*? Doing so makes no more sense than turning on the radio and then hitting the mute button.[15] *House* probably indicates a one-room Judean house; *all* parallels the universal expressions *earth* and *world.*

Christ's words recall 4.16 and what He said about those sitting in darkness. Darkness doesn't dispel darkness, only light dispels darkness. Disciples, by their love, provide light and participate in the mission of He who is the *Light of the world* (John 9.5).

5.16 Let your light so shine before men, that they may see your good works and glorify your Father in heaven.

---

[15] See this point applied to parables, 13.13.

This transitional verse, which summarizes vv 14–15 and introduces vv 17ff, explains that when disciples make love incarnate, they are the *light of the world*, making it possible for the unforgiven to see God. The world is weary of love that's all talk; the world is looking for love in deed and in truth (1 Jn. 3.18). In what follows, Christ illustrates what kingdom love looks like in practice.

For the first time in Matthew, God is referred to as *Father*—which is one of the key revelations in the Gospel (6.9). Important here is the revelation that disciples represent more than themselves; they represent Christ and His cause; Christians stand for Christ in this world. His honor, His reputation, and His success, in a real sense, depends on us.[16,17] Disciples are to shine, but the Father is to be seen.

Excursus on Salt of the Earth/Light of the World

At the age of eighty, John Quincy Adams met a man on a Boston street. "Good morning," said the friend, "and how is John Quincy Adams today?" The ex-president replied. "John Quincy Adams himself is well, quite well, I thank you. But the house in which he lives at present is becoming dilapidated. It is tottering upon its foundations. Time and the seasons have nearly destroyed it. Its roof is pretty well worn out. Its walls are much shattered and it trembles with every wind. The old tenement is becoming almost uninhabitable and I think John Quincy Adams will have to move out of it soon. But he himself is quite well, quite well" (qtd. by Fosdick, *The Meaning of Being a Christian*, 65).

When a man's body is working well, he is healthy because he is free of disease and debilities. But when his body is broken, he is limited and hampered. The church is the body of Christ (Col. 1.18); just as a man uses his body to express himself—to make himself heard, felt, understood, relate to others, etc.—so Christ uses the church to make Himself known; He expresses Himself through His church.

But when the body doesn't work well—when it is deaf, dumb, blind, crippled, devil-possessed—Christ is hindered in revealing Himself and furthering His work.

---

[16] "Believers don't have to be Jesus to get the world's attention. Most will forgive them their failings, but they must be honest failings, and there must be honest confession and contrition when appropriate. The most persuasive salesman in the world couldn't persuade anyone to buy aftershave or perfume when he smells like sewage water" (McGuiggan, *Jesus, Hero of My Soul*, 97).

[17] Daniel Webster once said that the strongest argument for religion he knew was an old aunt of his who lived up in the New Hampshire hills.

Christians are to live holy lives amid unbelief and unholiness, shining the light of Christ in a dark world. When beset by hatred and persecution, disciples are to love. May we ever be true to this.

BODY, 5.17–7.12

Preface, 5.17–20

Notes

The body of the sermon (5.17–7.12) begins with a preface (vv 17–20) containing three explanations and two admonitions. Christ's authority takes center stage: *I say unto you* appears twice in the preface (vv 18,20) and six more times in what follows (vv 21–48). Christ presents Himself as One greater than Moses, who authoritatively interprets Moses (vv 21–32), corrects false interpretations (vv 33–47), and will judge all men on the last day (7.24–27, 17.5). Verse 20 and its teaching on *exceeding righteousness* (v 20) is one of the key verses in Matthew.

5.17 "Do not think that I came to destroy the Law or the Prophets. I did not come to destroy but to fulfill.

In their attempts to destroy Christ, the Jewish establishment will accuse Him of breaking the Law (9.3,11, 15.2; Acts 6.11–14). Anticipating this, Christ launches a pre-emptive strike, defining His relationship to the OT in three statements.

First, *do not think that I have not come to destroy the Law or the prophets. The Law or the Prophets* is an idiom for the OT (7.12, 11.13, 22.40). *Destroy* (*kataluō*) means get rid of, cancel, abolish, break, not keep (24.2, 26.61, 27.40). In no way did Christ seek to diminish the integrity or authority of the OT.

Second, Christ *fulfilled* the OT. *Fulfill* (3.15) recalls the fulfillment quotations previously encountered (1.22, 2.15, etc.). Christ fulfilled the OT's verbal and nonverbal prophecies (types); He was the substance that cast the shadow (Jn. 5.39; Gal. 3.24; Heb. 10.1–20), the culmination of the Abrahamic and Davidic covenants (1.1), who in every respect upheld the eternal principles of the Law and Prophets (v 21ff).[18]

---

[18] A careful reading of Jeremiah 31.31–34 would have told the Jews that by predicting a *new covenant*, the Mosaic covenant recognized its own insufficiency and predicted its end. See this developed in Hebrews 8–10.

5.18 For assuredly, I say to you, till heaven and earth pass away, one jot or one tittle will by no means pass from the law till all is fulfilled.

Assuredly (*amēn,* truly, verily), *I say to you* conveys confidence, certainty.[19] The transition from Moses to Christ was one of continuity rather than contradiction, for Christ completed Moses (v 17). But at the same time, Christ superseded Moses (Heb. 3); He was a second Moses — a lawgiver — who infallibly interpreted the Law and the Prophets and authoritatively critiqued all other interpreters.

Third, until Christ fulfilled the OT (v 18), the OT remained in force; but once fulfilled, it ended. *It is easier for heaven and earth to pass away than one tittle of the law to fail* figuratively emphasizes the certainty of the OT's fulfilment (Lk. 16.17). But once fulfilled, the Law and Prophets would *pass away* (*parerchomai,* end, terminate, disappear; 2 Cor. 5.17).

No part of *the Law* and *the Prophets* was dispensable. A *jot* (*iota*) was the Gr. equivalent of the *yodh,* the smallest letter of the Heb. alphabet;[20] a *tittle* was the smallest part of a letter, the serif or flourish that distinguished some Heb. letters from others. In this memorable saying, Christ insists on the sacredness and relevance of every word, letter, and part of a letter in the OT (4.4).

5.19 Whoever therefore breaks one of the least of these commandments, and teaches men so, shall be called least in the kingdom of heaven; but whoever does and teaches *them,* he shall be called great in the kingdom of heaven.

Two admonitions follow the explanations.

First, in contrast to Christ, who kept the Law and Prophets, there were those who disregarded various areas of the OT and taught others to do so as well. In any family, all the rules are important, but some are more important than others. The rule to make your bed is important, but the rule to not play with matches is more important. And so it is in the kingdom. *Least* (*elachistos*) means small, insignificant, the opposite of *great* (2.6, 11.11, 25.40; v 22); *break* (*luō,* loose, set aside) means to free from restraints, downplay, or reduce the obligations of something (16.19, 18.18). *Luō* (*break*) is a cognate of *kataluō* (*destroy*) in v 17, implying that the Law and the Prophets are *destroyed* when their commands — even the seemingly trivial — are broken. When a

---

[19] "The prophets tend to say 'saith the Lord' and the apostles 'It is written,' but Jesus uses 'I say unto you'" (Bengle, qtd. by Morris, 109).

[20] In some Bibles, the *yodh* can be seen in Heb. script before Ps. 119.73.

child, out of willfulness, disrespect, or pride, refuses to make his bed, he is a rebel engaged in insurrection against his parents, even if he doesn't play with matches. Jewish rabbis classified OT commandments as *light* or *weighty* based on the effort required to keep them and the reward gained by keeping them. Jesus makes a similar distinction in 23.23, but there He excoriates the Jewish establishment for keeping the lighter commands to the neglect of the weightier ones.[21] All of God's commands are important, but some are more important than others. And when situations arise wherein two commands seem to conflict, we must choose the greater of the two, *approving the things that are excellent* (vv 23–24, 9.13; Lk. 10.42; Phil. 1.10). Not every choice is between good and bad; sometimes we must choose between the good, the better, and the best.

They who *break* the *least commandments* and *teach others to do so* well characterized the scribes and Pharisees (vv 20,33–35, 15.3–9). And yet, the Jews honored them as scholars (23.2) and considered them "in many senses the most outstanding people of the nation. …The average man said to himself, 'Ah, there is very little hope of my ever being as good as the scribes or the Pharisees'" (Lloyd-Jones, 201–202). In a family, anyone who breaks family rules and encourages other family members to do so as well is contributing to the ultimate failure of the family; such a person is small. But within Israel, those who picked and chose which laws they kept were thought great and were even given teaching responsibility. The consequences of such a course will be profusely illustrated in this Gospel.

Beginning in v 21, Christ shows how the Jewish clergy *destroyed* God's word. Others may give the scribes and Pharisees high marks, but not Christ (15.12–14). They who were thought the greatest were in reality the leastest.[22]

5.20 For I say to you, that unless your righteousness exceeds the righteousness of the scribes and Pharisees, you will by no means enter the kingdom of heaven.

Second, to enter the kingdom, one's righteousness *must exceed the righteousness of the scribes and Pharisees. Here is found the key human response taught in Matthew,* and we must understand it (*Notes*, 1.1).

---

[21] "The Rabbis quote Deut. xxii. 6 'Thou shalt not take the mother-bird with the young' as an example of a light precept, Deut. v. 16 'Honour thy father and thy mother' as an example of a grave one; but it is pointed out that the same reward 'length of days' is assigned to both" (Smith, *Matthew, Cambridge Greek Testament,* 97).

[22] It's possible that *least in the kingdom* should be translated *least by the kingdom*, with the Gr. preposition *en* rendered as an instrumental rather than a locative. Men might put the

What this verse doesn't teach is that if the Pharisees fasted twice each week (Lk. 18.12), Christians must fast at least three times each week—*exceeding* righteousness isn't measured by quantity (13.8,23; Lk. 21.1–4). Rather, as Christ will show (vv 21–48), *exceeding righteousness* refers to an obedience to God's will that is driven and governed by a love for Him and for men (22.36–39). Love isn't characterized, primarily, by what it doesn't do (legalists are just as good as trying not to be bad can make them) but by what it does. Love is characterized by an effusive, superabundant spirit that willingly overflows its obligations in service and sacrifice. Love is the attitude behind Christian action, the reality that propels the response. And love has a redemptiveness about it—a lifting power—that doesn't depend on the gratitude or appreciation of others and doesn't stop if resisted or opposed. Love never fails but persists for the sake of the one loved.

Men encounter God when they come in contact with men who love as He loves (v 16). Apart from love, no one can keep enough rules or do enough deeds to put himself in the kingdom (1 Cor. 13.1–3).[23]

Righteousness, 5.21–48

Notes

Kingdom love is illustrated by six situations introduced by the format *You have heard that it was said ... but I say to you.* To be determined is what Jesus meant by *you have heard that it was said*: is He referring to what Moses said, to the scribal/Pharisaic interpretations of Moses, or to something else?

From what follows, it doesn't seem that one size fits all. In some instances, Christ exegetes the full implications of Moses; with others, He exposes scribal perversions of Moses; for all, He stresses the love that underlies the law. Christ taught the highest level of goodness ever taught. To Him, hating is murder, impure desire is adultery, and harboring a grudge against an enemy or being insincere in philanthropy or prayer is sin. We must forgive our fellow, said He, but be so severe with ourselves that we would cut off a hand or remove an eye before we would sin. And

---

scribes and Pharisees at the top, but vis-à-vis the rule of God—the kingdom—they are at the bottom.

[23] "It was a hard thing as Christ taught it to be a Christian, and it was not so very difficult to be a creditable Pharisee; but it was better to die trying to be a Christian than to live having succeeded in becoming a perfect Pharisee" (J. Watson, *Respectable Sins*, 117).

He taught His followers not to be nitpickers who look for sawdust in other's eyes, while ignoring the tree trunks in their own eyes. *Hard on yourself, easy on others* was the way of Jesus.[24]

Murder, 5.21–26

5.21 "You have heard that it was said to those of old, 'You shall not murder, and whoever murders will be in danger of the judgment.'

Luz says that the Jews believed that when the Messiah appeared, He would give an infallible interpretation of the Law, which Christ does this throughout the Sermon. Here, He begins with the two sins that sit atop nearly everybody's list of sins: *murder* and *adultery*.

The second half of the Ten Commandments revealed that God is affected by how men treat each other, so it's not surprising to see the prohibition/condemnation of murder. *Will be in danger of the judgment* refers to a murderer's liability in a court of law.[25]

5.22 But I say to you that whoever is angry with his brother without a cause shall be in danger of the judgment. And whoever says to his brother, 'Raca!' shall be in danger of the council. But whoever says, 'You fool!' shall be in danger of hell fire.

Christ's take on murder went far beyond that of the scribes and Pharisees, who "did not extend the law of God to the thoughts; so that with them, evil desires and purposes were not sinful if they did not express themselves in overt acts."[26] But He who came to fulfill the Law and Prophets goes behind the act to the attitude that spawned the act; according to Christ, attitude is as important as action. If a man doesn't hate, he will not kill; if he doesn't lust, he will not fornicate; if he's honest, he will not break his oath; if evil thoughts do not control his heart, he will do no evil.[27] It does no good to knock down the cobweb if we're not going to kill the spider.

Anger is the emotion that tips the first domino that leads to murder. *Angry without a cause* implies that not all anger is sinful. Anger isn't usually thought of as a Christian virtue, but it should be, for it is a necessary

---

[24] "Hyperbole," Fosdick said, "was [Christ's] native language."

[25] Josephus, *Ant.* iv.8.14–16, *Wars* ii.20.5.

[26] R. Watson, *Exposition of the Gospels of St. Matthew and St. Mark. Thou shalt not covet*, however, was a sin that could occur only in the mind, which pious Jews would have acknowledged as sin (Rom. 7.7).

[27] Civil overnments make judgments based on attitude and uncompleted action. I may

catalyst in the righting of wrong (Mk. 3.5; Jn. 2.17). But anger is a volatile emotion that can easily get out of hand and turn sinful (Eph. 4.26–27).

A first step toward murder, then, is when we regard another contemptuously. And when we do, our speech usually gives us away (15.19). *Raca* transliterates an Aramaic word that was a common term of disrespect (cf. our *worthless* or *birdbrain*). To use this insult made one answerable to the *council* (*sunedrion*)—the Sanhedrin—which seems unusual, considering that courts like the Sanhedrin didn't concern themselves with private affronts (like calling someone an idiot).[28]

Fool (*mōros*, moron) was a stronger term of disrespect than *raca*. To conclude that Christ here bans the use of the word *fool* overlooks the fact that He called men fools (23.19; Lk. 11.40) and worse (16.23; Jn. 6.70). In fact, He will conclude this Sermon by drawing a distinction between the wise and foolish (7.24–27). Jesus taught us to *not call anyone on earth your father* (23.9), but there are people we rightly call *father* without violating Christ's injunction. There's nothing innately sinful in the words *fool* or *father*, but they can be sinful depending on how and why they are used. There are times when anger is wrong and times when it isn't; and there are times when *fool* is used demeaningly and times when it is used accurately. When it is expressive of hateful contempt, the one using it is in danger of *hell* (*gehenna*[29]) *fire*.

On *I say unto you*, see v 18.

Many commentators see here a progression of sin that moves from mere disdain to deeper levels of contempt, with punishment meted out proportionally at each step. The problem with this is that if the punishment for calling a brother a *fool* is *hell fire*, what worse punishment could be imposed for actual murder? I think it better to understand the references to verbal abuse, unjustified anger, and murder as substantially

---

shoot a man dead, but if there is no malice in my act, I will not be found guilty of homicide rather than murder. Or, I may intend to kill a man, shoot at him and miss without harming a hair of his head, yet the law will convict me of *attempted murder*.

[28] There have, however, been times when government was intimate, close to the governed. In the early 19th century, it was not unusual for American presidents to have visitors throughout the day who sought the president's personal intervention in private matters.

[29] *Gehenna* was a ravine on the south side of Jerusalem that had been the site of horrific pagan rites, including child sacrifice (2 Chron. 33.6, Jer. 7.31). During the reign of Josiah, it was thoroughly desecrated to make it unfit for idolatry, and thereafter it served as the city's garbage dump. Whether from the sacrificial fires of Moloch or from the tradition that garbage constantly smoldered there, *Gehenna* eventually came to represent hell, the place of eternal punishment.

equivalent, making the point that even the mildest manifestation of hatred puts one into the same category as a horrendous murderer (1 Jn. 3.15). Demeaning another might be thought less egregious than killing another (v 19), but God condemns sin (not just crime) regardless of its degree or expression.

Christ doesn't contradict what *was said to those of old* but showed how the heart is involved in the ramp-up to murder. "Is 'be not angry,'" asked Chrysostom, "contrary to 'do not kill'? or is not the one the perfecting and filling out of the other?"[30]

5.23 Therefore if you bring your gift to the altar, and there remember that your brother has something against you,

The implications of love go far beyond not hating or not murdering. Love may involve negatives, but it always involves positives. Not only does it insist that we refrain from wrong attitudes, it demands that we pursue right relationships.

Jesus describes a worshiper on his way to the temple to offer a sacrifice— we would say that he is *going to church*. On the way, he remembers a brother who is upset with him about something. Whether the complaint is justified, the result of a misunderstanding, or something else is irrelevant; the mere fact that brotherliness has been disrupted imposes a responsibility of love (v 9) that takes precedence over ritual.

5.24 leave your gift there before the altar, and go your way. First be reconciled to your brother, and then come and offer your gift.

In such cases, our priority is to be *reconciled* (*diallassō*, to make peace; only here in the NT). To be a peacemaker, humility and meekness are needed (vv 3,5), and no amount of worship can offset a refusal to seek reconciliation or to be reconciled (1 Sam. 15.22).[31]

Two adverbs, *first* and *then*, identify love's priority when estranged. Love goes first, it takes the *first* step in reconciliation (1 Jn. 4.10,19). Love finds an offended brother and seeks to restore the relationship. Only *then*, after love has done what it can do to be reconciled, should ritual resume.

---

[30] "What a sweeping law this is! My conscience might have been easy as to the command 'Thou shalt not kill,' but if anger without just cause be murder, how shall I answer for it? 'Deliver me from bloodguiltiness, O God, thou God of my salvation!'" (Spurgeon).

[31] "Do you think that Matt. 5.23–24 would almost empty some church buildings if the elders asked everyone who needed to observe these verses to leave quietly? Is not the duty of reconciliation as clear as Acts 2.38?" (Bales).

Reconciliation, of course, takes two; *be reconciled to your brother* should be read in light of 23.37.

5.25 Agree with your adversary quickly, while you are on the way with him, lest your adversary deliver you to the judge, the judge hand you over to the officer, and you be thrown into prison.

When there is trouble between brothers, God expects a speedy resolution. Delay can allow resentment to grow and hearts to harden. It's rare for legal counsel to advise its client to choose the uncertainty of a trial over an out-of-court settlement (first-century courts would imprison debtors until their debt was paid[32]); before a matter is brought before a judge, a mutual resolution between the involved parties is advisable.

5.26 Assuredly, I say to you, you will by no means get out of there till you have paid the last penny.

When in the heavenly court and standing before the Judge, divine law will decide the fate of those who did not pay their debt of love (Rom. 13.8).[33]

Adultery, 5.27–30

5.27–28 "You have heard that it was said to those of old, 'You shall not commit adultery.' But I say to you that whoever looks at a woman to lust for her has already committed adultery with her in his heart.

As with the sixth commandment (vv 21–22), so with the seventh—*you shall not commit adultery* forbade more than the physical act. Love (5.20) works to avoid all that might contribute to adultery, starting with lust in the heart. Adulterous thoughts that never reach the surface still are considered adulterous by God.[34]

Men are aroused by sight (*whoever looks*), women by touch (vv 29–30, *eye* and *hand*). *Looks* (*blepon*) is present tense, indicating a deliberate look—to stare—rather than an inadvertent glance. The preposition *to* (*pros*) can

---

[32] The imprisonment of Charles Dickens' father for debt was a trauma that affected Dickens throughout his life.

[33] When the Spanish Armada was preparing to sail, its commander-in-chief, the Duke of Medina Sidonia, gave an order, which was to be read three times a week as long as the voyage lasted, that "proclaimed a truce in all existing quarrels or disputes, to last the whole time of the expedition and a month afterwards. For violation of it the penalty was death on the ground of treason" (Howarth, *The Voyage of the Armada*, 49).

[34] Although Christ discusses adultery from the man's perspective, His gender-specific language nevertheless applies to women, who can be as guilty of lust as men. The gen-

indicate purpose or intent (6.1, 23.5, 26.12; 2 Pet. 2.14, *their eyes cannot look at a woman without lust* [JBP]). *Lust* is morally neutral and can refer to desire that is good (Lk. 22.15) or evil (Gal. 5.16). Sexual desire is a God-given appetite, but when a man *looks to lust*—when he fantasizes about committing the sexual act with another man's wife—he commits *adultery* in his heart (Job 31.1–4,9). *Adultery* (*moicheuō*) is sexual intercourse with another's spouse. Sexual desire is God-given, but man is more than an animal and desire is to be controlled.[35] And control begins in the mind— "Thou shalt not think adultery" (Jones, 149).[36]

5.29 If your right eye causes you to sin, pluck it out and cast *it* from you; for it is more profitable for you that one of your members perish, than for your whole body to be cast into hell.

Rooting out sin can require stern measures—*if your right eye causes you to sin, pluck it out and cast it from* you. These words have been literally interpreted by some to authorize physical dismemberment or mutilation,[37] but such is absurd. First, adultery occurs in the heart, not the eye (a dead man's eyes cannot lust). Second, even if adultery occurred in the eye, removing the *right* one wouldn't stop the left from lusting; even the blind have an imagination capable of lust. Third, Paul taught that the amputation that deals with sin is moral and spiritual, not physical (Col. 2.11–12, 3.5–9). Fourth, Paul also taught that hurting the body is of no value in warding off temptation (Col. 2.23), for bodily surgery doesn't touch the soul.

Christ's solution for that which *offends* (*skandalizō*, to entrap, trip up)— evil desire—is illustrated by the strong hyperbole of amputation. "If the literature we read, or the art we see, or the music we hear, or the theaters we patronize, or the games we play, or the friends with whom we associate, or the jobs we hold cause us to stumble, Jesus urges that we cut them off and cast them from us" (Ernest Ligon, qtd. by Bales, *Christ: The Fulfillment of the Law and the Prophets*, 108). Plucking out an eye is an act of self-denial, but self-denial is an act of self-interest—better to lose something than to lose everything, than to have our *whole body cast into hell.*

---

der-specific *brother* in v 23 includes a *sister* who has something against us.

[35] Parents may give their child something—a car, a firearm, etc.—with the understanding that the gift is to be used responsibly and kept under control.

[36] "The statement many times repeated cannot be repeated too often: Sow a thought and you reap an act, sow an act and you reap a habit, sow a habit and you reap a character, sow a character and you reap a destiny" (Jones 149).

[37] Origen cited this verse and 19.12 as justification for castrating himself.

5.30 And if your right hand causes you to sin, cut it off and cast *it* from you; for it is more profitable for you that one of your members perish, than for your whole body to be cast into hell.

The two-fold reference to the *right* is significant. *Right* (as opposed to left) symbolizes what is good, treasured, or important. To avoid sin, we must willingly surrender any *valued* thing, even something as valuable as our right hand. Doing so doesn't handicap our life but enhances it.[38]

Pluck it out and *cut it off* refer to soul surgery.[39] Kingdom righteousness is holistic, not admitting any dichotomy between inner and outer or between imagining and acting. Eyes and hands are never right when they lead us wrong.

Excursus on Lust as a Ground for Divorce

Given that Christ equated lust with *moicheia*, *adultery*—which clearly constitutes sexual immorality—and that in v 32, *sexual immorality* (*porneia*) is a ground for divorce, does lust, in which there is no physical contact with another, constitute a legitimate basis for divorcing one's spouse (v 32, 19.9)?

In answer, note that Jesus does with adultery what He just did with murder: in each case, He expands the sin by addressing the attitude behind the act. But the parity between murder and adultery suggests something regarding the question in the previous paragraph: if lust constitutes grounds for divorce, does hatred constitute grounds for hanging?[40] Hate is as sinful as murder (1 Jn. 3.15), but does it carry the same legal ramifications as actual murder? Under the Law of Moses, the act of adultery carried far more serious temporal consequences than lust, though both act and attitude are sinful. Friendship with the world constitutes adultery in James. 4.4, but does anyone seriously believe that having a worldly spouse is a ground for divorce? And if *adultery* is to be pressed literally in v 28, should the rememdies in v 29 likewise be taken literally? I agree with Wayne Jackson's assessment of those who try to twist lust into an acceptable ground for divorce: "Incredibly, a few inept students have attempted to sustain this ludicrous position! But such is absolutely untenable" (*The Christian Courier*).

---

[38] "Many of us would commit a score of sins, rather than lose an eye or hand. But to the mind of Jesus no loss which may come to the body is to be compared with the loss which comes to the soul by breaking the law of God" (Jefferson, *Things Fundamental*, 236).

[39] I would argue that the OT policy of ḥērem, wherein God ordered the extermination of certain peoples who were a threat to Israel, had a purpose similar to the rationale behind Christ's call for amputation in this passage.

[40] "The doctrine here taught in relation to adultery is identical with that laid down in v. 22 repsecting murder" (Alexander, *The Gospel According to Matthew*, 141).

Divorce, 5.31–32

Notes

The third antithesis involves the controversial subjects of divorce and remarriage. The literature on this section is vast; the interpretations are varied. As Luz suggests, the interpreter's sexual morals are often the progenitor to the interpreter's exegesis.[41]

5.31 "Furthermore it has been said, 'Whoever divorces his wife, let him give her a certificate of divorce.'

The third illustration of kingdom righteousness expands the discussion of sexual sin to the area of divorce. Deuteronomy 24.1 instructed a man who was divorcing his wife to give her a *certificate of divorce (apostasion,* only here, 19.7, and Mk. 10.4; a general word for relinquishing rights). But as Christ makes clear in v 32 and 19.1–9, God never meant for Deuteronomy 24 to be an "out" or escape hatch for a husband who was tired of his wife; rather, Deuteronomy 24 was meant to minimize the fallout when a husband divorced his wife (19.7–8); it didn't command divorce but was damage control necessitated by men (19.8) who despised Genesis 2.24 and willingly exposed their wives to economic and social hardship by divorcing them. As a rule (see 1.19), the *certificate of divorce* said more about the husband using it than about the wife it was used against. Adding insult to injury was the scribal and Pharisaic emphasis on keeping the letter of the law involving the certificate—rather than upholding the sanctity of marriage, their concern was that the right form be filled out in triplicate. "They made Deuteronomy 24 a cloak for evil when it was a scream against their evil" (McGuiggan).

5.32 But I say to you that whoever divorces his wife for any reason except sexual immorality causes her to commit adultery; and whoever marries a woman who is divorced commits adultery.

Jewish husbands divorced their wives for everything imaginable, but so long as they provided their wives a *certificate of divorce,* they legalistically congratulated themselves on their fidelity to Scripture.

Again (v 28), the emphasis is on a man's actions. *Causes her to commit*

---

[41] During the reign of Augustus, for the first time in Roman history, adultery was made a criminal act "with stronger penalties inevitably for the errant wife, who potentially faced banishment; and an obligation for the wronged husband to institute immediate divorce proceedings" (Matthew Dennison, *The Twelve Caesars,* 61).

adultery is passive tense.[42] It's a difficult construction. Of course, Christ isn't saying that a wife becomes an adulteress merely by her husband wrongfully divorcing her; the final clause explains that she becomes an adulteress *if* she remarries.[43] A similar construction occurs in 23.15 where Jesus uses the passive to say that the scribes and Pharisees *make* their proselytes the sons of hell, but a scribal or Pharisaic convert became a son of hell only if he embraced Pharisaic doctrine. Christ's point is that wrongful divorce puts a stone of stumbling before one's spouse that may contribute to them entering an unlawful relationship. Husbands who do this expose themselves to terrible judgment (18.6).

Except—there is an exception that makes divorce justifiable; namely, the case of a spouse's *sexual immorality* (*porneia*). *Porneia*, like *moicheuō* (*adultery*, v 28), refers to sexual sin. Christ doesn't explain why He used this word, but two possibilities are suggested by Luz: "(1) In the tradition of biblical language the root *moich*—is more likely used of men, the root *porn*—more of women. (2) The two roots do not have different meanings; instead, *moicheia* is a specific form of *porneia* so that the two words can also appear as synonyms" (I, 255). The *porneia* that justifies divorce, therefore, is *moicheuō* (adultery)—sexual relations with one other than your spouse.

Whoever marries a woman who is divorced commits adultery—to marry someone whose divorce was not due to their spouse's adultery is to commit adultery in the second marriage. "The only reason why this remarriage can be regarded as adulterous is that the first marriage is still intact in God's sight. Illegitimate divorce does not dissolve the marriage bond, and consequently, the fact of such divorce does not relieve the parties concerned from any of the obligations of their marriage. They are still bound to one another in the bonds of matrimony and a marital relation or any exercise of the privileges and rights of the marital relation with any other is adultery" (Murray, 25). No matter what civil government or human tradition says, God has the final say on marriage and divorce—a marriage isn't over until He says it's over.

It needs to be strongly urged that a spouse's adultery does not exempt one from mercy (v 7), reconciliation (vv 9,23–24), turning the other cheek,

---

[42] It should be noted that the passive only appears in *Sinaiticus* and *Vaticanus*; the Majority Text uses a present infinitive form of the verb.

[43] The use of the passive may simply mean to show the wife as an object in this discussion, in order to better focus attention on the unrighteousness of the husband who wrongly divorces her.

or going the second mile (vv 39,41). Rather, a spouse's infidelity is an opportunity to display redemptive love that glorifies God (vv 16,20).

It also needs to be said that it is a mistake to think that God's total teaching on marriage, divorce, and remarriage is exhausted in this passage or in 19.9. As 1 Corinthians 7 shows, Paul didn't think that what Jesus said while on earth covered everything heaven had to say on the subject. Further, 1 Corinthians 7 doesn't simply repeat what is found in the Gospels; Paul gives revelation on marriage and divorce not found in the Gospels. Any discussion of marriage that doesn't include 1 Corinthians 7 (or any other text on the subject) will likely draw a conclusion that doesn't reflect Biblical teaching.

Excursus on Divorce

In too many Christian marriages, once romantic love has run its course from infatuation to unhappiness, some spouses are more interested in getting out of their marriage than in restoring their first love (Rev. 2.4). Should their spouse commit a v 28- or v 32-type sin, they feel Scripturally released from their vow to take their spouse for better or *worse*. A marriage begins when two people make promises to each other that they'd likely never make if they knew the difficulties and perils involved in keeping them. But still, they make promises. And having made them, God expects them to keep them! The promise is not to do your best to keep your promise, the promise is to keep your promise! Yet, in times of marital conflict, when a chance to show redeeming love presents itself, far too many only want out. If you want to know what it means to keep a promise when the bottom drops out, read chs 26 to 27.

No one wins by walking away from a fixable situation—not the couple, not the children, not the extended families, not society. The greater problem is never one's spouse's unfaithfulness, rather (I'm leaning on McGuiggan here), the problem is that we are too easily tired, too quickly impatient, too self-righteous, and too self-centered to love redemptively. Just as 18.15–20 wasn't written to teach us how to be rid of those who sin against us, so vv 28–32 wasn't written to tell us how to get rid of a spouse who has broken our heart. Despite the introduction of soul-crushing sin, blessing will come when beatitude character is brought to bear on a broken relationship.

Oaths, 5.33–37

Notes

Lying is a fundamental sin. Since our souls are invisible and cannot be seen by others, we signal to one another our inner intent by words and deeds. Lying sends out a false signal, and when discovered, it creates cynicism and distrust for other signals we send out, undermining the whole system of trust on which human relationships depend. Because of a lie's destructiveness, Christ insisted on utter truthfulness. People should always be able to believe what we say.

5.33 "Again you have heard that it was said to those of old, "You shall not swear falsely, but shall perform your oaths to the Lord.'

Telling the truth and keeping promises is as necessary to a stable society as are solid marriages. To *swear* or take an *oath* is to call God as a witness to our veracity. One who takes an oath is asking, essentially, that God strike him dead—or some such thing—if he isn't telling the truth (26.74). Oaths are not ironclad guarantees that the truth is spoken (perjury is possible), but an oath seeks to increase the probability of this by reminding the individual of the eternal consequences if he lies (Heb. 6.16–18).

5.34–36 But I say to you, do not swear at all: neither by heaven, for it is God's throne; nor by the earth, for it is His footstool; nor by Jerusalem, for it is the city of the great King. Nor shall you swear by your head, because you cannot make one hair white or black.

When children cross their fingers, it means they are not bound by anything they say while their fingers are crossed. The scribes and Pharisees played this game by holding that some oaths, depending on the formula used, were less binding than others (23.16–22).

Against such dishonesty, Jesus says, *do not swear at all* (Jas. 5.12). Sages of old agreed with Him: Sophocles, Menander, Epictetus, and others urged people to be trustworthy in themselves, not needing to reference any outside authority to convince another of their truthfulness.

The prohibition against swearing is explained in four clauses. *Heaven, earth,* and *Jerusalem* are matching terms. *By heaven* and *by earth* were formulas used by Jews who didn't want to use the name of God in an oath; instead, they used something associated with God. *Jerusalem* could be included in this category, since it was the city where God put His name.

If oaths obliquely connected to God are prohibited, how much more are oaths connected to men (*nor shall you swear by your head*) who lack the power to change the color of a single hair on their head.

5.37 But let your 'Yes' be 'Yes,' and your 'No,' 'No.' For whatever is more than these is from the evil one."

In Gr. (and other languages), doubling a word intensifies it (7.21). *Yes, Yes* and *No, No* mean *really yes* and *really no*. Love understands that because we live and speak in the presence of God, we are always obligated to tell the truth.

Does Christ prohibit any speech that involves more than *yes* and *no*? In the OT, oaths were authorized (Lev. 19.12), and God swore by Himself (Heb. 6.16–18). Christ went beyond a simple *yes* and *no* whenever He used the term *amēn* (*assuredly*, v 26), and He would later testify under judicial oath (26.63). In the Epistles, Paul, on numerous occasions, invoked God as a witness to his truthfulness and/or sincerity (Rom. 1.9; 2 Cor. 1.23; Gal. 1.20; Phil. 1.8), and in 1 Thessalonians 5.27, he placed the entire Thessalonian church under oath (*I charge/adjure you*; contrast this with his *urging* and *exhorting*, 1 Thes. 5.12,14). When all the evidence is considered, it seems that Christ didn't prohibit oaths in all situations. There is nothing intrinsically evil about the word *swear* (cf. v 22, *fool*). I do not believe Christ is teaching that a disciple must *affirm* rather than *swear* when giving testimony in court or when asked to give a deposition. "In a court of law," wrote James Hastings, "we take the oath to convince our fellow men, who cannot see our heart and judge our regard for truth, of our good faith. That is a very different thing from thinking that we are not required to speak the truth unless bound by an oath; and it is the latter view that Christ condemns in His dictum upon swearing" (*A Dictionary of Christ and the Gospels* II, 255).

In our secular, pluralistic world, the reality is that appeals to God carry little weight. Unbelievers don't ascribe to God any role in guaranteeing truth; accordingly, public oaths have lost much of their value as instruments of verification. This wouldn't be a problem if people understood that they are obligated by God Himself, not talismanic words invoking Him, to tell the truth.

Evil, 5.38–42

Notes

Resist not evil has sometimes been taken out of context and made to say something it doesn't say. If *resist not evil* is an absolute guideline by which Christians should live, then "a woman would have to submit to rape without even a word of protest, for words are a form of resistance. The heretic should not be rebuked … nor should a false teacher be opposed in any way, for these would be forms of resistance to him that is evil" (Bales, *Christ: The Fulfillment of the Law and the Prophets*, 118).

There was never a moment when Jesus didn't resist evil! Even when telling us not to resist evil, He is resisting evil. But He isn't resisting evil with evil. What Christ is teaching is that evil is to be resisted with love and its superabundant spirit (v 20; Rom. 12.21). The temptation to respond to evil with evil, to meet hate with hate, and violence with violence is a mindset that should never be found in the kingdom.

The principle *resist not evil* is amplified in four pictures involving a personal attack, litigation, Roman law, and a loan. The last picture contains a double imperative that gives it a special emphasis. Understanding the historical context for each picture isn't difficult; the greater challenge is understanding the principle's contemporary application.

5.38 "You have heard that it was said, 'An eye for an eye and a tooth for a tooth.'

An eye for an eye and a tooth for a tooth (Ex. 21.24; Lev. 24.19–20; Deut. 19.21) is the law of justice and isn't unfair. In the OT, *quid pro quo* legislation was meant to guide Israel's judges in ensuring that the punishment fit the crime (Heb. 2.2, *every transgression and disobedience received a just reward*). The sentence given one who killed his neighbor's cat wasn't the same given one who killed his neighbor. Punishment was to be proportional.

There is some evidence that in Christ's time the Sadducees called for the literal observance of this law (Fosdick, *The Man from Nazareth*, 91). The general practice among the Pharisees, however, was financial compensation—a victim could only exact an aggressor's eye only if it was exactly like his own in size and color (Baba Kamma 83b). Since this was virtually an impossible condition to meet, monetary compensation enabled Jews to enforce the principle of an eye for an eye without its more gruesome features.

5.39 But I tell you not to resist an evil person. But whoever slaps you on your right cheek, turn the other to him also.

In contrast to proportional retaliation, Christ enjoins nonretaliation—*resist not evil* (KJV). The historical interpretation of these words runs the gamut from the absurd (such as the man who let the lice eat on him rather than he kill the lice) to pacifists (Francis of Assisi, the followers of Wycliffe, the Anabaptists, Quakers, Tolstoy, Albert Schweitzer, Gandhi, Martin Luther King, et al.) who renounce all forms of resistance, including that wielded by civil or military authorities.[44] To understand what Christ meant by *resist not* (*anthistēmi*, only here in Matt.; to stand against, oppose, withstand), we must look at the examples He gives.

Slaps you on your right cheek seems to go beyond the verbal abuse of v 22 to physical violence, but Christ is likely speaking of verbal assault rather than physical battery. To be slapped on your right cheek, an assailant facing you must either hit you with his left hand or backhand you with his right, which signifies an insult.[45] But whether physical injury or emotional insult is meant, love *turns the other cheek*, refusing to retaliate, respond in kind, render evil for evil (Rom. 12.17), or insult for insult (1 Pet. 3.9). "Of all expressions of brotherliness, the most common is active, practical service; far less common is the ability to bear injuries without being vengeful, to be reviled and to revile not again, to be wronged and instead of 'getting even' to help the offender. This is brotherliness in a most noble and difficult form" (Fosdick, *The Manhood of the Master*, 20).

A classic OT example of turning the cheek is seen in Isaac redigging his wells (Gen. 26.15–22).

5.40 If anyone wants to sue you and take away your tunic, let him have *your* cloak also.

The setting is a debtor's trial. A *tunic* was an undergarment (*chiton*, shirt) that could be awarded a creditor in payment for a debt; a *cloak* (*himation*, 21.7) was an outer garment (9.16) that was an inalienable right, a nontransferable possession (Ex. 22.26–27). It's obvious that we are to see more here than a literal interpretation, for giving a man your tunic and cloak might leave you naked, and it's unlikely that's what Christ meant. Nor is Christ saying that it's wrong to appeal to Caesar—the judicial

---

[44] Surely it isn't wrong to appeal to the civil power to do the very things the civil power was ordained of God to do (Rom. 13.3–6).

[45] But in 1 Esdras 4.30, a left-handed blow is also meant as an insult.

system—for protection from scoundrels or injustice. The point, again, is that love recognizes a standard of behavior above the level of legal justice that involves the surrender of one's rights. In the kingdom, rights are not insisted upon in a way that precludes reconciliation (vv 23–25) or hinders the influence of the gospel (v 16, 17.24–27, 26.53; 1 Cor. 9.4–6). Love understands there are things in life more important than one's rights.

5.41 And whoever compels you to go one mile, go with him two.

The third illustration alludes to the hated Roman policy of *compulsion* (27.32) that required people of occupied lands to serve Roman officials and soldiery—by carrying their equipment or luggage, giving directions, escorting, etc.—for a distance of one *mile* (*milion*, a thousand paces; only here in the NT).[46] The Jews bitterly resented this rule, and many who heard Christ say this must have bristled at the thought of trudging an extra mile for a Roman. Love, however, goes above and beyond the call of duty to the higher plane of *grace* with a willingness that exceeds obligations. Law walks the first mile, grace the second (1 Pet. 2.18–20). In life, the sting of compulsion leaves only when we are willing to do more than we are forced to do. Such a gracious spirit will save us from bitterness (Phile. 14).

5.42 Give to him who asks you, and from him who wants to borrow from you do not turn away."

The final illustration involves a double imperative about lending that serves as a transition to the next paragraph. In context, the borrower is an *evil* person (v 39; Lk. 6.35) whom we wouldn't ordinarily be inclined to help. From such people, however, love does *not turn away*.

What Christ says here isn't unqualified—disciples aren't expected to support professional beggars, enable the lazy (2 Thes. 3.10), or loan themselves into poverty (Prov. 22.26). Rather, this vignette, like the three others, enjoins a spirit of grace that goes beyond what is expected and does more than justice demands. "It is this audacious offensive of love that forces the man to go further. ... He tries to break your head, and you, as a Christian, try to break his heart. ... Allowing a man to smite you on one cheek, and letting him have the coat, and submitting to him when he

---

[46] The Roman practice was borrowed from the Persians who implemented it in connection with their pony express postal system. To maintain the system, it was legal for an individual to be impressed as a guide or for his horse to be used.

compels you to go one mile does little or no good. It is the other cheek, the cloak also and the second mile that do the trick" (Jones, 172–173).

Enemies, 5.43–48

Notes

Hate your enemy was the Graeco-Roman norm. When Xenophon eulogized his hero Cyrus the Younger, he climaxed his praise by saying that no one ever did more good to his friends or more harm to his enemies. The Roman philosopher and politician Cicero so hated his enemy Clodius that two years after Clodius's death at the (so-called) Battle of Bovillae, Cicero was dating his letters, "The 560th day after Bovillae... ."

We can imagine how the words *love your enemy* went over with Jews who chafed at the insulting, compulsive, humiliating Roman yoke. Hated by Rome, they hated Rome in return.

5.43 "You have heard that it was said, 'You shall love your neighbor and hate your enemy.'

You shall love your neighbor comes from Leviticus 19.18 (22.39). *Hate your enemy* appears nowhere in the OT but may be an inference that rabbis drew from passages such as Deuteronomy 20.16–18 or from a narrow interpretation of the word *neighbor* (Lk. 10.29).[47] "For all practical purposes hating enemies is what happens when one understands the love command in a particularistic or popular ethical sense" (Luz I, 288).[48]

Love your enemy, however, was illustrated in the Law even if not explicitly stated. Examples would be the requirement to help an enemy's ox or donkey (Ex. 23.4–5), David's attitude toward Saul at En-gedi (1 Sam. 24), the command against rejoicing when your enemy falls (Prov. 24.17–18), and the command to give your enemy bread to eat and water to drink (Prov. 25.21–22).[49]

---

[47] "How shall I admire, how laugh, how rejoice, how exult, when I behold so many proud monarchs and fancied gods groaning in the lowest abyss of darkness; so many magistrates, who persecuted in the name of the Lord, liquefying in fiercer fires than ever they kindled against the Christians; so many sage philosophers blushing in red-hot flames, with their deluded scholars; so many celebrated poets trembling before the tribunal, not of Minos, but of Christ!" (Tertullian).

[48] "The Bible tells us to love our neighbors, and also to love our enemies; probably because they are generally the same people" (G. K. Chesterton).

[49] *Love your enemy* was urged by Gr. philosophers on the basis that every person shares in the same divine origin.

5.44 But I say to you, love your enemies, bless those who curse you, do good to those who hate you, and pray for those who spitefully use you and persecute you,

In first-century Judea, the Jews hated the Romans, the Romans hated the Jews, the scrupulous and elite hated the lower classes (Jn. 7.48–49), and everybody hated tax collectors. As defined by Christ, our enemy is anyone who harbors ill will toward us as expressed in *cursing, hatred, spiteful mistreatment,* or *persecution.* Disciples, however, are to break the cycle of hate by loving the haters.

It's far easier to respond in kind to an enemy than to love him. But love returns kindness—*blessing, doing good, praying*—for wrong. To respond this way, our will must overrule our emotions to where we act lovingly toward an enemy even when we don't feel very loving. How we live should never be determined by another's conduct. Booker T. Washington, who endured many humiliations in his life, said, "I will not let any man reduce my soul to the level of hatred."

5.45 that you may be sons of your Father in heaven; for He makes His sun rise on the evil and on the good, and sends rain on the just and on the unjust.

Loving our enemies makes us like the God who loves His enemies (Rom. 5.10) and demonstrates His love by His common grace—causing the sun to rise and the rain to fall on the *evil* and *unjust* (*adikos,* unrighteous), as well as on the *good* and *just.* "His is no 'if' love (I'll love you if you do what I say!). His is more than 'because' love (I love you because …). His is an 'anyway' love (I love you no matter how you are!)" (McGuiggan, *The God of the Towel,* 10). The sunshine and rain give no clue to a man's character; the sons of God are not known in this life by any partiality their heavenly Father shows them in nature. It will be at the end of this age that the sons of God are fully revealed (13.42–43). In Semitic thought, to be a *son* figuratively expressed "the idea that a person shares the quality or nature of the source specified" (Hare, 60). To be *sons of the heavenly Father,* we must love like the heavenly Father. The true test of love righteousness is not how we treat the innocent but how we treat the guilty. "Loving means to love that which is unlovable, or it is no virtue at all" (Chesterton).

5.46–47 For if you love those who love you, what reward have you? Do not even the tax collectors do the same? 47 And if you greet your brethren only, what do you do more *than others?* Do not even the tax collectors do so?

The key phrase here is *what do you more*, which renders the same word translated *exceeds (perisson)* in v 20. Having called on us to do more (v 20), the question is: what are we doing that is more? *Reciprocal love* (sending Christmas cards to those who send Christmas cards to us) isn't doing more. In the first century, tax collection in the Roman provinces was often outsourced to private vendors, and in Judea, *tax collectors* were usually Jews who were often guilty of extortion (9.9; Lk. 15.12, 19.8) and who were viewed as collaborators. But even despised tax collectors practiced ordinary levels of friendliness.

5.48 Therefore you shall be perfect, just as your Father in heaven is perfect."

Therefore concludes these pictures of love righteousness by stating that the goal of all is *perfection*. *Perfect (teleios,* complete, entire) doesn't here mean sinlessness but *completeness in love*. "Jesus is not frustrating his hearers with an unachievable ideal" (Blomberg, 115) but is setting before us the ideal of loving as God loves. *Perfect* individuals are those who have "attain[ed] the end for which God has made them" (Morris, 134), which, in this context, is universal, unconditional love. *Perfection* isn't some special quality possessed by a small core of exceptional Christians but is the norm for all who would be under the rule of God.

Bales was right when he wrote that the principles in 5.21–48 "are among some of the most difficult passages to live up to" (*Christ: The Fulfillment of the Law and the Prophets*, 125–126). But Christ lived them and thereby showed that we can too.

Excursus on Love (George Matheson)

"It is not enough that you give to your brother what he has a legal right to; you must impart to him that to which he has no legal right. It is comparatively easy to remember him in the things wherein he is rich—in the things which are his own. But to remember him when he is poor, to sympathise with him in that which he is in want of—that is difficult. You have done well to respect his person, to keep your hands form his property, to abstain from calumniating his name. But after all, that is only a *refraining* of the hand. Is there no outstretching of the hand! Are you content with doing your brother no wrong! Is there no good that you can do him! You have not killed your brother; but have you enlarged his life! You have not stolen; but have you added to his store! You have not defamed; but have you spread his virtues! You have brought him no domestic dispeace; but have you brought him domestic joy! You have refused to covet his possessions; but have you ever coveted possessions *for him!*" (George Matheson, "Distinctiveness of Christian Morality," *Messages of Hope*, 186–187).

CHAPTER 6

Hypocrisy, **6.1–8**

In Benevolence, **6.1–4**

Notes

Verses 1–18 are the center of the sermon, and the Lord's Prayer (vv 6–13) is the center of the center—which is significant because of the revelation it contains.

When the modern mind looks to the heavens, two questions stand at the fore: is there someone out there? and if so, is he friend or foe? The incarnation speaks to the first of these questions; the revelation in the Lord's prayer to the second. To demonstrate how the second issue is addressed, I quote these lines from C. S. Lewis in his introduction to George MacDonald's *Phantastes*: "From his own father, [MacDonald] said, he first learned that Fatherhood must be at the core of the universe." This is stunning in its profundity for the core fact of reality, embedded into the very center of Christ's gospel, is that the universe was created and is sustained and governed by a *Father* who is loving, good, and just (7.11). They who lose sight of this invariably miss the goodness in the gospel that Christ proclaimed.

Few things constitute a more despicable attack on love than hypocrisy and its shameful exploitation of godly things for selfish goals (1 Pet. 1.22). *Hypocrisy*—the attempt of a mean thing to pass itself off as a mighty thing (Boreham)— permeated Pharisaic piety in the areas of benevolence (vv 2–4), prayer (vv 5–8), and fasting (vv 16–18). In discussing these, Christ uses a negative (*when you do … do not*) and a positive (*when you do … do*) to set up a contrast between public and private, men and God, and present and future reward. Several sayings in this section have become proverbial, including *blowing your own horn* and *let not your left hand know what your right hand is doing.*

6.1 "Take heed that you do not do your charitable deeds before men, to be seen by them. Otherwise you have no reward from your Father in heaven.

If the Majority Text reading (*eleēmosunē*, alms,[1] KJV) is right, this verse is a topic sentence for vv 1–4; if the variant reading (*dikaiosunē, acts of righteousness*, NASB, NIV, et al.) is right, this is a title for vv 1–18.

Charitable deeds are acts of kindness or benevolence. At first glance, *do not do your charitable deeds before men to be seen by them* seems to contradict *let your light shine before men, that they may see your good works* (5.16). The apparent conflict, however, is resolved by understanding that *something can be done publicly without being done for publicity*. For good works to cause the unforgiven to glorify God, the unforgiven must be aware of them. But a right thing can be done for the wrong reason, and good things done to glorify the worker carry no eternal reward. When man's applause is what we seek, man's applause is all we get.

6.2 Therefore, when you do a charitable deed, do not sound a trumpet before you as the hypocrites do in the synagogues and in the streets, that they may have glory from men. Assuredly, I say to you, they have their reward.

Social services for the poor were rare in antiquity; charity depended on the goodness of individuals. And in this, *hypocrisy* saw an opportunity. The help that hypocrites gave the unfortunate wasn't motivated by love (5.20) but by a desire to advertise themselves. There is no historical evidence that Pharisees actually blew a horn to call attention to some kindness they performed; *sound a trumpet* is likely meant as irony or caricature, but it well illustrates the ulterior motive of those who parade their kindness in order to promote themselves (1 Cor. 13.4).

Hupokrite (lit. one who answers) was the Gr. word for *actor*. Eventually, the word migrated from theatrics to ethics, but with a negative connotation that described a phony—one who wasn't what he appeared to be.[2] Its use in v 2 is fitting given that *seen* in v 1 translates *theaomai*, from which comes the word *theater*. Hypocrites may not have blown a horn, but they touted their compassion by practicing charity in public venues like *synagogues* and *street corners*. Note that a hypocrite isn't one who is inconsistent in

---

[1] *Alms* is an Eng. corruption of *eleēmosunē*, acts of mercy.
[2] Jesus is the only person in the NT who uses the word *hypocrite*.

life or succumbs to temptation—if so, we all are hypocrites. Rather, a hypocrite is one who wants to be noticed and praised but lives by a double standard: excusing in himself what he condemns in others (7.1–5,12.27, 23.4, 27.63, 28.11–14), breaking the will of God in the name of God (15.2–9), and masking wickedness as worship (22.15–17). "Hypocrisy is the tribute vice pays to virtue." Not only can sin occur in the absence of a bad deed (5.22,28), it can occur in the doing of a good deed (vv 1,5,16). "You can call attention to yourself in religion with such emphasis that you succeed in announcing only your spiritual death" (Jones 204).

Have (*apechō*) is a commercial term for a receipt showing that a bill had been paid in full. *Reward* (*misthos*, pay for service) referred to earned wages. One way Jewish hypocrites were paid for their hypocrisy was by being allowed to sit next to the rabbi (Luz I, 300; 23.6). Among the Greeks, self-promoters often finagled to see their name in an inscription or have a statue raised in their honor (cf. *seeing your name in lights, getting top billing*). "If a subtle desire to be seen of men runs through your doing of religious things, then the deed dies with the moment, there is no lasting quality. You wanted the praise of men—you got it. That settles the account, there is no reward with your Heavenly Father" (Jones, 206).

6.3 But when you do a charitable deed, do not let your left hand know what your right hand is doing,

Do not let your left hand know what your right hand is doing has become a common saying, whose meaning is the opposite of *sounding a trumpet*. It is a hyperbole that indicates a lack of consciousness or pretense. The judgment scene in 25.37–39 illustrates what is meant. As Hendriksen wrote, the righteous in that passage are so unpretentious about the mercy they have shown that they "are represented as being totally unaware of their own past benevolent deeds" (321).

6.4 that your charitable deed may be in secret; and your Father who sees in secret will Himself reward you openly.

Showing mercy *secretly* means that mercy is to be devoid of dishonesty or artifice. Mercy is done for the glory of God, who is aware of everything we offer in worship to Him (9.13,22; Heb. 6.10) and who will *openly* (*phanerō*, plainly, evidently) *reward* (*apodidōmi*, give away, recompense) our love.

Nothing is hidden from God now; nothing will be overlooked then.

"Half the misery in the world comes from trying to look, instead of trying to be, what one is not" (George MacDonald, *The Flight of the Shadow*, 5).

Excursus on Hypocrites in the Church

"Before you condemn Christians for being hypocrites, and our religion for being a gigantic system of cant, I think you must show either that Christ is responsible for the hypocrite and that His religion leads naturally to hypocrisy, or else that the hypocrite represents the large body of his brethren. It would be a little difficult, I think, to do either. If there was one thing Christ insisted on more stringently than another, it was reality, and any person whom he denounced more severely than another, it was a hypocrite. He was sorely tried by hypocrites in the shape of the Pharisees while He was living on earth, and at last they nailed Him to the Cross. It is very hard upon my Master that He should be still followed by hypocrites, and that on that account He should be put to shame. Twice put to shame by the same kind of people. Once when they were against Him; once because they insisted on joining Him. Be sure of this, if you know a hypocrite, Christ did not make him one, and Christ does all He can to prevent men being hypocrites, so do not on that account reject [Christ]" (J. Watson, *Reasonable Sins*, 128–129).

In Prayer, **6.5–15**

Notes

Jewish and pagan prayer practices are contrasted with prayer that pleases God. There is a great difference between *praying* and *saying your prayers*. In true prayer, God is acknowledged, not as a idea in our mind, but as a reality in our life. By contrast, *saying our prayers* is *pray-acting* — going through the motions of a stereotyped, lifeless ritual maintained by force of habit rather than true devotion. Genuine prayer is vital, for by it, the children of God lay hold of their Father's blessings.

The point about mercy (vv 1–2) is applicable to prayer: it is not to be an instrument of pride.

6.5 "And when you pray, you shall not be like the hypocrites. For they love to pray standing in the synagogues and on the corners of the streets, that they may be seen by men. Assuredly, I say to you, they have their reward.

Pray appears frequently in the Bible as the word for communication with

God—in prayer, men speak to God. "Prayer"—which Fosdick called "the soul of religion"—"is *not* prayer if it is addressed to anyone else but God" (Barth). "Prayer that has another agenda, whether it be showing off our skill with language or trying to preach to your fellow worshippers, fails to qualify as real prayer" (Gardiner, 123). On *hypocrites*, see v 2. Devout Jews typically prayed at morning, midday, and evening (Acts 3.1); and when a Jew decided to pray, he would do so wherever he happened to be. According to Christ, location factored heavily into where hypocrites prayed. Seeking to maximize the size of their audience, they gravitated to synagogues and street corners (*plateia*, main street, in contrast to an unspecified road) for prayer as well as benevolence (v 2). When hypocrites were praised for how well they prayed, they were paid in full, with nothing more to come (v 2).

6.6 But you, when you pray, go into your room, and when you have shut your door, pray to your Father who *is* in the secret *place*; and your Father who sees in secret will reward you openly.

Go into your room (*tameion*, a storage room found in Judean farmhouses; an inner room not visible from the street) parallels *do not let your left hand know what your right hand is doing* (v 3). *Shut your door* is a figurative way of describing the disposition of our heart when we pray. Even when done in public, prayer is to be *in private* (v 4). Any place, posture, or prose chosen to impress men is sinful. God has a bigger vocabulary than we do, so trying to impress Him with stained-glass oratory is useless. And He knows whether pride or poverty (5.3) motivates us; He knows if we're standing on the inside even if kneeling on the outside. Prayer is "to be undertaken with a single eye on God, not with a side glance at people who could be impressed" (Morris, 141). God's omniscience insures that He will not miss anything we say to Him.[3]

Reward you openly doesn't mean God rewards us immediately or gives us the answer we want (26.36–42); it means He blesses true devotion and will eventually do so in a way that will be known by all. On *reward*, see v 4.

6.7 And when you pray, do not use vain repetitions as the heathen *do*. For they think that they will be heard for their many words.

Cousin to hypocritical prayer is *heathen* prayer that was characterized by

---

[3] "When thou hast shut the door and darkened thy room, say not to thyself that thou art alone. God is in thy room" (Epictetus).

vain repetitions (*battalogeō*, a rare word whose etymology is uncertain; it probably traces to a word that meant *to stutter*, and then to the repetition of meaningless syllables[4]); if *many words* (*polulogia*) parallels *vain repetitions*, we have the meaning of *battalogeō*.[5] *Do not use vain repetitions* doesn't mean that words or ideas cannot be repeated in our prayers—until the human predicament changes, our petitions will remain essentially unchanged (26.42). But Christ contradicts the aphorism (popular among the heathen) that the squeaky wheel gets the grease. The heathen "by endless repetition and many words [would] try to tire out their gods and weary them into granting requests" (Vos 59; Seneca called this "fatiguing the gods," *Epistulae Morales* 31.5; cf. 1 Kgs. 18.26; Lk. 11.5–8, 18.1–8). Long prayers are not prohibited (the prayer in vv 9–13, has 66 words, the prayer in Jn. 17 has about 600 words, and in 14.23–25, Christ prayed all night[6]), but a prayer's length never obligates God to send the answer sought.

6.8 Therefore do not be like them. For your Father knows the things you have need of before you ask Him.

The reason *many words* in prayer are unnecessary is because God knows what we need before we pray; indeed, how could an omniscient God not know?

For your Father knows the things you have need of before you ask Him have caused some to ask, "If God knows what I need before I ask, why ask? Doesn't His omniscience make my prayer unnecessary? And if God is truly good and loving, doesn't it follow that He will supply my needs without me asking?"

Although such reasoning might seem logical, *revelation* and *reason* expose its illogic. Regarding revelation, in 7.11 Christ says that God gives good things *to those who ask Him*—His knowledge of our needs doesn't release us from our obligation to pray. The first miracle Christ performs after the sermon—cleansing leprosy (8.2–4)—demonstrates this; Christ could have healed the leper without the leper saying a word, but it was

---

[4] Verse 7 is notable for the rare words it contains: *battalogeō, polulogia, ethnikos,* and *eisakouō*.

[5] Protestants have often understood the Catholic rosary as an example of babbling prayer. The gibberish of charismatic prayers might also be considered an example of pagan-type praying.

[6] The Gettysburg Address had 272 words and took about two minutes to deliver. Given the tendency of minds to wander, those who lead public prayers should remember that it doesn't take long for a speaker to lose his listeners. There comes a point where a prayer's length can become counterproductive to attentiveness.

only when the leper asked that his leprosy was cleansed. Regarding reason, when the subject is changed from *prayer* to *work*, the necessity of prayer becomes clear.

To illustrate: does God know what we need before I ask? Yes. Does He have the goodness and love and power to give me what I need? Absolutely. Does it follow, then, that *working* for what I need is unnecessary? Why should I work if a loving God knows what I need and can give it to me without me working? It's because there are some blessings God gives when we *cooperate* with Him, and the primary ways by which we cooperate with Him are *thinking*, *working*, and *praying*. God knows we need *bread* (v 11), but who is so foolish as to think that God's knowledge exempts us from *working* for our bread? James tells us to pray for wisdom (Jas. 1.5), but that doesn't mean we don't have to study or think. Mark 6.5 says that Christ *could do no mighty work* in Nazareth, *except that He laid His hands on a few sick people and healed them*. Great as Christ's power was, it was limited by a lack of cooperation, a lack of faith. There are things that God will not do for us (even though He could) unless we *believe*; and there are things He will not do for us unless we pray. He wants to bless us, but He does so in response to our asking (7.11; Jas. 4.2).

The Lord's Prayer, 6.9–15

Notes

At the center of the sermon is the *Lord's Prayer*,[7] flanked on both sides with sections discussing righteousness.

"God, being infinite can never be fully comprehended by our minds; whatever thought of him be there, his real nature must still transcend: there will yet be deep after deep beyond, within that light ineffable; and what we see, compared with what we do not see, will be as the raindrop to the firmament. Our conception of him can never *correspond with the reality* ... but can only *represent the reality*, and *stand for God* within our souls, till nobler thoughts arise and reveal themselves as his interpreters" (James Marineau, *Prayers in the Congregation and in College*).

To think of God, we must use images with which we are familiar—we

---

[7] I call it this based on tradition, not interpretation. "The best-known prayer of our Lord is almost universally misnamed. It is called the Lord's Prayer when it is clearly a prayer designed for the use of His followers. It is actually the *Disciple's Prayer*" (Trueblood, *The Lord's Prayers*, 45).

must take something close at hand, lift it up as high as we can, and say, "God is like this." This is what Christ does for us when He speaks of God as a *father*.

There are times when God is nothing more than a conclusion at the end of an argument, a being posited to explain the universe. So long as God is but a concept in a syllogism, He is external to us. For Christianity to begin within us, the God we outwardly reason about must be inwardly experienced. Thinking of God as *our Father* is meant to move us in that direction—"The experience of religion consists in the perception of the supreme goodness or loveliness or friendliness or trustworthiness of the ultimate nature of things" (Baille, *And the Life Everlasting*, 191). We must believe that the ultimate reality—God—is supremely good, lovely, trustworthy, and gracious (Heb. 11.6), and thinking of God as our *father* is meant to move toward this thought.

The problem is that even the best human father is flawed. Thus, the real model for God's fatherhood—the real way to think of Him—is as Jesus (Jn. 14.9)—Christ is the best clue we have to the kind of God that God is. Based on Christ, God is One who "loves us better than we love ourselves. Our deepest interests are safer—beyond imagination safer—in His hand than they would be, had we ourselves the most unrestricted guardianship over them. And all the things that matter in the universe are safer in His hands than they could ever be in ours. Justice is safer. Friendship is safer. Love itself is safer. The cherished gains of the past are safer; and so also the promise of the future. 'So the All-great were the All-loving too.' The Omnipotence behind the universe is our Father and our Friend" (Baille, *And the Life Everlasting*, 194). No pagan philosopher ever imagined a God more glorious than the One revealed in Christ.

The *Lord's Prayer* is a prayer template—*In this manner … pray*—that divides into two parts: vv 9–10 contain three second-person petitions for God; vv 11–13 contain three first-person petitions for ourselves. The brevity of these petitions leaves them somewhat ambiguous, but far from being a detriment, in this lies their strength. "Countless human beings have been able to find a home in the Lord's Prayer for their own hopes and petitions" (Luz I, 314).

In true prayer, God comes first—His majesty, rule, and will have priority. Only after we have addressed His wants should we proceed to ours.

The tenses in the petitions encompass all our needs: *give us* concerns the present, *forgive us* concerns the past, and *lead us not* looks to the future. Furthermore, these petitions imply each being in the Godhead: asking for daily bread makes us think of the Father who provides for His children (7.9–11); asking for forgiveness makes us think of the Son who saved us from our sins (26.28); and asking for guidance causes us think of the Spirit, who leads us through His Word (4.8–10).

This prayer was never meant as a talisman to be mindlessly regurgitated. "How sad that Christ's very attempt to help men to escape from meaningless rote should sometimes become meaningless rote" (Trueblood, *The Lord's Prayers*, 48). A prayer that means nothing to us, means nothing to God.

6.9 In this manner, therefore, pray: Our Father in heaven, Hallowed be Your name.

I've previously referenced Barclay's observation that we define words by our experience, and this is particularly true, I think, with the term *father*. Because I had a loving father, this word is for me one of the most wonderful in my vocabulary. But not everyone had my father; there are some for whom *father* is a synonym for *devil*. How, then, does Christ want us to understand *father*?

Father has two primary meanings. It can indicate *paternity,* describing a male responsible for the birth of a child. But it is possible to sire a child without ever seeing the child. The deeper meaning of father, therefore, is *fatherhood*, which implies a *relationship* of love, intimacy, and trust. Although I believe that God is our father in the *paternal* sense (as our creator), I think it is the *fatherhood* sense that's meant here. God is everyone's *father* by virtue of creation; but in a special way, He is the *Father* of the new creation (2 Cor. 5.17).

The word *abba* gets at the idea. In Gethsemane, Jesus prayed *Abba, Father* (Mk. 14.36), and Paul twice said that Christians can pray to God this way (Rom. 8.15; Gal. 4.6). "The word *abba* ... was the word by which a little child in Palestine addressed his father in the home circle. ... There is only one possible English translation of this word in any ordinary use of it, and that is 'Daddy'" (Barclay, *The Beatitudes & The Lord's Prayer for Everyman,* 169). The relationship implied by *daddy* indicates God's approachability;[8] our *Father* and *Abba* close the gap between God and man. God is no capricious despot who is approached only under threat of death (Est. 4.16), but is One as accessible to us as a loving father (7.7–11).

Our is plural, indicating this prayer is suitable for a group of Christians. *In heaven* implies the transcendence of deity, without negating the imminence of *Father*. John Updike's observation in his autobiographical memoir, *Self-Consciousness*, is worth repeating: "Our brains are no longer conditioned for reverence and awe" —the familiarity implied by *Father* must never breed contempt for our Father's majesty.

Hallowed goes back to the earliest Eng. versions of the Bible; newer versions have replaced it with *holy, revered, honored, venerated*. To *hallow* God is simply to give Him the highest esteem and devotion of which we are capable.

To us, a *name* is nothing more than what a person is called, but in Bible times, a *name* signified what a person was—his character. *Those who know Your name will put their trust in You* (Ps. 9.10); *I have manifested Your name to the men whom You have given Me out of the world* (Jn. 17.6). Does this petition ask God to hallow His own name, or does it mean we are to hallow it? If the first, Christ's resurrection was the supreme example of such; if the second (Isa. 29.23–24), we do so by living lovingly (6.34). Instead of a case of either/or, this is likely a case of both/and.

6.10 Your kingdom come. Your will be done on earth as *it is* in heaven.

The *kingdom* was a central theme of Christ's gospel (3.2, 4.17). Older Restoration Movement commentators tended to interpret *your kingdom come* almost exclusively as referring to the establishment of the church on Pentecost[9]; but to see this request only that way limits its scope.

Kingdom is typically thought of as a certain area or territory (e.g., the Kingdom of Saudi Arabia), but as used by Christ, it primarily conveys the idea of *kingship*—God's rule, the authority He possesses and exercises. The *kingdom comes* in its truest sense when we bow to God's authority and do His will, thus incorporating His will *within* us (Lk. 17.20–21). The kingdom, however, is not within everyone, for not everyone is ruled by

---

[8] By *daddy* I do not mean *buddy*; even with fathers there is a line of decorum separating loving respect and disrespect.

[9] "This is a petition for the inauguration of the kingdom which Jesus came to establish" (McGarvey, 64). "Since his kingdom has been established, his children now pray for the 'spread of the kingdom'" (Boles, 160).

God. I think it perfectly valid, therefore, to pray *your kingdom come* as a petition that God's rule come to men who have shut Him out. Until God governs the hearts of all, this petition remains relevant.

Your will be done is how God's kingdom comes; He rules when He is obeyed. Prayer isn't something we engage in so that our will be done; we pray asking that God work through us to do what He wants done. Gethsemane sheds light here (26.42)—*Your will be done* reached its summit when Christ became obedient unto the death of the cross.

On earth as it is in heaven reverses the order of the original: "as in heaven and [or, also] on the earth" is how the Gr. reads. Heaven is the pattern for earth (16.19); the obedience found there is to be duplicated here. The only way we can have "heaven on earth" is when God's will is obeyed.

6.11 Give us this day our daily bread.

After addressing God's concerns, Christ turns to man's. As obvious as the meaning of the words *give us this day our daily bread* might seem, more has been written about this petition than any other because of the word *daily* (*ton epiousion*). *Epiousios* is the rarest of Gr. words, not being found in any extra-Biblical document.[10] It's a compound word whose literal meaning is something like *upon our substance* or *above our substance*. How it has been interpreted ranges from the figurative (the Lord's Supper or "the invisible bread of the Word of God," Augustine) to the literal. Some translators see a future element (*our bread for the morrow*, NEB, RSV margins).[11] I understand *bread*, here, as a metonymy for our physical needs. Throughout Christian history, there has been concern for bodies as well as for souls (as exemplified in the building of hospitals), an emphasis justified by the fact that man, who is body and spirit, requires physical sustenance (4.3,11). People need ideas for their minds, and they need food for the bodies. Because God gave us a body, it's no surprise that a petition for our body is in this prayer.

This request for bread would be especially important in an economy in which having enough food was not a given. To miss a day's work might mean that an individual or his family didn't eat that day (20.7). This

---

[10] An exception to this may be a single, late, and textually uncertain instance in a Hawara (Egyptian) papyrus accounting book, which is now lost. See Luz I, 319. The only other occurrence of the word is in Lk. 11.3.

[11] A. T. Robertson has a splendid discussion of *epiousios* in his comments on this verse in his *Word Pictures in the New Testament*.

petition would also have special significance for those whom Christ sent out to preach (10.10).

The verb *give* is a divine word (Jn. 3.16), characteristic of a loving God who richly gives us all things to enjoy (1 Tim. 6.17). God can provide for our physical needs apart from our involvement (4.11, 14.17–20, 15.34–38), but when we ask Him for bread, we understand that if we do nothing more than pray, we will likely starve. God has ordered life so that His blessing comes because of His giving and our doing.

The pronouns *us/our* continue the community aspect of this prayer, which isn't surprising, for love has an *us/our* outlook, rather than a selfish *I/my* perspective.

The precise meaning of the adjective *daily* may be uncertain,[12] but translators overwhelmingly believe that it indicates *now* or *today* rather than *then* or *tomorrow*. We are to live with a daily focus; day by day we ask God for what we need to get us through the day (v 34). I don't believe *bread* here implies a wide-screen TV, microwave, or smartphone; in the West, we're often concerned with luxuries, whereas God promises necessities (v 25). When He supplies seed for the sower (2 Cor. 9.10), this request is being answered.

6.12 And forgive us our debts, as we forgive our debtors.

Forgiveness was an important part of Jewish prayers. Man needs bread, but man doesn't live by bread alone (4.4); to truly live, man needs forgiveness (5.4). By including this petition, Christ expected this prayer to be endlessly necessary. They who understand the power of sin know that forgiveness is an ongoing need. Sin is represented in Scripture as a trespass or transgression (v 14), but here it is a *debt* we cannot repay (18.24ff).

Debt implies that God is owed something, namely, our total obedience (3.15). Through disobedience, we become indebted to Him, and present obedience can never pay off past disobedience for present obedience is the minimum requirement of the present, leaving nothing left over to apply to the past or store up for the future. Eliminating our spiritual debt is thus a moral impossibility for us, but not for God (19.25–26). When we ask Him to *forgive* (*aphiemi*, send away, let go), we are asking that our debt be cancelled (18.27), our sins covered, and our iniquities not imputed (Ps. 32.1–2, 103.12). And all this our loving Father does.

---

[12] "The petition for bread continues to be impossible to interpret with certainty" (Luz I, 319).

As we forgive our debtors involves a critical element. Our relationship with God cannot be right when our relationship with a brother is wrong (5.21–26; 1 Jn. 4.7–11). Just as mercy is shown the merciful (5.7; Jas. 2.13), so forgiveness is given the forgiving. We shouldn't expect to receive from God what we are unwilling to give to others. Forgiving another doesn't put God in our debt (nothing we do puts God in our debt), but an unforgiving spirit can block Him from forgiving us. So critical is this truth that Christ comments on it further in a postscript (vv 14–15) and parable (18.23–35).

6.13 And do not lead us into temptation, but deliver us from the evil one. For Yours is the kingdom and the power and the glory forever. Amen.

The previous petition dealt with *sin*, but this one deals with *situations*.

The term *temptation* is ambiguous. Depending on the context, it can indicate an attempt or endeavor (Acts 16.7), an examination or test (2 Cor. 13.5, Rev. 2.2), an external trial (Jas. 1.2), or an internal seduction to sin (4.1; Jas. 1.13). Because God never tempts us to sin, I think the third of these definitions (trial) best fits the context.

Trials are situations into which the Lord leads us (4.1) or allows us to find ourselves. They are an inescapable part of our existence. As Origen pointed out, the Septuagint version of Job 7.1 could be translated: *is not man's life on earth one continuous temptation?* (*On Prayer*, Ch 19). Trials can be times when pain seems perpetual, wounds incurable, healing impossible, God a liar (Jer. 15.18), and the loss of faith a possibility. God doesn't allow these situations because He wants us to fail, but that our faith in Him be strengthened, matured, and enriched. *When He has tested me, I shall come forth as gold* (Job 23.10). *Count it all joy when you fall into various trials, knowing that the testing of your faith produces patience* (Jas. 1.2–3). *In this you greatly rejoice, though now for a little while, if need be, you have been grieved by various trials, that the genuineness of your faith, being much more precious than gold that perishes, though it is tested by fire, may be found to praise, honor, and glory at the revelation of Jesus Christ* (1 Pet. 1.6–7).

What does it mean, then, to ask God to lead us not into temptation? "To take a very simple human analogy … we can easily imagine a student saying to his teacher … 'Go easy with me! Don't push me too hard!' It may well be that this is the best way in which to approach this petition; it may be best simply to see in it the instinctive appeal of the man who knows how weak he is and how dangerous life can be, and who takes his own peril to the protection of God" (Barclay, *The Beatitudes & The Lord's Prayer for Everyman*, 251). The superscription to Psalm 102 reads: *A Prayer of the afflicted, when he is overwhelmed and pours out his complaint before the LORD.* During such times, *lead us not into temptation* is a plea that God keep His promise of 1 Corinthians 10.13 and not allow the ordeal to exceed our strength or endurance. Like Habakkuk, we ask that God in His wrath remember mercy (Hab. 3.2).

It would be wonderful if, when we came to Christ, we found the power to forever destroy the pull of temptation. But life doesn't work that way. Temptation is ever present; victory involves not its elimination, but rather an unceasing struggle against it, refusing to be subjugated to it, and thus remaining unconquered by it. To be rid of a sinful appetite in one conclusive battle would be welcome, but rarely does this happen. Should God ordain for our eternal good that we spend time in the shadow of death, our plea is that He deliver us from all dangers encountered. And in this, He excels (2 Tim. 4.18; 2 Pet. 2.9).

The concluding doxology recalls David's prayer in 1 Chronicles 29.10–13. To God alone belongs the rule (v 10), the power (to answer our prayers and govern our lives), and the glory. Glory is a more than human word. We loosely use it to indicate honor and fame, but glory, truly, speaks of the divine and celestial majesty of God (17.1–8, 2 Pet. 1.16), the Greatest Great.

6.14–15 "For if you forgive men their trespasses, your heavenly Father will also forgive you. But if you do not forgive men their trespasses, neither will your Father forgive your trespasses

This postscript reinforces the warning that an unforgiving man cannot be in fellowship with God (v 12). What was first called a *debt* now becomes a *trespass* (*paraptōma*, a false step, a blunder). One reason why this addendum is necessary, I think, is that Biblical forgiveness involves *reinstating a sinner in the relationship against which he sinned* — which makes forgiving another one of the heaviest demands made on a disciple of Christ. Reconciliation isn't hard when another's behavior only bruises us and the wound is easily dismissed; it's when another's sin breaks us, shattering our trust and leaving our heart in pieces that the difficulty of forgiveness is seen. Opposing forgiveness (5.23–25) are the forces of bitterness, anger, and malice. The fact that forgiveness is undeserved, that the innocent is the one hung on a cross, that it costs the giver more than the receiver—only enhances its difficulty. Chesterton's observation that "Christianity has not been tried and found wanting, it has been found difficult and left untried," well applies here.

Without superabundant love there will be no forgiveness. And without forgiving, our forgiveness is impossible.

In Fasting, 6.16–18

6.16 "Moreover, when you fast, do not be like the hypocrites, with a sad countenance. For they disfigure their faces that they may appear to men to be fasting. Assuredly, I say to you, they have their reward.

A third piety is *fasting*, which is not a religious ritual but a cry to God (Jer. 14.12). Fasting is when one abstains from one thing (usually food, 15.32) to concentrate on another thing (17.19–21). It isn't something manufactured but something that comes naturally. Fasting is an intensification of mourning—an emotional italicizing or underscoring—that stresses the seriousness of our appeal to God (2 Sam.12.16–22). The Law of Moses required fasting only on the Day of Atonement (Lev. 16.29–31; Acts 27.9), but the Jews turned it into a religious ritual (Zech, 7.1–7; Lk. 18.12). Though Christ fasted for nearly six weeks in the wilderness (4.2), His regular practice differed noticeably from that of most Jews (9.14–17).

Sad countenance (*skuthrōpos,* only here and Lk. 24.17; sullen, with a dark look, gloomy) is frequently found in Gr. literature in reference to members of strange cults. When a Jew fasted, it was common for him to put on sackcloth, forego usual hygiene, and cover his head with ashes—devices tailor-made for those who sought attention. As with almsgiving and prayer, fasting done to impress men receives its full reward when men are impressed.

6.17–18 But you, when you fast, anoint your head and wash your face, so that you do not appear to men to be fasting, but to your Father who *is* in the secret *place;* and your Father who sees in secret will reward you openly.

Christ offers no rationale for Christian fasting (Mk. 2.20) but assumes His followers will do so out of a desire to be properly oriented toward God (9.15, 17.21; Acts 13.1–3, 14.23). Because God sees the *secret places* of a man's heart (v 6), He knows whether piety or pride is the motive.

When Christians fast, they are to wash their face and perform their daily hygiene, outwardly appearing the same. We don't become righteous by looking ridiculous.

Christ's teaching against hypocrisy resounds "through the ages as the most awful challenge to all veneer, all seeming, all double-mindedness, all unreality in religion" (Jones, 217).

Unrighteousness, 6.19–34

Wealth, 6.19–24

Notes

Any prophet who attempts to reform society must address the problem of riches. In our scale of values, only one thing can be first, and Christ minces no words in declaring that God is to be first, with all else taking a back seat. This is consistent with the order of *the Lord's Prayer* (see Notes, v 9). Nothing good is missed by putting God first; love, health, comfort, recreation, money, and all other things are elevated when made subservient to Him.[13] True wealth isn't found in money but in character; they who put cash above character make it impossible for the gospel to ennoble their life (13.22) and will suffer for their mistaken priority (1 Tim. 6.10; Jas. 5.1–3).[14]

---

[13] *"To dress, to call, to dine, to break / No canon of the social code, / The little laws that lacqueys make, / The futile Decalogue of Mode, — / How many a soul for these things lives / With pious passion, grave intent! / And never ev'n in dreams has seen / the things that are more excellent!"* William Watson, *The Things That Are More Excellent.*

[14] "Take Henry Ryecroft as a case in point; and Henry Ryecroft was the last man in the world to despise the value of money. On the contrary, 'You tell me,' he says, almost savagely, 'you tell me that money cannot buy the things most precious. Your commonplace proves that you have never known the lack of it. When I think of all the sorrow and the barrenness that has been wrought in my life by want of a few more pounds per annum than I was able to earn, I stand aghast at money's significance. What kindly joys have I lost—those simple forms of happiness to which every heart has claim—because of poverty! Meetings with those I loved made impossible year after year; sadness, misunderstanding, nay, cruel alienation arising from inability to do the things I wished, and which I might have done had a little money helped me; endless instances of homely pleasure and contentment curtailed or forbidden by narrow means. Solitude often cursed my life because I was poor.' And yet, towards the close of his life, he marshalled, in grateful retrospect, all the most joyous and delightful experiences he had ever known. And, in doing so, the thing that surprised him most was the fact that the pleasures that stood out most prominently in his memory were the pleasures that had come to him without money and without price. His strolls in country lanes; his long, familiar chats with congenial companions; his relish of common foods and simple fruits; his enjoyment of certain books picked up cheaply at a second-hand stall; his memoires of gorgeous sunsets that transfixed sea and land, of moonlight nights when the fields sparkled with the frost, and the river was like a stream of molted silver, of the russet

The section from 6.19 to 7.11 is virtually the same length as 5.21–48. It divides into two parts: vv 19–34 deals with possessions; 7.1–11 is harder to categorize, but it basically discusses criticism (of self and others) and prayer. *Destroy* in v 19 is the same word (*aphanizō*) translated *disfigure* in v 16; and *eye* in vv 22–23 anticipates 7.3–5. Following an exhortation and explanation (vv 19–20), Christ states three propositions (vv 21, 22–23, 24a–c), followed by a conclusion (v 24d). Principles discussed here are illustrated in 19.16–22.

6.19–20 "Do not lay up for yourselves treasures on earth, where moth and rust destroy and where thieves break in and steal; but lay up for yourselves treasures in heaven, where neither moth nor rust destroys and where thieves do not break in and steal.

The Gr. words for *lay up* and *treasures* are forms of *thesaurus* (deposit, wealth), which continues the reward motif from vv 1–18. *Don't store up* (BECK) doesn't mean that savings accounts are sinful but warns against prizing what will perish. "To 'lay up treasure on earth' does not mean being provident but being covetous" (Stott, *The Message of the Sermon on the Mount*, 155).

Corrupt is the same word translated *disfigure* in v 16. Earthly treasures can be corrupted in a variety of ways, such as the destruction of clothes by insects ("Oriental wealth often consisted in embroidered garments or fabrics," Vos, 61), coins rusting (*brōsis*, the act of eating, to gnaw or corrode), and the theft of property (Jas. 5.1–3).[15] *Break through* reflects the a first-century reality that thieves would sometimes dig through a mud brick wall to get at what was inside.

What doesn't last makes a poor treasure; a better spending of life is to live for the eternal rather than the fleeting. The one great thing we have to invest in life is our life, and we should invest it in ways—"holiness of character, obedience to all of God's commandments, souls won for Christ, and disciples nurtured in the faith" (Blomberg, 123)—that will give us the eternal when the temporal is no more.

---

tints of autumn and the delicate sweetness of spring—it was a medley of such images that rushed back upon his mind as he took stock of life's lordliest treasure" (Boreham, "Ian Melville's Will," *The Nest of Spears*, 217–219.

[15] "Lay not up for yourselves treasures upon the earth, where falling markets and depreciating bonds doth consume, and where dishonest directors and promoters break through and steal" (Jones, 225).

6.21 For where your treasure is, there your heart will be also.

Whatever gets our attention gets us. What we value—treasure (vv 19–20)—defines us. What a man is isn't determined by any opinion he professes but by the things he prizes. To invest in the temporal is to waste life on what will not last, but to invest life in the eternal is to travel a path of ever increasing enrichment (Prov. 4.18).

Having warned against false goodness (vv 1–18), Christ warns against false gods. Our god is whatever is most important to us, and if anything other than God is enthroned in our heart, we are idolaters, living in a spiritual darkness that ends in eternal darkness.

6.22 The lamp of the body is the eye. If therefore your eye is good, your whole body will be full of light.

The danger in valuing earthly treasure is illustrated by the figure of a bad eye. *The lamp of the body is the eye* is a general maxim that likely means that the eye is the opening—the window—that lets light in and sight out. If the eye is *good* (*haplous*, sound, clear, healthy; only here and Lk. 11.34), light is admitted, the body benefits, and we can function normally. *A good eye* is a way of looking at life (Col. 3.1–2). If we look at life through eyes of generosity, our entire being will be wonderfully affected; we will know, for instance, the joy of giving (Acts 20.35) and will delight in the blessings of mercy (Matt. 5.7).

6.23 But if your eye is bad, your whole body will be full of darkness. If therefore the light that is in you is darkness, how great *is* that darkness!

But if your eye is bad (*ponēros*, in poor condition, sick) *your whole body will be full of darkness*. The ailment here is moral, not physical. If our eye is bad—selfish—everything we touch is tainted: family relationships, friendships, work, money, etc. When we look at life through selfish eyes, we deteriorate as an individual and our life increasingly becomes dark. And if the light that is in us is darkness, how great is that darkness (Matt. 6. 23). When our good becomes bad, we are very bad indeed.

There is an important warning here: namely, we cannot take a wrong attitude in one part of our life without it affecting the rest of our life. Embracing wrong in one area eventually affects all areas. All it takes for the whole body to be poisoned is to ingest just a little bit of poison. In our attitude about possessions, our entire humanity is at risk.[16]

---

[16] "It is a well-known fact that lack of sufficient light makes it difficult to see things. Yet,

6.24 No one can serve two masters; for either he will hate the one and love the other, or else he will be loyal to the one and despise the other. You cannot serve God and mammon.

Christ reaches the climax of His argument by pointing out that a slave cannot be equally dedicated to two masters. First-century slaves were not American employees who worked eight hours and then went to a second job; slaves totally belonged to their owner, and to belong *totally* to one precludes belonging *partially* to a another. "*Hate* here, as often in the Bible, carries a comparative sense, not necessarily of active dislike so much as of displacement by a higher loyalty" (France, 139; cf. Mal. 1.2–3).

We must choose whom we will serve (Josh. 24.15): God or mammon (*mamōnas*, an Aramaic word meaning stock, provision, supply; sometimes used for riches or wealth).[17] One symptom of covetousness is that most people see no tension between pursuing money and serving God. But money can easily supplant God in our priority system. "Our materialistic civilization ought to be well aware of the bewitching power of money and possessions, but acquisitiveness has become so much a part of the air we breathe that we lack the distance necessary for a proper critique. We piously affirm that we have chosen to serve God, not mammon, but in our daily life it is mammon that sets our priorities and determines our choices. We would like to show a more bountiful eye toward the poor, but we cannot, because we need so much for ourselves. We plan to be more charitable in the future, but at the moment there are too many things we have to buy. We work overtime or at a second job rather than spend time with our children, because there is so much that we want to get for them" (Hare, 73).[18]

It's one thing to have earthly treasure; it's another thing when earthly treasure has us.

---

a sound eye quickly adjusts to the darkness. But if the eye itself is in poor condition, the darkness will be great indeed. In that case, even if the sun were shining, not much would be gained" (Hendriksen, 347).

[17] "Mammon, n. The god of the world's leading religion" (Ambrose Bierce, *The Devil's Dictionary*, 85).

[18] "The greatest single factor that keeps men from going on to perfection is the deceitfulness of riches, for no one ever feels that it is a danger to him. A Roman Catholic priest said that he had heard every sin in the catalogue confessed in the confessional, but not the sin of covetousness" (Jones, 230).

Worry, **6.25–34**

Notes

In times of global, economic, and personal unrest, *do not worry* seems incredibly naïve and possibly the most unrealistic thing Jesus ever said. This command might easily be dismissed, except for the fact that He who said it had plenty to worry about. The shadow of the cross, the dullness of the disciples, the hatred of His enemies, and a thousand other things provided Jesus constant opportunities for worry. Yet He never displayed the anxiety He condemns; instead, He met the tension of every day by trusting in God. "When words like 'Be not anxious' are spoken, it makes all the difference in the world what kind of person says them" (Fosdick). Christ has already taught that our outlook should never be determined by another's conduct (5.38–48); now He says that our outlook should never be determined by life's circumstances.

C. S. Lewis was right when he has Screwtape write to Wormwood that "There is nothing like ... anxiety for barricading a human's mind against the Enemy" (*The Screwtape Letters*, New York: Macmillan, 34), but not all anxiety indicates a defect of faith (see 26.37ff); anxiety can be an affliction rather than a sin.

An introductory prohibition (v 25) is followed by three arguments with two illustrations from nature (vv 26,28), concluding with a summarizing admonition and explanation (vv 31–34).

6.25 "Therefore I say to you, do not worry about your life, what you will eat or what you will drink; nor about your body, what you will put on. Is not life more than food and the body more than clothing?

The meaning of this verse hinges on its first word. *Therefore*—since we cannot serve two masters—*do not worry about your life*. Worry so concentrates our attention on our self that we make a god of our self. And we can no more serve God and self than we can serve God and mammon. Christ isn't forbidding foresight or planning (cf. Joseph's preparations for the lean years in Egypt; 7.24–27, 2 Cor. 11.28, 1 Jn. 4.18), but the debilitating, obsessive, life-controlling anxiety that is often the stepchild of covetousness.

Worry comes from the Old Eng. *wyrgan*, which means to *strangle*—an apt description for what anxiety can do to our soul (13.22). The Gr. word for *worry* (*merimnaō*) conveys an element of fear; to live with the unrelenting, paralyzing fear of loss is torture indeed (1 Jn. 4.8).

Against worry, Christ urges that the God who gives the greater—*life*, *body*—can be trusted to give the lesser—*food*, *clothing*. To resist this reasoning is to doubt our Father's love (v 9).

6.26 Look at the birds of the air, for they neither sow nor reap nor gather into barns; yet your heavenly Father feeds them. Are you not of more value than they?

If God cares for us individually—if, as Augustine said, "He loves us every one as though there were but one of us to love"—we have reason enough to pray and not worry. Two examples from nature, involving birds and flowers, illustrate God's care.

One reason we might doubt God's care comes from our smallness, our insignificance compared to the universe (Ps. 8.4). But comparative value isn't judged by size—if it were, a penny would be worth more than a dime. To assure us of God's concern for the small, Christ directs our attention to birds; despite their smallness and insignificance, they are known by God and are under the aegis of His oversight.

It seems odd that Christ would say that birds do not sow, reap, or store—of course they don't. But He is teaching by contrast: if God providentially cares for birds that do not sow, reap, or store, how much more does He care for people who do sow, reap, and store? This conclusion is strengthened when we remember that it is a loving Father, not a detached Creator, to whom we look to for bread (v 11). *Are you not of more value than they* is an *a fortiori* (lit., for a still stronger reason, all the more) form of comparative reasoning Christ used in His teaching (v 30, 7.11). The old woman who lived in a shoe might have had so many children that she didn't know what to do, but this is never the case with God.

6.27 Which of you by worrying can add one cubit to his stature?

Inserted between the two witnesses to God's care is a statement about human futility. *Stature (helikia)* can refer to one's *age (which of you by worrying can add a single minute to his life?* WMS; Heb. 11.11), but more likely refers to one's *height* (Zacchaeus *was of short stature,* Lk. 19.3) because *cubit (pēchus)* "is not used figuratively of time" (Luz I, 344). Worry's futility is seen in that no amount of it can make us taller.

6.28–29 So why do you worry about clothing? Consider the lilies of the field, how they grow: they neither toil nor spin; and yet I say to you that even Solomon in all his glory was not arrayed like one of these.

A second illustration from the lesser to the greater reinforces the first (v 26). *Consider* (*katamanthanō*, observe well, note carefully; only here in the NT) implies close study for the purpose of learning something. *The lilies of the field* are wild flowers of uncertain identity, but like all flowers, they do not engage in domestic work (*neither toil nor spin*). Solomon was proverbial for the amount of stuff he possessed (2 Chron. 1.13–17, 9.3–6,20–28), but when it came to sheer beauty, he couldn't match the magnificence in which God clothes a lily.

6.30 Now if God so clothes the grass of the field, which today is, and tomorrow is thrown into the oven, *will He* not much more *clothe* you, O you of little faith?

Wild flowers, despite their beauty, are nothing but *grass*—the vegetation that in fuel-starved Judea was used as kindling. If God lavishes such beauty on that which ends up as fuel, He can be trusted to care for those who are served by fuel.

Little faith is not a little fault but an inexcusable rejection of God's loving care. The term occurs five times in the NT, four of which are in Matthew (8.26, 14.31, 16.8). Each time it describes people who should know and do better. Disciples have sufficient reasons to trust God even when they can't understand life. To have *little faith* is to be weak in trust, which makes us easy pickings for worry (13.22).[19]

6.31–33 Therefore do not worry, saying, 'What shall we eat?' or 'What shall we drink?' or 'What shall we wear?' For after all these things the Gentiles seek. For your heavenly Father knows that you need all these things. But seek first the kingdom of God and His righteousness, and all these things shall be added to you.

Therefore summarizes the argument—if God cares for His lower creation, it follows that He, a loving Father (v 9), cares for His highest creation. The questions posed illustrate the kinds of things worriers worry about. Worry comes naturally for *Gentiles*—unbelievers—who have no *heavenly Father* who knows what His children need, even when they don't know what they need or how to articulate it (Rom. 8.26–27; Phil. 4.6, 1 Pet. 5.7).

"Preoccupation," said Fosdick, "is the most common form of failure" (*Twelve Tests of Character*). To be absorbed with trivialities is to fritter

---

[19] Don't tell me that worry doesn't do any good. The things I worry about never happen!

away one's life. Jesus demands a revolution in our standards of value. He expects us to put first things first and to properly subordinate all else. Worry is a form of idolatry in which we make a god of our self. *Seek* means to try to obtain, indicating a desire to possess, and what we are to seek involves two inseparable ideas: the *kingdom of God* (3.2) and *righteousness* (3.15, 5.6,20). Nothing will banish the relentless ache of anxiety more than rechanneling our life to a constant awareness of God's rule and bringing our lives into agreement with His will.

All these things do not promise that Christians will never be in need (2 Cor. 11.23–28), but that God, who knows our needs better than we do, will give us what we need (4.4).

6.34 Therefore do not worry about tomorrow, for tomorrow will worry about its own things. Sufficient for the day *is* its own trouble.

They who trust God live one day at a time. The anxiety and fear that comes from pursuing the earthly cannot avert tomorrow's problems but it can nullify our daily blessings by draining us of the spiritual and emotional energy needed to tackle daily problems. The strength we have today is to be spent on today's issues. *Its own trouble* refers to difficulties and hardships. If this observation seems to end the section pessimistically, at least it ends it realistically.

Things are bad enough as they are; don't borrow trouble.

CHAPTER 7

In Judging, 7.1–6

Notes

Criticizing others is easy; criticizing self is hard. And in possibly no area are we more prone to hypocrisy than in the area of criticism. The enticement of criticism, wrote Stanley Jones, is that it provides satisfaction in two areas: "(1) toward the one criticized, in that it is done for his good, and (2) toward one's self, in the self-satisfaction of being superior to the one criticized" (*The Way*, 145).

This section consists of two parts in which an admonition (vv 1–2) is followed by an illustration (vv 3–5). Two questions focus attention on how hypocrisy can insinuate itself into our assessments of others. Verse 6 summarizes a principle that has been woven into the text since 6.1. The threefold mention of *brother* indicates that at issue here is how love (5.20) behaves in the area of criticism.

7.1–2 "Judge not, that you be not judged. For with what judgment you judge, you will be judged; and with the measure you use, it will be measured back to you.

Judge (*krinō*) has a wide array of meanings, ranging from *decide* to *condemn*; the parallel in Luke 6.37 indicates that condemnation is the idea here. "Judge not" doesn't mean we are to suspend our critical thinking skills or that there is never a time when judging is in order. In v 5, Christ says we are to judge ourselves; in v 6 He expects us to have enough discernment to recognize people who behave like dogs and hogs; and in v 20, He tells us false teachers can be known by their fruit, which implies at least enough critical acumen to distinguish good men from bad men (fruit refers to one's life, behavior). "If we give up judgment we give up almost everything which dignifies human life" (Trueblood, *The Humor of Christ*, 60).

The judging here prohibited is the *judgmentalism* that is characterized by rash conclusions and disparaging comments often said under the breath or behind the back (5.21–22). Forbidden is hypercritical or hypocritical judgment, nitpicking, employing a double-standard. The Pharisees thought it their moral duty to correct people by criticism. Sometimes their criticism was verbal (e.g., 9.11), sometimes nonverbal; they would give a cold shoulder to those they didn't think were living right; I guess you could call this "conversion by avoidance." After all, sin separates a man from God, and what better way to drive that home to a sinner than to act like they don't exist! Christ, however, condemns the mindset that delights in finding fault and refuses to extend the benefit of the doubt (1 Cor. 13.6–7).

That you be not judged doesn't mean that if we are nonjudgmental about others they will be nonjudgmental about us. It's natural to form opinions about others, but to form an unjustified, uncomplimentary opinion invites retaliation. The yardstick we use to criticize will be used against us. "If we give ourselves to criticism, criticism will come back to us with deadly aim" (Jones, 247–248). Even if the target of our unfairness doesn't respond in kind, God's judgment of us will take into consideration our judgment of others (5.22; Jn. 8.7). Every judgment, in a real sense, is a self-judgment (26.52).

7.3–4 And why do you look at the speck in your brother's eye, but do not consider the plank in your own eye? Or how can you say to your brother, 'Let me remove the speck from your eye'; and look, a plank *is* in your own eye?

Trueblood said that when he read these verses to his young son, the boy burst out laughing: "He laughed because he saw how preposterous it would be for a man to be so deeply concerned about a speck in another person's eye, that he was unconscious of the fact his own eye had a beam in it" (*The Humor of Christ*, 9). Maybe you've seen an old Three Stooges' clip in which Curly is carrying a ladder, and every time he turns, the ladder swings around hitting Moe and Larry. That is the picture in this figure.

A *plank* (*dokos*, a log, joist) is a piece of lumber too big to miss. One who is blind to the obvious — who can't see his own sins or flaws — isn't qualified to identify a *speck* (*karphos*, a little piece of anything, something tiny) in another's eye. It is "a curious feature of the human race [that] a profound ignorance of oneself is often combined with an arrogant presumption of knowledge about others, especially about their faults" (Morris, 167).

The mention of *brother* reminds us that brotherly love doesn't rush to judgment or believe the worst about another (1 Cor. 13.7).

7.5 Hypocrite! First remove the plank from your own eye, and then you will see clearly to remove the speck from your brother's eye.

We are always to scrutinize our own life before turning our sights on anyone else. Few parts of the body are more sensitive than the eye; operating on it requires great skill. And skill is needed in helping a brother overcome his faults. We help him because we love him, but the skill to help comes from experience gained in judging self (2 Cor.13.5). To claim the acuity to spot and fix another's small problem while failing to recognize and fix our big problems is hypocritical. *First* and *then* establish priority (5.24, 6.33); before diagnosing another, we first critically examine our self, for only then are we qualified to help another. Specks in our eye are irritating; we want them removed, but not by a doctor who has cataracts. If we can't see our self for what we are, what we are will be pointed out to us when we try to tell others what they are. Sin should be rebuked, but not by those who practice it.

7.6 "Do not give what is holy to the dogs; nor cast your pearls before swine, lest they trample them under their feet, and turn and tear you in pieces."

Commentators are all over the map on the interpretation of this verse (Luz, who is exegetically perceptive in many ways, goes so far as to say that it is a puzzle that doesn't belong in this Gospel).

Two striking pictures make the point that precious things shouldn't be wasted on the indiscriminate and undiscerning. The language is farcical, as in vv 3–4. In first-century Judea, *dogs* could be dangerous scavengers. *Holy* likely refers to sacrificial meat that wasn't fully consumed on the altar; rabbis thought it profane to allow dogs to eat the remains of sacrificial animals. *Swine* were unclean in the extreme, whereas pearls were costly treasures; nobody would deck out a pig in pearls. But Christ is talking about people, not animals. A common view is that He is introducing a subject that He discusses in 10.13–14—namely, attempts to reach the unreachable are a waste of time (15.14). The problem with this interpretation is that it introduces something new into the context. There may be some similarity between not giving pearls to pigs and shaking the dust off one's feet, but Christ has been talking about living the gospel, not preaching it. Accordingly, I think another view is preferable.

Two things seem clear: first, Christ makes a sharp contrast between two groups, and second, there should be no point of contact between the things contrasted (*give not, cast not*). Leading up to this, He has distinguished between noble and shameful things: prayer/self-promotion, treasures in heaven/treasures on earth, faith/worry, compassion for a brother/criticizing a brother, etc. It seems to me that the hyperbole in this verse summarizes the point that we should "recognize what is holy and valuable and treat it accordingly" (McGuiggan). Holy things (e.g., prayer) are not to be handled in a profane way (e.g., self-promotion). Before we judge another to be a dog or hog, let's make sure we're not handling the holy things (truth, blessings, etc.) God gives us in a dog or hog fashion.

Prayer, 7.7–12

Notes

This section concludes the middle part of the Sermon (5.17–7.12), assuring us that what Christ expects, He enables. Anyone, for example, who has tried to break the chokehold of worry knows how difficult the task is, but God makes possible what He commands (19.26).

7.7–8 "Ask, and it will be given to you; seek, and you will find; knock, and it will be opened to you. For everyone who asks receives, and he who seeks finds, and to him who knocks it will be opened.

God decrees not only the end (blessing) but the means (prayer). A three-fold command to pray is followed by the promise that our prayers will be answered. Ask, seek, and knock are synonyms for prayer. We are to pray for what we need, but remember two caveats implicit in the Biblical doctrine of prayer. The first is that God will answer our prayer *if He so wills* (Jas. 4.15). All prayer must be subordinated to His will, and He might say yes, no (26.39–44, 2 Cor. 12.7–9), or wait. The second caveat is that God may answer our prayer by giving us an opportunity. We ask for bread, and He gives us a job (20.1); we pray for patience, and He sends us a problem (Jas. 1.2–5); etc.[1] It's right to ask for bread, forgiveness, guidance (6.9–13), but we should remember that more often than not, we play a critical role in the answer to our prayer (9.38, 25.14–30).

7.9–11 Or what man is there among you who, if his son asks for bread, will give him a stone? Or if he asks for a fish, will he give him a serpent? If you then, being evil, know how to give good gifts to your children, how much more will your Father who is in heaven give good things to those who ask Him!"

Two images from everyday life reinforce v 8 and the certainty that God answers prayer. When a son asks his father to pass the rolls, his father doesn't give him rocks (some stones resemble small, rounded loaves of bread, 4.3); or when his boy asks for a sardine, the father doesn't give him a snake. When a son is hungry, a loving father provides what nourishes, not what mocks or is dangerous; not even an *evil* (*ponēros*, bad, wicked) father would be this evil. *Evil* is used here in a comparative rather than moral sense (6.24); compared to the heavenly Father, human fathers are evil, imperfect in a thousand ways (Heb. 12.10). But if imperfect fathers do what's best for their children, *how much more* (*a fortiori*, 6.26) can a completely good Father be trusted to give what is best to His children.

To those who ask Him establishes the connection between prayer and blessing—God's power is accessed by prayer. Prayer doesn't change God's intention, but it can change God's action. Just as He doesn't give us some things unless we work (e.g., a paycheck), so there are blessings He doesn't bestow unless we pray (Jas. 4.2).

7.12 Therefore, whatever you want men to do to you, do also to them, for this is the Law and the Prophets.

As with the *beatitudes* (5.3–12) and the *Lord's Prayer* (6.9–13), here is another section of the Sermon known by its own label: *The Golden Rule*.

Therefore introduces the conclusion to the middle part of the Sermon. *Whatever you want men to do to you* means love—we want to be loved and be shown love. *Do also to them* is a command to love others as we wish to be loved.

Love takes the initiative (1 Jn. 4.10), as implied in the emphatic *do*. Love

---

[1] *I asked the Lord that I might grow, / in faith, and love and ev'ry grace, / might more of his salvation know / and seek more earnestly his face. Twas he who taught me thus to pray, / and he I know has answered prayer, / but it has been in such a way / as almost drove me to despair* (John Newton).

at its best is not an effect but a cause, generating rather than responding, treating others as we would be treated. The *golden rule* makes the love we have for self a standard in our dealings with others (22.39; Eph. 5.29).

The Law and the Prophets introduced the main body of the Sermon (5.17) and now concludes it. *Love* is what fulfills the Law and Prophets; on love *hangs* the Law and the Prophets (love *is the essence of all true religion*, 22.40, JBP). Love is both the divine essence and the hermeneutical key that unlocks all Scripture.

Conclusion, 7.13–29

Two Ways, **7.13–14**

Notes

Christ concludes the sermon by identifying two possible ways to live life under the figures of two ways (vv 13–14), two teachers (vv 15–23), and two builders (vv 24–27).

7.13–14 "Enter by the narrow gate; for wide *is* the gate and broad *is* the way that leads to destruction, and there are many who go in by it. Because narrow *is* the gate and difficult *is* the way which leads to life, and there are few who find it.

Life reduced to its essence offers only two alternatives that Christ characterizes as a *narrow gate* and *difficult way* or a *wide gate* and *broad way*. *Gate* and *way* are synonyms. Gate (*pulē*) refers to the entrance to a city or temple; *narrow* (*stenos*, strait, KJV; only here and Lk. 13.24) means *restricted* or *difficult* (*tethlimmenē*, to squeeze, press, encumber, afflict).

The way to life is the road less traveled, for most choose the *wide gate/ broad way* that avoids the hard decisions that attend the narrow gate/ difficult way (Gal. 6.12). But the wide gate/broad way leads to *destruction* (*apoleia*, damnation, perdition)—"a fact that its popularity does nothing to alter" (Morris, 174–175). "All life concentrates on man at the crossroads"; the life/road we choose is literally a matter of life or death.

Two Teachers, **7.15–23**

Notes

Ideas have consequences. Ideas a man holds in theory may be difficult to categorize or analyze, but eventually, his ideas will unfold in his life, and his fruit — his living — will reveal his ideas and character, showing him for who he truly is.

The work of *false prophets* swells the numbers of those on the broad way (Jer. 14.13–14), and because of this, it's important that they be recognized for the agents of hell they are. Aas noted by Christ, their *fruit* is one of the best ways to *know them*.

In structure, v 15 introduces the problem of false prophets, vv 16–20 gives a rule for testing prophets (1 Jn. 4.1), v 21 states the rule for entering the kingdom, and vv 22–23 apply the rule of v 21 to prophets.

7.15 "Beware of false prophets, who come to you in sheep's clothing, but inwardly they are ravenous wolves.

We must be careful to whom we listen. *Beware* (*prosechō*, to turn to, *take heed*, 6.1) introduces the threat of *false prophets* (*pseudoprophētēs*, one who characterizes error as truth; 24.11,24; Jer. 27.15). The issue here is not in defining the term *false prophet*, but in identifying a false prophet. We often attempt to do this by scrutinizing a man's beliefs, but Christ says that a better test is a man's behavior.

*The first characteristic mentioned is the disparity between the ex*ternal and internal (the basic trait of a hypocrite). Outwardly, false prophets wear a wool suit (*sheep's clothing*)[2] that implies they are one of the flock, nonthreatening and peaceful (2 Cor. 11.13–15). But inwardly, they have the heart of a wolf (*harpax*, devouring, predatory, voracious; Acts 20.29). Because their outer appearance doesn't match their inner reality, they are hypocrites.

7.16a You will know them by their fruits.

The test for a false prophet is their *fruits*, a common metaphor for how one lives his life (12.33–35, 21.43; Jas. 4.13–18). *You will know them by their fruits* is a law of nature for like produces like (Gen. 1.24; Jas. 3.11–12). The Lord doesn't mention any specific fruits or deeds here, but surely, every matter Christ has introduced since 5.21 (anger, reconciliation, sexual purity, truth-telling, etc.) is an inspectable area of life. *Works* aren't a foolproof means for determining character (v 22; 1 Tim. 5.24), but they are a valuable test nevertheless.

---

[2] Sheep's clothing has traditionally been interpreted as indicating humility, mercy, simplicity, and the like.

7.16b–18 Do men gather grapes from thornbushes or figs from thistles? Even so, every good tree bears good fruit, but a bad tree bears bad fruit. A good tree cannot bear bad fruit, nor *can* a bad tree bear good fruit.

The answer to the rhetorical question—*Do men gather grapes from thornbushes?*—is no; good things don't come from bad people! It sometimes happens that a false teacher (or ungodly man) is excused and tolerated because he is doctrinally orthodox, but false teachers are a danger even if doctrinally correct.

7.19–20 Every tree that does not bear good fruit is cut down and thrown into the fire. Therefore by their fruits you will know them.

Christ shifts from fruit to fate by repeating verbatim the warning of John the Baptist (3.10). They who lead others to destruction (vv 13–14) will be destroyed. "People who run orchards do not put up with rotten trees" (Morris, 178), for at best, bad trees take up valuable space, and at worst, their disease may spread to other trees. A tree isn't bad just because it produces one bad apple—it's bad when it *doesn't produce* good fruit. In a kingdom of love (v 12; 5.20), to not act lovingly is bad (v 12). Like the scribes and Pharisees, we might judge ourselves righteous for what we don't do—we don't murder, fornicate, or so forth—but the greater question is, what do we do out of love?

Verse 16 is repeated for emphasis—just as fruit is the test of a tree, so deeds are the test of a prophet.[3]

7.21 Not everyone who says to Me, 'Lord, Lord,' shall enter the kingdom of heaven, but he who does the will of My Father in heaven.

On the surface, *not everyone* seems to encompass more than just prophets. Without denying the universality of the principle involved, in context, the application is to those cited in vv 16–20.

On *Lord,* see 3.3. Naturally, a Christian prophet would acknowledge Jesus as *Lord* (1 Jn. 2.22), and *Lord, Lord* is especially expressive and imploring; the double appeal seems sincere and faith-based. But as vv 22–23 show, appearances can be deceiving. *Enter the kingdom of heaven* recalls 5.20. The righteousness that exceeds the righteousness of the scribes and

---

[3] The *Didachē,* or *The Teaching of the Twelve Apostles,* is a noncanonical, late first-century treatise. In it, false prophets are defined as those who do not practice what they preach, who stay more than two days in a community, who do not go to the synagogue, who gossip too much, and who charge money for their prophecies.

Pharisees is preeminently a matter of loving obedience to the will of God (6.10). This isn't salvation by meritorious works but involves the paradox that obedience and grace work together (Jas. 2.18).

7.22–23 Many will say to Me in that day, 'Lord, Lord, have we not prophesied in Your name, cast out demons in Your name, and done many wonders in Your name?' And then I will declare to them, 'I never knew you; depart from Me, you who practice lawlessness!'"

In that day is a Hebraism for the last day, the day of judgment. On judgment day, false prophets (the referent of *many*) whom Christ has warned about will plead a right to the kingdom on the basis of miraculous and stupendous things (prophesy, exorcisms, wonders) they had done in the name of Jesus (*Lord, Lord*). But Christ says He never knew them—He didn't recognize them; no relationship existed between Him and them for they *practiced lawlessness*. *You who practice* translates a present participle indicating continuous action, one's habitual practice; they who are unknown by Christ are the chronically *lawlessness*—believing and behaving in ways not sanctioned by God (v 21, 28.19). Lawlessness is the bad tree/bad fruit/fake life that Christ has discussed throughout most of the Sermon. The proof that a man is under the influence of the Holy Spirit has never been the *gifts of the Spirit* (1 Cor. 12.7–11) but the *fruit of the Spirit* (Gal. 5.22–23, loving obedience). Neither preaching in Christ's name, casting out a demon, nor dynamic works are enough to open heaven's gates. Apart from lovingly doing the Father's will on earth as it is done in heaven (v 21, 6.10), nothing we do counts for anything (5.20ff; 1 Cor. 13.1–3).[4]

The fate of the lawless was given in v 19. *Depart from Me* signals total rejection. Throughout Matthew, the reality of judgment (the idea appears in more than sixty places: v 2, 5.21, 10.15, 11.22–24, 12.36,41, 13.36–42,47–50, 21.28, 22.14) is often described in stark figures (outer darkness, weeping, gnashing of teeth, burned in fire, unquenchable fire, worm dies not, etc.) and is used to encourage righteousness (Rom. 11.22ff). "This hell fire and brimstone imagery is unwelcome if not repugnant to a modern generation that has lost a sense of sin and that does not give credence to

---

[4] The Apostle John further develops the tests for distinguishing between the true and the false in his discussion of obedience, belief, and love. To fail in any of these is to fail of the kingdom. For a commentary on 1 John, I recommend Robert Law's *The Tests of Life*. Charles Erdman, in his *The General Epistles*, and John R. W. Stott, in *The Letters of John*, follow Law's analysis.

God's recompense for sin" (Garland, 222). Hell's imagery will become a reality for those who live outside God's will (25.41–46; Lk. 6.46).

Two Builders, **7.24–27**

Notes

The choice before every man concludes with a discussion of two builders who illustrate the importance of *hearing* and *doing* the will of God. No one was ever made better just by hearing a sermon (Jas. 1.21–25).

Regardless of how a man lives, he will experience trouble. Sin can cause suffering, but we can never conclude that suffering is the result of sin (the book of Job was written to refute this idea). The righteous face the same storms as the unrighteous, but with an entirely different outcome.

7.24–27 "Therefore whoever hears these sayings of Mine, and does them, I will liken him to a wise man who built his house on the rock: and the rain descended, the floods came, and the winds blew and beat on that house; and it did not fall, for it was founded on the rock. But everyone who hears these sayings of Mine, and does not do them, will be like a foolish man who built his house on the sand: and the rain descended, the floods came, and the winds blew and beat on that house; and it fell. And great was its fall."

In 5.19, Christ stressed the importance of obedience to God, and at the close of His sermon, He returns to this theme (v 21). Love righteousness *responds* properly to God's *revelation* (28.19). It's not enough that a person merely acts (5.20)—*what* is done (*these sayings of Mine*) is as important as *why* it's done. Christ's *sayings* tell us what must be done, but it is in the *loving doing* of His word that one finds blessing (Jas. 1.25) and glorifies God (5.16).

The wise man—who *hears these sayings of Mine, and does them*—is discussed first. Biblically, the opposite of ignorance isn't knowledge but obedience. An obedient man is pictured as a *wise* (*phronimos*, prudent, sensible, intelligent) *man* who builds his house on rock. Storms (rain, *broche*, in the NT, only here and v 27, and wind) are common OT figures for trouble and ordeals. *Beat* (*proskoptō*, to strike one thing against another; 4.6), when applied to the wind, indicates a cyclone, which says something about the intensity of the trouble that can come our way. To survive the storms of life, we must be built on rock—on Christ (16.16; 1 Pet. 2.6; Isa. 28.16), fortified by the blessings and promises He gives (5.3–12; 19.28–29).

To be a *hearer* only invites catastrophe (Jas. 1.22). No builder in his right mind would build a house on a foundation of dirt or sand,[5] but in life, people do things that are against all reason. To build on sand is to live on the basis of something other than Christ (e.g., money, 6.19–24, self, 6.25–32), and such a life is headed for a *great fall*. Those *foolish* enough to live disregarding the will of the Father (v 21) will be swept away.

On Christ the solid rock I stand: all other ground is shifting sand.

Epilogue, **7.28–29**

Notes

The sermon has ended, and Matthew describes its effect with words that recall 5.1–2 (*ochlos, multitudes, people; didaskō,* taught). The term *authority* will be expanded in the next section, where Christ's *sayings* are backed up by miraculous signs (9.6,8; 10.1). *When Jesus had ended these sayings* is the phrase that concludes the five major discourses in Matthew (11.1, 13.53, 19.1, 26.1).

7.28–29 And so it was, when Jesus had ended these sayings, that the people were astonished at His teaching, for He taught them as one having authority, and not as the scribes.

Never was there so great a preacher and never did He deliver so great a sermon. The hearers were *astonished*, which translates a strong verb (*ekplessō*, to strike out of one's senses)—the audience was stunned, for Christ's teaching was radically different from anything they had heard. Jesus spoke in His own name—*I say unto you*—what He said didn't derive from Moses or the traditions of the elders but from Himself. Barclay says that *exousia* (out of one's substance or property) was a wide-ranging word that indicated prestige, rank, a free hand, the right to do something, power and control over people and circumstances (*By What Authority*, 79). The scribes taught using footnotes, basing their teaching on the opinions of teachers before them. But Jesus' teaching was based on Himself; He spoke with a ring of authority that was divine. And the people noticed it. "The motif of Jesus' authority, which appears here for the first time, will recur repeatedly (8.9; 9.6; 10.1; 21.23), until we finally reach the climactic declaration of the Great Commission, 'All authority in heaven and on earth has been given to me' (28.18)" (Hare, 87).

---

[5] "Utterly improbable cases have to be supposed in parables to illustrate human folly" (A. B. Bruce, quoted by Morris, 183).

Excursus on Foundations

There is an old adage that "what goes up, must come down," and the job of a foundation is to offset the downward pull.

The science of seismology unanimously attests that the best foundation is rock. In *Peace of Mind in Earthquake Country*, Peter Yanev writes, "During the early morning 1906 San Francisco quake, some people living on top of the famous hills of that city were not even awakened by the enormous tremor, and numerous un-reinforced masonry buildings located on these bedrock hills survived the earthquake without significant damage. On the other hand, in homes atop the landfill along the bay and the alluvial soils between the hills of San Francisco, people were thrown out of bed by the shock and found themselves unable to get on their feet during the sixty seconds that the motion lasted. Many of the buildings on these flat, thick-soiled areas totally collapsed; structures built on solid rock near the fault or epicenter of an earthquake fared better than more distant buildings on soft soils." Soil foundations are dangerous for two reasons, the first being their instability. "The shock waves of an earthquake are amplified by soft soil, and strong shocks can cause compaction of the clay and settlement of the ground surface." The second reason is called *liquefaction*. "Soil which is stable under normal conditions and apparently quite suitable for a building foundation can suddenly change to 'soup' and flow like a liquid when shaken in an earthquake. This effect, called 'liquefaction,' can cause the most dramatic failures; complete buildings may sink or topple over, and large areas may be subjected to landslides."

Because people, as well as bridges and buildings, are liable to collapse when the storms of life hit, a solid foundation is essential. *When the storm has swept by, the wicked are gone, but the righteous stand firm forever* (Prov. 10.25, NIV).

CHAPTER 8

8.1–9.35: Through Works

Notes

In antiquity, a king would place his seal on a communication as a sign to the recipient that the message sent was authentic—that it really came from the king and not from an impersonater. For this system to work, the seal had to be unique, recognizable, and something only the king possessed.

Miracles were the divine seal—supernatural acts that made them unmistakeable signs because they were unique (9.33), recognizable (Acts 4.16), and explainable only by positing God (Jn. 3.2). They were to the unseen what lighting is to electrified air: visible evidence of the invisible. "A miracle," said Anthony Flew, "is something which would never have happened had nature, as it were, been left to its own devices" (N. Geisler and F. Turek, *I Don't Have Enough Faith to Be an Atheist*, 201). "A higher form of existence manifests itself in higher accomplishments and powers" (Bales, *The Biblical Doctrine of Christ*, 17). Knowing that extraordinary claims demand extraordinary proof, Christ didn't leave His claims in the realm of the unverifiable, but confirmed them by miracles (9.2–8; Jn. 5.36; Acts 2.22; Heb. 2.3–4).[1]

Four words in the NT describe supernatural acts: *miracle* (*dunamis*), something mighty or powerful; *wonder* (*teras*), the impression made on witnesses (9.8); *work* (*ergon*), an objective, concrete act; and *sign* (*semainō*), an indicator that points to something beyond itself (Jn. 20.30–31). Christ's miracles were characterized by their *extent* (encompassing nature, v 26, 14.25; material elements, 14.15–21; all disease, 4.23, 9.35; men, 9.4, Lk. 4.28–30; demons, vv 28–32, 12.22–29; death, 9.23–25), *success* (Jesus never lost a

---

[1] "Experience leads us to realize that the arrogation of authority to oneself apart from a substantial basis for the claim ends in exposure to ridicule. The higher the claim the greater the risk" (Harrison, 97).

patient or failed in His attempt to work a miracle), *immediacy* (occurring instantly, vv 3,14–15),[2] and *visibility* (performed publicly without props, set up, or accomplices). Christ's miracles were so obviously devoid of dishonesty that not even His enemies could deny them (Jn. 11.47). But more than merely displaying divine muscle, miracles were revelatory, giving insight into Christ's heart.

Verses 1–17,18–34, and 9.2–34 are self-contained units marked by topographical and geographical indicators. In v 1, Jesus comes down from the mountain; in v 18, He crosses the Sea of Galilee; in 9.1, He recrosses the Sea of Galilee.[3]

Excursus on Miracles

"We should probably agree that though the 'works of healing' may well have been miracles in the eyes of the disciples of Jesus, they would not so appear to us. As a matter of fact, it is rather doubtful whether at the time they were considered so very wonderful. They seem to have differed only in degree from cures performed by other men. They were sufficient to call forth delight and astonishment, love and reverence, but they were not 'signs from heaven.'"

So writes Donald Hankey, an author whose devotional writings I admire, in *The Lord of All Good Life* (165). I include this excerpt because it is representative of those who believe the validity of Christianity is unconnected to the reality of Christ's miracles. The problems with this view are many, but let me point out just one.

The miracles in Matthew seem to have been selected with an eye to refuting any attempt to explain them naturally. Mind over matter isn't involved when advanced symptoms of leprosy disappear instantaneously. And nature has no explanation for how a servant is cured of paralysis at the very time Jesus, from a distance, pronounces him cured. It's true, as Hankey admits (168) "that sudden storms do sometimes subside as quickly as they arise," but it is not true that there is a *great calm* on the sea as soon as a storm blows itself out. And it has never been shown that pigs are susceptible to psychosomatic suggestion.

The miracles in Matthew defy all attempts to explain them by nature or magic, which isn't surprising, for they really were miraculous.

---

[2] In the single exception to this rule — Mark 8.22–26 — Jesus healed in two stages to teach a point about the disciples' spiritual acuity.

[3] "The believers in miracles accept them (rightly or wrongly) because they have evidence for them. The disbelievers in miracles deny them (rightly or wrongly) because they have a doctrine against them" (G. K. Chesterton, *Orthodoxy*).

LEPROSY, 8.1–4

8.1 When He had come down from the mountain, great multitudes followed Him.

Verse 1 is a transition from the Sermon on the Mount to its aftermath. *Great multitudes followed Him* repeats 4.25. Having gone up the mountain to preach the gospel, Christ comes down to practice it.

8.2 And behold, a leper came and worshiped Him, saying, "Lord, if You are willing, You can make me clean."

Leprosy has long been regarded a metaphor for sin; that it is the first specific disease Christ heals in this Gospel suggests the deeper truth that He came to deal with sin and not just sickness (1.21).

Behold appears over sixty times in the book; it's purpose is to focus attention. The term *leprosy* has been applied to various skin diseases, but here, it's the disease described in Leviticus 13 to 14—the most terrible disease known to the Jews, thought to be as difficult to cure as it would be to raise the dead (Luz II, 5).[4] If leprosy could be cured—something considered impossible—surely it would signify the Messiah's arrival (11.5). Luke the physician (5.12) says this man was *full of leprosy*, indicating an advanced case. This leper would have been utterly repulsive: his body falling apart, open sores, a smell so vile you could taste it, all who saw him reacting with fear and disgust—a living picture of one seemingly cursed by God. But the leper displayed a daring faith in approaching Christ, worshiping Him (2.2), calling Him *Lord* (7.21), and asking for help (7.7–8). *If You are willing* is a third-class conditional sentence (undetermined, but with the prospect of being determined) expressing doubt, not about Christ's strength, but about His sympathy—"Are you willing to heal one like me?"[5]

---

[4] Modern leprosy is a mildly infectious disease caused by the *Mycobacterium lepae* bacillus. *Lepros* (a scale) refers to dermatological symptoms that include swellings, scabs or spots below the surface of the skin; the skin and hair within the infected area turning white and, in advanced cases, raw flesh (Lev. 13).

[5] In *Village of the Outcasts*, Robert M. Wulff, who spent many years treating lepers in Thailand, described these symptoms: hands and feet of which nothing was left except rough, uneven stumps; faces puffed up and badly deformed; noses caved in and almost flat with the face due to the collapse of the nose bridge; fingers and toes that had withered away; muscular contractions that produced the 'claw hand' and 'drop foot'; ears that were pendulous and puffy; sores oozing pus that covered the whole body; and ulcerations that went to the bone. He also described the terrible stench that attended lepers. Leprosy is the least contagious of the infectious diseases, but it produces the greatest number of bacteria; when the dead

8.3 Then Jesus put out His hand and touched him, saying, "I am willing; be cleansed." Immediately his leprosy was cleansed.

When Jesus *touched* the man, it undoubtedly brought a gasp from the crowd, for contact with a leper rendered one unclean (Lev. 5.2–3). Some rabbis taught that no one should come within six feet of a leper (100′ if downwind; Lev. 13.45), and Jews were known to throw rocks at lepers who got too close (Edersheim I, 495). But while others stood back, disgusted and nervous at being so close to one so unclean, Jesus touched the man ("It must have been years since the man had experienced such contact with anyone who did not have the disease," Morris, 189). The significance of this is enormous. Christ didn't have to touch a sick person in order to heal (vv 5–13), but He touched this leper, and in so doing, identified with him in his sickness (a touch is one of the most tangible ways by which we communicate love). Christ came to share our predicament, taking on Himself our infirmities and weaknesses (v 17; Heb. 2.11). Identifying with the sick, the hurting, and the unclean is what love does (but the last thing legalism does, 9.11). By a touch, the Lord breached the buffer zones that society and religion put around lepers, not turning from the stench of putrefaction, the risk of contamination, or the stigma of association with the repulsive (9.9–13). By a touch, Christ took upon Himself the man's uncleanness.[6]

"Are you willing?" the leper asked. "Of course I'm willing!" Jesus answered; "Don't ever think otherwise!" — and doesn't this speak volumes about the kind of God Christ is? *Be cleansed* was the command, and the disease obeyed: the rotting skin disappeared, the face returned to normal, and the odor of death was gone.

8.4 And Jesus said to him, "See that you tell no one; but go your way,

---

bacilli are exuded through the skin they produce a nauseating stench that has been likened to "the smell of death." As cruel as it seems, the physical side of leprosy was the good news. The worst part of leprosy was not the mechanical breakdown of the cells, but the emotional and psychological trauma—the sensory deprivation—that resulted from being unwanted. "I know it is fashionable in America nowadays to refer to leprosy as Hansen's disease and to minimize the misery and suffering it causes, but to my mind it is one of the most horrible afflictions a person can have. In addition to the physical deformity the patients suffered mentally. They had been shunned by their society and cast out. They knew they were ugly and unwanted, and I thought I could detect in their eyes a loss of hope" (27). Hansen's disease primarily acts as an anesthetic on the body's nervous system, numbing the pain cells of the hands, feet, eyes, etc. Lacking the sensation of pain, sufferers often abuse their bodies in such a way that results in the destruction and decay of tissue.

[6] In Psalm 38, David uses the language of leprosy to describe how he was treated after some unspecified sin.

show yourself to the priest, and offer the gift that Moses commanded, as a testimony to them."

Why Jesus told some not to tell others about His miracles is puzzling, and it may be that no single explanation covers all instances. Christ's miracles were meant for public consumption (9.6; Jn. 20.30–31), and as Luke 5.15 shows, news of this incident spread like wildfire. Despite Christ telling people not to talk about a miracle He performed (9.30, 12.16, etc.), word always got out. "Jesus recognized early on that the excitement generated by miracles did not readily convert into life-changing faith" (Yancey, *The Jesus I Never Knew*, 166). "How strange it is that even though Jesus charged them with silence, they published it abroad. Yet we who are charged to publish glad tidings are so derelict in doing so" (Hobbs, 114).

Here, *see that you tell no one* may have indicated priority—before he did anything else, the man needed to honor the Law (5.17–18). Christ tells him to present himself to the priest *as a testimony to them*. In OT times, should leprosy go into remission and its symptoms disappear, the leper was to appear before a priest. Part of the ceremony certifying the leper's cleanness involved killing a clean bird, draining its blood into a bowl and mixing it with water (Lev. 14.6–7). The priest then took another clean bird and plunged it into the blood and water, thus turning it into a red bird, covered with blood. This bird was then set free. All of this, of course, was a foreshadow of Christ.

But even more, this leper's cleansing was a sign to the very group involved in putting Christ to death at the end of the Gospel—the priests. Unwittingly (Acts 3.17) and ironically, the Jewish priesthood would play a critical role in making possible their own cleansing by putting Christ to death (1.21, 26.28). Assuming Christ told every leper He cleansed to do what was told this leper, the priests had a steady stream of evidence that exposed the egregious nature of their murderous intent (Acts 6.7). Yet, in it all, the wrath of man would praise God (Ps. 76.10).

PARALYSIS, 8.5–13

Notes

Christ's first miracle blessed a Jew; His second blessed a Gentile. His first miracle signified His intention to save from sin; His second signified His intention to save Gentiles, as well as Jews, from sin. To the Jew first but also to the Greek; the Abrahamic promise included all (1.1).

This is the most detailed encounter in this section. Conversation and discourse dominate. The scope of mercy is emphasized and the gospel's universal theme advanced (1.1, 28.19); Christ's center of operations may have been Galilee, but His horizon was the world. "It was the breadth of Jesus' ideas and sympathies which first brought him into conflict with his countrymen. The Jews as a people were proverbially narrow and bigoted. ... The Jews were an exclusive and haughty and aristocratic race, constantly thanking God that they were superior to all other nations. But the spirit of Jesus was different" (Jefferson, *The Character of Jesus*, 122). "People ... who divide the world into 'us' and 'them,' don't know what they're talking about when they talk about God" (Stephen Mitchell, *Jesus, What He Really Said and Did*, 23).

8.5 Now when Jesus had entered Capernaum, a centurion came to Him, pleading with Him,

On *Capernaum*, see 4.13. *Centurion* is the Lat. word for *hekatontarchēs*, a noncommissioned officer in charge of one hundred men. Centurions were the backbone of the Roman Army and the character of those cited in the NT agrees with their ancient reputation (27.54; Acts 10.1–2, 22.25–26, 27.1–3).[7] This centurion was probably stationed in Capernaum because of its location as a border city and customs post.

8.6 saying, "Lord, my servant is lying at home paralyzed, dreadfully tormented."

The centurion appeals for his servant, who is suffering from paralysis (diseases such as muscular dystrophy and cerebral palsy would fall into this category). *Dreadfully* (*demos*, terribly, fearfully; only here and Lk. 11.53) *tormented* (*basanizō*, torture) indicates the servant's extremity.

That the centurion was concerned for his servant and that he was deferential to a Jewish preacher were extraordinary—Roman concern for slaves was the exception rather than the rule. Just as it's more economical to buy a new toaster than repair an old one, so it was cheaper to dispose of sick slaves and acquire healthy ones. This man, however, had compassion

---

[7] Polybius described the ideal centurion "as possessing the faculty for command, steady and serious; not prone to rush into battle nor eager to strike the first blow, but ready to die in defence of their posts if their men are overborne by number and hard pressed" (*Dictionary of Christ and the Gospels* I, 276).

for his servant (5.7) and humility before Christ; instead of ordering Jesus to help (5.41), he *pled* for help.

8.7 And Jesus said to him, "I will come and heal him."

I will come and heal him not only recalls v 3, but true to the Abrahamic promise (1.1), puts Gentiles as well as Jews within the scope of Christ's mercy.

8.8–9 The centurion answered and said, "Lord, I am not worthy that You should come under my roof. But only speak a word, and my servant will be healed. For I also am a man under authority, having soldiers under me. And I say to this *one,* 'Go,' and he goes; and to another, 'Come,' and he comes; and to my servant, 'Do this,' and he does *it.*"

The centurion suggests an alternate plan. Because he felt unworthy (see 18.4) and because he felt it unnecessary, he said there was no reason for Jesus to visit his house. The reason he thought this was because he understood authority: *I also am a man under authority, having soldiers under me. And I say to this one, 'Go,' and he goes ... 'Come,' and he comes ... 'Do this,' and he does it.* Authority means that when a superior gives an order, it is obeyed by those under him. Believing Christ had authority over disease, all that was needed was for Jesus to *speak a word*—give the order—and the paralysis would obey (v 32).

8.10 When Jesus heard *it,* He marveled, and said to those who followed, "Assuredly, I say to you, I have not found such great faith, not even in Israel!

Environment shapes expectations—for one reared in hereditary paganism, the centurion had an extraordinary understanding of Christ (which would be matched by another centurion at the end of Matthew's story, 27.54). In a town that Jesus would curse for its arrogance and unbelief (11.23–24), here was a Gentile making a faith-based appeal. Those who heard the Sermon on the Mount were astonished at the authority with which Christ taught (7.28–29), but this Roman was fully convinced of Christ's authority.

It's astonishing to see Jesus astonished, but the faith of this foreigner stopped Christ in His tracks and caused Him to marvel (*baumazō,* to wonder at, admire).[8] "It isn't a rare thing to hear Christians confess one to

---

[8] Only twice in the Gospels does Jesus marvel: at a Gentile's belief and at Jewish unbelief (Mk. 6.6).

another that sometimes 'outsiders' show more love and compassion than the people we worship with" (McGuiggan, *Heading Home with God*, 39). Given his background, there were a hundred reasons why the centurion should never have asked what he did; but he did ask, and it's almost as if Christ asked him, "How did you do that?" "Neither Matthew nor Luke gives a psychological study of Christ on this occasion but it's not hard to see and sense his joy. 'Can you beat that?' we can hear him say to the following crowd. He understood very well that faith is God's work in us but it isn't coercive work; the believer's not turned into a choiceless robot, he or she must personally and freely give themselves in the process. And people can choose not to believe (see Mark 6.6) so when we come across a believer we come across someone who has gladly allowed God to have his way with them" (McGuiggan, "Faith in God, Stupid or Heroic?"). The contrast between him and what Jesus was finding among the Jews was so stark, that Christ said, *I have not found such great faith, not even in Israel.*[9]

8.11 And I say to you that many will come from east and west, and sit down with Abraham, Isaac, and Jacob in the kingdom of heaven.

To *sit down with* means *to recline at a table* and is a common Bible figure for eating together, sharing a meal. This table fellowship picture reflects the truth taught in Ephesians 2.12,19 when Paul said that the Gentiles, who were *aliens from the commonwealth of Israel, are no longer strangers and foreigners, but fellow citizens with the saints and of the household of God* (Eph. 3.5–6). The inclusion of Gentiles with Jews under the Messianic blessing agrees with the universal theme of 1.1, 21.43, 28.19, etc. They *who are of faith are blessed with believing Abraham* (Gal. 3.9), and because of his faith, the centurion was blessed (1.1).

8.12 But the sons of the kingdom will be cast out into outer darkness. There will be weeping and gnashing of teeth."

The sons of the kingdom—the Jews—would lose their place in God's kingdom. Contrary to what the Jews thought, they had no hereditary right to the kingdom (3.7–12); unless they had the faith of Abraham, they would not be found with Abraham (Lk. 16.19ff), but would be expelled—*cast out into outer darkness* where there is *weeping and gnashing* (*brugmos*, grating,

---

[9] The centurion is not the last Gentile in Matthew who will be praised for great faith (15.28).

grinding; 4.15–16, 22.11–13) *of teeth* (13.42,50, 24.51).[10] "The kingdom is open to all but guaranteed to none. Only those who believe as the centurion believed will sit at table with Jesus and Abraham" (Gardner, 147).

8.13 Then Jesus said to the centurion, "Go your way; and as you have believed, *so* let it be done for you." And his servant was healed that same hour.

The prayer of faith was rewarded (7.8); the centurion's request was granted. *Go home now, and everything will happen as you have believed it will* (JBP).

FEVER, 8.14–15

NOTES

When love sees a need, it acts to meet the need (1 Jn. 3.16–18, 4.10,19). Lepers, Gentiles, slaves, and women might have occupied the bottom rungs in Israel, but in Christ there "is a chance for the man who is supposed to have no chance" (Jefferson, *The Character of Jesus*, 128).

8.14 Now when Jesus had come into Peter's house, He saw his wife's mother lying sick with a fever.

This third miracle involved another outcast—a mother-in-law.[11] After a Sabbath synagogue service (Mk. 1.29–30, Lk. 4.38), Jesus goes to Peter's house and sees his mother-in-law bedridden with an infection (*fever, puresso*, to be on fire).[12]

8.15 So He touched her hand, and the fever left her. And she arose and served them.

Matthew gives a minimum of detail but leaves no doubt that at Jesus' touch (v 3) the woman was instantly healthy. When fevers break, it usually

---

[10] In His warnings about hell, Christ invokes every form of terror (fear of the dark, loneliness, existential pain) to describe the fate awaiting unbelievers (7.13).

[11] Women were generally despised in the Roman Empire and held equally contemptible in Jewish thought. A daily rabbinic prayer was: "Blessed be Thou, O Lord God, who has not made me a woman." Cf. Josephus: "For saith the Scripture, 'A woman is inferior to her husband in all things' (*Against Apion*, 11.24; Josephus was no Bible scholar, this quote is not in Scripture).

[12] Commentators have often noted that Peter was a married man. Jerome thought that all the apostles were married, except for John. "Why then is it that the Roman popes took away the wives from the bishops and the other servants of the church?" (Bullinger). This question has never been adequately answered.

takes a while for the body to regain strength, but this fever vanished so completely that the woman could immediately arise and *serve*. And this is quite possibly the reason this miracle is included by Matthew, for *serve* is what people do who have been touched by Christ. In John 13—one of the clearest revelations of God that Christ ever gave—He ties a towel around His waist, pours water into a basin, and washes the disciples' feet. Luke tells us (22.27) that Jesus said: *I am among you as the One who serves*. In His serving, Christ revealed a servant God—a thought never thought by the pagan god-makers. As Philippians 2.6 indicates, Christ didn't *exchange* the form of God for the form of a servant, He *revealed* the form of God in the form of a servant. No act terminating in itself constitutes greatness; greatness is when God-given strength is lovingly used to serve others.

PROPHECY, 8.16–17

Notes

Verse 16 summarizes the first three miracles; v 17 connects Christ's miraculous healings to prophecy.

8.16 When evening had come, they brought to Him many who were demon-possessed. And He cast out the spirits with a word, and healed all who were sick,

The healing of Peter's mother-in-law occurred on the Sabbath (Mk. 1.32), and *when evening had* come—after sundown when the Sabbath ended and the first day of the week began—more sick people are brought to Jesus. That families waited until after sundown, undoubtedly, to avoid conflict with scribal and Pharisaic regulations about the Sabbath.

Christ's healings in vv 1–15 can be summarized in three ways. First, they were but a sample of the *many* healings He performed. Second, in addition to physical illnesses, Christ dealt with metaphysical demon possession (v 32). Third, with Christ, there was no such thing as an incurable disease—He *healed all who were sick*.[13]

8.17 that it might be fulfilled which was spoken by Isaiah the prophet, saying: "He Himself took our infirmities and bore our sicknesses."

---

[13] "A total of thirty-five miracles are described in some detail in the Gospels; in addition, several mass or general headings are recorded. Those in Matthew alone include 4.23–24; 8.16; 9.35; 11.20–24; 12.15; 14.14,36; 15.30; 19.2; 21.14" (Vos, 71).

On *that it might be fulfilled,* see 1.22 (this is the first time the quotation formula has been used since the prologue). Jesus' healing fulfilled Isaiah 53.4, a prophecy of Christ's atoning work. Because Isaiah 53 speaks primarily of what Christ accomplished by His death rather than what He did in His life, the "use of Isa. 53.4 in Matt. 8.17 has led to much debate over the relationship of Jesus's ministry and death to physical healing" (Turner, *Matthew*, 235).

Here are four views on the subject, followed by my own.

First, a common belief among Pentecostals is that there is *healing in the atonement*—the remission of sins and the healing of the body go together. Two considerations, however, argue against this. First, believers in the NT were not always healed of sickness (1 Tim. 5.23; 2 Tim. 4.20). In 9.2, Christ forgives a paralytic's sins, but the man's paralysis isn't healed until Christ performs a miracle (9.6–7). Second, many who believe the *healing-in-the-atonement* doctrine have not been healed of their physical debilities; given their premise, it would follow that they haven't been forgiven.

Second, Luz offers the view that everything in Isaiah 53 speaks of Christ's vicarious atonement *except* for 53.4, the part quoted by Matthew.

Third, Edward Young writes that "The reference in Matthew 8.17 is appropriate, for although the figure of sicknesses here used refers to sin itself, the verse also includes the thought of the removal of the consequences of sin" (*The Book of Isaiah* III, 345). Young then references Hengstenberg "who correctly states that the servant bears sin in its consequences, and among these sicknesses and pains occupy a prominent place."

Fourth, Bales believed that Christ's healings fulfilled Isaiah 53.4 in a *sympathetic* way. "The only conclusion which can be drawn ... is that Matthew is guided to use the spiritual figures of Isaiah 53 *illustratively* of the physical healing ministry of Christ" (*Miracles or Mirages,* 109–110). Young and Bales may be saying the same thing in different ways.

Clearly, Christ's miraculous healings were prophesied by Isaiah—*griefs* in 53.4 translates *choliy,* which means sickness, disease (Deut. 7.15, 1 Kgs. 17.17). "Healing work was part of the whole Christ-event" (McGuiggan, "Matthew 8.16–17 & Suffering"). Disease, of course, has a spiritual aspect to it for it is a consequence of sin (Gen. 3.19). "Disease in a specific individual is a specific outworking of the universal curse that God brought on humanity ... a specific application of a universal judgment" (McGuiggan). When Christ thus dispelled disease, which is ultimately the result of sin, it signaled His larger intent to deal with the entirety of the curse, which He would accomplish by His death (Col. 2.13–15).

INTERLUDE: DISCIPLESHIP, 8.18–22

Notes

Christ seeks disciples who trust and obey. Here are two reactions that fell short of what a disciple should be.

There are two paragraphs in this section. In v 18, Jesus commands His disciples to follow; in vv 19–22, He admonishes two—an overeager scribe and an undermotivated disciples—whose following was flawed.

8.18 And when Jesus saw great multitudes about Him, He gave a command to depart to the other side.

Jesus commands His inner group of disciples (v 25, 5.1) to sail to the eastern side (v 28) of the Sea of Galilee.

8.19–20 Then a certain scribe came and said to Him, "Teacher, I will follow You wherever You go." And Jesus said to him, "Foxes have holes and birds of the air *have* nests, but the Son of Man has nowhere to lay *His* head."

Before departing, Christ is approached by a scribe (2.4) who professes a readiness to follow Him wherever He goes (Rev. 14.4). It was common practice in the first century for students to attach themselves to a rabbi or philosopher whose teachings they admired.

When dealing with individuals, Christ always spoke to the person's deepest problem (Jn. 2.25), and He knew this man needed a reality check about discipleship. *Has nowhere to lay His head* means that Christ, essentially, was a vagrant who lived below the poverty line. He who is the hope of outcasts was Himself an outcast (v 34, 2.20), without home, health insurance, retirement fund, computer, smartphone, etc. Following Christ meant accepting heretical views, breaking the closest of earthly ties, facing the certainty of contempt and the probability of violence. No one follows Christ theoretically; discipleship involves a decision that reaches to the depths of commitment. Any who want to be His disciple should read the fine print before signing on the dotted line (5.10–12, 13.20–21; Lk. 14.25–33).[14]

---

[14] "Miracles create enthusiasts who need to learn the difficulties connected with disciple-

For the first time, Christ refers to Himself as *the Son of Man*, which became His favorite self-designation. Of the eighty-one times it appears in the Gospels, it is used by Christ every time except in John 12.34. This wasn't a designation Christ coined but was generally understood, based on Daniel 7.13, to be a messianic title.[15] Gould (*Dictionary of Christ and the Gospels* II, 659–654) suggests three reasons for its use by Christ. First, it was already accepted by the Jews as a Messianic title. Second, it allowed for a suffering Messiah. The Jews had great difficulty conceiving of a suffering Messiah (Jn. 12.34), but that the Messiah would be a man provided a logical opening for suffering (16.13–21; Heb. 2.9). Third, it linked Christ to humanity without any nationalistic or political implications. More than the *son of David* or the *son of Abraham,* Jesus was the *Son of Man* — "He who is called by it has the nature and the qualities of mankind, and that he who calls Himself by it claims thereby relationship with men everywhere."

8.21–22 Then another of His disciples said to Him, "Lord, let me first go and bury my father." But Jesus said to him, "Follow Me, and let the dead bury their own dead."

In contrast to the scribe who volunteered to follow, Jesus commands a man already a *disciple* to follow (Lk. 9.59). In response, the man asks for bereavement leave to bury his father.

Burying a parent was a priority for Jews, and Jesus spoke of the importance of honoring parents (Mk. 7.9–13). Priests, who were required to avoid defilement through contact with the dead, were exempted from this rule when an immediate family member died (Lev. 21.1–3). When Elijah put his mantle on Elisha, Elisha was given permission to tell his parents goodbye (1 Kgs. 19.19–21). In first-century Judea, burial was carried out quickly, which means it was unlikely that this man would have been long delayed from catching up with Christ (unless he was executor of his father's estate).

Considering the importance of burying a deceased parent, *let the dead bury their dead* sounds harsh, and interpreters have long tried to soften Christ's words. Some have argued that *bury my father* meant something other than what it says. "The father was not dead," wrote Hobbs, "but according to custom a son was supposed to stay with his father until his

---

ship before they start on the journey" (Mounce, 77).

[15] There is no indication in the Gospels that Christ's disciples or the wider public were unfamiliar with the designation.

death. Then after his death he was free to live his own life" (99). France notes that "K. E. Bailey gives ample evidence of the colloquial use of 'to bury' in the sense of 'to look after until death', which was a son's clear duty to his father" (160). Possibly the most popular suggestion is that Christ is saying "let the spiritually dead bury the physically dead" — "those who have not found life of the Kingdom of God in Jesus can attend to matters of burial" (Hill, 165).

Thus, in various ways, when Christ dares apply the principle of Luke 14.26, men don't turn Him down, they tone Him down.

So are disciples forbidden from burying a parent? Of course not. Christ's command is in the category of the *prophetic symbolic action commands* found throughout the OT. *Let the dead bury the dead* is like the command prohibiting Jeremiah from marrying (Jer. 16.1–9); it is exacting (and probably painful) in a way that Ezekiel understood when God wouldn't allow him to mourn his deceased wife (Eze. 24.15–18). "This harsh saying of Jesus was not intended to give general instructions about how people should act any more than the demand to give up everything and to follow Jesus was a requirement for everybody" (Luz II, 19–20). Christ's command illustrates what Hankey articulated: "Once a man has got a true sense of perspective, he will realize that, if God matters at all, He matters so much that nothing else matters in the least by comparison with Him" (Hankey, *The Lord of All Good Life,* 33). A common failure of character is to allow the crowding out of things that really matter by things that do not matter as much. It is important in life that we put first things first.

Fosdick imagined a scene involving the great Italian patriot Garibaldi. "If Garibaldi, leading his men to the liberation of Italy, had found a devotee who said, 'I believe in you; I love to read your deeds, and often in my solitary, meditative hours I am cheered by the thought of you' — one can easily imagine the swift and penetrating answer! … 'no one believes in me who does not share my purpose; the army is afoot, great business is ahead, the cause is calling, he who believes follows.'" Such a spirit was Christ's, and so He says to those who would postpone Him.

STORM, 8.23–27

Notes

The next twenty-four hours in Christ's life involve a series of interruptions: while sleeping in a boat, He is aroused from slumber; while teaching in a house, He pauses to heal; while attending a feast, He is forced to explain; while on His way to raise the dead, He is delayed by a diseased woman.

8.23 Now when He got into a boat, His disciples followed Him.

Lest would-be disciples question the wisdom of following Jesus, an incident on the Sea of Galilee confirms that the One who requires unchallenged loyalty (v 22) is Lord of all.[16] *Boat* (*ploion*) refers to a sizable, lake-going vessel.[17]

8.24 And suddenly a great tempest arose on the sea, so that the boat was covered with the waves. But He was asleep.

The Sea of Galilee, whose surface lies 700' below sea level, is encircled by mountains. When cool mountain air descends in the evenings, it sometimes collides with warm, moist air rising from the lake. The clash of these air masses can trigger violent storms that beat the lake into a fury. The severity of this storm is stressed by the adjective *great* and Matthew's use of *seismos* (*tempest*, shaking), the word used for earthquakes (21.10, 24.7).[18] *Covered* (*kaluptō*, to hide, remove from sight) indicates that waves were breaking over the boat (Mk. 4.37), putting it in danger of sinking.

The storm, however, didn't keep Jesus from sleep (6.25–33); "his trust in his great Father was so firm, that, rocked in the cradle of the deep, he slept peacefully. Winds howled, and waters dashed over him, but he slept on" (Spurgeon). Over the centuries, readers have seen in this an analogy to their own turbulent life and in Christ's sleep have glimpsed— and yearned for—the *peace that passes understanding* (Phil. 4.7).

8.25 Then His disciples came to *Him* and awoke Him, saying, "Lord, save us! We are perishing!"

The disciples, some of whom were professional fishermen and thus familiar with the storms that hit the Sea of Galilee, were convinced that they were going to drown. Paradoxically, in their anxiety, they cause the Lord more disquiet than did the storm. With a shout of desperation that

[16] "The ancient church correctly spoke here of the deity of Jesus" (Luz II, 20).

[17] In 1986, a boat was discovered at the bottom of the Sea of Galilee that appears to date from the NT period. It was 26.5 feet long, 7.5 feet wide, and 4.5 feet in height, room enough for over a dozen passengers. There were places for two oars on each side, a mast, and a steering oar.

[18] Mark 4.37 uses the word *lailaps*, windstorm, squall.

was heard above the tempest, they cry, *Lord, save us; we are going down!* (wms). When men are sinking, they get to the point quickly.

8.26 But He said to them, "Why are you fearful, O you of little faith? Then He arose and rebuked the winds and the sea, and there was a great calm.

Christ awakens and does two things. First, He rebukes the disciples. Initially, it seems their appeal was an act of faith—when their skill as sailors proved unavailing, they called on a carpenter to save them—but the Lord criticized them for having *little faith* (6.30). *Why are ye fearful* uses a word (*deilos*, in the NT, only here, Mk. 4.40, and Rev. 21.8) that means *cowardly*; their fear was a cowardice borne of inadequate faith. *Little faith* is the despair of those who have taken a risk on God but fear it will end badly (1 Pet. 2.5).

Had the disciples carefully listened to what Jesus said, they would have realized there was no need for panic. Jesus said, *Let us cross over to the other side* (Mk. 4.35), not, "Let's go to the middle of the lake and drown." Our soul doesn't grow from merely hearing the Lord or even following Him, but from *trusting* Him. Jesus knew that people do not learn faith from a lecture but in the laboratory of life. The storms of life supply the pressure that turns spiritual coal into diamonds, and the disciples' reaction showed that they lacked the level of trust needed for storms yet to come. Patiently, Jesus will cultivate their faith, working to instill in them the ability to trust Him no matter how greatly the odds seemed to be stacked against Him.

After rebuking the disciples, Christ *rebuked* (*epitimaō*, to reprove, censure; 17.18) the storm, and there was an immediate calm—one minute there was a threatening sky, raging winds, and crashing waves; the next, still waters, without even the residual rolling of waves that occurs after the wind dies out.

8.27 So the men marveled, saying, "Who can this be, that even the winds and the sea obey Him?"

The disciples knew how storms behaved on the Sea of Galilee, and they knew that what just happened could be explained only on the basis of divine power. *Who can this be, that even the winds and the sea obey Him?* In the OT, a singular evidence of God's power was that the sea obeyed Him (Ps. 107.23–31, Jon. 1.15–16), and this isn't lost on the disciples. The next time Christ stills a storm, they will have no doubt about who He is (14.33).

DEMONS, 8.28–34

Notes

As stormy as it was upon the sea, it was stormier on shore. Christ encounters two men possessed by demons. The implications of Christ's exorcisms are explained in 12.25–30, but here, hell's impotence and Christ's power are demonstrated in that a legion of demons could not withstand a single word from Jesus (vv 8,16).

8.28 When He had come to the other side, to the country of the Gergesenes, there met Him two demon-possessed *men*, coming out of the tombs, exceedingly fierce, so that no one could pass that way.

The location involves "one of the most puzzling manuscript differences in the gospels" (Foster I, 152). Matthew uses *Gergesenes*, Mark 5.1 and Luke 8.26 say *Gadarenes*, and some manuscripts for Mark 5.1 have *Gerasenes* (NASB). Current thought is that the location was Gergesa, a small village on the eastern shore of the Sea of Galilee, located within a political district whose capital was Gadara, an important trade center and center of philosophy that was five or six miles to the southeast. Matthew's term refers to the area, not the village: the *country* (district, territory) *of the Gergesenes*.[19]

Upon landing, Christ is accosted by two demoniacs (v 16) who live in the cemetery (rock-hewn tombs or burial caves)—the archetypical unclean place. They were especially savage (*chalepos*, difficult, dangerous; only here and 2 Tim. 3.1), terrorizing any who *dared to use that road* (JBP). They had scared everybody off—until now.

8.29 And suddenly they cried out, saying, "What have we to do with You, Jesus, You Son of God? Have You come here to torment us before the time?"

Fear and insolence characterized the demons. *What have we to do with You?* means *Let us alone!* (BECK). *Have you come here to torment us before the time?* Whether by *here* they meant earth or the country of the Gergesenes isn't clear. They recognize Jesus as the *Son of God* (even if the Gergesenes didn't;

---

[19] "Until recent times no one knew where the long-forgotten Gergesa was. W. M. Thomson gave a fascinating discussion of its discovery and location at a point midway on the east shore of Galilee. It was a ruin in Thomson's time, called *Kersa* or *Gersa* by local Arabs. Whatever one may think about the manuscript evidence and whatever explanation is preferred for the three names—Gerasenes, Gadarenes, Gergesenes—the only location for the incident so far proposed which fits the narrative must be the ruined Kersa" (Culver, 142).

4.3,6; Jas. 2.19) and suspect that He will destroy them (*torment, basanizō,* torture) before *the time*—whether final judgment or a set time allowed them for possessing men isn't stated (Zech. 13.2).

8.30 Now a good way off from them there was a herd of many swine feeding.

Nearby was a herd of hogs (Mk. 5.13). It isn't known whether the animals belonged to Jews or Gentiles—arguments can be made for either possibility.

8.31 So the demons begged Him, saying, "If You cast us out, permit us to go away into the herd of swine."

The demons realize their *rest* (12.43–45) is about to be interrupted, and desperate for a host, ask permission to enter the swine.

8.32 And He said to them, "Go." So when they had come out, they went into the herd of swine. And suddenly the whole herd of swine ran violently down the steep place into the sea, and perished in the water.

Jesus says the same thing to the demons that He said to the devil: *Go* (*hupagō,* begone, depart; 4.10, 16.23); it was a command, not mere consent—*Away with you!* When the demons leave the men and enter the swine, the herd stampedes down a steep slope, plunge into the sea, and drown.[20] Whether the spirits foresaw this and hoped it would prejudice the district against Jesus, or whether they thought they could control the pigs as they had controlled the men, or whether they didn't foresee what would happen and the joke is on them isn't stated.

Critics have criticized Christ for allowing for the mistreatment of animals and the destruction of private property. "There is the instance of the Gadarene swine, where it certainly was not very kind to the pigs to put the devils into them and make them rush down the hill to the sea. You must remember that [Christ] was omnipotent, and He could have made the devils simply go away; but He chose to send them into the pigs" (Bertrand Russell, *Why I Am Not a Christian,* 18–19). Russell is right; Jesus could have exorcised the demons without allowing them to enter the swine; "the terrible things which possess men do not need, when they are eliminated in one place, to go to another" (Trueblood, *Confronting Christ,*

---

[20] Neither the healing of the centurion's servant (v 13) nor the stampede of pigs was coincidental; Christ's words caused the healing and stampede.

39). That He allowed the demons to enter the herd tells us more is going on here than just an exorcism. Jesus saw this as a teachable moment; but what lesson is taught?

For one, the destruction of the herd demonstrates that demon possession was not a psychosomatic disorder but an actual, objective phenomenon. Pigs do not suffer from chemical imbalances, low serotonin, or other instances of insanity. Broadus says, "Swine are extremely averse to entering deep water, and require to be forced into it" (192); something real and objective drove the pigs into the sea.

Second, it's curious that men question why Christ permitted the demons to enter the pigs but not why He allowed them to enter the men? Men are of more value than pigs (12.12), and it's no compliment to us if we leave this text thinking more about the animals lost than about the men set free.

Third, there are two instances in which Christ's miracles are destructive: this and the cursing of the fig tree (21.18–22). With the fig tree's withering, God's judgment on Israel's spiritual barrenness was illustrated. With the herd's drowning, hell's chaos and destructiveness are illustrated, but without men being destroyed in the process. What occurred here is no different than what happens with lab animals; it's better to see how a drug affects an animal before it is given to a man. When hell is in control, panic, havoc, and ruin ensue.

8.33–34 Then those who kept *them* fled; and they went away into the city and told everything, including what *had happened* to the demon-possessed *men*. And behold, the whole city came out to meet Jesus. And when they saw Him, they begged Him to depart from their region.

The swineherds report every detail, and the entire town goes out to ask Jesus to leave. Matthew doesn't say whether this was due to anger over the loss of property (if so, this offers a commentary on 6.21–23) or out of fear over Christ's power. Fear is instinctive when men realize they are in the presence of the supernatural (Lk. 5.8), and the Gadarenes' request may have been analogous to our concern if we were told a nuclear waste dump was to be located next to our property; although we recognize its necessity, we might prefer that it be built elsewhere. Some people are more comfortable with the demons they know than with a power they cannot comprehend.

It was a sad thing that the city asked, but Jesus complied (9.1). He did not, however, leave Himself without witness. Left behind were two men who were to tell their *friends … what great things the Lord has done for you, and how He has had compassion on you* (Mk. 5.19). That they did so might explain why the next time Christ visited this region, His reception was overwhelming (15.30).

"O Lord, I thank thee that thou didst not go away from me, when I, in my unregenerate condition wished thee to let me alone!" (Spurgeon).

CHAPTER 9

SCRIBES, 9.1–8

Notes

The opposition to Christ that first appeared in ch 2 reappears. In every incident in this chapter, Jesus is questioned or criticized by the religious establishment. From here on, the antagonism between Him and Israel's leaders grows until it ends in His death.[1]

In 1846, French mathematician Urbain LeVerrier predicted and computed the size, position, and orbit of a previously unseen and unknown planet to explain disturbances and irregularities he had witnessed in the orbit of the planet Uranus. LeVerrier sent his coordinates to the German astronomer Johann Gottfried Galle, and on the very day Galle received the letter, he spotted Neptune within 1° of the position LeVerrier had plotted.

Men believe in gravity, the wind, and electrons not because they have seen them, but because there are things inexplicable without them. Man has the ability to reason inductively, from effect to cause, and it was

---

[1] "The resentment of the religious leaders has been likened to that of the medical profession against an unregistered practitioner who seems to be meeting with great success" (Harrison, 126–127). "The people who hanged Christ never accused Him of being a bore—on the contrary; they thought Him too dynamic to be safe. It has been left for later generations to muffle up that shattering personality and surround Him with an atmosphere of tedium. We have efficiently pared the claws of the Lion of Judah, certified Him 'meek and mild,' and recommended Him as a fitting household pet for pale curates and pious old ladies. To those who knew Him, however, He in no way suggested a milk-and-water person; they objected to Him as a dangerous firebrand. True, He was tender to the unfortunate, patient with honest inquirers, and humble before Heaven; but he insulted respectable clergymen by calling them hypocrites; He referred to King Herod as 'that fox'; He went to parties in disreputable company and was looked upon as a 'gluttonous man and a wine bibber, a friend of publicans and sinners'; He assaulted indignant tradesmen and threw them and their belongings out of the Temple; He drove a coach-and-horses through a number of sacrosanct and hoary regulations; He cured diseases by means that came handy, with a shocking casualness in the matter of other people's pigs and property. ... He was emphatically not a dull man in His human lifetime, and if He was God, there can be nothing dull about God either" (Dorothy Sayers, "The Greatest Drama Ever Staged," *Letters to a Diminished Church*, 4).

by this means that Christ authenticated His deity. Jesus of Nazareth didn't look the way a god is supposed to look (Isa. 53.2–3); to men, God appeared as a man (v 3).[2] To prove that He was more than a man, Christ did what only God can do, thereby giving a basis for believing in His deity (v 6; Jn. 20.30–31). It is indeed true *that the seen can enable us see the unseen* (Rom. 1.20).

9.1 So He got into a boat, crossed over, and came to His own city.

Leaving the country of the Gergesenes (8.28), Jesus returns to Capernaum, *His own city* (4.13).

9.2 Then behold, they brought to Him a paralytic lying on a bed. When Jesus saw their faith, He said to the paralytic, "Son, be of good cheer; your sins are forgiven you."

A *paralytic* (8.6) is brought to Christ, but instead of healing him, Jesus tells him to take courage (*tharseō*, be confident, bold; Christ, alone, uses this word) for *your sins are forgiven* (1.21; Eph. 3.20).

9.3 And at once some of the scribes said within themselves, "This Man blasphemes!"

And so it begins. We don't know what the paralytic or his friends thought when Christ pronounced forgiveness, but we do know what the scribes thought. The opening salvo between Jesus and the Jewish establishment was a silent slander (*said within themselves*) in which some scribes interpreted Jesus' statement as *blasphemy* (*blasphemeō*, to revile, libel, speak against). *Blasphemy* was a broad term that covered a variety of offenses including slander, cursing God, disrespect to God, and claiming to be God—which, under Mosaic law, was a capital crime (Lev. 24.10–23; 1 Kgs. 21.9–14; Acts 6.8–11, 7.58). Blasphemy is the first accusation leveled against Christ, and it will be the last (26.65). Although what they thought about Jesus was wrong, the scribes were right in thinking that forgiving sin is a divine prerogative (Mk. 2.7; Lk. 5.21).

9.4 But Jesus, knowing their thoughts, said, "Why do you think evil in your hearts?

Why do you think evil in your hearts? You would have thought Christ's sudden exposure of their thoughts would have caused the scribes pause.

---

[2] The Transfiguration, of course, being the exception.

When Jesus revealed something to Nathanial that was known only by Nathaniel, his reaction to just a snippet of omniscience was to acclaim Jesus as the Messiah (Jn. 1.48–49; cf. Nebuchadnzzar's dream, Dan. 2; Jn. 7.19). Not only was the scribes' conclusion wrong, it was wrong because they were evil—hardhearted (7.17, 15.18). Christ's miracles were signs of deity, not blasphemy. The scribes' thinking said more about them than about Jesus.

9.5 For which is easier, to say, '*Your* sins are forgiven you,' or to say, 'Arise and walk'?

To demonstrate that He had the right to forgive, Christ asks: *which is easier, to say, "Your sins are forgiven you," or to say, "Arise and walk"?* "It is generally thought that the answer to Jesus' question … is 'Take up thy bed and walk.' Quite the opposite is the case. Perhaps it is easier to restore a sick man to health than to forgive sin, but Jesus' question has to do, not with acts but with *claims*; Jesus asks not 'Which is easier?' but 'Which is easier to *say*?' Clearly, it is easier to *claim* to be able to forgive sin than to be able to miraculously restore a palsied man to health, for the former is a theological affirmation which cannot *per se* be subjected to verification" (Montgomery, *Crisis in Lutheran Theology* 1, 40). It is easier to claim the unverifiable than to claim something that can be checked out. To assert that a thousand angels can stand on the head of a pin can't be proven or disproven, but to claim that a thousand angelfish can stand on the head of a pin can be empirically tested. Forgiveness, which takes place in the mind of God, cannot be objectively confirmed, but telling a crippled man to rise and walk can.

9.6 But that you may know that the Son of Man has power on earth to forgive sins"—then He said to the paralytic, "Arise, take up your bed, and go to your house."

Jesus doesn't leave His God-claim in the realm of the unverifiable but links it to a concrete test. *But that you may know that the Son of Man has power* (*exousia*, authority, 7.29, 28.18) *on earth to forgive sins*—to back up the invisible (forgiveness), Christ does something visible (heals)—to convince the scribes of what they couldn't see, Jesus does something they can see. The proof offered was consistent with the claim made— to prove His divine prerogative to forgive, Jesus displayed His divine power to heal. *Turning to the paralyzed man, He said to him—"Get up, pick up your bed, and go home"* (wms).[3]

9.7–8 And he arose and departed to his house. Now when the multitudes saw *it*, they marveled and glorified God, who had given such power to men.

Instantaneously healing paralysis is beyond the reach of man, but at Christ's command, the paralytic *sprang to his feet and went home* (jbp)—without further physical therapy required. They who saw it *marveled and glorified God*, which is the reaction miracles were meant to produce (*Notes*, 8.1).

In this healing, the multitudes saw the hand of God, but this didn't necessarily mean that Jesus was God, for throughout Israel's history, God worked miraculously through men. Supernatural deeds attest to a supernatural being, but they do not necessarily imply that the one performing the deed is supernatural. Why, then, should we believe that Christ's miracles proved Him to be God and not just a man through whom God worked? On the basis of His explanation! For isn't the one who works a miracle in the best position to explain its significance (Acts 4.8–10)? If Jesus says His miracles prove His deity, who are we to argue?

PHARISEES, 9.9–13

Notes

Having demonstrated His authority to forgive sin, Christ further shocks the Pharisees by fraternizing with sinners. Their idea of holiness, as their name implied (3.7), was to stay separate, segregated from sinners. Christ's socializing with sinners was a drastic departure from their religious worldview.

This section has three parts: Matthew's call (v 9), the Pharisees' question (vv 10–11), and Christ's answer (vv 12–13).

9.9 As Jesus passed on from there, He saw a man named Matthew sitting at the tax office. And He said to him, "Follow Me." So he arose and followed Him.

---

[3] Christ's bestowal of forgiveness was especially offensive to the scribes and Pharisees, but Christianity is worthless without forgiveness. Religion says, "Be good and some day you will become worthy of meeting God"; Christianity says, "Repent, and—unacceptable though you are—you will be accepted by God this day."

After leaving the house where the paralytic was forgiven and healed (vv 1–8), Jesus passes by the *office* of a tax collector named *Matthew* (*gift of Jehovah*; called *Levi* by Mark and Luke),[4] whose job would have been to collect toll on goods entering his district. Though tax collectors are never popular, in first-century Judea they were especially loathed when they were Jews who represented Roman power. A tax collector's money was looked upon as tainted and wasn't accepted in synagogue offerings; his oath was worthless and wasn't accepted in court; and if a man made a promise to a tax collector, he wasn't bound to keep it. Tax law was as bewildering then as now, making it easy for crooked collectors to overcharge and pocket the surplus, becoming wealthy in the process (Lk. 3.13, 19.8; the size of Matthew's party suggests that he was well off, v 10). The Jewish clergy lumped tax collectors in the same category as sinners and prostitutes (5.46, 9.10, 21.31).

There is no indication that Matthew had any prior exposure to Jesus, but it's hard to imagine anyone in Capernaum who hadn't heard of Him by th is time. When called to follow, Matthew responded immediately, probably at great loss to himself financially and professionally.[5]

9.10 Now it happened, as Jesus sat at the table in the house, *that* behold, many tax collectors and sinners came and sat down with Him and His disciples.

One of the first things Matthew did following his call was to invite Jesus to a gathering of acquaintances and coworkers (Spurgeon said that these would be more likely to come to a supper than to a sermon). *Sinners* was a pejorative used by holier-than-thou Jews (Isa. 65.5) to describe the irreligious, immoral, and those who ignored orthodox conventions and shibboleths.

9.11 And when the Pharisees saw *it*, they said to His disciples, "Why does your Teacher eat with tax collectors and sinners?"

"From the outside a group of Pharisees watched the scene and snarled" (J. Watson). Matthew doesn't tell us how the Pharisees knew about this

---

[4] *Matthew* is a perfect name for the one who gave us the gift of a Gospel.

[5] Matthew's employer would "surely never take him back again if he later decided he wanted to return. The fishermen might go back to their fishing, but the tax collector would not be able to return to the levying of customs duties; his lucrative post would soon be filled. And if he tried to get another job, who would want to employ a former tax collector?" (Morris, 220).

gathering; my guess is that after the incident involving the paralytic (vv 1–6), Christ was under constant surveillance by the guardians of the faith. If so, what the Pharisees saw confirmed their suspicions; they are aghast that Jesus ignored their scruples about eating with the unclean. They viewed separateness as the price of survival for a holy people and contemptuously suggest that anyone who associated with the irreligious must be irreligious. *Why does your Teacher eat with tax collectors and sinners?* implies that birds of a feather flock together, and that you can tell a man by the company he keeps (11.6,19). It's the kind of criticism a preacher might garner today if he met and had dinner at a casino with a bartender he was trying to lead to Christ. The Pharisees believed it was legitimate for a rabbi to teach sinners, but to eat or socialize with them was tantamount to endorsing their sin. *Teacher* was how outsiders designated Jesus (8.19). Christ, significantly, not only accepted dinner invitations from unrighteous sinners but from self-righteous Pharisees (Lk. 11.37).

9.12 When Jesus heard *that,* He said to them, "Those who are well have no need of a physician, but those who are sick.

Though not addressed to Jesus, the question was aimed at Him, and He answers it. To the slander, "You associate with sinners because you are a sinner," He replies: "I associate with sinners because I'm a doctor." Doctors are found in the company of sick people;[6] a doctor who refuses to see the sick is no doctor at all. *What* Christ was determined *where* He was, and since He was a doctor, He spent time with those who needed doctoring. "The Pharisees," by contrast, "were pseudo-physicians who were afraid of germs" (Hobbs, 109). Christ—the Great Physician—was more concerned about His responsibility than His reputation. "His interest was in the welfare of broken and needy men, not in the trivial determination to keep His own skirts clean or His reputation unsullied" (Trueblood, *Confronting Christ*, 14–15).

9.13 But go and learn what *this* means: 'I desire mercy and not sacrifice.' For I did not come to call the righteous, but sinners, to repentance."

"Hosea 6.6 was a saying highly treasured by our Lord" (Kidner, *Hosea,*

---

[6] The absurd and lethal doctrines of some cults that condemn the use of doctors or medical measures is answered by this passage. God accomplishes many things through means and instrumentalities, including healing the sick. It is not unspiritual to be under a doctor's care. Christ said the sick need a physician.

67), but the Pharisees didn't understand it, as implied by *go and learn*—a phrase, said Richard Watson, used by the Jews when they were about to explain a text of Scripture, draw out an argument, or get at its sense. In Hosea 6.6, *sacrifice* refers to the Mosaic sacrificial system, which is used as the lesser element in a comparative. By quoting Hosea 6.6, Christ didn't discount sacrifice any more than He discounted mint, anise, and cummin in 23.23. Rather, He is pointing out that when mercy and sacrifice cannot simultaneously occur (Jn. 7.23), mercy takes precedence over sacrifice (5.23–24).[7] And if mercy takes precedence over God-ordained ritual, it certainly takes precedence over man-made rules.

To be salt and light, disciples must be in contact with the world. As Christ shows, it's possible to associate with sinners without sinning; there is middle ground between avoiding sinners and joining them in their sin. Christ was at Matthew's party because mercy dictated He be there for a redemptive purpose. Christ could help the *unrighteous* who knew they needed help, but He could never help the *righteous*—a satire on Pharisaic self-righteousness—who thought they needed no help.

E. Stanley Jones thought this statement about calling sinners was the most precedent-shattering thing Jesus ever said. "In the Christian conception we do not find God at the topmost rung of the ladder, but at the bottommost. For we do not get to God—God comes to us. He comes to us in Incarnation and meets us on our level. He meets us where we are and takes us where He is. He meets us on the level of our sin, not on the level of our attained righteousness. 'I came not to call the righteous, but sinners,' is the absolutely new thing in the Gospel. That verse shatters all our attempts to climb to God. He has come to us on our level, the level of our deepest need—our sin. This idea is breath-taking and precedent-shattering. It is new, so new that it could be called nothing else except the Good News— the Gospel" (*Christian Maturity*, 131). *I desire mercy and not sacrifice* is a hard concept for legalists to grasp, but it is at the heart of Christ's message.

JOHN'S DISCIPLES, 9.14–17

Notes

John the Baptist's austerity (3.1,4) was a long way from Matthew's feast, and some good people were as perplexed as the Pharisees by

---

[7] A Chaldee paraphrase reads, "For in those that exercise mercy is my delight, more than in sacrifice."

Christ's behavior. The fasting approach to religion often has a hard time understanding a time for feasting (Eccl. 3.4).

The section contains a principle (vv 14–15) followed by an illustration (vv 16–17).

9.14 Then the disciples of John came to Him, saying, "Why do we and the Pharisees fast often, but Your disciples do not fast?"

The disciples of John (11.2; Jn. 3.25–26) ask: *Why do we and the Pharisees fast often, but Your disciples do not fast?* On fasting, see 6.16–18. As often happens in our application of divine principles, we tend to make our application the standard by which we judge others. Pharisees fasted twice a week, and they measured the spirituality of others by their practice (Lk. 18.12).

9.15 And Jesus said to them, "Can the friends of the bridegroom mourn as long as the bridegroom is with them? But the days will come when the bridegroom will be taken away from them, and then they will fast.

Whatever Christ was, He wasn't gloomy. In his preaching, John had spoken of himself as the best man and of Christ as the bridegroom (Jn. 3.29), and the Lord uses this metaphor to state that when a groom is with his friends it is a time for feasting; fasting is appropriate when a groom and his friends part. Jesus offers no further explanation on *when the bridegroom will be taken away*, but the allusion is clearly to His death. So long as He is with them—healing disease, exorcising demons, forgiving sins, showing mercy—feasting was in order. Men should feast when appropriate and fast when appropriate. When fasting becomes nothing but a ritual instead of an aid to a genuine relationship with God, its purpose has been perverted.[8]

9.16–17 No one puts a piece of unshrunk cloth on an old garment; for the patch pulls away from the garment, and the tear is made worse. Nor do they put new wine into old wineskins, or else the wineskins break, the

---

[8] See Zechariah 7.1–7. "Instead of answering the question immediately, the prophets' message from God relativizes the entire question about fasting and goes to the heart of the matter (7.4–7). Implied in the query from Bethel is the suggestion that they had been pleasing God all these years in engaging in these fasts. God doesn't accept that claim and tells them that when they fasted or feasted it was their own agenda they were furthering. They had structured their lives in fasts of feasts with their eye on themselves (7.5–6). This is a tough response to what on the surface appears to be a pious enquiry, but receiving it as the word from the Lord, it must have been on target" (McGuiggan, *Zechariah, The Day of Small Things*, 81).

wine is spilled, and the wineskins are ruined. But they put new wine into new wineskins, and both are preserved."

In the context, this double-saying illustrates the impropriety of fasting when it isn't called for. To put *a piece of unshrunk cloth on an old garment* already shrunken by many washings solves nothing, for when the new cloth is washed, it will shrink to where it no longer fits the hole it was meant to cover.

Similarly, *new wine* (unfermented grape juice) is not put into *old wineskins*. A common explanation for this is that any expansion caused by new wine fermenting would burst skins already stretched to the breaking point by previous fermentation. This answer, however, doesn't agree with chemistry. Sugar in grape juice can produce carbon dioxide forty to fifty times its original volume, which is more than enough to burst new skins much less old ones (Job 32.19; fermenting wine has been known to burst wooden barrels bound by metal hoops). New wine was put into new skins because old skins were brittle, cracked, and contained dregs that precipitated fermentation in fresh juice (McGuiggan, *The Bible, The Saint & The Liquor Industry*, 39,113). There are some things you just don't do.

Christ's comments may also imply something about the incompatibility between the old (represented by the scribes, Pharisees, and disciples of John) and the new (represented by Jesus and His disciples). A *tear, break*—rupture—has opened up between Jesus and the establishment that will become more evident as the story continues. There is no patch to mend this breach; there is only the new way, Christ's way.

DEATH, I, 9.18–19

Notes

By the miracles in vv 18–34, Matthew accomplishes two things. First, he ties together all the threads introduced since 8.1: the thread of faith (8.10,13, 9.22,28–29), discipleship (18.18–27; 9.27), sleeping and rising (8.25–26, 9.24–25), Pharisaic criticism (9.2–17, 34), etc. Second, by the end of ch. 9, Matthew will have cited at least one example of each miracle mentioned in 11.5–6.

9.18–19 While He spoke these things to them, behold, a ruler came and worshiped Him, saying, "My daughter has just died, but come and lay

Your hand on her and she will live." [19] So Jesus arose and followed him, and so *did* His disciples.

While still at Matthew's house, Christ is contacted by a ruler with a critically ill daughter. So great was his concern that the ruler ignored the growing chasm between Jesus and men of his type. Synagogue rulers were responsible for seeing that synagogue services were done decently and in order, assigned duties for those assisting in the service, etc. On *worshiped*, see 2.2. By the time he reached Christ, his daughter had *just died*, but with a father's love, he clung to the hope that Jesus could help. Without a word, Christ arose and followed him. Christ's compassion needed no other inducement beyond "that of the man's broken heart" (Morgan, 96).

HEMORRHAGE, 9.20–22

9.20–21 And suddenly, a woman who had a flow of blood for twelve years came from behind and touched the hem of His garment. For she said to herself, "If only I may touch His garment, I shall be made well."

Many of those with whom Christ interacted were persons whose names we don't know. They were otherwise inconspicuous people, and often, unfortunate people, whom Christ thought significant. An example of this occurs here with a delay caused by another hopeless situation (Mk. 5.26)—a woman who for twelve years had suffered from a hemorrhage (*haimorreoō*, a menstrual disorder). Block believes that the *uncleanness* in Deuteronomy 24.1 refers to this sort of a condition, which put a woman in "a constant state of impurity, curtailing many normal marital activities (cf. Lev. 12.2–8) and rendering her incapable of bearing children" (*Deuteronomy*, 558). Menstruating women were not allowed to participate in the Passover. This woman's ritual uncleanness would result in religious and social segregation (Lev. 15.25–33), which likely explains why she *came from behind and touched the hem of His garment.* Though unwelcomed by those around Christ, her faith was such that she believed that even the slightest contact with Him would make her whole. Faith requires an object—this woman didn't have faith in faith or a superstitious belief in Christ's tassels—her faith was in Christ. *Hem* refers to the tassels Jews wore on their clothes to remind them of the Law (23.5; Num. 15.37–41).

9.22 But Jesus turned around, and when He saw her He said, "Be of good cheer, daughter; your faith has made you well." And the woman was made well from that hour.

The woman makes a dash for it, so to speak, but her attempt to go unnoticed fails. Christ immediately turns around and confronts her. She only wanted to *touch His garment*, but He felt not so much a touch as a plea. Without rebuke or irritation, He tells her to *be of good cheer* (v 2). *Daughter* is "a term of affectionate endearment, something like 'Maiden,' or 'Little girl,' or even 'Sweetheart'" (Pritchard, *Keep Believing*, 82). Because of faith, it took only a piece of fringe and the touch of a finger to establish a connection between a sufferer and the Savior. In her touch, faith sent its request and, Christ's response to her faith *made her well* (*sozō*, to save, deliver; Mk. 5.30). Heaven rewards faith's risk (Ps. 86.15–16).

The whole incident probably took only a minute or two, but for the ruler, it must have seemed like hours.

DEATH, II, 9.23–26

9.23 When Jesus came into the ruler's house, and saw the flute players and the noisy crowd wailing,

By the time Jesus reaches the ruler's house, the professional mourners— *flute players* and *noisy crowd*—had begun their lament.[9] Because the Jews didn't embalm corpses, decomposition was rapid, and funerals were held within hours of death.

9.24–25 He said to them, "Make room, for the girl is not dead, but sleeping." And they ridiculed Him. But when the crowd was put outside, He went in and took her by the hand, and the girl arose.

Jesus tells the bereavement brigade to get out (*anachoreō*, depart); they were proclaiming death's victory too soon. When Christ announces that *the girl is not dead, but sleeping*, the mourners became scorners (*katagelaō*, to laugh down; laughter aimed at humiliating; Heb. 12.3); to them, the idea of a doctor (v 12) who couldn't diagnose death was a joke. The secular mindset always laughs at the claim that Christ is the answer to man's needs. Psychiatry, so believes modern man, can help, or medical science or philosophy, but not Christ.

---

[9] "Professional mourners were hired even by the poorest families (Mishnah *Ketuboth* 4.4 specifies 'not less than two flutes and one wailing woman')" (France, 171).

Christ knew the girl was dead (v 18), and He also knew what He would do (Jn. 11.11–14). His description of her condition as *sleep* better described the situation than what is meant by death. After the mourners leave, Jesus *went in and took her by the hand,* and raised her from the dead.

9.26 And the report of this went out into all that land.

Death could not keep its prey, and the news spread like wildfire. If healing a cripple argues for Christ's authority to forgive sins (v 6), how much more does healing an incurable disorder or raising the dead! It's incredible to think that anyone who heard about this miracle could have remained undecided about Jesus.[10]

BLINDNESS, 9.27–31

9.27 When Jesus departed from there, two blind men followed Him, crying out and saying, "Son of David, have mercy on us!"

After leaving the ruler's house, Jesus is met by two blind men who appeal for *mercy*—the very thing God delights to show (v 13). These two are the first in Matthew to address Jesus as the *Son of David*, but they are not the last (20.30–31). There are no instances in the OT of blindness being miraculously cured, but Isaiah 35.5 foretold a day when it would happen. That day had arrived, and the blind—physically and spiritually (4.16)—were made to see.

9.28 And when He had come into the house, the blind men came to Him. And Jesus said to them, "Do you believe that I am able to do this?" They said to Him, "Yes, Lord."

Do you believe I am able to do this? It would seem that the risk of faith for the blind men was small, since in their appeal to Christ they had nothing to lose and everything to gain. But as John 9.34 reveals, a serious price could be paid for being healed by Christ.

Without hesitating, they answer, *Yes, Lord.*

9.29 Then He touched their eyes, saying, "According to your faith let it be to you."

According to your faith let it be to you indicates that *blessing comes in proportion to faith.* Faith may be great (8.10) or little (8.26). If little, it is a self-limitation

---

[10] "Christ personally ridicules death … and calls it sleep. … My tomb is (in reality) my bed … I do not die; I sleep" (Martin Luther, qtd. by Luz II, 44).

that keeps us from God's full scope of blessing (recall that the Christ slept peacefully through a storm the disciples feared). God rewards faith (17.14–18, Mk. 9.24), not unbelief (Mk. 6.5).

9.30–31 And their eyes were opened. And Jesus sternly warned them, saying, "See that no one knows it." But when they had departed, they spread the news about Him in all that country.

And their eyes were opened gets to the goal of Christ's work (Lk. 24.31,45); opening blind eyes reflected what Jesus wanted to do for blind hearts.

Sternly warned translates *embrimaomai* (only five times in the NT; to roar, charge sternly, vehemently; used in classical texts of horses snorting and of Cerberus howling; Jn. 11.33) and indicates that what follows wasn't said with a sly wink. *See that no one knows* is difficult to interpret, but see 8.4.

EXORCISM, 9.32–35

9.32–33 As they went out, behold, they brought to Him a man, mute and demon-possessed. And when the demon was cast out, the mute spoke. And the multitudes marveled, saying, "It was never seen like this in Israel!"

The emphasis in this paragraph is not on the miracle but on reactions to it.

A man unable to speak (*kophos*, blunted or dull; can refer to dumbness or deafness) due to demon possession is healed by Christ, who always treated the cause, not the symptoms. And they who saw it *marveled* (*thaumazō*, to be amazed). This doesn't mean that they responded in faith but rather that the miracle got their attention, prompting a confession that such power was unprecedented in Israel. "The scribes taught and nothing happened. Jesus spoke and demons fled, storms were settled, dead were raised, sins forgiven" (G. E. Ladd, qtd. by France, 173–174).

9.34 But the Pharisees said, "He casts out demons by the ruler of the demons."

Not everyone was favorably impressed by Christ's miracles; some were angered. The Pharisees, unable to deny Christ's power, attributed it to Satan. So sure were they in their presuppositions that they adamantly refused to reevaluate them in the light of new evidence. Their explanation for the evidence was inane—to say that evil is cured by evil is a contradiction in terms; error doesn't eliminate error, for error *is* error; you can't cover up red paint with red paint. Error is overcome only by truth; hell is overcome only by heaven. It was a serious charge and shows how quickly the rift introduced in vv 3 has widened. For now, Christ allows the slander to pass, but when repeated in 12.24, He expose sits stupidity and the evil behind it.

Matthew thus closes this first section on Jesus' miracles by noting a difference in attitude between the common people and the Jewish leadership.

9.35 Then Jesus went about all the cities and villages, teaching in their synagogues, preaching the gospel of the kingdom, and healing every sickness and every disease among the people.

This verse is virtually identical to 4.23, but the end of ch 9 puts us at a different point from where we were at the end of ch 4. Because of chs. 5 to 9, we know what is meant by *the gospel of the kingdom* and the role of the healings. But we also know that Israel's response to its Messiah, in many cases, fell short of what it should have been. The resistance to these early miracles foreshadows the rejection of the supreme miracle at end of the story.

9.36–11.1: Through Disciples

Notes

This section, sometimes called the *discourse on missions*, tells of the selection of twelve *apostles* (10.2) to assist Christ in His work. Numerous threads continue: the sending out of the Twelve to preach (10.1,7) corresponds to Christ's going out to preach (4.17); the miracles given the Twelve parallel Christ's miracles; the reception given the Twelve would reflect the reception given Christ, etc.

The discourse is introduced by 9.36 to 10.4 and is followed by two subsections. The first of these (10.5–23) is bookended by references to *Israel* (10.6,23) and can be subdivided into two parts: vv 5–15 and vv 16–23. Each part begins with a reference to the *going* or *sending* of the disciples and to *sheep* (9.36, 10.2), and each ends with an *amēn* (*assuredly*) saying and a reference to judgment (10.15,23). The second section (10.24–42) is a bit harder to structure and contains an interesting didactic technique Christ used on several occasions.

"It is of the nature of oppressive societies," wrote Paul Johnson, "to induce a feeling of hopelessness among those who live in them" (*The Birth of the Modern*, 303); this is true religiously as well as politically. And in this paragraph, Christ speaks to the hopelessness in Israel.

CHRIST'S CONCERN, 9.36–38

9.36 But when He saw the multitudes, He was moved with compassion for them, because they were weary and scattered, like sheep having no shepherd.

This section on the sending out of the disciples begins with a statement of Christ's compassion for the disheartened. *When He saw the multitudes* recalls 5.1. While on a tour through Galilee (v 35), Jesus is stirred by the desperate situation of people who were *weary* (*skullō*, to flay, lacerate, torment, oppress) and *scattered* (*hriptō*, to throw off, throw away; Polybius used this word to describe exhausted men lying prostrate on the ground). The common people were so emotionally battered and worn down by their leaders that they resembled *sheep having no shepherd* (Num. 27.17; 1 Kgs. 22.17; Eze. 34.5, etc.). Although Jesus makes no direct reference to the scribes, Pharisees, or priests (Eze. 34), they are the ones He meant.

What Christ saw *moved Him with* compassion—He was stirred to His depths with emotion. The word *splagchnizomai* (the bowels, intestines, guts; Acts 1.18) is the strongest term for pity in the Gr. language. "Jesus' compassion is a favorite theme for Matthew, who employs the corresponding verb more often than any other Gospel writer" (Hare, 182). What follows is the result of the Good Shepherd arriving on the scene, assessing the situation, and supplying good shepherd leadership.

9.37 Then He said to His disciples, "The harvest truly *is* plentiful, but the laborers *are* few.

Although the metaphor of *harvest* often stands for judgment (13.30,39), it can also refer to conversions (13.3–8; Jn. 4.36–38). Christ sees the masses as grain ripe for harvest—people who needed the gospel and were ready to respond to it. Many in Israel had hearts receptive to His message, but there was a teacher shortage; few were available to "bring in the sheaves."

9.38 Therefore pray the Lord of the harvest to send out laborers into His harvest."

Mercy leads to action, and the first action was to pray. That Christ resorted to prayer indicated His own sense of need. No one is more interested in saving souls than God, *the Lord of the harvest*, and so to God, Christ prayed. Matthew has already laid out the importance of prayer in accomplishing God's will (6.9–13, 7.7–12); if any attempt to reach the lost is to succeed, prayer must be the vanguard.

CHAPTER 10

CALL, 10.1–4

Notes

To reach the majority, Christ used a minority, a small company of the committed who would ultimately be given a great commission (28.19) to preach the great commandment (22.36–40). "In every realm the pathfinders have been few and the truths that at last triumphed were at first the possession of the minority" (Fosdick, "The Hope of the World in Its Minorities," *An Answer to Real Problems*, 2).

Rome's genius lay in this: when it wanted to Romanize a province, it took Roman people and planted them in the province as a colony. Initially, the colony was a small minority, but by standing for Roman law, Roman justice, Roman belief, and Roman custom, the colony gradually permeated and influenced the entire region. Paul called the Philippian church *a colony of heaven* (3.20, MOFFATT). The believers in Philippi were pioneers in an unchristian society who represented the ideals, belief, and life of a higher realm. The strategy of the colony is how Christ sought to redeem the world.

The first paragraph in this chapter concludes the introduction to the second discourse (9.36–10.4). Christ identifies twelve men to expand His outreach. By sending them out, He kept His promise to the first disciples He called to make them *fishers of men* (4.19).

10.1 And when He had called His twelve disciples to *Him*, He gave them power *over* unclean spirits, to cast them out, and to heal all kinds of sickness and all kinds of disease.

Those Christ told to pray for laborers to bring in the harvest (9.38) were the answer to their prayer. It is often the case that for our prayer to be answered, we must do something.

Before sending out the disciples, Christ equipped them[1] with authority that reflected His own (4.23, 9.35). *Twelve* appears in vv 1,2,5; a number that recalls the tribes of Israel (19.28).

10.2–4 Now the names of the twelve apostles are these: first, Simon, who is called Peter, and Andrew his brother; James the *son* of Zebedee, and John his brother; Philip and Bartholomew; Thomas and Matthew the tax collector; James the *son* of Alphaeus, and Lebbaeus, whose surname was Thaddaeus; Simon the Cananite, and Judas Iscariot, who also betrayed Him.

Apostle (*apostolos*, only here in Matt.) refers to one *sent out* on a mission (v 5). This is the first of four apostolic rosters in the NT (Mk. 3.16–19; Lk. 6.13–16; Acts 1.13). Some names vary among the lists, which probably means some were known by more than one name (9.9). Matthew groups his list in pairs—note the *and* within each pair and its omission between each pair—which was his way of saying that the apostles went out two by two (Mk. 6.7; Lk. 10.1). *Two are better than one* (Eccl. 4.9ff); at least two are needed to confirm testimony (18.16, Deut. 19.15), and six groups vastly extended Christ's area of operation.

The four called in 4.18–22 are named first. In each apostolic list, Simon Peter (Jn. 1.42) appears first, Philip fifth, James the son of Alphaeus ninth, and Judas Iscariot last. Since the sixteenth century, controversy has centered on the placement of the word *first* before Peter's name. The Catholic church argues that it indicates Peter's primacy. Contextually, however, it surely means nothing more than that Peter was the first one called by Jesus to be a disciple; someone had to be first, and it was Peter. Peter's given name was *Simon* (Simeon); He was nicknamed Peter (rock) by Christ in John 1.42.

Andrew (4.18) was the first disciple of John to follow Jesus (Jn. 1.35ff). Apart from the apostolic lists and his introduction to Christ in John 1, he appears in only three other places: Mark 13.3, John 6.8, and John 12.22.

On three occasions, *James* (4.21–22; Heb. Jacob), along with Peter and John, accompanies Christ separately from the other disciples (17.1, 26.37; Mk. 5.37). The nickname *Boanerges* (*sons of thunder*, Mk. 3.17), given him and his brother John by Christ, indicates a volatile temperament. He was martyred by Herod Agrippa I circa AD 44 (Acts 12.2).[2]

---

[1] Disciples who try to preach before they are ready to preach can create more problems than they solve.

[2] There's a possibility that James and John were Christ's cousins; cf. the names in 4.21,

John, James's brother, was the third member of Christ's innermost circle and wrote more of the NT than any of the Twelve (a Gospel, three epistles, and the Revelation). An early tradition associates him with Ephesus and maintains that he was the only apostle to die a natural death (but see 20.20–23).

Philip was from Bethsaida, the hometown of Peter and Andrew (Jn. 1.44), and was one of Christ's earliest followers. Apart from the apostolic lists, he is mentioned in only four places (Jn. 1.43–46, 6.5–7, 12.20–22, 14.8–11) and should be distinguished from Philip the evangelist (Acts 6.5, 8.26–40, 21.8).

Bartholomew (son of Toimai, Ptolemy) may be a surname. He is thought to be the Nathanael of John 1.43–51 and 21.2.

Thomas (known as *Didymus*, Gr. *twin*, Jn. 11.16) is famous for his doubting (Jn. 20.24ff). His was not a gullible faith but one that insisted on concrete evidence before believing. His skepticism, which was only overcome by overwhelming evidence, is a strong argument for the honesty and integrity of the apostles.

On *Matthew*, see 9.9. "Only in the Gospel of Matthew is Matthew called the tax collector. It reflects the author's amazement that Jesus would call into his service one who had served in such a disreputable occupation" (Mounce, 91).

James the son of Alpheus distinguishes him from Zebedee's son (v 2). Because Matthew's father was also named Alpheus (Mk. 2.14), some speculate that he and Matthew were brothers. In Mark 15.40, he is called *the Less*, a term that may reflect his age, size, or prominence in relation to the other James.

Lebbaeus, whose surname was Thaddeus (warmhearted), is called *Judas the brother of James* in Luke 6.16. His only other mention outside the apostolic lists is in John 14.22 where he is called *Judas (not Iscariot).*

Simon the Canaanite was a zealot (Lk. 6.15). Though nothing is known about him personally, a great deal is known about the zealots, who were Jewish terrorists bent on ridding Judea of Romans (Josephus, *Ant.* xviii.1.6). That Christ included him in the same group with a tax collector demonstrates the power of love. Matthew was the kind of person targeted by zealots for assassination, but in Christ, natural enemies are integrated in peace (Isa. 11.6–9).

27.56, Mk. 15.40, and Jn. 19.25.

Whenever *Judas Iscariot* is cited in the lists, he is linked to the infamous deed forever associated with his name—his betrayal of Jesus.[3] *Iscariot* means *the man from Iscaria/Kerioth,* a town in southern Judea (Josh. 15.25; Jer. 48.24,41; Am. 2.2). He was a thief (Jn. 12.6) who, after betraying Christ, regretted his deed and committed suicide (27.1–10; Acts 1.18).

"The outstanding thing about these men is that they were not outstanding. To the casual observer they may appear to be a rather motley group. But they were just ordinary men chosen to do an extraordinary task in the service of God" (Hobbs, 119).

COMMISSION, 10.5–15

Notes

The orders given the apostles recall Christ's ministry. Their work and proclamation were to reflect His; they were to perform His deeds. This section consists entirely of imperatives, concluding with an *amēn* (v 15).

10.5 These twelve Jesus sent out and commanded them, saying: "Do not go into the way of the Gentiles, and do not enter a city of the Samaritans.

In rapid-fire order, Christ gives the apostles their marching orders (*commanded, paraggellō,* referred to the orders given by a military commander). The first order to not go to Gentile or Samaritan territory seems exclusivist but is consistent with God's promise to the patriarchs (Acts 3.26, 13.46; Rom. 1.16).[4] First-century Galilee was a cosmopolitan area; Gentile enclaves existed around Tiberias and Magdala on the northwestern side of the Sea of Galilee, at Scythopolis south of the Sea, and at Sepphoris north of Nazareth, as well as elsewhere in the region.

10.6 But go rather to the lost sheep of the house of Israel.

---

[3] Only once is the technical term for *betrayer* used of Judas (Lk. 6.16). Elsewhere, the term is *paradidōmi,* which means to deliver or hand over. It is the same word used to describe Christ's voluntary self-sacrifice (Gal. 2.20) and the Father's giving of His Son (Rom. 8.32).

[4] Samaria was the political district situated between Judea and Galilee and the former center of the northern kingdom of Israel. The Samaritans were descendants of Jews who had intermarried with Gentiles (2 Kgs. 17.24,29). "The origins of the Samaritans of the NT as a distinctive group should probably not be sought before the start of the Hellenistic period (end of the 4th century BC), when Shechem was rebuilt after a long period of desolation" (*New Bible Dictionary,* 1062). This prohibition against preaching to the Samaritans should be balanced by Jn. 4 and Lk. 10.

The lost sheep of the house of Israel, who are contrasted with Gentiles and Samaritans, were not the sinners, outcasts, and downtrodden referenced in 9.10,36, but *all* Israel—all the chosen people were *lost* (*apollumi*, utterly destroyed, perish; Rom. 3.23) and needed saving.

10.7–8 And as you go, preach, saying, 'The kingdom of heaven is at hand.' Heal the sick, cleanse the lepers, raise the dead, cast out demons. Freely you have received, freely give.

The apostles were to proclaim the same message preached by John and Jesus: *the kingdom of heaven is at hand* (3.2, 4.17). As did Jesus, they were to work miracles: *heal the sick, cleanse the lepers, raise the dead, cast out demons.* As with Jesus, the miracles confirmed the message (9.1–8), and both were to be freely bestowed—the apostles' powers had not been purchased and were not to be sold.

10.9–10 Provide neither gold nor silver nor copper in your money belts, nor bag for *your* journey, nor two tunics, nor sandals, nor staffs; for a worker is worthy of his food.

After telling the Twelve what to preach, Christ tells them how to pack. *Provide* (*ktaomai*) means to procure or obtain; they were to waste no time on preparations usually involved in making a trip but were to start on their mission with just the clothes on their back, travelling light, leaving their care and support to God (6.25–33). They were not to take money (*gold, silver, copper*), luggage (*bag*), extra shoes (*sandals*), or staff (*rabdos*, a general word for sticks of all kinds; a staff was handy for fending off attacks by dogs or other animals). The apostles' needs would be met by people who honored the principle that a workman deserves compensation (Deut. 25.4; 1 Cor. 9.14; 1 Tim. 5.18). Surely, those blessed by the apostles' ministry would not begrudge them support.

These instructions should not be taken out of context and made into absolute rules for preachers. Christ no more forbids missionaries from preparing for a trip than He forbids sermon preparation (v 20). These instructions were specific to the Twelve, identifying them with Christ's poverty and homelessness (8.20). Other situations, however, might require different preparations (Acts 18.3–4). Preachers should prepare for and be supported in their work in whatever scriptural way is most expedient for advancing the gospel (1 Cor. 9.1–18).

10.11 "Now whatever city or town you enter, inquire who in it is worthy, and stay there till you go out.

Upon arriving in a village or city, the apostles were to find lodging with a *worthy* (*axios*, deserving, congenial) family—those who welcomed the message brought by the Twelve. Christ had already preached throughout Galilee (9.35), and the apostles, most likely, were revisiting towns and villages who knew of Jesus and had been blessed by Him. When the Twelve *inquired* (*exetazō*, scrutinize, examine; careful questioning) *who was worthy*, they were asking about those in town favorably inclined toward Christ.

Once settled in, they were to stay put until their work was finished in the area.

10.12–14 And when you go into a household, greet it. If the household is worthy, let your peace come upon it. But if it is not worthy, let your peace return to you. And whoever will not receive you nor hear your words, when you depart from that house or city, shake off the dust from your feet.

After deciding where to stay, they were to pronounce a blessing of peace, indicating God's favor on the house or family (Lk. 10.5). *Peace* is pronounced on those who assist those who proclaim *the gospel of peace* (v 41; Rom. 10.15).

If the household turned against the apostles, possibly as a result of intimidation or peer pressure by those hostile to Christ (vv 21–22; Jn. 9.18–23), the blessing was revoked, thus indicating that the former hosts were now outside God's blessing. They who are not with Christ are against Him (12.30). *Shaking off the dust from his feet* symbolized the family or town's loss of blessing (Acts 13.51, 18.6; cf. *washing the hands*, 27.24; 2 Jn. 10–11).

10.15 Assuredly, I say to you, it will be more tolerable for the land of Sodom and Gomorrah in the day of judgment than for that city!

With shocking hyperbole, Christ says that those who reject His gospel will fare worse at the judgment than Sodom and Gomorrah, towns proverbial for their wickedness (11.20–24, 18.7; Gen. 18–19).[5] Although some have decried the so-called judgmental spirit of vv 14–15, Christ reminds us that the gate and way to eternal life is narrow (7.13–14).

---

[5] *Arndt-Gingrich* mention an inscription found at Pompeii that reads *Sodoma Gomora* (766), thus indicating a widespread reputation for these cities.

CONFLICT, 10.16–23

Notes

This section has three parts: an introduction (v 16), a conclusion (introduced by *assuredly*), and an intervening discussion (vv 17–22) consisting of an imperative (v 17a), two pronouncements introduced by *will deliver* (*paradidōmi*, vv 17b–18, 21–22) and two instructions introduced by *but when* (vv 19–20, 23a).

The use of the future tense in vv 17,21 (*will deliver*) introduces a curiosity in Christ's teaching whereby He sometimes shifts, quite suddenly, from His present topic to a cognate topic (12.22–32, 16.27–28, chs 24–25). Here, He shifts from the *limited commission* (vv 5–14) to the *great commission* (vv 15–22, 28.19), and then back to the limited commission (v 23ff).

10.16 "Behold, I send you out as sheep in the midst of wolves. Therefore be wise as serpents and harmless as doves.

The mention of sheep amid wolves introduces something ominous. Prior to this, the only hint of opposition involved unreceptive hosts (v 14), but now, predatory violence from *wolves* in the religious establishment (v 17), civil government (v 18), and one's family (v 21) is said to be a possibility.

The weapon of believers is that they are weaponless—sheep aren't sent to fight with wolves, but to love them, reason with them, and persuade them. To this end, the disciples were to be as *wise as serpents and as harmless as doves* (5.43–48). To the Jews, the dove was a symbol of defenselessness and *harmlessness* (*akeraios*, unmixed, guileless), but as far back as Genesis 3, the *serpent* has been a symbol for Satan. It's possible, though, for one to be serpent-like without being Satan-like. To be *wise* as serpents indicates that this is a wisdom exhortation (*wise, phronimos,* thoughtful, shrewd; this is the word used in the Septuagint for *cunning* in Gen. 3.1). Christ is telling the Twelve to be prudent and pure—invaluable qualities in tense situations (Acts 17.5–10, 23.13–24, Rom. 16.19). A serpent's "only wisdom is displayed in escaping from danger" (McGarvey, 91; cf. v 23, *when they persecute you in this city, flee to another*). Disciples were to avoid harm, while doing no harm.

10.17 But beware of men, for they will deliver you up to councils and scourge you in their synagogues.

Beware of men was no idle caution. Open hostility lay ahead. The disciples would be *delivered* (fn 2) to Jewish councils (*sunedrion,* sanhedrin, a deliberative or adjudicating body) who would *scourge* (*mastix*, a whip or lash used in beatings) them in their synagogues.[6] *Scourging* refers to the punishment of forty lashes (23.34; Acts 5.40, 22.19; 2 Cor. 11.24); mistreatment the disciples received would mirror what Christ received.

10.18 You will be brought before governors and kings for My sake, as a testimony to them and to the Gentiles.

Opposition would come from *Gentiles* as well as Jews, which indicates that Christ is here envisioning a mission for the Twelve beyond the scope of v 6. When brought before *governors* (e.g., Gallio, Acts 18.12–17, Felix and Festus, Acts 24–25) and *kings* (e.g., Agrippa I, Acts 12.1, Agrippa II, Acts 25.22–27, and Caesar, Acts 25.11–12) *for My sake* (5.10–11), the apostles were to use their arraignment as an opportunity to *testify*. When hauled into court, instead of defending themselves, they were to preach Christ. Persecution opened doors to reach authorities the Twelve might otherwise have missed. It is possible that because of Paul's appeal to Caesar (Acts 25.11, 28.19) that even Nero heard a sermon or two.

10.19–20 But when they deliver you up, do not worry about how or what you should speak. For it will be given to you in that hour what you should speak; for it is not you who speak, but the Spirit of your Father who speaks in you.

Christ promises that when the apostles appeared before officials, *the Spirit of your Father* (an expression unique to Matthew) would give them the words to speak (Acts 4.29). If evil spirits could use human vocal cords to speak (8.29), how much more could the Holy Spirit. There was no need for the apostles to be accomplished orators (1 Cor. 2.1–5) or to prepare their thoughts ahead of time, for *it is not you who speak*. They were but the instrument the Holy Spirit would use (Jn. 14–16).

10.21 "Now brother will deliver up brother to death, and a father *his* child; and children will rise up against parents and cause them to be put to death.

The coming hostility would disrupt family life (w 34ff). Under the

---

[6] "Matthew uses *synagogue* more frequently than any other Gospel, always in a negative way. The word is always modified by *their* (4.23; 9.35; 10.17; 12.9; 13.54), except when the context indicates that the synagogue belongs to *the hypocrites* (6.2; 23.6, 34). For Matthew the Jew, the synagogue has become an alien institution in which he no longer belongs" (Hare, 114).

pressure of religious persecution, sacred ties of flesh and blood would erode. Family members would betray believing relatives, informing the authorities against them, exposing believers to possible death.

10.22 And you will be hated by all for My name's sake. But he who endures to the end will be saved.

Because disciples would be hated by their families, disciples would be tempted to compromise or abandon the faith (v 13, 26.69–75; Gal. 6.12). But Christ expected His followers to *endure* (*hupo-menō*, patience), maintaining their faith despite persecution, even if it led to death (Heb. 11.35ff; Rev. 2.10, 12.11). Only overcomers receive a crown (Rev. 2.10).

10.23 When they persecute you in this city, flee to another. For assuredly, I say to you, you will not have gone through the cities of Israel before the Son of Man comes.

Reference to *the cities of Israel* suggests that Christ now reverts back to the limited commission (vv 5–15). Being driven from one city would lead to opportunity in other cities; when the apostles encountered opposition, they were to change their place but not their preaching.

Other texts help interpret the phrase *you shall not have gone through the cities of Israel before the Son of man comes*. In Luke 4.43, Christ told the crowds that He *must preach the kingdom of God to the other cities also, because for this purpose I have been sent*. Something similar is said when the Seventy were sent out *into every city and place where He Himself was about to go* (Lk. 10.1). The *coming of the Son of Man*, here, has nothing to do with Christ's second coming but refers to a preaching tour Jesus was about to make through Israel, as 11.1 indicates: when He *finished commanding His twelve disciples ... He departed from there to teach and to preach in their cities* (11.1). Christ thus sends the Twelve out (just as God sent John the Baptist) to prepare people for His visit to their city/area. If they encountered resistance in one town, they were to go to the next—not as cowards fleeing trouble but rather as advance men, preparing the way for the coming King.

COURAGE, 10.24–33

NOTES

This paragraph connects the two halves of the chapter. Its topic involves *disciples* (vv 1,42), *persecution* (vv 16–23), and a disciple's *response* to persecution. Two parallel statements are followed by a concluding statement and explanation.

10.24–25 "A disciple is not above *his* teacher, nor a servant above his master. It is enough for a disciple that he be like his teacher, and a servant like his master. If they have called the master of the house Beelzebub, how much more *will they call* those of his household!

A disciple is not above his teacher, nor a servant above his master reflected a Jewish proverb: subordinates are not treated better than their superiors (Lk. 6.40; Jn. 13.16, 15.20; 2 Tim. 3.12).[7] If the master is betrayed, scourged, arraigned, and killed, his followers should expect no less (vv 17,18,19,21).

Christ isn't speaking hypothetically, for in 9.34 the Pharisees associated Him with *the ruler of the demons.* Beelzebub "means something like 'lord of the (heavenly) dwelling' or 'lord of the temple,' [and] is probably the original name of the Baal of Ekron" (Luz II, 90; 2 Kgs. 1.2).[8] This name is known primarily from the NT (12.24; cf. 9.34); it isn't found in the OT and appears in only a single Jewish text on magic. It's unclear whether it refers to Satan or one of his underlings, but it was a label clearly meant to link Christ to Satan. *If they have called* is followed by a double accusative—*master of the house, household*—and indicates a surname, or, as in this case, a blasphemous nickname.

10.26a Therefore do not fear them."

The prospect of betrayal, scourging, hatred, hounding, and execution can scare the staunchest, but disciples are to not fear—three times, in quick succession, Jesus forbids it (vv 26,28,31).

10.26b–27 "For there is nothing covered that will not be revealed, and hidden that will not be known. Whatever I tell you in the dark, speak in the light; and what you hear in the ear, preach on the housetops.

Warned about their fate, the disciples needed to be fortified against the fear that would assault their faith. Four reasons are given for courage.

First, their faith would be vindicated. *There is nothing covered that will not be revealed* reflected a well-known Gr. proverb similar to our *time will tell.* In life, evil can pass for goodness and goodness for evil, but the time will come when good and evil will be truly seen (1 Tim. 5.24), and

---

[7] Dating back to the time of Elijah, a prophet's disciples also functioned as his servants.

[8] Thayer translates it *lord of dung;* BAGD, *lord of flies.*

goodness will be vindicated and wickedness exposed (Rom. 2.16; Rev. 6.10–11, 18.1–24).

Disciples, therefore, should act appropriate to the final revelation of character, which here means that the gospel Jesus taught them privately (*in the dark, in the ear*) must be proclaimed publicly (*in the light, on the housetops*[9]).

10.28 And do not fear those who kill the body but cannot kill the soul. But rather fear Him who is able to destroy both soul and body in hell.

A second reason for courage is the limitations of the enemy. Believers might die at the hands of persecutors, but the persecutors' power did not extend beyond this life. God, however, has sovereignty over our entire being—*soul and body*. The *fear of God* is a familiar theme in the OT and permits of various accentuations. *Fear of God* and *love of God* are often linked for they converge in obedience to the will of God (Deut. 10.12). When *fear of God* is connected, as here, with *hell*, motivation comes from the threat of punishment (Heb. 12.28–29).

"If we die in God's battle we live in the grandest sense, for by loss of life we gain life" (Spurgeon). As was said of the *Immortals*, the vanguard of Napoleon's army, Christians know how to die but not how to surrender.

10.29–31 Are not two sparrows sold for a copper coin? And not one of them falls to the ground apart from your Father's will. But the very hairs of your head are all numbered. Do not fear therefore; you are of more value than many sparrows.

A third reason for courage is God's concern. The Lord of body and soul is a loving, omniscient Father (6.9), whose concern extends to every part of His creation, including the insignificant.[10]

Copper coin (*asarion*) refers to a small denomination Roman coin, the value of which depends on the source you consult. Regardless of its precise value, a *copper coin* wasn't worth much; that you could buy *two sparrows* with one shows how cheap sparrows were.[11] God's omniscience is further underscored by His knowledge of the trivial, such as the number of *hairs on our head*.

---

[9] On Friday, before the beginning of the Sabbath, a synagogue servant would blow a horn from the highest roof in town.

[10] One of the best texts that enumerates the goodness of God and all implied by His goodness is Ps. 86.

[11] Sparrows, the cheapest birds sold in the market, were the poultry of the poor.

You are of more value than many sparrows (6.26). If God is aware of the death of nearly worthless birds, and if He is so acquainted with us that He knows how much hair we have, it follows that we will receive individual and loving care from Him.

10.32–33 Therefore whoever confesses Me before men, him I will also confess before My Father who is in heaven. But whoever denies Me before men, him I will also deny before My Father who is in heaven."

A fourth reason for courage is that Jesus will *confess* (*homologeō*, to say yes, to agree, to stand publicly with someone) before God those who confess Him before men. A disciple's fundamental confession is that *Jesus is Lord* (Rom. 10.9–10), with all that implies. In this context, confession is made before judges and courts, but our entire life should confess Christ (v 28).[12] "In effect Jesus says that the person who says before men, in word and in deed, 'He is mine,' of him Christ will say before the Father, 'He is mine'" (Hobbs, 126).

Everything Christ says here is meant to assure us and encourage us to not value our life too highly. In the eyes of moderns, death is a tragedy; in the eyes of Jesus, it is never a tragedy, unless we fail to confess Him in our life.[13]

PRIORITY. 10.34–42

Notes

Here is a reality check that returns to the subject of family conflict (v 21) and provides an example of what it means to confess Jesus as Lord (Lk. 14.26). Truth doesn't always unite—sometimes it divides, and Jesus wants no one caught by surprise. Would-be followers must count the cost of discipleship (8.19–20), which may involve breaking the family circle.

Verses 34–36 deal with Jesus; vv 37–39 with His followers.

---

[12] "It is told of J. P. Mahaffy, the famous scholar and man of the world from Trinity College, Dublin, that, when he was asked if he was a Christian, his answer was: 'Yes, but not offensively so.' He meant that he wished to make it quite clear that he did not propose to allow his Christianity to interfere with the society he kept and the pleasures he loved" (Barclay I, 403).

[13] "By the time of Lucian, Christians have apparently become renowned for their fearlessness: 'The poor wretches have convinced themselves, first and foremost, that they are going to be immortal and live for all time, in consequence of which they despise death and even willingly give themselves into custody, most of them' (*The Passing of Peregrinus*, qtd. by Garland, 117).

10.34 "Do not think that I came to bring peace on earth. I did not come to bring peace but a sword.

Three times in succession Christ speaks of His coming. The Jews believed their Messiah would bring peace (Isa. 9.5–6, 11.5–10; Mal. 3.23–24), but Christ says that He came to bring war. *Sword* (*machaira*, a large knife, sabre) is a metaphor for conflict (Lk. 12.51, *division*). The bringing of peace between God and man can sever the closest of ties with those who do not wish to be at peace with God.[14] "In the act of producing the peace of heaven [Christ] arouses the rage of hell" (Spurgeon).

10.35–36 For I have come to 'set a man against his father, a daughter against her mother, and a daughter-in-law against her mother-in-law'; and 'a man's enemies *will be* those of his *own* household.'

But even in this Jesus fit the Messianic profile, for Micah 7.6 predicted family divisions between believing and unbelieving spouses (1 Cor. 7.15; 1 Pet. 3.1–2), parents and children (1 Sam. 20.30–34), etc.

10.37 He who loves father or mother more than Me is not worthy of Me. And he who loves son or daughter more than Me is not worthy of Me.

In Christ's kingdom, the first commandment has priority over the fifth (8.21–22). Family love is fully affirmed in Matthew (15.3–6, 19.19), but this doesn't preclude conflict between believers and unbelievers within a family. Should conflict come, Christ must be first (12.46–50). Rather than making this point using *hate* as a comparative, as He did in Luke 14.26, Christ here uses *love.* To love son or daughter more than He is to have a skewed priority system.

Not worthy here speaks of judgment (vv 32–33, 40–42). Those who consign Christ a lower level off allegiance will be condemned in the last day. Given this, it's better to divide a family (or a friendship or a church) with truth than to leave it united in error.

10.38 And he who does not take his cross and follow after Me is not worthy of Me.

This is the first of two references in Matthew to *taking one's cross* (16.24–25), and its meaning has been often debated. One view is that it refers to suffering or bearing pain. Another is that it indicates an act of sealing (Eze. 9.4–6; Rev. 7), as a tattoo or brand might indicate one's allegiance (cf.

---

[14] A close family and clan ties were no small things in Jewish culture.

the Crusaders *taking of the cross*). The most likely view, however, is that it refers to the Roman custom of requiring the condemned to carry their cross to the place of execution (27.32).[15] It is a two-part argument from the greater to the lesser: if the master must carry His cross to His death, disciples should expect to do the same; and if disciples should be willing to die, how much more should they be willing to suffer. To suffer and die for Christ is part and parcel of confessing Him (32).

10.39 He who finds his life will lose it, and he who loses his life for My sake will find it."

The challenge to take up one's cross is backed by the promise that *he who finds his life will lose it, and he who loses his life for My sake will find it.* This statement appears six times in the Gospels (16.25; Mk. 8.35; Lk. 9.24, 17.33; Jn. 12.25), offering the alternatives of *finding* (sparing) life or *losing* (sacrificing) it. For those who *lose their life for Christ's sake*—who make Him their highest priority, even if it means the loss of their own life—they shall find a rich reward awaiting them at death. But they who *find their life*— who compromise their faith in order to avoid persecution or suffering— will lose it (*apollumi, destroy* in v 28; perish). What appears to be an act of self-preservation can be an act of self-condemnation.

  Losing life "is that inner resolve to make Jesus Lord of all! And when this life is over and we go home to live forever with the Master we'll be glad we lived 'sacrificially.' We'll rejoice eternally that we chose with a deliberate choice to cast ourselves from the throne and place Jesus there as Lord" (McGuiggan, *The God of the Towel*, 191–194).

10.40–41 "He who receives you receives Me, and he who receives Me receives Him who sent Me. He who receives a prophet in the name of a prophet shall receive a prophet's reward. And he who receives a righteous man in the name of a righteous man shall receive a righteous man's reward.

Four sentences of increasing length are followed by a relative sentence that concludes with an *amēn*.

  The background for these verses is the *emissary rule*, whereby an emissary or ambassador represents the full authority of the one who

---

[15] Crucifixion was one of the *intensified death penalties* under Roman law, which also included drowning, burning, and *ad bestias*—being thrown to wild animals. Simple executions were carried out by sword.

commissions him. To receive an apostle is to receive Christ,[16] and to receive Christ through the apostles is to be given *the right to become children of God* (Jn. 1.12). To come in contact with Jesus through the apostolic word is how one comes in contact with God.

Not everyone is a prophet (23.34, one who speaks by inspiration from God; "others may comment on what God has said, but the prophet can say, 'Thus saith the Lord,'" Morris, 270), but everyone can receive a prophet's reward by accepting and welcoming a prophet's message (Heb. 11.31). Showing hospitality to a representative of Christ is to show hospitality to Christ (25.34–40).

Some believe the reference to *a righteous man* indicates the existence in the early church of some special group of pious believers. Based on 5.20, however, I think it more likely that *a righteous man* refers to all true followers of Christ.

10.42 And whoever gives one of these little ones only a cup of cold *water* in the name of a disciple, assuredly, I say to you, he shall by no means lose his reward."

The scope of Christ's representatives is broadened to include *little ones* (18.6–14). In Judaism, *little ones* referred to "the socially weak, the childish and immature, and the pious. … In early Christianity the term is used in Mark 9.42 to refer to ordinary, insignificant Christians" (Luz II, 121). Ordinary Christians represent God (5.16) and are valued by God (v 31); the smallest act of kindness practiced by an insignificant follower of Christ is noted and rewarded by God.

Assuredly, I say to you, he will by no means lose his reward. The reward, which is God's solemn promise, is of grace—giving a single (*only*) cup of water doesn't seem particularly significant, but when done from love, there is an ocean of heaven in a cup of water. The fact that the poor are always with us (Jn. 12.8) means that there is ever-present opportunity to show love to Christ.

CONCLUSION, 11.1

11.1 And it came to pass, when Jesus had made an end of commanding his twelve disciples, he departed thence to teach and to preach in their cities.

---

[16] The importance of this principle for the authority of the Epistles cannot be understated.

Matthew finishes this discourse with words similar to 7.29 and picks up the narrative where he left it at 9.38. *Teach* and *preach* are active infinitives indicating what Jesus did constantly. We're not told how the apostles fared on their mission; Matthew's emphasis is on Christ.

CHAPTER 11

11.2–16.20: Reactions to the Revelation

11.2–15: John the Baptist

Notes

Matthew 11.2 to16.20 concludes the first major section of the Gospel, and it has three subsections: 11.2 to 12.50 contains examples of belief and unbelief, 13.1–52 is a collection of parables meant to explain the kingdom, and 13.53 to 16.12 contain further examples of belief and unbelief. At the outset, Jesus is asked, *are you the Christ?* (11.3, KJV); at the conclusion comes the answer: *Thou art the Christ* (16.16, KJV).

Chapter 11 has two parts: vv 2–19 center on John the Baptist, and vv 20–30 include a condemnation of Jewish unbelief (vv 20–24), an important Christological text (vv 25–27), and a great invitation (vv 28–30).

The first part begins with a question (vv 2–3) and answer (vv 4–6) that isn't a yes or no, but a rehearsal of facts that implies the answer. Six short clauses mention five of Christ's miracles (each of which is illustrated in chs 8 to 9) and His message (chs 5–7).[1]

Matthew has already mentioned John's imprisonment (4.1–12), which illustrated what Christ predicted in 10.16–26.

11.2–3 And when John had heard in prison about the works of Christ, he sent two of his disciples and said to Him, "Are You the Coming One, or do we look for another?"

"Dark thoughts may come to the bravest when pent up in a narrow cell" (Spurgeon), and being a caged bird was hard on John. From prison, he sent some of his followers (9.14) to ask Jesus: *Are you the One who was to come, or should we keep on looking?* (WMS).[2] Josephus (*Ant.*, xviii.5.2) says John was

---

[1] For similar replies see Mk. 2.19 and Lk. 10.23–24.

[2] This is the first of a string of questions in this section that involve Jesus' identity: 13.54–

imprisoned in the castle of Macherus, which was "a Hasmonaean fortress on the E shore of the Dead Sea, rebuilt by Herod the Great" (*Baker's Bible Atlas*, 308).

Bible students have long puzzled over why John questioned Christ's messiahship, especially after 3.14–17. Early commentators didn't want to ascribe any doubt to him and suggested that his question was for the benefit of his disciples (e.g., Origen, Chrysostom, Augustine). But if this was the case, it isn't obvious from the text. In v 4, Jesus tells those sent to *go and tell John*. Considering the Baptist's imprisonment and impending execution, it rings psychologically true that he would have doubts. From his perspective, there must have seemed a disconnect between what he predicted about Christ (3.10–12) and what Jesus was doing (why hadn't Jesus secured his release? why hadn't He laid the ax to the root of Herod? etc.) For one who had served Christ in such a singular way (vv 9–10), John must have been baffled. When fortune is reversed and injustice reigns, when it seems like the wicked are getting away with murder, bewilderment is to be expected (Ex. 5.1–23).[3]

11.4–5 Jesus answered and said to them, "Go and tell John the things which you hear and see: *The* blind see and *the* lame walk; *the* lepers are cleansed and *the* deaf hear; *the* dead are raised up and *the* poor have the gospel preached to them.

Jesus doesn't scold John or answer him directly but says that the evidence speaks for itself. *Go and tell John the things you hear and see*, from which John could draw his own conclusion (16.17; Jn. 7.3).

Each miracle Christ mentions is illustrated in chs 8 to 9: *the blind receive their sight* (9.27–31), *the lame walk* (9.2–8), *lepers are cleansed* (8.1–4), *the deaf hear* (9.32–34), *the dead are raised* (9.18–26). And the poor — the downtrodden who counted for little in the eyes of the world — were hearing the gospel (chs 5–7), all of which pointed to Jesus as the Messiah.[4]

---

55 and 16.13–15. See also 14.2,33 and 15.22.

[3] "For Matthew, this material was well-suited to introduce the section before us. First of all, the question that John raises in verse 3 is the question that all of Israel must answer. It thus sets the stage for the responses to Jesus and his mission in the narratives to follow" (Gardner, 185).

[4] Numerous OT texts lie in the background to vv 4–5: Isa. 29.18–19, 35.5–6, 42.18, and 61.1. The healing of lepers and the raising of the dead in the time of Elijah and Elisha might also be cited (1 Kgs. 17.17–24; 2 Kgs. 4.18–37, 5.1–27).

11.6 And blessed is he who is not offended because of Me."

Every man must decide if he is with Christ or not (10.32–33; 12.30). *Offended* (*skandalizō*) means to set a trap, erect an obstacle, lead to ruin, seduce to sin. Here, it "is a passive with a meaning like 'is not stumbled, is not tripped up on account of me'" (Morris, 277). Jesus frequently rattles our assumptions about who He is and what He does (9.10–17) and at such times, "the temptation will be to remove the cause of offense by making Jesus over in our image so that he fulfills our agenda. Or, the temptation will be to remove him altogether" (Garland, 126).

Jesus' answer to John is His answer to all who struggle with the problem of evil. Christ doesn't explain how John's imprisonment fits into heaven's plan, nor does He offer to secure John's release. Instead, He reminds John of the reasons for believing in things most surely believed (Lk. 1.4). "The humble worshiper has abundant reason to believe in God. If, then, he runs into some difficulty, even a difficulty as great as the problem of evil, he does not, for that reason, give up his faith. The reasons for his faith are so great that they can weather a few storms" (Trueblood, *Philosophy of Religion,* 244). "Blessed is he who can be left in prison, can be silenced in his testimony, can seem to be deserted of his Lord, and yet can shut out every doubt" (Spurgeon).

11.7–9 As they departed, Jesus began to say to the multitudes concerning John: "What did you go out into the wilderness to see? A reed shaken by the wind? But what did you go out to see? A man clothed in soft garments? Indeed, those who wear soft *clothing* are in kings' houses. But what did you go out to see? A prophet? Yes, I say to you, and more than a prophet.

This paragraph begins two subsections about John. The first (vv 7–11) is introduced by three rhetorical sentences and concludes with an OT quotation introduced by an explanation (*this is he*). The second (vv 12–15) is Jesus' tribute to John in which He uses John's situation to presage events involving Himself, before asking three questions meant to correct any false impression anyone might have about John.

Had people gone out to the wilderness (3.1,5) to see a reed shaking in the wind? No! Reeds were plentiful around the Jordan, and a shaking reed suggested a fickle, vacillating, no-backbone individual.[5] Had people

---

[5] "[Gerd] Thiessen has pointed out that Herod Antipas, in his first period ... had coins

gone out to see courtiers decked out in dainty (*malakos*, effeminate, 1 Cor. 6.9; "silks and satins," wms) apparel such as might be found in genteel society? No! People need a good reason to leave their home and trek to a deserted place; Jews flocked to John because they rightly believed he stood in the line of God's prophets. They didn't, however, understand that he was *more* (*perissoteron*, sufficient, over and above, abundant; only here in Matt.) *than a prophet*.

11.10–11 For this is *he* of whom it is written: 'Behold, I send My messenger before Your face, Who will prepare Your way before You.' Assuredly, I say to you, among those born of women there has not risen one greater than John the Baptist; but he who is least in the kingdom of heaven is greater than he.

The comparatives *more than a prophet* and *among those born of women there has not risen one greater* refer not to John as an individual, but to the *role* he played. Something similar is found in Luke 1.28 where Gabriel greets Mary by saying, *blessed are you among women*, which is similar to *among those born of women there has not risen one greater than John the Baptist*. But in Luke 11, when a woman in the crowd shouts *blessed is the womb that bore You, and the breasts which nursed You* (11.27), Christ tells her that she's missed a larger point: *more than that, blessed are those who hear the word of God and keep it* (v 28), which parallels *but he who is least in the kingdom of heaven is greater than he.* Heaven gave to Mary and John singular roles, but there is something better than being Christ's mother or messenger, and that is to be His follower, doing the will of God (7.21–23, 12.49–50).

11.12 And from the days of John the Baptist until now the kingdom of heaven suffers violence, and the violent take it by force.

"The original meaning of the 'violence saying' that follows is one of the greatest riddles of the exegesis of the Synoptics" (Luz II, 140). For a detailed discussion of the verb *biazō* (*suffers violence*, only here and Lk. 16.16) and the noun *biastēs* (*the violent*), critical commentaries can be consulted. The three most popular interpretations are that: the kingdom suffers violence in the sense that political activists are trying to establish it by violent means[6];

---

imprinted with the personal emblem of a reed." Based on this, Luz suggests that the reference to a reed might be thinly veiled ridicule of Herod—i.e., "You did not go out to see this (well-known) windbag and sissy!" (Luz II, 138).

[6] Cf. John 6.14–15. "The verse refers to the eagerness of the people to enter by violence

the kingdom is being sought and entered with forceful enthusiasm (*from the days of John the Baptist until the present moment the kingdom of heaven has been continuously taken by storm*, WMS); the kingdom is being persecuted (5.10–12).

The last of these best fits the context. Persecution is the norm for prophets and preachers. John and Jesus were persecuted by the political class and religious establishment. John was in prison and would soon be executed (14.1–12), he and Jesus were slandered (vv 18–19, 9.34), the Twelve would be persecuted (10.16ff), attempts had already been made on Christ's life (2.16; Lk. 4.28–29), and He will shortly be targeted for death by the Jewish leadership (12.14). Almost from the start of John's ministry, men opposed God's rule (3.7) and resorted to violence to stop it (23.29–39). The kingdom suffered violence the same way the church suffered havoc (Acts 8.1,3) — via the persecution of evil men.

13–14 For all the prophets and the law prophesied until John. And if you are willing to receive *it,* he is Elijah who is to come.

For all the prophets and the law prophesied until John indicates John was the last OT prophet; *for* likely reaches back to v 11 to carry that thought forward. Though vitally connected with the Messiah, John prophesied and died under the Mosaic system. *Prophets* may here precede the *law* in word order because Christ was discussing the *prophet* John. John was thus a hinge in history, wherein the shadow gave way to the substance.

11.15 "He who has ears to hear, let him hear!

Jesus identifies John as the Elijah of Malachi 4.5. John was not Elijah redivivus (17.3ff; Jn. 1.21), but he resembled Elijah in severasl points (Lk. 1.17), particularly in his insistence that Israel decide for God (1 Kgs. 18).

He that has ears to hear, let him hear is a call to pay attention (13.9,43; Rev. 2.7,11). God never fails to speak as He should, but we sometimes fail to listen as we ought. *Ears* refer not to what hangs on either side of our head but to the receptiveness of our heart. Hearing and doing what Jesus said is the challenge facing every man (7.24–27).

---

into the privileges and honors of the kingdom — a disposition which arose from the mistaken idea that it was to be a political or military kingdom. The kingdom is compared to a walled city, and these men who wished to set up the kingdom by military force, to an army besieging the city" (McGarvey, 98).

11.16–30: Galilee

Notes

Christ responds to the growing opposition.

This section has two parts: vv 16–19 consist of a parable and its interpretation, and vv 20–24 contain an introduction (v 20) and two parallel statements of judgment (vv 21–24), each of which contains a woe, a reason, and a threat.

To willfully close our eyes to light (4.12–16; Rom. 1.18) is the gravest of sins (13.10–17). By all human canons, Sodom was synonymous with depravity, but according to Christ, to be a Capernau-mite is worse than being a Sodomite. The contrast and condemnation Jesus pronounces on the Jewish cities is reflected in Paul's argument in Romans 1 to 2, showing that the Jews bore greater guilt than the Gentiles. The mention of Chorazin and Bethsaida, which have not previously appeared in Matthew, hint at John's statement that there were many things Jesus did that were not written in the Gospels (Jn. 20.30, 21.25).[7] Thematically, the ending of v 23 corresponds to 28.15, and vv 25–30 are similar to 28.16–20.

11.16–17 "But to what shall I liken this generation? It is like children sitting in the marketplaces and calling to their companions, and saying: 'We played the flute for you, And you did not dance; We mourned to you, And you did not lament.'

Thinking out loud, Christ asks what metaphor made the point He wished to make about the current generation of Jews, The one He selects involves a common scene in the *marketplaces*, the center of community life (20.3), where children played while parents shopped. Popular games were *wedding* and *funeral* (9.23), in which children mimicked events they regularly witnessed in their village. Jesus had invited the Jews to play, but they would neither dance (as if at a wedding) nor lament (as if at a funeral; Lk. 8.52). Instead, they were passive, obstinate killjoys.[8]

11.18 For John came neither eating nor drinking, and they say, 'He has a demon.'

---

[7] "It is a reminder of how little we know about the life of Jesus that we have only this one reference to what was evidently an extensive ministry during the course of which a number of miracles were performed" (Morris, 288).

[8] *I danced for the scribes and the Pharisees / They wouldn't dance, they wouldn't follow me / I danced for the fishermen James and John ' They came with me so the dance went on.* Sydney Carter, *The Lord of the Dance*

Dance and mourning are opposites, as were the methods that characterized Jesus and John. John lived an austere life, ate a plain diet (3.4), and was so noticeably different from most that he was thought mentally unhinged.

11.19 The Son of Man came eating and drinking, and they say, 'Look, a glutton and a winebibber, a friend of tax collectors and sinners!' But wisdom is justified by her children."

By contrast, Jesus was more mainstream—He *came eating and drinking*. This, however, didn't gain Him acceptance, for He was slandered as a *glutton* and a *winebibber*. In their personal habits, John and Jesus were a study in contrasts, but both were verbally accosted (v·12), with John labeled insane and Jesus immoral.[9]

The real problem was with those who did the labelling. A hardened heart is impervious to any didactic method; in such cases, enough evidence is never enough. It's impossible to reason a person out of a position they weren't reasoned into (12.22–27, 16.1–4).

But wisdom is justified by her children. In Judaism, *wisdom* personified was an expression of God's benevolent rule shown in creating the world, directing history, and governing humanity. In setting themselves against John and Jesus, the Jews set themselves against God's wisdom (v 2), which would be ultimately *justified*—vindicated—by Christ's resurrection.

11.20 Then He began to rebuke the cities in which most of His mighty works had been done, because they did not repent:

God's wisdom was meant to produce repentance (3.2, 4.17), but Jews who heard Jesus and saw His miracles remained impenitent in droves. In His strongest condemnation yet, Jesus *began to upbraid* (*oneidizō*, denounce, reproach, heap insults on, 5.11, 27.44) three Galilean cities with a front-row seat to the drama of the ages, but refused to respond in faith: Chorazin, Bethsaida, and Capernaum.

11.21 "Woe to you, Chorazin! Woe to you, Bethsaida! For if the mighty works which were done in you had been done in Tyre and Sidon, they would have repented long ago in sackcloth and ashes.

Chorazin (modern Kerazeh) was located two and a half miles north of Capernaum. *Bethsaida*, the home of Peter, Andrew, and Philip (Jn. 1.44, 12.21),

---

[9] What they called Christ was a slander, but it could never have gained any traction unless Christ was noted as one who *ate His food with gladness* (Acts 2.46).

was on the northern shore of the lake. Upon these cities Jesus pronounced a corporate *woe* (*ouar*, a lament for the dead, a word of complaint; a familiar OT interjection of doom and calamity; "How terrible it will be for you!"). To stress the depth of their guilt, Christ contrasts Chorazin and Bethsaida with Tyre and Sidon, Phoenician cities pilloried in the OT for their opulence and arrogance (Isa. 23; Eze. 26–28; Amos 1.9–10). *Sackcloth and ashes* were Eastern symbols of grief and penitence (15.28; Est. 4.3; Jon. 3.5–6).

11.22 But I say to you, it will be more tolerable for Tyre and Sidon in the day of judgment than for you.

Galilee would fare worse than the Gentiles; come the judgment, Tyre and Sidon would be in a better situation than Chorazin and Bethsaida. To Jews who prided themselves on being God's chosen, few things Christ said could have been more shocking.

Some believe the comparative *more tolerable* indicates degrees of punishment in hell. Bales, for instance, commenting on 23.14 writes, "If 'greater condemnation' is the same as 'condemnation', is not 'greater' meaningless? If some receive greater condemnation than others, does not this indicate grades or degrees of punishment? There are, in other words, degrees of punishment. Men's lot in the world to come will have degrees proportioned to their advantages in this world. Men will be judged and punished according to their opportunities of knowing truth and duty" (*Woe unto You?* 80–82). Lending support to this is the fact that the Law of Moses insisted that punishment fit the crime (5.38).

If this view is correct, and there are degrees of punishment in eternity, I have no clue how they will be distinguished from one another.

Another possibility is that Christ is using hyperbole (23.15), teaching neither degrees of torment (25.41–46 indicates that the unrighteous all suffer the same fate), nor suggesting that Tyre and Sidon had been treated unfairly by being denied evidence that would have brought them to repentance. Instead, He may simply be arguing from the lesser to the greater: if Tyre and Sidon, with less information, were justly condemned for unbelief, where does that leave the unbelief of Chorazin and Bethsaida that had far greater information (12.41–42, Rom. 2.1)?

11.23 And you, Capernaum, who are exalted to heaven, will be brought down to Hades; for if the mighty works which were done in you had been done in Sodom, it would have remained until this day.

It would be hard to name a city in history more privileged than Capernaum. "For two years the Master lived among its people, homely and accessible, easy to be entreated and friendly with all. They could hear Him in the synagogue or in the open air; they could speak with Him on the street or in His lodgings. There was no kind of mighty work He did not perform in Capernaum" (J. Watson, *The Life of the Master*, 115). Because Capernaum's privileges were great, so was her responsibility. *Exalted to heaven* echoes the self-important description of the king of Babylon in Isaiah 14.13–14; Babylon and Capernaum were legends in their own mind. Capernaum was Jesus' adopted home (4.13, 9.1) and the scene of many of His greatest miracles (8.5ff), but despite these advantages the town, as a whole, was stubbornly impenitent. The *mighty works* Capernaum witnessed are listed in v 5. Her "refusal to acknowledge [Christ's] miracles as evidence of God's reign will bring about her utter humiliation in judgment" (Hill, 203). *Hades* often indicates the realm of the dead, the state of death, but here it likely refers to hell, the place of eternal damnation.

11.24 But I say to you that it shall be more tolerable for the land of Sodom in the day of judgment than for you."

Sodom is first mentioned in Matthew 10.15, and no judgment is mentioned more often in Scripture than Sodom's, being cited in Genesis, Deuteronomy, Isaiah, Jeremiah, Lamentations, Ezekiel, Amos, Zephaniah, Matthew, Luke, 2 Peter, Jude, and Revelation. When God rained fire and brimstone on the city, He burned the deepest hole on earth's surface. Capernaum, undoubtedly, thought itself far superior to Sodom, but Christ told Capernaum to think again.

INVITATION, 11.25–30

Notes
Christ is still addressing the Galilean cities, but condemnation now gives way to invitation.

11.25–26 At that time Jesus answered and said, "I thank You, Father, Lord of heaven and earth, that You have hidden these things from *the* wise and prudent and have revealed them to babes. Even so, Father, for so it seemed good in Your sight.

Answered, which connects this section to the unbelief just described (vv 21–24), can mean *reply*, but it can also indicate *solution*, and here Christ offers heaven's solution to Jewish unbelief.

He begins with a prayer of thanksgiving to the *Father* (6.9), the *Lord of heaven and earth* (6.10), for two things: first, that He had *hidden these things from the wise and prudent*, and second, that He had *revealed them to babes*. The antecedent of *these things* are Christ's *mighty works* (vv 4–5) that confirmed His deity and that should have led Chorazin, Bethsaida, and Capernaum to repent. *Wise and prudent* are how these cities would have described themselves (vv 21,23), but for God to have entrusted the gospel to the safekeeping of such Jews would have been to cast pearls before swine (7.6). Christ isn't thanking God for Jewish blindness and unbelief but rather is thanking God for not giving the gospel treasure to the arrogant and haughty (v 23) who would have trampled it underfoot and used it to destroy rather than deliver (23.15).

Christ thanks God that the gospel was committed to *babes* (*nēpios*, an infant, child, 18.3–4)—the unsophisticated and humble (like the disciples) who could be trusted to communicate it faithfully and fully.

11.27 All things have been delivered to Me by My Father, and no one knows the Son except the Father. Nor does anyone know the Father except the Son, and *the one* to whom the Son wills to reveal *Him*.

All things, in context, refers to *these things* in v 25—that is, the gospel.

Three propositions are offered. First, God *delivered all things* (the gospel) to *the Son*. Second, this was not a delivery from a superior to an inferior, as occurred when a prophet was inspired to speak, but was a sharing/handing over between equals—*no one knows the Son but the Father*. It was the knowledge of like by like; God's own knowledge known by God (1.23; 1 Cor. 2.11).[10] Third, *all things* that God delivered to Christ have been revealed to *babes* (vv 25,29), *to whom the Son wills to reveal Him*. Let the Pharisees criticize Christ's selection of Matthew the tax collector (9.14) or any other; Christ delivered what He received from God to those whose faith and allegiance were beyond question (*Notes*, 16.21).

11.28 Come to Me, all *you* who labor and are heavy laden, and I will give you rest.

[10] "This verse stands out as a more explicit statement of [Christ's] relationship with the Father than any other in the Synoptic Gospels" (France, 199).

For those whose hearts are open (v 27), there is an invitation, a promise, and an explanation. When one is physically tired, he can sleep until the weariness is gone; but what can be done for spiritual weariness? How is weariness of the soul dispelled?

Come to Me, all you who labor and are heavy laden and I will give you rest. Labor (*kopiaō*, to toil, grow tired, weary; Lk. 5.5) and *heavy laden* (*phrotizō*, to be loaded with a burden) refer to the spiritual and emotional exhaustion that comes from sin and guilt, which is exacerbated by man-made rules and tradition that guts the gospel of the grace of God (Acts 20.34). Like the woman whom Christ healed in 9.20–22, we can consult the *wise and prudent* until we have spent all we have and are no better for it (Lk. 8.43). There used to be (and maybe still are) doctors who advertised a cure for cancer. From far and wide the desperately ill would come, buy their medicine, go home, take the medicine, and die of cancer. The scribes and Pharisees were physicians who peddled such cures; they could kill, but they could not save.

But Christ saves! To all who would *come* to Him—in faith and worship—He gives a twice-repeated promise of *rest* (*anapauō*, repose, relief, peace). On the seventh day God rested from His work of creating, and every seventh day, the Jews recalled God's rest by observing a day of rest (*sabbath*). When we come to Christ, we enter into the rest of grace—not a soul-exhausting system of self-justifying legalism in which we try to earn our standing with God.

11.29 Take My yoke upon you and learn from Me, for I am gentle and lowly in heart, and you will find rest for your souls.

Two illustrations expand the invitation. A *yoke*, a wooden frame laid on the necks of oxen, was a common metaphor in Scripture signifying submission or subjugation (Jer. 27.1–15), which eventually took on a religious meaning—at the end of a synagogue service, rabbis would often urge the audience to submit to the *yoke of the law*. The yoke of Pharisaism, however, involved *heavy burdens, hard to bear, laid on men's shoulders*, which the scribes and Pharisees *would not move with one of their fingers* (23.4). Fosdick said that the scribes and Pharisees, in addition to the 600-some commandments they counted in the Law of Moses, created more than 2,000 rules Jews were expected to observe. Whereas Moses simply told Jews not to work on the Sabbath, Pharisaism identified thirty-nine categories of work, specifying what should and should not be done on the Sabbath (e.g., swallowing mouthwash was permitted; spitting it out wasn't). Further, just like politicians today, the scribes and Pharisees often exempted themselves from the rules they imposed on others (23.4). Pharisaism was a guilt-imposing, hope-robbing, dictatorial system that wearied (9.36) but never refreshed. *Why do you test God by putting a yoke on the neck of the disciples which neither our fathers nor we were able to bear?* (Acts 15.10).

Learn from me changes the figure from a farmer and oxen to a teacher and students, for it is in learning and living Christ that His yoke is borne (Eph. 4.17–20). It is Christ's teaching that is to be learned (28.19)—not church tradition, the practices of pioneer preachers, or the ways of those around us (1 Sam. 8.9).

But why will Christ's yoke give rest? Because of what He is—*gentle and lowly in heart.* Any first-century observer would have noted an obvious difference between the meek and lowly Christ and the religious clergy who loved *the best places at feasts, the best seats in the synagogues, [and] greetings in the market places.* Their judgmental censoriousness (9.3,10–11) contrasted sharply with His ever-present restraint, unfailing kindness, and compassionate lowliness (*tapeinos,* humility, a despised quality in the ancient world; Eph. 4.2; 1 Pet. 5.5). The scribe and Pharisees bound burdens (23.4); Christ bore burdens (Isa. 53; 1 Pet. 2.24); the rabbis wouldn't move its burdens with their little finger; Christ took on Himself the sins of the world.

11.30 For My yoke *is* easy and My burden is light."

Christ's yoke isn't easy and the burden He asks us to bear isn't light because He asks little of us. On the contrary, He demands our all (22.37). The ease and lightness of Christ must refer, I think, to the end result of following Him. Only when we live and think within His frame of reference, place ourself under His authority, accept His limits, know that there are things from which we must abstain, thoughts we must not think, and impulses that must not impel us will we find His rest. Only by repudiating the *freedom* that enslaves us to our fancies, appetites, and ambitions will we find His peace (1 Jn. 5.3). Man's center is not himself; he was made to serve some end greater than himself. Whenever man makes himself the measure of all things, he is headed for the worst sort of bondage.[11] "All his true disciples unite in the testimony, that his 'service is perfect freedom'" (R. Watson).

---

[11] "No horse gets anywhere till he's harnessed, no steam or gas drives anything until it's confined, no Niagara ever turned anything into light or power until it's tunneled, no life ever

CHAPTER 12

12.1–14: Pharisees

SABBATH, 12.1–14

Notes

At no point was Christ's conflict with the religious establishment more obvious than in regard to Sabbath observance. The Pharisees—who failed to see that people are more important than *things* or *rules*—had made an idol out of the Sabbath. In Pharisaism, instead of the Sabbath being a means to an end, it was an end in itself.

In the remaining part of Matthew's first section (12.1–16.12), Christ increasingly *withdraws* from orthodox Judaism. *Anachōreō* appears three times (*withdrew*, 12.15; *departed,* 14.13, 15.21), and separation is expressed in other ways in 13.36 and 16.4. In each case, a debate between Jesus and the Jewish establishment precedes the withdrawal.

Chapter 12 echoes the structure of ch 11: a description of Christ's miracles is followed by a warning, a pronouncement of judgment, and a statement about salvation. The opening paragraph flows out of 11.25–30: the Pharisees are *the wise and prudent* who missed the truth, and the disciples are the *babes* who welcomed it. The incident involving the Sabbath illustrates this, as well as the lightness of Christ's yoke (11.30).

12.1 At that time Jesus went through the grainfields on the Sabbath. And His disciples were hungry, and began to pluck heads of grain and to eat.

At that time connects this to the preceding. Details are sparse except to note that the events occurred in a *grainfield* on a *Sabbath*. Christ and the disciples are, presumably, on a wayside (13.4), and the disciples, being hungry, grab some handfuls of grain to eat, as the Law allowed (Deut. 23.25).

---

grows great until focused, dedicated, and disciplined" (Fosdick).

12.2 And when the Pharisees saw *it*, they said to Him, "Look, Your disciples are doing what is not lawful to do on the Sabbath!"

In Matthew, the Pharisees (3.7) appear as Christ's initial opponents, and it seems that due to previous incidents (9.10ff), they now have Jesus under constant surveillance. When they see His disciples plucking grain, they pounce. Pharisaic tradition said that plucking grain on the Sabbath was allowable, but rubbing grain in one's hands was threshing, which was work forbidden on the Sabbath.[1]

12.3–4 But He said to them, "Have you not read what David did when he was hungry, he and those who were with him: how he entered the house of God and ate the showbread which was not lawful for him to eat, nor for those who were with him, but only for the priests?

Jesus' response is threefold. First, He points out the *Pharisees' inconsistency* by referring to David in 1 Samuel 21. *Have you not read* had to grate on those who considered themselves the best-read men of their day; the Pharisees had read 1 Samuel 21, but you couldn't tell it. While fleeing Saul's murderous rage, David ordered Abimelech, the high priest, to supply him and his men with bread, even if it meant giving them the consecrated loaves in the tabernacle (1 Sam. 21 doesn't mention the Sabbath, but Lev. 24.8 points in that direction). Consequently, David ate that which *was not lawful for him to eat*, thus violating God's Law — but Jewish rabbis didn't stigmatize David as a lawbreaker. Their usual defense of him was that *necessity knows no law* — David's life-threatening predicament took precedence over Sabbath law. The Pharisees' attitude toward hungry David and their accusation of Jesus' hungry disciples (v 1) revealed a double standard. Some see Christ's reference to David as an appeal to historical precedent and situational ethics, but this wasn't Jesus' point. He who refused to go beyond His Father's word to satisfy His hunger (4.2–4), and He who condemned those who broke the least of God's commandments (5.19) is making an *ad hominem* argument that exposed a glaring discrepancy in Pharisaism.[2]

---

[1] "Modern Jewish scholars point out that there was a wide diversity of opinion on such matters among first-century interpreters. The Mishnah does not list 'plucking' among the thirty-nine varieties of prohibited labor. It is suggested that the view expressed by these Pharisees represents not ordinary Jewish opinion but that of extreme sabbatarians, such as those responsible for the Dead Sea Scrolls and the book of *Jubilees*, for whom the Sabbath could not be violated even to save a life (see I Macc. 2.29–41)" (Hare, 131).

[2] "If Christians may violate law when its observance would involve hardship or suffer-

12.5–6 Or have you not read in the law that on the Sabbath the priests in the temple profane the Sabbath, and are blameless? Yet I say to you that in this place there is *One* greater than the temple.

Second, Christ reminds the Pharisees that in the Law, some things took precedence over other things. When the priests, for instance, offered sacrifices on the Sabbath (Num. 28.9–10), they weren't violating the Sabbath prohibition against work.

Christ mentions something that took precedence over the Sabbath. Here I must depart from the NKJV reading, for the translators' insertion of *One*—*there is One greater than the temple*—is indefensible. The Gr. uses the noun *meizon*, which is neuter and rightly translates as *something* [not *someone*] *greater than the temple is here* (NASB; so also BECK, WMS, NEB, CEV, GOODSPEED, BARCLAY, JBP, ASV margin, etc.)—Christ has in mind some *thing*, not some *one*. He's not saying that He is greater than the temple but is referring to something else as being greater than the temple.[3] If the temple was greater than the Sabbath, then anything greater than the temple is greater than the Sabbath! If sacrifice takes precedence over the Sabbath, how much more does that which is greater than sacrifice take precedence over the Sabbath.

12.7 But if you had known what *this* means, 'I desire mercy and not sacrifice,' you would not have condemned the guiltless.

And what is *greater* than sacrifice? *Mercy!* It is greater than the sacrificial system, which makes it greater than anything sacrifice is greater than, such as the Sabbath. To interpret Sabbath law in a way that disallows mercy completely misses God's will (23.23).[4] For a second time, Christ goes to Hosea 6.6 (9.13) and its teaching that God is more concerned with mercy (which is difficult to practice) than with sacrifice (which is easy to produce). The Pharisees didn't understand Hosea 6. It didn't disannul the law of sacrifice (5.17), but it explained that neither temple services nor Sabbath rest prohibited acts of mercy. Note here that simple hunger falls within Christ's definition of need (v 12, 15.32). Anyone who claims to be within the circle of Christ and is insensitive to human need is a

---

ing, then there is an end of suffering for the name of Christ, and an end even of self-denial" (McGarvey, 104).

[3] *Temple* is here used metonymically for the temple service, which included sacrifices.

[4] The Essenes "during the Sabbath left a 'living human being lying in a water hole' or 'any other place,' if saving the person was possible only with a ladder or a rope" (Luz II, 184).

heretic at heart. Had the Pharisees understood this, they wouldn't have condemned the innocent—Christ's disciples.

12.8 For the Son of Man is Lord even of the Sabbath."

Third, Christ asserts the sovereignty He claimed in the Sermon on the Mount when He said, *but I say to you* (5.22,44). *The Son of Man is Lord even of the Sabbath!* As in 5.21–48, Christ isn't contradicting the Law but explaining it. If anyone understood the Sabbath law, it was He, and He affirms that Sabbath law was subordinate to mercy, not the other way around (Mk. 2.27).

12.9–10 Now when He had departed from there, He went into their synagogue. And behold, there was a man who had a withered hand. And they asked Him, saying, "Is it lawful to heal on the Sabbath?"— that they might accuse Him.

Illustration follows explanation, but because the Pharisees regarded the Sabbath as an end in itself, their anger toward Jesus rose to a murderous rage.

Leaving the field, Jesus entered *their*—the Jew's—synagogue (Rev. 2.9). Christ had nothing to learn by going to a synagogue service, but it was His custom to attend the synagogue on the Sabbath (Lk. 4.16).

The Pharisees, determined to exonerate themselves, ask a loaded question. Rabbinic law allowed medical attention on the Sabbath in life-or-death situations, but *a withered hand*,[5] though dysfunctional, wasn't an emergency; its healing could easily wait until the next day.[6] Behind this question is the Pharisaic assumption that healing would violate the Sabbath law prohibiting work (v 2). *Is it lawful to heal on the Sabbath?* was

---

[5] "A withered hand ... is a terrible handicap. It is not merely the loss of a limb; it is an impoverishment of the entire personality. The hand is, to many people, the organ of self-expression. The soul of the painter may be flooded with beauty, the soul of the pianist may be overflowing with music; but, if the hand be hurt, the beauty will never be seen and the music will never be heard. With the shriveling of the hand, all the energies and activities of life undergo diminution and decay. A withered hand represents a lessened receptivity; it represents an impaired fellowship; it represents a vanished sufficiency; it represents a limited degree of usefulness and service" (Boreham, *The Nest of Spears*, 81–82).

[6] Geikie explains that the Pharisees' "fine-spun casuistry had elaborated endless rules for the treatment of all maladies on the sacred day. A person in health was not to take medicine on the Sabbath. For the toothache, vinegar might be put in the mouth, if it were afterwards swallowed, but it must not be spat out again. A sore throat must not be gargled with oil, but the oil might be swallowed. The school of Shammai held it unlawful to comfort the sick, or visit the mourner on the Sabbath" (*The Life and Words of Christ* II, 99–100).

asked because they were sure they knew how Christ would answer, and they intended to use His answer as a ground for an *accusation* (*katēgoreō*, to charge in court).

12.11 Then He said to them, "What man is there among you who has one sheep, and if it falls into a pit on the Sabbath, will not lay hold of it and lift *it* out?

Jesus answers their question with a question involving a scenario much discussed in Judaism: "Is it permitted to save an animal that has fallen into a ditch on the Sabbath?" For legalistic Jews, the answer was an unequivocal no. But many rabbis took a less harsh approach and taught that an owner could help the animal (putting blankets and padding under it, feeding it, etc.), so long as the animal came out of the ditch by itself (Luz II, 187).

Possibly the best way to understand Christ and the Sabbath is to put it in a family context. Suppose there is a family rule that the kids are to be home from dates by 10 pm, but then comes a night when a child doesn't show up until 11 pm. The parents have sat up, concerned and worried, and when the child finally gets home they immediately question him and learn he was late because he had come upon an accident and had stopped to assist the injured. The parents in such a situation would conclude that any *rule-breaking* was irrelevant and would heap praise on a child who manifested the spirit of family love by showing compassion. Helping the hurting is more important than and supercedes a be-home-by-10 pm rule. Acts of mercy did not violate the spirit of the Sabbath for they reflected the spirit of God. Pharisees in ivory towers might debate the lawfulness of pulling a sheep out of a ditch on the Sabbath, but no Jewish shepherd was in no doubt about what he would do if it were his *only sheep* in the ditch.[7]

12.12 Of how much more value then is a man than a sheep? Therefore it is lawful to do good on the Sabbath."

Mercy was the answer to Christ's question. If compassion could help a sheep on the Sabbath, how much more could it help a man (Mk. 3.4). Christ's answer applied Hosea 6.6 and illustrated what the *weightier matters of the law* allowed (23.23). By this healing, Jesus showed that mercy isn't limited to life-or-death situations (which many scribes and Pharisees would have allowed) but includes everyday situations (9.9–13). *Mercy*

---

[7] There may be an allusion here to Nathan's fable in 2 Sam. 12.3.

isn't something on the periphery of God's Law—meant for emergency use only—but is at the very heart of God.

12.13 Then He said to the man, "Stretch out your hand." And he stretched *it* out, and it was restored as whole as the other.

Almost incidental to the story was the miracle. Jesus commands, the man obeys, and his hand was miraculously healed in a manner to which all could attest. Jesus did good on the Sabbath day because God delights in mercy (Mic. 7.18).

12.14 Then the Pharisees went out and plotted against Him, how they might destroy Him.

Christ could have waited until after the Sabbath, or have performed the healing more discretely in some place other than a synagogue. That He did what He did when He did it and where He did it threw down the gauntlet, deliberately challenging the heresy that subordinated mercy to ritual.

The Pharisees double down. *Went out and took counsel against Him* signals a major shift in the narrative. The split between Jesus and the establishment will not be resolved. For the first time in Matthew, the story's end directly comes in view. Jesus will die at the prompting of the Pharisees.[8]

12.15–21: Withdrawal

Notes

Four brief clauses (vv 15–17) introduce a quotation from Isaiah 42.1–4 (vv 18–21) that is the longest OT quotation in Matthew. It is a difficult passage to interpret in context. An obvious connection occurs between vv 16 and 19, but in v 16, Jesus warns the healed man to keep quiet, whereas in v 19, it is the Messiah who keeps quiet. If Matthew was concerned only with stressing the quiet and modest reserve of Jesus, Isaiah 42.2 would have sufficed; that he includes a larger excerpt suggests that he wants to remind His readers of other aspects of Christ's ministry besides the fact that He was not a sensation-monger.

---

[8] "Each of the Evangelists refers to this fact that it was because of our Lord's attitude toward the Sabbath that these men decided to kill Him" (Morgan, 128).

12.15 But when Jesus knew *it*, He withdrew from there. And great multitudes followed Him, and He healed them all.

Jesus knows of the Pharisees' conspiracy (v 14), and He leaves the area, "not because He was afraid to die, but because it was not time for Him to die" (Foster I, 104). He is as popular with the multitudes as ever, and great crowds follow, hoping for a cure. And He didn't disappoint—*He healed them all.*

12.16–17 Yet He warned them not to make Him known, that it might be fulfilled which was spoken by Isaiah the prophet, saying:

Christ *warns* (*epitimaō*, rebuke, censure, speak seriously) *them not to make Him known* (8.4), which is surprising since His name was on the lips of everyone in the land. As Matthew explains, the Lord's avoidance of self-promotion was predicted by the prophets.

12.18 "Behold! My Servant whom I have chosen, My Beloved in whom My soul is well pleased! I will put My Spirit upon Him, And He will declare justice to the Gentiles.

God calls attention to His *Servant* (*pais*). The usual meaning of *pais* is *child*, but in the NT, it is often translated *servant*. Whether *child*, *son*, or *servant*, Christ was God's *beloved* in whom He was *well pleased*, which recalls 3.17.

Four clauses follow.

First, God *will put [His] Spirit upon Him*, which recalls Jesus' baptism. The bestowal of the *Spirit* (v 28) empowered Christ for His work (Jn. 3.34).

Second, the Messiah *will declare justice* (*krisis*) to *the Gentiles.* Luz says that "in secular Greek *krisis* never means 'justice,' and Matthew also has used the word thus far only for the final judgment and will continue to do so."[9] If *judgment* rather than *justice* is the meaning here, Isaiah is simply saying that the Spirit-endowed Servant of God would reveal to the Gentiles the fact of a *final* judgment—but, as implied in vv 20–21, with a happy connotation. The idea of a final judgment was a novel idea in Greco-Roman society. "For the philosophers and historians of Greece and Rome, history had no beginning and would have no end" (Montgomery, *The Shape of the Past*, 42). "When the Apostle Paul announced to the Athenians that God had 'appointed a day in which He will judge the word in righteousness' [Acts 17.31] he declared a truth

---

[9] 23.23 being the only exception.

which in such comprehensiveness was utterly new in the thought of the Greek and Roman world" (Smith, *Therefore, Stand*, 438). It was the Hebrew religion that introduced to the world the thought of a day of reckoning. Christ not only confirmed this, but taught that for some, the day of judgment will be a day of glory.

12.19–20 He will not quarrel nor cry out, nor will anyone hear His voice in the streets. A bruised reed He will not break, and smoking flax He will not quench, till He sends forth justice to victory;

Third, the Messiah *will not quarrel nor cry out*, which suggests a peaceful demeanor. Whether attacked (v 24) or ignored (*nor will anyone hear His voice in the streets*), God's Servant would not resort to violence or shouting (1 Pet. 2.23).

The referents for *bruised reed* and *smoking flax* have been variously interpreted. From a domestic standpoint, bruised reeds and smoking flax were useless items. Reeds are long, thin plants that grow near water (11.7) that, in antiquity, were used for yardsticks, pens, and flutes. They were so plentiful and cheap that when broken, they were simply discarded and replaced. Flax is a fibrous plant material that was used for lamp wicks. When it doesn't burn properly, it gives off more smoke than light, and when this occurs, the fire is put out and the defective flax is thrown away. Smoking flax was the equivalent of a burned-out lightbulb.

Metaphorically, reed and flax refer to people whom society deems disposable, dispensable—the weak, immature, uncertain, irritating, sin-burdened (1 Thes. 5.14). The significant thing here is how the Messiah deals with such: *He will not break … He will not quench*. Because He is meek, kind, merciful, and loving, He binds what is broken (Lk. 4.18) and fans embers back into flame.[10]

Fourth, the Messiah will *send forth justice to victory*—which, again, I believe, speaks of the final *judgment* (v 18) that will bring death to some (vv 32,36) and life to others (7.14, 25.31–40; Jn. 5.29).

---

[10] "As the victor over temptation, the Servant would have every right to break the bruised reed and to quench the dimly burning wick. Israel, and we ourselves, have failed and disobeyed. Justice demands that we should be finally broken, that our faint light should be quenched. But *he will not*. This is the amazing message of the prophecy. He will not quench what light there is. There is something ineffably tender in the Servant's compassion; he will stoop over us, he will not quench us, he will spend his own life to heal the bruised reed, to revive the flaming wick. There is only one word for this—*grace*. What a promise, what grace, to us bruised reeds and fainting wicks!" (Henri Blocher, *Songs of the Servant*, 32–33).

12.21 And in His name Gentiles will trust."

The judgment predicted for the Jews was dire (11.21–24), but for the Gentiles it was hopeful (vv 41–42). The Jewish Messiah was One in whom the Gentiles could put their *trust* (*elpizō*, hope; only here in Matt.; 2.2). Though Jesus' fate has been determined by the Jews (v 14), He—*His name*, character—was the basis for the Gentile's hope.

12.22–37: Blasphemy

Notes

Now that open conflict between Christ and the Jewish clergy has broken out, Matthew shows how Jesus routed Pharisaic premises using Scripture and reasoning.[11]

12.22 Then one was brought to Him who was demon-possessed, blind and mute; and He healed him, so that the blind and mute man both spoke and saw.

The exorcism of a demon—which had rendered its victim unable to see or speak—set the stage for what follows.

12.23 And all the multitudes were amazed and said, "Could this be the Son of David?"

The difference between the people and the Pharisees, first noted in 9.32–34, reappears and intensifies. There, the people *marveled* (*thaumazō*, wonder, admire); here, they were beside themselves (Mk. 3.21; *existēmi*; *the whole crowd went wild with excitement*, JBP). There, the people knew they had witnessed something unique; here, it begins to dawn on them that Jesus was the Messiah, *the Son of David*.

12.24 Now when the Pharisees heard *it* they said, "This *fellow* does not cast out demons except by Beelzebub, the ruler of the demons."

The Pharisees move quickly to squash this idea by repeating their previous slander that Jesus did what He did by the power of *Beelzebub* (9.34, 10.25). Nothing they said was more perverse than this; only utter depravity could accuse One completely untouched by the devil of acting by the devil's

---

[11] Vernon K. Robbins (*Rhetorical Composition and the Beelzebub Controversy*) notes that Christ's argument here contained all the steps that, according to Hermogenes, are necessary for a complete rhetorical argument.

power! But the Pharisees were desperate; for the people to think that a man they branded by them a blasphemer and heretic might be the Messiah was a reflection on their leadership.

12.25–26 But Jesus knew their thoughts, and said to them: "Every kingdom divided against itself is brought to desolation, and every city or house divided against itself will not stand. If Satan casts out Satan, he is divided against himself. How then will his kingdom stand?

Jesus never had to use a man's spoken words as an index to the man's thoughts, for every person's hidden depths were open to His omniscience (Jn. 2.25), making Him the superior and sovereign party in every encounter. To reduce the Pharisees' charge to absurdity, He applies the test of reason.[12]

It is an axiom that internal strife leads to disaster; no society — earthly or otherworldly — beset by civil strife can survive. Yet, civil war is precisely what the Pharisees affirmed for Satan if he empowered Jesus to cast out demons. "Whatever faults the devils have, they are not at strife with each other; that fault is reserved for the servants of a better Master" (Spurgeon).

12.27 And if I cast out demons by Beelzebub, by whom do your sons cast *them* out? Therefore they shall be your judges.

Various sources attest that exorcism, so-called, was a recognized profession in Jewish society, but Jewish exorcists employed magic rituals rather than an authoritative, divine word (8.32). Josephus reflected common superstition when he wrote that God " enabled [Solomon] to learn that skill which expels demons, which is a science useful and sanative to men. … he left behind him the manner of using exorcisms, by which they drive away demons, so that they never return, and this method of cure is of great force unto this day; for I have seen a certain man of my own country whose name was Eleazar, releasing people that were demoniacal in the presence of Vespasian. … The manner of the cure was this: — He put a ring that had a root of one of those sorts mentioned by Solomon to the nostrils of the demoniac, after which he drew out the demon through his nostrils" (*Ant.* v.2.5).[13] According to Christ, some within the Pharisees'

---

[12] "This charge [that Christ's power was Satanic] persisted as a common view of Jesus among Jews in the early centuries of the Christian era. They did not deny the genuineness of his miracles but ascribed his power to the devil, so that he was branded a sorcerer (e.g., *b. Sank.* 107b; *b. Sabb.* 104b) and worthy of death *(m. Sank.* 7.4)." (Blomberg, 201).

[13] See Edersheim II, 775–776; also, Acts 19.13.

ranks (*your sons*, disciples, 23.15) practiced exorcisms. Without pausing to evaluate the validity of this claim, Jesus asks why He has been singled out—how did they know He cast out demons by a power different from that used by their disciples? *They shall be your judges* means that which proves the Pharisees' case against Christ proves too much. *By their fruits you will know them* (7.20)—if casting out demons meant Christ worked by Satanic power, why didn't it mean the same for the Pharisees' disciples? Hypocrites are adept at criticizing those outside their circle while ignoring similar behavior within their clique. For the Pharisees, exoneration or condemnation often depended on who their friends were.

12.28 But if I cast out demons by the Spirit of God, surely the kingdom of God has come upon you.

But (*de*) is a disjunctive particle (serving or tending to disjoin or divide) that introduces the real reason for Christ's power over demons. Considering that Isaiah prophesied that the Spirit would be upon the Messiah (v 18), and that Jesus didn't exorcise demons by the power of the devil (vv 25–26), it followed that His power was divine (19.24, 21.31,43). *Has come* translates the aorist form of *phthanō*, but the past tense of this verb doesn't contradict the future sense of the kingdom as preached in 4.17—there was a sense in which the kingdom had begun, even while there was a sense in which it was still future.[14]

12.29 Or how can one enter a strong man's house and plunder his goods, unless he first binds the strong man? And then he will plunder his house.

A rhetorical question backs the point made in v 28. Satan is a strong man unable to defend his property (*goods, skeuos*, a vessel, implement, equipment; a reference either to demons, the demonized, or both) against a break-in by a stronger man (Isa. 49.24–25). Christ's argument is that He can cast out demons because He is stronger than the devil—which is the only explanation that explains! Man hasn't the power to extricate himself from the devil, but—thank God!—there is One who can set captives free (Lk. 4.18).

12.30 He who is not with Me is against Me, and he who does not gather with Me scatters abroad.

Here is a call to decision. It isn't directed at the Pharisees, for they have

---

[14] Though an aorist normally indicates past action, there are exceptions. In 1 Thes. 2.16, 4.15, a past tense verb (*ephthae*) denotes a future event.

made their decision (v 14); more likely, it's addressed to the undecided among the people (v 23). Parallel statements set out the alternatives: one either *gathers*/is with Christ or *scatters*/is against Him. *Gathers* could refer to a harvest (3.12, 9.38, 13.28–29), to a shepherd collecting his flock (Isa. 40.11), or to God calling His people (23.37). *Scatters* indicates an adversarial position. Though it is the one against Jesus who is said to scatter, Scripture also teaches that those who set themselves against Christ will be scattered, just like a defeated army is demolished and scattered (Zech. 1.19,21).

12.31–32 Therefore I say to you, every sin and blasphemy will be forgiven men, but the blasphemy *against* the Spirit will not be forgiven men. Anyone who speaks a word against the Son of Man, it will be forgiven him; but whoever speaks against the Holy Spirit, it will not be forgiven him, either in this age or in the *age* to come.

Throughout ecclesiastical history, devout individuals have been tortured by the fear that they have committed the unforgivable sin. Augustine, in one of his sermons (71), said that the meaning of the twice-repeated words *will not be forgiven* may be the most difficult and most important question in the Bible. What makes it difficult is the seeming suggestion that *the blasphemy against the Holy Spirit* puts a limit on grace.

Therefore introduces the conclusion to Christ's rejoinder (v 24). *I say to you* indicates the solemnity of what follows, in which a distinction is made between two types of *blasphemy* (*blasphēmia*, slander, speech injurious to another's good name). According to Christ, to speak against the Son (v 24, 9.34), no matter how vile or debased, is forgivable; but to speak against the Spirit is unforgiveable. What does this mean?

Athanasius thought that the blasphemy against the Holy Spirit is the denial of the divinity of Christ by unbelievers or heretics. Origen believed it a sin that could be committed only by Christians (because the Spirit dwells only in Christians) who apostatize (Heb. 6.4–6). Augustine believed that the sin was committed when one was impenitent and cut himself off from the church, the source of forgiveness.

Here's what I think. The Pharisees, clearly, blasphemed Jesus when they accused Him of casting out demons by the power of Beelzebub—and for this they could be forgiven (Lk. 23.34). After the Lord returned to the Father, He sent the Holy Spirit to equip the apostles in their work (28.18–20; Jn. 16.6ff), which included revealing the terms of forgiveness for those who had blasphemed the Son (Acts 2.37–38). In the parallel text in Luke 12, the warning about blaspheming the Spirit is followed by *and when they bring you to the synagogues and to magistrates and authorities, do not worry about how or what you will answer, or what you will say. For the Holy Spirit will teach you in the same hour what you ought to say* (vv 11–12) — which implies that *blaspheming the Spirit* occurs when the apostles' Spirit-inspired words are rejected. If the gospel of grace revealed by the Holy Spirit through the apostles is refused, there is no other means of salvation. When men repudiate the apostolic word, they blaspheme the Spirit and put themselves beyond the reach of forgiveness (Acts 7.51, 13.45–46).

Blasphemy against the Holy Spirit, then, is not a particular word, set of words, or act — it is a hardened heart that closes the mind and shuts out God. Blaspheming the Holy Spirit isn't God refusing to forgive, but man refusing to be forgiven.[15]

12.33 Either make the tree good and its fruit good, or else make the tree bad and its fruit bad; for a tree is known by *its* fruit.

This is a metaphorical call for repentance (7.16–18). If men are to avoid blaspheming the Spirit, they must change their hearts. The character of a tree is judged by the nature of its fruit, but the character of the tree determines the nature of the fruit.

12.34–35 Brood of vipers! How can you, being evil, speak good things? For out of the abundance of the heart the mouth speaks. A good man out of the good treasure of his heart brings forth good things, and an evil man out of the evil treasure brings forth evil things.

Using an image employed by John (*brood of vipers*, 3.7, 23.33), Christ calls the Pharisees a bunch of snakes because their *fruit* — their hypocritical lives and blasphemy of Christ — showed they were inwardly evil (as Matthew's Gospel amply confirms). This conclusion follows from the truism that *out of the abundance of the heart the mouth speaks*. Like produces like; the words of the mouth reveal the character of the heart (Tit. 1.10–11).

12.36–37 But I say to you that for every idle word men may speak, they will give account of it in the day of judgment. For by your words you will be justified, and by your words you will be condemned."

---

[15] Scripture, in several places, speaks of defiance toward God as unforgivable (Num. 15.30–31; 1 Sam. 3.14; Isa. 22.14).

These verses conclude Christ's response to the Pharisees' blasphemy. *Word* translates *rhēma* (rather than *logos*), which indicates the spoken word. *Idle* (*argos*) means lazy or unemployed when used of a person (20.3,6); when used of things, it means unproductive, useless. Jesus isn't talking about slang interjections, verbal exclamation points, or euphemisms—the vocal shorthand found in every language for expressing emotion (*wow, oops, shucks*, etc.). His concern is with real evil such as blasphemy (v 24). Judgment will be based on the character of our heart, not on harmless interjections from a good heart.

12.38–45: Unbelief

Notes

Christ sees evil behind the request for a sign (v 38) and for the first time speaks of the ultimate sign—the sign of Jonah—followed by a warning to those who don't believe in Him. His resurrection would be the ultimate answer to unbelief.

12.38 Then some of the scribes and Pharisees answered, saying, "Teacher, we want to see a sign from You."

Answered (11.25) connects this section to the previous. Some scribes and Pharisees, stung by Christ's exposure of their inanity (vv 24ff), attempt to recover their credibility by indicating that they would believe if Jesus supplied credible evidence for His claims. In asking for a *sign* (*sēmeion*, a mark, a token, indication; something visible by which something not visible can be known; 16.1–4; 1 Cor. 1.22), it isn't clear what they expected. In John 6.30–31, the multitude asks for a sign that would enable them to believe Christ's claims, and they suggest something along the line of manna from heaven. Seven times in John 6, Christ refers to Himself as the one *who comes down from heaven* (vv 33,38,41,42,50,51,58), which means that He Himself is the sign! Christ had been performing one spectacular miracle after another to demonstrate His deity (vv 22–23), but hard-hearted Jews couldn't see what was staring them in the face! "The demand for a sign was a cruel and studied insult. It reflected upon the miracles already wrought; it implied that Jesus lacked credentials, it intimated that he was making claims he could not vindicate. It is echoed today by men who claim that they have not proof enough for believing in Christ" (Erdman, 99).

12.39–40 But He answered and said to them, "An evil and adulterous generation seeks after a sign, and no sign will be given to it except the sign of the prophet Jonah. For as Jonah was three days and three nights in the belly of the great fish, so will the Son of Man be three days and three nights in the heart of the earth.

The scribes and Pharisees weren't truth seekers but *evil* men with closed minds who stood condemned (7.17–18, 12.34–35). The adjective *adulterous* is interesting. The prophets often identified idolatry as adultery (Hos. 1–3; Eze. 16.38; Jer. 13.26–27); after the Jews returned from exile, they never returned to formal idolatry. But by elevating their tradition above God's word and having hearts far from God (15.3,8), they had broken covenant with God and, by definition, were as idolatrous as their forebears.

The sign of the prophet Jonah refers to Jonah's *three days and three nights* in *the belly of the great fish* (Jon. 1–2). Something would happen to Jesus that paralleled Jonah's experience—He, like Jonah, would survive an unsurvivable situation. But instead of being in a fish, Jesus would be *in the heart of the earth*, indicating death and burial. Jesus offers no further specifics, but anyone who knew the story of Jonah would understood that something stupendous was meant. Conquering death would be Christ's ultimate vindication (1 Tim. 3.16).[16]

The KJV uses the word *whale* in v 40, but the better translation is the NKJV's *great fish* (*ketos*, sea monster, huge fish, Jonah 1.17, 2.1).

A great deal of ink has been expended on the phrase *three days and three nights* because of contemporary man's attempt to impose Western methods of reckoning on first-century reckoning. To the Jews; *three days and three nights* was a figure of speech that didn't necessarily mean seventy-two hours. In 27.63–64, the Pharisees (of all people!) are concerned about Christ's prediction of His resurrection; instead of *three days and three nights*, they use two different expressions—*after three days* and *until the third* day—interchangeably. The textual evidence indicates that Jesus was in the grave two nights, one whole day, and parts of two other days—which, for the Jews, constituted *three days and three nights*. As Thomas Cooper noted, "We did not make the ancient languages, and we cannot

---

[16] The exchange in Jn. 10.24–38 is helpful here. The authorities surround Jesus and challenge Him to tell them *plainly* (publicly, verbally) if He was the Christ. Christ replies that He has already answered their question by His works/miracles (vv 25,37–38). Actions speak louder than words; if a mind is so closed that it refuses to see the significance of a supernatural work, no spoken word will likely succeed in bringing enlightenment.

be accountable for any method of reckoning time that was in use by an ancient nation. Many of their usages differed from ours; and among the rest, their way of reckoning time" (*The Verity of Christ's Resurrection from the Dead*, 79).[17]

Neither Christ nor Matthew showed much interest in the precise amount of time that Jesus would spend in the grave; what is paramount is that He died and then arose.

12.41–42 The men of Nineveh will rise up in the judgment with this generation and condemn it, because they repented at the preaching of Jonah; and indeed a greater than Jonah *is* here. The queen of the South will rise up in the judgment with this generation and condemn it, for she came from the ends of the earth to hear the wisdom of Solomon; and indeed a greater than Solomon *is* here.

Two statements contrasting Jews and Gentiles reintroduce the subject of judgment. Each case—*Nineveh* and the *queen of the South* (Sheba, 1 Kgs. 10.1–13)—involves Gentiles who turned to God on less evidence than was available to the Jews. The belief of these Gentiles utterly rebuked the unbelief of the Jews.

12.43–45 When an unclean spirit goes out of a man, he goes through dry places, seeking rest, and finds none. Then he says, 'I will return to my house from which I came.' And when he comes, he finds *it* empty, swept, and put in order. Then he goes and takes with him seven other spirits more wicked than himself, and they enter and dwell there; and the last *state* of that man is worse than the first. So shall it also be with this wicked generation."

An illustration involving an exorcism emphasizes the fate facing the *evil and adulterous generation* (v 39, 41,42). A demon is cast out of a man and wanders through deserted places seeking rest (11.28–29)—another victim—but without success.[18] Frustrated, it revisits the old neighborhood and finds its former house (victim) is *empty* (*scholazō*, from which comes our Eng. *school, scholar*), *swept, and put in order*. Nature, said Aristotle, hates

---

[17] "Suppose any of our kings reigned ten years and one week—we should say he reigned ten years. But, in the ancient canon of Ptolemy, which scholars reckon to be a most valuable piece of ancient chronology, the odd week entitles the dead king to be set down as having reigned eleven years. It was a prevailing custom among ancient nations to reckon in this manner" (Cooper, 80).

[18] In 11.28, Jesus offers *rest*, which demons seek (the same word is used in both passages).

a vacuum, and the demon moves back in with a vengeance, taking *seven* (the Heb. number for completeness, fulness) other demons more fiendish than itself. Consequently, the man ends up worse off than ever. Satan can tolerate a temporary remission if it leads to evil metastasizing.

So it also makes the point. It didn't matter if the Jews had rid the land of idols, or attended synagogue every Sabbath, or kept the great feasts—if they rejected their Messiah, their spiritual, moral, and eternal situation would be worse than ever.[19] Judgment was coming, and Israel needed to repent.

12.46–50: Belief

Notes

Following the condemnation of unbelief in vv 22–45 is a commendation of belief. Chapter 12 follows the format of ch 11, in that a section condemning unbelief (vv 7–24) is followed by a section encouraging belief (vv 25–30).

12.46 While He was still talking to the multitudes, behold, His mother and brothers stood outside, seeking to speak with Him.

Not only was there a divide between Jesus and the Jews, but at this point, there was a divide between Him and His family, which is suggested by the fact that they *stood outside*. The appearance of Christ's mother and brothers (13.55) may have been prompted by their concern that *He was out of His mind* (Mk. 3.21). So they sought Him out, thinking He was still submissive to them, but they were to find out otherwise.

That Christ's sisters aren't mentioned (13.56) reflects the Jewish custom that would have remain at home. That Joseph isn't mentioned likely implies he was dead.

12.47–49 Then one said to Him, "Look, Your mother and Your brothers are standing outside, seeking to speak with You." But He answered and said to the one who told Him, "Who is My mother and who are My brothers?" And He stretched out His hand toward His disciples and said, "Here are My mother and My brothers!

But a defining characteristic of demons is that they don't want the rest Christ offers.

[19] In context, it is Christ's generation of Jews to whom these words apply, but it's hard not to make an individual application as well. When sin is replaced with its righteous alternative, a relapse will likely occur and the individual will return to his former vice to a deeper degree than ever (2 Pet. 2.20–22).

Christ's response to His family's arrival is a question: *Who is My mother and who are My brothers?* The answer is surprising—so much so, that some consider it a slap in the face to Mary and her family. With a gesture (*He stretched out His hand toward His disciples*) and a declaration (*Here are my mother and My brothers!*), Jesus defined His family as consisting of the community of believers (Heb. 2.11).

12.50 For whoever does the will of My Father in heaven is My brother and sister and mother."

This is one of the critical verses in Matthew defining discipleship—a disciple is *whoever does the will of My Father who is in heaven.* Doing God's will is what we are to pray for (6.10), it is what enables the lost to see God (5.16), it is what Christ lived (26.42), it is to be proclaimed worldwide (28.20), and it is that by which all will be judged (7.21–23).

And when one is obedient, he is part of Christ's family. The Athenian philosopher Isocrates wrote, "The man who shares our highest thoughts is a Greek in a truer sense than he who shares merely our blood." In the kingdom, obedience is thicker than blood.

CHAPTER 13

13.1–53: Parables

IN PUBLIC, 13.1–35

Notes

There is a noticeable difference between Christ's teaching in the Sermon on the Mount and His teaching here, in parables (v 10). His teaching in the Sermon was direct; His teaching with parables, it was indirect, but still effective for the purpose He had in mind.

To Christ, *kingdom* meant something very different from the popular understanding. To explain what He meant, He used a new style of teaching (but one that had a literary history) known as the *parable* (*parabolē*, to put one thing alongside another for the purpose of comparison; the term occurs seventeen times in this discourse). Three blocks of parables—13.3–52, 21.28 to 22.14, and 24.42 to 25.30—are found in Matthew.

A parable's purpose, wrote Hobbs, "was to take some situation which was found in everyday life and *cast it alongside* a spiritual truth to enable the hearers to comprehend the latter" (162). Parables were stories that used familiar events to move the listener from the known to the unknown, instructing him inj subjects he didn't understand. A parable embodies the maxim that a picture is worth a thousand words, that illustration is better than explanation. They were windows that let in light to where a student could say, "I see it!"

Historically, Christ's parables have been subjected to reckless allegorizing, wherein man's imagination has been unbridled. In response, some have gone to the opposite extreme to argue that each parable contains only a single point. Although this may be true in some cases, it isn't true in all, for there are parables where the details bear significance beyond mere window dressing.

This kingdom discourse falls into two parts: a public section (vv 1–36a) and a private section (vv 36b–52). Each part contains four parables (if v 52 is considered a parable). The first section was spoken in the presence of the multitudes (v 36a), with an extended aside for the disciples (vv 10–23). Throughout, the exhortation is *to hear* (thirteen times), which means to *understand* (six times).

The parable of the sower has three parts: the parable (vv 3–9), a question-and-answer section (vv 10–17), and the explanation (vv 18–23).

The Sower, 13.1–23

13.1 On the same day Jesus went out of the house and sat by the sea.

Verses 1–2 are the introduction. *The same day* connects this section to the preceding. On *sat*, see 5.1.1

13.2 And great multitudes were gathered together to Him, so that He got into a boat and sat; and the whole multitude stood on the shore.

Once again, a large crowd gathers (12.23), and Jesus gets in a boat to address everyone.

13.3 Then He spoke many things to them in parables, saying: "Behold, a sower went out to sow.

The first part of this verse is a general comment on Jesus' use of parables that corresponds to vv 10,13,34,53. *Parabolē*, in Heb. thought, meant an illustration, a saying, fable, proverb, or riddle; in Gr. thought, it meant a comparison.

Behold, a sower went out to sow. The first parable describes how Judean farmers planted—walking back and forth over a field, broadcasting seed by hand in all directions. With the command, *Behold!—Look!*—Christ may have directed attention to a farmer planting in a nearby field. Alexander, though, says that the use of the definite article (*ho speirori, the sower*) and aorist verb (*exelthen, went out*) indicate that Christ was envisioning an ideal individual of the class *sower* (352).

13.4 And as he sowed, some *seed* fell by the wayside; and the birds came and devoured them.

---

[1] "The teacher *sat*, and the people *stood*: we should have less sleeping in congregations if this arrangement still prevailed" (Spurgeon).

During planting, seed invariably fall where it wasn't meant to go, such as *the wayside*. Waysides were paths that ran through and around fields that had been compacted by constant traffic into dirt sidewalks. Seed falling on hard soil couldn't penetrate the ground and would lay on the surface, becoming easy pickings for birds.[2]

13.5–6 Some fell on stony places, where they did not have much earth; and they immediately sprang up because they had no depth of earth. But when the sun was up they were scorched, and because they had no root they withered away.

Stony places isn't ground littered with rocks but ground where a thin layer of soil covers a substratum of rock. Germination for seeds falling on such soil would be normal, but plant emergence would seem quicker because the seeds were covered by a minimum of dirt. The shallowness of the soil, however, would preclude root development and uptake of water, and the plants wouldn't survive.[3] Soon up; soon down.[4]

13.7 And some fell among thorns, and the thorns sprang up and choked them.

Some seed fell among thorns (*akantha*, 27.29) and had to compete for sunlight and nutrients; vigorous weeds choke out desired plants by sapping their sources of nourishment.[5]

13.8 But others fell on good ground and yielded a crop: some a hundredfold, some sixty, some thirty.

Some seed fell on good (*kalos*, beautiful) soil—loose, deep, weed-free— and produced *a hundredfold, some sixty, some thirty*.

Note that this parable doesn't say only a quarter of the total amount of seed was productive, but only the seed that fell on bad ground. Further, the hundred, sixty, and thirty speak of the kernels of grain produced by an individual seed, not the total yield of the field. I grew up in the Midwest

---

[2] "And the prince Mastêmâ sent ravens and birds to devour the seed which was sown in the land, in order to destroy the land, and rob the children of men of their labours. Before they could plough in the seed, the ravens picked [it] from the surface of the ground" (Book of Jubilees 11.10).

[3] The *Talmud Kilayim* 7.1 had rules on the depth of soil required before seed should be planted.

[4] I thank Craig Roberts, PhD, professor, state forage specialist, University of Missouri, Columbia, MO, for information on shallow soil.

[5] Jeremiah 4.3 tells what to do about thorny ground.

cornbelt where farmers talk about "bushels per acre," not "kernels per ear." But in this parable, the emphasis is on the number of kernels produced by a single seed.

13.9 He who has ears to hear, let him hear!"

On *he who has ears to hear, let him hear!* (see 11.15) is Christ's way of saying, "Understand!"

13.10–11 And the disciples came and said to Him, "Why do You speak to them in parables?" He answered and said to them, "Because it has been given to you to know the mysteries of the kingdom of heaven, but to them it has not been given.

The enmity between Jesus and the Jewish leadership is now obvious, but not so apparent is the break between Christ and the crowds. He continues to turn to the people, and they seem open to His ministry, but there is a distance between them that will grow and be overt by the end of the Gospel. Here, Christ acknowledges the fact of the breach.

It appears that Jesus is no longer in the boat. The disciples' question goes back to v 3 and asks why Christ was using parables.

It has been given to you to know the mysteries of the kingdom of heaven, but to them it has not been given recalls the distinction in 11.25–27. At first glance, it seems that Christ was arbitrarily withholding something from the crowds, but as He explains, this wasn't the case.

For the first time in the NT, the word *mystery* (*mustērion*, hidden thing, secret) appears. It refers to knowledge that cannot be known through reason or research (empirical investigation) but only through revelation (16.17). *Mysteries of the kingdom* is a synonym for *gospel of the kingdom* (4.23, 9.35) and *word of the kingdom* (v 19). What Jesus taught was to be *known* (*ginōskō*, perceive), understood, by His disciples.

Christ isn't withholding truth from the crowds; if He meant to do this, He wouldn't have spoken to them at all (vv 2–3,13). Christ used parables because *the truth wasn't getting through to people*. The problem wasn't with the truth or the way He taught it, but with the hearts of the hearers.

13.12 For whoever has, to him more will be given, and he will have abundance; but whoever does not have, even what he has will be taken away from him.

There's a reason why the rich get richer and the poor poorer—or, in this context, why some have understanding and some don't. God doesn't give static blessings; if we don't use what He gives, we will lose what He gives (12.43–45, 25.14–30). The crowds following Jesus had received tremendous blessings from Him (especially healings), but these had not led them to a deeper commitment to Christ (Lk. 17.11–19).

13.13 Therefore I speak to them in parables, because seeing they do not see, and hearing they do not hear, nor do they understand.

Christ answers the question of v 10: He spoke to the crowd in parables *because seeing they do not see, and hearing they do not hear, nor do they understand* — they listened, but without comprehension (vv 19,23). It is absurd to think Christ used parables to increase confusion and misunderstanding; a parable's purpose was clarity, not concealment. Jesus didn't light a candle just to hide it (5.15). When people fail to understand, the failure is theirs, not His.

13.14–15 And in them the prophecy of Isaiah is fulfilled, which says 'Hearing you will hear and shall not understand, and seeing you will see and not perceive; for the hearts of this people have grown dull. *Their* ears are hard of hearing, and their eyes they have closed, lest they should see with *their* eyes and hear with *their* ears, lest they should understand with *their* hearts and turn, so that I should heal them.'

At the heart of the crowd's ignorance was a sinful heart, just as Isaiah diagnosed. Isaiah 6.9–10 (which Christ quotes using the fulfillment formula, 1.22) is the classic OT statement on unbelief (Jn. 12.39–40; Acts 28.26). Israel's lack of understanding was due to a *dull* (*pachunō*, to make thick, fat, impermeable) *heart* in which the word of God could not lodge. The awful truth is that a man can deaden his intellect, emotions, and volition and choose to be blind and deaf. Even worse is that they who refuse to see eventually become unable to see.

13.16–17 But blessed *are* your eyes for they see, and your ears for they hear; for assuredly, I say to you that many prophets and righteous *men* desired to see what you see, and did not see *it*, and to hear what you hear, and did not hear *it*."

In contrast to unseeing and unhearing unbelief, a blessing is pronounced on those who see and hear (i.e., believe). This didn't mean the disciples perfectly understood everything Christ said, for they didn't (16.8–9,

Mk. 4.13), but they had a teachable heart—a mind open to Him and His doctrine (11.4). Under Christ's patient instruction, a true student can be led to understanding (14.33).

13.18 "Therefore hear the parable of the sower:

For blessing to come in many areas in life, there must be cooperation between God and man. God sows good seed, but nothing happens if there isn't a corresponding effort by the hearer to receive what is sown. It takes at least two to get the truth told; the task of the teller is a serious one, but equally important is the task of the listener. As Christ explains in His first parable, certain conditions limit receptivity. Hearing is serious business, and we are to take what we hear seriously.

Despite the emphasis of some commentators on the *soils* rather than the *sower*,[6] Jesus "knew the purpose of His own parable, and He called it *the parable of the sower*" (Bales, *The Sower Goes Forth*, 20–21). This doesn't mean there aren't lessons to be learned about the soils, but that the primary aim of the parable was to instruct and encourage those who communicate the gospel. When the Twelve went out (ch 10, 28.18–20) they would encounter the kind of people Christ describes, and they needed to know that "evangelism must be pursued enthusiastically in spite of what appear to be meager results" (Hare, 154).

13.19 When anyone hears the word of the kingdom, and does not understand *it*, then the wicked *one* comes and snatches away what was sown in his heart. This is he who received seed by the wayside.

The word—the gospel of the kingdom (4.23–7.27, 9.35; Lk. 8.11)—is the seed sown. No farmer has the power to make a seed grow; the power is God's, but man, by his labor, gives God's power a chance (1 Cor. 3.6). The wayside soil, however, shuts the door to God's power. It represents the person who hears but doesn't understand due to a *dull*—closed, hardened—*heart* (v 15; Heb. 5.11). Impenetrable soil stands for an unreachable mind. In giving us self-will, God gave us the power to be unreasonable and irrational, closing our mind to logic, suppressing the truth about God, and leaving ourselves *empty*, *darkened*, and *blind* (Rom. 1.18ff; Eph. 4.18). *The wicked one*, the devil, is represented by birds who feed on exposed seed; it is the devil who

---

[6] E.g., Carson: "The focus of the parable is not the sower, but the soils" (305) and France: "The 'title' of the parable can be misleading. *The sower* himself is not the focus of attention, nor is he identified in what follows. It is the seed and the soils which are the subject" (218).

snatches away (*harpazō*, to catch up, take by force, pluck) the word from the heart. How this happens isn't explained here, but numerous texts speak to the matter (Eph. 4.17–19; Col. 2.8).

13.20–21 But he who received the seed on stony places, this is he who hears the word and immediately receives it with joy; yet he has no root in himself, but endures only for a while. For when tribulation or persecution arises because of the word, immediately he stumbles.

The wayside soil represents the *stubborn* heart, and the stony soil the *superficial* heart. A common figure in Jewish wisdom literature is that the wise person is like a tree with strong roots located near a stream, whereas the ungodly are like a tree without roots that quickly withers.[7] An emotional reaction can be a shooting star that briefly burns brightly, but then cools and disappears. There are those who quickly respond to the word with *joy* (*chara*, gladness; 1 Thes. 1.6), but their emotion isn't backed by their will, as revealed by their reaction to *tribulation* (*thlipsis*, a pressing together, pressure, trouble, anguish[8]) and *persecution* (*diōgmos*, to pursue, follow; suffering that is often set in a religious context, Acts 26.11). Christ had previously spoken of hostility to Him and His message (5.10–12, 10.23) and will mention it again (23.34, 24.9,21,29). The devil can use buffeting (2 Cor. 12.7) as well as blindness (2 Cor. 4.4) to damn. "There is a vast difference between a joy which springs from a life committed to Christ and one which springs from the rocky soil in which there is no depth of conviction but only the shallowness of a temporary emotional response" (Bales, *The Sower Goes Forth*, 75).

13.22 Now he who received seed among the thorns is he who hears the word, and the cares of this world and the deceitfulness of riches choke the word, and he becomes unfruitful.

To *stubborn* and *superficial* hearts is added the *strangled* heart where the seed falls onto preoccupied ground (6.33). Since Genesis 3.18, *thorns* have symbolized the curse. Here, they represent the *cares of this world and the deceitfulness of riches [that] choke the word*. Busyness or concentration on

---

[7] "But the prolific brood of the ungodly will be of no use, and none of their illegitimate seedlings will strike a deep root or take a firm hold. For even if they put forth boughs for a while, standing insecurely they will be shaken by the wind, and by the violence of the winds they will be uprooted" (Wisdom of Solomon, 4.3–4).

[8] "The English word is from the Lat. *tribulum*, the roller used by the Romans for pressing wheat. Cf. our 'steam roller'" (Robertson, 106).

not unworthy things but on less worthy things can sap our attention to supreme things. This warning recalls the admonition in 6.10–34 about *riches* and *worry*. *Cares* (*merimna*, to be drawn in different directions; anxiety) result from the *deceitfulness* (*apatē*, lusts; *illusions*, JBP) *of riches*. And few things are more deceitful than wealth. In C. S. Lewis's story, *The Lion, the Witch, and the Wardrobe*, the Witch Queen gave Edmund some Turkish Delight to eat. Though he ate it and thought it delightful, Edmund always felt hungry and wanted more. Though abundant and tasty, the Turkish delight was never satisfying.

Such is wealth. The worry it brings can choke the joy out of life. "The devil is delighted if he can keep the seed from being sown. However, if the seed is sown, he does not give up. He welcomes the existence of the wayside hearts from which he can snatch the seed. If the seed sprouts, the devil does not accept defeat, for he recognizes that some can be turned away from Christ through tribulation and persecution. If persecution fails, the devil tries something else, for he realizes that there are hearts with depth of soil, which can nevertheless have the word crowded out by different things. If the devil wins, it is obviously a small matter to him whether he wins through one avenue or another" (Bales, *The Sower Goes Forth*, 79).

13.23 But he who received seed on the good ground is he who hears the word and understands *it*, who indeed bears fruit and produces: some a hundredfold, some sixty, some thirty."

A composite picture from the Gospels identifies the *good ground* as the heart that reacts to the word intellectually (hears/listens), emotionally (accepts, welcomes; Mk. 4.20), and volitionally (keeps/obeys; Lk. 8.15). *Understanding* (*suniēmi*, to put together, comprehend) receives major emphasis in Matthew (15.10, 16.12, 17.13). In the kingdom, *hearing*, *understanding*, and *obeying* are inseparable, for until one comprehends, embraces, and practices the message of Christ, he cannot be fruitful in every good work (Col.1.9–10; Tit. 3.8), and to not be fruitful puts us into the fellowship of false prophets (7.16–23).

On *hundredfold, sixty, and thirty* see v 8. These numbers refer to the grains produced by a single seed. A seed that produces 30 grains is fruitful; it may not be 100-grain fruitful, but it is still fruitful. A servant with but a single talent is as important to the master as one who has five talents (25.14–30).

The Tares, 13.24–30

Notes

Although terms and figures found in the parable of the sower are used in the parable of the tares, it's important to pay attention to the definitions Christ assigns.[9] The story breaks into two parts: vv 24–26 give the story, and vv 27–30 give the sense; the interpretation is found in vv 37–43.

13.24–26 Another parable He put forth to them, saying: "The kingdom of heaven is like a man who sowed good seed in his field; but while men slept, his enemy came and sowed tares among the wheat and went his way. But when the grain had sprouted and produced a crop, then the tares also appeared.

Another parable He put forth to them introduces the parable of the tares. *Put forth* translates *paratithēmi*, which Carr said was used by Homer to describe setting food before a guest (189). *Is like* means *may be compared to* (NASB); every time this expression is used (vv 31,33,34,44,45,47), it refers to the parable as a whole. "We might paraphrase, 'This is what it is like when God is at work'" (France, 225).

A farmer sows *good seed in his field*, but during the night, an enemy sneaks in and sows *tares*. *Tares* (*zizaniori*) probably refers to *darnel*, a noxious weed containing a poisonous fungus that is virtually indistinguishable from wheat in the early stages of growth. When ingested, darnel can induce dizziness, drowsiness, and vomiting. "Sowing darnel in a field for purposes of revenge was a crime under Roman legislation. The necessity for a law on the subject suggests that the action was not infrequent" (*New Bible Dictionary*, 948).

13.27–28 So the servants of the owner came and said to him, 'Sir, did you not sow good seed in your field? How then does it have tares?' He said to them, 'An enemy has done this.' The servants said to him, 'Do you want us then to go and gather them up?'

When it becomes evident the field is infested with tares, the servants ask, *Where did all these weeds come from?* (JBP).[10] The owner knows an enemy (*echthros*, hated, hostile; 5.43) is responsible. The servants' eagerness

---

[9] After the emphasis on hearing and understanding found in the parable of the sower, it's amazing how many fail to hear and understand the parable of the tares.

[10] Without pausing here to develop the idea, the farmer's allowing the tares to coexist with the wheat has bearing, I think, on the coexistence of good and evil in this world.

to undo the mischief—*Do you want us then to go and gather them up?*—is understandable, because pulling weeds is something farm hands do.

13.29 But he said, 'No, lest while you gather up the tares you also uproot the wheat with them.

That this story doesn't reflect normal farming practice is obvious when the owner declines his servants' offer out of concern that the wheat might be damaged in an attempt to remove the tares.[11]

13.30 Let both grow together until the harvest, and at the time of harvest I will say to the reapers, "First gather together the tares and bind them in bundles to burn them, but gather the wheat into my barn."'

Typically, after the grain is gathered, remaining weeds were cut down or burned; but here, it is the other way around—the tares are gathered, bound, and burned (3.12) before the wheat is harvested. In Jewish thought, a harvest often symbolized judgment.

The Mustard Seed, 13.31–32

Notes

This and the following parable are characterized as a *double parable* (vv 44–45). In Scripture, repetition is used to emphasize, and here the emphasis is on the *expansion* or *growth of the kingdom*.

13.31–32 Another parable He put forth to them, saying: "The kingdom of heaven is like a mustard seed, which a man took and sowed in his field, which indeed is the least of all the seeds; but when it is grown it is greater than the herbs and becomes a tree, so that the birds of the air come and nest in its branches."

Mustard was an herb with several usages—its leaves were cooked as greens, and its kernels were used as spice, medicine, and food for birds. The mustard seed was proverbially the smallest seed found in Jewish gardens (seeds were about four-hundredths of an inch in diameter; *Mishna Niddah*, 5.2). But despite its diminutive size, mustard seed produced a plant ten feet in height and sturdy enough to provide a roost for birds. What's unusual here is that the farmer sows only a single seed, which

---

[11] Some sources indicate that when wheat and tares grow in the same area, their root systems become entwined, making it difficult to pull up tares separately.

seems to bring in a point of emphasis beyond the mere identification of the seed as the gospel (v 19).

Because Christ doesn't interpret this parable, we should be cautious in our interpretation[12]—but considering the small size of mustard seed, the point seems to involve an entity that appears incapable of producing the resulting effect. Who would think, after looking at a mustard seed, that a tree-sized plant could come from it? And who would think that a universal, eternal kingdom (Dan. 2.35,44) could come from a King who was despised, rejected (Isa. 53.3), and put to death by His own (12.39; Jn. 1.11)?

The Leaven, 13.33

13.33 Another parable He spoke to them: "The kingdom of heaven is like leaven, which a woman took and hid in three measures of meal till it was all leavened."

Christ moves from the garden to the kitchen. The use of leaven (*zumē*, a fermenting agent) to make bread rise was common domestic practice. The amount of flour cited is unusual, for three measures (about three pecks) of dough would produce roughly 110 lbs. of bread, which is considerably more than Judean wives normally made. Even more surprising is that Jesus used leaven in a positive way; used metaphorically, leaven typically represented something evil or insidious (16.6,11; 1 Cor. 5.7)[13] and was left out of Passover ritual (Ex. 12.15–20, 23.8, 34.25).

A final surprise is that Jesus uses the word *hid* (*egkruptō*, to conceal in something) rather than the word for kneading. The leaven is *hidden* in the flour, but its influence spreads (the idea of *hiddenness* reappears in vv 35,44). In the kingdom, quality is more important than quantity; Christ will spend more time with His disciples than with the multitudes, for reaching the many (the world, 28.19) will depend on Him reaching the few (the

---

[12] Numerous commentators interpret the birds roosting in the branches of the mustard plant as referring to bringing in Gentiles into the church. I think, however, that the interpretation given by Hilary of Poitiers (ca. 310–367) is more in keeping with what is meant by the *kingdom of heaven*. He understood the mustard seed to be Christ, who was sown in the ground (killed, buried), but whose influence and power were mighty and glorious precisely because He was sown. An intriguing interpretation is to see the *cross* rather than the *church*.

[13] It is not unheard of for Scripture to use the same figure in contrasting ways. In 10.16 the apostles are exhorted to be "as serpents," but in 3.7 and 12.34 the Pharisees are the serpents. In 1 Pet. 5.8. Satan is a lion, but in Rev. 5.5, Christ is a lion. The same figure can be used to describe different entities; context determines the meaning.

disciples). Utilizing just a few sowers (10.1), the kingdom would wield influence and produce results far beyond what anyone thought possible.

Conclusion to Public Section, 13.34–35

13.34–35 All these things Jesus spoke to the multitude in parables; and without a parable He did not speak to them, that it might be fulfilled which was spoken by the prophet, saying: "I will open My mouth in parables; I will utter things kept secret from the foundation of the world."

Matthew summarizes vv 1–33 by using Psalm 78.2 to show that Christ's use of parables was part of the Messianic profile. Everything Jesus said to the crowd in this discourse has been in parables, by which He *uttered things kept secret from the foundation of the world. Uttered* translates the rare word *ereugomai* (only here in the NT; to make noise, belch, expel, spit or spew out; used of streams); the *things kept secret from the foundation of the world* refers to the truth—mysteries (v 11) of the kingdom—Christ proclaimed. Clearly, the purpose of the parables was to reveal, not conceal; to make known, not to keep secret or hidden.

IN PRIVATE, 13.36–53

The Tares Explained, 13.36–43

13.36 Then Jesus sent the multitude away and went into the house. And His disciples came to Him, saying, "Explain to us the parable of the tares of the field."

Dismissing the multitude (v 2) may be an application of 10.13–14. Despite their having followed, the multitude was *not worthy* (10.13)—they didn't understand Jesus beyond a superficial level (v 13). As in John 2.23–24, many believed in Christ, but not in a way that allowed Him to believe in them. Sending the multitude away and then entering the house with the *disciples* underscored the divide between Jesus and the masses.

Once in the house, the disciples, who want to understand, ask Christ to explain (*phrazō*, expound, indicate plainly; in NT, only here and 15.15) the parable of the tares.

13.37–39 He answered and said to them: "He who sows the good seed is the Son of Man. The field is the world, the good seeds are the sons of

the kingdom, but the tares are the sons of the wicked *one*. The enemy who sowed them is the devil, the harvest is the end of the age, and the reapers are the angels.

Christ's answer consists of two parts: in vv 37–39, He provides a lexicon for interpreting the parable; in vv 40–43, He gives the interpretation.

The sower is Christ, *the Son of Man* (8.20). *The field is the world.* But because v 41 equates the field to the *kingdom*, many jump to the conclusion that Christ is talking about the church, since it is often assumed that "the church is the kingdom and the kingdom is the church." There are three problems with this view. First, Jesus says the field is *the world*, and the world is not the church. A better interpretation is that Christ makes a universal claim for His rule—which is consistent with the fact that Christians are *the light of the world* (5.14) and that the great commission is worldwide in scope (28.18). Christ has authority over the entire world, and He seeks the submission of the world. Second, to make the *field* the *church* sets the nonintervention of vv 29–30 against the intervention of 18.15–17 (and other passages, e.g., 1 Cor. 5; 2 Thes. 3.14). In v 30, the bad is to be left with the good, but in 18.15–17 the bad is not to be left with the good (1 Cor. 5.6). Third, to make the field the church puts children of the devil in the kingdom. Though the devil's children may enjoy the fellowship of a local church (1 Cor. 5.5), they are outside the kingdom (7.21–23, 8.12). The Lord knows those who are His even if we sometimes don't (2 Tim. 2.19).[14] Whereas in the parable of the sower, *the good seed* was *the word of the kingdom*, in the parable of the tares, *the good seeds are the sons of the kingdom.* It is the righteous (v 43), the sons of the kingdom, who are sown in the world, which recalls the role of disciples in 5.13–16. *The tares are the sons of the wicked one*, and *the enemy who sowed them is the devil.* Satan works in the world through his followers, just as Christ works in the world through His. *The harvest*, consistent with standard Jewish metaphor (Jer. 51.33; Joel 3.13), is *the end of the age*, and *the reapers are the angels* (25.31; angels regularly figure as God's helpers in portrayals of judgment; 16.27, 24.31). *Age* (*aiōn*) translates the Gr. word indicating forever or eternal, but also means that which pertains to an aeon or era. The *age* intended here is the time God has allotted for man on earth.

---

[14] Luz offers a fascinating discussion of the historical problems associated with interpreting the field as the church rather than the world—for example, the Catholic dilemma on how to handle heretics, and the Reformation dilemma on how to regard the pope (II, 271–274).

13.40–43 Therefore as the tares are gathered and burned in the fire, so it will be at the end of this age. The Son of Man will send out His angels, and they will gather out of His kingdom all things that offend, and those who practice lawlessness, and will cast them into the furnace of fire. There will be wailing and gnashing of teeth. Then the righteous will shine forth as the sun in the kingdom of their Father. He who has ears to hear, let him hear!

Consistent with the title of the parable (v 36), the emphasis is on the judgment of the *tares*, the wicked. Just as a farmer at harvest burns the tares, so the *sons of the wicked one* will be *burned in the fire at the end of this age* (3.12). Christ will have the angels gather out of the world (His kingdom) *all things that offend, and those who practice lawlessness. All things that offend* (*skandalon*, a noose, snare, the trigger of a trap, something that trips up, a stumbling block) are not defined here, but in ch 18, the term refers to anyone who contributes to another's sin. *Those who practice lawlessness* recalls 7.23, which leans more toward ethical evil than doctrinal error, although doctrinal error does fall under the umbrella of *lawlessness*. Judgment (*fire*) will fall on those who traffic in evil and live outside God's will; disobedience will result in unspeakable anguish (*wailing and gnashing of teeth*). God presently allows the wicked to coexist with the righteous, and sometimes the wicked are hard to identify (18.6–7, 19.16–26; 2 Cor. 11.13–15; 1 Tim. 5.24), but God knows who they are and will ultimately deal with them.[15]

Once the wicked are judged, the righteous—who obey the Father's will (6.10)—will be openly vindicated (6.4), shining (*eklampō*, resplendent; only here in the NT) like the sun. *He who has ears to hear, let him hear!* The reality of judgment/punishment gives urgency to the importance of understanding, receiving, and obeying Christ (v 23).

The Treasure in the Field, 13.44

Notes
The parables of the hidden treasure and pearl of great price constitute the second set of double parables (vv 31–33). Apart from some minor variations (e.g., the parable of the treasure is present tense, the parable of

---

[15] It is sometimes said that in every parable of judgment in the NT, the wicked were not condemned for what they did (commission) but for what they didn't do (omission). In the parable of the tares, however, men are condemned for what they did (v 41).

the pearl is past tense), they are structured much the same. Each begins with a title, followed by a story containing the verb *found*. A significant difference is that in v 44, the kingdom of heaven is like *treasure hidden in a field*, whereas in v 45, the kingdom of heaven is like a *merchant seeking treasure*. Contextually, *treasure* parallels the Father's will that is dismissed by *the sons of the wicked one* (v 38), and the *merchant* corresponds to *the sons of the kingdom* who understand the value and importance of doing God's will.

13.44 "Again, the kingdom of heaven is like treasure hidden in a field, which a man found and hid; and for joy over it he goes and sells all that he has and buys that field."

The threat of war, thieves, the confiscatory power of the state, and the absence of a reliable banking industry led many in the ancient world to bury their wealth (25.18; e.g., the Qumran community's hiding of the Dead Sea Scrolls), which caused people to dream of finding forgotten or buried treasure.

In this parable, a man stumbles upon such a treasure, joyfully reburies it (presumably, in a safer place, where it wouldn't be found by another), and liquidates his entire holdings to buy the field containing the treasure. Some have a problem with the buyer's ethics, but the legality/morality of the action is no more in view here than in Luke 16.1–8 or Luke 18.1–8. The emphasis is on *what the man does* to obtain the treasure. If the *treasure* represents God's will and His blessing on obedience (v 43), every effort should be made (6.33) and every temporal concern repudiated to possess the eternal (16.24; Lk. 14.33); no sacrifice should be thought too great (Phil. 2.5–8).

The Merchant, 13.45–46

13.45–46 "Again, the kingdom of heaven is like a merchant seeking beautiful pearls, who, when he had found one pearl of great price, went and sold all that he had and bought it.

In this parable, the kingdom isn't likened to treasure but to one seeking treasure. *Merchant* (*emporos*, emporium; one on a journey seeking merchandise) refers to a wholesaler. Since the time of Alexander the Great, *pearls* (imported from India) had been a staple luxury for the upper class (Luz II, 278). To the Jews, they figuratively represented the Law, Israel, or an insightful thought and were used of God's blessings on the pious (7.5).

The twice repeated *sells all that he has/sold all that he had* is the key to both parables. Together, they teach the importance of seizing an opportunity (25.1–30). For the will of God to be done, opportunity must be recognized and action taken. Finding a treasure presented an opportunity, but to take advantage of it, the man and the merchant had to realize that the opportunity was worth everything they had, and that they needed to spring into action to obtain the treasure (8.22, 19.21–22, 22.36–40). They didn't allow the *cares of this world* or *the deceitfulness of riches* (v 22) to prevent them from seeing what was before them. The kingdom is worth more than anything else in this life.

The Net, 13.47–50

Notes
This parable begins with a short introduction, followed by a brief narrative, and a concluding interpretation. It is often interpreted similar to the parable of the tares.

13.47–48 "Again, the kingdom of heaven is like a dragnet that was cast into the sea and gathered some of every kind, which, when it was full, they drew to shore; and they sat down and gathered the good into vessels, but threw the bad away.

The parables discourse opened with Jesus by the seaside (vv 1–2), and now, although spoken in a house (v 36), He gives a parable based on a practice commonly seen by the seaside. *Dragnet* (*sagēnē*, only here in the NT) refers to a large seine that could be hundreds of feet long by a few feet wide, with weights attached to the bottom of one of the long sides and floats (of cork or wood) to the top side. Ropes were attached to each end. After being unloaded into the water, the net was drawn to shore (Lk. 5.4–7), and it wasn't unusual for it to snare fish *of every kind* (*genos*, lit., of every race; a strange way to talk about fish, but not men[16]). This required the fishermen to sort the fish, keeping the good, and throwing away the unusable.

13.49–50 So it will be at the end of the age. The angels will come forth, separate the wicked from among the just, and cast them into the furnace of fire. There will be wailing and gnashing of teeth."

---

[16] "The Sea of Galilee is said to contain 54 different species" of fish (Mounce, 136).

The *kingdom of heaven*—the rule of Christ—is the *dragnet* (the church, if we are to see it at all in this parable, would be the *good* fish). In language that in some ways parallels vv 40–43, this is a parable of judgment, discussing what happens *at the end of the age.* The *angels* (not the apostles, 4.19) are the fishermen who bring in and separate (*aphorizō,* to mark off from others by boundaries, to exclude) the catch. As previously established, whether one is *wicked* or *righteous,* clean or unclean, usable or not depends on his response to the *word of the kingdom* (v 23). *Wailing and gnashing of teeth* are figures meant to indicate the agony visited upon the *wicked* at the judgment (8.11–12).

The Understanding Scribe, 13.51–53

Notes
The parables discourse concludes with a question asked the disciples, followed by a short parable that speaks to the matter of understanding *the kingdom of heaven.* The difficulty with this paragraph is in determining its relationship to the context. Why, at the end of the parables discourse, does Jesus speak of a scribe?

13.51 Jesus said to them, "Have you understood all these things?" They said to Him, "Yes, Lord."
Have you understood all these things?—do you see what these parables have to do with life and fruit bearing (v 23)? The disciples answer *Yes,* but they gave themselves too much credit; they were a long way from understanding some critical matters Christ was teaching (15.15–16; Mk. 4.10). They had a heart for understanding (vv 16–17), but they didn't yet understand.

13.52 Then He said to them, "Therefore every scribe instructed concerning the kingdom of heaven is like a householder who brings out of his treasure *things* new and old."
If the disciples understood as they claimed (v 51), they had a responsibility. *Scribe,* in the Gr. sense, indicated a clerk or secretary (Acts 19.35, *city clerk*), but to the Jews, the term indicated a "'man learned in the Torah, a 'rabbi,' an 'ordained theologian'" (J. Jeremias, *Theological Dictionary of the New Testament* I, 740). Jewish *scribes* were considered Bible experts (23.2). The disciples—who were being *instructed* (*mathēteuō,* to be a disciple of one, to follow precepts and instruction) and schooled (v 11) were to be like

a *householder* (*oikodespotēs*, v 27, homeowner, master of the house) who brings out of his *treasure* (*thēsauros*, v 44, 6.21, 12.35; a storehouse of good things, a repository) things new and old. Just as a homeowner managed his house, so the disciples would manage the *treasure* committed to them (2 Cor. 4.7). Christ doesn't identify the treasure, but I think 5.21–48 is an example of what it means to bring out things *new* and *old*: by showing the continuity between the OT and the gospel, by interpreting OT prophecies in light of the gospel, by making contemporary and relevant application of the principles of the gospel, etc. Disciples are not weary of the old or afraid of the new. They are to be experts in relating, unfolding, and expounding the relationship between Christ (new) and Moses (old). "The First Gospel, especially in its proof from Scripture, shows us the scribe at work" (Jeremias, op. cit., 742).

13.53 Now it came to pass, when Jesus had finished these parables, that He departed from there.

And it came to pass is Matthew's customary way for concluding a discourse (7.28, 19.1)

13.54–58: Nazareth

Notes

The final part to the first section of Matthew's Gospel (4.17–16.12) begins here and contains several allusions to chs 10 to 12, as well as some repetition.

As to allusions, the death of John in 14.1–12 picks up 11.2–6; the stilling of the storm in 14.22–33 recalls 8.23–27 (but the scene is heightened when Peter walks on water); in several ways, 15.1–20 reminds of 13.3–23, but goes beyond it in its judgment on the Pharisees (15.13–14); and in 15.24, we recall 10.5–6. Regarding repetitions, there are two feeding miracles (14.13–21, 15.32–39), two confessions of Jesus as the Son of God (14.33, 16.16), two withdrawals of Jesus from Judea (14.13, 15.21), and two healing summaries (14.34–36, 15.29–31).

In this section, the disciples grow in understanding to where they confess Jesus as the Son of God. The Jewish leadership, however, only grows in its malice and opposition. The people are challenged to understand (15.10) but fail to do so; although the disciples confess Jesus as God's Son, the crowds think that He is just a prophet (16.14).

Peter is prominent in this section for his little faith (14.28–31), insightful faith (16.16–18), lack of faith (16.22–23), and desire to understand (15.15, 17.24). Not until Christ's passion will he again occupy such a prominent role.

Verses 54–58 are taken up with questions asked by Jesus' former neighbors in Nazareth. Two *where* questions bookend three negative questions. The mention of Jesus' physical family recalls 12.46–50.

13.54 When He had come to His own country, He taught them in their synagogue, so that they were astonished and said, "Where did this *Man* get this wisdom and *these* mighty works?

His own country refers to Nazareth (2.23). At the start of His Galilean ministry, Christ visited Nazareth but left after an attempt was made on His life (Lk. 4.16–30). Now, nearing the end of His Galilean work, He makes a final visit. Upon arriving, He teaches in *their* synagogue. This is Christ's last recorded visit to a synagogue, and the use of the possessive *their* (12.9) indicates a distance between Himself and His home congregation. After the incident in Luke 4, it's surprising that He was allowed to speak, but the Jews had a custom known as "the freedom of the synagogue,"[17] and it was nothing out of the ordinary for Jesus to be allowed to say a few words. When He does, the congregation is *astonished* at His *wisdom* (which they heard firsthand) and *mighty works* (of which they had heard, v 58, 7.28, 22.33), but Nazareth's reaction was still largely negative.

13.55–56 Is this not the carpenter's son? Is not His mother called Mary? And His brothers James,[18] Joses, Simon, and Judas? And His sisters, are they not all with us? Where then did this *Man* get all these things?"

Hometowns are often eager to bask in the reflected glory of a favorite son, but not the Nazarenes. They couldn't reconcile Christ's *wisdom* and *works* with either his father's profession as a *carpenter* (*tektōn*, craftsman) or their acquaintance with Him. To Nazareth, Jesus was ordinary, His extraordinary words and deeds to the contrary (thus showing the power of presuppositions to silence conflicting evidence). His mother and brothers

---

[17] Israel Abrahams, *Studies in Pharisaism and the Gospels*, 1–14. https://archive.org/details/studiesinpharis01abrauoft.

[18] James the brother of Jesus was a leader in the Jerusalem church (Acts 15). According to Josephus, he was condemned by the High Priest Ananus as "a breaker of the law" and was stoned to death ca. AD 62 (*Ant.* xx.9.1).

had typical Jewish names, and His sisters, unnamed and unnumbered, were still living in the area (*with us*).[19]

13.57 So they were offended at Him. But Jesus said to them, "A prophet is not without honor except in his own country and in his own house."

By not understanding what they saw and heard, Nazareth illustrated the problem described in vv 13–15. They were not lacking data, but their minds were closed to the implications of the data. Instead of honoring Christ, they were dismissive of Him (v 41, 11.16). His explanation for their reaction is that familiarity breeds contempt—prophets are not valued by those closest to them. As the incident in Luke 4 illustrates, Jesus, in keeping with all true prophets, shattered the peace of Jewish self-contentment by speaking what they were unwilling to accept. And in so doing, He incurred Nazareth's opposition.

13.58 Now He did not do many mighty works there because of their unbelief.

The Nazarenes don't try to kill Jesus this time, but they reject His message (v 23)—their *unbelief* reflected the unbelief of the Jews in general. It wasn't that Jesus *couldn't* do miracles in Nazareth but that He *wouldn't*; His sovereignty wasn't limited by their unbelief, but since they didn't' ask, they didn't receive (7.7–11). Having done what He could, Christ follows His own advice and leaves (10.12–14).

---

[19] The controversy over the reference to Jesus' *brothers* and *sisters* is fueled by Catholic dogma, not Scriptural data. There are times when *adelphoi/ adelphai* (brothers/sisters) refers to cousins, but there is no reason to think such is the case here; if it were. To argue that the brothers and sisters of Jesus were Joseph's children by a prior marriage or more distant relatives of Christ is utterly without Scriptural warrant.

CHAPTER 14

14.1–12: Herod Antipas

Notes

This section is both flashback and portent—what happened to John was but another Jewish atrocity in a long line of atrocities (vv 3–5, 23.30–31) that would culminate in the death of Jesus.

The setting is given in vv 3–5, Herodias's daughter's dance is in vv 6–8, and Herod's granting of her wish is in vv 9–11; v 12 concludes with John's burial.

14.1–2 At that time Herod the tetrarch heard the report about Jesus and said to his servants, "This is John the Baptist; he is risen from the dead, and therefore these powers are at work in him."

At that time connects this paragraph to Christ's visit to Nazareth (13.53–58). *Herod the tetrarch*, whose given name was Antipas, is the third Herod to appear in the Gospel (Herod the Great, 2.1–12,16–19; Archelaus, 2.22). Cornfeld wrote, "He was perhaps the most talented ruler and politician and ultimately the most unfortunate of the sons of King Herod. Inheriting the northern part of his father's domain, he ruled firmly, though sometimes foolishly, over his tetrarchy[1] from 4 BC to 39 AD, the longest reign of any Jewish ruler of the period" (*The Historical Jesus*, 91).

When Herod hears about Jesus, he concludes that John the Baptist has risen from the dead (Lk. 9.7). We're not told why he thought this, but a guilty conscience and superstitious fear were the likely culprits. Many Jews, such as the Pharisees, believed in resurrection, and Josephus said

---

[1] *Tetrarch* strictly means *ruler over a fourth part* but served as a generic term the Romans used to denote petty rulers. "It denoted a status below that of ethnarch (2 Cor. 11.32), which in turn was below that of a king. Precisely what the reasons were for bestowing any of these titles and the exact differences they denoted are not now clear; probably the size of the territory to be ruled and the measure of independence that Romans allowed were significant factors" (Morris, 369).

that some in the ruling class believed in ghosts (*Wars*, i.30.7; v 26). Herod had enough conscience to scare him, but not enough to change him.

14.3–5 For Herod had laid hold of John and bound him, and put *him* in prison for the sake of Herodias, his brother Philip's wife. Because John had said to him, "It is not lawful for you to have her." And although he wanted to put him to death, he feared the multitude, because they counted him as a prophet.

Here begins a flashback about the fate of John the Baptist (4.12, 11.2).

Herod's first wife was the royal princess of the neighboring Nabatean kingdom of Aretas IV (2 Cor. 11.32). After marrying her, Herod became infatuated with his niece Herodias, who was then married to his half-brother Philip.[2] Herodias left Philip (with no known objection on his part) and married Herod, thus violating Mosaic law on several counts—it might have been considered an incestuous relationship between near kinsmen (although this isn't certain; Lev. 18.6,12–14, 20.19–20) or a forbidden marriage between in-laws (Lev. 18.16, 20.21; levitate marriage being the exception, Deut. 25.5, Matt. 22.24). It was certainly adulterous (5.32, 19.9; Ex. 20.14; Lev. 20.10), and it elicited the protest of John, who didn't mince words: *"It is not lawful for you to have her."* For this rebuke, Herod *wanted to put John to death.* "Herod laid hold on John, because John's word had laid hold on Herod" (Spurgeon). Herodias bore a grudge against John for his criticism (v 8), but ultimate responsibility for John's death belonged to Herod. What kept him from immediately executing John was his fear of the multitude who considered John a holy man. Restraint due to fear of the multitude reappears in 21.46, when the Pharisees are stymied in their effort to kill Jesus because *they feared the multitudes, who took Jesus for a prophet.* The Jewish tradition of murdering prophets thus continued with John and Jesus (5.12, 17.12, 21.33–41, 22.3–6, 23.29–36).[3]

---

[2] Herod Philip (Mk. 6.16) is to be distinguished from another half-brother of Herod's by the same name, who ruled the neighboring tetrarchy of Batanaea and Trachonitis, located north of Galilee (Lk. 3.1), and whose name is reflected in the city Caesarea Philippi (16.31). Herodias's husband was one of the unambitious Herods, who enjoyed living in the luxury of Rome.

[3] Both John and Jesus were handed over (*paradidōmi*, 4.12, 27.2,18,26), seized (*krateō*, v 3, 26.4,48,50), and bound (*deō*, v 3, 27.2). Just as Herod was reluctant to execute John, so Pilate was reluctant to execute Jesus (27.11–26). And the wives of both men played a behind-the-scenes role (27.19). Despite some sympathy for their victims, Herod and Pilate both caved to expediency.

14.6–7 But when Herod's birthday was celebrated, the daughter of Herodias danced before them and pleased Herod. Therefore he promised with an oath to give her whatever she might ask.

At a feast celebrating Herod's birthday (a Hellenistic rather than Hebrew custom), his stepdaughter[4] *danced* (*orcheomai*, Eng. orchestra) for the guests. Luz says that the role she played would normally have been assumed by courtesans or prostitutes (II, 307), which would fit the depraved morals of the Herodians. When she finished, Herod (likely under the influence of alcohol; how else explain such an extra-large reward for such low-level lust) swore *with an oath* to give her whatever she asked, up to half his kingdom (Esth. 5.3,6).

14.8–11 So she, having been prompted by her mother, said, "Give me John the Baptist's head here on a platter." And the king was sorry; nevertheless, because of the oaths and because of those who sat with him, he commanded *it* to be given to *her*. So he sent and had John beheaded in prison. And his head was brought on a platter and given to the girl, and she brought *it* to her mother.

The girl is *prompted* (*probibazō*, to bring forward, induce; only here in the NT) by her mother to make the grisly request for John's head on a platter. Herod hadn't anticipated this, and it made him *sorry* (*perilupos*, grieved all around, intensely sad).[5] His regret, however, seems to have been as much for himself as for John, as implied by the comment, *because of those who sat with him at the table*. Too embarrassed to renege on his promise in front of his cronies, John—who had the courage to protest wickedness in places of power—will be executed because of Herodias's scorn and Herod's cowardice.

It was against Jewish law to execute a man without a trial, but Herod was a law unto himself;[6] tyrants think lightly of murder.[7] Herod acted

---

[4] Salome, Josephus, *Ant.* xviii.5.4.

[5] "Herod: Come, Salomé, be reasonable. I have never been hard to you. I have ever loved you. … It may be that I have loved you too much. Therefore ask not this thing of me. This is a terrible thing, an awful thing to ask of me. Surely, I think you are jesting. The head of a man that is cut from his body is ill to look upon. It is not meet that the eyes of a virgin should look upon such a thing. What pleasure would you have in it? None. No, no, it is not what you desire" (Oscar Wilde, *SALOMÉ, A Tragedy in One Act*).

[6] "It is not the last time that a man has been more afraid of a sneer than a crime," Erdman, 112.

[7] Klemens von Metternich, the Austrian ambassador to France, told Napoleon that a campaign he was contemplating would cost a million men. "What are a million men to me?"

by proxy (*he sent and beheaded John*), but God held him accountable for the deed.

In AD 39, at the urging of Herodias, Antipas went to Rome to request the title of *king*, which had been granted to Herodias's brother Agrippa (Acts 25.13). When Agrippa heard of this, he accused Antipas of treachery. Despite protestations of loyalty, Caligula sentenced Antipas to exile in Gaul (France). Herodias joined him (she may have had no choice), and there they died.

14.12 Then his disciples came and took away the body and buried it, and went and told Jesus.

This macabre story ends with the burial of John's body by his disciples. Because John and Jesus were so closely identified with one another, it's not surprising that John's disciples found Jesus and told Him what had happened.[8]

14.13–21: Five Thousand

Notes

Of the thirty-five miracles of Jesus recorded in the Gospels, the feeding of the five thousand is the only one mentioned in all four (Mk. 6.35–44; Lk. 9.12–17; Jn. 6.1–14). The reason for this is isn't stated. One possibility is that this miracle marked the zenith of Christ's popularity with the multitudes; hereafter, His following ebbs to where the Jewish leadership will risk putting Him to death.

Narrative (vv 13–14) is followed by a conversation between Jesus and His disciples (vv 15–18), which is followed by the actual miracle (vv 19–20), concluding with an additional comment from Mathew (v 21). The feeding of the five thousand, like the parables, has been subjected to heavy allegorizing. In Catholic tradition, the five loaves are the five books of Moses, the two fishes are the prophets and writings, the twelve baskets of food are the apostles, the wilderness represents the Gentiles, etc.

14.13–14 When Jesus heard *it*, He departed from there by boat to a deserted place by Himself. But when the multitudes heard it, they

Napoleon replied.

[8] I think Herod's fulfillment of his rash vow bears on the interpretation of Judges 11. Whatever Jephthah did, I don't believe that he—a man of faith (Heb. 11.32)—did that which put him into the same murderous category as Herod Antipas. Rash oaths are to be repented of, not acted on.

followed Him on foot from the cities. And when Jesus went out He saw a great multitude; and He was moved with compassion for them, and healed their sick.

When Jesus heard about John's death, it became an occasion for Him to again *depart* (12.15). Matthew doesn't give the location of the *deserted place* to which He went, but to get there, Christ and the disciples traveled by boat across the Sea of Galilee. The ever-present *multitudes* followed on foot, which implies they were able to keep Jesus in view from shore.

George Macdonald said, "Nothing makes a man strong like a cry for help." Christ was seeking rest and relaxation with His disciples (Mk. 6.31), but His mercy could not ignore the multitude's pleas. Rather than being annoyed or impatient, *He was moved with compassion* (*splagchnizomai*, to be moved to one's bowels, a strong term for mercy; being stirred to the depths of one's being). "The needs of people mean far more to him than his own convenience and ease" (Hendriksen, 593), and consistent with His mercy, He healed the sick.

14.15–18 When it was evening, His disciples came to Him, saying, "This is a deserted place, and the hour is already late. Send the multitudes away, that they may go into the villages and buy themselves food." But Jesus said to them, "They do not need to go away. You give them something to eat." And they said to Him, "We have here only five loaves and two fish." He said, "Bring them here to Me."

The disciples are concerned that everyone will miss supper. *Evening* (*opsios*) could refer to any time from late afternoon to the beginning of night (v 23, 27.57).[9] The disciples remind Jesus that they are in *a deserted place, and the hour is already late*. They suggest that the people be dismissed so they can go to nearby villages to get food.

Christ has a different idea: *they don't need to go away ... give them something to eat* (BECK). He said this to challenge His disciples, testing their understanding (13.51). But they didn't have a clue about what to do; the available resources (a boy's lunch[10]) were too meagre. As is too often the case with us, it never occurred to them that Christ was the solution to the problem.

---

[9] "In the Jewish division of the day there were two evenings. According to the most probable view the space of time called 'between the evenings' (Ex. xii.6) was from the ninth to the twelfth hour (Jos. *B.J.* vi.9.3). Hence the first evening ended at 3 o'clock, the second began at sunset. In this verse the first evening is meant, in *v.* 23 the second" (Carr, 199).

[10] Bread and salted or pickled fish was a common meal for the common people.

14.19 Then He commanded the multitudes to sit down on the grass. And He took the five loaves and the two fish, and looking up to heaven, He blessed and broke and gave the loaves to the disciples; and the disciples gave to the multitudes.

The Lord orders the crowd to sit (*anaklinō*, lean back, recline; the customary posture for eating) on the grass, nature's carpet. The mention of the grass indicates springtime, when the grass would be lush due to the seasonal rain (Mk. 6.39). Using resources the apostles deemed inadequate (five loaves and two fishes), Jesus, *looking up to heaven*, thanked God (*blessed*) and broke off pieces of *the loaves* (and fish, Mk. 6.41), which were distributed to the people.[11]

14.20 So they all ate and were filled, and they took up twelve baskets full of the fragments that remained.

This was more than an appetizer—*all ate and were filled* (*chortazō*, to fatten, gorge; Rev. 19.21). There was so much food that twelve baskets (*kophinos*, a knapsack-type basket) were needed to hold the leftovers (Eph. 3.20).

14.21 Now those who had eaten were about five thousand men, besides women and children.

The number fed was *about five thousand men, besides women and children.* The seating arrangement enabled an accurate count (Mk. 6.40); when the women and children were added in, the actual number fed was much higher than five thousand.

It should be stressed that this miracle occurred because Jesus was *moved with compassion*. This wasn't a life-or-death situation; nor were the disciples being hard-hearted when they suggested the crowd be sent away (v 15); it was a reasonable suggestion. And Jesus didn't work a miracle here just to work a miracle; He worked a miracle because His mercy was deep. He saw hungry people, and it hurt Him to allow them to leave hungry (12.1–7). Seeing need, He met need. Love is *kind* (1 Cor. 13.4); there are things Jesus did for no other reason than that He was kind.

The Exodus generation asked: *Can God prepare a table in the wilderness?* (Ps. 78.19). God's answer is always yes (Ex. 16)! They who are in a desert place emotionally or spiritually need to remember how much Jesus can do with very little.

---

[11] Cf. the feeding miracle of Elijah in 2 Kings 4.42–44.

14.22–33: The Disciples

Notes

This paragraph transitions from the feeding of the five thousand to what follows. In v 24, a storm is described, in v 32 it is stilled, and in between is an episode involving Jesus (vv 25–27) and Peter (vv 28–31) walking on water. The disciples' confession of faith (v 33) concludes the story. A lesson here is that a little faith, like a little knowledge, can be a dangerous thing.

14.22 And immediately Jesus made His disciples get into the boat and go before Him to the other side, while He sent the multitudes away.

After the miraculous meal, Jesus *made* (*anagkazō*, to force; occurs only here in Matt.) the disciples depart in the boat, after which He *sent* (*apoluō*, to let go, dismiss) *the multitudes away*. The scene recalls 8.23, except that Jesus isn't in the boat.

14.23 And when He had sent the multitudes away, He went up on the mountain by Himself to pray. Now when evening came, He was alone there.

Once alone, Jesus prays. This is one of only two times when Matthew describes Christ in private prayer (26.36–46). Few things in Christ's life bring Him closer to us than His praying. Despite His perfection, He didn't feel self-sufficient. The self-sufficient do not pray. Prayer was especially appropriate considering that the feeding of the five thousand coincided with a crisis in Christ's ministry (Jn. 6.25–66).

14.24 But the boat was now in the middle of the sea, tossed by the waves, for the wind was contrary.

The scene shifts to the disciples in the boat. They had made it to the middle of the lake but were finding further progress difficult due to a strong headwind (*contrary*, *enantios*, dead against). *Tossed* translates *basanizō*, which means to torture: according to *Arndt-Gingrich*, it is seldom used in reference to a thing but more commonly refers to human distress, affliction, and sickness. Those familiar with the Psalms know that troubled water, storm, and night are used to represent human fear and distress.

It would have been easier for the disciples to turn about and run with the wind, but Jesus had ordered them to *the other side*, and to the other side they were determined to go. The belief that the presence of agonies or difficulties means one is outside the will of God finds no support here. The disciples were facing rough going precisely because they were obedient to the will of Christ.

14.25 Now in the fourth watch of the night Jesus went to them, walking on the sea.

For guard-duty purposes, the Romans divided the night into four watches of three hours each.[12] During the fourth watch (3 to 6 AM; roughly the time when He would leave His grave), Christ goes to the disciples by *walking on the sea*—Jesus doesn't always come to us the way we expect.[13]

In the OT, men passed *through* the sea (Ex. 14; Josh. 3–4), but there are no examples of men walking on the sea. Greek literature contains references to this phenomenon[14] but makes it clear that the ability was divine, not human.

14.26 And when the disciples saw Him walking on the sea, they were troubled, saying, "It is a ghost!" And they cried out for fear.

The disciples' conclusion (*It is a ghost!*) and reaction (*they cried out for fear*) are understandable. Their reaction was similar to the fear and cowering of an animal, like a rabbit or opossum, when a human being walks up to release it from a trap in which it is caught. They saw something supernatural, and fear is a normal reaction to an encounter with a higher being. Whether they saw Jesus by moonlight or the light of dawn isn't stated, but they were unnerved by what they saw.

14.27 But immediately Jesus spoke to them, saying, "Be of good cheer! It is I; do not be afraid."

Jesus speaks above the wind, telling them not to fear but to *be of good cheer!* (*tharseō*, courage; 9.2). *It is I* translates the emphatic *egō eimi* —*I AM*—which is the name of God (22.32).[15] Christ's deity, of course, was why He could walk on water.

14.28–29 And Peter answered Him and said, "Lord, if it is You, command me to come to You on the water." So He said, "Come." And when Peter

---

[12] Mk. 13.35 names these periods as *even, midnight, the crowing of the rooster*, and *morning*.

[13] Just as God doesn't always answer our prayers the way we expect (cf. Hab. 1.5–11, Rom. 1.10).

[14] See Isocrates's *Panegyricus*, 89.

[15] E.g., Deut. 32.39; Isa. 41.4, 43.10.

had come down out of the boat, he walked on the water to go to Jesus.

This is the first of five vignettes Matthew includes about Peter not found elsewhere (15.15, 16.17–19, 17.24–27, 18.21). Peter responds to Christ by saying *if it is You*, a first-class condition that assumes that it is, in fact, Jesus (4.3). For reasons not explained, but probably to show off his faith (v 27), Peter says that he will leave the boat and walk to Jesus if so ordered. And Christ so orders: *Come.*

14.30 But when he saw that the wind *was* boisterous, he was afraid; and beginning to sink he cried out, saying, "Lord, save me!"

Talking is easier than walking (9.5). What seemed possible to Peter inside the boat seems less certain outside it. Initially, he walked on water, but instead of gaining confidence from this, his attention shifted from Christ to the force of the gale (*when he saw that the wind was boisterous*), *and he was afraid* (*panicked*, JBP) and began to sink (*katapontizō*, 18.6, *drowned*). All who have felt insecure and endangered understand Peter's desperation. With words reminiscent of Psalm 69.2,15–16, he cries, *Lord, save me!* When you're sinking, you get to the point quickly.

14.31 And immediately Jesus stretched out *His* hand and caught him, and said to him, "O you of little faith, why did you doubt?"

Jesus reaches Peter, and then teaches Peter—explaining that he sank due to *little faith* (6.30). Following Jesus doesn't mean life's storms are eliminated; it means that when we risk obedience and move away from our securities that God is *a very present help in trouble* (Ps. 46.1). *Little faith* mixes doubt with trust (*why did you doubt?*) that comes when we look at the situation rather than the Savior. "If it be right to trust Jesus at all, why not trust him altogether?" (Spurgeon).

14.32–33 And when they got into the boat, the wind ceased. Then those who were in the boat came and worshiped Him, saying, "Truly You are the Son of God."

As soon as Jesus and Peter enter the boat the wind stops (*ceased, kopazō*, to grow weary or tired, to rest from fatigue) and the disciples' reverence reaches a new high (on *worship*, see 2.2).[16] The deeper significance of the

---

[16] Edmund Burke, who wrote *Philosophical Enquiry into the Origin of our Ideas of the Sublime and Beautiful*, possibly the most influential essay on aesthetics ever published, included the following as qualities of the sublime: Astonishment, Terror, Power, Vastness, Infinity, Mag-

miracles is breaking through. The first time Jesus calmed a storm they wondered *What kind of man is this?* (8.27); now they confess: *Truly You are the Son of God.* Despite their little faith and limited knowledge, the disciples see (13.16) the crucial truth of the gospel (16.16).

The German writer Goethe loved this incident and said, "It expresses the noble doctrine that man, through faith and hearty courage, will come off victor in the most difficult enterprises, while he may be ruined by the least paroxysm of doubt" (*Conversations of Goethe with Eckermann and Soret*, 506). Storms have often been used to represent the insecurities of life, the unfathomable, the fear of death, failure, meaninglessness, the unfinished, etc. The thing needed when we must walk on water is absolute trust in a loving Father who is with us in the storm (1.23).

14.34–36: The Sick

14.34 When they had crossed over, they came to the land of Gennesaret.

The scene shifts from the Sea of Galilee to *the land of Gennesaret*, which is presumed to be the plain along the western side of the Sea of Galilee (8.28). Josephus described it as a garden spot where "nature is [as] wonderful as its beauty" (*Wars* iii,10.8).

14.35 And when the men of that place recognized Him, they sent out into all that surrounding region, brought to Him all who were sick, and begged Him that they might only touch the hem of His garment. And as many as touched *it* were made perfectly well.

As soon as the *men* (*anēr*, a male) *of that place* realize Jesus is in the vicinity, they send word to the sick, and many came seekin only to touch *the hem of Christ's garment* (*himation*, 5.40), which recalls the healing of the hemorrhaging woman (9.20–21; 4.24, 8.16). Touching the hem wasn't a superstitious belief in Christ's clothes, but reflected the thought that even marginal contact with Christ could bring health. And they weren't disappointed. Christ delivered many from their personal storms that day.

---

nificence, Magnitude, Difficulty. Such qualities characterized Christ's miracles and explain why men who saw the miracles fell to their knees in worship or shrank back in fear (Lk. 5.8).

CHAPTER 15

15.1–20: Tradition

Notes

The topic in vv 1–9 is Pharisaic tradition, and in vv 10–20 it is ethical purity, but several considerations indicate that these sections go together. Verse 20, for instance, looks back to the issue of hand washing introduced in vv 1–2, and vv 12–14 continue Christ's criticism of the Pharisees begun in vv 1–9.

15.1 Then the scribes and Pharisees who were from Jerusalem came to Jesus, saying,

Then, during the visit to Gennesaret (14.34), Christ is met by some *scribes and Pharisees,* who reappear for the first time since 12.38–45. The mention of *Jerusalem* recalls 2.4.

15.2 "Why do Your disciples transgress the tradition of the elders? For they do not wash their hands when they eat bread."

The Jews waste no time getting to the point—they want to know why Jesus' disciples *transgress the tradition of the elders.* Since rabbis were held liable for their follower's behavior (12.2), this was really a criticism of Christ. *The tradition* (*paradosis,* a handing down) *of the elders* referred to a body of rabbinic oral commentary that was considered authoritative by the Pharisees, but not the Sadducees.[1] These traditions were originally meant to be a hedge around the Law, removing all ambiguity and gray areas

---

[1] When Pharisaic tradition was written down in the second century AD, it was called the "Mishnah, meaning to repeat or study, since it was originally memorized and regurgitated. Mishnah consisted of three elements: the midrash, that is the method of interpreting the Pentateuch to make clear points of law; the halakhah ... the body of generally accepted legal decisions on particular points; and the aggadah or homilies, including anecdotes and legends used to convey understanding of the law to the ordinary people" (Johnson, *A History of the Jews,* 152).

in the interpretation of the Law in order that men might avoid breaking the law. Eventually, however, they were accorded *ex cathedra* status, and the scribes and Pharisees believed that to ignore their traditions was equivalent to breaking Scripture.

The tradition in question involved handwashing before eating, which Mosaic law didn't address; in fact, the earliest reference to this ritual is this incident in the Gospels. The only OT texts even remotely relevant were Leviticus 15.11, which had to do with hygienic washing to prevent the spread of germs, and the texts instructing priests to wash their hands and feet at the laver before serving at the altar (Ex. 30.19). The Pharisees believed, though, that "people became unclean by contact with any sort of ceremonially unclean object or person [such as a Gentile]. To ensure purity, [they] would go through a rather elaborate ritual of purification before they ate" (Mounce, 148). "Discussions of the issue of clean and unclean eventually yielded enough material to fill twelve tractates in the Mishnah" (Gardner, 235). Matthew, writing from a Jewish perspective, apparently assumes his readers know what he's talking about and doesn't explain the ritual, but Mark gives more detail (Mk. 7.1–5).

15.3 He answered and said to them, "Why do you also transgress the commandment of God because of your tradition?

Jesus never allowed Himself to be placed on the defensive and now goes on the offensive by answering the accusation with an accusation. He offers no defense for His disciples, but instead charges that Pharisaic tradition, far from encouraging obedience to God's Law, violated it. Throughout this exchange, Jesus maintains a sharp contrast between what the Pharisees said (*your tradition*) and what God said (*the commandment of God*). The Pharisees, not Jesus or His disciples, were the problem.

15.4 For God commanded, saying, 'Honor your father and your mother'; and, 'He who curses father or mother, let him be put to death.'

An example substantiates Christ's charge. The fifth commandment — *honor your father and your mother* (Ex. 20.13) — was a fun-damental obligation in Judaism. *Honor* implies the ideas of support, welfare, and physical care; parents care for children in the child's infancy, and children care for parents in the parents' infirmity. So important was this responsibility that its violation was a capital crime (Ex. 21.17).

15.5–6 But you say, 'Whoever says to his father or mother, "Whatever profit you might have received from me *is* a gift *to God"* — then he need not honor his father or mother.' Thus you have made the commandment of God of no effect by your tradition.

Exactly what the Pharisees did isn't clear, but they had a rule wherein they could declare their assets *a gift* (*dōron*, a gift; equivalent to the Heb. *corban*, Mk. 7.11), which meant they were earmarked for the temple or service of God and couldn't be used for anything else, such as supporting a parent. What thus seemed a pious act was in reality a fraud, for some rabbis employed a great deal of casuistry in allowing situations in which something given to the temple could still be used by the giver — a humanly devised loophole that exempted Jews from the debt of love they owed their parents. What they characterized as devotion to God, God said was worthy of death. Whenever man tries to pass off what he says (v 6) as something *God* says (v 5), the duplicity and unrighteousness seen here is usually replicated.

15.7–9 Hypocrites! Well did Isaiah prophesy about you, saying: 'These people draw near to Me with their mouth, and honor Me with *their* lips, But their heart is far from Me. And in vain they worship Me, Teaching *as* doctrines the commandments of men.'"

Christ applies Isaiah 29.13 to the Pharisees. They were *hypocrites* who talked one way (*draw near with their mouth*) but acted another (*their heart is far from Me*).[2] Agitated about unwashed hands, they laid ungodly hands on God's word and perverted it. Any talk they did about honoring their parents was just talk. Lacking true honor for their parents, these children of the devil (Jn. 8.41) hatched a scheme that made them look like angels (2 Cor. 11.14–15). They filled out the paperwork that ostensibly "gave" something to God that God said should have gone to their parents.

"When a man could teach the law as to permit a son to leave his old parents destitute in spite of what the law explicitly said, that man 'knew' the law too well! We have all heard of lawyers who made use of the law to enable crooks to escape punishment; who used the law to their own private advantages. It was their very 'knowing' of the law which served their wicked ways and their 'knowledge' of that law was a greater condemnation for them" (McGuigan, *The Book of Romans*, 111).[3]

---

[2] "O God … save us from a worship of the lips while our hearts are far away" (W. E. Orchard).

[3] "To [wash pots and cooking utensils] as a religious ceremony, and to require others to

15.10–11 When He had called the multitude to *Himself*, He said to them, "Hear and understand: Not what goes into the mouth defiles a man; but what comes out of the mouth, this defiles a man."

Jesus calls the crowd together because He has something to say that everyone needed to hear. Two words—*not/but*—frame the contrast: *not what goes into the mouth defiles the man* (the Pharisaic view), *but what comes out of the mouth defiles a man* (God's view). The Pharisees taught that purity was determined by externals like clean hands; Jesus taught that purity was an internal matter, a clean soul. The Pharisees lost sight of the fact that OT purity laws were meant as a *primer* on morality (Lev. 20.22–26). True purity or defilement is determined what's in the heart, not food in the belly or the person one touches.[4]

15.12–14 Then His disciples came and said to Him, "Do You know that the Pharisees were offended when they heard this saying?" But He answered and said, "Every plant which My heavenly Father has not planted will be uprooted. Let them alone. They are blind leaders of the blind. And if the blind leads the blind, both will fall into a ditch."

An ax has been laid at the root of Pharisaic doctrine, and the Pharisees don't like it. When the disciples report this to Jesus, He pronounces a judgment on the Pharisees that recalls the parable of the tares (13.37–43). The figure of a *planting* echoes Jeremiah 45.4 and God's election of Israel as a community of salvation, but Pharisaism—with its traditions that vacated God's Law—wasn't planted by God! Pharisaism was a noxious weed growing in God's field that would *be uprooted* (13.41). Christ's denunciation couldn't have been more pointed.

Let them alone—the disciples were to have nothing to do with the Pharisees. Regardless of how they advertised themselves (Rom. 2.19), they had committed the real sin unforgiveable—a hardened heart. They were blind guides (in contrast to Jesus who healed the blind) who created sins that weren't sins, proposed solutions that didn't solve, and consistently misinterpreted and misapplied the Law (5.19–20, 23.16–26).

---

do them on the same grounds, is to bind where God has not bound. It is to put human authority on an equality with God's authority, and that is to bring God's authority down on an equality with man's. But people are not so different today. They develop certain customs that become sacred to them. Such people, like the Pharisees, think it strange that any one claiming to be religious will disregard their customs. As respects custom and tradition, none of us are free from danger" (Whiteside, *Biblical Studies, The Interwoven Gospels*, 274, 276).

[4] See 8.3, 9.21,25, 14.36; Mk. 7.19; 1 Tim. 4.3–4.

There are some with whom we are not obligated to debate or argue (Tit. 3.10–11).

15.15 Then Peter answered and said to Him, "Explain this parable to us."

This is the second of the Matthean scenes involving Peter (14.28). Speaking for the disciples, he asks for a clarification of the *parable*—what Christ had just said (v 11, 13.10,36).

15.16 So Jesus said, "Are you also still without understanding?

In a mild rebuke, Jesus asks why men who claimed to understand (13.51) didn't understand.

15.17–18 Do you not yet understand that whatever enters the mouth goes into the stomach and is eliminated? But those things which proceed out of the mouth come from the heart, and they defile a man.

Externals are not evil, but if a man is missing the internal reality, no external can bring him closer to God. True religion leads to life with God, and life with God leads to the love of our fellows. Food that *goes into the stomach* and travels through the digestive system doesn't determine the quality of the *heart* ("the source of a man's true character, the true person as he really is," France, 245). It is the content of the heart, not the contents of the stomach, that defiles a man before God (23.25; Ps. 24.4). Pharisaic tradition—indeed, all tradition—elevated the irrelevant.

15.19 For out of the heart proceed evil thoughts, murders, adulteries, fornications, thefts, false witness, blasphemies.

Here are seven deadly sins (Mk. 7.21–22) that reflect the second part of the Ten Commandments. On *evil thoughts,* see vv 3–6 and 9.4; on *murders,* see 5.21–22; on *adulteries,* see 5.27–28; on *fornications,* see 5.31–32; on *thefts, false witness,* and *blasphemies,* see 12.31–32. The plural nouns encompass every instance of sin in each category.

15.20 These are *the things* which defile a man, but to eat with unwashed hands does not defile a man."

Christ answers the question with which the section began (v 2), affirming that *to eat with unwashed hands does not defile a man.* Handwashing involves external hygiene that does nothing to sanitize the soul (1 Pet. 3.21). Fellowship with God is determined by a pure heart that expresses itself in righteous words and deeds.

Excursus on Modern Pharisaism

"It was not a Pharisee but a New England Puritan who said that to hold a wedding banquet or any similar activity on the Lord's day was 'as great a sin as for a Father to take a knife and cut his child's throat. It was a twentieth-century denominationalist who wrote that to eat breakfast before partaking of Holy Communion was a sin comparable with fornication'" (Fosdick, *The Man from Nazareth*, 73). "When a certain Captain Kemple returned, after being three years at sea, he was greeted by his wife at the doorsill. In his joy at reunion, he kissed her right there—publicly. And for this wrong, he was placed in the stocks" (Phillip Clarke, "Christ and our Morals").

15.21–28: Canaanite Woman

Notes

For a third time, Christ makes a strategic withdrawal (12.15, 14.13)—this time, to illustrate His teaching on purity and uncleanness. John Watson's observation that Jesus' life "was full of arranged accidents" applies here. A superficial reading sees Christ's encounter with the Canaanite woman as one of the most unsettling scenes in the Gospels. F. W. Beare, for instance, characterized His behavior here as "atrocious, insolent, and chauvinistic."

15.21 Then Jesus went out from there and departed to the region of Tyre and Sidon.

Went out from there refers to Gennesaret (14.34). *The region of Tyre and Sidon* was fifty miles northwest of Gennesaret and corresponded to ancient Phoenicia (modern Lebanon). Hebrew prophets condemned the area's depravity (11.21–22; Isa. 23; Eze. 27–28), and the Pharisees would have regarded the region as off-limits, making it an ideal place for Christ to practice what He had just preached (vv 11–20).

15.22 And behold, a woman of Canaan came from that region and cried out to Him, saying, "Have mercy on me, O Lord, Son of David! My daughter is severely demon-possessed."

A woman of Canaan (*Chananaios*, only here in the NT[5]) indicates descent from aboriginal stock. Her cry (imperfect tense: constant crying) not only reveals the magnitude of her distress but is full of Biblical flavor. *Have*

---

[5] "'Phoenician' is the Gr. translation of 'Canaanite': *phoenix* is Greek and is derived from the adjective *phoinos* = red. ... 'Into the Hellenistic period' Canaan designated 'the Syrian

mercy on me is a common supplication in the OT (Ps. 30.10, 123.3, etc.); *Lord* is the term of address used by the disciples and others (8.2); and *Son of David* shows a familiarity with the Jewish Messiah who healed His hurting people. Her appeal is for her *severely demon-possessed daughter*.

15.23–24 But He answered her not a word. And His disciples came and urged Him, saying, "Send her away, for she cries out after us." But He answered and said, "I was not sent except to the lost sheep of the house of Israel."

Christ knew the great faith that resided in this woman (Jn. 2.25), and He wanted to showcase it. To do so, He became a dramatic foil by placing before her three obstacles.

The first was *silence*; few trials are harder to endure than silence. There are times when no news isn't good news, and fear can transform silence into panic or hopelessness.

The second obstacle was *exclusivity*. Not for the first or last time, the disciples play a less-than-cordial role (14.15, 19.13). *Send her away, for she cries out after* us—no she wasn't, she was crying after Jesus (there's a lesson here for disciples who have a high sense of self-importance). They weren't asking that Jesus get rid of her by granting her request—to them she was a nuisance they wanted gone. Disciples who lack the compassion of Christ can do great damage to the cause of Christ. Blessed is he who allows no Christian to discourage or keep him from Christ.

I was not sent except to the lost sheep of the house of Israel (10.6) was said to the disciples and seems to endorse their request. These words are analogous to an insurance agent telling a client who has suffered a great loss that his policy doesn't cover his claim.

15.25 Then she came and worshiped Him, saying, "Lord, help me!"

Love doesn't quit. Twice rebuffed, the mother *worships* (8.2, 9.18, 14.33) and again begs for her child. Again she calls Jesus *Lord*. Again she implores using language that echoed Peter's cry: *help me* (boetheō, come to the aid of; 14.30).

15.26 But He answered and said, "It is not good to take the children's bread and throw *it* to the little dogs."

The third obstacle was *rudeness*. "One would think that this would have broken Jesus' heart" (Hobbs, 205), but Christ responds with an insult: *It is*

coast, the area where the *kinachchu*, red purple, is produced" (Luz II, 338).

not good to take the children's bread and throw it to the little dogs. The diminutive form for *dog* (*kunarion,* little dog) refers to pet dogs—household dogs, not wild scavengers. But even if we're talking about toy poodles, this was still a verbal slap. This woman was a *dog* (Gentile), not a *child* (Jews), and children are fed first. (For another perspective on this woman's humility, see 18.4.)

15.27 And she said, "Yes, Lord, yet even the little dogs eat the crumbs which fall from their masters' table."

The woman doesn't disagree, but notes that even pet dogs get to eat *crumbs which fall from their master's table.*

15.28 Then Jesus answered and said to her, "O woman, great *is* your faith! Let it be to you as you desire." And her daughter was healed from that very hour.

Christ can maintain the ruse no longer; He becomes "like himself again" (McGarvey, 139) and declares her pursuit of Him to be *great faith* (8.10), which He rewards by granting her request *that very hour. Great faith* persists despite cold shoulders, rudeness, and insult. God can use resistance and adversity to important ends, for the strongest faith is developed in those who have to overcome the most. "Hardly an outstanding champion of faith," said Fosdick, "can be found who has not won and confirmed it in the face of trouble."

As mentioned in the *Notes* to this section, many find this a disturbing exchange in which Christ seems *unchristian.* Attempts to explain His behavior have spanned the spectrum. Some consider the story a fabrication; others believe that it reveals Jesus "as a Jewish man of his day, chauvinistic toward women and non-Jews" (Hare, 177). Still others see it as a statement to economically wealthy Phoenicia that "charity begins at home" (Garland, 165). A more ingenious explanation understands Christ's words as lighthearted repartee. "We must remember that words are made very different in connotation by the tone of the voice and by the look in the eye of the speaker. There are things which we can say with a smile, but which cannot be said, without offense, with a straight face. … That Jesus was indulging in this kind of banter about racial and national differences is the only logical alternative to the insufferable hypothesis that He was being intentionally chauvinistic and rude" (Trueblood, *The Humor of Christ,* 123).

I, however, don't believe that Christ engaged this woman with a sly wink; I think what He said sounded as jolting as it reads.

It's true that there are lessons here on the importance of prayer and faith, and that Christ is anticipating the gospel being preached to the Gentiles, etc.; but contextually, the best explanation for Christ's behavior is that He acted as a Pharisee would have acted in the situation. How better expose the despicableness of human tradition (vv 1–20) than by seeing it in action? *By their fruits you will know them.* Abstractions that look good in theory can take on an entirely different cast when made concrete. When the Pharisaic view of purity was acted out, it was seen to be an arrogant, rude, unmerciful attitude antithetical to the love of God. "So Jesus played this role of tradition to the hilt, as in an acted parable He unmasked it before His disciples for the vicious thing that it is" (Hobbs, 203).

15.29–39: Four Thousand

Notes

The feeding of the four thousand has never elicited much interest from commentators, for most think that everything that could be said about it was said in the feeding of the five thousand (14.13–21). Scripture, however, repeats for emphasis. Matthew wanted to summarize, for the last time in his Gospel, the blessings Jesus brought to Israel. Christ's healings and feedings were not one-time phenomena, but characteristic of His ministry. Which makes His rejection by His Israel all the more unfathomable.

Geographical references frame this section (vv 29,39). Against the notion that this is a retelling of the feeding miracle in ch 14 are two considerations. First, though similarities exist, the events diverge on several key details: the number fed (5,000 vs. 4,000), the time frame (the 5,000 fed on the day of their arrival, the 4,000 after being with Jesus for three days), the quantity of leftovers (twelve baskets vs. seven), and the sequel (Jesus sent the disciples away without Him vs. leaving with them). Second, and most impor-tantly, Jesus identified them as separate incidents (16.9–10). Based on v 33, this miracle says as much about human nature as about divine power.

15.29 Jesus departed from there, skirted the Sea of Galilee, and went up on the mountain and sat down there.

Leaving *the region of Tyre and Sidon* (v 21), Christ returned to *the Sea of Galilee* and an unspecified *mountain* in the area.

15.30–31 Then great multitudes came to Him, having with them *the* lame, blind, mute, maimed, and many others; and they laid them down at Jesus' feet, and He healed them. So the multitude marveled when they saw *the* mute speaking, *the* maimed made whole, *the* lame walking, and *the* blind seeing; and they glorified the God of Israel.

A magnet always attracts—Christ never lacked an audience, and the response to Him is overwhelming—*great multitudes came* bringing their sick, *and He healed them all.* From Mark 7.31 we know that Jesus is in the region of Decapolis. The last time He was in this area He was asked to leave (8.28–34), but now His reception is entirely positive. It would seem that the testimony of the demoniac Jesus commissioned had its intended effect (Mk. 5.18–20).

The miracles caused the crowd to *marvel* (*thaumazō*, admiration; Acts 2.22) and *glorify the God of Israel*—recalling the language of the Psalms (Ps. 106.48; Lk. 1.68).

15.32 Now Jesus called His disciples to *Himself* and said, "I have compassion on the multitude, because they have now continued with Me three days and have nothing to eat. And I do not want to send them away hungry, lest they faint on the way."

For a third time, Matthew notes that Christ is deeply moved by the plight of people (9.36, 14.14; this is the only place where Jesus says, *I have compassion*; in every other place the pronoun is in the third person). Any food the people had brought with them was gone, and Jesus was unwilling to send them home (some lived a long way off, Mk. 8.3) on an empty stomach.

15.33 Then His disciples said to Him, "Where could we get enough bread in the wilderness to fill such a great multitude?"

The disciples' obtuseness is embarrassing (14.21). Despite the miracle of the five thousand, they have no idea how to feed such a multitude in the wilderness. Erdman is worth quoting here: "Some commentators insist that such doubt is incredible and that this portion of the story, at least, must have been borrowed by the writer from the former narrative. Some of us are too conscious of similar unbelief in ourselves, in spite of repeated miracles of grace, to wonder long at the blindness of the apostles" (127).

15.34–35 Jesus said to them, "How many loaves do you have?" And they said, "Seven, and a few little fish." So He commanded the multitude to sit down on the ground.

Christ takes the initiative and asks about available resources, which turn out to be seven loaves and a few fishes. Jesus commands the crowd to sit on the ground (rather than the grass, 14.19), which likely places this scene in summer when the grass has been burnt brown by the heat.

15.36 And He took the seven loaves and the fish and gave thanks, broke *them* **and gave** *them* **to His disciples; and the disciples** *gave* **to the multitude.**

Christ *gave thanks*, using a word (*eucharisteō*, to express gratitude) that reappears in 26.27 when He institutes the Lord's Supper. Breaking off pieces of food, He hands them to the disciples who distribute them to the people.

15.37 So they all ate and were filled, and they took up seven large baskets full of the fragments that were left.

Where need abounds, supply much more abounds (Rom. 5.20). No matter how sparse or meager the resources (14.21), Christ meets our need. And when His people imitate His liberality, they prove the truth of the proverb: *One man gives freely, yet grows all the richer* (Prov. 11.24, RSV). *Baskets* (*spuris*, Acts 9.25) refers to a container that was larger than the *kophinos* used in 14.20. "To waste food which we do not need, when some live at starvation level, is an insult to the divine giver" (F. F. Bruce, *The Gospel of John*, 145).

15.38 Now those who ate were four thousand men, besides women and children.

If women and children are included, the number fed could easily have approached 10,000.

15.39 And He sent away the multitude, got into the boat, and came to the region of Magdala.

As in 14.22, after the meal the crowd is dismissed and Jesus recrosses the Sea of Galilee. This time, the boat lands at *Magdala*, which seems to have been located on the western shore of the lake (modern Khirbet Mejdel). The name derives from the Heb. word for *tower* (*migdal*, Josh, 19.38).

CHAPTER 16

16.1–12: Pharisees and Sadducees

Notes

Fosdick tells of some women "who climbed an Alpine height on an autumn day, when the riot of color in the valley sobered into the green of the pines upon the heights, and over all stood the crests of eternal snow, and who inquired in the full sight of all this, 'We heard there was a view up here; where is it?'" (*The Meaning of Prayer*, 79–80). As the first paragraph in this chapter illustrates, an inability to see what is right in front of you is a characteristic of the hardened heart.

This section (vv 1–12) concludes the first major division in Matthew wherein the emphasis is on God's revelation of the Christ. Almost everything here is familiar. The Pharisees' and Sadducees' hatred of Jesus outflanks their partisanship, and they unite, as in 3.7 and 12.38–40, to request a sign. They might as well have asked for a bucket of water from the sea to prove that the sea is wet; just as water is wet (its essential nature is wetness), so Christ is divine, as His miracles attested.

16.1 Then the Pharisees and Sadducees came, and testing Him asked that He would show them a sign from heaven.

It's not unusual for dogs that fight among themselves to stop long enough to chase the same rabbit. The Pharisees and Sadducees despised each other, but their hatred of Christ was strong enough to make them strange bedfellows (3.7, 22.23). The location is *Magdala* (15.39), and this joint committee asks Jesus for *a sign from heaven*—some sort of cosmic or atmospheric demonstration that would be more stupendous than an earthly miracle. That the Jews still asked for a sign after all the miracles Christ had performed points to hardened hearts. They weren't asking for something to see but were setting a trap (*peirazō*, put to proof, 4.7) to ensnare Christ.

16.2–3 He answered and said to them, "When it is evening you say, '*It will be* fair weather, for the sky is red'; and in the morning, '*It will be* foul weather today, for the sky is red and threatening.' Hypocrites!

You know how to discern the face of the sky, but you cannot *discern* the signs of the times.

"Red sky at night, sailor's delight / red sky in morning, sailors take warning."[1] Jesus lampoons their request by pointing out that they could use physical evidence to forecast the weather but couldn't use supernatural to read *the signs of the times* and know that the Messianic era had dawned. The spiritually blind wouldn't recognize a sign from heaven if it ran over them. Only here and in Mark 10.22 does the NT use the word translated *threatening* (*stugnazō*, used in Mk. 10.22 of the rich young ruler's gloomy, cloudy countenance).

16.4 A wicked and adulterous generation seeks after a sign, and no sign shall be given to it except the sign of the prophet Jonah." And He left them and departed.

The problem wasn't a lack of evidence but the Pharisees' and Sadducees' rejection of the evidence. Jesus repeats 12.39 about *the sign of Jonah* and walks off; discussion was useless (15.14). He will have no further communication with the Jewish leadership until He returns to Judea for the last time (19.3, 22.23).

16.5 Now when His disciples had come to the other side, they had forgotten to take bread.

This paragraph follows a chiastic outline in which vv 5–6 correspond to vv 11–12 and v 7 corresponds to vv 8–10.

And when his disciples were come to the other side may imply that Jesus was by Himself in vv 1–4 and the disciples just now catch up. The disciples had forgotten to pack a lunch, which became an occasion to expose a misunderstanding (13.51).

16.6–7 Then Jesus said to them, "Take heed and beware of the leaven of the Pharisees and the Sadducees." And they reasoned among themselves, saying, "*It is* because we have taken no bread."

---

[1] "As clouds move from west to east, the dawn sunlight will tint them in the west, portending rain as the day progresses. In the evening, the same phenomenon suggests that the clouds have almost disappeared, bringing good weather instead" (Blomberg, 247–248).

Jesus warns about the Jews, but the disciples think *beware of the leaven of the Pharisees and of the Sadducees* was a criticism of them for failing to bring something to eat.

16.8–10 But Jesus, being aware of *it*, said to them, "O you of little faith, why do you reason among yourselves because you have brought no bread? Do you not yet understand, or remember the five loaves of the five thousand and how many baskets you took up? Nor the seven loaves of the four thousand and how many large baskets you took up?

Christ is aware of the disciples' discussion (*they reasoned among themselves*) and chides them—not for misunderstanding, but for the *little faith* their misunderstanding revealed. Some misunderstandings are understandable, but not this one. He who fed five thousand and four thousand with next to nothing could surely feed the disciples if necessary, and their failure to see this was inexcusable. Crises of faith occur when former mercies are forgotten (Ps. 77).

16.11–12 How is it you do not understand that I did not speak to you concerning bread?—*but* to beware of the leaven of the Pharisees and Sadducees." Then they understood that He did not tell *them* to beware of the leaven of bread, but of the doctrine of the Pharisees and Sadducees.

Christ repeats His warning, and the disciples finally get it (*suniēmi*, understand, to join or bring together). By *leaven*, Christ meant *doctrine*, not bread (1 Cor. 5.6); ideas are like leaven—they can influence and spread. The Pharisees and Sadducees taught different things, but Christ warns of their *doctrine*, singular. It's not their distinctive teachings that are in view but rather their shared opposition to Him. There are many ways of going wrong, including embracing the errors of the right to avoid the errors of the left, or vice versa. In opposing error, it's important to avoid extremes.

16.13–20: Jesus Is the Christ

Notes

Not only is this passage the center of Matthew's Gospel, but it summarizes the argument made since 4.17 that Jesus is the Christ, Immanuel, the Son of God (1.21,23). The disciples may have been fuzzy on the metaphorical use of *leaven* (vv 6–12), but unlike the Jewish clergy, they understood who Jesus was.

274 | *Christ Revealed*

For the first time, the word *church* (*ekklēsia*) appears, and beginning with v 21, Christ will speak in increasing detail about the holy society He was creating.

This section breaks into three parts: vv 13–16 contain two questions that Jesus asks and the disciples answer; in vv 17–19, Christ enlarges on the answer given His second question; and in v 20, He gives the disciples a command.

16.13–16 When Jesus came into the region of Caesarea Philippi, He asked His disciples, saying, "Who do men say that I, the Son of Man, am?" So they said, "Some *say* John the Baptist, some Elijah, and others Jeremiah or one of the prophets." He said to them, "But who do you say that I am?" Simon Peter answered and said, "You are the Christ, the Son of the living God."

Christ and the disciples travel north to *Caesarea Philippi*, near a source of the Jordan River. The town was originally called Paneas, after a nearby grotto dedicated to the Greek god Pan. Philip the tetrarch (Lk. 3.1) had rebuilt the city and named it after himself and Caesar Augustus.

Who do men say that I, the Son of Man, am? By this question, the distinction Christ made in 11.25 and 13.13,16 between those who understand and those who didn't is reintroduced. Those who didn't understand Jesus answered variously: *some say John the*

Baptist (14.1–2), *some Elijah, and others Jeremiah*[2] *or one of the* prophets. The disciples could have added that some believed Jesus was *the Son of David* (12.23, 15.22), which was the most accurate assessment made about Him thus far; why they omitted this isn't stated. And for some reason, they don't mention any hostile opinions (11.19, 12.24, 13.55). Of the several things that could be said about these answers, the main thing to be said is that they were wrong—complimentary, but wrong nevertheless.[3]

After the polls are noted, Jesus asks the disciples: *but who do you say that I am?* The critical thing is not what others said but what the disciples said.

---

[2] Based on Mal. 4.5–6, the mention of Elijah is understandable; less understandable is why some thought Jesus to be Jeremiah, but some of the intertestamental apocryphal books predicted the reappearance of Jeremiah (2 Esdr. 2.16–18; 2 Macc. 15.13–16,22).

[3] "One day when Jesus propounded the question, 'Who do men say that I am?' the disciples told him that men had different opinions in regard to him. Some said he was John the Baptist, some said he was Elijah, others said he was Jeremiah, while others unable to give his exact name felt convinced he was one of the old prophets. This is remarkable! They went to the grave in order to find a man to whom they could liken him. There was no man then living with whom he could be compared" (Jefferson, *The Character of Jesus*, 49).

If they knew the answer to Christ's question, maybe they were equal to the task for which they had been chosen.

In the third Matthean scene involving Peter (14.28), he speaks for the rest, formally and solemnly repeating a confession they had previously made (14.33; Jn. 6.69): *You* (in contrast to the prophets who were servants of God) *are the Christ* (Israel's Messiah), *the Son of the living God* (the true God who acts in history in contrast to the dead gods of the Gentiles).[4]

16.17 Jesus answered and said to him, "Blessed are you, Simon Bar-Jonah, for flesh and blood has not revealed *this* to you, but My Father who is in heaven.

"Mrs Keller... Mrs Keller. … She knows!" is how Annie Sullivan shouted her excitement when she realized that her pupil, Helen Keller, finally "got it" — understood what she was trying to teach her (*The Miracle Worker*). And Christ is no less excited when His chosen pupils show they have gotten the central truth He was trying to teach them. To express His delight, He pronounces a *blessing* (5.3) on Peter using the Aramaic formulation of his name, *Simon bar-Jonah* (*son of Jonah*, Jn. 1.42, 21.15). Peter's confession wasn't based on arguments or evidence supplied by *flesh and blood* (a Semitic colloquialism for *man*, 1 Cor. 15.50; Gal. 1.12), nor had Peter received some special revelation given to him and no one else. Peter simply stated the logical conclusion from what Jesus had said and done (Jn. 5.31–39; a special revelation is given Peter in 17.1–5, which he recalls in 2 Pet. 1.16–18). Whereas the Pharisees and Sadducees continued to ask for proof, Peter and the other disciples had seen enough to know that Jesus was God's Son.

16.18 And I also say to you that you are Peter, and on this rock I will build My church, and the gates of Hades shall not prevail against it.

Peter (*petros*, rock) was a nickname Christ gave Simon at their first meeting (Jn. 1.42), and Christ now explains its significance. In time, Peter would become a man of strength and stability, rocklike in character (Acts 4.10), but he had a way to go before reaching that point. His confession, though, showed he was headed in the right direction.

On this rock I will build my church is the first of only two places in the Gospels where the *church* is mentioned (18.17). The Eng. word *church*

---

[4] In the Gr., Peter's answer contains ten words, including a fourfold use of the definite article: *the* Christ, *the* Son, *the* living, *the* God.

derives from the Gr. *kuriakōn* (the *Lord's* or *the Lord's house*) and through long usage has become the standard translation for *ekklēsia* (the word Jesus used), a collective noun that means *called out* (2 Thes. 2.14). In the first century, *ekklēsia* described a *group of people* assembled for virtually any purpose (civil, Acts 19.39; religious, Acts 7.38; illegal, Acts 19.32,41). What is significant is not that Jesus spoke of an *ekklēsia*, but that He spoke of *His ekklēsia—My church*. The *church* is Christ's group, His crowd, comprised of those who confess Him as Lord (Rom. 10.9–10). Here, *ekklēsia* is used in a general sense to include everyone who confesses Christ's lordship, builds their life on Him, and stands in right relationship to Him. In 18.18, *ekklēsia* is used in a specific sense, referring to believers in a certain congregation who have banded together for worship and fellowship.

I will build indicates the church hadn't yet been built. Using the image of a building to represent the people of God was nothing new, for the OT spoke about *the house of Israel* (Ex. 16.31; Matt. 10.6, 15.24). The first part of a building that's built is the foundation, which is a force sufficient to withstand any pressure placed upon it. A foundation's job is to make sure that what goes up doesn't come down (7.24–25). Modern engineers have greatly refined the methods of construction, but they have never improved on rock as the best foundation on which to build. Men, as well as buildings and bridges, need a sure foundation, "a place to stand" (Archimedes), and for a foundation, nothing is better than rock.

But what did Jesus mean by *this rock*? The answer to this was called by Barclay, "one of the storm-centres of New Testament interpretation." Historically, there have been four major explanations. (1) The *Catholic* interpretation asserts that *Peter is the rock*, which is the basis for its doctrine of papal supremacy. (2) The *disciple* interpretation understands *rock to be every disciple*, of whom Peter is representative. (3) The *confession* interpretation believes the *rock is the faith Peter expressed*. (4) The *Christological* interpretation understands the *rock to be Christ*.

The Roman Catholic interpretation is based on a wordplay in the Gr. between *petros* (*Peter*) and *petra* (*rock*, *petros* being the masc. and *petra* the fem. form of the root *petr*). Starting with this, Rome has constructed an elaborate ecclesiology that regards Peter as the first pope, whose primacy has been passed to his successors. "By the word 'rock' the Saviour cannot have meant Himself, but only Peter, as is so much more apparent in Aramaic in which the same word (Kipha) is used for 'Peter' and 'rock'. His statement then admits of but one explanation, namely, that He wishes to make Peter the head of the whole community of those who believed in Him as the true Messias; that through this foundation (Pe-ter) the Kingdom of Christ would be unconquerable; that the spiritual guidance of the faithful was placed in the hands of Peter, as the special representative of Christ. It is also clear that the position of Peter among the other Apostles and in the Christian community was the basis for the Kingdom of God on earth, that is, the Church of Christ. Peter was personally installed as Head of the Apostles by Christ Himself. This foundation created for the Church by its Founder could not disappear with the person of Peter, but was intended to continue and did continue (as actual history shows) in the primacy of the Roman Church and its bishops" (*The Catholic Encyclopedia*, XI, 1911 ed., 746).[5] The Anglican scholar George Salmon scarcely understated the matter when he wrote, "It takes one's breath away to read a commentary which finds so much more in a text than lies on the surface of it. If our Lord meant all this, we may ask, why did He not say it?" (*Infallibility of the Church*, 334).

There are several problems with the Catholic interpretation. First, contrary to Catholic claims, their interpretation cannot be substantiated patristically—the current Catholic position making Peter the foundation of the church is relatively recent; it did not become dominant until the sixteenth and seventeenth centuries. The *rock* = *Peter* interpretation was needed by the popes in their controversies with the Protestants "for their own legitimation against the Protestant use of the hitherto standard Augustinian and Easter interpretations of the text" (Luz, *Matthew in History,* 62). Although the church in Rome early on laid claim to special authority (which was mostly ignored by other churches), the earliest unambiguous historical connection between vv 17–19 and the papal office was made in the mid-third century by Stephanus, bishop of Rome. Prior to this, there is no evidence in the postapostolic era of successors to Peter holding authority over the church universal. Second, if granting singular authority to Peter is the crucial point of this text, why isn't v 18 repeated in Mark 8.29 or Luke 9.20? Third, if Christ gave apostolic primacy to Peter, why did the disciples continue to argue about which of them was the greatest (18.1, 20.21)? Fourth, it is highly improbable that Jesus, having to fight the religious hierarchy at every turn, would establish one of His own.

---

[5] Verse 18 is inscribed in the dome of St. Peter's Church in Rome in large letters.

The disciple interpretation was advocated by Origen: "For a rock is every disciple of Christ of whom those drank who drank of the spiritual rock which followed them, 1 Corinthians 10.4, and upon every such rock is built every word of the church, and the polity in accordance with it; for in each of the perfect, who have the combination of words and deeds and thoughts which fill up the blessedness, is the church built by God" (*Commentary on the Gospel of Matthew*, Book XII.10).

The confession interpretation was a variant of Origen's view and was widespread in the postapostolic age, being advocated by Tertullian, Theodore of Mopsuestia, Ambrose, and others.[6]

The Christological interpretation was held by Augustine[7] and was "the dominant interpretation of the church in the Middle Ages" (Luz, *Matthew in History*, 60). For the following reasons, I believe it is the correct interpretation.

Semantically, every standard Gr. lexicon distinguishes between the meaning of *petros* and *petra*. *Arndt-Gingrich*, for instance, define *petra* as *rock* (7.24) and *petros* as *stone* (660). Kittel's says "The fem., petra is predominantly used in secular Gk. for a large and solid 'rock.' The masc. petros is used more for isolated rocks or small stones" (VI, 95). Robertson *says petra* is "a ledge or cliff of rock like that in 7.24. *Petros* is usually a smaller detachment of the massive ledge" (131). Alexander adamantly insists that "The classical use *of petros and petra* is entirely distinct, the latter answering to *rock and* the former to *stone*, the two being scarcely ever interchanged even by poetic licence" (439).[8] There is no rule in Gr. that precludes agreement between substantives of different genders (1 Cor. 10.4), but the use of two different forms for *rock* in v 18 implies that they should be distinguished from each other. If Christ meant to name Peter as

---

[6] Luz comments that in the disciple and confession interpretations, there was no anti-Catholic accent. "The reason for this was that the Roman interpretation of our text was so marginal and unknown that it was not necessary to be preoccupied with it" (*Matthew in History*, 59).

[7] Augustine was a "Doctor of the Church, ... a philosophical and theological genius of the first order, dominating, like a pyramid, antiquity and the succeeding ages. ... Compared with the great philosophers of past centuries and modern times, he is the equal of them all; among theologians he is undeniably the first, and such has been his influence that none of the Fathers, Scholastics, or Reformers has surpassed it" (*The Catholic Encyclopedia*, Vol. II, 1907 ed., 84).

[8] It is frequently asserted that because Jesus spoke Aramaic He used the same word for *Peter* and *rock*, since in Aramaic both are the word *kef ha*. This view is entirely hypothetical and doesn't change the fact that it is a Gr. text that we must interpret.

the *rock*, He could have simply said, "You are *Petros* and on *this petros* I will build my church," or, "You are *Petros* and on *you* I will build my church." But by using the demonstrative pronoun *this* rather than the personal pronoun *you*, He points away from Peter to another antecedent—namely, Peter's confession that Jesus is the Son of God (v 16).[9] The church is built upon *deity*, not humanity.[10] Concerning the wordplay between *petros* and *petra*, there is similarity, but there is also dissimilarity. "'*Petros* has given utterance to a *petra*, but *the petra* is not *Petros*.' The similarity is 'in the sound and general sense.' The dissimilarity is in the meaning or specific reference" (C.C. Caragounis, qtd. by Garland, 170).

Patristically, contrary to Catholic revisionism, the identification of Peter as the *rock* was a minority view in the postapostolic era. "The most elaborate examination of the opinions of the Fathers is in an Epistle by the French Roman Catholic Launoy, in which, besides the interpretation that Peter was the rock, for which he produces seventeen Patristic testimonies, he gives the interpretations that the rock was the faith which Peter confessed, supported by forty-four quotations; that the rock was Christ Himself, supported by sixteen; and that the Church was built on all the Apostles, supported by eight" (Salmon, 335). Sixty-eight of eighty-five ancient commentators (including Origen, Chrysostom, Gregory of Nyssa, Isidore of Pelusium, Cyril of Alexandria, Hilary, Theodoret, Theophanes, Theophylact, John of Damascus, Augustine, Jerome, and Gregory the Great)—80 percent—believed that *Peter was not* the rock.

Scripturally, and importantly, three considerations point to *Christ* as the *rock*. First, "if we trace the figurative use of the word 'Rock' throughout the Hebrew Scripture, we find it is never used symbolically of man, but always of God. The Hebrew word is *Tsur*, and we find it occurring at least forty times figuratively in the Old Testament. Twice it is used of false gods in Deuteronomy 32, as they are put into contrast with the Rock of Israel, Who is the living God. In every other instance the figurative use of the word applies to God" (Morgan, *Peter and the Church*, 17). "In all these places [where *rock* is used figuratively] the term is applied directly either to Jehovah or to Christ. Nor is it ever applied, even by the strongest figure, to a merely human subject. This remarkable usage is at least sufficient

---

[9] "The demonstrative pronoun 'this' logically should refer to something other than the speaker or the one spoken to and would be appropriate only if 'Jesus were speaking about Peter in the third person and not speaking directly to him'" (Garland, 170).

[10] See Campbell and Purcell, *Debate on the Roman Catholic Church*, 104.

to create a strong presumption, that the figure here is not applied to any mere man" (Alexander, 438). Second, when Peter wrote and spoke about the church's foundation, he never identified himself as the *rock*. In 1 Peter 2.4–8, for instance, he applies a catena of OT prophecies about rocks and stones exclusively to Christ (Acts 4.10–11). Third, Paul taught, *for no other foundation can anyone lay than that which is laid, which is Jesus Christ* (1 Cor. 3.11). The depiction of the apostles and prophets as the foundation of the church in Ephesians 2.20 is a metonymy—it is their inspired message, not their person or office, on which the church rests (28.19). Scriptural testimony, augmented by semantic and patristic considerations, strongly argues that the church's one foundation is Jesus Christ her Lord.

The gates of Hades (11.23) *shall not prevail* (*katischuō*, to have the upper hand, be superior to, stronger than) *against it* assures us that death will not stop Christ from building His church. *Hades,* the place of the dead, should be distinguished from *gehenna,* which refers to the fate of the wicked. The death of a leader often signals the end of a movement, but not for Christ's movement; death would neither stop Him from building it (vv 21–22; Acts 2.24,27), nor spell defeat for those whose lives are predicated on Him (vv 24–27) for, paradoxically, the church could not be built without His death (v 21)! *Gates of Hades* was a standard expression for death or mortal danger (Isa. 38.10; 3 Macc. 5.51, *and cried out in a very loud voice, imploring the Ruler over every power to manifest himself and be merciful to them, as they stood now at the gates of death*). The disciples would forget this promise in the coming weeks, but neither their failing nor Christ's death would stop what heaven was doing.

16.19 And I will give you the keys of the kingdom of heaven, and whatever you bind on earth will be bound in heaven, and whatever you loose on earth will be loosed in heaven."

Entering a building often requires a key, and to Peter (*you*, sing.) would be given *the keys of the kingdom of heaven*. In popular lore, Peter is often pictured as the gatekeeper at the pearly gates of heaven, but his gatekeeping duties were earthly, corresponding to the manager of a building.

The figures of *binding* and *loosing* were rooted in Jewish thought. According to C. P. S. Clarke in *Church History from Nero to Constantine*, "The power to bind and loose … was the regular Jewish expression for making the rules or bye-laws of the synagogue—in other words, for legislation" (xiv). The terms were sometimes used in a judicial sense meaning to *condemn* or *acquit*. But more commonly, they were used by rabbis meaning to *forbid* or *permit*, referring to what was Scriptural or unScriptural. In 23.13, Jesus accuses the scribes and Pharisees of closing (forbidding people to enter) the kingdom (*you lock people out of the kingdom*, BECK), which in Luke 11.52 becomes: *you have taken away the key of knowledge.* Pharisaic interpretations of the Law kept people from the kingdom (15.1–20), but, by contrast, Peter would use the gospel to open the way into the kingdom. Peter showed people how to enter the kingdom (Acts 2), shut the door to the unrighteous (Acts 5), and opened the door to Gentiles (Acts 10). *The keys of the kingdom* refer to the knowledge revealed through Peter and the apostles that instructed men in the nature of the kingdom (13.11), including the knowledge of how to enter it.

Possessing the *keys of the kingdom* didn't mean Peter (or anyone else) had arbitrary authority to create, impose, or define kingdom law. The will of God is kingdom law (6.10). The grammatical form of the verbs *bind* (*deō*) and *loose* (*luō*) is future perfect passive, which are translated in the NASB as *whatever you shall bind on earth shall have been bound in heaven, and whatever you shall loose on earth shall have been loosed in heaven.* This statement "takes away the responsibility of human choice, and therefore uninformed choice, and represents St. Peter as acting in these solemn binding and loosing matters always under the infallible guidance of the Holy Spirit" (N. Turner, quoted by Morris, 426; 1 Cor. 2.9–10). We are to only teach on earth what God has willed in heaven (6.10).

Though it might seem from v 19 that to Peter alone was given the keys to the kingdom, in 18.18, *binding* and *loosing* authority is extended to believers in local churches.[11]

16.20 Then He commanded His disciples that they should tell no one that He was Jesus the Christ.

This section ends abruptly with Christ's command that the disciples not tell anyone that He is the Christ (v 16). Though the disciples understood this truth, as v 21 shows, they didn't understand it to where they were ready to expound it. The time would come when Christ would send them out to proclaim Him as Lord (28.19–20), but until then, they needed to keep their mouths shut and their eyes and ears open.

---

[11] Here, the *binding* and *loosing* refer to teaching; in 18.18, to judging.

16.21–27.66: Christ Builds His Church
16.21–20.34: Preparing for the Cross
16.21–17.21: The First Prediction

Notes

From that time on marks a turning point in the narrative. "On the deep level of the Matthean story we have now entered the realm of the church" (Luz II, 378), and a major truth to be grasped by the church is the centrality of the cross. F. F. Bruce makes the valuable observation that "in the Synoptic record, it was not until the apostles, in the face of all appearances to the contrary confessed [Jesus] spontaneously as Messiah, through the lips of their spokesman Peter, that Jesus 'began to teach them that the Son of man must suffer many things" (*Gospel of John*, 78). It was only those whose faith and allegiance were beyond question that Christ admitted to the inner mystery of His person and purpose. In this section, which con-centrates on Christ and His disciples (16.21–20.34), Christ's enemies appear only in 19.3, and the crowds make a substantial appearance only in 19.2 and 20.29–31.

The characterization of the Gospels as "passion narratives with an extended introduction" is accurate. The death of Jesus is referred to over 170 times in the NT. In the Gospels, the emphasis (with a few exceptions, e.g., 20.28) is on the *historical fact* of Christ's suffering; in the Epistles and the Revelation, the emphasis is on the *spiritual meaning* of His suffering. Both emphases are needed, for "the central fact in history and the life of every individual, if he but knew it, is the death of Christ" (W. Ramsay).

16.21 From that time Jesus began to show to His disciples that He must go to Jerusalem, and suffer many things from the elders and chief priests and scribes, and be killed, and be raised the third day.

This verse helps explain v 20, with Jesus looking ahead to the central event of history—His death and resurrection—about which the disciples were woefully ignorant.

Though previously hinted at (v 4, 9.15, 12.40), for the first time, Jesus speaks openly about His approaching death (17.9,12, 22–23, 20.18–19,28, 21.38–39, 26.2). *Show* translates the relatively rare word *deiknuō* (to expose to the eyes). Christ's use of *must* (*dei*, it is necessary) indicates a divine necessity (Jn. 4.4), but one that in no way excused the Jews for their malice and murderous intent (12.14).[12,13] Christ gives five details about what *must* occur: (1) He must *go to Jerusalem*, (2) where He will *suffer many things* (3) at the hands of *the elders and chief priests and scribes*, (4) ending with Him being *killed,* and (5) then being *raised again the third day. Suffer (paschō)* was a general word for a wide variety of pains and distresses. The *elders* have appeared previously in Matthew only in 15.2; originally, they were the heads of the tribes, tribal subdivisions, cities, and families. When the Sanhedrin came into existence, prominent elders "shared with the chief priest the power of determining religious affairs and, if necessary, of expulsion from the synagogue" (*New Bible Dictionary,* 314; on chief priests and scribes, see 2.4.) As noted in v 1, mutual enemies will bury the hatchet long enough to kill Christ, and the Lord didn't want His disciples in any doubt about what lay ahead. But He assured them that the *gates of Hades* would not prevail for He would rise from the dead (vv 4,18, 12.40). Christ never spoke of His death without speaking of His resurrection, but the disciples consistently missed this.

16.22 Then Peter took Him aside and began to rebuke Him, saying, "Far be it from You, Lord; this shall not happen to You!"

Peter *took Jesus aside*[14] and *rebuked (epitimaō,* to chide, fault, reprove) *Him saying, "Far be it from You, Lord,"* concluding with the double negative *not never shall this be to You.* Translators differ on how the Gr. for *far be it from you* should be rendered, but most take it as a mild form of *God forbid!* or *may God prevent it!* We can only speculate about Peter's reasoning, but two possibilities are that he thought Christ was being pessimistic,[15] or that he was pained at the thought of his Lord suffering injustice. Peter illustrates how Satan can co-opt the goodness of love for an evil purpose.

---

[12] In Gr. literature, *must* was used of blind, impersonal fate, but for Christ, it referred to the course determined for Him by God (20.28, 26.28).

[13] Jesus was active in accomplishing His death at Jerusalem, but the passive verbs He uses point to the actions of others, whether the Jews, Romans, or God.

[14] The only known examples of this phrase, as cited in *Arndt-Gingrich,* are here and Mark 8.32.

[15] "Contemporary Jewish thought found no reference to a suffering Messiah in the Hebrew Scriptures, and the idea is absent from the vast literature of Jewish apocrypha and pseudepigrapha, including the Dead Sea Scrolls. Nothing in their background prepared Jesus' disciples for the notion that Israel's champion should suffer a shameful death. The Messiah was expected to inflict suffering and death on Israel's enemies and on the wicked within Israel, not to experience it himself" (Hare, 194).

16.23 But He turned and said to Peter, "Get behind Me, Satan! You are an offense to Me, for you are not mindful of the things of God, but the things of men."

A dear friend becomes a dire foe. With a scathing response reminiscent of the third temptation (4.10), Christ turns His back on Peter and says, *Get behind me, Satan.* The cross was so critical, so central to God's eternal plan that to oppose it, for even the best of reasons, was to side with the devil.[16] Peter the *rock* (v 18) had become a rock of *offense* for his suggestion was an unwitting attempt to thwart Christ's mission. But as in ch 4, so here: Christ resisted the devil (Jas. 4.7). Christ's cross wouldn't crush Him, it would lift Him (Jn. 12.32)!

DISCIPLESHIP, 16.24–28

16.24 Then Jesus said to His disciples, "If anyone desires to come after Me, let him deny himself, and take up his cross, and follow Me.

Salvation is free, but discipleship is costly (8.22). *Then,* after summarily rejecting Peter's protest, Jesus continues His shock therapy by listing three implications for *anyone who desires to come after* Him. Here, the Lord unpacks what it takes to enter the narrow gate (5.13). First, a man must *deny himself,* which is an idiom originated by Christ. The verb used (*aparneomai*) basically means to say "No" — in this context, not to things but to self. "We all know what Peter's Christ-denial was: I know not the man. This too must be involved in self-denial! We must learn to say of ourselves: I know not the man!" (McGuiggan, *Revelation*, 178). If confessing Christ is one side of the coin, *self-denial* is the other. Saying "No" to self is more than merely practicing Christian rules; it involves a complete reorientation of life, a shift from self to God as the ruling principle of life.

Second, a man must *take up his cross,* which interprets and intensifies *self-denial.* Biblically, *cross-bearing* refers *not* to enduring the discomforts and hurts of life, but to *self-sacrifice,* choosing death — killing sin (cf. 5.29–30) — as a way of life (20.20–28; Rom. 6.6; Gal. 5.24; Col. 3.5). There is only one way to a crown (19.28) and that is by a cross. Third, a man must *follow* (9.9). Christ uses a present imperative that means *keep on following* (1 Pet. 2.21). The way of Christ isn't easy, but the highest nobility of which man is capable is to accept the suffering involved and to freely choose to follow the Lord.

---

[16] Peter "did not realize that he was asking for his own eternal damnation" (Hendriksen, 656).

16.25 For whoever desires to save his life will lose it, but whoever loses his life for My sake will find it.

The most unforgettable people are those who forget themselves. Only by *losing* life—by self-denial, cross-bearing, and following (v 24)—can one save life. To *save life*—reject self-denial, cross-bearing, and following—is to lose one's life in every way that counts. For the self-denier, cross-bearer, and follower, however, *death shall not prevail*. Far from destroying a man (or the church), death is how victory comes. Because the world defines sacrificial living as wasting life, self-preservation takes a high priority. Resurrection (v 21), however, completely changes this equation and makes the way of the cross the way to life eternal (7.13–14; Gal. 2.20).

16.26 For what profit is it to a man if he gains the whole world, and loses his own soul? Or what will a man give in exchange for his soul?

Two rhetorical questions drive home the paradox (v 25). Suppose a man were to gain the whole world—would that compensate (*profit, ōpheleō*, to assist, be useful, advantageous) for the loss of his soul? Never! *Soul* (*psuchē*, translated *life* in v 25) "had a wide range of meaning to the Greek; it was 'life' in all its extent, from the mere vegetative existence to the highest intellectual life. Christianity has deepened the conception by adding to the connotation of *psuchē* the spiritual life of the soul in union with Christ" (Carr, 214). One's *soul* is one's *life*—not simply earthly life, but essential, eternal life. Eternal life doesn't start at death (1 Jn. 5.13); if a man is eternal at all, he is eternal now. Let a man live as though he were not going to die, and the spiritual values of which Christ spoke—self-denial, cross-bearing, and following/obedience—take on a new importance. "One can hardly think too little of one's self. One can hardly think too much of one's soul" (G. K. Chesterton, *Orthodoxy*, 174).

16.27 For the Son of Man will come in the glory of His Father with His angels, and then He will reward each according to his works.

This is the third consecutive verse that begins with *for*, which indicates a tightly reasoned argument. There is coming a day when the loss one sustains by *saving his life* will be apparent—namely, the day when the *Son of Man* (8.20) *comes to reward each according to his works* (*praxis*, deed, behavior; Rom. 2.6; 2 Cor. 5.10). Peter confessed Jesus as the *Son of God* (v 16), but Jesus refers to Himself as the *Son of Man*, which, in Matthew, relates both to Christ's earthly situation (8.20) and to His heavenly exaltation (26.64). Understanding this is helpful when interpreting v 28.

The mention of *works* (self-denial, cross-bearing, following) recalls 7.21–27 and the truth that confession (*Lord, Lord*) without obedience (*does the will of My Father*) is useless. The references to *coming in glory* and *angels* are common prophetic symbols for divine judgment both temporal (24.30–31) and eternal (25.31). In apocalyptic language, any great intervention of God in history is regarded as a *coming*. He who lives to gain the whole world might gain it, but a temporally oriented life receives nothing further at the judgment (6.2,5,16). At the judgment, it will be those who sought heaven through self-denial, cross-bearing, and following who will be blessed beyond their ability to comprehend (19.29).

16.28 Assuredly, I say to you, there are some standing here who shall not taste death till they see the Son of Man coming in His kingdom."

Alexander calls this verse "one of the most difficult and disputed in the whole book" (446). If so, it's because of attempts to impose meanings it that do not fit the context.

On *Son of Man*, see 8.20. Verses 27 and 28 both speak of the coming of the Son of Man. *Coming* is a prophetically freighted word that speaks of divine judgment. As noted in v 27, the language there seems to point to Christ's second, final coming to judge (Heb. 9.28).

In this verse, however, Christ says that His coming would occur within the lifetime of some present: *some standing here shall not taste death till they see the Son of Man coming in His kingdom*. Because the generation alive at the time Jesus spoke these words is long gone, the coming of this verse cannot be the final coming. So, which *coming* is it?

I think the best possibility is the judgment on the Jews that occurred ca. AD 70, about forty years in the future from when Christ spoke and within the lifetime of some standing around (24.1–35; Lk. 21.20–32). In 26.64 there is another reference to a coming of Christ in judgment that also seems to refer to AD 70. Jesus will indeed judge all men at the end of time (25.31–46; Acts 17.31), but before that judgment there would be a historical judgment on Israel (23.34ff). Those not built on rock, nationally or individually, would not stand (v 18, 7.24–27).

CHAPTER 17

TRANSFIGURATION, 17.1–13

Notes

Peter spoke the *central fact* of Christianity in 16.16, but the disciples' conception of the Chrst was badly flawed—so much so, that five verses later Peter objected to the *central act* of Christianity (16.21). A larger understanding was needed, and so a greater revelation was given. Atop a mountain, Christ "opened a little of his deity and showed the divinity within" (Chrysostom). The revelation consisted of a *vision* (v 9, *horama*, "a noun used elsewhere in the New Testament [all in Acts] only for apparently 'inward' experiences," France, 262), but on this occasion it refers to an objective, empirical event. Luke says it was seen by the disciples after they had awakened from sleep (Lk. 9.32). Peter was so moved by the sight that he proposed building physical huts (v 4), and in 2 Peter 1.16–18, he affirmed the reality of the event.

The subject that alarmed the disciples—Christ's death—is discussed by Jesus, Moses, and Elijah and is characterized as a *decease* (*exodus*) that He would accomplish (*pleroō*, fulfill; Lk. 9.31). Christ was born to die; His death was the culmination of an eternal plan. "Undoubtedly the transfiguration meant much to Jesus, but it is nevertheless probable that it was chiefly an educative instrument for the benefit of the disciples. They did not need to be convinced of the divine sonship of Jesus, Peter had confessed that, and there is no indication of dissent. The need was for light on the mission of their Master, not on his person" (Harrison, 153).

This section has two parts: vv 1–9 and vv 10–13, with v 9 serving as a transitional hinge. Elements of previous scenes are recalled: the heavenly voice (3.17), a high mountain (4.8), and John the Baptist (11.12–14, 14.3–12). Other features look forward, anticipating Christ's passion. The chapter opens and ends with embarrassing statements by Peter.

17.1 Now after six days Jesus took Peter, James, and John his brother, led them up on a high mountain by themselves;

And after six days—one week after Caesarea Philippi (16.13–28)—Jesus takes Peter, James, and John with Him *up on a high mountain by themselves.*[1]

17.2 and He was transfigured before them. His face shone like the sun, and His clothes became as white as the light.

Transfigured (*metamorphoō*, changed, transformed; Rom. 12.2; 2 Cor. 3.18) means Christ's outer form changed into the appearance of a heavenly being: *His face shone like the sun* (13.43) and *His clothes became as white as the light* (28.3) "This was not a light shining upon Jesus from without. It was His deity shining forth from within. The wick of His essential deity, which from His birth had been turned down low, was suddenly turned up to burn in the brightness of His true glory" (Hobbs, 230). Thus, the three disciples *beheld His glory* (Jn. 1.14; 2 Pet. 1.16–17).

17.3 And behold, Moses and Elijah appeared to them, talking with Him.

It's often said that *Moses* and *Elijah* appear as representatives of the Law and prophets, but the text doesn't say this. And how the disciples recognized the OT figures isn't stated; possibly they overheard Christ address them by name. The departures of *Moses* and *Elijah* from this world were accomplished in unusual ways (Deut. 34; 2 Kgs. 2), but their appearance with Christ said a great deal about life beyond the grave (16.21). If men long departed could still live, maybe Christ's death wouldn't be as fatal to Him or His kingdom as His disciples feared (16.18; Lk. 24.26–27).

17.4 Then Peter answered and said to Jesus, "Lord, it is good for us to be here; if You wish, let us make here three tabernacles: one for You, one for Moses, and one for Elijah."

There are moments we want to last forever, and perhaps something like this was behind Peter's suggestion to build three *tabernacles* (*skēnē*, huts,

---

[1] Morgan notes that on the three occasions when Christ separated Peter, James, and John from the rest of the disciples, each time it was in the presence of death (26.37; Mk. 5.37). Morgan believed this was because the three needed their false notions about death corrected (*The Crises of the Christ*, 247–250). A better interpretation, I think, is that in Jairus's house, the three disciples saw Jesus power over death; on the Mount of Transfiguration, they learned He would be glorified through death, and in Gethsemane they saw Jesus surrender to death. These lessons were very important to the apostle who would be the first to die (James), the last to die (John), and one who would suffer great persecution before dying (Peter).

temporary shelters made of branches). Luke 9.33 says that Peter said this *not knowing what he said*—not realizing how preposterous it was. Peter didn't know what to say, but he said it anyway.[2]

17.5–6 While he was still speaking, behold, a bright cloud overshadowed them; and suddenly a voice came out of the cloud, saying, "This is My beloved Son, in whom I am well pleased. Hear Him!" And when the disciples heard *it*, they fell on their faces and were greatly afraid.

God interrupts Peter to interpret the significance of the event. Speaking from *a bright cloud* that *overshadowed* all, He said: *This is My beloved Son, in whom I am well-pleased. Hear Him!* Christ ranks above Moses and Elijah and is to be heeded (the tense of the verb is linear: *keep on listening to Him!* wms), believed, and obeyed (even if the disciples disagreed with what He said, 16.21). The theophany overwhelms the disciples, and in a natural reaction to the supernatural, they fall on their faces in fear (8.25–27, 14.26–33).

17.7–8 But Jesus came and touched them and said, "Arise, and do not be afraid." When they had lifted up their eyes, they saw no one but Jesus only.

While still terrified with their faces to the ground, the three feel a touch (8.3) and hear the words *Arise, and do not be afraid.* When they open their eyes, Moses and Elijah are gone, and they see Jesus in His human form. The three could not bear the power of unmediated deity, but the appearance of the man, Christ Jesus, reassured them.

17.9 Now as they came down from the mountain, Jesus commanded them, saying, "Tell the vision to no one until the Son of Man is risen from the dead."

On the way down the mountain, Christ puts the disciples under a temporary gag order (16.20), telling them not to speak of what they had seen until after *the Son of Man is risen from the dead.* The transfiguration should have given the disciples a better understanding of Christ's mission, but as subsequent events show, they were slow to see its implications.

---

[2] I think we're guilty of the same in our speculations on various topics for which we have no point of contact. As an example: "I heard NT Wright, following others, speak of "heaven" as "God's space". I think we only talk that way because we don't know what we're talking about but we're not able to stay silent" (Jim McGuiggan, "Why I Thought I Was Going to Heaven").

They needed more instruction and experience (cf. vv 24–27) before they could be entrusted with a great commission.

17.10 And His disciples asked Him, saying, "Why then do the scribes say that Elijah must come first?"

Elijah's appearance (vv 3,4) prompts a question about the Jewish expectation that Elijah would precede the Messiah (Mal. 4.5), for it seemed to the three that the Messiah (16.16) had preceded Elijah. Were the scribes wrong in what they taught about Elijah?

17.11 Jesus answered and said to them, "Indeed, Elijah is coming first and will restore all things.

The scribes had it right: *Elijah is coming first* to do his work of spiritual *restoration* (*apokathistēmi*, to reconstitute, restore to a former state, 12.13) prophesized in Malachi 4.6.

17.12 But I say to you that Elijah has come already, and they did not know him but did to him whatever they wished. Likewise the Son of Man is also about to suffer at their hands."

Not only would Elijah come first, but he had come first—John the Baptist was the Elijah predicted by Malachi (11.4). Though many thought John a prophet (14.5), his Elijah role wasn't recognized by the Jews and *they did to him whatever they wished*—an allusion to his death (14.1–12), for which God held the nation accountable (23.34–36).

What happened to John would happen to Christ; His path involved death, and the disciples needed to *hear* (v 5)—understand—and believe Jesus on this, just as they believed what He said about John being Elijah.

17.13 Then the disciples understood that He spoke to them of John the Baptist.

They understood what Jesus said about John, but understanding what He said about Himself would take considerably longer."

THE DISCIPLES' FAILURE, 17.14–21

Notes

This section consists of three parts: frustration (vv 14–17), miracle (v 18), and explanation (vv 19–21). The teaching turns on the contrast between *could not* (vv 16,19) and *nothing impossible* (v 20).

Several elements recall the incident with the Canaanite woman (15.21–28): a parent pleads for a demonized child, a parent addresses Jesus as *Lord*, there is a complication involving the disciples, and Christ casts out a demon. A contrast is that the Canaanite woman is praised for her *great faith* (15.28), whereas the father in this story confesses his struggling faith (Mk. 9.24, *Lord, I believe; help my unbelief!*).

17.14–16 And when they had come to the multitude, a man came to Him, kneeling down to Him and saying, "Lord, have mercy on my son, for he is an epileptic and suffers severely; for he often falls into the fire and often into the water. So I brought him to Your disciples, but they could not cure him."

A scene of frustration and defeat awaits Jesus when He *came down from the mountain* (v 9). A man respectfully approaches, *kneels*, calls Him *Lord* (15.22), and asks for *mercy* for his son. *Epileptic* (*lunatic*, KJV) translates the rare verb *seleniazomai* (to be affected by the moon; in the NT, only here and 4.24), but the text makes clear that the boy's problems were the result of *demon* possession (v 18) rather than mere physical illness. *Seleniazomai* reflected the popular belief that seizures were caused by the moon goddess Selene; Matthew uses the word to summarize the symptoms (seizures) rather than the cause. The boy's condition was serious (*suffers severely*) — when the demon stirred, the boy might collapse and fall into whatever was nearby, including *fire* and *water*.

The most distressing aspect of the story is that when the man asked the nine disciples who had remained behind for help, they utterly failed, despite having been given power over demons by the Lord (10.1,8).

17.17 Then Jesus answered and said, "O faithless and perverse generation, how long shall I be with you? How long shall I bear with you? Bring him here to Me."

With a stinging rebuke, Christ criticizes His disciples for their failure. The adjectives *faithless and perverse* (*diastreophō*, crooked, corrupt) are sharp; if Christ didn't hesitate to call Peter *Satan* (16.23), neither would He hesitate to accurately characterize the others. The mention of *generation* reveals the truth that disciples often reflect the spirit of the age (12.39; Rom. 12.2). Two *how long?* questions express the Lord's irritation. *How long shall I be with you?* may mean that the time was growing short for the disciples to be with Christ and it was imperative that they understand what He was telling them.[3]

17.18 And Jesus rebuked the demon, and it came out of him; and the child was cured from that very hour.

After rebuking His disciples, Christ casts out the demon (this is the last of Christ's exorcisms in Matthew), and the boy is healed.

17.19–21 Then the disciples came to Jesus privately and said, "Why could we not cast it out?" So Jesus said to them, "Because of your unbelief; for assuredly, I say to you, if you have faith as a mustard seed, you will say to this mountain, 'Move from here to there,' and it will move; and nothing will be impossible for you. However, this kind does not go out except by prayer and fasting."

The disciples are puzzled by their failure and *privately* ask about it (vv 16,19). Christ tells them they failed because they *believed not*.[4] On other occasions, the disciples were marked by *little faith* (8.26, 14.31, 16.8), but here, they lacked faith entirely, for had they possessed even a smidgen of it (*as a mustard seed*), they would have dispatched the demon. Lacking faith, they failed publicly and embarrassingly.

What constituted their *unbelief*? It wasn't atheistic in the least, and it wasn't for a lack of trying (vv 16,19, 7.22). A more likely explanation is that their earlier success (Lk. 10.17) had given them a sense of self-sufficiency; they tried to exorcise the demon without reliance on God.[5] The power is of God (6.13), and their failure to access His power through prayer constituted their *unbelief*. Trusting in themselves rather than God, they were unable to move the demonic *mountain*. When used metaphorically, a *mountain* is an obstacle illusion—to think that any problem we encounter cannot be resolved or surmounted is a delusion (14.13–21, 15.32–38). If we *trust* God, we will *pray* to Him, giving Him an opportunity to unleash power (7.11) on the problem (Jas. 5.13–18).[6] But prayer, which is an expression of dependence on God, must be sincere, even to the point of

---

[3] "What must our Lord feel as He looks at powerless believers today?" (Wiersbe, *Meet Your King*, 120).

[4] Paradoxically, the father's unbelief did not preclude his son from being healed, but the disciples' unbelief precluded them from effecting the healing.

[5] A malady from which Samson suffered (Judg. 16.19–21).

[6] "Shortly after I became a Christian," wrote Howard Hendricks, "someone wrote in the flyleaf of my Bible this couplet: 'When I try, I fail. When I trust, He succeeds'" (*Standing*

fasting (6.16)—forgoing other activities—in order to bring a matter to God. When properly related to God through trust, prayer, and fasting, *nothing will be impossible for you*. This isn't a guarantee that circumstances will change; it may be that we need to change. But with God's help, we will be able to meet whatever comes our way.

This kind does not go out except by offers some insight into the nature of demons and problems. Some demons were, apparently, more insidious and resilient than others and could not be exorcised casually. And so it is with problems; some are easily handled; others are more entrenched and *impossible* for us to resolve on our own (12.29). It is when we encounter *this kind* that our need for God becomes apparent (Jn. 15.5). Problems persist not for lack of divine power but for lack of human prayer. We plan, we labor, we work; we do everything except pray. Consequently, we have not, because we ask not.

Excursus on the Impossible

Just because the age of miracles has passed doesn't mean the age of doing the impossible has passed. In life, we encounter situations beyond our ability to affect, control, or change. But what is *impossible* to us isn't to God. We are to pray about impossible things—a child imprisoned in sin, incurable illness, the opening of a closed heart, for rulers to maintain the peace (1 Tim. 2.2), etc.—in the confidence that though we are insufficient, God is able (14.16–21, 15.33–38; Dan. 3.17). God can work providentially without working miraculously (vv 27). With miracles, God worked supernaturally and directly; with providence, He works naturally and indirectly. And what He does providentially may be as unlikely or unexpected as what He did miraculously. Unbelief doesn't ask for the impossible, but faith does; it makes extraordinary claims on God's power. If we're unwilling to ask God for the impossible, then perhaps we, too, have been shaped by the perversity of our generation.

17.22–20.16: The Second Prediction

17.22–23 Now while they were staying in Galilee, Jesus said to them, "The Son of Man is about to be betrayed into the hands of men, and they will kill Him, and the third day He will be raised up." And they were exceedingly sorrowful.

Together, 50).

Christ's final journey to Jerusalem has begun. He and the disciples have left *Caesarea Philippi* (16.13) and returned to Galilee, and for a second time (16.21), He predicts His death. Instead of *must* (16.21), He now says *is about to be*, indicating nearness rather than necessity. *The Son of Man* will *be betrayed into the hands of men*—Matthew has already alerted us to this treachery (10.4).[7] Despite repeated attempts to reassure the disciples with the promise of His resurrection on *the third day*, the disciples are *exceedingly sorrowful* (*crushed with grief*, WMS), which indicates that they are still not *hearing* what Jesus was saying (v 5). Their presuppositions about the Messiah didn't allow them to entertain thoughts of His death (Mk. 4.20; Jn. 12.34).[8]

THE TEMPLE TAX, 17.24–27
Notes

This section contains two parts, beginning with a question some tax collectors ask Peter (vv 24–25a), followed by a question Jesus asked Peter (vv 25b–27). The extraordinary miracle in this section should have also served to ease the disciples' fears regarding Christ's predictions of His death.

17.24–25a When they had come to Capernaum, those who received the *temple* tax came to Peter and said, "Does your Teacher not pay the *temple* tax?" He said, "Yes."

This is the fourth of five Matthean scenes involving Peter (14.28). When Jesus and the disciples returned *to Capernaum*, they who collected *the temple tax* (*kēnsos*, a tax or the coin with which the tax was paid) ask Peter if his *Teacher* (Christ) paid the half-shekel tax imposed on every Jewish male, twenty years old and up, for temple upkeep (Ex. 30.11–16). It is uncertain whether this was a one-time or annual tax.[9] The question seems as if it might be setting up a controversy, but nothing sinister follows, and without hesitating, Peter answers *Yes*.

---

[7] In the NT, several disparate parties are said to have betrayed or delivered (*paradidōmi*) Jesus to death: Judas (obviously, 10.4), but also the Jewish people (Acts 3.13), the chief priests and elders (27.2), and Pilate (27.26). The most amazing revelation of all is that *paradidōmi* is used to describe God's giving of His Son (Rom. 8.32) and Christ's giving of Himself (Gal. 2.20).

[8] "He sugared the bitter pill of his death with the sweetness of his assured resurrection" (Spurgeon).

[9] Most of our information on the collection of this tax comes from the Mishnah tractate *Sheqalim*.

17.25b And when he had come into the house, Jesus anticipated him, saying, "What do you think, Simon? From whom do the kings of the earth take customs or taxes, from their sons or from strangers?"

Peter probably thought no more about the matter until Christ probes his understanding. After entering a *house* (Peter's? 8.14, 13.1,36), Jesus asks Peter: *From whom do the kings of the earth take customs or taxes, from their own sons or from strangers?*

17.26 Peter said to Him, "From strangers." Jesus said to him, "Then the sons are free.

It was an easy question to answer: rulers tax their subjects (*strangers*) not their sons (*the sons are free*). So if Christ is God's Son, as Peter confessed (v 5, 16.16), why did Peter give the answer He gave?

It was because Peter wasn't thinking. The contradiction involved in his answers hadn't dawned on him anymore than had his silly proposal in v 4.

17.27 Nevertheless, lest we offend them, go to the sea, cast in a hook, and take the fish that comes up first. And when you have opened its mouth, you will find a piece of money; take that and give it to them for Me and you."

Christ was indeed God's Son (v 5), but He lived as a servant (5.40, 16.24; Phil. 2.6). This scene illustrates this and becomes a preview of what He would do in Jerusalem, where He would give up His rights not just as God's Son (26.53), but to justice and life itself.

How payment of the tax is arranged is fascinating. Blomberg calls this incident "the strangest in Matthew's Gospel" (271), but is it any stranger than the scene that opens this chapter? This incident, every bit as much as the transfiguration, was a demonstration of deity, for deity alone is sufficient to explain what happened.

Peter the fisherman is told to go fishing. That Christ, for the only time in the NT, uses the word for *hook* (rather than *net*) is significant—He is increasing the odds *against* the possibility of the event He will describe; the odds of catching a single fish with a coin in its mouth are much less than the odds of a fish with a coin in its mouth being caught in a net. But impossibilities disappear when God steps in (v 20). Christ tells Peter that the first fish he catches will have in its mouth *a piece of money* (*statēr*, a silver coin sometimes called the *tetradrachmos*, four drachma), which would cover the tax owed by Peter and Himself. By knowing that Peter would catch a single fish that would have a coin in its mouth that would be the exact amount needed to pay two temple tax bills, etc., Christ gave a memorable demonstration of His divine omniscience and omnipotence at a time when the disciples needed reassurance that He was, indeed, the *Son of God* (vv 22–23).

CHAPTER 18

DISCOURSE ON BROTHERLY LOVE, 18.1–35
Give No Offense, 18.1–14

Notes

This is the fourth discourse in Matthew ending with the formula: *and it came to pass, when Jesus had finished these sayings* (7.28, 11.1, 13.53, 19.1, 26.1). The subject is brotherly love—the disciples understood that Christ came first, but they didn't understand that everyone else came next. In vv 3–4, Christ identifies the essential quality in brotherliness, and then shows that people who possess this quality neither *give offense* (vv 1–14) nor *take offense* (vv 15–35), Relationships involve at least two, and sometimes we have to live together before we are fit to live with. To appropriate an idea intellectually may happen relatively quickly, but to appropriate an idea practically in our thoughts, feelings, and behavior, which have long been under the dominion of of sin, takes longer. Humility is what makes us fit to live with; love holds us together during and after the process.

18.1 At that time the disciples came to Jesus, saying, "Who then is greatest in the kingdom of heaven?"

At that time provides a timeframe (3.1, 12.1, 14.1). Christ has spoken of a cross (16.24), but the disciples dream of crowns and ask, *Who then is greatest in the kingdom of heaven?* It was a question they wouldn't have asked if they were imbued with humility. By *who*, they meant, *who within our group*; by *greatest*, they mean who would be given the most authority in Christ's government (viceroy, ambassador, etc.). Christ uses their question to again instruct them in the lowliness that characterizes His kingdom (11.28–30).

18.2–3 Then Jesus called a little child to Him, set him in the midst of them, and said, "Assuredly, I say to you, unless you are converted and become as little children, you will by no means enter the kingdom of heaven.

What Jesus did and said had to jolt (insult?) the disciples. He *called a little child* and *set him in the midst of them, and said, "Assuredly, I say to you, unless you are converted and become as little children, you will by no means enter the kingdom of heaven."* The goal for a follower of Christ is to achieve a childlike spirit, which, for most, involves a change of character so radical that it requires a *conversion* (*strephō*, to turn, reverse; a synonym for *repent*). The disciples' question showed they did not have a child's attitude.[1]

Historically, *become as little children* has been a blank slate on which commentators have filled in their own ideas, not of what little children are *like*, but of *what they should be like*—the *ideal* child. "Every age to a great degree has read into the text its own understanding of what a child is" (Luz II, 427). Most commentators say that to *become as a little child* means to be innocent, gentle, simple, etc. Little children "follow their father, love their mother, do not know how to think evil of their fellow humans, have no interest in wealth, are not impudent, do not hate, do not lie, believe what they are told, and regard whatever they hear as true."[2]

18.4 Therefore whoever humbles himself as this little child is the greatest in the kingdom of heaven.

Christ explains what He meant by *little children*. *Whoever* is here a true universal—everyone without exception. *Humbles* translates a word that indicates a willingness to put one's self at the bottom (*tepeinoō*, to make low), "to be nothing" (Andrew Murray, *Like Christ*, 140). In Graeco-Roman society, children had no legal standing. *Paidion*, translated *child*, was also used for *slave*. Children were not considered full humans but incomplete beings who needed to learn and mature. To become a little child thus meant to exchange position and standing for insignificance and powerlessness. Two Gentiles in this Gospel illustrate the idea Christ has in mind. The first is the centurion who said, *Lord, I am not worthy that You should come under my roof* (8.8); the second is the Canaanite woman who said, *Truth, Lord: yet the dogs eat of the crumbs which fall from their masters' table* (15.27, KJV). Because they thought themselves *least*, Christ thought their faith *great* (8.10, 15.28).

Philippians 2.3–8 is undoubtedly the greatest passage in the Epistles exegeting kingdom humility. *Let nothing be done through selfish ambition or conceit, but in lowliness of mind let each esteem another better than himself*

---

[1] *Becoming a little child* is the next step after one is *born again* (Jn. 3.3).

[2] Hilary of Poitiers, a doctor of the Roman Catholic Church, qtd. by Luz II, 427.

(v 3). It was by such self-abasement, making himself nothing, that Saul of Tarsus went from being *advanced in the Jews' religion* (Gal. 1.14, ASV) to regarding himself as the *chief of sinners* (1 Tim. 1.15) and *less than the least of all saints* (Eph. 3.8).

The kingdom doesn't operate by worldly standards (20.25–28); it isn't for the *wise and prudent* (arrogant know-it-alls) but for *babes* (11.25), *little children*, who are lowly in heart (11.29).[3]

18.5 Whoever receives one little child like this in My name receives Me.
To drain one's self of all pride is to be like Christ who *emptied Himself* (Phil. 2.7), and to embrace the nothings of this world is to *receive* (*dechomai*, take by the hand, show hospitality, grant fellowship) Jesus (25.31–46).

The fourth Matthean discourse thus begins like the first, with a call to a radically different life (5.3). Believers are to orient themselves down, not up. Kingdom greatness involves lowliness, scorn, humility, and service (20.25), not power, influence, and prestige.

18.6 Whoever causes one of these little ones who believe in Me to sin, it would be better for him if a millstone were hung around his neck, and he were drowned in the depth of the sea.
In a selfish world, it is the nothings who are exploited, actively and passively. Pride has no problem sinning against the insignificant, whether by injuring or ignoring. And such unloving behavior can cause a little one to sin. *Whoever* (again, a true universal) causes a little one to sin commits a sin so egregious that *it would be better for him* (the offender) *if a millstone were hung around his neck, and he were drowned in the depth of the sea.* Millstone (*mulos onikos*, a donkey stone) refers to the larger upper grindstone on a mill that was turned by a donkey, horse, or slaves. Shapes varied, but *millstones* were always large, heavy, and solid. Every man is ultimately responsible for his actions (16.27), but we can adversely affect the actions of others (Lk. 15.8). They who contribute to another's sin deserve to be put in a concrete overcoat and drowned at

---

[3] In Phil. 2.3, *tepeinoō* appears in the phrase *lowliness of mind*, which Barclay contrasts with personal prestige. "It is in many ways true to say that prestige is for many people an even greater temptation than wealth. To be admired, to be respected, to have a platform seat, to have one's opinion sought, to be known by name and appearance, to be listened to, to have a certain degree of fame, and even to be flattered, are for many people most desirable things. But the aim of the Christian is not self-display, but self-obliteration" (*The Letters to the Philippians, Colossians, and Thessalonians*, 39–40).

sea—a gruesome fate for one who contributes to the eternal destruction of the vulnerable (*little ones, mikros,* small, little; Rom. 14.15).

18.7 Woe to the world because of offenses! For offenses must come, but woe to that man by whom the offense comes!

Disciples are to *give no offense* (*skandalizō,* to ensnare, *cause to sin*; the root of this word occurs six times in vv 6–9). Love doesn't help another sin; it doesn't push one towards hell, and a double *woe* (11.21) is pronounced on those who do. *Offenses* (v 5) refers to actions that encourage sin. In a sin-cursed world, *offenses must come*—in various ways men will promote sin in others t(13.40–43). Such can happen even in the church—where you'd least expect it (Eph. 6.12).

18.8–9 If your hand or foot causes you to sin, cut it off and cast *it* from you. It is better for you to enter into life lame or maimed, rather than having two hands or two feet, to be cast into the everlasting fire. And if your eye causes you to sin, pluck it out and cast *it* from you. It is better for you to enter into life with one eye, rather than having two eyes, to be cast into hell fire.

Life is a struggle, and it may be that to survive, some things must be relinquished so that others can be gained and kept. Temporal losses, however, are nothing when seen from the perspective of eternity.

The hyperbole of 5.29–30 reappears, but this time with a different application. In the Sermon on the Mount, the figure of self-amputation was used in a sexual context; here, it involves anything that prompts another to sin. The antecedent of the second person possessive pronouns (*your*) isn't clear (at least not to me): is Christ warning the *offender* who might tempt another to sin (v 6) or is He warning the *little one* who might be tempted to sin? We need not decide, for the principle applies to both. Whatever tempts us to sin by hurting another is to be dealt with ruthlessly. To Christ, the soul is of supreme value (10.28); so much so, that any sacrifice necessary to save it eternally should be made. In sinning, we are playing with *hell fire.* On *everlasting,* see 19.29.

18.10 Take heed that you do not despise one of these little ones, for I say to you that in heaven their angels always see the face of My Father who is in heaven.

Do not despise one of these little ones is the attitude behind offending a *little one* (v 6, 5.21ff). The verb *kataphroneō* is weaker than *skandalizō* and carries the nuance of *to disregard* or *not be concerned with.* In any group, especially among those who have made themselves nothing, there are those easily overlooked. But Christ insists that no one be unnoticed, unattended, or undervalued; we are to make ourselves insignificant, but no one should be insignificant to us (1 Cor. 12.21–23).

Three propositions expand Christ's teaching. The first is that *little ones* have friends in high places. The mention of *their angels* has generated centuries of speculation about *guardian angels*, but Christ says nothing further about this. *Angels* who *see the face of My Father* is a figure from a royal court (2 Kgs. 25.19; Est. 1.14, 4.11) that signified access to and familiarity with the king. The point is that if angels who enjoy direct fellowship with God have interest in the insignificant, shouldn't we also?[4]

Excursus on Guardian Angels

Belief in guardian angels has a long history in Gentile and Jewish traditions. Among the ancients, the Persians called them *fravashis*, the Romans called them the *genius* (a spiritual entity that would follow each man from the hour of his birth until the day he died), and the Greeks called them the *daimon.* "The idea that each individual has a personal guardian angel [became] widespread for the first time in rabbinic Judaism" (Luz II, 441). The Roman Catholic Church affirms the existence of guardian angels in its *Cathechism* 336: "From its beginning until death, human life is surrounded by their [angels'] watchful care and intercession. 'Beside each believer stands an angel as protector and shepherd leading him to life.'" The Reformation, however, for the most part, rejected this view.

Matthew 18.10, Acts 12.15, Hebrews 1.14, and other passages indicate that Christians are the object of angelic attention. See especially the entirety of Psalm 91, the passage quoted by Satan in 4.6, which says as much about the *protection* angels provide believers as any passage in Scripture. I would caution that any view one forms about angelic protection must be balanced by the paradox of Luke 21.16,18 where *not a hair of the believer's head is lost*, even as family members hand them over to be put to death.

---

[4] "It is a serious thing to live in a society of possible gods and goddesses, to remember that the dullest and most uninteresting person you can talk to may one day be a creature which, if you saw it now, you would be strongly tempted to worship. In the light of [this] overwhelming [possibility], it is with the awe and circumspection proper to them, that we should conduct all our dealings with one another, all friendships, all loves, all play, all politics. There are no *ordinary* people. You have never talked to a mere mortal" (C. S. Lewis, *The Weight of Glory: And Other Addresses*).

There is no doubt that the Bible teaches the existence of angels and that they serve mankind in various ways, but modern doctrines of *angelology* and *guardian angels* are highly speculative and outrun the Biblical evidence. "Nowhere in Scripture or Jewish tradition of the NT period," writes Carson, "is there any suggestion that there is one angel for one person" (401).

18.11–13 For the Son of Man has come to save that which was lost. What do you think? If a man has a hundred sheep, and one of them goes astray, does he not leave the ninety-nine and go to the mountains to seek the one that is straying? And if he should find it, assuredly, I say to you, he rejoices more over that *sheep* than over the ninety-nine that did not go astray.

Second, *little ones* are so important to *the Son of Man* (8.20, 16.27–28) that He came to *save* them (1.21). To underscore this, Christ tells a story about a *sheep gone astray*, a common occurrence with which His listeners would have been familiar (*goes astray/straying* appears three times in this paragraph). To get at its emotional depth, consider these lines from Fosdick: "When a mother prays for her wayward son, no words can make clear the vivid reality of her supplications. Her love pours itself out in insistent demand that her boy must not be lost. She is sure of his value, with which no outward thing is worthy to be compared, and of his possibilities which no sin of his can ever make her doubt. She will not give him up. She follows him through his abandonment down to the gates of death; and if she loses him through death into the mystery beyond, she still prays on in secret, with intercessions which she may not dare to utter, that wherever in the moral universe he may be, God will reclaim him. ... whether that mother has ever argued out the theory or not, she still prays on. Her intercession is the utterance of her life; it is *love on its knees*" (Fosdick, *The Meaning of Prayer*, 191).

The story is introduced by the question *What do you think?* (Christ expects us to think, to use our mind) followed by two conditional clauses. The first, *if a man has a hundred sheep, and one of them goes astray*, is followed by a rhetorical question, *does he not leave the ninety-nine and go into the mountains to seek the one that is straying?* Yes! A single sheep is important enough that when one *strays* (*planaō*, planet, wander) away, the shepherd's entire routine is altered. Though only a single sheep is missing, it becomes a priority and the shepherd leaves the flock to find it. To *stray* is to wander from Christ and into to sin (v 11). As the next clause indicates, eternal loss (v 8, *everlasting fire*; v 9, *hell fire*; v 14, *perish*) results if the lamb doesn't return to the fold.

If he should find it,[5] the shepherd's joy is greater for the one than for the ninety-nine who didn't stray (Lk. 15.22–32). This wasn't said to devalue the ninety-nine but to stress the value of the one.[6]

Christ's love insists that little ones not be lost. He is sure of their value, and no sin they commit can make Him doubt their value. He will not give them up but will follow them in their straying to the gates of death. In Luke 19.10, this language refers to unsaved sinners, but here, it is believers (little ones) who wander into sin (vv 6,8). What changes might occur in our churches about those who have "fallen away" if we viewed them as does the Lord.

It's worth mentioning that this section is not addressed to shepherds or elders of the church as a distinct group, but to disciples in general; every disciple is to lovingly value every other disciple.

18.14 Even so it is not the will of your Father who is in heaven that one of these little ones should perish.

The third argument is that *it is not the will of your Father that one of them perish*. The *will of the Father* recalls 7.21 and its stress on obedience as a condition for salvation. Because it's not God's will that little ones *perish* (*apollumi*, to destroy, abolish, ruin), we are to be attentive to all, especially those thought unimiportant (*despised*, v 10). Not despising means *do not neglect the straying*. Ignoring those who stray is an expression of contempt incompatible with love. The angels, Christ, and the Father, therefore, are a threefold testimony to the importance of *little ones* and our responsibility to them.

Take No Offense, 18.15–35

Notes

The perspective shifts from instruction on sinning against another to what to do when another sins against us. "Matthew 18 was not written to teach us how to get rid of offenders but how to win them back. The section

---

[5] A third-class subjunctive (doubtful) condition that recognizes that the search might not end in success.

[6] "When one is dealing with things, it is impressive to maintain a 99 percent average. But the statistical approach does not work when one is dealing with persons. God is never willing to say, 'We have most of them.' In a family, the one who is missing is never compensated for by the ones who are present" (Garland, 190).

teaches that every single person matters to God and that when we lovingly pursue the offender to bring about reconciliation, we're doing something that pleases God. The transgressor is worth the trouble! To dismiss him without a loving pursuit is to say that his life is of no consequence to us, that we wouldn't miss him, that nothing in or about him matters enough to us to motivate us to go the distance with him" (McGuiggan, *Where the Spirit of the Lord Is*, 15). Offenders are not generally viewed as *little ones*, but even when a brother lacks lowliness of heart, he is to be loved, not despised.

This text breaks into three sections: vv 15–20 detail the process for resolving problems between individuals; vv 21–22 asks a question about forgiveness; and vv 23–35 is a parable that illustrates heaven's perspective on forgiveness.

In vv 15–20, the phrases, *I say to you* and *again, I say to you,* divide this subsection into three parts: vv 15–17 are spoken to an individual, v 18 is spoken to the church, and vv 19–20 affirms the legitimacy of church action.

18.15 "Moreover if your brother sins against you, go and tell him his fault between you and him alone. If he hears you, you have gained your brother.

We are not to despise (v 10) those who sin against us. In life, there are sins against us that we can deflect without lingering effect. The greater our love for another, the greater will be the number of sins he or she commits against us that fall into this category (1 Pet. 4.8).

But sometimes a sin against us rises to where we can't let it go. In such cases, reconciliation is required (5.23–25), and the first step in this is for the aggrieved to take the initiative to resolve THE matter[7]: *go and tell him his fault* (Lk. 17.3–4). *Fault* translates *elegchō*, which means *to take to task, call to account*. This conversation is to be private, *between you and him alone*, which helps minimize the offender's defensiveness or embarrassment. The end sought is the *gaining of your brother*—a reinstatement of the brotherly relationship that existed prior to the sin (6.14–15).[8] He who sins against us is to be regarded as of value, as worth bothering with, as one to be forgiven.

18.16 But if he will not hear, take with you one or two more, that 'by the mouth of two or three witnesses every word may be established.'

---

[7] Love always takes the initiative (1 Jn. 4.10).

[8] "How often personal confrontation is the last stage rather than the first in Christian complaints! It frequently seems as if the whole world knows of someone's grievances against us before we are personally approached" (Blomberg, 278). "A great deal of tension in Chris-

If reconciliation fails at this stage, the matter is put before *one or two more*, consistent with the ancient rule that *by the mouth of two or three witnesses every word may be established* (Deut. 19.15). In the Deuteronomy text, the *witnesses* were actual witnesses of the incident in question, but here, there is no indication that they witness in this sense, but function more as jurors who hear both sides of the story and render an opinion. If they agree with the aggrieved (v 15), it is hoped that their joint conclusion will persuade the offender to repent and be reconciled. It goes without saying that *witnesses* should be regarded by the offender as people of integrity.

If the offender rejects their judgment, he reveals himself as one who isn't lowly (v 4) and who has strayed (vv 12–14).

18.17 And if he refuses to hear them, tell *it* to the church. But if he refuses even to hear the church, let him be to you like a heathen and a tax collector.

If reconciliation fails at step two, the matter is brought before the church. Except for 16.18, this is the only other occurrence of *ekklēsia (church)* in the Gospels. In 16.18, *church* is used in a general sense to describe all who believe in Christ; here, it refers to a congregation of believers (e.g., the church at Corinth, Rome, Thessalonica, etc.).

Tell it to the church means that the aggrieved (v 15) makes the matter public before the entire congregation—not just a select few, such as the elders or the evangelist. *If he refuses to hear the church* implies that step two (v 16) is repeated on a larger scale. If—after the congregation hears both sides and agrees with the aggrieved—the offender *refuses (parakouō, to disobey, ignore)* to accept the church's verdict, he is to be regarded *like a heathen and a tax collector*, that is, he is considered unconverted (Lk. 22.32). No hint of vindictiveness or ill-will should be present. Christ loved the *heathen* and *tax collectors* (9.10–11), and His followers should too. Love should govern all interaction with the offender.

The pronoun *you* in *let him be to you*, is singular, which has led some to think that the instruction to *let him be to you like a heathen and a tax collector* applies only to the aggrieved (v 15). Note, though, that both uses of *ekklēsia*

tian congregations would be eased if we obeyed this plain command of Jesus: 'Go and tell him his fault between you and him alone.' Instead of having the courage to face a person with his fault, frankly but privately, we whisper behind his back and poison other people's minds against him. The whole atmosphere of the church becomes foul" (Stott, *Confess Your Sins*, 34).

(*church*) are singular. Since *church* is a collective noun (a noun that names a group), it would take a singular pronoun if thought of as a unit, which I believe is the case here. A congregation is to be united in regarding the impenitent as a straying sheep who has left the flock (v 13); there is to be an increase in the social pressure brought to bear on an offender. 1 Corinthians 5.1–5 and 2 Corinthians 2.6 testify to the effectiveness of loving pressure imposed by the church on a straying brother.

A further consideration about the antecedent of the singular *you* is that in the next verse, the plural *you* is used, which seems to confirm that the church, not just the aggrieved individual, is the one implied in *let him be to you*.

18.18 "Assuredly, I say to you, whatever you bind on earth will be bound in heaven, and whatever you loose on earth will be loosed in heaven.

Assuredly introduces a solemn pronouncement: *I say to you … whatever you bind … whatever you loose*. Contextually, *bind* and *loose* refer to the decision reached by the church in v 17. The future passive perfect form doesn't mean heaven automatically endorses arbitrary church decisions, but that God's will in the matter of a straying believer is to be done on earth as it is in heaven (16.19). *Whatever you forbid on earth must be already forbidden in heaven, and whatever you permit on earth must be already permitted in heaven* (wms). When a private matter is brought before the church, the church is to apply the will of God to the matter.

18.19–20 Again I say to you that if two of you agree on earth concerning anything that they ask, it will be done for them by My Father in heaven. For where two or three are gathered together in My name, I am there in the midst of them."

Again restates v 18 for emphasis. Christ isn't talking here about a quorum needed to hold a valid church service, nor is He making a statement about effectual prayer. Contextually, the *two or three* are those mentioned in v 16. When two or three, or the entire church, are asked to weigh in on a disagreement between brothers, the matter should be undertaken seriously, fairly, and Scripturally. God's guidance should be sought through prayer. Once the evidence is heard, the Lord's will is sought, and a conclusion is reached (*agree on earth, sumphoneō, symphony, to be harmonious, concur*), and Christ is with His church in its decision (1.23).

This is one of the strongest text in Scripture asserting the validity of human action done according to the will of God. Men are fallible, and their judgment sometimes flawed, but when the teaching of vv 15–17 is followed, the decision reached reflects heaven's judgment in the matter.

18.21 Then Peter came to Him and said, "Lord, how often shall my brother sin against me, and I forgive him? Up to seven times?"

The last of Matthew's five unique scenes involving Peter (14.28) picks up on v 15 by asking whether there is a limit to forgiveness—*how often do I have to forgive my brother?* (BECK). Rabbis traditionally limited forgiveness to three times (*b. Yoma* 86b–87a), but Peter is more generous and asks if seven times is sufficient.[9] But as Christ shows, any limitation on forgiveness is far removed from the love that *keeps no score of wrongs* (1 Cor. 13.6, NEB).

18.22 Jesus said to him, "I do not say to you, up to seven times, but up to seventy times seven.

In the Gr., the negative is emphatic: *not I say to you until seven times, but up to seventy times seven.* The use of *seven* and *seventy* figuratively represents a quality rather than a quantity—the quality of love that abundantly forgives (Lk. 17.3–4). *Seventy times seven*[10] doesn't limit forgiveness to 490 times but is a memorable way of teaching that forgiveness is to be a way of life. Measured mercy is incompatible with exceeding love (5.20). "A man cannot forgive up to four hundred and ninety times without forgiveness becoming a part of the habit structure of his being. Forgiveness is not an occasional act; it is a permanent attitude" (Martin Luther King).

There are some who protest that *seventy times seven* forgive-ness is liable to abuse (e.g., being taken for granted, exploited by the unscrupulous), and they are right (probably all reading this have abused it), as shown in the following parable—but the possibility of abuse doesn't change the rule (5.39–41).

18.23 Therefore the kingdom of heaven is like a certain king who wanted to settle accounts with his servants.

---

[9] Luz wrote that "The sevenfold forgiveness that Peter suggests is by no means trivial. Seven is the traditional number of perfection. That Peter suggests forgiving seven times does not mean, therefore, that he wants to grant his brother only a limited forgiveness. Instead, the sense of Peters question is: 'Is perfect forgiveness expected of me?'" (II, 465). I tend to think that this gives Peter's perceptiveness more credit than it deserves.

[10] Gen. 4.24.

Seventy times seven forgiveness is illustrated by a parable. Verse 23 introduces the parable, v 35 states the lesson, and in between are three scenes. The first involves a *king* and a *servant* (vv 24–27), the second, the *servant* and a *fellow servant* (vv 28–30), and the third, the *king* and the original *servant*, vv 31–34.

18.24–27 And when he had begun to settle accounts, one was brought to him who owed him ten thousand talents. But as he was not able to pay, his master commanded that he be sold, with his wife and children and all that he had, and that payment be made. The servant therefore fell down before him, saying, 'Master, have patience with me, and I will pay you all.' Then the master of that servant was moved with compassion, released him, and forgave him the debt.

Nothing here is difficult to understand. A ruler wants to settle accounts with his servants—he wants to see how they have handled the responsibilities entrusted to them, including those involving money (25.19). *Servant* (*doulos*) is a broad term that can include any type of slave.

During the audit, a *servant* is found who has somehow lost *ten thousand talents*. How he did this isn't explained.[11] In Gr., *ten thousand* (*murioi*) was the highest possible number, and *talent* was the highest valued coin. Considering the number of variables involved, there's no way to know how much *ten thousand talents* would be in today's dollars, but estimates have ranged from several million (NIV marg.) to a trillion dollars. Regardless of the amount, *ten thousand talents* was a sum far beyond the servant's ability to repay.

When it's determined that the servant cannot repay this amount, the king commands that he, his family, and his possessions be sold to recover some of the loss (5.26; 2 Kgs. 4.1).

Desperate men will promise anything to get out of a jam. Falling prostrate (*proskuneō*, to kiss the hand towards one, to worship), the servant pleads for *patience*, asking time to repay. It was a delusional request, but

---

[11] "The parable seems to be faulty in this, that it makes the servant answerable for such a debt as it seems impossible for any man to run up. The difficulty is met by the suggestion that the debtor is a person of high rank, like one of the princes whom Darius set over the kingdom of Persia or a provincial governor of the Roman Empire. Such an official might very soon make himself liable for the huge sum here specified, simply by retaining for his own benefit the revenues of his province as they passed through his hands, instead of remitting them to the royal treasury. That it was some such unscrupulous minister of state, guilty of the crime of embezzlement, whom Jesus had in His eye, appears all but certain when we recollect what gave rise to the discourse of which this parable forms the conclusion. The

we repeat it every time we promise God that if He will let us off the hook this time, we won't get back on it.[12]

The servant asked for *patience*, but the king, moved by *compassion* (9.36), *forgave him the debt* (*daneion*, loan, only here in the NT; the verb *aphiēmi*, *forgive*, appears more often in Matthew than in any other NT book)—which was exceedingly and abundantly above all the servant asked or hoped.[13] God *has not dealt with us according to our sins, nor punished us according to our iniquities* (Ps. 103.10). God doesn't deal with His debtors as Scrooge dealt with his, inflexibly demanding interest on every penny owed. Rather, He freely releases us from that which we cannot pay (Rom. 3.24, 5.6).

18.28–30 But that servant went out and found one of his fellow servants who owed him a hundred denarii; and he laid hands on him and took *him* by the throat, saying, 'Pay me what you owe!' So his fellow servant fell down at his feet and begged him, saying, 'Have patience with me, and I will pay you all.' And he would not, but went and threw him into prison till he should pay the debt.

What happens next is unconscionable. The forgiven servant brutally accosts a *fellow servant* (not an inferior, but an equal), *laying hands on him and taking him by the throat*, demanding payment of the paltry sum of one hundred denarii—which was less than a third of an average laborer's yearly salary—"an amount that even a poor farmer could scrape together in the course of a year" (Luz II, 473). The second servant pleads the same as did the one accosting him: *have patience with me, and I will pay you all*—a promise that wasn't unrealistic and that should have caused the first servant to remember the judgment he had just escaped. But *he would not*— instead of showing mercy, the first servant has his fellow thrown in jail.

18.31–34 So when his fellow servants saw what had been done, they were very grieved, and came and told their master all that had been done. Then his master, after he had called him, said to him, 'You wicked

---

disciples had disputed among themselves who should be greatest in the kingdom. Here, accordingly, their Master holds up to their view the conduct of a great one, concerned not about the faithful discharge of his duty, but about his own aggrandizement" (A. B. Bruce, *The Training of the Twelve*, 210–211).

[12] "O my soul, humble thyself as thou answerest the question, 'How much owest thou?'" (Spurgeon).

[13] The measure of the forgiveness was not the servant's sense of need but the king's depth of compassion.

servant! I forgave you all that debt because you begged me. Should you not also have had compassion on your fellow servant, just as I had pity on you?' And his master was angry, and delivered him to the torturers until he should pay all that was due to him.

When other servants learn of this, they *told* (*diasapheō*, say point blank, make clear; only here in the NT) *their master all that had been done*. The king immediately summons the *wicked servant* (to be unmerciful is to be wicked[14]; 5.7) and informs him that being forgiven his debt was not merely a bookkeeping matter but was meant to enlarge his soul, making him merciful toward others. *Should you not also have had compassion on your fellow servant, just as I had pity (eleeō,* to have mercy on) *on you?*

Two principles—*forgive us our debts, as we forgive our debtors* (6.12) and *with what judgment you judge, you will be judged* (7.2)—are applied. The *master angrily* retracts his forgiveness and remands the unmerciful servant to the *torturers* (*basanistēs*, one who tortured debtors, thus putting pressure on the man's family to pay off the debt; only here in the NT). As his debt was unpayable, this man likely died in prison (5.26).

18.35 So My heavenly Father also will do to you if each of you, from his heart, does not forgive his brother his trespasses."

We will never forgive as much as we have been forgiven, and a spirit that is unmerciful and unforgiving has no place in Christ's kingdom. Situations calling for our *mercy* and *forgiveness* always test whether we have *humbled ourselves as little children* (v 4), esteem others better than self (Phil. 2.3), and reflect the love of God.

The bluntness of direct address—*will do to you*—grabs our attention. Christ is speaking to His church (v 17); His forgiveness precedes and is to prompt our forgiveness (v 15, 6.14–15).

The forgiveness we grant is to be *from the heart*, where true *righteousness* is found (5.20). And forgiveness is to result in reconciliation (v 15, 6.14–15). An unforgiving spirit is not simply a fault; it is unutterably mean.

"God can forgive the passing sin of the hot heart but not the inherent sin of the cold. Even he has no mercy for the unmerciful" (John Ruskin).

---

[14] "The lord did not call him 'wicked servant' when he owed him the 'ten thousand talents,' but he did call him a 'wicked servant' for such harsh and cruel treatment toward his fellow servant" (Boles, 382).

CHAPTER 19 .

DIVORCE, 19.1–12

Notes

Jesus has told His disciples that He must return to Jerusalem where He will be killed (16.21, 17.22–23), and 19.1 to 20.34 narrates this final trip. A great deal more happened on this journey than is told by Matthew (events recorded by Luke fill ten chapters), but what Matthew tells contains important teaching for Christians and sets the stage for the climactic scenes of his Gospel.

Chapter 19 divides into three sections centered around three issues: divorce (vv 1–12), children (who are often the victims of divorce; vv 13–15), and possessions (vv 16–30).

The paragraph on divorce has three subsections: the opening, which sets the scene (vv 1–2); the middle, involving an encounter with the Pharisees (vv 3–9); and the conclusion, where Jesus answers a question asked by the disciples (vv 10–12). The middle scene has two short paragraphs (vv 3–6, 7–9), each of which begins with a question from the Pharisees.[1]

As previously noted (5.32), any study that doesn't take into account the totality of God's revelation on marriage, divorce, and remarriage, including 1 Corinthians 7, will likely fall short of a conclusion that reflects God's will on these subjects (4.4).

19.1–2 Now it came to pass, when Jesus had finished these sayings, *that* **He departed from Galilee and came to the region of Judea beyond the Jordan. And great multitudes followed Him, and He healed them there.**

Christ's fourth discourse (18.1–19.2) concludes with the usual ending: *and it came to pass, when Jesus had finished these sayings* (7.28, 11.1, 13.53).

---

[1] This section is an example of how Christ revealed truth from within His cultural milieu. In the Gospels, every discussion of marriage and divorce is presented from the male point of view and address only male hearers, which makes it appear to modern readers as if only women commit adultery and only men get a divorce.

Passover is approaching, and Jesus and the disciples leave Galilee for Judea. *Beyond Jordan* indicates that they traveled down the east side of the Jordan (Mk. 10.1). *Great multitudes* were also going to Jerusalem for Passover, and on the way Christ continued His miraculous healings.

19.3 The Pharisees also came to Him, testing Him, and saying to Him, "Is it lawful for a man to divorce his wife for *just* any reason?"

"The questions relating to marriage/divorce/remarriage will never go away until Jesus returns" (McGuiggan).

Somewhere on the road, Christ is approached by a group of Pharisees (last seen in 16.1–4) who ask a question about marriage and divorce.[2] Their motive was malicious—they sought to *test* (trap) Jesus in a way that would destroy His influence.

Is it lawful for a man to divorce his wife for just any reason? Matthew doesn't concern himself with any rabbinic or cultural background to this question, but ample historical evidence indicates that in the first century, there was a split among Jews on the subject of divorce.

According to David Instone-Brewer, the division traced to a disagreement over the meaning of the phrase *some uncleanness* (or *matter of indecency*) in Deuteronomy 24.1. Two competing rabbinic schools, one that followed the teachings of Rabbi Shammai and the other the teachings of Rabbi Hillel, differed on the interpretation of this unusual phrase (the Heb. expression appears in only one other place, Deut. 23.14). Those who followed Hillel believed *matter of indecency* "referred to two different grounds for divorce—'indecency' and 'a matter.' This meant one could base a divorce on an act of 'indecency' or on 'a matter,' which meant 'any matter.' Because 'any matter' encompassed all other grounds for divorce, this single ground could be used by anyone seeking a divorce. The Shammaites took the two words to mean 'a matter of indecency,' by which they understood the phrase to mean 'adultery.'"[3] *For just any reason*, therefore, was rabbinic semantics—the Pharisees were asking whether Moses allowed *no-fault* divorce. John the Baptist had lost his head for taking a strict view of marriage and divorce (14.3–12); maybe the Pharisees

---

[2] In the Gospels, Christ's teaching on marriage and divorce is found in four passages: Matt. 5.31–32, Matt. 19.3–9, Mk. 10.11–12, and Lk. 16.18. Of these, Matt. 19.3–9 is the most comprehensive.

[3] David Instone-Brewer, *Divorce and Remarriage in the Bible: The Social and Literary Context* (Kindle ed.), location 1209.

thought Jesus would meet a similar fate if He followed John's lead. The uniform testimony of linguists is that, here, *divorce* correctly translates *apoluō* (to loose from, set free, let go, dismiss, repudiate).

19.4–6 And He answered and said to them, "Have you not read that He who made *them* at the beginning 'made them male and female,' and said, 'For this reason a man shall leave his father and mother and be joined to his wife, and the two shall become one flesh'? So then, they are no longer two but one flesh. Therefore what God has joined together, let not man separate."

Since the Pharisees were fond of tradition (15.1–2), Christ answers by citing the oldest tradition on marriage—the one from the *beginning*. *Have you not read* is a slap at their boasted knowledge of the Law and implied that if they knew their Bible (13.14–15), they would have known the answer to their question. The Scriptures referenced are Genesis 1.27 and 2.24, which say that God *made them male and female,* with the expectation that *a man shall be joined to his wife* and *become one flesh,* which indicates a unity wherein two halves form a whole. Since God, at the beginning, made no provision for anything other than marriage, *what God has joined together, let not man divide.* In marriage, a man and woman are *joined* (*suzeugnumi,* to yoke, unite; only here and Mk. 10.9), but divorce destroys this unity. In creating man and woman and bringing them together, God declared His ideal for marriage. "'The first human male and female were intended solely for each other' (there was no one else to marry) and this norm of an indissoluble union was intended for each succeeding pair" (A. H. McNeile, qtd. by Mounce, 180). Marriage is the primary human relationship ordained and governed by God, not a private, arbitrary convention originating with man and subject to subjective whims.

Christ's answer to the Pharisees' (v 3) is an unmistakable: "No! A man may not divorce his wife for every cause!"

19.7 They said to Him, "Why then did Moses command to give a certificate of divorce, and to put her away?"

Christ's answer (v 6) elicits a second, logical question from the Pharisees: *Why then did Moses command to give a certificate of divorce, and to put her away?* The reference is to Deuteronomy 24.1. On *some uncleanness,* see v 3, 5.31. *A certificate of divorce* was a document that officially severed the marriage

314 | *Christ Revealed*

bond.[4] "Extrabiblical data suggest the document included (1) a dissolution of marriage formula, 'I am not/no longer your husband, and you are not/no longer my wife' (cf. Hos. 2.2) ... (2) an explicit declaration of release, authorizing the woman to return home to her father's household or to remarry ... (3) a declaration of the return of the dowry" (Block, *Deuteronomy*, 558). The Pharisees' point is that if Genesis 1–2 teaches the indissolubility of marriage, why did Deuteronomy 24 allow (*command*) for dissolution?

19.8 He said to them, "Moses, because of the hardness of your hearts, permitted you to divorce your wives, but from the beginning it was not so.

"Moses *permitted* you to divorce your wives, but this permission was not part of God's original blueprint."[5] Deuteronomy 24.1–4 wasn't a positive moral permission but a divine response to human sin, a reaction to failure made necessary by *hardened hearts* (*sklērokardia*, a "term that in general refers to the inner dimension of sin, particularly against God. It reflects an unwillingness to repent, being closed to God, stubbornness" [Luz II, 490]). Sin, therefore, is what occasioned the *certificate of divorce*. The Pharisees "came assuming that to line one's life up with a correct interpretation of Deuteronomy 24.1–4 was to line one's life up with the full will of God" (McGuiggan, *Divorce and Matthew 19*). But they were wrong. The *certificate of divorce* was a contingency necessitated by hard-hearted Jewish husbands who were determined to separate what God had joined together, regardless of what God had ordained *from the beginning*. Deuteronomy 24 wasn't an escape hatch to Genesis 1–2; God wasn't saying that what was previously unlawful was now okay. Deuteronomy 24 was meant to limit the personal and social fallout of divorce by protecting victimized wives who were forced into difficult situations when wrongfully dismissed by unrighteous husbands. Considering the spiritual, emotional, and economic devastation of divorce, only a warped mind would ever think that God desired or commanded it.[6] "The norm for marriage remains the vision embodied at the outset of creation, not later concessions made to deal with human failure" (Gardiner, 289).

---

[4] In the OT, the term *document of separation/divorce* is only found in Deut. 24.1, Isa. 50.1, and Jer. 3.8.

[5] Note that between Matt. 19.7–8 and Mk. 10.4–5 the verbs are switched: *command/permitted, permitted/precept* (i.e., command). Deut. 24.1–4 is both a *command* and *permission*.

[6] I can't locate the transcript, but I remember a Paul Harvey radio monologue that went something like this: "When you see the worried look on a child's face, wondering if there's

19.9 And I say to you, whoever divorces his wife, except for sexual immorality, and marries another, commits adultery; and whoever marries her who is divorced commits adultery."

And I say to you recalls the authoritative pronouncements in the Sermon on the Mount (5.32). What Christ says is clear: *divorce is forbidden except for sexual immorality*. To divorce—or be divorced (5.32)—for any reason other than *sexual immorality*, and then remarry, is to *commit adultery*.[7] The reason remarriage in such cases constitutes *adultery* is because the couple, under God's law, are still married no matter what their civil marital status (1 Cor. 7.10–11). Only when divorce is due to a spouse's fornication does a subsequent remarriage not involve adultery—which is the implication of the word *except* (*ei mē*, see Gal. 6.14) and repeats the teaching of 5.32.[8] Although the prospect of divorce is absent in Genesis 1–2, Christ authorizes it for the reason stated; He recognizes situations wherein impenitent sin makes divorce permissible.

On *sexual immorality* (*porneia*), see 5.32. Attempts to broaden this term beyond actual adultery to include any and every sort of sexual uncleanness (e.g., lust, 5.28) reduces Christ's teaching to the absurd (see 5.30, *Excursus on lust as a ground for divorce*). *Porneia* can function as a general term for immorality, but in this context its meaning is narrow—so much so that the disciples conclude it is better not to marry than to be bound by such stringent limitations (v 10). The Pharisees asked whether one could divorce *for any and every reason* (v 3, NIV)—does anyone seriously believe that the one reason Christ allows is so broad and expansive that virtually

---

going to be a dad or mom in his life any more, *you'll know*. When you see the love in a child's eyes when his dad comes to get him, and his tears at having to say goodbye to his mom, *you'll know*. When you see the anger in a child's eyes, wondering why his parents don't love each other, *you'll know*. When you see a mother trying to be a father, shouldering spiritual, physical, and emotional burdens she wasn't meant to bear, *you'll know*. When you've felt the loneliness, heartache, devastation of abandonment, and betrayal, *you'll know*. When you see grandparents trying to fill the void their children have created in their grandchildren's lives, *you'll know*. When you understand the effects of divorce on children, how they continue even after the child reaches maturity and has difficulty in forming relationships, *you'll know*. When you hear of the emotional and physical abuse that is heaped on step-children, *you'll know* why God says, 'I hate divorce!'"

[7] This constitutes a major difference between Christ's teaching and Deut. 24.1–4, which allowed for the remarriage of the dismissed wife.

[8] Numerous interpreters (in the postapostolic age and the Roman Catholic Church) do not admit remarriage for any reason, even after the sexual infidelity of one's spouse, but as Turner states, "If divorce [for *porneia*] does not convey freedom to remarry, it is essentially meaningless" (*Matthew*, 462).

every married person could legitimately divorce their spouse (for if Jesus allows divorce for lust—as some contend based on 5.28—the vast majority of married persons have grounds for divorce). Under Moses, adultery was a capital crime (Lev. 20.10; Deut. 22.22; Jn. 8.5) but lust wasn't. From heaven's perspective, lust is adultery (5.28) and hatred is murder (5.21–22; 1 Jn. 3.15), but actions that have the same result in eternity can have different consequences now. To think otherwise throws open the door to easy divorce, which is the exact opposite of God's will. The *porneia* that allows for divorce is actual adultery—not lust or other sexually-linked uncleanness, as bad as these sins are.

Christians have been called to a love righteousness (5.20) that is redemptive and sacrificial. When a spouse steps over love's cheating line, it's not the time to see Matthew 19.9 as an *out*, but a time to show the superabundant love God expects of His people. Marriage is a commitment, not a contract; it is a relationship in which sinners (a husband and wife) are redeemed by their love for each other in which they repeatedly turn the other cheek, go the second mile, forgive seventy times seven, etc. (5.39–42, 5.43–48, 18.10–35, etc.).[9]

Excursus on Divorce in the Old Testament

Attempts to reconstruct divorce procedures under the Law of Moses are limited by the lack of a single clear-cut example of divorce in the OT involving Deuteronomy 24.1–4. Judges 19.1–2 tells of a concubine who left her husband and returned to her father's house; some believe Hosea 2.1–4 provided guidelines for a divorce formula; and in Ezra 10, postexilic Jews were commanded to put away their Gentile wives. Other than this, information about OT divorce is scant. Throughout the OT, there is a divine aversion to divorce that culminates with the Malachi 2.16 statement that God *hates divorce*!

But what is it about divorce that makes it so unacceptable to God? Strong reasons are listed in Malachi 2.10–16.

First, in the context of Malachi—in which the Jews are accused of boredom and malpractice in worship, 1.6–14; priestly corruption, 2.1–9; intermarriage with pagans, 2.10–12; cynicism and contempt for the Lord, 2.17–3.4,13–14; abusive conduct toward the vulnerable, 3.5–6; and robbing God, 3.7–12—divorce betrays a general lack of reverence and respect for God.

---

[9] It was said of Henry Ward Beecher, an American Congregationalist minister, that no one ever felt the full force of his kindness until he did Beecher an injury.

Second, it is an act of treachery (deceit) against one's spouse—a breach of the covenant (2.14) that puts it into the same category as intermarriage, which was an act of treachery against the entire Jewish community and social structure (2.10).

Third, it endangers the spiritual well-being of future generations (2.15) by lessening the chance that they will be a *godly seed* (*godly children*, NLT) devoted to the Lord. The physical functions of procreation can be performed apart from the marital relationship, but a stable marriage and home are indispensable for the continuance of a people of faith.

Fourth, a man's treachery against his marriage covenant absolves God of His promises to the man (2.15–16; see 18.23–35). To wrong a spouse by breaking one's marriage vows (e.g., "for better or for worse … till death do us part") invites the judgment of God (Heb. 13.4, 1 Pet. 1.7).

Fifth, *take heed to your spirit*, says God (2.15). Marital treachery arises in the heart before it appears in the act. God isn't fooled by external worship from a heart filled with adulterous thoughts and intents that violate the marriage covenant (Heb. 4.12).

Nowadays, people spend much time talking about their *right* to a divorce when they ought to spend more time talking about why God hates it and what can be done to save a troubled marriage.

19.10 His disciples said to Him, "If such is the case of the man with *his* wife, it is better not to marry."

The Pharisees have disappeared; only the disciples remain, and they offer a conclusion. Most likely, they had been culturally conditioned by the easy divorce of the time and were amazed at the restrictiveness of Christ's teaching, concluding that it would be better to remain single than to enter a relationship in which the marriage-knot wasn't a slip-knot.[10]

19.11 But He said to them, "All cannot accept this saying, but only *those* to whom it has been given:

The antecedent of *this saying* is Christ's teaching in vv 3–9. He admits that *all men cannot accept* His teaching, except *those to whom it has been given*. *Accept* (*chōreō*, to make room) involves intellectual and emotional acceptance—wrapping one's head and heart around something. Those who accept Christ's teaching are the ones to *whom it has been given*. A similar construction occurs in 13.11, where Jesus said that His disciples

---

[10] Surveys indicate that today, most Americans who marry don't expect to stay married.

had been given to know the mysteries of the kingdom, but to others this knowledge *had not been given*. This doesn't mean the disciples were stuffed with divine knowledge apart from their will, but that they understood Christ because they wanted to understand; they were good soil (13.23) with minds and hearts were open to Him (even if imperfectly so). And the same point is made here. The reason *all men cannot accept* Christ's teaching is because some have closed their hearts to truth (v 8); His teaching is *given* only to those willing to receive it.

19.12 For there are eunuchs who were born thus from *their* mother's womb, and there are eunuchs who were made eunuchs by men, and there are eunuchs who have made themselves eunuchs for the kingdom of heaven's sake. He who is able to accept *it*, let him accept *it*."

Based on what Christ said, the disciples aren't sure that marriage was worth the bother (v 10), but Jesus, rather than softening His teaching, reinforces it by acknowledging that *accepting* it might involve celibacy. Although celibacy was not part of God's ideal *at the beginning* (v 4), there are times when it's a reality of life. Some men, for instance, are *eunuchs* (celibate) *from their mother's womb*—for some reason, physically or psychologically, they are impotent and unable to sire children. Some *were made eunuchs by men*, having been castrated (which was common in antiquity for attendants of a royal harem; Acts 8.27). And then there are some *who have made themselves eunuchs for the kingdom of heaven's sake*. John the Baptist, Jesus, and Paul (1 Cor. 7.32–38, 9.5; Acts 21.9) were in this category. In this context, however, Christ seems to refer to the divorced who would commit adultery by a remarriage (v 9; 1 Cor. 7.10–11); rather than enter a relationship God disallows (v 9), they choose celibacy in order to be under His rule. *He who is able to accept it, let him accept it* is an exhortation to embrace this teaching. Celibacy comes with its own set of challenges (1 Tim. 5.11), but it is consistent with the principle that obedience to Christ is better than being cast into hell fire (v 29, 5.29–30, 18.8–9).[11]

CHILDREN, 19.13–15

19.13 Then little children were brought to Him that He might put *His* hands on them and pray, but the disciples rebuked them.

---

[11] See also v 28 where Christ promises an incredible reward awaiting the faithful that is out of all proportion to what they gave up for the sake of the kingdom.

The transition from marriage to children is natural. *Little children (paidia,* small children; per Hippocrates, under seven years of age) are brought that Jesus might *put His hands on them and pray.* In the OT, *putting* or *laying on of hands* was done to sacrificial animals (Lev. 1.4), at Joshua's ordination (Deut. 34.9), and in parental blessing (Gen. 48.14–18). This paragraph recalls 18.1–5 and is likely meant to underscore the importance of the lesson taught there. The disciples, characteristically (15.23), see the children as a nuisance and shoo them away.

19.14–15 But Jesus said, "Let the little children come to Me, and do not forbid them; for of such is the kingdom of heaven." And He laid *His* hands on them and departed from there.

Jesus stops the disciples, telling them that children are not to be kept from Him,[12] *for of such is the kingdom of heaven.* As taught in 18.4, children are an example of lowliness for those who desire to be under the rule of God. To *forbid them* is to forbid the very type of spirit and status Christ seeks.

Excursus on Infant Baptism

Jesus blessed children, but He didn't baptize them. Historically, advocates of infant baptism have used this passage as a proof text. Their argument doesn't rest on the fact that children were baptized here (for they weren't) but rather on the words, *do not forbid* them. To see infant baptism in the phrase *do not forbid them* is tenuous indeed.

There is no example, command, or implication of infant baptism in the NT, and 1 Corinthians 7.14 affirms the holiness of unbaptized children. In debates between the Reformers (e.g., Luther, Zwingli) and the Anabaptists, the Anabaptist Peter Walpot made a point that has been repeated many times since by noting that baptism is of no value apart from faith. Since their youth precludes intelligent faith, baptizing children serves no purpose. Luz notes that the use of Matthew 19.13–15 to support infant baptism "illustrates how little a biblical text can accomplish against the weight of tradition and liturgy. ... It is exegetically certain that Matt 19.13–15 does not provide a basis for infant baptism" (II, 507).[13]

---

[12] Spurgeon said that *Let the little children come to Me* "is the banner of the Sunday school."

[13] An interesting footnote on this verse in Restoration history is found in the *Memoirs of*

POSSESSIONS, 19.16–30

Notes

Jesus dealt with individuals as individuals, and because He always knew the person's greatest need, He knew what to address (Jn. 2.25). Any attempt to take Christ's specific instructions spoken to a specific individual about a specific problem and expand them into a general rule should be done with extreme caution; see comments in 8.21–22 on *prophetic symbolic action commands*.

This section consists of three parts. It begins with an encounter between Jesus and a young man (vv 16–22), is followed by Christ teaching His disciples about wealth (vv 23–26), and concludes with Christ answering a question asked by Peter (vv 27–30).

In the first paragraph (vv 16–22), there is an introduction (v 16a), a conclusion (v 22), and a middle containing three questions and answers (vv 16b–21).

19.16 Now behold, one came and said to Him, "Good Teacher, what good thing shall I do that I may have eternal life?"

Possibly no scene in the Gospel better illustrates how Christ dealt with men on an individual basis than this incident involving a *rich* (v 22) *young man* (v 20), whom Luke identifies as a *ruler* of the Jews (Lk. 18.18; see 9.18). The question he asks, on the surface, has much to commend it: *Good Teacher, what good thing shall I do that I may have eternal life?* In asking about *eternal life*, he asked about the right thing, and in asking Jesus, he asked the right person—synagogue rulers didn't customarily ask Jesus how to

Alexander Campbell. Thomas Campbell "went on to announce, in the most simple and emphatic terms, the great principle or rule upon which he understood they were then acting, and upon which, he trusted, they would continue to act, consistently and perseveringly to the end. 'That rule, my highly respected hearers,' said he in conclusion, 'is this, that WHERE THE SCRIPTURES SPEAK, WE SPEAK; AND WHERE THE SCRIPTURES ARE SILENT, WE ARE SILENT.' At length, a shrewd Scotch Seceder, Andrew Munro arose and said: 'Mr. Campbell, if we adopt *that* as a basis, then there is an end of infant baptism.' This remark, and the conviction it seemed to carry with it, produced a profound sensation. 'Of course,' said Mr. Campbell, in reply, 'if infant baptism be not found in Scripture, we can have nothing to do with it.' Upon this, Thomas Acheson, of Washington exclaimed, laying his hand upon his heart: 'I hope I may never see the day when my heart will renounce that blessed saying of the Scripture, "Suffer little children to come unto me, and forbid them not, for of such is the kingdom of heaven."' Upon saying this he was so much affected that he burst into tears, and while a deep sympathetic feeling pervaded the entire assembly, he was about to retire to an adjoined room, when James Foster, not willing that this misapplication of Scripture should pass unchallenged, cried out, 'Mr. Acheson, I would remark that in the portion of Scripture you have quoted *there is no reference, whatever, to infant baptism*'" (Richardson, 236, 238).

obtain eternal life, for they thought they already knew the answer (Rom. 2.17–20). For this ruler to ask Jesus this question was to risk his reputation and position. In asking *what good thing shall I do?* the man showed that he appreciated the need for obedience. Contrary to some who criticize him for trusting in *works righteousness,* he understood that men must *do* something to be saved (Acts 2.37).

19.17 So He said to him, "Why do you call Me good? No one *is* good but One, *that is,* God. But if you want to enter into life, keep the commandments."

Christ zeroes in on his core problem. *Why do you call Me good?* Jesus wouldn't accept empty praise or an insincere compliment from one not convicted about Him and His cause; He insisted that men speak out of true devotion (16.16–17, 22.16,18).

If this man wished to use God's vocabulary, he must use God's dictionary: *no one is good but One, that is, God.* If Christ is truly good (and not a liar or lunatic), He must be God as He claimed to be. And if Jesus is God, then this young man must respond accordingly. If he truly believed Christ to be good—and thus God—to reject Christ's answer was to reject God.

If you want to enter into life, keep the commandments fully upheld the Law and the prophets (5.17) and the teaching that the kingdom is for those who obey God's will (7.21–27).

19.18–19 He said to Him, "Which ones?" Jesus said, "'You shall not murder,' 'You shall not commit adultery,' 'You shall not steal,' 'You shall not bear false witness,' 'Honor your father and *your* mother,' and, 'You shall love your neighbor as yourself.'"

The man asks for specifics, and Christ cites the sixth, seventh, eighth, ninth, and fifth commandments, concluding with Leviticus 19.18, *love your neighbor as yourself,* which summarized the commandments just mentioned (22.39). We are to love ourselves well (Eph. 5.28–29) and others every bit as much.

19.20 The young man said to Him, "All these things I have kept from my youth. What do I still lack?"

According to Philo, a *young man* was one between the ages of twenty-one and twenty-eight. *I've kept all these* (BECK) is presumptuous. As I've tried to show in my comments on the Sermon on the Mount, the second half of the

Ten Commandments was demanding and not easily checked off. But this man was undoubtedly sincere. As men are wont to do, he believed, based on his morally creditable life and the avoidance of major failings, that he was blameless in regard to his neighbor.

And yet his inner syntax still told him something was missing—*What do I still lack?* As Christ's next words will show, this man was, indeed, too good to be true.

19.21 Jesus said to him, "If you want to be perfect, go, sell what you have and give to the poor, and you will have treasure in heaven; and come, follow Me."

Christ goes for the jugular (Heb. 4.12). Without questioning the man's claim (v 20), the Lord tells him, *If you want to be perfect, go, sell what you have and give to the poor*—which is entirely consistent with the statement in Luke 14.33: *whoever of you does not forsake all that he has, he cannot be My disciple.* Christ knew what was in this man's heart, and the challenge He places before him brought the truth to the surface. This man's outer correctness hid an inner covetousness that valued stuff above God, and he who values anything higher than God can never be *perfect* (*teleios*, completeness, wholeness; 5.48). It entirely misses the point to conclude that to be a disciple one must sell out lock, stock, and barrel and give everything to the poor. A man can bestow *all his goods to feed the poor* and still be imperfect before God (1 Cor. 13.3). Zacchaeus only promised to give the poor *half* his goods, yet Christ told him, *Today salvation has come to this house* (Lk. 19.8). It's not the amount of the check but the amount of the commitment that matters. When Christ looked into the heart of Zacchaeus, He saw unrivaled love (Lk. 14.33); when He looked into the heart of the rich young ruler, He saw an idol—and no man can serve two masters (6.24).[14]

19.22 But when the young man heard that saying, he went away sorrowful, for he had great possessions.

The man's reaction revealed that he was ruled by possessions rather than God (6.21). At the level where one must be to be in Christ's kingdom, he failed. He didn't love God or his neighbor (25.31–46), and he left *sorrowful* (*lupeō*, grieving, in heaviness; cf. the joy in 13.44–46). But it wasn't godly

---

[14] Cf. Christ's statement in Lk. 14.12: "When you give a dinner or a supper, do not ask your friends, your brothers, your relatives. ... "

sorrow; he sorrowed over the fact the kingdom wasn't big enough to accommodate his idol (7.13–14). Consequently, his goodness (v 21)—which was largely predicated on what he hadn't done—did him no good.[15]

19.23–24 Then Jesus said to His disciples, "Assuredly, I say to you that it is hard for a rich man to enter the kingdom of heaven. And again I say to you, it is easier for a camel to go through the eye of a needle than for a rich man to enter the kingdom of God."

The man's reaction illustrates how wealth can capture the heart to where *it is hard (duskolōs,* difficult) *for a rich man to enter the kingdom of God*—so hard, in fact, that one of Christ's most memorable metaphors is used to describe it: *it is easier for a camel to go through the eye of a needle than for a rich man to enter the kingdom of God.* A camel was the largest animal in Judea and the eye of a needle the smallest domestic opening. To talk about a camel going through a needle's eye was to talk about an impossibility; it's impossible for one who *trusts* in riches (Mk. 10.24) to enter the kingdom. Some have tried to soften this statement by claiming Christ used the word for *cable* (as in ship rigging) rather than for *camel,* or that the *eye of a needle* referred to a certain low gate in the wall of Jerusalem, but no evidence exists for either.[16]

19.25 When His disciples heard *it,* they were greatly astonished, saying, "Who then can be saved?"

For a second time in this chapter, the disciples are startled by Christ' teaching (v 10). If the rich can't enter the kingdom, *who then can be saved?* As explained by Carson, "Most Jews expected the rich to inherit eternal life, not because their wealth could buy their way in, but because their wealth testified to the blessing of the Lord in their lives" (425). But according to Christ, riches can indicate a curse rather than a blessing (13.22).

19.26 But Jesus looked at *them* and said to them, "With men this is impossible, but with God all things are possible."

There is hope for the rich, but it is in God, not gold. If the rich will humble themselves and become as a little child (v 14, 18.3–4), they can gain by

---

[15] "In the New Testament, joy is the fruit of giving up having, while sadness is the mood of the one who hangs onto possessions" (Erich Fromm, *To Have or To Be?* 105).

[16] The textual variant that has *kamilos* (cable, rope) rather than *kamelos* (camel) is very weak and very late. And there was never a city gate in Jerusalem known as the *eye of the needle.*

grace what money can't buy. Gold and the gospel seldom agree (6.24; 1 Tim. 6.17), but when a man who trusts in riches becomes poor in spirit and fill his heart with love, you'll see a camel go through the eye of a needle.

19.27 Then Peter answered and said to Him, "See, we have left all and followed You. Therefore what shall we have?"

There is no question that the disciples paid a price to follow Jesus, and the mention of *treasure in heaven* (v 21) occasions a question from Peter. Christ had previously spoken of a heavenly reward (5.12,46, 6.1–18, 10.41–42), and Peter realizes that he and the disciples have done what Christ asked of the young man (v 21)—they had left their livelihoods and were away from their families a great deal, thus, *what shall we have?*

19.28 So Jesus said to them, "Assuredly I say to you, that in the regeneration, when the Son of Man sits on the throne of His glory, you who have followed Me will also sit on twelve thrones, judging the twelve tribes of Israel.

The certainty of future reward is introduced by *assuredly*. *Regeneration* (*paliggenesia*, only here and Tit. 3.5) was a word used by the Stoics to describe the renewal of the world after its destruction by fire. It means born again, rebirth, or renovation ("the restoration of a thing to its pristine state," Thayer, 474) and has no Heb. equivalent. In Titus 3.5, it refers to the spiritual renewal that comes through forgiveness, and most likely that is its meaning here. A passage that sheds some light is Acts 3.19,21, where Peter uses the phrases *times of refreshing* and *times of restoration* to describe the gospel era. Understanding the time since Acts 2 as one of *regeneration* fits with Christ's statement that it will be a time when *the Son of Man sits on the throne of His glory* (Acts 2.33–36). *You who have followed Me* refers to the disciples (vv 27,28); the promise that they *will sit on twelve thrones judging the twelve tribes of Israel* is remarkable and unexplained. The imagery is undeniably Jewish, as *the twelve tribes* is an ancient designation for the nation of Israel. Christ and the Twelve were in the process of being judged by Israel, but the greater reality is that Israel would be judged by the word revealed by Christ and the apostles.

In interpreting Christ's promise, note that similar statements are found in Revelation 2.26 and 3.21. Disciples share in Christ's rule and authority over the world; the prayers of disciples affect the world (Rev.

8.3–5); and God's revelation through the Twelve is the basis by which God will judge the world (7.21–27; 1 Cor. 6.2–4).

19.29 And everyone who has left houses or brothers or sisters or father or mother or wife or children or lands, for My name's sake, shall receive a hundredfold, and inherit eternal life.

When we give up something for the kingdom's sake, we often focus on how much we lose; Christ, though, wants us to be impressed with how much we gain.[17]

The Lord broadens the promised reward beyond the Twelve to include *everyone* who leaves something for His sake (v 12). The all-loving and all-good heavenly Father will bestow unimaginable—*a hundredfold*—reward (13.44–46) on those who follow His Son.

Everlasting life is the Christian hope. According to Gibbon in his *Decline and Fall of the Roman Empire*, "the doctrine of a future life" was one of the five primary reasons for the rapid growth of Christianity in the Empire (ch XV). *Everlasting* (*aiōnios*) is a term that goes back to Plato and means pertaining to an aeon, pertaining to an age, lasting for an age. Plato applied the term to that which has no beginning or end and that is subject to neither change nor decay.

In the NT, *everlasting life* refers to the reality found in Christ and in life under His rule. It never refers to mere unending existence but indicates a new dimension of life. In the writings of John, *everlasting life* is a certain quality of life that is entered in the present, with a fuller aspect awaiting in the future (Jn. 5.24–25, 17.3; 1 Jn. 3.14). In Christ, a man can take hold now of something that is above the struggle, weariness, and disappointment of temporality. In Christ, a man can enjoy wealth and blessing that will one day broaden into a reality wonderful beyond our ability to imagine.[18]

19.30 But many *who are* first will be last, and the last first.

Christ has turned the normal evaluation of life upside-down. His kingdom includes those who become like little children (18.2), but it excludes those who trust in riches (v 25). They who think themselves great by men's

---

[17] It was with a vision of what is to be gained that David Livingston, after his terrible sufferings in Africa, said, "I never made a sacrifice in my life."

[18] Our thoughts of heaven are surely inadequate, perhaps so inadequate that not a detail of them is true, bearing no more similarity to the facts than a child's sand castle does to the Parthenon.

standards do not rate by heaven's standards. Those ranked last by men can rank highly in heaven. Contextually, the *last* who will be *first* refers to the disciples who will *sit on twelve thrones, judging the twelve tribes of Israel*; whereas the *first* who will be *last* refers to those such as the *Pharisees* (v 3) and the *young man* (v 22). In the next section, however, Christ makes an application of the *first* and *last* that challenges us every bit as much as the challenge put before the rich young ruler.

CHAPTER 20

THE PARABLE OF THE FIRST AND THE LAST, 20.1–16

Notes

If the parable that opens this chapter teaches anything, it teaches that Christ's kingdom is governed by grace.

Structurally, the parable has two parts. Verses 1–7 occur during the day and involve five scenes wherein a farmer hires workers for his vineyard. In the first scene (vv 1–3), the farmer promises to pay the workers a *denarius*; in the second (vv 3–4), he promises to pay *whatever is right*; in the three remaining scenes (vv 5–7), a wage isn't mentioned, except with the last group hired.

The second part (vv 8–15) occurs in the *evening* and contains two sections. In vv 8–9, the farmer orders the workers be paid, beginning with the last ones hired; in vv 10–15, the farmer is challenged by disgruntled workers. As at the end of the parable of the prodigal son, so at the end of this parable, there occurs a conversation that clarifies the point. Several parallels can, in fact, be drawn between this parable and the prodigal son: both include those who think they deserved more than they got, those who got more than they deserved, and the jealousy that evoked a protest. It's likely that Matthew's original readers thought of the *vineyard* as Israel and the *landowner* as God (Isa. 5.1–7; Jer. 12.10; Amos 9.13–14).

20.1–2 "For the kingdom of heaven is like a landowner who went out early in the morning to hire laborers for his vineyard. Now when he had agreed with the laborers for a denarius a day, he sent them into his vineyard.

For links this parable (found only in Matthew) to 19.30. On *the kingdom of heaven is like*, see 13.24; something in this story is meant to illustrate a truth about the kingdom. It is a familiar Jewish setting. *Early in the morning* (the workday began at sunrise), a vineyard owner goes out to hire day laborers. These were cheaper than slaves, and a denarius was the customary wage for a day's work (18.28). Christ doesn't indicate whether it was pruning time, weeding time, or harvest time.

20.3–5 And he went out about the third hour and saw others standing idle in the marketplace, and said to them, 'You also go into the vineyard, and whatever is right I will give you.' So they went. Again he went out about the sixth and the ninth hour, and did likewise.

The Jewish day consisted of twelve hours proportionally divided between sunup and sundown. The length of a day varied depending on the time of year, but the *third hour* would be around 9 AM. The Jewish *marketplace* was the center of business and community activity and a place where employers could find laborers. Left unexplained is the meaning of *whatever is right*, but the workers apparently believe they would receive a fair wage. A foray to hire more workers is repeated at *the sixth* (noon) and *ninth hours* (3 PM).

20.6–7 And about the eleventh hour he went out and found others standing idle, and said to them, 'Why have you been standing here idle all day?' They said to him, 'Because no one hired us.' He said to them, 'You also go into the vineyard, and whatever is right you will receive.'

It's unusual that workers would be hired at the *eleventh hour*—one hour before sundown. But still needing workers, the owner finds some men and asks, *Why have you been standing here idle all day? Idle* (*argos*, inactive) can mean either *unemployed* or *lazy*. The answer leans away from laziness: *because no one hired* us, but no reason for this is given (were they too old? too sick? had the owner miscalculated his needs?). The owner hires them with a promise to pay *whatever is right* (v 4). Though unusual in real life, hiring laborers at the last hour reveals something important about God and His kingdom.

20.8–9 So when evening had come, the owner of the vineyard said to his steward, 'Call the laborers and give them *their* wages, beginning with the last to the first.' And when those came who *were hired* about the eleventh hour, they each received a denarius.

When evening had come, the owner of the vineyard orders his *steward to* pay the workers their *wages* (*misthos*, dues paid for work), which was common practice (Lev. 19.13, Deut. 24.15). Surprisingly, the *steward* is to work backwards, paying first those who were hired last. Even more surprisingly, those who worked the least received the pay promised those who worked the most—illustrative of the hundred-fold reward just described (19.29). (Might not the thief on the cross be considered an eleventh-hour laborer [Lk. 23.39–43]?)

20.10 But when the first came, they supposed that they would receive more; and they likewise received each a denarius.

The owner's generosity with the one-hour workers raises the expectations of the all-day workers. They think they'll be paid more, but instead, receive only what was promised.

20.11–12 And when they had received *it*, they complained against the landowner, saying, 'These last *men* have worked *only* one hour, and you made them equal to us who have borne the burden and the heat of the day.'

The all-day workers aren't happy with this turn of events and *complain* (*gogguzō*, to murmur, mutter, grumble in a low tone) that they had been treated unfairly. *You made them equal to us who have borne the burden and heat of the day! Heat of the day* (*kausōn*) can refer to direct sunlight, the sirocco wind, or both (Lk. 12.55, "It's going to be a scorcher"). "Little seems more unequal than the equal treatment of unequals!" (Blomberg, 303).

20.13–14a But he answered one of them and said, 'Friend, I am doing you no wrong. Did you not agree with me for a denarius? Take *what is* yours and go your way.

The owner addresses one of the grumblers as *friend* (*hetairos*, a term used only by Matthew and only of those acting unfriendly; 22.12, 26.50) and defends his action on the basis of the contract and compassion. With the all-day workers, there was a contractual agreement—they agreed to work for a denarius, and a denarius they received. They had no legal basis for expecting more and needed to take their pay and go home.

20.14b–15 I want to give to this last man the same as to you. Is it not lawful for me to do what I want with my own things? Or is your eye evil because I am good?'

Further, the owner could dispose of his property anyway he wanted—a right recognized in every legal system and culture. "If what is mine belongs to me, may I not then give it to whom I wish?" (Plato). The owner did no wrong: he kept his word with the all-day workers and showed compassion to the one-hour workers (19.21).

Because the grumblers weren't protesting a broken promise or a man's right to show mercy, some other reason had to be behind their complaint, and the owner identifies it: *is your eye evil because I am good?* Using the metaphor of the *evil eye* (6.23), the owner identifies the real problem as envy or jealousy. "The grumblers were not complaining of some evil action that the householder had done; they were not saying that they had been cheated out of the wages they agreed on. They were objecting to an act of sheer generosity that he had displayed toward other people" (Morris, 504).

20.16 So the last will be first, and the first last. For many are called, but few chosen."

This verse repeats 19.30 with a slight modification — the order corresponds to the parable, speaking first of the ascent of the *last* and then of the descent of the *first*.

The general rule for parables is that they are true-to-life stories, but here is an exception. Equal pay for unequal work didn't reflect normal business practice in first-century Judea. But it is in this departure from the norm that the lesson is found. "Jesus' story makes no economic sense, and that was his intent. He was giving us a parable about grace, which cannot be calculated like a day's wages. The employer in Jesus' story did not cheat the full-day workers. No, the full-day workers got what they were promised. Their discontent arose from the scandalous mathematics of grace. They could not accept that their employer had the right to do what he wanted with his money when it meant paying scoundrels twelve times what they deserved. Significantly, many Christians who study this parable identify with the employees who put in a full day's work, rather than the add-ons at the end of the day. We like to think of ourselves as responsible workers, and the employer's strange behavior baffles us as it did the original hearers. We risk missing the story's point: that God dispenses gifts, not wages. None of us gets paid according to merit, for none of us comes close to satisfying God's requirements for a perfect life. If paid based on fairness, we would all end up in hell" (Yancey, *What's So Amazing About Grace*, 61–62).

Legalists take note: the kingdom of heaven operates by mercy (*hundredfold*, 19.29), not merit. Being first according to human yardsticks (19.16ff) places no lien on God. And if those who think themselves more deserving resent God for not agreeing with them, it's because they are unrighteous.

Throughout His ministry, Jesus championed outcasts—lepers, publicans, sinners, a prophet who dressed in camel's hair and ate locusts, women, Gentiles (Lk. 13.29–30), a thief (Lk. 23.39–43), and others. Those who objected—kings, Pharisees (Bible scholars), priests, rich young rulers, disciples (vv 20–21)—did not understand mercy. For us to claim in regard to the commandments of God, *All these things I have kept* (19.20), is a delusion borne of ignorance—we are deluded about the *quality* of our obedience and ignorant of the fact that even when we *have done all those things which are commanded*, our fallibility is such that the best we can say is, *We are unprofitable servants* (Lk. 17.10). We, who so easily think in terms of merit, may be in for many surprises when the God of grace bestows His rewards at the judgment.

20.17–34: The Third Prediction

Notes

Christ's third explicit prediction about what awaits at Jerusalem is framed by the verbs: *will be betrayed* and *will rise.* In between, simple sentences describe the stages of the ordeal, detailing both Jewish and Roman involvement.

20.17–19 Now Jesus, going up to Jerusalem, took the twelve disciples aside on the road and said to them, "Behold, we are going up to Jerusalem, and the Son of Man will be betrayed to the chief priests and to the scribes; and they will condemn Him to death, and deliver Him to the Gentiles to mock and to scourge and to crucify. And the third day He will rise again."

Going up was the usual way Jews described any trip to Jerusalem and doesn't necessarily indicate that the actual ascent has begun. What Jesus says is said only to His disciples. The emphasis is on the *Son of Man* (8.20) and what will happen to Him in Jerusalem.

The predictions are so precise that they could serve as a table of contents for the passion narrative in chs 26 to 27. At Jerusalem, Christ would be *betrayed to the chief priests and* scribes, who would *condemn Him to death and deliver Him to the Gentiles.* The Gentiles would *mock, scourge,* and *crucify* Him. *Crucify*—a means of execution reserved for the worst of the worst— introduces a new detail not mentioned in 16.21 or 17.22–23. It is not a glorious martyrdom that awaits Jesus, but a horrible, humiliating execution.

TWO DISCIPLES, 20.20–28

Notes

One of the ways by which historians assess the veracity of a document is "the embarrassment test"—does the narrative contain events or details that are embarrassing to the author? This principle assumes that most people leave out information that makes them look bad, and if something embarrassing is included, it is probably true. "How does the New Testament measure up to the principle of embarrassment? Let's put it this way: If you and your friends were concocting a story that you wanted to pass off as the truth, would you make yourselves look like dim-witted, uncaring, rebuked, doubting cowards?" (Geisler, 276).

Nothing better illustrates the embarrassment principle and the obtuseness of the disciples than this scene involving James and John. After the teaching of 18.1–4, the disciples should have been striving to be the lowest, but instead, they are still wanting to be the greatest.

This section divides into two parts. The first (vv 20–23) involves a question asked Jesus by the mother of James and John; the second (vv 24–28) is Christ's response to the indignation of the Ten over the question asked by the Two.

Despite Christ's teaching, the disciples haven't accepted the fact of His death, for "no man asks to sit on the right hand and left of a man who is going to the gallows" (Morgan, 246).

20.20 Then the mother of Zebedee's sons came to Him with her sons, kneeling down and asking something from Him.

Matthew doesn't say what prompted the *mother of Zebedee's sons*[1] (4.21) to approach Jesus, but considering that Jesus speaks directly to James and John in vv 22–23, the implication is that they put her up to it ("A mother can usually be counted on to do almost anything on behalf of

---

[1] It is possible that *the mother of Zebedee's sons* was the sister of Mary the mother of Jesus (i.e., Salome). See 27.56, Mk.15.40 and Jn. 19.25.

her children," Harrison, 145). The request reveals inexcusable ignorance, made more shocking by the fact it not only came from members of the Twelve, but from members of the Three (17.1, 26.37; Mk. 5.37).

James and John's mother's manner is respectful (*kneeling down*); she doesn't speak until encouraged to do so.

20.21 And He said to her, "What do you wish?" She said to Him, "Grant that these two sons of mine may sit, one on Your right hand and the other on the left, in Your kingdom."

James and John want privileged positions in Christ's government. It's an impudent request, but not entirely irrational considering Christ's statement in 19.28, and the fact that the brothers belonged to Jesus' innermost circle (17.1, 26.37). The *right* and *left* seats were places of honor (23.6). According to the Mishna, when a rabbi was walking in public, he should be in the middle, with the older pupil on his right and the younger on his left. In Middle Eastern courts, the right-hand seat was often reserved for the crown prince (Ps. 110.1).

20.22 But Jesus answered and said, "You do not know what you ask. Are you able to drink the cup that I am about to drink, and be baptized with the baptism that I am baptized with?" They said to Him, "We are able."

Jesus brushes the request aside and says it was asked out of ignorance: *you don't know what you're asking* (BECK). After 19.30 to 20.16, the brothers should have understood that *first place* was a precarious position. To re-emphasize this, Christ asks a question that says, in essence, be careful what you ask for. *Are you able to drink the cup that I am about to drink, and be baptized with the baptism that I am baptized with?* The *cup* was prophetic metonymy for God's wrath (Jer. 25.15–16; Jn. 18.11; Rev. 16.1); *to drink the cup* was to be under His judgment. *Baptism*, which parallels *drink the cup*, was used in the papyri to mean being immersed in or overwhelmed by something. Assuming that James and John understood the significance of the figures, they courageously answer, *We are able*. Any hardships they anticipated were probably understood as the fighting required to establish a political kingdom; they certainly weren't thinking of the redemptive suffering meant by Christ that resisted not evil (5.38). "The mood here is one of heroism, a self-assured gutsy readiness to act nobly for a noble cause" (Gardiner, 304).

20.23 So He said to them, "You will indeed drink My cup, and be baptized with the baptism that I am baptized with; but to sit on My right hand and on My left is not Mine to give, but *it is for those* for whom it is prepared by My Father."

The brothers spoke better than they realized. *You shall indeed drink My cup* foretold suffering in their future, but not in the way they expected. James would be the first apostle to die (Acts 12.2), and it is likely that John also died a martyr's death (Tertullian, in his *Prescriptions against Heretics*, said that John was "immersed in boiling oil without harm, [and then] was banished to an island"; Rev. 1.9). Their willingness to suffer, however, gave them no advantage, for *to sit on My right hand and on My left is not Mine to give*. It was not Christ's prerogative to assign places of honor; such responsibility belonged to God. In this world, favors are often doled out on the basis of friendship, nepotism, tenure, etc., but in the kingdom, places of honor are for the truly honorable (Phil. 2.29) — the loving and lowly.

20.24 And when the ten heard *it*, they were greatly displeased with the two brothers.

The other disciples fume because James and John had beaten them to the punch (18.1; Lk. 22.24).

20.25–27 But Jesus called them to *Himself* and said, "You know that the rulers of the Gentiles lord it over them, and those who are great exercise authority over them. Yet it shall not be so among you; but whoever desires to become great among you, let him be your servant. And whoever desires to be first among you, let him be your slave—

Christ ends the squabble by presenting a contrast. Contrary to the power structures of earthly kingdoms and *rulers* who *lord it over* (*katakurieuō*, only here, Mk. 10.42, Acts 19.16, and 1 Pet. 5.3) *them and exercise authority over them,*[2] His followers would be characterized by *service*. In the political world, the goal is to be served, and rank is measured by how many serve you. *Yet it shall not be so among you.* Instead of laying out an alternative path to greatness, Christ is saying that in His kingdom, there is no mindset to be great at all! The goal in Christ's kingdom is to serve. *Servant* (*diakonos*) appears here in Matthew for the first time (v 28, 25.44). In a Gr. context,

---

[2] It is the very nature of secular authority, even democratic authority, to demand obedience from the constituency and use the full force and power of government to enforce compliance.

it often referred to a personal servant (valet) or house servant (butler);[3] *slave* (*doulos*) was a broader term that often included more menial or demeaning servitude.

Christ thus reverses the popular measure of greatness. There are no lords or bosses in his kingdom, only servants. Regrettably, the desire to boss others sometimes plagues churches (3 Jn. 9) and elderships (1 Pet. 5.3). To lord it over rather than serve under is a powerful temptation (4.8–10), but it is utterly unChristlike.[4]

Verse 27, for emphasis, repeats v 26.

20.28 just as the Son of Man did not come to be served, but to serve, and to give His life a ransom for many."

A paragraph that began with the suffering Son of Man (v 18) ends on the same note. *Just as the Son of Man* means that disciples are to follow Christ's example; the character of the kingdom is determined by the character of the King. Christ's *service* is the model to which His followers orient themselves. At this point, when the disciples thought of His service, they likely thought of Jesus' healing ministry, miraculous feedings, etc. Christ, however, is thinking of His death—His best and highest act of service would be *to give His life a ransom for many.* He has spoken of His death (vv 18–19, 16.21, 17.22–23) and introduced the idea that discipleship involved the surrendering of one's life (10.38–39, 16.24–26), but now, for the first time, He describes His death as a *ransom* (*lutron*, to loose; only here and Mk. 10.45).

A *lutron* was the price paid to free a slave or to save the condemned from capital punishment (Ex. 21.30). It was a substitutionary transaction wherein something (money) or someone took the place of another. Implicit is the idea of substitutionary or vicarious atonement.[5] This is one of the clearest statements in the NT about the redemptive nature of Christ's death. *Many* recalls the great sacrificial prophecy of the OT, Isaiah 53.11–12, and as 1 Timothy 2.6 shows, *many* is a synecdoche for *all* (*gave Himself a ransom for all*; v 16, 26.28).[6]

---

[3] *Diakonos* "may [have] come from *dia* and *konis* (dust), to raise a dust by one's hurry, and so to minister" (Robertson, 162).

[4] Isn't it ironic that a word meant to indicate a servant—*minister*—can refer to one who is anything but?

[5] See Leon Morris's excellent discussion of *lutron*/ransom in *The Apostolic Preaching of the Cross*, 11ff.

[6] One of the best illustrations of where *many* means *all* is seen by comparing Mk. 1.32–34

TWO BLIND MEN, 20.29–34

Notes

The last paragraph in Matthew's run-up to Jerusalem gives us the place and setting (v 29), followed by an exposition (vv 30–33) in which Jesus is engaged by two blind men who appeal to Him for help, concluding with a miracle of compassion (v 34). The healing of the blind and their acclamation *Son of David* transition to the next section and the cry of the triumphal entry (21.9).

20.29–31 Now as they went out of Jericho, a great multitude followed Him. And behold, two blind men sitting by the road, when they heard that Jesus was passing by, cried out, saying, "Have mercy on us, O Lord, Son of David!" Then the multitude warned them that they should be quiet; but they cried out all the more, saying, "Have mercy on us, O Lord, Son of David!"

For the first time since He left Galilee (19.1), Matthew pinpoints Jesus' location. Jericho was in the Jordan Valley on the west bank of the river, about fifteen miles northeast of Jerusalem, 1300' below sea level. At the time of Christ, OT Jericho was identified with a large mound known as Tell es-Sultan. A second site also called *Jericho* was located a mile to the south. Because of its warm winters, Jericho was a resort city where Herod the Great had built a spectacular palace after the Roman style (it was destroyed during the Jewish Rebellion of AD 66–70).

The *great multitude* that accompanied Christ from Galilee was still with Him. After leaving Jericho (see *Excursus* following), two blind beggars (Lk. 18.35)—undoubtedly hoping for alms from well-to-do worshipers on their way to Passover—hear a commotion and learn that Jesus is passing by. They can't see Him, but readers are asked to see them—*Behold.* It's likely that they had heard of Jesus' earlier healings of blindness (9.27–31, 12.22, 15.30–31), and so they cry out, *Have mercy on us, O Lord, Son of David!* In Matthew, *Lord* was the usual term of address by a supplicant (14.30, 15.22, 17.15, 18.26) and *Son of David* was a popular designation for the Messiah (1.1). The crowd tells them to *be quiet*, but this only elicits further shouts—*they cried out all the more* (*krazō*, to scream, shriek) *saying, "Have mercy on us, O Lord, Son of David!"* They were not going to keep quiet; they might never have this chance again.

---

with Matt. 8.16. Whereas Mark says that they *brought to Him all who were sick and He healed many*, Matthew says, they *brought to Him many and he healed all who were sick*.

20.32–34 So Jesus stood still and called them, and said, "What do you want Me to do for you?" They said to Him, "Lord, that our eyes may be opened." So Jesus had compassion and touched their eyes. And immediately their eyes received sight, and they followed Him.

They get Christ's attention (He *stood still*). *What do you want Me to do for you?* and they answer, *we want our eyes opened.* Misery provides mercy an opportunity, and Christ, moved by *compassion* (*splagchnizomai*, to be moved to one's bowels, a gut reaction) restores to them the light of sight. *And they followed Him*, which is what men do who see Christ clearly.

This miracle occupies a strategic place in this Gospel. Not only is it "the end of the account of Jesus' itinerant ministry" (France, 294), but it typifies the central place of mercy (v 15) and service (v 28) in the kingdom. "The request of the disciples [v 21] shows their blindness: the request of the blind men shows their vision—of who Jesus is and what he can do" (Michael Green, qtd. by Morris, 516).

Excursus on the Healing of the Blind Men

Skeptics often cite Christ's encounter with the blind men as an example of a contradiction that disqualifies the Gospels as credible historical records.

By definition, a contradiction exists only when it is impossible to reconcile two statements. If a plausible explanation exists, a contradiction cannot be claimed; whether or not we like the explanation is irrelevant. So long as it is logical and accounts for all the data, no contradiction exists. From a legal standpoint, the variations in the Gospels strengthen their credibility, for they are precisely what we would expect from independent accounts of the same event. "In point of fact, discrepancies are all in favor instead of against the truth of the New Testament. Nothing is more commonly known in the department of civil jurisprudence than that testimony, given by different witnesses whose statements too closely resemble each other, is invalidated thereby. It looks like collusion; it casts suspicion of fraud, and really jeopardizes what might have otherwise been a good cause" (Moses Lard, "The Resurrection of Christ," *Lard's Quarterly*, 5.312–313).

Objections to the healing of the blind men focus on two issues.

First, did Jesus heal one blind man (Mk. 10.46; Lk. 18.35) or two (v 30)? The obvious answer is that Mark and Luke mention only Bartimaeus, the more conspicuous of the two (Mk. 10.46). They didn't say Jesus healed *only* one blind man; their lack of reference to the second man in no way precludes his presence (cf. the Gospel accounts of the demoniacs in 8.38, the blind men in 9.27, and the donkeys in 21.2–7).

Second, were the blind men healed before Jesus reached Jericho (Lk. 18.35) or after He left it (v 29)? Various solutions have been offered to explain this discrepancy (see Culver, 212), but the simplest is that Matthew probably refers to the mound of OT Jericho (v 29) and Luke to the city built by Herod the Great (Josephus, *Wars* IV.viii.3). Somewhere between these two locations is where Jesus encountered the blind men.

CHAPTER 21

21.1–25.46: The Jews Tried by Jesus

    21.1–17: Sunday

ENTRY INTO JERUSALEM, 21.1–11

Notes

The time has come for Christ to complete His work on earth, and to do so He returns to Jerusalem (Lk. 9.31,33). Of the 1071 verses in Matthew, 389—more than a third—are dedicated to the final week of Christ's life. Such emphasis isn't surprising for the most important event in history.

Chapters 21–22 can be thought of as an ad hoc trial in which Judaism is arraigned before Jesus, the judge. The verdict reached is *guilty!* (ch 23), followed by sentencing (chs 24–25).

Establishing a timeline for Christ's final week isn't easy, but I think a likely scenario for the first three days is this: Sunday, 21.1–17; Monday, 21.18–19; Tuesday, 21.20 to 25.46.

Jesus' first day back in Jerusalem (vv 1–17) is framed by geographical references (vv 1a, 17), between which are scenes prior to Christ's entry (vv 1b–9), after His entry (vv 10–11), and in the temple (vv 12–16).

21.1–3 Now when they drew near Jerusalem, and came to Bethphage, at the Mount of Olives, then Jesus sent two disciples, saying to them, "Go into the village opposite you, and immediately you will find a donkey tied, and a colt with her. Loose *them* and bring *them* to Me. And if anyone says anything to you, you shall say, 'The Lord has need of them,' and immediately he will send them."

The *Triumphal Entry* is one of the most remarkable events in Christ's earthly career. It is found in all four Gospels and is quite unlike anything else said of the Lord up to this point. Prior to this, Jesus didn't court attention—He did not *cry out, no one heard His voice in the streets* (12.19);

He often told people not to tell what He had done (8.4, 9.30, 12.16, 16.20, 17.9). But the entry into Jerusalem changes all this. So demonstrative and public is the event that even the Pharisees must admit, *the world has gone after Him!* (Jn. 12.19).

The reason for this change is that the Scriptures must be fulfilled (v 4). The major crisis of Christ's life has been reached, and His entrance was fully intended to proclaim His Messiahship. No longer will He charge people to not make Him known; now He accepts the acclamations of the people and silences the remonstrations of the establishment (vv 15–16, Lk. 19.39–40). Wise men testified in Jerusalem to the *king of the Jews* early on (ch 2), and now at the end, the King testifies to Himself as the king of Israel.

From rabbinic sources, we know that *Bethphage* (house of unripe figs) was a village east of Jerusalem on the Mount of Olives. After arriving there, Jesus takes the initiative to ensure that what must happen, happens. "Any prudent person in the circumstances of Jesus would have tried to slip into the city unseen; the last thing he would have tried to do would have been to court publicity. But Jesus entered Jerusalem in a way that was designed to focus every eye upon him" (Barclay, *By What Authority*, 187).

Two disciples are sent *into the village opposite*—Bethphage—to requisition a donkey and colt. "Jesus had walked all the way from Galilee, and surely did not *need* to ride a donkey for only the last two miles" (France, 296), but riding a donkey into Jerusalem was a deliberate Messianic gesture, and Christ means to portray Himself as Israel's Messiah.

As evidence of His command of the situation, Jesus anticipates an objection by the animals' owner. "It is unlikely that a stranger might walk into a village, untie an animal, and walk off with it without being challenged" (Morris, 519). When challenged, the disciples were to say *the Lord has need of them*, and they would be allowed to proceed. Trueblood makes the intriguing observation "that Christ's cause had some of the features of an underground movement. ... The colt was deliberately tied in a prearranged location and a password had been established in case of difficulty" (*Confronting Christ*, 104). Although this may be a stretch, there were elements of mystery involved in fetching the animals.

21.4–5 All this was done that it might be fulfilled which was spoken by the prophet, saying: "Tell the daughter of Zion, 'Behold, your King is coming to you, Lowly, and sitting on a donkey, A colt, the foal of a donkey.'

This is the only time in Matthew when a prophecy is quoted *before* its fulfillment. The manner of Christ's entry *fulfilled* (1.22) Zechariah 9.9,[1] which depicted Israel's king riding into Jerusalem (*daughter of Zion*, a metaphor for Jerusalem, Isa. 62.11) astride a donkey.[2]

The use of a donkey sent several messages. One of the things that was to mark out Israel as a peculiar people was the absence of the horse. In contrast to Egypt (Ex. 14.23, 15.1), the kings of Canaan (Josh. 11.4), or Assyria (Isa. 36.8), the kings of Israel were not to multiply horses for themselves (Deut. 17.16). *Some trust in chariots, and some in horses; but we will remember the name of the LORD OUR GOD* (Ps. 20.7). The king of Israel was to be sharply distinguished from the kings of the Gentiles (20.25–26), and the manner of Christ's entry symbolized this. He didn't ride into town astride a warhorse or in a horse-drawn chariot, but entered *on a donkey*, a beast of burden that symbolized His *lowliness* (*praus, lowly*, meek, 5.5, 11.29, 18.4) and servant character.[3]

J. C. Ryle noted another message conveyed by Christ's entry: "No Roman soldier in the garrison of Jerusalem, who, standing at his post or sitting in his barrack-window, saw our Lord riding on an ass, could report to his centurion that He looked like one who came to wrest the kingdom of Judea out of the hands of the Romans, drive out Pontius Pilate and his legions from the tower of Antonia, and achieve independence for the Jews with the sword" (qtd. by Mauro, "Christ's Entry into Jerusalem"). I think it probable that Pilate knew of Christ's entry and drew on it to conclude that He posed no military threat to Rome.

Sitting on a donkey, and a colt, the foal of a donkey seems to indicate that Christ rode astride two animals. The other Gospels, however, make it clear that He rode on the colt (Mk. 11.7; Lk. 19.35; Jn. 12.15). Matthew's account may indicate that the animals were yoked or tied together, as the second mention of a *donkey* translates *hupozugion*, which in "early Greek … is a general term for a yoked animal, but in Koine it means 'donkey'" (Luz III, 8).

In Mark's account, the Lord describes the colt as one *on which no one has ever sat* (Mk. 11.2). This is a striking statement — to ride serenely on an

---

[1] Only Isaiah (8.17) and Jeremiah (2.17) are mentioned by name in introductions to OT fulfillment quotations. Unnamed are Micah (2.5), Hosea (2.15), Asaph (13.35), and Zechariah.

[2] Some believe Matthew blends two prophecies here. "The quotation is partly from Zechariah, partly from Isaiah. The first clause, *eipate te thugatri Sion*, is the LXX rendering of Is. lxii.11. The remainder is an abbreviated citation from Zech. ix. 9" (Carr, 241).

[3] In contrast to Christ's lowly ride here, see Him in Rev. 6.2, 19.11 on the *whit horse*.

unbroken colt was a marvel that spoke of Christ's authority over creation and recalls other things that spoke of His uniqueness, such as the fact that He was born of a virgin and buried in a new tomb *in which no one had yet been laid* (Jn. 19.41).

21.6–7 So the disciples went and did as Jesus commanded them. They brought the donkey and the colt, laid their clothes on them, and set *Him* on them.

The disciples do as they are told. When they return with the animals, they place some *clothes* (*himation*, outer cloak, 5.40) upon the colt and hoist Jesus onto it (v 5).

> *When fishes flew and forests walk'd*
> *And figs grew upon thorn,*
> *Some moment when the moon was blood*
> *Then surely I was born.*
> *With monstrous head and sickening cry*
> *And ears like errant wings,*
> *The devil's walking parody*
> *Of all four-footed things.*
> *The tatter'd outlaw of the earth,*
> *Of ancient crooked will;*
> *Starve, scourge, deride me: I am dumb,*
> *I keep my secret still.*
> *Fools! For I also had my hour,*
> *One far fierce hour and sweet:*
> *There was a shout about my ears,*
> *And palms before my feet.*
> G. K. Chesterton, *The Donkey*

21.8–9 And a very great multitude spread their clothes on the road; others cut down branches from the trees and spread *them* on the road. Then the multitudes who went before and those who followed cried out, saying: "Hosanna to the Son of David! 'Blessed *is* He who comes in the name of the Lord!' Hosanna in the highest!"

The entry into Jerusalem is known as the *Triumphal Entry*. It's true that vv 8–9 describe homage that might have been shown a king or conquering general,[4] but no one present would have mistaken Christ's entry for the

---

[4] 1 Macc. 13.51 describes the entrance of Simon the Maccabee into the temple with palm

splendor of a Roman *triumph* or *ovation*.[5] Just as Christ memorialized His death before He died (26.26–29), so the *triumphal entry* anticipated His ultimate victory (28.6).

The implication of Jesus' mount wasn't lost on the crowd, and they gave Him the red-carpet treatment. Spreading branches on the ground was a common act of respect and homage (2 Kgs. 9.13; Rev. 7.9).

Hosanna was originally a heaven-sent sos that meant *Save now!* or *Please help!* but here it is a cry of praise and acclamation. By *Son of David*, the *multitudes* were acknowledging Jesus as the Messiah, even though they were woefully ignorant of the Messiah's true nature. *Blessed is He who comes in the name of the Lord* comes from Psalm 118.26 and was a greeting with which priests would welcome pilgrims to the temple; there is no indication that the Jews saw it as a singularly Messianic phrase (v 42). *Hosanna in the highest*, or *in the heights*, may be understood as a call to the angels to join in the hosanna cry. "Let heaven itself join us in acclaiming him!" (Gardner, 313).

21.10–11 And when He had come into Jerusalem, all the city was moved, saying, "Who is this?" So the multitudes said, "This is Jesus, the prophet from Nazareth of Galilee."

When Jesus entered Jerusalem, *all the city was moved.* This was no minor event for *moved* translates *seiesthai,* from which comes *seismic,* which is used to describe the shaking caused by earthquakes. This word described Herod's and Jerusalem's apprehension over Jesus' birth (2.3), and the guards' quaking at Jesus' resurrection (28.4). The word often denotes fear, and here it likely refers to the apprehension caused in Jerusalem by the excitement of the Passover pilgrims (v 8).

Jerusalem asks *Who is this?* and the answer is, *Jesus, the prophet from Nazareth of Galilee.* Even if the crowd only meant Jesus was *a* prophet (14.5, 16.14), not implying that He was the Messiah, their excitement over Him was enough to keep the Jewish leaders from immediately carrying out their murderous intent (vv 26,46).

---

branches, shouts of jubilation, hymns, and songs.

[5] A wonderful description of the Roman triumph is found in Frances Elliot's *Pictures of Old Rome,* 195–216.

CLEANSING THE TEMPLE, 21.12–17

Notes

The popular impression of Jesus as a "pale Galilean" (Swinburne)—sad, anorexic, effeminate—doesn't hold up before a text like this. Here, and at other times in the final week (ch 23), Christ was noticeably angry. Because our anger is often born of selfishness, it often ends in shame and remorse. Jesus, however, was never angry over any wrong done to Him as an individual; His wrath was always unselfish, directed at dishonor toward God and injustices toward men. And there was no conflict between His anger and His lowliness. He had a capacity for moral indignation that we will never approach, and yet, when spat upon, mocked, scourged, and crucified He didn't utter a word of anger or resentment at the brutality He received. *When He was reviled, He did not revile in return* (1 Pet. 2.23). George Matheson, who wrote the hymn "O Love That Will Not Let Me Go," once confessed, "There are times when I do well to be angry, but I have mistaken the times"—Christ never mistook the time, and He was never angry over personal mistreatment.

21.12 Then Jesus went into the temple of God and drove out all those who bought and sold in the temple, and overturned the tables of the money changers and the seats of those who sold doves.

The reverence of the temple has been replaced by a flea market atmosphere that elicits two responses from Christ: He *drove out all those who bought and sold and overturned the tables of the moneychangers*, and He healed *the blind and the lame*. It's surprising that the temple police didn't try to stop Him. Possibly, something in the Lord's demeanor occasioned a restraint similar to the scene in John 18.6, when those who went to arrest Christ *drew back and fell to the ground.*

For pilgrims coming to Passover, it was easier to buy sacrificial animals after reaching Jerusalem than to bring them from home. Worshippers would also need to convert their regional currency into the Jewish half-shekel in order to pay the temple tax (17.24).[6] There was nothing wrong with providing animals or currency exchange services, but historical sources show that the priests and Sadducees controlled these businesses, and they

---

[6] Various sources indicate that foreign money was converted into Tyrian currency. According to Israel Abrahams, the Tyrian coins "were so emphatically the legal tender in the Temple that they were termed Jerusalemite as well as Tyrian" (*Studies in Pharisaism and the Gospels*, 83).

allowed transactions to be conducted in *the temple of God,* which here refers to the Court of the Gentiles that encompassed about twenty-five acres in Herod's temple. Because the priests and Sadducees had a monopoly, the rates they charged vendors were exorbitant. *Moneychangers (kollubistēs,* banker) is literally "one who takes a commission." The mention of *those who sold doves* indicates that the poor, in particular, were hard hit by the inflated prices, as doves were the sacrifice of the poor (Lev. 5.7). That Jesus drove out *all* the buyers and sellers indicates that this was no minor disruption.

21.13 And He said to them, "It is written, 'My house shall be called a house of prayer,' but you have made it a 'den of thieves.'"

Christ defends His actions with an *It is written* (4.4), citing Isaiah 56.7 and Jeremiah 7.11. The religious establishment had perverted the purpose of God's *house*[7,8]—instead of *a house of prayer* that encouraged a worshipper's approach to God, the temple had become *a den of thieves*—a cave in a mountain—where criminals lurked. Greed had supplanted God, and huckstering hampered worship.

21.14 Then *the* blind and *the* lame came to Him in the temple, and He healed them.

This last reference in Matthew to Christ's miraculous healings presents a contrast that says a great deal about the true use of the temple. Jesus, in anger, drove out the buyers, sellers, and moneychangers, but in mercy, *healed the* blind and the lame who are always welcome in the house of God (9.12–13).

21.15–16 But when the chief priests and scribes saw the wonderful things that He did, and the children crying out in the temple and saying, "Hosanna to the Son of David!" they were indignant and said to Him, "Do You hear what these are saying?" And Jesus said to them, "Yes. Have you never read, 'Out of the mouth of babes and nursing infants You have perfected praise'?"

The *wonderful things (thaumasios,* marvelous; only here in the NT) *that Jesus did* (v 14) aroused the malevolence of *the chief priests and scribes.* Nothing is said about their reaction to the cleansing of the temple (v 12); instead, they

---

[7] Cf. 15.5 where the custom of *corban* completely reversed the intent of the fifth commandment.

[8] "Soon after the time of Jesus, Rabbi Shimeon ben Gamaliel [Acts 5.34] protested vigorously against excessive charges for sacrificial birds" (Israel Abrahams, *Studies in Pharisaism and the Gospels,* ch 11).

are *indignant* that the blind and lame are healed in the temple and that *children* joined in the shouts of *Hosanna to the Son of David* (v 9).

The chief priests and scribes ask Jesus a question that elicits a question: *Do you not hear? ... Have you never read?* This is the first mention of children since Christ entered Jerusalem. Presumably, the reference is to actual *children* in the sense of 18.2–5 and 19.13–15, but the reference to Psalm 8.2, *out of the mouth of babes and nursing infants*, recalls 11.25–27 and those to whom are given the mysteries of the kingdom. The irony is unmistakable: because Israel's religious establishment opposed Israel's Messiah, it was left to children to *perfect* (*katartizō*, to mend [4.21], repair, put in order) *praise*—to render to Christ His due.

21.17 Then He left them and went out of the city to Bethany, and He lodged there.

Everything Christ had done this day—His entry into Jerusalem, cleansing the temple, miracles, validating the children's cries—presented Him as Israel's Messiah. He left the chief priests, scribes, and Jerusalem on edge (v 10) to spend the night (*lodged, aulizomai*, to pass the night) in Bethany, a village on the southeastern side of the Mount of Olives.

21.18–19: Monday

Notes

Again, identifying the individual days of the last week isn't easy, but I think we're on firm ground to see a break between v 17 and v 18. I'm less sure about when the day beginning in v 18 ends. Considering that in Mark 11 the cursing of the fig tree occurs on one day (v 14), but its withering isn't noticed until the next (vv 20–21), I'm including only vv 18–19 as occurring on Monday of the final week.

THE FIG TREE, 21.18–19

21.18–19 Now in the morning, as He returned to the city, He was hungry. And seeing a fig tree by the road, He came to it and found nothing on it but leaves, and said to it, "Let no fruit grow on you ever again." Immediately the fig tree withered away.

The next morning, on the way back to Jerusalem, Jesus *was hungry*. Seeing *a fig tree by the road*, He went to pick some fruit for breakfast but found nothing except foliage (Mk. 11.13). A peculiarity of fig trees is that the fruit appears either in advance of leaves or simultaneously with them.[9] Since this tree had leaves, it should have had fruit. When Christ found the tree barren, He pronounced a curse: *Let no fruit grow on you anymore forever. And immediately* (*parachrēma*, instantly, soon) *the fig tree withered away* (see Mk. 11.14–21[10]).

Those who are shocked by what seems a pique of anger miss the symbolism. Miracles always point beyond themselves, and this incident previewed the judgment coming to Israel (vv 33–44) when God would pour out His wrath on those who killed His Son (11.21–24, 12.41–42). This tree "fairly represented the Jewish nation. It made great pretense of service to God, but it was pretense only. Jesus had already pronounced the doom of that nation; and like the fig tree it would soon wither and die" (Whiteside, *Reflections*, 465).

21.20–25.46: Tuesday

21.20–22 And when the disciples saw *it*, they marveled, saying, "How did the fig tree wither away so soon?" So Jesus answered and said to them, "Assuredly, I say to you, if you have faith and do not doubt, you will not only do what was done to the fig tree, but also if you say to this mountain, 'Be removed and be cast into the sea,' it will be done. And whatever things you ask in prayer, believing, you will receive."

When the disciples see what happened to the fig tree, they *marvel* (*thaumazō*, to wonder) at the rapidity with which it died. But instead of using the occasion to make a point about judgment, Jesus makes a point about faith. In the coming days, the disciples' faith would be tested beyond anything they had encountered up till then, and strong faith was needed (on *moving mountains*, see 17.20). *All things*, contextually, refers to the challenges the disciples would face in the coming days, and they needed a faith equal to

---

[9] "When the young leaves are appearing in spring, every fertile fig will have some *taksh* [underdeveloped fruit] on it, even though the season for edible figs (Mk. 11.13, AV) has not arrived. When the leaves are fully developed the fruit ought to be mature also. But if a tree with leaves has no fruit, it will be barren for the entire season" (*International Standard Bible Encyclopedia*, II, 302).

[10] *Immediately* (v 19) indicates that tree died instantly, but it wasn't obvious until the next day. Blomberg believes the withering occurred over a twenty-four-hour period rather than at once. "By horticultural standards, this still qualifies as 'immediately.'" He also cites Louw and Nida's *Greek-English Lexicon of the New Testament*, which "emphasizes *parachrēma* as often meaning *suddenly* more than *strict immediacy*" (317).

the challenge. God equips us with the wherewithal to meet our problems; not, necessarily, by giving us things that are good, but by giving us what we need to be good.

THE BAPTISM OF JOHN, 21.23–27

Notes

From 21.23 to 22.46, five clashes occur between Jesus and His enemies involving question and answer—a common rabbinic debate format. "These controversies, sprung upon Him unaware and without warning ... never found Him unprepared, nor at a loss what to say in self-defense, or in retort. His method of dealing with cavilers and objectors was exactly suited to the situation. The result of these controversial encounters shook public confidence in the scribes and Pharisees, while enhancing His own authority with the people and with His own disciples. And it drew forth from Jesus some of His brightest and most characteristic utterances" (E. Griffith-Jones, qtd. by Bales, *Christian, Contend for Thy Cause*, 16–17). Following hard on the cleansing of the temple, these controversies constitute the second round between Christ and His opponents.

We know more about what Jesus said and did on this day than on any other day in His life. He is in the temple—Judaism's center—teaching the teachers and the people alike.

21.23 Now when He came into the temple, the chief priests and the elders of the people confronted Him as He was teaching, and said, "By what authority are You doing these things? And who gave You this authority?"

In the *temple*, Jesus does what should be done there (v 13)—He *teaches*. While thus engaged, He is approached by *the chief priests and the elders of the people*—the highest representatives of the temple and nation. *Chief priests* were leaders of the priestly families; the *elders* were aristocratic laymen who represented the people and would likely have been Pharisees (v 45); these two groups will play a major role in securing Jesus to death (26.3,47, 27.1). Apparently believing that anyone teaching in the temple needed their imprimatur, they ask two questions: *By what authority are you doing these things?* and *Who gave you this authority? These things* likely include everything Jesus had done since arriving at Jerusalem: cleansing the temple (v 12), healing (v 14), and teaching.

21.24 But Jesus answered and said to them, "I also will ask you one thing, which if you tell Me, I likewise will tell you by what authority I do these things:

Jesus knew these men were beyond reason and reach (13.15). Nevertheless, He agrees to answer their question if they will answer His. The chief priests and elders could hardly object, for they recognized question/ counter-question as a legitimate way to get at truth.

21.25–26 The baptism of John—where was it from? From heaven or from men?" And they reasoned among themselves, saying, "If we say, 'From heaven,' He will say to us, 'Why then did you not believe him?' But if we say, 'From men,' we fear the multitude, for all count John as a prophet."

The baptism of John, where was it from? From heaven or from men? Implicit in this question is that Jesus' authority derived from the same source as John the Baptist's (3.1–12). It was a simple question for which there were only two possible answers. But either answer would hang the respondents on the horns of a dilemma. If they said John's authority came from God, Jesus would have said that His authority also came from God (11.27), for the credentials He offered far exceeded John's (Jn. 10.40–42). If His authority was from God, the temple establishment could not claim jurisdiction over Him. Further, this answer would have been self-incriminating for these were they who *did not* believe—they were the *brood of vipers* (3.7) who didn't respond to John's preaching or submit to his baptism.

If they said John's authority came *from men*, they opened themselves to a backlash from those, especially the pilgrims in town for the Passover, who believed John to be a prophet.

21.27 So they answered Jesus and said, "We do not know." And He said to them, "Neither will I tell you by what authority I do these things.

Because neither answer was politically expedient, they replied, *We do not know*. If they thought this got them off the hook, they were wrong. "The question they asked Jesus was based on the assumption that they were qualified to examine a man's credentials and tell whether he had proper authority. John had generated a great deal of attention, but they said that they were unable to make up their minds about him. In other words, they were too incompetent to evaluate the credentials of those who professed to be sent of God. This being the case they really denied their own right to ask

Jesus for His credentials. Thus, they disqualified themselves" (Bales, *Jesus, The Master Respondent*, 8–9). "If ever men stood self-condemned, they stood self-condemned; they ought to have known; it was their duty to know. It was part of the duty of the Sanhedrin, of which they were members, to distinguish between true and false prophets, and they were saying that they were quite unable to make that distinction" (Barclay II, 285).

Men unable to draw a conclusion about John were in no position to question Jesus. Because they refused to answer, He refused to answer; He would not cast pearls before swine (7.6).

TWO SONS, 21.28–32

Notes

Three parables follow involving two sons, wicked tenants, and a wedding feast. The first and second begin with a question that asks for an opinion that Jesus will use as a conclusion. The third parable is more pointed than the first two, but all three are related by content; they belong together and interpret one another in warning of judgment coming on Israel.

21.28–30 "But what do you think? A man had two sons, and he came to the first and said, 'Son, go, work today in my vineyard.' He answered and said, 'I will not,' but afterward he regretted it and went. Then he came to the second and said likewise. And he answered and said, 'I *go*, sir,' but he did not go.

What do you think? (18.12). This parable involves a father who asks his two sons to go work in his vineyard (20.1ff). The first adamantly refuses—*I will not*—but later *regrets* (*metamellomai,* to change one's mind; v 32, 27.3, 2 Cor. 7.8, Heb. 7.21) his insolence and does as his father asked.[11]

The second son initially promises obedience and shows respect. Morgan says that *I go, sir,* "is idiomatic and suggests that this son put himself into contrast with the other one, who said he would not go, as though he said, You may depend on *me* sir!" (Morgan, 260). But though he drew near with his mouth, his heart was far from his father (15.8), and he didn't do as promised.

21.31–32 Which of the two did the will of *his* father?" They said to Him, "The first." Jesus said to them, "Assuredly, I say to you that tax collectors

---

[11] "It was rude, rebellious, ungrateful, unfilial; but it was hasty; and when a little interval had elapsed, quiet reflection brought the wayward boy to a better mind" (Spurgeon).

and harlots enter the kingdom of God before you. For John came to you in the way of righteousness, and you did not believe him; but tax collectors and harlots believed him; and when you saw *it*, you did not afterward relent and believe him.

Jesus asks: *Which of the two did the will of his father?* and Christ's opponents correctly answer, *the first*, thus setting the stage for Christ's point. *Assuredly* indicates the seriousness of the matter. The sons represent two extremes: those at the high end of the religious scale and those at the low end. *The tax collectors and harlots* were like the first son and would be ranked at the bottom of the spiritual barrel; but those at the bottom can enter the kingdom if they *do the will of the Father* (7.21, 12.50, 13.23, 20.16). Sins of the flesh (extortion, whoring) are bad, but sins of the spirit (legalism, pride, no mercy) are worse. The chief priests and elders were like the second son who was all talk. As in the parable of the prodigal (Lk. 15.2,11–32), the unrighteous find a seat at the feast, while the self-righteous stand outside, refusing to enter.

John came to you in the way of righteousness answers the question about John's baptism: it was from God. The Jewish leadership, despite its big talk, rejected God's prophet and message, whereas tax collectors and harlots who believed and obeyed entered the kingdom.

WICKED TENANTS, 21.33–46

Notes

"No parable interprets itself more clearly than this" (Carr, 247), but many commentators have a problem with a landowner who initially accepts the mistreatment and murder of his slaves with the utmost restraint, and then jeopardizes his son's life when he has the power to destroy the criminals. But such behavior isn't surprising for a landowner who loves his enemies (5.43–48), is patient, compassionate, and unwilling that any should perish (2 Pet. 3.9).

This parable extends the thought of the previous one by showing that the Jewish leadership had gone beyond passive disobedience to active malice. Here, Jesus asserts a rank and authority (v 23) that surpasses the prophets and lets the Jewish leaders know that their time is running out. The story, with elements similar to 20.1–16 (a landowner, a vineyard), falls into two parts: the narrative (vv 33–39) and the conclusion (vv 40–46).

21.33 "Hear another parable: There was a certain landowner who planted a vineyard and set a hedge around it, dug a winepress in it and built a tower. And he leased it to vinedressers and went into a far country.

Christ's enemies would understand the major figures in this parable (Ps. 80.12–14, Isa. 5.1–7)—the owner was God and the vineyard was Israel (v 43). The owner did everything necessary for a successful crop. He put a *hedge around* his vineyard to keep out wild animals (the hedge could be a wall of stone, wood, reeds, or other plants); he *dug a winepress*, which would have consisted of two stone basins (the grapes were crushed in upper; the juice flowed into the lower); and he *built a tower* from which servants could watch for thieves. With everything ready, he *leased* out (*ekdidōmi*, can be used as a technical term meaning "to let for hire") the vineyard and left until it could reasonably be expected to bear fruit.

21.34–36 Now when vintage-time drew near, he sent his servants to the vinedressers, that they might receive its fruit. And the vinedressers took his servants, beat one, killed one, and stoned another. Again he sent other servants, more than the first, and they did likewise to them.

At harvest, the owner *sent his servants to the vinedressers, that they might receive the fruit of it.* An agreement between an owner and his tenants could involve a fixed percentage (usually 25–50 percent), a fixed amount of fruit, or cash rent. The tenants, however, have no intention of giving the owner his due. They brutalize the servants, *beating* (*derō*, to flay, smite) one, *killing* a second, and *stoning* a third. The mistreated servants represented the prophets (Amos 3.7; Zech. 1.6; Jer. 7.25–26), and the mention of stoning would have recalled the fate of Zechariah in 2 Chronicles 24.21, which Jesus references in 23.35.

Displaying extraordinary patience (2 Chron. 36.15–16, 2 Pet. 3.9), the owner gives the renters another chance by sending a second, larger group of servants, who suffer the same treatment as the first group. Christ is rehearsing how Israel treated the prophets of God (23.34,37; Acts 7.51–53).

21.37–39 Then last of all he sent his son to them, saying, 'They will respect my son.' But when the vinedressers saw the son, they said among themselves, 'This is the heir. Come, let us kill him and seize his inheritance.' So they took him and cast *him* out of the vineyard and killed *him*.

As a last resort, the owner *sent his son*, hoping the tenants would *respect* him. It was an act of patience, but it was also an ultimatum. But even with this, evil worked itself to its bitter end. When the tenants see the son, they decide to kill him and confiscate his inheritance (as Jacob's sons did with Joseph, Gen. 37.20). We're not told how the tenants thought they could get away with it all; their actions reflect the irrationality of those whose consciences have been deadened by sin. When the son arrived, *they caught him, cast him out of the vineyard, and killed* him, anticipating what would be done to Jesus.

21.40–41 Therefore, when the owner of the vineyard comes, what will he do to those vinedressers?" They said to Him, "He will destroy those wicked men miserably, and lease *his* vineyard to other vinedressers who will render to him the fruits in their seasons."

Christ ends the story by again (v 31) challenging the chief priests and elders to answer a question: *When the owner of the vineyard comes, what will he do to those vinedressers?* In reply, the Jews condemn themselves: *He will miserably destroy those wicked men and lease his vineyard to other vinedressers who will render to him the fruits in their seasons.*

Oh wad some power the giftie gie us / To see oursel's as others see us! (Robert Burns). In the abstract, the Jews recognized their evil (2 Sam. 12.1–6), but they, like the sharecroppers, had fatally miscalculated — they had killed (or ignored, v 32) the servants and the son, but they hadn't killed the owner, who would even the score. The judgment they deserve is addressed in the next parable (22.7).

21.42 Jesus said to them, "Have you never read in the Scriptures: 'The stone which the builders rejected has become the chief cornerstone. This was the Lord's doing, and it is marvelous in our eyes'?

Jesus substantiates the Jews' answer with Scripture. *Did you never read in the Scriptures* jabs at them for their ignorance of the Bible (v 16, 12.3,5, 19.4). In His controversies during the final week, Scripture is Christ's constant recourse (4.4,7,10).

The passage quoted is Psalm 118.22 (a text often associated with other messianic *stone* texts, such as Isa. 8.4 and 28.16; see 1 Pet. 2.4–8), which is especially significant, considering that it immediately precedes the Hosanna passage quoted in v 9. The self-professed *builders* (chief priests, elders, Pharisees) thought that the perfect *cornerstone* (Christ) was unsuitable as a cornerstone.[12] It's the same mentality they displayed when they accused Satan's greatest foe of acting by Satanic power (9.34, 12.24).

21.43–44 Therefore I say to you, the kingdom of God will be taken from you and given to a nation bearing the fruits of it. And whoever falls on this stone will be broken; but on whomever it falls, it will grind him to powder."

Here is further confirmation and interpretation of the Jews' answer in v 41: v 43 expands on v 41b, and v 44 takes up v 41a. *Therefore*—for this reason—connects v 43 to the preceding. *The kingdom of God* was something Israel's establishment had possessed, but would lose. Since Sinai, a special relationship had existed between God and Israel, but it was coming to an end, and the kingdom would be *given to a nation bearing the fruits of it* (v 41b). This recalls 8.11–12, with the understanding that the *nation* that received the kingdom consisted of the obedient, who honored God by their fruits of repentance (v 29, 3.8).

Verse 44 unpacks v 41a, but Christ changes the stone imagery of v 42 (which one commentator called a "curious incongruity"). Cornerstones don't fall on people, but here is a *stone* that falls on people and *grinds them to powder*. If there is an OT allusion here, it likely is Daniel 2.34ff, especially v 44, which uses the figure of a stone that crushes the kingdoms of the world. As Morgan noted (262), "there is a touch of mercy" here; they who fall on the stone will be broken—brought to repentance and forgiveness (5.3, 18.3–4, 19.14). *But on whomever the stone falls* there is only pulverizing—judgment.

21.45–46 Now when the chief priests and Pharisees heard His parables, they perceived that He was speaking of them. But when they sought to lay hands on Him, they feared the multitudes, because they took Him for a prophet.

The points of comparison are unmistakable, and it dawns on *the chief priests and Pharisees* (*elders of the people*, v 23) that Jesus is talking about

---

[12] A cornerstone was an especially square, well-chiseled stone that would have anchored one of the four corners of a building. "The cornerstone of a building, in addition to being part of the foundation and therefore *supporting* the superstructure, *finalizes* its shape, for, being placed at the corner formed by the junction of two primary walls, it determines the lay of the walls and crosswalls throughout. All the other stones must adjust themselves to this cornerstone" (Hendriksen, 787).

them. They are the son who said yes but didn't obey, they are the tenants who killed the servants and the son, they are the builders who rejected the cornerstone, and they are the ones who will be ground into powder. All this had to especially infuriate them for they couldn't even accuse Jesus of being wrong in predicting His death at their hands!

They wanted to seize Christ on the spot but were stymied by their fear that the multitude will turn on them. Thus, they bide their time and will move in for the kill when circumstances are more favorable.

CHAPTER 22

THE WEDDING FEAST, 22.1–14

Notes

Verse 1 connects this parable about a wedding feast to the two preceding parables (21.28–46). The actual story occupies vv 2–13. Verse 2 is a heading, followed by two parts: vv 3–7 and vv 8–13. Each part begins with a king sending out his servants to invite guests to a wedding. The first invitation is ignored, but not the second, and both scenes end with a judgment. In the first case, judgment is visited on all who were invited; in the second, judgment falls on a single guest. Verse 14 is the conclusion. The twice-mentioned sending out of servants (vv 3–4) recalls 21.34,36. A *banquet* was a standard metaphor in Jewish tradition for the Messianic era.

22.1 And Jesus answered and spoke to them again by parables and said:

Answered indicates that this parable is Christ's response to the thoughts of the chief priests and Pharisees in 21.45–46. The plural *parables* is likely Matthew's way of indicating that this one is to be grouped with the two previous ones.

22.2 "The kingdom of heaven is like a certain king who arranged a marriage for his son,

The kingdom of heaven is like tells us that this story teaches something about the kingdom. It involves a wedding feast a king prepares for his son. After 9.15, Matthew's readers understand the bridegroom to be Christ (25.1–13).

22.3–6 and sent out his servants to call those who were invited to the wedding; and they were not willing to come. Again, he sent out other servants, saying, 'Tell those who are invited, "See, I have prepared my dinner; my oxen and fatted cattle *are* killed, and all things *are* ready.

Come to the wedding."' But they made light of it and went their ways, one to his own farm, another to his business. And the rest seized his servants, treated *them* spitefully, and killed *them*.

Servants are sent out (21.34,36) to call the *invited* to the wedding. In Christ's time, it was customary for an invitation to be sent out early, followed by a second invitation at the time of the wedding (Est. 5.8, 6.14). In this parable, when the second invitation goes out, they who had initially accepted the invitation *were not willing to come* (21.30, 23.37).

Patiently, the king sends other servants to tell the invited that *all things are ready; come to the wedding*—enticing them with a description of the *dinner* that has been prepared. *Fattened* (*sitistos*, only here in the NT) referred to "animals especially fed and in prime condition" (Morris, 548); the king would serve his guests nothing but the best.[1]

But those invited refuse to come. *They made light* (*ameleō*, to be careless of, neglect) of the invitation, ignoring it and going about their business. Some reacted violently, *seizing the servants, treating them spitefully* (*hubrizō*, to injure), even committing murder (21.34–36). This "brutality fits Jesus' remarks about how the prophets were received (5.11–22; 23.29–31,37) and his warnings about what will happen both to him (16.21, 17.22–23; 20.18–19; 26.2) and to his disciples (10.7–25; 20.23; 23.34)" (Garland, 220).

The king's servants represent the prophets who were ignored, persecuted, and killed by the Jews (5.10–12, 10.23, 23.34).

22.7 But when the king heard *about it,* he was furious. And he sent out his armies, destroyed those murderers, and burned up their city.

The servants' reaction to the king's invitation was an act of insanity. The king's patience runs out, and in language that recalls 21.41, he exacts vengeance by sending soldiers to destroy the *murderers* and their *city*—not just the leadership, but Jerusalem itself will be judged (23.34–39). This is not a prediction of the final judgment but of the historical judgment detailed in chs 24–25.

---

[1] Among the letters of Pliny the Younger is found this: "To Septicius Clarus. What a fellow you are! You promise to come to dinner and then fail to turn up! Well, here is my magisterial sentence upon you. You must pay the money I am out of pocket to the last farthing, and you will find the sum no small one. … You have done violence to yourself. You have grudged, possibly yourself, but certainly me, a fine treat. Yes, yourself! For how we should have enjoyed ourselves, how we should have laughed together, how we should have applied ourselves!" (*Epistulae* 1.15).

22.8–10 Then he said to his servants, 'The wedding is ready, but those who were invited were not worthy. Therefore go into the highways, and as many as you find, invite to the wedding.' So those servants went out into the highways and gathered together all whom they found, both bad and good. And the wedding *hall* was filled with guests.

Those initially invited proved *unworthy* of the honor shown them. The king, however, is determined to hold a wedding banquet for his son, so he directs his servants to invite (continuously invite) the previously uninvited. *Into the highways* (*diexodous tōn hodōn*) occurs only here in the NT; Luz says that the Gr. "means a starting or ending point, for example, the most distant part of a territory" (III, 55), but the word's meaning as an intersection or crossroads (where people gather) is ancient. The invitation was to be indiscriminate: *as many as you find invite to the wedding.* If the city in v 7 refers to Jerusalem, and by association, Israel, the invited here are Gentiles, the *nation* of 21.43.

The servants do as ordered, and the feast is filled with a motley group that includes the *good* and the *bad* (such as tax collectors and harlots, 21.31–32; 13.47–48).

22.11–13 But when the king came in to see the guests, he saw a man there who did not have on a wedding garment. So he said to him, 'Friend, how did you come in here without a wedding garment?' And he was speechless. Then the king said to the servants, 'Bind him hand and foot, take him away, and cast *him* into outer darkness; there will be weeping and gnashing of teeth.'

Christ adds an element that didn't appear in the two previous parables. From one aspect, what He depicts seems unreasonable, but when interpreted in the light of the previous parables, it sounds a warning to those who accept His invitation.

After the feast is filled (v 10), the king—with an eye that sees all and overlooks nothing—*came in to see the guests* and spots a man *who did not have on a wedding* garment, which isn't surprising for someone who came straight from the street into a banquet. Ancient sources do not indicate that guests wore special clothing (analogous to our *Sunday best*) to a wedding; a clean, everyday garment was sufficient. But a man suddenly invited to a party was still expected to wash up and put on some clean clothes. One man at the feast hadn't done this. When confronted by the king about his appearance, his neglect is so indefensible that *he was speechless* (v 34, *put to silence*). On *friend*, see 20.13.

The consequence is swift and severe—the king orders that the man be cuffed hand and foot like a common criminal and *cast into outer darkness,* a synonym for hell (8.12; 13.42,50; 24.51, 25.30).

Whereas vv 1–7 warn unbelieving Jews of coming judgment, vv 8–13 warn believers of the same (Rom. 11.18–21). By comparing the three parables beginning at 21.28, the *wedding garment* corresponds to doing the will of the Father (5.20, 7.21–23, 21.31)/ bringing forth fruit worthy of the kingdom (21.41,43)/the good works (5.16) that will be honored at the final judgment (25.31–46).

Israel's fate is a warning to the church—all unbelief and disobedience, whether by Jew or Gentile, will be judged by God (Rom. 11.20–22).

22.14 For many are called, but few *are* chosen."

Many are called, but few are chosen sets up a contrast (7.13–14) that warns of judgment against unrighteousness—not just for Jews, but for all.[2] There's a difference between being *called* and being *chosen*—to be *called* is simply to be invited; to be *chosen* is to be accepted. An invitation doesn't guarantee acceptance. Those originally invited were not accepted because they refused to accept the invitation. The responsibility was theirs. Even answering the call doesn't guarantee that one will finally be among the chosen (remember Judas). God chooses those who choose Him and rejects those who reject Him (23.37).

QUESTION ABOUT TRIBUTE, 22.15–22

Notes

The parable section (21.23–22.14) is followed by a controversy section (vv 15–46) involving four episodes between Jesus and the Jews, who try to *entangle Him in His talk* (v 15) by asking loaded questions. Just as sacrificial lambs had to be examined and pronounced free of blemish (Lev. 1.3), so too did the Lamb of God (Heb. 9.14), and the following controversies were a means by which Christ's blamelessness was established. In each case, His answers leave His enemies stymied, lacking a comeback. Christ was

---

[2] *Many* doesn't imply here Calvinistic election. The primary dictionary definition of *many* is a large, indefinite number; the secondary definition means the greater part of a number. In v 9, *many* clearly implies *all*; when God goes searching for wedding guests, He invites all without exception (Mk. 16.15).

never caught off guard, was never confused, and never failed to see the weakness in His opponent's argument. He never appealed to prejudice or resorted to special pleading to extricate Himself from a tight spot. They who tried to entrap Him ended up caught in their own trap and finally stopped asking Him questions (v 46).

Verse 15 summarizes what follows; the actual debates begin in v 16.

22.15 Then the Pharisees went and plotted how they might entangle Him in *His* talk.

This isn't the first-time Christ's enemies try to trap Him in talk—possibly in no area is it easier to get in trouble than by talking (Lk. 11.53–54; Jas. 3.1–2). And so, the Pharisees plot how to *entangle* (*pagideuō*, to trap, snare; only here in the NT) Jesus in debate. Then, as now, two volatile topics were politics and religion.

22.16–17 And they sent to Him their disciples with the Herodians, saying, "Teacher, we know that You are true, and teach the way of God in truth; nor do You care about anyone, for You do not regard the person of men. Tell us, therefore, what do You think? Is it lawful to pay taxes to Caesar, or not?"

The Pharisees send their *disciples* (see 12.27, 23.15), accompanied by *Herodians*, to set the trap. The only thing known about the Herodians is what might be inferred from their name. Likely, they were supporters of the Herodian family, which means their politics would have placed them at odds with the Pharisees. The Herods were puppets of Rome who supported Roman taxes and the Roman presence in Judea, both of which the Pharisees despised. The common antagonism of the two groups to Christ, however, momentarily overshadowed their partisan strife, and they bury the hatchet long enough to consolidate their attack.

Beginning with false flattery (v 18), they acknowledge Jesus as a *Teacher* who taught *God's truth* regardless of what anyone else thought.[3] Their question involves a sensitive issue in first-century Judea: *is it lawful to pay taxes to Caesar, or not? Taxes* refers to the census tax that was "introduced in Judea in A.D. 6 [that] every inhabitant from age 12 (or 14) to 65 was required to pay" (Gardiner, 326). In AD 6, *Judas of Galilee* (Acts 5.37) led a revolt against payment of Roman taxes (Josephus, *Ant.* xviii.1.1), and after

---

[3] "Never compromise your integrity because of what others might think."

that, any refusal to pay the Roman tax was viewed as an act of sedition. If Jesus answered the question *Yes*, He would alienate Jews who chafed at the thought of Roman taxes; if He said *No*, the Herodians would report Him to the Romans (Lk. 20.20). If He refused to answer, He would be charged with political cowardice. No matter what He did, the Pharisees thought they had Him.

22.18–21 But Jesus perceived their wickedness, and said, "Why do you test Me, *you* hypocrites? Show Me the tax money." So they brought Him a denarius. And He said to them, "Whose image and inscription *is* this?" They said to Him, "Caesar's." And He said to them, "Render therefore to Caesar the things that are Caesar's, and to God the things that are God's."

The Lord knew their motive was *wicked* (*ponēria*, evil; a strong word applied to the devil in 13.19,38 and to *this generation* in 12.45, 16.4), and He unmasked them on the spot, exposing them for the *hypocrites* they were.

He asks for a coin, and the one given Him was likely the Tiberius denarius (*dēnarion*, lit. consisting of ten; a Roman silver coin), which was stamped with the head of the emperor and the inscription: "Ti Caesar Divi Aug F Agustus" (Caesar Augustus Tiberius, son of the Divine Augustus). *Whose image and superscription is this?* Christ asked; *Caesar's*, they answer. In one of His most famous sayings, Jesus adds, *render therefore to Caesar the things that are Caesar's.* The Pharisees and Herodians used a verb that meant *give* (*didōmi*, to pay), but Jesus uses a verb that meant *give back* (*apodidomi, render,* return). By using coins minted by Caesar (Rome), the Jews tacitly acknowledged his role in their economy, and one who facilitated their economy was worthy of being recompensed for doing so. Christ simply says that the Jews should pay taxes to Caesar as payment for services rendered. They who benefit from government should support government (Gen. 41.33–36,46–49).

But Jesus doesn't stop with Caesar: *give to God the things that are God's.*[4] The larger concern, as the preceding three parables made clear, is that the Pharisees—who were made in God's image (Gen. 1.27, Jas. 3.9)—were not returning to God the devotion and obedience due Him. This should have been their chief concern, but it wasn't.

---

[4] These "words gave to the civil power, under the protection of conscience, a sacredness it had never enjoyed and bounds it had never acknowledged: and they were also the repu-

22.22 When they had heard these words, they marveled, and left Him and went their way.

The Pharisees' and Herodians' question presented a *false dilemma*, in which only two alternatives were thought to exhaust all possibilities. They expected an either/or answer and were unprepared for a both/and answer—*fear God, honor the king* (1 Pet. 2.17). Realizing the validity of Christ's reply, the questioners *marvel* and leave, as did the devil in 4.11. (On the way back, someone probably asked, "Who thought up that dumb question anyway?")

QUESTION ABOUT RESURRECTION, 22.23–33

Notes

The Sadducees come to the rescue, but in doing so "They made a fatal mistake" (Foster, *The Final Week*, 95). Verse 23, which introduces them and states their premise, is followed by an exchange that divides into two parts involving a question (vv 24–28) and answer (vv 29–32). Christ's answer divides into two subsections that deal first with the hypothetical presented by the Sadducees (vv 29–30) and then with their denial of resurrection (vv 31–32). Both the Sadducees and Christ quote Scripture, but once again, Christ backs an opponent into a corner from which there is no escape (21.25–27).

The importance of this encounter is attested by the fact that all three synoptic Gospels give it in full with little variation. The afterlife is a question no thoughtful person can avoid. We are all going to die and what happens next should concern us all (Ps. 89.48).

22.23 The same day the Sadducees, who say there is no resurrection, came to Him and asked Him,

On *Sadducees*, see 3.7. Most of our information about them comes from Josephus, who tells us that they rejected the idea of a future resurrection, believed "that souls die with the bodies" (*Ant.* xviii.1.4; Acts 4.1–2, 23.8), emphasized free will, accepted only the written Law (not the traditions of the Pharisees), and were the party of the rich.

22.24–27 saying: "Teacher, Moses said that if a man dies, having no

---

diation of absolutism and the inauguration of freedom" (Lord Acton, qtd. by Trueblood, *Confronting Christ*, 120).

children, his brother shall marry his wife and raise up offspring for his brother. Now there were with us seven brothers. The first died after he had married, and having no offspring, left his wife to his brother. Likewise the second also, and the third, even to the seventh. Last of all the woman died also.

The Sadducees also address Jesus as *Teacher* (v 16) and pose a hypothetical situation based on Deuteronomy 25.5–6 (Gen. 38.6–11) that they thought reduced belief in resurrection to the absurd. "If, for the sake of argument, there is an afterlife, what would happen in a case like this?" Moses legislated that a man marry his brother's childless widow;[5] so what happens if seven brothers each, in turn, marry their childless sister-in-law and then each of them dies? *Marry* (v 24, *epigambreuō*), here, isn't the standard word for marriage but a technical term that meant to marry the next of kin.

22.28 Therefore, in the resurrection, whose wife of the seven will she be? For they all had her."

In the resurrection, whose wife of the seven will she be? For they all had her — considering that she was legally married to each brother in this life, couldn't each brother claim her in a future life and dispute the claims of the others? The argument rests on the assumption that a future life would be a continuation of the present life — with all its problems and pettiness, including jealousy, and quarreling — only on a higher plane. The Sadducees had likely used this question to silence the Pharisees, and they thought it would work equally well on Jesus.

22.29–30 Jesus answered and said to them, "You are mistaken, not knowing the Scriptures nor the power of God. For in the resurrection they neither marry nor are given in marriage, but are like angels of God in heaven.

Christ says that they are *mistaken* (*planaō*, to planet, stray) because they limited God's power and denied God's word.

First, not only did the Sadducees' hypothetical (vv 24–28) rest on an unproven assumption (how did they know a future life would be a continuation of the present?), it denied God's power. The God powerful enough to create life is surely powerful enough to transform it. And this He will do *in the resurrection [where] they neither marry* (*gamousin*, referring

---

[5] Cf. Isa. 4.1, seven women; Tob 3.8–15, Sarah and her seven husbands; 2 Macc. 7, seven brothers.

to men) *nor are given in marriage* (*gamizontai*, referring to women), *but are like the angels of God in heaven.*[6] Angels are spirit beings without sexuality; if God can create such a situation with angels, He can do the same with men. And should any Sadducee dispute Christ's right to speak about conditions in the afterlife, he could come back Sunday and continue the discussion with Christ.[7,8]

But Christ isn't finished. Just as the Sadducees tried to use Scripture to reduce His belief in resurrection to the absurd, Jesus will give them a dose of their own medicine by using Scripture to reduce their denial of resurrection (v 23) to the absurd.

22.31–32 But concerning the resurrection of the dead, have you not read what was spoken to you by God, saying, 'I am the God of Abraham, the God of Isaac, and the God of Jacob'? God is not the God of the dead, but of the living."

All Christ needed to shred the Sadducees' position on the resurrection was a single verse from the Law. *Concerning the resurrection of the dead, have you not read?* didn't imply that the Sadducees hadn't read Exodus 3.6, but that they didn't understand it.[9] Not only was Exodus 3.6 the foundational text of Judaism affirming God's covenantal relationship with Israel, but it taught the reality of the resurrection—not by direct statement but by inference.

Exodus 3.6 was spoken hundreds of years after the patriarchs had died. According to the Sadducees, when someone died, they, like Rover, were dead all over. Given this, does *I am the God of Abraham, Isaac, and Jacob* mean, *I am the God of the nonexistent*? For God to tell Moses, *I am* (not, *I was*) *the God of Abraham, Isaac, and Jacob* implies a *relationship* with them,

---

[6] If we will be like the angels in regard to marriage, might we not also be like them in regard to friendship? C. S. Lewis made the lovely comment that friendship "is the sort of love once can imagine between angels" (*The Four Loves*, 77).

[7] Limiting God's power lies behind many questions about the future life, such as "How can I be happy in heaven knowing that I have loved ones in hell?"

[8] "Before endeavoring to answer a question one ought to consider whether or not the question is based on a false assumption and therefore presents a false issue. There are times when one tries to think about the answer to the question without asking whether the question is answerless because it presupposes a situation which does not in reality exist" (Bales, *Jesus the Master Respondent*, 42).

[9] Since the Sadducees only accepted the books of Moses as authoritative, any argument for the resurrection based on the Psalms or Prophets would have fallen on deaf ears. See Edersheim, Vol II, 397–398.

which implies their *existence*! Men may claim an actual relationship with the nonexistent—"I am the next-door neighbor of the Easter Bunny"—but if they do so, they are insane. God affirmed a relationship with the patriarchs, but if there was no sense in which the patriarchs lived, His statement was sheer nonsense. *God is not the God of the dead*—in the way the Sadducees understood death—*but of the living*.[10,11] As soon as Christ points this out, the people saw it (v 33). His "argument," said Baille, "is unanswerable" (*And the Life Everlasting*, 162). Indeed!

But Christ said Exodus 3.6 proves the resurrection of the body, not just the immortality of the soul after death. How does it do this?

The answer is that God is the God of the whole person. "'Man' as God made him is an 'embodied' being. If 'man' is to survive as 'man' he must be *embodied*. So plain is this to Jesus and his opponents that all he has to do is to show that Abraham has survived death and lives unto God in order to establish the resurrection of the dead" (McGuiggan, *The Book of 1 Corinthians*, 265). "The thoughtful reader may have observed that the conclusion of this argument falls short, in its terms of the demands of the subject. The subject is the resurrection of the dead, while the conclusion affects only the question whether the spirit is of the dead are still alive… How, then, does the Savior's proof that spirits continue to live apart from the body, include proof of a resurrection? … [H]uman spirits, having been originally created for the exercise of their powers through the organs of a body, must, unless their original nature be changed, which is an inadmissible supposition because unsupported by evidence, be dependent for their highest enjoyment on the possession of a body. This being so, the continued existence of spirits after the death of the body creates a demand for the resurrection of the body" (McGarvey, *A Commentary on Matthew and Mark*, 192). If man is to continue as *man* after death, at some point he must have a body, which even the Sadducees had to concede.

22.33 And when the multitudes heard *this*, they were astonished at His teaching.

The multitudes were astonished at the brilliance of Christ's response (7.28, 13.54). I don't know whether the Lord's argument caused any Sadducees to

---

[10] If God could have a fulfilling relationship with the nonexistent, why create man in the first place?

[11] See Edward J. Young's excellent study on the implications of the present tense *I AM* in "The Call of Moses," *Westminster Theological Journal*, 1967 XXIX (2).

become resurrectionists, but at the very least, it exposed the vacuity of their reasoning so forcefully that it's unlikely they ever used their riddle again.

QUESTION ABOUT THE GREAT COMMANDMENT, 22.34–40

Notes

When Jesus is asked about the greatest commandment, His answer did more than make sin illegal, it made sin difficult, for nothing is harder than sinning against love.

Structurally, this passage begins with a transitional verse (v 34), followed by a question (v 35) and answer (vv 36–40).

22.34–36 But when the Pharisees heard that He had silenced the Sadducees, they gathered together. Then one of them, a lawyer, asked *Him a question*, testing Him, and saying, "Teacher, which *is* the great commandment in the law?"

When the Pharisees heard that Christ had put the Sadducees to silence (*phimoō*, muzzle, gag; v 12, *speechless*), they were undoubtedly delighted (and probably thinking, "Why didn't we think of that?"). One of them, with an ulterior motive (*testing Him*), asks, *Teacher, which is the great commandment of the Law?* According to the rabbis, the Law of Moses contained 248 positive commands and 365 prohibitions; speculating about which of these was the greatest was a favorite scribal pastime.

22.37–38 Jesus said to him, "'You shall love the Lᴏʀᴅ your God with all your heart, with all your soul, and with all your mind.' This is *the* first and great commandment.

All the ages and angels, said Stanley Jones, must have bent down to hear Christ's answer for it forever fixed man's highest priority. As declared by Christ, the highest essence of life involves a double priority, having not one but two requirements. There are two *firsts* that are alike in that both command *thou shalt love*.

Christ first quotes Deuteronomy 6.5 (which wouldn't have surprised His hearers) and its call for the *total* man (*heart, soul, mind*) to love God *totally* (*all*). In Jewish thought, *with all your heart* spoke of undivided obedience.[12] *With all your soul*, in some translations, becomes *with all your life* (ʙᴇᴄᴋ) and may carry the thought of unreserved commitment, even martyrdom

---

[12] Ironically, Jonah, the prophet whose experience singularly predicted Christ's death

(10.28, 16.24; Lk. 14.26; 1 Cor. 13.3). *With all your mind* indicates a thinking, intellectual approach to God—a religion that appeals only to the emotions and imagination and not to the mind is woefully inadequate (8.8–9).

Love is to life what combustion is to an engine—it is the impulse that is to drive us (5.20ff). The distributive use of *all* intensifies love's depth; all that man is, is to love God (1 Thes. 5.23). "God's whole-hearted love must not be answered in a half-hearted manner" (Hendriksen, 809).

Two incidents from the Gospels illustrate total love. In 26.7, a woman shows no hesitation in *wasting* (26.8) a precious ointment to anoint Christ. So significant did Christ deem her action that He said that wherever the gospel is preached, what she did is to be told. Why such a big deal about such a seemingly trivial thing? It's because the woman's act exemplified the profuse, extravagant love that is due God.

Then, in Luke 21, Christ is moved by a poor widow (5.3) who made a tiny contribution to the temple treasury—but who, in so doing, gave all that she had. The Lord didn't need to create a parable for the point He wished to make, for the widow's action personified the total commitment of a loving soul. That Christ called attention to her shows that heaven measures love qualitatively, not quantitatively.

This is the first and great commandment "because God is the Supreme Being; and to fail to acknowledge our proper relationship to Him is to cut the ground out from under other commandments and obligations" (Bales, *Jesus, The Master Respondent*, 66).

22.39 And *the* second *is* like it: 'You shall love your neighbor as yourself.'

Christ's answer is not wider than the question. The *second first* (*homoios, the second is like, homoios*, the second is of equal importance with the first, *Arndt-Gingrich*, 169), on equal standing with the first *first*, comes from an unlikely place—the book of Leviticus. Leviticus 19.18 shows that if the love of God is not associated with practical concern for our fellows, we cannot love God. In the kingdom, it's impossible to separate the love of God from the love of man. Love of God without love of man or love of man without love of God is selfish and enthrones the human will. It is impossible to love God in the abstract without loving our neighbor in the concrete.[13] "When Jesus gave His doctrine of Love in its final form, one is struck by a

---

and resurrection, exemplified the ugliness of the individual who gives God his mind and will, but not his heart.

[13] "When I say 'love is good,' or 'justice is good,' I mean that love as realized in a personal

startling omission. He laid on His disciples the repeated charge of Love to one another, [but] He did not once command them to love God. While His preachers have in the main exhorted men to love God, Jesus in the main exhorted them to love their fellowmen. This was not an accident … it was an intention—the revelation of Jesus' idea of Love" (J. Watson, *The Mind of the Master*, 164). The love of God and neighbor stands or falls together; if we love God, we will love people, and we cannot love God if we don't love people (1 Jn. 4.20). Biblically, *neighbor* encompasses everybody (see 25.40).

As yourself is an important modification to the command *love your neighbor*, for *as yourself* brings the golden rule into the equation (7.12). Loving our neighbor cannot be done distinct from loving ourself, for to love our neighbor properly we must use the guidelines by which we love ourself. In its true form, self-love is a self-concern that involves *nourishing* (feeding) and *cherishing* (which includes guarding, protecting; Eph. 5.29). When we love our neighbor as ourself, we will put ourself into his place and feel with his heart. Without doing so, the chances increase that we will do him wrong.

22.40 On these two commandments hang all the Law and the Prophets."
To say that *all the law and the prophets* (5.17, 7.12) *hang* (*kremannumi*, to suspend, Acts 5.30) on the commands to love God and neighbor means that all of God's laws, somehow or other, are express love. Love is the interpretive key that unlocks the OT. Just as "all roads lead to Rome," so all Scripture leads to love.

QUESTION ABOUT THE CHRIST, 22.41–46

Notes
The encounters that began in v 15 conclude with Christ again turning the table on His opponents.

22.41–42 While the Pharisees were gathered together, Jesus asked them, saying, "What do you think about the Christ? Whose Son is He?" They said to Him, *"The Son* of David."

---

life is good, that justice as manifested in a man's character or in a social order is good. I do not mean that the mere abstract quality of love or justice is good. The mere quality love, conceived abstractedly and without any reference to its realization in personal life, is not good… Good cannot be predicated of the abstract. It belongs only to the concreted … to persons" (W. R. Sorley, *Moral Values and the Idea of God*, 139–140).

The Pharisees, who had regathered in v 34, are still standing around, and Jesus—speaking to them for the last time—asks a question that is at the center of their controversies with Him.

What do you think about the Christ? In Matthew, *Christ* with the article (*the*) is used as a title (1.17, 2.4, 11.2, 16.16,20); Jesus isn't asking about Himself specifically (16.13–16), but about the Messiah abstractly—*Whose Son is He?*

The Pharisees answer, *the Son of David,* and they are right (1.1, 21.9)—but they are still wrong for they only understood part of the truth about the Christ. We can believe what is true and still be wrong by failing to consider all truth (4.4). The Pharisees were trying to prove that Jesus wasn't the Christ when they didn't understand the Christ; they accused Jesus of being outside the box without knowing what was in the box.

22.43–45 He said to them, "How then does David in the Spirit call Him 'Lord,' saying: 'The Lord said to my Lord, "Sit at My right hand, Till I make Your enemies Your footstool"'? If David then calls Him 'Lord,' how is He his Son?"

Jesus asks a follow-up question: *How then does David in the Spirit call Him 'Lord'?* which references Psalm 110.1, the most quoted OT passage in the NT. "You say that the Christ is the Son of David, implying He is David's inferior; if that's so, why did David refer to the Christ as His *Lord*, implying He is David's superior? How can the Messiah be lesser than David (his Son) and greater than David (his Lord) at the same time?"

22.46 And no one was able to answer Him a word, nor from that day on did anyone dare question Him anymore.

As Matthew has shown, the Messiah is David's *Son* and *Lord* because in Him are blended deity and humanity (1.1–25, 26.63–64). Because the Pharisees didn't understand this, *no one was able to answer Him a word.* They could have asked Jesus to explain, but they weren't interested in an explanation and *from that day on no one dared to ask Him anymore questions.* Their own Bible was closed to them, and they didn't care to open it.

The Jewish examination of Jesus is concluded. The time has come for Jesus to examine the Jews.

CHAPTER 23

THE SCRIBES AND PHARISEES, 23.1–12

Notes

"Of the teachings of the past, whose sayings have been preserved," said the English essayist and historian Sir John Seeley, "Mohammed would be regarded by most as the type of unrelenting severity, and yet we may read the Koran from beginning to end, without finding words expressive of more vehement condemnation than those attributed to Christ."

Since I've not read the Koran, I can't say whether Seeley exaggerates, but when he penned this, he may have had in mind Matthew 23, for few passages in literature offer invective as scathing as that found here. There is no bright spot in Christ's denunciation of the scribes and Pharisees; it only moves from dark to darker.

Because of this, it isn't unusual for writers to accuse Jesus of being unsympathetic and unfair—it is "the unloveliest chapter in the Gospel" (Benedict Viviano). Undoubtedly, Matthew 23, more than any other part of the Gospels, contributed to *Pharisee* becoming a synonym for *hypocrite*. Some protest that Jesus painted with too broad a brush, making all of the Pharisees "black sheep" (Luz III, 105). Commentators who object to Christ's characterization of the Pharisees will list passages from rabbinic literature where Pharisees warn about the same errors and excesses cited by Christ. It's highly presumptuous, though, to think that He who knew the hearts of men is guilty of the false judgment He condemned (7.1).

Christ teaches is that one can use correct and pious words, appear in religious garb, receive deference from people, appear important, and be far from the kingdom. Religiosity, far from being evidence of righteousness, may indicate one's depravity.

This chapter has three sections: an introduction (vv 1–12), a series of eight woes (vv 13–33), and a conclusion (vv 34–39). In the first, Christ speaks to the crowds and His disciples; in the second, to the scribes and Pharisees; and in the third, to the crowds and to Jerusalem.

In the first section (vv 1–12), v 1 sets the stage, followed by vv 2–7, wherein Jesus talks about the scribes and Pharisees, and vv 8–12, where He warns His disciples not to be like the scribes and Pharisees.

23.1 Then Jesus spoke to the multitudes and to His disciples,

Although the scribes and Pharisees are present (22.34,41, Christ doesn't speak to them, for as a class they were beyond reach. Here, He *speaks to the multitudes*, who were friendly to Him, *and to his disciples*, who followed Him.

23.2 saying: "The scribes and the Pharisees sit in Moses' seat.

This is the only place in Matthew where each group has a separate article—*the scribes, the Pharisees*—but it is certain that Matthew viewed them as a unit who constituted the main opposition to Jesus. *Moses' seat*— the teacher's chair—was literal and metaphorical. "Perhaps the most interesting single object from the Chorazin synagogue is this large stone seat, now preserved in the Archaeological Museum in Jerusalem... On the seat back there is a rosette in a circle, and on the front an inscription. ... Such an elaborate seat as this was probably occupied by the chief official in the synagogue, perhaps 'the ruler of the synagogue.' As such it was probably the 'Moses' seat' of Mt 23.2" (Finegan, *The Archaeology of the New Testament*, 58). The *Moses' seat* was a chair on which a rabbi *sat* to teach officially; a modern counterpart would be *professorial* or *endowed chairs* in colleges and universities. Neither the scribes nor Pharisees had been appointed by God as teachers; that was something they assumed for themselves.

23.3 Therefore whatever they tell you to observe, *that* observe and do, but do not do according to their works; for they say, and do not do.

Whatever they tell you to observe, that observe and do is surprising, if not shocking, considering that in 15.1–9, Christ condemned the scribes' and Pharisees' tradition-laced doctrine and in 15.10–14 called them blind guides who were to be avoided. In 16.6–12, He explicitly warned His disciples about their teaching, and in this chapter (vv 13,19), He again says they are *blind*. And in vv 8–10, He claims to be the only true teacher. Truth, of course, is binding regardless of who teaches it, but based on Christ's castigation of scribal and Pharisaic teaching elsewhere, I think He is here engaging in some sanctified sarcasm (26.45), as tipped off by His command to observe *whatever* (*panta*, everything) they teach.

23.4 For they bind heavy burdens, hard to bear, and lay *them* on men's shoulders; but they *themselves* will not move them with one of their fingers.

We believe in no man's infallibility, but we do believe every man is capable of integrity. To fail to practice what we preach is a common shortcoming, but with the scribes and Pharisees, it was a characteristic that destroyed their character and was made more egregious because of the position they assumed as teachers (v 3; Jas. 3.1). *Bind* (*desmeuō*, to tie; 16.19, 18.18) means to impose, or obligate. *Heavy burdens, hard to bear* could refer to any of several things: the traditions of the elders (15.2–11), *the weightier matters of the law* (v 23), or a legalistic system (Acts 15.10; Gal. 3.10–11). Regardless, what the scribes and Pharisees imposed stood in contrast to the easy yoke and light burden of Christ (11.30). Hypocrites are noted for a double standard that exempts them from rules they bind on others. *They will not move them with one of their fingers* has no proverbial saying behind it, but its meaning is clear: hypocrites exempt themselves from the onerous regulations they impose on others.

23.5 But all their works they do to be seen by men. They make their phylacteries broad and enlarge the borders of their garments.

Hypocrisy cares little for character so long as respectability is maintained. *All their works they do to be seen by men* recalls 6.1–18. In that passage, the *hypocrites* are not identified, but Christ now makes clear who He had in mind. He also shows that hypocrisy involves a contradiction not only between word and deed but between motive and deed.

Two examples of Pharisaic hypocrisy are cited. *Phylacteries* (*phulaktēria*, only here in the NT) were leather straps to which were attached cube-shaped pouches containing verses from the OT (e.g., Deut. 6.8, 11.18; Ex. 13.16). Some phylacteries would be worn around the head where they were easily visible; others were worn under the arm. According to the Talmud, the Pharisees almost always wore phylacteries, but the common people didn't. To make a phylactery *broad* was to make it more conspicuous. Based on Qumran discoveries, this was done by making a container large enough to hold more than one passage of Scripture.

Enlarge the borders of their garments refers to tassels or fringes sewn onto a garment to remind the wearer of the commandments of God (Num. 15.38–40; Deut.22.12). The length of these was not prescribed, but hypocrites made sure theirs were long enough to be noticed.[1]

23.6–7 They love the best places at feasts, the best seats in the synagogues, greetings in the marketplaces, and to be called by men, 'Rabbi, Rabbi.'

Extrabiblical sources reveal that strict rules existed within Judaism about seating arrangements based on age and rank. *To love the best places at feasts* and *the best seats in the synagogue* indicated a desire to be noticed. The scribes and Pharisees wanted to be up front, where everyone could see them and think them important.

According to Luz (III, 104), it was during the first century that the term *rabbi* transitioned from a general term of respect to a title for learned men, becoming the equivalent of our terms *reverend*, *professor*, or *doctor*.

23.8–10 But you, do not be called 'Rabbi'; for One is your Teacher, the Christ, and you are all brethren. Do not call anyone on earth your father; for One is your Father, He who is in heaven. And do not be called teachers; for One is your Teacher, the Christ.

But you refers to Christ's disciples—*do not be called "Rabbi," do not call anyone on earth your father, do not be called teachers.* The words *rabbi, father,* and *teacher* are not the issue (5.22); the issue is the motive behind their use. On *rabbi*, see v 7. *Father* is sometimes used figuratively as a term of respect for older persons or benefactors, and *teacher* (*kathēgētēs*) means guide or leader. In the kingdom, there are no titles that distinguish disciples from one another. Instead, the threefold use of *one* states that there is but *one* authority, and that is God. Teaching and blessing come from Him (6.9–13), and titles or rankings among disciples that suggest any hierarchy other than that disciples are *brethren* are wrong.[2] Christians are part of a family in which they are equals, not a school in which some are freshmen and some are seniors, or a company in which some are blue-collar and

---

[1] "In India I have seen men sitting on beds of spikes, have seen them beating their backs with chains that had knives attached to them, have seen men hang head-down over a fire swinging through the flames, have seen men sitting in a row of silence—speechless. But all of these were where men could see them and admire them and, in many instances, given them divine honors. And they received these honors as their due" (Jones, *Christian Maturity*, 274).

[2] See 1 Cor. 4.14–17; 1 Thes. 2.11; 1 Tim. 1.2.

others white-collar. God word is to be taught by men (v 34; Eph. 4.11), and anyone who chooses to teach God's word should do so with all humility and caution (Jas. 3.1ff).[3]

23.11–12 But he who is greatest among you shall be your servant. And whoever exalts himself will be humbled, and he who humbles himself will be exalted.

Taking up the principle of 20.26, Christ unpacks the implications of the word *brethren*. To be brothers and sisters in a family means renouncing privilege and prestige and embracing reciprocal service. The kingdom involves the total reversal of authority and power found in secular settings (20.26). *The only "superior" among you is the one who serves the others* (JBP). Modern religious groups, with their special offices, hierarchies, titles, clothing. and authority structures find no sanction in Christ's gospel.

WOES, 23.13–33

Notes

The middle part of this discourse contains a Screwtapian octave consisting of eight *woes*.[4] *Woe* can be a lament over a bad situation (18.7, 24.19) or a foreboding of judgment on the wicked; it's in this latter sense that Christ uses it in this chapter. Except for the third entry (v 16), each statement begins with *Woe to you, scribes and Pharisees, hypocrites!* and is followed by a causative *for* (because). The accusations are increasingly severe. The first three (vv 13,14,15) cite examples of how the scribes and Pharisees negatively affected others, the next three (vv 16–22,23–24,25–26) cover scribal and Pharisaic heresies, and the final two (vv 27–28,29–31) address scribal and Pharisaic priorities. Fittingly, references to *hell* (vv 15,33) bracket the section.

First Woe

23.13 "But woe to you, scribes and Pharisees, hypocrites! For you shut up the kingdom of heaven against men; for you neither go in *yourselves*, nor do you allow those who are entering to go in.

---

[3] "Frederic W. Farrar has quoted, with documentation, some of the extravagant claims made for rabbis. 'Rashi on Deut. xvii. 111, says, "The Rabbis are to be believed even when they say that right is left, and left is right"'" (Bales, *Woe unto You*, 52).

[4] Many recent versions, based on the uncial manuscripts rather than the Majority Text, completely omit or footnote v 14: e.g., NIV, NASB, NRSV, etc. The authenticity of the verse, however, is beyond doubt, being found in Mark 12.40 and Luke 20.47.

On *hypocrite*, see 6.2. *Hypocrites*, more than being ungodly people, are people who live a contradiction. The scribes and Pharisees, who ostensibly helped people find the kingdom (v 2), in fact kept people from the kingdom—*shutting up the kingdom,* means they made it difficult, if not impossible, for men to come under the rule of God. In this, they are the antithesis of Peter who was given *keys* with which to open the kingdom and make it accessible to men (16.19). Instead of being stepping stones, the scribes and Pharisees were stumbling stones, obstacles to spiritual advancement.

Second Woe

23.14 Woe to you, scribes and Pharisees, hypocrites! For you devour widows' houses, and for a pretense make long prayers. Therefore you will receive greater condemnation.

The scribes and Pharisees were social predators who wronged the vulnerable. Widows are often cited in Scripture as objects of care and concern (Ex. 22.22–23, Jas. 1.27), but instead of protecting them, the scribes and Pharisees exploited them by *devouring* (*katesthiō,* to consume by eating) *their houses* (by foreclosure? betraying financial trust? home repair scams?). Their long prayers ("they are said to have remained three hours in prayer," Boles, 446) were a cover-up for their rapacity.

Third Woe

23.15 Woe to you, scribes and Pharisees, hypocrites! For you travel land and sea to win one proselyte, and when he is won, you make him twice as much a son of hell as yourselves.

A *proselyte* (*prosēlutos,* one who approaches, a worshiper) was a Gentile who became a member of the Jewish nation (for a male, this involved circumcision). There is no extrabiblical evidence suggesting the Jews aggressively pursued missionary activity, certainly not like Christian preachers in the book of Acts, so this may be another example of Christ's use of hyperbole (see *Notes,* ch 5). But though the Pharisees proselytized, they didn't save. When they made an effort (*go about on land and sea*) to convert a Gentile to Judaism, they left him worse off than he was in his Gentileism—*twice as much a son of hell as yourselves.* How they were worse off isn't explained. But by embracing a legalistic system, a proselyte was less likely to understand or accept a system of grace (Acts 20.24). And converts to a cause are often more zealous than their mentors—"The more converted, the more perverted" (H. J. Holtzmann).[5]

Fourth Woe

23.16,18 Woe to you, blind guides, who say, 'Whoever swears by the temple, it is nothing; but whoever swears by the gold of the temple, he is obliged *to perform it.'* [18] **And, 'Whoever swears by the altar, it is nothing; but whoever swears by the gift that is on it, he is obliged** *to perform it.'*

This woe departs from the introductory formula for the others (*Notes*) to characterize the scribes and Pharisees as *blind guides* (vv 17,29,34,26)—a label Christ first gave them in 15.14. *Blindness*, according to Jesus, is disobedience (15.1–11) and a failure to understand fundamental truths (15.16–20). In this woe, scribal and Pharisaic blindness is illustrated by their casuistry and dishonesty involving oaths (5.33–37).

Oaths are formulas that have been devised in every culture to assure others of our truthfulness by asking God to hold them accountable.[6] But instead of swearing by God or invoking His name, the Jews (who thought it profane to mention God's name) would swear by something connected with God, such as *the temple* or *the altar* (v 18). Despite the Law's insistence on truthful and honest speech (Lev. 19.12; Deut. 23.23), some oath formulas, with rabbinic blessing, were regarded as not binding. "With all solemnity they would make oaths that to the other party appeared to be binding, but [they] had certain kinds of mental reservations which made the oath mean 'nothing'" (Vos, 157).

Christ cites two examples of such blatant dishonesty: *whoever swears by the temple, it is nothing; but whoever swears by the gold of the temple, he is obligated … whoever swears by the altar, it is nothing; but whoever swears by the gift that is on it, he is obligat-ed*. It's bizarre to think that swearing by part of the whole imposed a greater obligation than swearing by the whole, but this illustrates the irrationality that goes with moral blindness (Rom. 1.21, Eph. 4.18).

---

[5] When Beethoven gained legal custody of his nephew Karl in 1816, his obsessive love made Karl's life a nightmare. In 1826, Karl tried to kill himself with a pistol, but failed in his attempt. His explanation to the magistrates was: "I have become worse because my uncle insisted on making me better" (Johnson, *The Birth of the Modern*, 122).

[6] William the Conqueror sought to control Harold, the last Anglo-Saxon king of England, "not by good faith, but by fear of holy relics on which he had sworn" (F. Warre Cornish, *Chivalry*, 358).

23.17,19 Fools and blind! For which is greater, the gold or the temple that sanctifies the gold? ¹⁹ Fools and blind! For which is greater, the gift or the altar that sanctifies the gift?

With two rhetorical questions, Christ exposes the inanity of Pharisaic reasoning: it was the altar that sanctified the sacrifice and the temple that sanctified the gold, not the other way around. An animal burnt on a campfire is just meal, but an animal burnt on God's *altar* is a sacrifice; a gold necklace around a woman's neck is just jewelry, but the gold in God's house is holy, set apart to Him. Pharisaic oaths reversed the proper order by making lesser things more important than greater things.

23.20–22 Therefore he who swears by the altar, swears by it and by all things on it. He who swears by the temple, swears by it and by Him who dwells in it. And he who swears by heaven, swears by the throne of God and by Him who sits on it.

To invoke the greater includes the lesser; to swear by the altar includes offerings placed on it; to swear by the temple includes the material of which it is made.

In v 21, Christ reverses the polarity to show that just as swearing by the greater includes the lesser, so swearing by the lesser includes the greater. *He who swears by the temple, swears by it and by Him who dwells in it.* Christ sweeps away the speciousness that thinks it can disconnect God from His house or creation. "The foot bone's connected to the leg bone, the leg bone's connected to the knee bone" is sound theology. Jewish oath formulas were nothing but a hypocritical cover-up for dishonesty.

Fifth Woe

23.23–24 Woe to you, scribes and Pharisees, hypocrites! For you pay tithe of mint and anise and cummin, and have neglected the weightier *matters* of the law: justice and mercy and faith. These you ought to have done, without leaving the others undone. Blind guides, who strain out a gnat and swallow a camel!

The Law of Moses required a tithe of seeds and fruit (Lev. 27.30), grain, wine, oil, and animals (Deut. 14.22–23). Tithes were an opportunity to celebrate and share the Lord's blessings. But as with nearly everything they touched, the scribes and Pharisees had perverted tithing, making it an external matter disconnected from loving devotion (22.36–39). *Mint, anise, and cummin* were spices; to tithe them would be like tithing basil, chives, and parsley. Preoccupied with tithing spices, the scribes and Pharisees *neglected* (*aphiēmi*, to send away, divorce) *weightier* (*barus*, heavy in weight, important) *matters* like *justice, mercy, and faith. Justice* (fair, evenhanded) was missing in the Pharisees' dealings with widows (v 14); they didn't mercifully ease suffering, they imposed suffering. *Faith* here is not faith in Christ, but trustworthiness and dependability in our dealings with others, which was lacking in Pharisaic oaths (vv 16–19).

These you ought to have done, without leaving the others undone. Christ taught us to respect the small things of the Law (5.18) without neglecting the big things. There are times when all that should be done cannot be done simultaneously (5.23–25; Lk. 10.39–42). When we must prioritize, we ought never choose the good over the better or the better over the best (Phil. 1.10, *approve the things that are excellent*). To fail in this is to major in minors: *straining out a gnat and swallowing a camel.* Because insects were unclean and nasty (Lev. 11.41), wine would be strained through a sieve or a cloth before being drunk. The scribes and Pharisees were scrupulous about the small, while egregiously violating the significant (27.6).

Sixth Woe

23.25–26 Woe to you, scribes and Pharisees, hypocrites! For you cleanse the outside of the cup and dish, but inside they are full of extortion and self-indulgence. Blind Pharisee, first cleanse the inside of the cup and dish, that the outside of them may be clean also.

The sixth woe recalls the discussion of purity in ch 15 and the distinction between outward and inward cleanness. The scribes and Pharisees *cleaned the outside of the cup,* they looked good outwardly, but they destroyed their character while maintaining their reputation, for inwardly they were full of *extortion* (*harpagē*, robbery, the act of plundering) and *self-indulgence* (*akrasia*, the opposite of self-control). *Akrasia* can refer to sexual incontinence or immoderate eating, but as used here, it involves a greedy, covetous spirit that robs others (v 14).

For the fifth and last time in this section, Jesus calls the Pharisees blind, but here the adjective is followed by an appeal: *first cleanse the inside of the cup and dish, that the outside of them may be clean also. First* (5.24, 7.5) establishes priority. To clean the inside of the cup is to repent (3.1, 4.17). God wants clean to reach the heart. That Christ, in a polemic condemning the scribes and Pharisees would include this appeal was an act of mercy that offered a way forward for these hypocrites.

Seventh Woe

23.27–28 Woe to you, scribes and Pharisees, hypocrites! For you are like whitewashed tombs which indeed appear beautiful outwardly, but inside are full of dead *men's* bones and all uncleanness. Even so you also outwardly appear righteous to men, but inside you are full of hypocrisy and lawlessness.

This woe repeats the contrast between outer and inner found in the sixth woe. In our vernacular, *whitewash* refers to a cover up, and this corresponds to Christ's meaning (Acts 23.3). In the first century, Jews would whiten tombs with lime dust so that pilgrims on their way to feasts could steer clear of them and avoid defilement (Num. 19.16; Lk. 11.44).[7] Christ's words, *appear beautiful outwardly*, recognize that while a gravestone can be a work of art, it is still a grave, a place of death. Christ is telling the Pharisees: "You aren't fooling anybody. Your long prayers and respectability no more convinces others of your goodness than a whitewashed tomb convinces men of its cleanness. You're painting rotten wood, and everybody knows it."

Eighth Woe

23.29–31 Woe to you, scribes and Pharisees, hypocrites! Because you build the tombs of the prophets and adorn the monuments of the righteous, and say, 'If we had lived in the days of our fathers, we would not have been partakers with them in the blood of the prophets.' Therefore you are witnesses against yourselves that you are sons of those who murdered the prophets.

The final woe condemns the scribes and Pharisees for following the example of past persecutors. Publicly, they venerated the prophets and righteous men of the long ago by *building the tombs of the prophets and adorning the monuments of the righteous*. There is no evidence that the scribes and Pharisees erected any tomb for any prophet, so Christ's words were likely meant to suggest similarity. Around the time of the first century, there appeared an apocryphal book known as the *Lives of the Prophets* that mentioned martyred prophets (Isaiah, Jeremiah, Ezekiel, Micah, Amos,

---

[7] In first-century Judea, people were not necessarily buried in cemeteries but were often buried in isolated graves near where they died.

and Zechariah) and the location of their graves. Then as now, tombs and memorials would be *adorned* (with flowers, etc.) to show respect and honor, but the scribes and Pharisees went beyond this, claiming they would have never committed the crimes their ancestors committed.[8] But they were wrong, for in killing Jesus, they would commit a crime that exceeded anything done by previous generations (21.35–39; Acts 7.51). In condemning their fathers' lesser guilt, they only judged their greater guilt.

23.32–33 Fill up, then, the measure of your fathers' *guilt.* Serpents, brood of vipers! How can you escape the condemnation of hell?"

Sounding like an ancient Hebrew prophet (16.13–14), Christ tells the Pharisees to *fill up the measure of your fathers' guilt. Measure* refers to the amount of sin God tolerates before acting in judgment (Gen. 15.16; Isa. 51.17; Jer. 25.15). "To fill up this measure is seldom the work of one age. Successive generations adopt the principles, and imitate the practices of their ancestor, adding 'sin to sin' and 'iniquity to iniquity,' until either by the natural consequence of such public vices as tend to subvert the strength and security of society, or by the special visitations of divine vengeance, now no longer corrective, but in the strictest sense penal, they receive the full reward of their sins" (R. Watson, *A Practical Exposition of the Gospels of Matthew and St. Mark*, 334). The last drop added to the cup of Israel's guilt would be the killing of God's Son (21.38–41).

The irony is that the scribes and Pharisees would do just as Jesus tells them to do—they would fulfill their father's guilt by killing Him (v 34, 10.17, 16.21, 17.22–23, 20.18–19). They were, just as John the Baptist (a murdered prophet) had said, *a brood of vipers* (3.7, 12.34). For their crime, they would end up where they led their converts: to *the condemnation* (*krisis*, justice, v 23) *of hell.*

The *woes* have come full circle (v 15). "Outwardly righteous but inwardly corrupt, [the scribes and Pharisees] will spend eternity with all of the unrighteous. So concerned about ceremonial cleanliness, yet they are consigned to the place symbolized by one where filth, dead animals, and the unclaimed dead bodies of executed criminals were thrown" (Hobbs, 329).

---

[8] "There was in the first century a great emphasis on building splendid tombs, including some for long-dead worthies (e.g., Herod's new marble monument over David's tomb, Josephus, *Ant.* xvi.179–82)" (France 329).

THE SENTENCE, 23.34–39

Notes

"The twenty-third chapter of Matthew, the most terrible outburst of the Master's wrath, ends with the most wonderful overflow of his love to be found in any one verse of the gospels: 'O Jerusalem, Jerusalem that killeth the prophets and stoneth them that are sent unto her! How often would I have gathered thy children together, even as a hen gathereth her chickens under her wings, and ye would not!' So like a terrific storm ending in a rainbow, Jesus' wrath comes to its close in love" (Fosdick, *The Manhood of the Master*, 42).

23.34 Therefore, indeed, I send you prophets, wise men, and scribes: *some* **of them you will kill and crucify, and** *some* **of them you will scourge in your synagogues and persecute from city to city,**

Therefore connects this to the preceding. Christ is speaking not of things past but of things present. Judgment would not fall immediately, for God would patiently (21.34–36, 22.3–6) send more *prophets* (who spoke by inspiration), *wise men* (whose knowledge of God's will came from their own study), and *scribes* (experts in God's word) preaching a gospel of grace (Lk. 23.34; Acts 20.24). But Christ knew that these righteous ones would fare no better than those who preceded them (v 30).

The scope of guilt is broadened to include the entire nation, for God's messengers were sent to the nation as a whole, not just to the religious establishment. Some commentators maintain that no evidence directly links the scribes and Pharisees to the persecution of Christians, but Luke and others say differently (Acts 8.1, 9.1–2). Scribes and Pharisees actively participated in the persecution and murder of Christians and supported others who murdered believers (v 35; Acts 2.23). And they couldn't have done so without the acquiescence of the nation.

23.35–36 that on you may come all the righteous blood shed on the earth, from the blood of righteous Abel to the blood of Zechariah, son of Berechiah, whom you murdered between the temple and the altar. Assuredly, I say to you, all these things will come upon this generation.

The blood of the murdered righteous cries for justice (Gen. 4.10; Rev. 6.10). Christ cites the list of persecuted prophets from A to Z—from *Abel* (Gen. 4.8) to *Zechariah* (2 Chron. 24.20–22), the first and last martyrs in the OT

(2 Chron. appeared last in the Jewish arrangement of the Heb. canon). "Zechariah ben Barachiah has been the subject of discussion for as long as there has been biblical exegesis. There appears to be a mistake somewhere" (Luz III, 154). The reason Luz says this is because in 2 Chronicles 24.20–22, Zechariah, the priest stoned by King Joash, is called the *son of Jehoiada* rather than the *son of Berechiah*. But a simple explanation might be that Jews often had more than one name (in 9.9, Jesus calls a tax collector *Matthew*, whom Luke 5.27 calls *Levi*). *Whom you killed* emphasizes the solidarity of the scribes and Pharisees with earlier prophet killers (v 31). For this, the accumulated punishment of the nation would fall on first-century Jews. This isn't a reference to the final judgment but to the judgment that came on Israel forty years after Christ's death (ch 24). In 22.7, Christ has hinted at the destruction of Jerusalem, but now He makes it plain. Israel had survived earlier divine judgments nationally intact, but the nation would not survive this judgment. In *filling up the measure of their fathers' guilt* (v 32), the time for Israel's national demise had come.

23.37 "O Jerusalem, Jerusalem, the one who kills the prophets and stones those who are sent to her! How often I wanted to gather your children together, as a hen gathers her chicks under *her* wings, but you were not willing!

These words come from a broken heart. Justice required the sentence of death, but there was nothing Christ wanted more than to justify those who merited death. The doubling of a name—*Jerusalem, Jerusalem*—is unusual in Greek and indicates intense emotion (*Lord, Lord,* 7.22; *Absalom, Absalom,* 2 Sam. 18.33). Jerusalem represented the nation, and Jesus grieved over His people's fate. A famous metaphor—*as a hen gathers* (9.37, 12.30) *her chicks under her wings*—portrayed the love, protection, and nurture Christ held out to His people.

How often would I ... and ye would not (KJV) summarizes the reality and tragedy of free will. Israel didn't want God, and for that, *O Israel, thou hast destroyed thyself* (Hos. 13.9, KJV).

23.38 See! Your house is left to you desolate;

Your house is the temple, which here represents the nation. In Ezekiel 10.18–19 and 11.22–23, God's glory leaves the temple, and it is no longer His house *but your*—the Jews'—*house*. *Desolate* (*erēmos*, lonely, uninhabited; translated *neglected* in v 23 and *left* in 19.27,29) means it is vacant, unoccupied by its owner (12.44).

23.39 for I say to you, you shall see Me no more till you say, 'Blessed *is* He who comes in the name of the LORD!'"

No more translates *ap arti*, which means *from now on* (26.29,64). These words signal a change that, on the surface, seem positive, anticipating the time when Israel would proclaim, *Blessed is He who comes in the name of the Lord* (21.9; Ps. 118.26). And it might be that Christ here shines a gleam of light into the gloom by looking forward to the time when those who killed Him would be offered the chance to repent and be forgiven (Lk. 23.34).

The context, however, is against this interpretation (21.43); the *woes* (vv 13–33), the persecution of God's messengers (v 34), the pronouncement of judgment on *this generation* (vv 35–36), and the declaration that God has left the temple (v 38) suggest not a turn to the Lord, but an admission of divine judgment similar to that found in Ezekiel 33.33: *when all these terrible things happen to them—as they certainly will—then they will know a prophet has been among them.* There comes a time when confessing Christ comes too late (7.21).

CHAPTER 24

JUDGMENT, 24.1–25.46

On Jerusalem, 24.1–36

Notes

This is the fifth and last of the great discourses in Matthew and the second longest after the Sermon on the Mount. It is often called the *Olivet* or *Eschatological Discourse*, because it was delivered on the Mount of Olives and deals with eschatology—teaching concerning the last days. What makes this chapter challenging is its apocalyptic language. *Apocalyptic*, which means *uncovering* or *revealing*, is a highly symbolic, figurative genre of biblical literature that was sometimes used by the prophets to depict God's judgment—His pouring out wrath on the wicked. On the surface, the language seems to portend end-of-the-world, final judgment phenomena, when, most usually, it refers to a historical judgment. Those familiar with OT symbolism will have little difficulty understanding Matthew 24.

The discourse has three parts. The first, 24.1–36, concerns God's judgment on the Jews; the second, 24.37 to 25.30, consists of parables on how to prepare for judgment (any judgment); the third, 25.31–46, describes the final judgment.

24.1 Then Jesus went out and departed from the temple, and His disciples came up to show Him the buildings of the temple.

That *Jesus went out and departed from the temple* is significant. Having declared that God had left His house (23.38), Christ leaves the temple, never to return. His public teaching is over; from here on, His instruction is solely for the disciples. The crucifixion is just three days away.

24.2 And Jesus said to them, "Do you not see all these things? Assuredly, I say to you, not *one* stone shall be left here upon another, that shall not be thrown down."

Do you not see all these things introduces a word picture describing the aftermath of the coming destruction of Jerusalem when *not one stone shall be left here upon another that shall not be thrown down.* Christ is specifically talking about the temple. "Just as the prophet Haggai described the building of the temple as 'a stone being laid upon a stone' (2.15), Jesus now expressed its destruction by the proverbial statement 'one stone not being left upon another'" (Paher, 78).

Excursus on the Temple

In 22 BC, Herod the Great summoned a national assembly and announced his plan to rebuild the Jewish temple. "The next two years were spent assembling and training a force of 10,000 workmen and 1,000 supervisory priests, who also worked as builder-craftsmen in the forbidden areas. The creation of the Temple as a functional place of sacrifice took only eighteen months, during which time elaborate curtaining screened the sanctuary from profane gaze. But the vast building as a whole needed forty-six years to complete. To achieve the grandiose effect he desired, Herod doubled the area of the Temple Mount by building huge supporting walls and filling in the gaps with rubble. Around the vast forecourt thus created he erected porticos; cash was spent profusely on the exterior, gates, fittings and decorations being covered in gold and silver plate. Josephus says the stone was 'exceptionally white', and the glitter of the stone and the gleam of the gold—reflected many miles away in the bright sun—was what made the Temple so striking to travelers seeing it from afar for the first time" (Johnson, *The History of the Jews*, 114–115). Johnson adds that some of the lower course stones were "45 cubits in length, 10 in height and 6 in breath, finished by imported craftsmen to an unusually high standard. The top 40 feet of the platform covered vaulted corridors and above them, on the platform itself, were the cloisters, with hundreds of Corinthian pillars 27 feet high and so thick, says Josephus, that three men with arms extended could hardly encompass them." The Roman general Titus wished to preserve the temple when he destroyed Jerusalem; it was against his orders when a Roman soldier fired it, sending it up in *flames* (Josephus, *Wars,* vi.4.6).

TWO QUESTIONS, 24.3

Notes

The first part of the judgment discourse (24.3–36) begins with v 3 and can be outlined according to the *when* and *what* questions the disciples ask.

Their *what* question is discussed in vv 4–31, first negatively (vv 4–14), then positively (vv 15–31); the *when* question is addressed in vv 32–36.

Prior to the advent of modern weaponry, the rules of war were quite clear that when a town refused to surrender, it should expect no mercy from the besieging army. Completely apart from the fighting, a besieging army was at risk of hunger and sickness. Because of the dangers faced by an investment on the outside, the garrison on the inside was often ruthlessly slaughtered once the walls were breached. The destruction Christ depicts is entirely consistent with the fact that the Jews refused to surrender to the Romans.

24.3 Now as He sat on the Mount of Olives, the disciples came to Him privately, saying, "Tell us, when will these things be? And what *will be* the sign of Your coming, and of the end of the age?"

When He reached the Mount of Olives, Jesus sat down (5.1, 13.2) and is asked two questions by His disciples: *Tell us, when will these things be? And what will be the sign of your coming, and of the end of the age?*

These things refers to the things in 23.35 to 24.2 that portended judgment. *Which* judgment is involved in this chapter has been much debated. *Your coming* and *the end of the age* have been interpreted as referring: (1) exclusively to God's first-century judgment on the Jews; (2) to God's first-century judgment on the Jews and His final judgment on the world; (3) exclusively to the final judgment on the world. For the following reasons, I consider the first option the correct one. First, it is likely that the disciples asked two questions rather than three, because in Mark 13.4 and Luke 21.7 only two questions are recorded. Matthew probably gave the questions in their entirety, whereas Mark and Luke distilled them to their essence. Second, in the Gr., a single article governs the two clauses (*the coming … end of the age*), which points to a single unit. Third, the phrase *end of the age* occurs six times in the NT, five times in Matthew (13.39,40,49, 28.20; Heb. 9.26) and means *the end* or *consummation of the age*. It can refer to the conclusion of any era, not just the final one. In this context, Christ's coming to judge the Jews is the focus.[1]; the destruction of the temple would certainly suggest the end of the Jewish era. Fourth, *coming* (*parousia*; 2 Cor. 10.10) was used to indicate the presence or arrival of a god or exalted person. When many think of the

---

[1] "How could the disciples have asked about [Christ's] second coming when they did not believe he would be killed? When Jesus told them that he would be killed during this visit to Jerusalem, and would rise again, 'They understood none of these things; and this saying

coming of Christ, they think of an actual descent from heaven as indicated in Acts 1.11, but in Scripture, *the coming of God* commonly expresses divine judgment against a nation through a human agency (Jer. 49.14; Hab. 1.5–11), an interpretation that fits well with the discussion here (Lk. 21.20,31). Nothing in the phrase *the end of the age* necessarily implies the end of the world, and in this text, Christ's *coming* and the *end of the age* point to the historical judgment on the Jews in the second half of the first century AD.

THE WHAT QUESTION, 24.4–31

What Is Not *the Sign*, 24.4–14

24.4–5 And Jesus answered and said to them: "Take heed that no one deceives you. For many will come in My name, saying, 'I am the Christ,' and will deceive many.

Christ answers the questions in reverse order. The answer to the *what* question falls into two parts: in vv 4–14, Jesus mentions seven things that will precede the sign but are not the sign; in vv 15–33, He identifies the sign and tells the disciples how to respond when it appears.

Take heed warns against being deceived by frauds. During times of turmoil, people are susceptible to fear-mongering and rabble-rousing, and first-century Judea was rife with turmoil. *I am the Christ* refers to messianic claimants (Josephus names quite a few, *Wars* i.13.4–5; Acts 5.36–37, 21.38).

24.6–8 And you will hear of wars and rumors of wars. See that you are not troubled; for all *these things* must come to pass, but the end is not yet. For nation will rise against nation, and kingdom against kingdom. And there will be famines, pestilences, and earthquakes in various places. All these *are* the beginning of sorrows.

In Jesus' time, Jewish nationalism was so rampant that Josephus wrote that "the nation began to grow mad with this distemper" (*Ant.* i.1.6). One attempted insurrection after another made the region a tinderbox. During Christ's childhood, Judas of Gamala led a revolt that marched on Sepphoris (the administrative center of Galilee, just a few miles north of Nazareth) and seized and held the arsenal. When Varus, the Roman

---

was hid from them, and they perceived not the things that were said.' (Luke 18.31–34.) They evidently held the Jewish idea that the Messiah would not be killed, but would abide here for ever. (John 12.32–34.). With their idea that the Messiah would not be killed, but would remain on earth forever, how could they have asked about his second coming?" (Whiteside, *Doctrinal Discourses*, 295–296).

general in Syria, arrived on the scene, he defeated Gamala's army, burned the city to the ground, and sold its populace into slavery. *Wars and rumors of wars* were the norm at that time in Judea[2] and have plagued the world in every century. Disciples were not to interpret political instability as the sign of imminent judgment.[3]

Exacerbating the unrest were natural calamities. A famine hit Judea during the rule of Claudius (Acts 11.28). "More than 30,000 died of pestilence in ancient Babylon and in parts of Judea and in Rome before AD 70" (Paher, 84). An earthquake is recorded in Acts 16.26, and others occurred in Antioch (AD 37), Phrygia (AD 53), Asia (AD 61), and the Lycus Valley (AD 61). But natural disasters were the *beginning*—not the end—*of sorrows*, the labor pains that would precede further stress and trouble.

24.9 Then they will deliver you up to tribulation and kill you, and you will be hated by all nations for My name's sake.

Christ talks about the fate of His disciples. *Then* is used eight times in this chapter (vv 10,14,16,21,23,30,40), and whether it means *at that time* (v 10, NIV), *after*, or *therefore* must be determined by the context. Here, it probably means *at that time*—at the time of the events alluded to in vv 5–7. *They will deliver you up to tribulation* recalls 10.17–21, and *kill you* recalls 10.28, 21.35, 22.6, 23.34,37. A time of persecution was coming when disciples would be *hated by all nations for My name's sake*—for no other reason than their faith in Christ (5.10–12; 1 Pet. 2.11–12).[4]

24.10–12 And then many will be offended, will betray one another, and will hate one another. Then many false prophets will rise up and deceive many. And because lawlessness will abound, the love of many will grow cold.

Persecution would exact a heavy toll. Hostility that began outside the church would emerge inside it, causing *many to be offended*—fall into sin

---

[2] "The history on which I am entering is that of a period rich in disasters, terrible with battles, torn by civil struggles, horrible even in peace. Four emperors fell by the swords; there were three civil wars, more foreign wars, and often both at the same time" (Tacitus, *Histories*, I.ii.3).

[3] "It would be easy to evince, by a catena of quotations from the earlier and later fathers, from the medieval writers, the reformers, and the protestant divines of the last three centuries, that this propensity to look on national commotions and collisions as decisive proof that the world is near its end, has never been extinguished in the church" (Alexander, *The Gospel According to Mark*, 349).

[4] Tacitus, in his Annals, refers to "the detestable superstition" of Christianity.

and leave the faith (18.6). Not only would the shallow (13.20–21) apostatize, but they would cause trouble for the faithful through *betrayal*[5] and *hatred*.

False prophets are mentioned a second time (vv 4–5) because of the role they would play in contributing to the apostasy of many (v 10, 7.15–20). "In retrospect it becomes clear why in 7.21–23 [Christ] confronts the false prophets so dramatically" (Luz III, 194).

Lawlessness (7.23, 13.41) is law-breaking behavior. In v 12, the law in view is the *great commandment*—the love commandment (22.36–40); nothing is worse than causing another to stop loving God or his fellows.

24.13–14 But he who endures to the end shall be saved. And this gospel of the kingdom will be preached in all the world as a witness to all the nations, and then the end will come.

Despite schisms, betrayals, lovelessness, and other forms of persecution, disciples must *endure to the end*. Endure (*hupomenō*, to remain under, persevere, patience) "is an aorist participle of a verb meaning to have an inner fortitude. It expresses the idea of one having the quality which enables him to withstand all that the enemy can throw against him, and still have the reserve power with which to counter-charge to victory" (Hobbs, 335; Rev. 2.7,10). To *endure* (from a Lat. word meaning *to last*)—to stay at one's post without panic or retreat—is one of the hardest assignments handed out by Christ (Rev. 2.10, 14.12).

Despite chaotic conditions, nothing would prevent the spread of the *gospel* (16.18), for it would *be preached in all the world as a witness to all the nations*. Christ would commission this in the last paragraph of the Gospel (28.18–19), and within thirty years, Paul would announce that the gospel had indeed reached every corner of the world (Col. 1.6,23). Only after the gospel had been preached to all would *the end*—divine judgment on the Jews—*come*.

What Is the Sign, 24.15–3

24.15 Therefore when you see the 'abomination of desolation,' spoken of by Daniel the prophet, standing in the holy place" (whoever reads, let him understand),

---

[5] "Tacitus in speaking of the persecution of Christians by Nero in A. D. 64, says, 'At first those who confessed were seized, afterwards, upon their information, a great multitude'" (Broadus, 484).

The sign (v 3) of the end would be *the abomination of desolation spoken of by Daniel the prophet, standing in the holy place* (Dan. 9.27, 11.31, 12.11). In the OT, *abomination* (*bdelugma*, a foul, detestable thing) "was Moses' favorite expression for the abhorrent nature of idolatry" (Block, *Deuteronomy*, 217). *Desolation*, recalling 23.38, means to lay waste, despoil, and describes the abomination's effect.[6] *Abomination of desolation*, therefore, referred to an idolatrous entity, which is how the Jews would view the Roman army — God's instrument of destruction.[7] *Holy place* translates the single word *hagios*. This word is elsewhere applied to the temple (Acts 6.13, 21.28), and many believe that is its referent here. Mark, however, talks about the abomination of desolation *standing where it ought not* (13.14), and Luke says the desolation is near *when you see Jerusalem surrounded by armies* (21.20). Based on these readings and the instructions in vv 16–20, I think it more likely that *hagios* refers to Judea, the holy *land* (v 16), rather than to the temple or city. Why would anyone wait until the enemy had breached the city walls and was ransacking the temple before fleeing (vv 16–20)? Christ is saying that when a hostile pagan force is seen approaching Jerusalem, the end is near, and it's time to leave.[8]

It's uncertain whether *whoever reads, let him understand* was spoken by Christ or Matthew, but regardless, the words are an admonition to readers to understand what Christ is saying.

Excursus on the Destruction of Jerusalem
Sacred and secular sources point to the devastation of Judea by the Romans during *the Great Revolt* of AD 66 to 70 as being the fulfillment of the judgment predicted in Matthew 23.34 to 24.36.

Enraged by a Greek pogrom in the Jewish quarter of Caesarea—about which

---

[6] *Abomination of desolation* is variously translated as: *the desolating sacrilege* (RSV), *the abomination that causes desolation* (NIV), *the destructive desecration* (WMS), *the appalling Horror* (MOFFATT), *the desolating abomination* (BARCLAY), and *the abomination that maketh desolate* (Carr, 268). Many Jews in the Maccabbean period believed the abomination of desolation to be a description of the Syrian ruler Antiochus Epiphanes, who in 168 BC had an image of Olympian Zeus erected in the temple and offered pagan sacrifices on the altar (1 Macc. 1.41–59).

[7] This was not the first time God used a pagan instrument to punish His people; see Habakkuk 1.5ff.

[8] "The Roman armies are called the abomination of desolation because, being heathen armies, they were an abomination to the Jews, and because they brought desolation on the country" (McGarvey, 207). Cf. Josephus, "In the very same manner Daniel also wrote concerning the Roman government, and that our country should be made desolate by them" (*Ant.* x.11.7).

the Roman authorities did nothing—militant Jews attacked and massacred the Roman garrison in Jerusalem. In response, Cestius Gallus, the Roman legate in Syria, assembled a large force at Acre and marched on Jerusalem but was routed by fierce resistance on the outskirts of the city. "Rome then took charge and reacted with enormous force, no fewer than four legions, the V, X, XII and XV, being concentrated in Judaea, and one of the empire's most experienced generals, Titus Flavius Vespasian, being given the command. He took his time, leaving Jerusalem severely alone until he had cleared the coast and secured his communications, reduced most of the fortresses held by Jews and settled the countryside. In 69 AD Vespasian was proclaimed emperor, and at the end of the year he left for Rome, leaving his eldest son, the twenty-nine-year-old Titus, in charge of the final phase of the campaign, the siege and capture of Jerusalem, which lasted from April to September 70 AD" (Johnson, *The History of the Jews*, 137).

24.16–20 "then let those who are in Judea flee to the mountains. Let him who is on the housetop not go down to take anything out of his house. And let him who is in the field not go back to get his clothes. But woe to those who are pregnant and to those who are nursing babies in those days! And pray that your flight may not be in winter or on the Sabbath. These verses clearly show that a historical judgment of God, rather than the final judgment, is in view. If the final judgment is meant, what difference would it make if it occurred in winter? And how could anyone expect to escape it by fleeing to the mountains? And why would anyone even think about returning to their home to fetch a coat? And how in the world would pregnancy, having small children, or the Sabbath be relevant?

Since the time of Lot (Gen. 19.17), the mountains in and around Judea had been a refuge for those on the run (Jer. 48.6), and it was to the mountains that believers in Judea should flee at the outbreak of the Jewish war. (For logistical reasons, armies try to avoid hilly terrain, which makes mountains a haven for those wishing to hide; Ps. 121.1.) The double use of *let him who is* (vv 17–18) stressed the urgency of flight—a man lounging on his patio roof (Acts 10.9) should leave without reentering his house, even to retrieve something as useful as a cloak (5.40).

Woe is here the woe of lament or sympathy (23.13). Especially to be pitied among the refugees would be pregnant women and mothers of small children, whose condition and responsibilities might slow them down. Wiersbe writes, "Alas, it would be the women and children who would suffer the most, a fact supported by history. The Romans attempted to starve the Jews into submission; and hungry men, defending their city, took food from their suffering wives and children and even killed and ate their own flesh and blood" (*Be Courageous*, 134). Flight *on the Sabbath* could bring its own set of problems from orthodox Jews who might impede travel (Acts 1.12). The suggestion of some that Jewish Christians would have had scruples about traveling farther than a Sabbath day's journey is unlikely; the instinct of self-preservation would surely have outweighed other considerations. Prayer (6.8) would never be more needed than when it came to surviving what was coming.

24.21–22 For then there will be great tribulation, such as has not been since the beginning of the world until this time, no, nor ever shall be. And unless those days were shortened, no flesh would be saved; but for the elect's sake those days will be shortened.

For connects these verses to vv 15–20. Although this seems to be end-of-the-world-language, Christ is still talking about the historical judgment ahead for the Jews. Hyperbole was a characteristic of Christ (*Notes*, 5.1), but there isn't much exaggeration here[9]—what happened to Jerusalem and the Jews in AD 70 was unparalleled in the nation's history to that point.

"No words can describe the unequaled horrors of the siege" (Carr, 269). Outside the city, hundreds of Jews were crucified; inside, civil war reigned as various factions spent more time fighting each other than the Romans; the temple courts were awash with the blood of this internecine hatred. The Roman blockade induced a state of famine so severe that mothers ate their children (Josephus, *Wars*, vi.3.4). Pestilence, starvation, slaughter, and monstrous atrocities were commonplace. By the time it ended on August 10, AD 70, 1.1 million Jews had fallen "by the edge of the sword" and 100,000 had been "led away captive into all nations" (Lk. 21.24). "There have been greater number of deaths—six million in the Nazi death camps, mostly Jews, and an estimated twenty million under Stalin—but never so high a percentage of a great city's population so thoroughly and painfully exterminated and enslaved as during the Fall of Jerusalem" (Carson, 501). "Accordingly, it appears to me, that the misfortunes of all men from the beginning of the world, if they be compared to these of the Jews, are not so considerable as they were" (Josephus, Preface to *Wars*, 4).

---

[9] See similar language in Jer. 30.7; Eze. 5.8–9; Joel 2.2; Rev. 16.18; also, see Ex. 10.4–6, 11.6; 1 Kgs. 3.12; 2 Kgs. 18.5; Dan. 9.12, 12.1.

Those days—the days of tribulation (v 21)—would be *shortened* (*koloboō*, to cut off, abridge; often used to indicate amputation). Rome always met uprisings with irresistible force, and it would not have been unusual for the legions to press the attack until *no flesh* remained alive in the Judean theater of operations. But in wrath, God remembered mercy (Hab. 3.2); He would not allow the desolation to run its full course. The presence of Christians—*for the elect's sake*—would temper His judgment (5.13; Gen. 18.23–32). "God's people bring a certain mercy to the people around them; while the unrepentant do not share in the ultimate salvation, yet something of good comes to them because of the presence of the elect in their communities" (Morris, 606).

24.23–26 Then if anyone says to you, 'Look, here *is* the Christ!' or 'There!' do not believe *it*. For false christs and false prophets will rise and show great signs and wonders to deceive, if possible, even the elect. See, I have told you beforehand. Therefore if they say to you, 'Look, He is in the desert!' do not go out; *or* 'Look, *He is* in the inner rooms!' do not believe *it*.

Unscrupulous men never let a crisis go to waste, and for a third time Christ warns against frauds—*false christs and false prophets*—(vv 4–5,11), including those who *show great signs and wonders* (7.22). According to the Law, more than a *sign* was needed to identify a true prophet. In Deuteronomy 13.2, if a man's message was at odds with prior revelation, he was not to be believed even if he worked a *sign or wonder that comes to pass*. Not all that glitters is gold; signs and wonders could be faked (2 Thes. 2.9, 2 Tim. 3.8). "Many deceivers and pretenders had appeared at the time of the previous siege of Jerusalem in 586 B.C. (Jer. 23.9–32, Ezek. 22.25–31). According to Eusebius and Jerome, one Jewish deceiver, Barchochebus (whose name meant 'son of a star'), pretended to vomit flames. He styled himself as having come down out of heaven to the Jews to bring them light amid their misfortunes. Josephus wrote that during the siege one false prophet persuaded 6,000 people to enter the temple to see signs of deliverance, and all of them perished" (Paher, 126–127). Forewarned is forearmed: *see, I have told you beforehand.*

24.27 For as the lightning comes from the east and flashes to the west, so also will the coming of the Son of Man be.

For connects this to v 26. Christ's *coming* would not be a clandestine event only a few would see but would be as obvious and unambiguous as a streak of lighting (Zech. 9.14).

24.28 For wherever the carcass is, there the eagles will be gathered together.
This proverb concludes the thought of the preceding verses. Newer versions have rendered *aetos* as *vultures* based upon the mistaken belief that "eagles are not normally carrion eaters" (Carson, 503). But *eagles* is a perfectly acceptable translation (golden eagles, especially, are opportunistic carrion feeders). I don't see here any allusion to the figures of eagles that were stitched on Roman legion standards. The thought recalls v 27: people will no more miss the coming of Christ than birds of prey overlook a dead skunk in the middle of the road.[10]

24.29 Immediately after the tribulation of those days the sun will be darkened, and the moon will not give its light; the stars will fall from heaven, and the powers of the heavens will be shaken.
It's easy to think Christ is speaking of some cosmic, world-destroying catastrophe here, but references to the *sun and moon being darkened and the stars falling from the sky* are rhetorical fireworks frequently used by the prophets to describe God's judgment on wicked nations (Acts 2.20; Rev. 6.12–13). McGuiggan is helpful: "Here is a judgment on the ungodly. It is not the end of time. … The language of judgment is ever similar. … This [language] is a characteristic of the prophets" (*Revelation*, 106[11]). Just as we today refer to celebrities as *stars* (and sometimes as *fallen stars*), so the prophets used the fall of celestial bodies to indicate the downfall or comeuppance of political and social luminaries. Matthew's original Jewish-Christian readers, who were familiar with the prophets, would not have struggled with language like this.

Immediately indicates that the fall of Jerusalem would quickly follow the hardships (*tribulation*) created by the war between the Jews and Rome.

24.30–31 Then the sign of the Son of Man will appear in heaven, and then all the tribes of the earth will mourn, and they will see the Son of

---

[10] A bird of prey feeding on a carcass is a figure frequently used by the prophets to describe God's judgment upon a nation (Deut. 28.49; Isa. 46.11; Jer. 19.7; Eze. 17.3; Hos. 8.1; Rev. 19.17–18).

[11] Christ is not mistaken in what He said, but we are sometimes mistaken in understanding what He meant. See Isa. 13.10, Babylon; 34.4–6, Edom; Eze. 32.7, Egypt; Joel 2.30–31,

Man coming on the clouds of heaven with power and great glory. And He will send His angels with a great sound of a trumpet, and they will gather together His elect from the four winds, from one end of heaven to the other.

Four events would attend God's judgment on Jerusalem. First, the *sign of the Son of Man would appear in heaven*, which contrasts with the false signs of the false christs and prophets (v 24). Christ, through the instrumentality of the Romans, was present in the war against Jerusalem and the Jews (v 33, 26.64).

Second, *all the tribes of the earth would mourn. Tribes of the earth* likely refers the *dispersion* (Jas. 1.1)—Jews who had migrated throughout the world and who, when they learned of Jerusalem's fate, were terribly saddened. News of Jerusalem's fall, however, elated many Gentiles. "The fall of Jerusalem was cited as evidence that Jews were hated by God. Philostratus asserted in his *Vita Apollonii* that when Helen of Judea offered Titus a victory wreath after he took the city that he refused it because there was no merit in vanquishing a people deserted by their own God" (Johnson, *The History of the Jews*, 140).

Third, *coming on the clouds* prophetically symbolized divine judgment (26.64; Ps. 104.3; Isa. 19.1; Jer. 4.13; Eze. 30.3–4; Rev. 14.14). When God sends a historical judgment, and pours out His wrath on nations and empires, it is a demonstration of His *power and great glory*. Decreation, as well as creation, reveals His majesty.[12]

Fourth, the *angels with a great sound of a trumpet would be sent to gather together God's elect from one end of heaven to the other.* The figurative language continues, recalling 8.11–12. The destruction of Jerusalem would not be a setback for God or His message. Not only would the gospel be preached prior to the war (v 14), it would be preached afterward. *Angels* may refer to gospel preachers (Rev. 1.20) whose message was a trumpet call to salvation throughout the world (*the four winds*, Jer. 49.36; Rev. 7.1). *Elect* (*eklektos*, chosen, 22.14) refers to the people of God (v 24, 22.14). Even when it is necessary for God to visit wrath on sinners, His work of redeeming the lost continues (vv 40–41).

Judah. Also, Isa. 24.23; Jer. 4.23–28; Dan. 8.9–10; Acts 2.19–20; Rev. 6.12–13.

[12] See Chilton, *The Days of Vengeance*, 196.

THE WHEN QUESTION, 24.32–36

24.32–33 Now learn this parable from the fig tree: When its branch has already become tender and puts forth leaves, you know that summer *is* near. So you also, when you see all these things, know that it is near—at the doors!

Jesus now answers the first question asked in v 3: *when will these things be?*

For the Hebrews, there were only two seasons: summer and winter.[13] Fig trees put on their leaves in April, which was late winter per Jewish calculation, right before the start of summer. When a fig tree had leaves, it meant summer was near. Similarly, *when you see* (v 15) *all these things, know that He is near, even at the doors. All these things* would include the things in vv 4–31, particularly the *abomination of desolation* (v 15). When the Roman army landed in Judea, *He,* the Son of Man (v 30) would be *near, right at the door* (NASB). Christ is the judge in this section; the Romans were only His hangman.

24.34–35 Assuredly, I say to you, this generation will by no means pass away till all these things take place. Heaven and earth will pass away, but My words will by no means pass away.

Assuredly—truly, guaranteed—introduces the answer to the *when question:* Christ would come (v 30)—to judge the Jews—before *this generation* passed away (16.28). Attempts to make *this generation* refer to the Jewish race, the church, or humanity are indefensible; in context, Christ is saying that the time when *not one stone shall be left here upon another* would occur within the lifespan of the present generation of Jews. A familiar idiom (*heaven and earth will pass,* 5.18; Ps. 102.25–27; Isa. 40.6–8; 1 Pet. 1.25) underscores the *certainty* of the coming judgment, which occurred forty years later in AD 68 to 70.

24.36 But of that day and hour no one knows, no, not even the angels of heaven, but My Father only.

This is a transitional verse that moves the discussion from God's judgment on the Jews to a section of *judgment parables* (24.37–25.30). The precise day and hour of Jerusalem's end was unknown to all except God; the best Christ can do, in His humanity, was give a general time frame for it (*this generation,*

---

[13] According to Luz, there was no Biblical Hebrew word for *spring.* In Modern Hebrew, the Biblical word for "ears whose kernels are still soft" has become the term for *spring* (III, 208, fn 8).

v 34). Only the Father—not the *angels, false prophets* (v 24), or even Christ (Mk. 13.32)—knows the day and hour when judgment would occur; when it would happen was as unpredictable as a bolt of *lightning* (v 27).

C. S. Lewis, in his wonderful essay, "The World's Last Night," calls this admission of ignorance by Christ "the most embarrassing verse in the Bible." If Jesus is God (as the incarnation affirms), then He is omniscient; but if He is omniscient, how could He be ignorant? Lewis continues, "The answer of theologians is that the God-Man was omniscient as God, and ignorant as Man. This, no doubt, is true, though it cannot be imagined. Nor indeed can the unconsciousness of Christ in sleep be imagined, nor the twilight of reason in his infancy. ... A generation which has accepted the curvature of space need not boggle at the impossibility of imaging the consousness of incarnate God. In that consciousness the temporal and the timeless were united. I think we can acquiesce in mystery at that point." I don't think anyone can frame the issue better. Contrary to the charge of many critics, Jesus was not wrong in v 34 when He predicted His coming within the lifetime of the generation then alive, for His coming referred to His historal coming against Jerusalem, not His final coming to judge the world. But there is no explaining His admission of ignorance, and the tortured attempts to explain it have been exercises in futility. It is indeed best to simply acquiesce to the mystery. "The doctrine of the two natures in one person transcends human reason. It is the expression of a supersensible reality, and of an incomprehensible mystery, which has no analogy in the life of man as we know it, and finds no support in human reason, and therefore can only be accepted by faith on the authority of the Word of God" (Berkhof, quoted by Gromacki, 106).

Excursus on the *Parousia of the Son of Man*

Four times in Matthew 24 (and nowhere else in the book), reference is made to the *parousia* (*coming*) of the Son of Man (vv 3,27,37,39). As every standard lexicon indicates, the basic meaning of the word is *presence* or *arrival*, and it was commonly used to describe the visit of a royal or official personage. Because of this, some maintain that two comings of Christ are involved in ch 24: the judgment on Jerusalem and the second coming of Christ. A typical comment to this effect comes from Turner: "Most scholars understand 24.15–28 to be speaking of events accompanying the destruction of Jerusalem in 70 CE. Some scholars ... see an additional eschatological fulfillment" (581).

I disagree with the two-coming view, believing only one coming—the historical judgment on the Jews—is discussed in 24.1–36.

Here are my reasons why.

An unprejudiced reading of Matthew 24 strongly favors the judgment-on-the-Jews interpretation. First, beginning in v 3, Christ expands on the judgment alluded to in 21.41, 22.7, and 23.34–39; He, not the Romans, will be the reason for their coming defeat (v 2) and the city's destruction (Dan. 1.2). Second, v 34 places the events of vv 4–33, including *the* parousia *of the Son of Man* in vv 27, within the lifetime of Jews then alive (*coming* in v 30 translates the more common verb *erchomenon*). "Verses 30 and 31 might seem to refer to events that would take place at the second coming of Christ, were it not that the events therein mentioned, as well as those mentioned in verse 29, were to take place … during the life of some of those then living. It must, therefore. mean that the destruction of Jerusalem would be such a striking fulfillment of the prophecy of Jesus that it would be a sight of his presence in the whole affair" (Whiteside, *Reflections*, 42–43). Lightfoot's observation on 24.34 was, "Hence it appears plain enough, that the foregoing verses are not to be understood of the last judgment, but, as we said, of the destruction of Jerusalem." Third, there is no grammatical reason why *parousia* cannot be a synonym for *erchomai* (v 30, 16.28) or refer to God's judgment against the Jews. The lexicons cite instances (e.g., Kittel's, V, 858–871; *Arndt-Gingrich*, 635; et al.) where the term was used in an abstract, nonliteral way; thus, to assert that *parousia* necessarily and always implies *actual* presence is not true. As noted in 10.41, the universally recognized *emissary rule* says that when an ambassador arrived at a foreign court, the sovereign he represented arrived (2 Cor. 5.18–20). Just as God *came* in human agents to judge nations in the OT (e.g., Isa. 19.1), so Christ would come in human agents to judge the Jews. And no law of language prohibits the Lord from using *parousia* this way.

Either *all these things* prior to v 34 were fulfilled before that generation passed away, or only *some* were. Because Christ said *all* rather than *some*, I believe *parosia* (v 27) should be interpreted ccordingly. *Context, not a dictionary or lexicon, determines a word's meaning.*[14]

For an in-depth study of this subject, see James Stuart Russell's *Parousia, A Careful Look at the New Testament Doctrine of the Lord's Second Coming* (accessible online).

---

[14] When used metaphorically, *leaven* ordinarily describes the insinuating influence of evil

PARABLES OF JUDGMENT, 24.37–25.30

Notes

Verse 37 begins an interlude in the discourse that consists of three sections: vv 37–41, vv 42 to 25.13, and 25.14–30. These grow increasingly longer, with the middle one bracketed by a call to watchfulness (v 42, 25.13).

24.37–39 But as the days of Noah *were*, so also will the coming of the Son of Man be. For as in the days before the flood, they were eating and drinking, marrying and giving in marriage, until the day that Noah entered the ark, and did not know until the flood came and took them all away, so also will the coming of the Son of Man be.

A comparison is drawn between the present generation and Noah's generation. Prior to the flood, life went on as usual. There was *eating and drinking, marrying and giving in marriage*. Though warned of what was coming (Heb. 11.7; 1 Pet. 3.20; 2 Pet. 2.5), the antediluvians were caught unprepared. History teaches that man learns nothing from history, but Christ gives a warning nevertheless.

24.40–41 Then two *men* will be in the field: one will be taken and the other left. Two *women will be* grinding at the mill: one will be taken and the other left.

Two cameos from ordinary life intensify the admonition. When Christ comes, men and women will be going about their usual chores *in the field* and *at the mill*, but a separation will occur wherein one is taken (v 31, spared) and one is left. *"Taken* is the same verb used, *e.g.*, in 1.20; 17.1; 18.16; 20.17; it implies to take someone to be with you, and therefore here points to the salvation rather than the destruction of the one 'taken'" (France, 348).

24.42–44 Watch therefore, for you do not know what hour your Lord is coming. But know this, that if the master of the house had known what hour the thief would come, he would have watched and not allowed

---

(16.6; Mk. 8.15; 1 Cor. 5.6–7), but in 13.33, *leaven* refers to a *righteous* influence. As far as I know, this is the only place where it has this meaning, but this is the meaning indicated by the context. Of the word *vision (horama)* in 17.9, France says it is "a noun used elsewhere in the New Testament [all in Acts] only for apparently 'inward' experiences" (262), but in 17.9, it refers to an objective event. Even if in every other instance *parousia* implies literal presence, if the context so indicates, it can have a nonliteral meaning, which I believe to be the case in Matt. 24.

his house to be broken into. Therefore you also be ready, for the Son of Man is coming at an hour you do not expect."

Here begins a section of three parables enclosed by the command *watch* (v 42, 25.13). "There was no word that Jesus Christ spoke oftener to His disciples than this word *Watch.* ... It is a word that He spoke with increasing frequency, as He drew near to His death" (Baillie, *Christian Devotion*, 52). To *watch* is to be alert, as illustrated by the contrast in vv 43–44. The coming of Christ is like a burglary (*to be broken into, diorussō*, lit. to dig through; the word had become a technical term for a break-in) in that no one knows when it will occur. The contrast is this: the homeowner didn't watch because he didn't anticipate what was coming (v 43), but disciples are to watch because they know what's coming (v 44). Uncertainty should lead to vigilance; to *watch* is to be ready at all times by carrying out responsibilities (vv 45–41), forethought (25.1–13), and seizing opportunities (25.14–30) to love our fellows (25.31–46). Because a sentry doesn't know when the enemy will attack or when an officer will inspect him at his post, he must stay awake and be on guard at all times. A glance at a concordance will show the drumbeat of *watch* in almost every NT book (1 Cor. 16.13; Col. 4.2; 1 Thes. 5.2; 2 Pet. 3.10; Rev. 3.3). *Therefore be ready, for the Son of Man is coming at an hour when you do not expect Him.*

First Parable, 24.45–51

24.45–51 "Who then is a faithful and wise servant, whom his master made ruler over his household, to give them food in due season? Blessed *is* that servant whom his master, when he comes, will find so doing. Assuredly, I say to you that he will make him ruler over all his goods. But if that evil servant says in his heart, 'My master is delaying his coming,' and begins to beat *his* fellow servants, and to eat and drink with the drunkards, the master of that servant will come on a day when he is not looking for *him* and at an hour that he is not aware of, and will cut him in two and appoint *him* his portion with the hypocrites. There shall be weeping and gnashing of teeth.

These parables (24.45–25.30) have four features in common: (1) an absentee major figure whose coming is delayed; (2) two groups, one that is prepared for the absentee's coming and one that isn't; (3) a definition of preparedness and unpreparedness; and, (4) reward for the prepared and punishment for the unprepared. The principles here are relevant to any judgment, whether historical, individual, or final.[15]

Who then is a faithful and wise servant recalls 7.24 (and anticipates 25.2–9,21,23) and challenges readers to examine themselves to see where they stand. This first parable involves a *servant* appointed by his master to give other servants their food ration. Blessing is pronounced on the servant who attends to his duties and is found performing his duties when his master returns (*comes*, v 30). His reward is a promotion to a position of greater responsibility and trust (25.21; cf. the story of Joseph).

In contrast to the dutiful servant is an *evil servant*, who, believing his master's return wasn't imminent, morally deteriorates (which *watching* is meant to prevent, 2 Pet. 3.3–4), beats his fellow servants, and engages in general carousing. But this servant egregiously miscalculated, for his master returns unexpectedly and catches him in his irresponsibility and wickedness. His punishment is a gruesome death that involves being cut in two (Heb. 11.37) and consigned with the hypocrites (which the wicked servant was; 23.29–38) to a place of suffering and pain (8.12).

---

[15] "Today we live in an even more difficult time to conceive of the end of history and the accompanying last judgment. Therefore, for many people the idea that Christ is coming again in judgment no longer has an impact on the way they live, while the idea of one's own death is an analogous experience that is inescapable. All can experience in their own death the reality that *their* time comes to an end even though time in general continues. Thus, the experience of one's own death emphasized in the history of interpretation is a hermeneutically interesting analogy in what the text is trying to say" (Luz III, 220).

CHAPTER 25

Second Parable, 25.1–13

Notes

The parable of the virgins is the second in a series of three providing guidance on how one should live given the uncertainty of life's end or the Lord's return. A number of themes—*wise, delay, ready, master, watch*—tie this parable to the preceding.

Contextually, Christ emphasizes the need for readiness in order to be prepared for His coming (24.42,44). Historically, the parable of the virgins has suffered from blatant allegorizing.

25.1–4 "Then the kingdom of heaven shall be likened to ten virgins who took their lamps and went out to meet the bridegroom. Now five of them were wise, and five *were* foolish. Those who *were* foolish took their lamps and took no oil with them, but the wise took oil in their vessels with their lamps.

Ten maidens are introduced who are alike in every way except one: all are virgins, all have lamps, all lamps are lit, all are present to meet the bridegroom, all fall asleep before the bridegroom arrives, all awake when the bridegroom's arrival is announced, and all arise and trim their lamps. The only difference is that five had enough oil for their lamps and five didn't. Those with enough oil are called *wise;* those lacking oil are called *foolish.*

Except for the information gleaned from passages like this, little is known of Jewish wedding customs in the time of Christ. Apparently, the wedding was held at the bridegroom's house. The ceremony would begin when the groom went to the bride's house to fetch his bride. If the wedding took place at night, friends would accompany the groom and form a processional lit by lamps or torches. The *lamps (lampas)* were not the small oil lamps used inside houses but outdoor torches of which there were two types. One involved a stick or pole around which were wrapped rags soaked in olive oil; the other involved a pole from which hung a container in which oil-soaked rags were placed. *Vessels* (*aggeion*, only here in the NT) refers to a flask or container that could be used to carry extra oil.

25.5–7 But while the bridegroom was delayed, they all slumbered and slept. And at midnight a cry was *heard:* 'Behold, the bridegroom is coming; go out to meet him!' Then all those virgins arose and trimmed their lamps.

For some unexplained reason, the bridegroom *tarried* (*chronizō*, 24.48, *delay*) and didn't arrive when expected (in contrast to 24.48–50, in which the master returned *before* he was expected). The five who didn't bring extra oil didn't use the delay to procure more oil' along with the wise virgins, they nod off to sleep. At *midnight*—the Gr. merely indicates the middle of the night[1]—the maidens are awakened by a *cry* (1 Cor. 15.52; 1 Thes. 4.16) signaling the bridegroom's approach. A flurry of activity follows as each trims (*kosmeō*, put in order) her lamp by adding oil to the rags.

25.8 And the foolish said to the wise, 'Give us *some* of your oil, for our lamps are going out.'

The lamps of the foolish cannot be relit for lack of oil, and they ask their companions to share some with them.

25.9 But the wise answered, saying, 'No, lest there should not be enough for us and you; but go rather to those who sell, and buy for yourselves.'

Here, the parable takes an unexpected turn. Neighborliness would dictate that the wise share their oil, but they refuse *lest there not be enough for us and you*; if they shared, they might all end up in the dark. The suggestion to *go rather to those who sell, and buy for yourselves* seems insensitive since it is the middle of the night. Clearly, the five without oil were in a predicament.

25.10 And while they went to buy, the bridegroom came, and those who were ready went in with him to the wedding; and the door was shut.

The foolish hurry off to find oil, and while they are gone, the bridegroom arrives. Those *who were ready*—the wise—*went in with him to the wedding,*

---

[1] The Gr. for 12 AM, *kata to mesonuktion* or *kata meson tēs nuktros* is found in Acts 16.25, 27.27.

for many are called, but few are chosen (22.14). All the virgins were invited to the wedding, but only the prepared got in.

This scene also departs from a normal Jewish wedding when the foolish find the door shut to them. Jewish weddings were usually celebrated by the entire village, which would make a closed (locked) door unnecessary. The shut door is ominous.

25.11–12 Afterward the other virgins came also, saying, 'Lord, Lord, open to us!' But he answered and said, 'Assuredly, I say to you, I do not know you.'

Instead of celebrating, the foolish virgins are judged. Two previous passages in Matthew help with the interpretation here.

The first is 5.16, and the suggestion that the lit lamps are the *good works* that glorify God. The obedience that points men to God is how one readies himself for the Lord's return.

The second text is 7.21–27, which is the only other place where Christ distinguishes between the *wise* and *foolish*. Both builders heard the Lord's words, both built, and to all appearances their houses were solid. But just as with the virgins, a crisis reveals a difference when one house withstands the storm, but the other falls. The difference between the wise and foolish builder was obedience: one heard and obeyed, the other heard but didn't obey.

The similarity between the builders and the virgins is suggested by the foolish virgins' double cry of *Lord, Lord* (7.21) and the response, *I do not know you* (7.23). *Obeying the Father's will* is what makes one *known* to Christ; obedience is the *oil* that readies us for the Lord's arrival. *But obedience is nontransferable*—it cannot be given to another, which explains the oddities in this parable already noted. The fact that the ones without oil did not take the opportunity during the delay to secure oil speaks to the deadening power of sin. Sin dulls us to the seriousness of our situation, robbing us of a sense of urgency until it becomes a matter of *too little, too late*.

25.13 Watch therefore, for you know neither the day nor the hour in which the Son of Man is coming.

Preparedness is critical, "because the bridegroom can come at any time, and the door can close at any time" (Luz III, 235). At any moment, it may be too late to do what we should have been doing all along.

Third Parable, 25.14–30

Notes

Stories in which an absentee king or master entrusts possessions to slaves for them to gainfully use were common in Jewish literature. In this parable, the first section briefly narrates the transfer of talents from master to slaves (vv 14–15), followed by a section describing the slaves' activity during the period between the master's departure and return (vv 16–18), and concluding with a reckoning between the master and his slaves (vv 19–30). The dialogue between the master and third slave (vv 24–30) takes up about two-fifths of the parable.

25.14–15 "For *the kingdom of heaven is* **like a man traveling to a far country,** *who* **called his own servants and delivered his goods to them. And to one he gave five talents, to another two, and to another one, to each according to his own ability; and immediately he went on a journey.** *Kingdom of heaven* is not in the Gr. text, but *like* (*hōsper*, just as, even as) ties this parable to the previous kingdom parable (v 1). It wasn't uncommon for a king or slave owner to assign management of his assets to his slaves. The Romans even had a word for it, *peculium*, whereby a slave was at liberty to invest an asset as he thought best.

One slave receives *five talents*, another *two*, and a third *one* (13.8,23). In the first century, a *talanton* was a unit of weight rather than a specific currency, whose value depended on whether it was gold, silver, or copper; here, the talents were silver (v 18). In our usage, *talent* refers to one's potential or ability, but in this parable, the talents are distributed to each slave *according to his own ability.* "Each had all he that he was capable of handling" (Robertson, 198). The master wasn't dispensing intellectual or business acumen but was assigning talents based on skills already possessed, giving the slaves an opportunity to show what they could do. God provides opportunities commensurate with *our* abilities.

25.16–18 Then he who had received the five talents went and traded with them, and made another five talents. And likewise he who *had received* **two gained two more also. But he who had received one went and dug in the ground, and hid his lord's money.**

The first two slaves get busy (note that it is the slaves, not the talents, who work). The first *trades* (*ergazomai*, to work, be active) his talents. In first-century Judea, a favorite way to increase holdings was by trading in commodities or speculating on land. However they did it, the first two slaves doubled their talents (increased their opportunities), recalling Christ's earlier teaching about bearing fruit (7.15–20, 13.18–23) and seeing opportunity in persecution (10.18–19).

The peculiar temptation of those who have only one talent is to do nothing because they can do so little, relatively speaking. Possibly reasoning this way, the third servant buried his talent.

25.19–23 After a long time the lord of those servants came and settled accounts with them. So he who had received five talents came and brought five other talents, saying, 'Lord, you delivered to me five talents; look, I have gained five more talents besides them.' His lord said to him, 'Well *done*, good and faithful servant; you were faithful over a few things, I will make you ruler over many things. Enter into the joy of your lord.' He also who had received two talents came and said, 'Lord, you delivered to me two talents; look, I have gained two more talents besides them.' His lord said to him, 'Well *done*, good and faithful servant; you have been faithful over a few things, I will make you ruler over many things. Enter into the joy of your lord.'

After a long time, the master returns and calls his servants to account (18.23, 21.34). *Settled accounts* (*sunairō*) is used only in Matthew and "may have been a business phrase familiar to Matthew the publican" (Carr, 278).

The first two servants are praised for their diligence. In words often cited as the welcome given the righteous upon their entrance into heaven, the master commends them for *well doing* as *good and faithful servants*. Morris likens the praise to our "Bravo!" (629). *Enter into the joy of your master* recalls v 10.

Faithful labor brings greater responsibility. The principle involved in *you have been faithful over a few things* (24.45–47), *I will make you ruler over many things* was illustrated by Moses and David, who learned to lead men by leading sheep.

25.24–25 Then he who had received the one talent came and said, 'Lord, I knew you to be a hard man, reaping where you have not sown, and gathering where you have not scattered seed. And I was afraid, and went and hid your talent in the ground. Look, *there* you have *what is* yours.'

The third servant's accounting is contradictory, insulting, and self-condemning. He accuses his master of being *a hard man*, who profited unjustly by *reaping where you have not sown, and gathering where you have not scattered* seed. Because the slave was *afraid* of how the master might react to a loss of his principal, he played it safe by hiding his talent in the ground.[2] *Look, there you have what is yours* comes across as insolent; how often is it the case that people who refuse to accept responsibility blame others for their irresponsibility?

25.26–28 But his lord answered and said to him, 'You wicked and lazy servant, you knew that I reap where I have not sown, and gather where I have not scattered seed. So you ought to have deposited my money with the bankers, and at my coming I would have received back my own with interest. Therefore take the talent from him, and give *it* to him who has ten talents.

The master's assessment differs markedly from the servant's (20.15). The real problem was that the servant was *wicked and slothful* (*oknēros* means hesitating or fearful). His fear of failing caused him to not even try. Fear paralyzes, precludes success, and robs us of productivity.

That the master repeats the slave's characterization of himself doesn't mean he agrees with it; readers of Matthew know that this master bestows an easy yoke and light burden (11.29–30). The master repeats the accusation to point out the irony in it: "If you really thought I was as greedy and unfair as you say, why would you think I'd be happy with you doing nothing? Why didn't you put my talent in the bank where it could have at least earned some interest?" (*tokos,* offspring, the offspring of money).[3]

The inconsistency in the slave's explanation exposed the truth, and his talent is taken away and given to the first servant.

25.29–30 'For to everyone who has, more will be given, and he will have abundance; but from him who does not have, even what he has will be taken away. And cast the unprofitable servant into the outer darkness. There will be weeping and gnashing of teeth.'

---

[2] "In rabbinic sources burying money is explicitly praised as a safe way to preserve things" (Luz III, 252). But as 13.44 shows, not even this provided absolute security.

[3] It appears that in first-century Judaism, the prohibition against charging interest was followed, so Christ's reference to *interest* may have alluded to doing business with Gentiles.

For to everyone who has, more will be given, but from him who does not have will be taken away even what he has recalls a principle previously encountered in Matthew (e.g., 13.11–16). Far from being a capricious, unreasonable master, Christ is a merciful master who gives heaven in exchange for the love that gives a cup of cold water (10.42), restores a hundredfold for anything given up for His sake (19.29), and graciously pays men what they haven't earned (20.10). *The* LORD WILL GIVE GRACE AND GLORY; *no good thing will He withhold from those who walk uprightly* (Ps. 84.11).

For the *unprofitable* (*achreios*, only here and Lk. 17.10), there awaits the horror of divine wrath. It's worth noting that whereas the joy of heaven is often described in general figures, references to hell and punishment are specific and terrifying: *outer darkness, weeping and gnashing of teeth* (8.12, 24.51).

This parable expands on the previous one. To increase talents is to increase opportunities (vv 14–15) for showing love and displaying faith (vv 34–40). But to increase opportunities requires engagement with others, a willingness to overcome fear and take risks, getting involved rather than standing back. We live wisely when we live lovingly and faithfully, seeing in every contact and relationship an opportunity to glorify the Father (5.16). But opportunity doesn't always come knocking; we must make our own breaks. Speaking to others, interacting with others,[4] and having eyes open to the needs of others (1 Jn. 3.16–17) will provide constant occasions for doing the will of God. While awaiting the Lord's return, we are to be busy, seeing opportunities where others see obstacles, working for the night is coming.

ON THE WORLD, 25.31–46

Notes

"What death is to man," wrote C. S. Lewis, "the Second Coming is to the wh ole human race," and the second coming/final judgment is woven throughout Matthew. The judgment in ch 24 could be avoided; but no one will avoid the judgment now discussed. John the Baptist alluded to the final judgment in 3.7–12, all the major discourses in the Gospel end with it (7.13–27, 10.39–42, 13.47–50, 18.23–35), and it is a key concept in chs 11 to 12 (11.20–24, 12.20,27,31–32,33–37,41–42). Figures of judgment include

---

[4] If we don't know our neighbor well enough to have him over for coffee, chances are we don't know him well enough to lead him to Christ.

wailing and gnashing of teeth (found six times), the *fire of gehenna* (5.22,29–30, 18.8–9), and *cast out into outer darkness* (8.12, 22.13, 25.30; Matthew wasn't shy about frightening his readers).

This section concludes Christ's last extended discourse in Matthew. It well deserves its designation as the *masterpiece of the Gospel*,[5] for it underscores love as the defining character God honors and accepts (22.36–40).[6] And this is another example wherein Christ's teaching on one subject occasions His comments on a related subject (*Notes*, 10.16)—a section on the judgment on the Jews now segues into a section on the judgment on the world.

Verses 31–33 are the introduction and v 46 the conclusion. In between are two dialogues, the first addressed to the *sheep*/righteous (vv 34–40), the second to the *goats*/wicked (vv 41–45). The point of emphasis unfolds in a fourfold repetition of the works of love.

25.31–33 "When the Son of Man comes in His glory, and all the holy angels with Him, then He will sit on the throne of His glory. All the nations will be gathered before Him, and He will separate them one from another, as a shepherd divides *his* sheep from the goats. And He will set the sheep on His right hand, but the goats on the left.

Christ ended His previous discourses with a reference to judgment (7.21–27, 10.39–42, 13.47–50, 18.23–35), and He does the same here, speaking as the Judge of all.

All the nations sometimes signifies only the Gentiles (24.9,14), but here it includes Jew and Gentile (24.14, 28.19), when each individual is held responsible (v 19; 18.24) for how he used his talents—invested his life (vv 16–18, 2 Cor. 5.10).

Judgment will involve a separation between two groups identified as the sheep and the goats. The sheep are placed on Christ's right (a position of honor, 20.21), and the goats on His left (a position of disgrace; 13.49, 20.23). There is no middle group.

---

[5] "The New Testament contains no scene of more impressive majesty than this which is sketched by the pen of Matthew alone" (Erdman, 201–202).

[6] Tolstoy's story *Where Love Is, There God Is Also*, was based on this text and is well worth locating and reading.

Sheep, 25.34–40

25.34 Then the King will say to those on His right hand, 'Come, you blessed of My Father, inherit the kingdom prepared for you from the foundation of the world:

The language goes from figurative (in the parables) to literal as the King speaks (this is the only place in Matthew where Jesus explicitly identifies Himself as King; 2.2, 21.5). Those on the right—the *blessed of My* Father—are invited to *come* (v 10, 11.28). *Blessed* (*eulogeō*, eulogy, to speak well of, praise; vv 21,23, 26.26) indicates God's approval and acceptance. *Inherit* means to receive an assigned or designated portion (Jn. 14.2–3). *The kingdom prepared for you from the foundation of the world* indicates that the kingdom was always in God's mind—it was always God's intent to have a relationship wherein those who loved Him and lived under His loving rule.

25.35–36 for I was hungry and you gave Me food; I was thirsty and you gave Me drink; I was a stranger and you took Me in; I *was* naked and you clothed Me; I was sick and you visited Me; I was in prison and you came to Me.'

Those on the right are blessed because they characteristically loved God by loving their neighbor (22.37–3; *Notes*, 5.3). They gave the Lord *food* when He was *hungry*, *drink* when He was *thirsty*, *shelter* when He was homeless, *clothing* when He was *naked*, *care* when He was sick, and *companionship* (by visiting) when He was imprisoned (first-century prisons were noted for their inhumanity, especially for the poor, who had no one to bring them extra food or other provisions, 24.25; 2 Tim. 4.13). These verses unpack what the servant was *doing* when his master returned (24.45–46), what constituted the *oil* and *watchfulness* of the wise virgins (v 4), and how the servants who were given five and two talents doubled them—namely, by practicing pure religion, characteristically showing mercy to the unfortunate and distressed (Jas. 1.27).

25.37–39 Then the righteous will answer Him, saying, 'Lord, when did we see You hungry and feed *You*, or thirsty and give *You* drink? When did we see You a stranger and take *You* in, or naked and clothe *You*? Or when did we see You sick, or in prison, and come to You?'

The king's six-fold repetition of *for I was … and you gave Me* catches the righteous by surprise; they couldn't recall having ever met Christ, much less ministering to Him. "Thoroughly unaware are these people of ever having performed any good deeds—which was exactly what made these deeds so good!" (Hendriksen, 889).[7]

25.40 And the King will answer and say to them, 'Assuredly, I say to you, inasmuch as you did *it* to one of the least of these My brethren, you did *it* to Me.'

Blessed are the merciful, for they shall obtain mercy.

Most Bible students are familiar with the concept of vicarious *sacrifice*, but here is vicarious *service*, wherein the *greatest*—Christ (10.40–42)—is represented by the *lowest* (*elachistos*, superlative of *short*; smallest, lowliest): the vulnerable, exploited, and poor. Significant here is that the smallest act of love shown to the least is love shown to Christ.

Commentators have long debated who is included by *My brethren*. Some limit the term to Christians (12.49–50) or to itinerate evangelists (10.40), but such narrowness smacks of the Pharisaism Christ condemned in the Sermon on the Mount (5.47). *Brethren* here includes all mankind; by taking on our nature, Christ became the brother of every man. "We are all neighbors in the eyes of God, and we must all become neighbors in our own eyes" (Johnson, *Jesus, A Biography from a Believer*, 164).

To miss this will result in missing it all.

Goats, 25.41–46

25.41–45 Then He will also say to those on the left hand, 'Depart from Me, you cursed, into the everlasting fire prepared for the devil and his angels: for I was hungry and you gave Me no food; I was thirsty and you gave Me no drink; I was a stranger and you did not take Me in, naked and you did not clothe Me, sick and in prison and you did not visit Me.' Then they also will answer Him, saying, 'Lord, when did we see You hungry or thirsty or a stranger or naked or sick or in prison, and did not minister to You?' Then He will answer them, saying, 'Assuredly, I say to you, inasmuch as you did not do *it* to one of the least of these, you did not do *it* to Me.'

---

[7] In L. Frank Baum's classic American fairy tale, *The Wonderful Wizard of Oz*, the Scarecrow thinks he doesn't have a brain, the Tin Woodman thinks he doesn't have a heart, and the Cowardly Lion thinks he has no courage, when, in fact, the Scarecrow was always the most intelligent person in the group, the Tin Woodman would cry if he stepped on an ant, and the Cowardly Lion risked his life repeatedly to protect his friends. The humility of these three, who were unaware of their virtues, is one of the great aspects of the story.

Christ tells those on the left to *depart from Me, you cursed, into the everlasting fire prepared for the devil and his angels*. Unlike the *kingdom prepared from the foundation of the world* (v 34), hell was prepared for the devil, not for man. But the children of the devil (Jn. 8.44) will share their father's fate. On *everlasting*, see 19.29; the term indicates quality rather than quantity.[8]

The explanation given the goats for their fate is the antithesis of that given the sheep—they weren't merciful to Christ for they weren't merciful to those they encountered who were in need. The goats protest that they had never seen the Lord, but He explains that they saw Him every time they met the hurting and needy. The goats are thus damned for lacking oil and burying their talent—for not seeing and grasping opportunities to love.

25.46 And these will go away into everlasting punishment, but the righteous into eternal life."

Everlasting and *eternal* translate *aiōnios* "and ought in both instances to have been rendered by the same English word. The fatal preference for variety of expression, in place of accuracy of representation" is unnecessary (Farrar, *Texts Explained*, 41). Robertson said that *aiōnios* "comes as near to the idea of eternal as the Greek can put it in one word" (202). *Punishment* (*kolasis*, only here and 1 Jn. 4.18) is detailed elsewhere (v 30, 24.51).

The standard by which men will be judged is love—not in the abstract but in concrete acts of mercy (Jas. 2.13). "When we show mercy spontaneously, gladly, freely, instantly, not thoughtlessly but unthinkingly and happily, we behave not just in kingly fashion but like God himself—it is the best way to show we are made in his image" (Johnson, *Jesus, A Biography from a Believer*, 167).

---

[8] Farrar says that *aiōnios* does not include "the conception of time, and sequence" at all (*Texts Explained*, 42).

CHAPTER 26

26.1–27.66: Jesus Tried and Crucified
26.1–16: Background to Betrayal
RIVAL PLANS, 26.1–5

Notes

The end is near. Passover and the sacrifice of the Lamb has arrived. Superficially, it will seem that the Jewish establishment has the upper hand in the events that unfold, but in reality, they play only a supporting role. It is Jesus who is in control.

This section is connected to what has preceded by predictions (16.21, 17.22–23, 20.18–19) and allusions (9.15, 12.14, 20.28) to Christ's death. Here is found the explanation for the enigmatic signals that appear early in the Gospel, such as the inclusion of women in the genealogy (1.2–16), the genealogy's forty-twoness (1.17), the name *Jesus* (1.21), the name *Immanuel* (1.23–24), the unity between Herod and the chief priests and scribes (2.3–4), the appearances of Gentiles (2.1–12, 8.5–13, 15.21–28), etc. All these curiosities have dimensions of meaning that are understandable only in light of the cross.

Chapters 26 to 28 are framed in some interesting ways: Christ is the speaker and dominant figure in the first (vv 1–2) and last paragraphs (28.18–20); His enemies plot His death in vv 3–5, but learn that their plot has failed in 28.11–15; a woman anoints Jesus in vv 6–13, but in 28.1 women find it unnecessary to anoint Jesus; etc.

The present paragraph introduces the main actors: Jesus and His disciples (vv 1–2) and the chief priests and elders (vv 3–5).

26.1–2 Now it came to pass, when Jesus had finished all these sayings, *that* **He said to His disciples, "You know that after two days is the Passover, and the Son of Man will be delivered up to be crucified."**

The standard formula with which Matthew ends a discourse is expanded by the word *all*: *when Jesus had finished all these sayings*. Although there will still be instruction that Christ gives His disciples, efforts to reach His enemies have ended. Over the next few days, Jesus will be silent, for the most part, before His opponents.

Jesus reminds the disciples of what He had already told them (16.21, 17.22–23, 20.18–19), but for the first time He provides a time frame. *After two days*, per Jewish usage, could be anywhere from just over twenty-four hours to forty-eight hours (12.40). If it is still Tuesday (*Notes*, 21.1), *after two days* would be Thursday or Friday.

Passover[1] occurred on the fourteenth day of the first month (Nisan, our March/April) in the Jewish calendar. It was the first of the three great Jewish feasts, along with Pentecost and Tabernacles, and commemorated the sparing of Israel's firstborn during the tenth plague (Ex. 12.1–14). It's uncertain whether Jesus referred to the day when the Passover lambs were killed, or the night when they were eaten (which, according to Jewish time, would be the following day, as Jewish days began at sundown), or both (a Roman day allowed for the killing and eating of the Passover lamb on the same day). What is certain is that in connection with Passover, Jesus would be *betrayed to be crucified*. The Gr. word translated *betrayed* (*paradidōmi*) has previously been used in Matthew of John the Baptist (4.12), Judas (10.4), the disciples (10.17–21), believers (24.9–10), and Jesus (17.22, 20.18). The disciples should have remembered that *crucifixion* wasn't the end of Christ's story, but they didn't.

26.3–5 Then the chief priests, the scribes, and the elders of the people assembled at the palace of the high priest, who was called Caiaphas, and plotted to take Jesus by trickery and kill *Him*. But they said, "Not during the feast, lest there be an uproar among the people."

While Jesus is predicting, His enemies are plotting. The scene shifts to the minor actors: *the chief priests, scribes, and elders of the people* (vv 47,57, 2.4, 27.1,3,12,20,41).[2] The mention of the *people* is ironic for the Jewish hierarchy, rather than representing the *people*, was afraid of them (v 5).

A meeting occurs in the *palace* (*aulē*, courtyard or buildings surround a courtyard, v 58) *of the high priest Caiaphas*. This was undoubtedly an ad

---

[1] "Tyndale has the merit of introducing into English the word 'passover,' which keeps up the play on the words in the original Hebrew (Exod. xii.1 1 and 13)" (Carr, 283).

[2] The *scribes* are omitted from Eng. versions not based on the Majority Text.

hoc gathering, for regular assemblies of the Sanhedrin were not held at the home of the high priest. *Joseph Caiaphas* was high priest from AD 18 to 37. He was removed from office at the same time Pilate was deposed. The length of his time in office, compared with the short tenures of his immediate predecessors, suggests he was a capable politician.[3]

Plotted (*sumbouleuō*) means to give advice, confer, consult, decide; the group had assembled to reach a decision. *Trickery* (*dolos*) was a legal term indicating malice aforethought. In Exodus 21.14, crimes committed with *treachery* (*dolō*) were capital crimes, which made the word germane to this meeting, for these men were plotting a murder.

But they feared the people. During Passover, the influx of pilgrims could swell Jerusalem's population as much as 500 times. Many visitors to the city were from Galilee where Jesus enjoyed popular support (21.8–16), and the leadership fears an arrest might trigger an uprising. To avoid this, *they said* (*they kept saying*, WMS; it was a point of emp.) *not during the feast.* They wanted Jesus dead, but could wait until after Passover. Their plan, of course, directly conflicted with Christ's (v 2), but it was His plan, not theirs, that was enacted,[4] which shows who was master of the situation. This is heaven's hour.

CHRIST HONORED, 26.6–13

Notes

Jesus and the Jews agreed that He should die, but disagree on when it should happen. To show how Christ implemented His schedule, Matthew backtracks to two incidents that probably occurred the previous Saturday (between chs 20 and 21; Jn. 12.1–13), involving a memorable act of devotion and a despicable act of betrayal.

In vv 7 and 13, attention is focused an unnamed woman who anoints Jesus; between these verses (vv 8–12) is an embarrassing exchange between Christ and His disciples.

26.6–7 And when Jesus was in Bethany at the house of Simon the leper, a woman came to Him having an alabaster flask of very costly fragrant oil, and she poured *it* on His head as He sat *at the table*.

So long as the bridegroom is with them, it is a time for feasting (9.15). The

---

[3] In 1990, the family tomb of Caiaphas was discovered south of Jerusalem.

[4] This recalls God's plan overriding Herod's plan to kill the infant Jesus in ch 2.

location is a house in *Bethany* belonging to *Simon the leper* (about whom nothing more is known), where a *supper* has been prepared (Jn. 12.2). During supper, Mary (Jn. 12.3), sister of Martha and Lazarus, brings in an *alabaster flask* containing a *very costly fragrant oil. Alabaster* was a yellowish gypsum, and the flask was probably a small bottle for holding ointments. *Fragrant oil (muron)* indicates a perfume. Matthew doesn't use the ordinary verb for *anoint (aleiphō)* but says the oil was *poured (katacheō*, to pour down, pour over) on Jesus' head.

26.8–9 But when His disciples saw *it*, they were indignant, saying, "Why this waste? For this fragrant oil might have been sold for much and given to *the* poor."

"In the passion narratives the disciples cut a particularly bad figure" (Luz III, 337). The contrast between them and Mary is stark: she pours, they protest. *Indignant (aganakteō*, very displeased; 20.24) indicates a strong reaction to what they deplored as a *waste* of money.[5] John 12.5 prices the oil at *three hundred denarii;* a footnote in the NKJV says this was "about one year's wages for a worker." The suggestion that the money could have been used by the poor is hard to dispute (9.13, 12.7, 19.21, 25.36–37); the disciples' reaction might well have been our own.

Mary doesn't explain why she did what she did, but Jesus will interpret her deed (v 12).

26.10–12 But when Jesus was aware of *it*, He said to them, "Why do you trouble the woman? For she has done a good work for Me. For you have the poor with you always, but Me you do not have always. For in pouring this fragrant oil on My body, she did *it* for My burial.

The women of the passion narratives come off more loving, loyal and brave than the men. Here, the men quibble over the propriety of a loving act, while a woman manifests the true spirit of love.

Jesus is *aware* of the disciples' complaint, and He rebukes them and defends Mary. The disciples' behavior is another example of how they sometimes bore little resemblance to the Christ they followed. They had *troubled (kopos*, a beating) Mary for doing a *good (kalos*, beautiful, choice,

---

[5] Trueblood makes the interesting comment that "Christianity does not teach moderation. … The unjust steward [Lk. 16.1–9] was commended by his employer for his prudence, but this does not mean that, in the Christian context, prudence is good" (*Confronting Christ*, 141).

suitable) *work*. Christ recalls Deuteronomy 15.11 and its statement about the poor—not to diminish the importance of helping the poor but to emphasize the significance of the moment.[6] Because of v 2, readers understand *Me you do not have always* as alluding to Christ's death, but the disciples missed it.

What Mary did was done for Christ's *burial*.[7] It was Jewish custom to anoint corpses with aromatics to mask the odor of decaying flesh (Mk. 16.1). Based on v 13, I understand Mary's deed as a conscious act of devotion done in light of Christ's imminent death. Mary had put herself in a position to understand (Lk. 10.39) and took the opportunity to express her love for Christ before He died (a good practice to follow). In it, she illustrated the extravagance and prodigality of love. Mary's economic situation is unknown, but to pour out a year's savings would be a major financial hit for most anyone in the middle class. But Mary didn't hesitate; faith counts the cost (Lk. 14.28), but love doesn't. It wouldn't surprise me to learn she gave Christ the costliest thing she had.

26.13 Assuredly, I say to you, wherever this gospel is preached in the whole world, what this woman has done will also be told as a memorial to her."

It's nearly impossible to tell the story of Christ's nativity without mentioning the devotion of the magi (2.1–11), but the story of His death is often told without mentioning the devotion of Mary—which is remarkable, seeing that Jesus saw such importance in what she did that He expressly said her story is to be told wherever His story is told.

After a solemn *amēn* (*assuredly*), Jesus turns attention to Mary; of those in the room, she alone is worthy of special recognition. This constitutes the first of two memorials in this chapter. The supper instituted in vv 26–29 would be in memory of Christ (1 Cor. 11.25), but what Mary did is to be told *as a memorial* (*mnēmosunon*, from *Mnemosyne*, the Gr. goddess of memory) *to her*. And what is to be remembered? Her illustration of the love involved in the great commandment (22.37) and her understanding that enabled her to see Christ's cross beforehand (v 12).

---

[6] So long as there are the poor, there are opportunities for showing love to the Lord (25.41–46).

[7] "She, and she first, believes that Christ should die" (J. Lightfoot, quoted by Morris, 649).

CHRIST BETRAYED, 26.14–16

Notes

Defection is a common human experience, but Judas is still an enigmatic figure. We know virtually nothing about him or his motives. We don't even know with certainty the meaning of his surname, *Iscariot*,[8] and yet, he is the poster child for treachery and betrayal. It would be hard to think of any other historical figure more reviled or maligned than he.[9]

The time of this action is uncertain; Matthew is more interested in telling the story than in providing a detailed timeline. Judas is the one who sets in motion what Christ predicted (v 2, 16.21, 17.22–23, 20.18–19); he will resurface in vv 21–25, 47–50, and 27.3.

26.14–16 Then one of the twelve, called Judas Iscariot, went to the chief priests and said, "What are you willing to give me if I deliver Him to you?" And they counted out to him thirty pieces of silver. So from that time he sought opportunity to betray Him.

Then would seem to indicate the same time frame as vv 6–13, but it may be that v 14 picks up the thread of v 5: at the very time when the chief priests and elders were plotting Jesus' death, Judas shows up. Attempts to absolve him of guilt by suggesting that he acted out of noble causes are certainly wrong (see Barclay, *The Mind of Jesus*, 205–206). Christ said that Judas did what he did because he gave in to the devil (Jn. 6.70, 17.12). Judas's own assessment will be, *I have sinned* (27.4).[10]

What are you willing to give me if I deliver Him to you? suggests greed as a motive, but if Judas was after money, it's hard to understand why he settled for just thirty pieces of silver. Thirty denarii would approximate a laborer's monthly wage—which seems a piddling amount for the service he offered, but some have sold their birthright for less (Heb. 12.16). The Jewish establishment had to be worried that Jesus was unarrestable (Jn. 7.30,32,45–47), and for one of His inner circle to offer assistance was more than they had dreamed. Undoubtedly, they would have paid more, but Zechariah

---

[8] The geographical interpretation *man from Kerioth*, is thought the most probable meaning. Kerioth was a village in Judea.

[9] In Dante's *Divine Comedy*, Judas is in the lowest part of hell, along with the traitors Brutus and Cassius.

[10] "The sad truth is that Judas was no inhuman monster but a warning example of what a man may do, who, while in daily fellowship with Jesus does not renounce or master his besetting sin. He was not the last professing Christian guilty of treason against the King" (Erdman, 206).

11.12 set the betrayal price at thirty pieces of silver (Matt. 27.9), and thirty pieces of silver (one tenth of what Mary spent, Jn. 12.5) it was. Whatever reasons compelled Judas to do the unthinkable, God foresaw it all.

From that time recalls the literary breaks at 4.17 and 16.21. The last major section of the Gospel—the account of Christ's suffering—has begun. A deal has been struck, and Judas, consistent with the caveat stated in v 5 (Lk. 22.6), looked for a time when Jesus could be arrested as quietly as possible.

26.17–56: Thursday

PASSOVER, 26.17–35

Notes

The crucifixion story begins with v 17, and a series of chronological notes (vv 17,20,31, 27.1,57,62, 28.1) move it along in an unbroken flow until 28.15.

The Passover meal (vv 17–29) consists of three scenes: preparation (vv 17–19), identifying the betrayer (vv 20–25), and instituting the Lord's supper (vv 26–29).

26.17 Now on the first *day of the Feast* of Unleavened Bread the disciples came to Jesus, saying to Him, "Where do You want us to prepare for You to eat the Passover?"

The Feast of the Unleavened Bread actually began the day after Passover (Num. 28.17), but in popular parlance the term was applied to the period surrounding the Passover (cf. "the Christmas season"), including the day on which the Passover lambs were killed and the meal eaten.[11] Because the Passover was to be eaten the evening of the fourteenth day of the month (Ex. 12.6–10), vv 17–19 would have occurred on the thirteenth day of the month.[12]

The disciples ask *Where do You want us to prepare for You to eat the Passover?*

26.18 And He said, "Go into the city to a certain man, and say to him, 'The Teacher says, "My time is at hand; I will keep the Passover at your house with My disciples."'"

---

[11] "This happened at the time when the feast of unleavened bread was celebrated, which we call the Passover" (Josephus, *Ant.* xiv.2.1).

[12] Although 28.1 seems to indicate that Matthew reckoned the beginning of a day at sunrise, I see no problem placing these events into the Jewish custom of beginning a day at sundown.

In answer, two *disciples* (Mk. 14.13) are instructed to go into Jerusalem (where the Passover was to be kept, Deut. 16.16), where they will find *a certain man* (*ho deina*, which could be rendered *so-and-so*). Christ's instructions were more specific than Matthew reveals, for as Luke indicates, the man would be *carrying a pitcher of water* (22.8), which would have made him stand out for doing a chore usually done by women. When they found him, they were to tell him that the *Teacher's time is at hand and He would keep the Passover with His disciples at the man's house.* Since it would have been difficult to reserve a large room during Passover at the last minute, it's reasonable to think Christ had made prior arrangements (Mk.14.15).

26.19 So the disciples did as Jesus had directed them; and they prepared the Passover.

The man is found, and preparations begin. Typically, preparing the Passover involved: (1) removing all leaven from the house (Ex. 12.15), (2) procuring a lamb (Ex. 12.5), (3) having it slaughtered by a priest and its blood poured on the altar, (4) roasting it whole, (5) baking unleavened bread, (6) preparing a dish of bitter herbs (Ex. 12.8), and (7) securing drink (v 27).

26.20 When evening had come, He sat down with the twelve.

Like v 17, this section begins with a chronological note. *When evening had come* agrees with Exodus 12.8, which stipulated that the Passover be eaten at night (thus, the fourteenth day of the month had begun, Ex. 12.6). *Sat down* (*anakeimai*) means to lie or recline. "We are not to envisage, with Leonardo da Vinci's famous Renaissance portrait of the last supper, one long table with people sitting on chairs on either side of it, but rather the *triclinium.* This was a square-cornered, U-shaped combination of three cushions, on which people would recline, lying on their sides with their bodies perpendicular to the cushions and stretched outward away from the center of the room. The food was placed in the middle of the 'U,' in between the couches" (Blomberg, 388).

26.21–22 Now as they were eating, He said, "Assuredly, I say to you, one of you will betray Me." And they were exceedingly sorrowful, and each of them began to say to Him, "Lord, is it I?"

At some point during the meal, Jesus drops a bombshell. Introduced by *assuredly* (indicating an important truth), He announces that someone in the room will betray Him. Hearing this, the disciples were *exceedingly sorrowful* (cf. vv 37). Eleven of them had never even imagined what Christ predicted—*Certainly not I? Could it be I?*—but they knew that Christ knew men, and they were humble enough to entertain self-doubt, trusting the truth of the Lord's words more than their own good conscience. It is noteworthy that none of the Eleven suspected anyone but himself. To paraphrase Spurgeon, we rarely do good by suspecting our brother; we often do good by suspecting our self.

26.23 He answered and said, "He who dipped *his* hand with Me in the dish will betray Me.

More specifically, *He who dipped his hand with Me in the dish will betray Me.* Luz notes that the verb is an aorist participle: "the one is meant who—just now—is reaching into the common bowl with Jesus" (III, 359). Even with this specificity, the disciples still aren't clear about who is meant (Jn. 13.28). *The dish* was a bowl holding either bitter herbs or the *charoseth,* a sop of crushed fruit and vinegar, sometimes added to the Passover meal to symbolize the mud the Hebrews used to make bricks in Egypt. Both mixtures were a salsa into which diners dipped their bread (Jn. 13.26). John was seated to Jesus' right (Jn. 13.23) and Judas, based on the fact that He and Jesus shared the same bowl, was on Christ's left in a place of honor (20.21).

26.24 The Son of Man indeed goes just as it is written of Him, but woe to that man by whom the Son of Man is betrayed! It would have been good for that man if he had not been born."

This verse contains three elements. First, Christ reaffirms His approaching death—*the Son of Man goes as it is written of Him.* He is not at the mercy of a traitor; He will not die "because he had strong enemies who were weaving a plot from which he could not escape" (Morris, 657), but because it was His Father's will that He die.

Second, though His death is God's will, Judas was not absolved of guilt. Judas was no pawn; he retained his free will, which God providentially used to bring about His Son's death. The *woe* pronounced recalls 18.7.

Third, *it would have been good for that man if he had not been born* underscores the enormity of the crime. The theory that has the wicked annihilated at death cannot explain this comparative; if Judas instantaneously went from existence to nonexistence, Christ's statement makes no sense.

26.25 Then Judas, who was betraying Him, answered and said, "Rabbi, is it I?" He said to him, "You have said it."

Judas doubtless felt that to not join with the others (v 22) would be suspicious, so he disingenuously asks, *Rabbi, is it I?* Instead of addressing Jesus as *Lord*, he calls Him *Rabbi*, the title coveted by self-righteous scribes (23.7–8). He is the only one who addresses Jesus this way (v 49). Whether consciously or unconsciously, it indicates that he is outside the group; Jesus is no longer his *Lord* or *Teacher* (v 18).

In answer, Christ laconically says *You have said it* — *Yes, it is you.* After being urged by Christ to make quick work of it (Jn. 13.27), Judas leaves to inform the Jews that he has been found out (vv 14–16,47; Jn. 13.30), and that if they wanted to take Him, they would have to act on the very day they didn't want to act (v 5).

26.26 And as they were eating, Jesus took bread, blessed and broke *it*, and gave *it* to the disciples and said, "Take, eat; this is My body."

Except for the reference to *the dish* (v 23), nothing is said about the Passover meal, for it isn't the focus. The emphasis is on Jesus who was the substance of the Passover shadow (Jn. 1.29,36; 1 Cor. 5.7; Heb. 10.1). "These are tremendously significant deeds and words. It is a pity that we are so familiar with them that they tend to lose their impact. For they throw floods of light on Jesus' own view of his death. By what he did with the bread and wine, and by what [he] said about them, he was visibly dramatizing his death before it took place and giving his own authoritative explanation of its meaning and purpose" (Stott, *The Cross of Christ*, 67–68).

As they were eating, Jesus took bread, blessed it and broke it, and gave it to the disciples. This would have been unleavened bread (Ex. 12.15). Pieces were broken off (15.36) and handed out. *Blessed* (*eulogēsas*) is a word of praise and thanksgiving; *it* is not in the Gr. — grammatically, the blessing could refer to God or the bread. In 14.19, the closest parallel to this text, praise and thanksgiving are directed to God. At Jewish meals, it was common for a thanksgiving to God to be spoken over the food (Lk. 22.19).

This is My body, to which Luke adds, *which is given for you.* It's certainly true that "The apostles picked up this simple concept and repeated it, sometimes making it more personal by changing it from the second person to the first: 'Christ died for us'" (Stott, *The Cross of Christ*, 63). But I think there's added truth here, which a Jewish reader would have seen.

In Leviticus, the first sacrifice discussed is the burnt offering (1.1–9) in which the *entire* animal is burned on the altar with nothing left over. "The burnt offering was the basic sacrifice that expressed devotion and dedication to the Lord" (Wiersbe, *Be Holy*, 28). By making the bread a symbol of His body, Christ commemorated that His sacrifice involved "the last full measure of devotion." The unreserved devotion He expected from and praised in others (vv 6–13, 19.21, 22.36–39) He supremely displayed. The typical significance of the *whole burnt offering* (Deut. 33.10, Ps. 51.19) was fulfilled in Christ's total giving of Himself.

On another level, "What trials, hatreds, struggles, and schisms," said the seventeenth-century Austrian theologian Johann Wolzogen, "have these few words evoked among Christians." Historically, controversy has centered on whether the copula *is* should be understood literally or figuratively.

Catholicism insists that *is* should be taken literally—that during the *Eucharist* (the giving of thanks, the Lord's supper), the bread and fruit of the vine are actually changed into the body and blood of Christ. Several considerations, however, are against this view.

First, if the bread and fruit of the vine are literally changed into flesh and blood, a miracle takes place. In the Bible, though, miracles were discernible by the physical senses. When Christ changed water to wine, the result tasted like wine, not water (Jn. 2.10). The Catholic Church admits that in the Eucharist no such change occurs. Second, while Jesus was speaking, His *body* held the *bread*—the two were distinct. "It would be hard for any thoughtful person to believe that Jesus was holding his literal body in his hands!" (Whiteside, *Reflections*, 508). Third, Christ elsewhere used cannibalistic language to speak of Himself; for example, *unless you eat the flesh of the Son of Man and drink His blood, you have no life in you* (Jn. 6.53).[13] No one thinks of literally interpreting other figures Christ used—*I am the door* (Jn. 10.9), for instance, doesn't mean He was changed into wood. Fourth, in 1 Corinthians 11, Paul says it is bread, not flesh, that is eaten: *as often as you eat this bread* (vv 26,27,28). Fifth, after Jesus said of the cup *this is My blood*, He called it *the fruit of the vine* (v 29); that is, after He said *this is My blood*, Christ still understood the contents of the cup to be grape juice. The natural interpretation of *this is my body* is that it is meant figuratively, not literally.

---

[13] 1 Jn. 3.24 is a good interpretation of the cannibalistic language that appears in the eating flesh and drinking blood texts. Compare *And he who keeps His commandments dwells in Him, and He in him* (3.24), with *He who eats my flesh and drinks my blood dwells in Me, and I in*

26.27–28 Then He took the cup, and gave thanks, and gave *it* to them, saying, "Drink from it, all of you. For this is My blood of the new covenant, which is shed for many for the remission of sins.

Life isn't possible without an adequate blood supply, and Christ now speaks to the life made possible by His blood. *Cup* metonymically represents its contents—grape juice, the *fruit of the vine* (v 29), which symbolizes the *blood of the new covenant, which is shed for many for the remission of sins*. The Eng. *covenant* comes from the Lat. *convenire*, which means an agreement. Every covenant implies at least two parties who are free moral agents; every covenant is made for the benefit of the parties involved; a covenant creates a special relationship between the parties; and a covenant creates *rights* and *responsibilities* held by each party.

In Exodus 24, at the ratification of the Sinai Covenant, Moses sprinkled blood on the altar (v 6) and the people (v 8), but the use of *blood* to ratify a covenant is somewhat obscure. The clues we have about this rite come from the other two incidents in the OT that involved sprinkling blood: the consecration of Aaron and his sons to the priesthood (Lev. 8.30) and the purification of a man healed of leprosy (8.4; Lev. 14.6–7). "From these two incidents … we get the principle that the sprinkling of blood is likely to signify the entry into a new state marked by cleansing from previous defilement and consecration to a holy purpose" (Morris, *The Apostolic Preaching of the Cross*, 76). Christ's blood makes it possible for sinners to enter a new state of innocence and fellowship with God.

Shed (*ekcheō*, to gush) implies a violent death, as happened with a sacrificial animal. Christ's death was sacrificial. *For many* recalls 20.28 (also 22.14) and Isaiah 53.12. The benefit gained by Christ's shed blood is *the remission of sins*—which takes us to the heart of His mission (1.21, 20.28). "Is it possible to exaggerate the staggering nature of this claim? Here is Jesus' view of his death. It is the divinely appointed sacrifice by which the new covenant with its promise of forgiveness will be ratified" (Stott, *The Cross of Christ*, 70).[14]

26.29 But I say to you, I will not drink of this fruit of the vine from now on until that day when I drink it new with you in My Father's kingdom."

The Lord's supper is not a funeral meal, for Christ says that He will

---

him (Jn. 6.56). Eating Christ's flesh and drinking His blood is but a vivid way of describing *obedience*.

[14] "I have only heard of one person, in all the ages, to whose stricken soul *the fifty-third of*

again eat it with His disciples. On *until that day when I drink it new with you*, see a similar structure in 23.39. In many ways, this verse recalls the opening of the Gospel and threads woven into the narrative thereafter. The celebratory nature of the supper is because Jesus *saves* His people from their sins (1.21) and *is with them* always (1.23, 28.20). Several texts have spoken of feasting and banqueting while Christ is with His people (22.2,11–12. 25.10–12; also, 20.20–23), as well as a time when Christ would not be with His followers (v 11, 9.15). The personal way in which Christ had enjoyed fellowship with them was ending, but it would resume in a new way. Bible students disagree on whether *new* should be understood as an adjective (*when I drink the new wine with you*, wms) or adverb (*when I drink it anew with you*, NIV). Both ideas may be present, for in the kingdom, not only does the fruit of the vine have a new significance as a memorial (1 Pet. 1.18–19), but the believer's eating and drinking with Christ are done in a new way (spiritually, not literally). Christ is present with us when we eat His supper; real communion involves an awareness of this.

Before moving on, note the following. First, the Lord's supper points to the centrality of Christ's death. Not His birth or life, but His death is what is specially remembered, for His death is the foundation of everything else. Second, Christ's death made possible the remission of sins, the key provision of the new covenant (Jer. 31.31–34). Third, eating the supper signifies participation in the saving power of Christ's death. Christians aren't spectators but guests participating in the feast and appropriating its benefits. "To every disciple he says, 'For *you* my body was wounded; for *you* my life was taken.' In receiving it the disciple says, 'Lord, I believe it. My life sprung from thy suffering; my joy from thy sorrows; and my hope of glory everlasting from thy humiliation and abasement event to death" (A. Campbell, *The Christian System*, 331).

26.30 And when they had sung a hymn, they went out to the Mount of Olives.

Isaiah brought no comfort at all; and that exception was a woman. For her *the fifty-third of Isaiah* gleamed with no Kindly Light: it was black with the darkness of midnight. *The fifty-third of Isaiah* was no antidote to the bitterness of *her* sorrow: it was sorrow's crown of sorrow. Mary, the mother of Jesus, it is said, could never bear to read *the fifty-third of Isaiah* herself, and she would never let her Divine Son read it. It was like a knife in her heart whenever she caught sight of the sublime passage. But the reason that made it as bitter as wormwood to her is the reason that has made it, to us, the fountain of all consolation and grace. For it was to *her* what it is to *us*—a glimpse into the heart that was to be broken at last upon the bitter Cross" (Boreham, *A Casket of Cameos*, 67).

Verse 30 is transitional and is followed by two predictions about stumbling and denying (vv 31–32,34) and two protests by Peter (v 33,35), which predictions are fulfilled in vv 56,69–75.

How courageous of Jesus to sing (Jas. 5.13)! We're not told which psalm was sung, but the Jews traditionally ended the Passover meal by singing Psalms 114 to 118, a section known as the *Hallel* (praise) psalms. After the hymn, Jesus and the disciples retire to the Mount of Olives.

26.31 Then Jesus said to them, "All of you will be made to stumble because of Me this night, for it is written: 'I will strike the Shepherd, And the sheep of the flock will be scattered.

Then—on their way out of Jerusalem—Jesus again shocks the disciples (v 23) by telling them that *all of you will be made to stumble because of Me this night.* Stumbled (*skandalizō*) is the word in 18.8,9; the very thing Christ warned against, He would occasion—He would somehow *offend* the disciples (18.6). To explain, Christ quotes Zechariah 13.7: *I will strike the Shepherd, and the sheep of the flock will be scattered.*[15] The Heb. for *strike* indicates a blow that can be fatal, and the one striking the Shepherd is God (9.36). The warning Jesus sent John the Baptist now applies to the disciples: *blessed is he who is not offended because of Me* (11.6). But they would be offended; their faith would fail. Paradoxically, however, the very thing that makes them fail had to happen to save them from their failure.

26.32 But after I have been raised, I will go before you to Galilee."

I will go before you sounds like shepherd language, indicating that Jesus would lead His disciples to Galilee, but based on 28.10, it's more likely that Jesus means that He will go to Galilee alone and await the disciples' arrival. *Galilee* recalls 4.12–25 and the start of Christ's ministry in the region.

26.33 Peter answered and said to Him, "Even if all are made to stumble because of You, I will never be made to stumble."

With characteristic bravado, Peter hears and reacts to only the first part of what Jesus said—the stumbling part. Peter was humble enough to admit

---

[15] "It's clear that God himself does the smiting. In the prophets it's always God who orders the sword to awake and strike (a sword in its scabbard is 'asleep'). And in 13.7 we're told that the Lord would turn his hand even against the little ones (lambs or shepherd boys) which would express the thoroughness of the judgment. In all this we are hearing that the innocent and the righteous suffer along with the guilty in the purging and judgment process." (McGuiggan, *Zechariah*, 123).

the possibility of betraying Christ (v 22) but with a bit of arrogance rejects Christ's prediction that he would stumble and distances himself from the rest—you may not be able to count on *them*, but you can count on *me*! In 28.7,10, the part Peter and the rest missed will be repeated by an angel and the Lord.

26.34 Jesus said to him, "Assuredly, I say to you that this night, before the rooster crows, you will deny Me three times."

Jesus knew Peter's bravery wouldn't match his bluster, and He confronts him with a sharp statement of fact. Not only would Peter stumble, but he would do so blatantly, denying his Lord three times! *Deny* (*aparneisthai*) recalls 10.32–33 and means to disavow, disown, repudiate, renounce. Further, Peter's denial would occur soon: *this night before the rooster crows. The rooster crows* was a phrase that referred to the time of night (early morning) when roosters crowed (vv 74–75), which, at this point, was just a few hours away.

26.35 Peter said to Him, "Even if I have to die with You, I will not deny You!" And so said all the disciples.

In 16.21–24, Peter tried to cause Christ to stumble by talking Him out of the cross; now, it is Peter who will stumble *because* of the cross. In 16.24, Jesus tells each disciple to deny himself; soon, Peter will deny Christ to save himself. Peter's courage cannot be questioned, but as events will show, talk is cheap. *And so said all the* disciples—the rest join Peter in professing their loyalty.

Origen, in his commentary, wrote that Peter "undertook to make a liar of our Lord." I think this unfair. It's true that Peter should have known better than to disagree with Christ, and his denial of Christ was a terrible thing, but Christ knew there was something deeper in Peter than failure. Just a few weeks later, Peter would say *Lord, You know that I love You* (Jn. 21.17), and in this he spoke truly. Even when we can't plead on the basis of our behavior, we can still plead our love. And thank God that He sees our love even when it's hard to see.

Could anything better illustrate Jesus' understanding and appreciation of Peter's love than that in the next paragraph, He asks Peter to be with Him during His deepest agony?

GETHSEMANE, 26.36–46

Notes

We will never fully understand Christ's sorrow in Gethsemane, but we can understand there was never a battle like it. What Jesus faced was not the ordinary experience of death by an ordinary (sinful) man, but the death of an innocent man who tasted death for every man. "He who was the 'true Light,' and had always dwelt in the bosom of God, Who *is* Light, was about to plunge into the thick darkness. He Who is the 'Prince of Life' was also to go into the realm of death, in utter weakness and self-abandonment. He Who was holy and absolutely sinless was about to be *"made sin"* (2 Corinthians 5.21), as well as to have the sins of all His people laid upon Him (Isaiah 53.6; 1 Peter 2.24)" (Philip Mauro, *The Prayer in Gethsemane*).

When a man prays as Jesus did in the garden, it's because he has a fight on his hands. Moreover, Christ prayed because He didn't feel self-sufficient; the self-sufficient do not pray. Fighting against His enemy and His emotions, Jesus sought through prayer the strength to be completely submissive to the will of God. And He found what He sought. Behind His restraint before Caiaphas, His calm before Pilate, and His trust on the cross lay the victory won in Gethsemane. Thought the battle continued until Christ drew His last breath, the outcome was determined in Gethsemane.[16]

This section opens with Christ taking the Three—Peter, James, and John—deeper with Him into Gethsemane, where He will then separate Himself from them. This is followed by three prayers, in which the Lord says nearly the same thing (vv 39–41, 42–43, 44–45a), followed by a rebuke (vv 45b–46).

But as for you, you meant evil against me; but God meant it for good, in order to bring it about as it is this day, to save many people alive (Gen. 50.20).

26.36 Then Jesus came with them to a place called Gethsemane, and said to the disciples, "Sit here while I go and pray over there."

Somewhere on the western side of Olivet was a garden Christ frequented known as *Gethsemane* (oil press, a place of crushing; there was probably a press on the property). Leaving the disciples behind, He walks away to pray.

Nowhere is Jesus' humanity more clearly on display. Before He suffers

---

[16] "Gethsemane—people generally let their voices drop when they reach that point in the story of the passion. It is so easy to find examples of people who died without a sense of

outwardly, He agonizes inwardly. He doesn't want to die, and He brings this plea to His Father. "Gethsemane portrays Jesus' final struggle with his God in complete, authentic humanity" (Luz III, 394–395).

26.37 And He took with Him Peter and the two sons of Zebedee, and He began to be sorrowful and deeply distressed.

Paradoxically, during times of sorrow, we sometimes don't want people around but we don't want to be alone. Jesus takes with Him Peter and James and John, *the sons of Zebedee. Immanuel, God with us,* asks His closest friends to be with Him. For those who had just professed a willingness to follow Him to death (v 35), it wasn't too much to ask. The three who saw Him in His glory (17.2–8) will now be with Him in His grief.

Jesus *began to be sorrowful and deeply distressed*—Matthew presses language to its limit to find words that adequately convey Christ's emotional state. *Began* indicates the onset of something (4.17, 16.21), *sorrowful (lupeō)* means distress or grief; *deeply distressed (ademoneō,* only three times in the NT, here, Mk. 14.33, Phil. 2.26) is an intensification that indicates Jesus was *crushed with anguish* (WEYMOUTH). These words "depict the utmost degree of unbounded horror and suffering. Lightfoot says that *ekthambeomai* 'describes the confused, restless, half-distracted state, which is produced by physical derangement, or by mental distress, as grief, shame, disappointment, etc.'" (Morris, *The Cross of Jesus,* 75–76).

26.38 Then He said to them, "My soul is exceedingly sorrowful, even to death. Stay here and watch with Me."

To the disciples, Jesus confides His anguish. *Exceedingly sorrowful* is a superlative *(perilupos,* sorrowfulest) intensified by *even to death.* This may only be a verbal attempt to express suffering never experienced by any human being, but it may also be that Christ sensed He was in danger of dying from shock or stroke. Emotionally, He was at the limit of His endurance.

In a very real way, Jesus' agony in Gethsemane is inscrutable, for it

---

dread, without the experience of intense anguish, or at least of people who approached death less anxiously than Christ. World history, national history, the history of culture, the galleries of great men dead will afford such examples. People read us their names and ask: What is your opinion? Are these who drink the hemlock courageously, who serenely approach death by the sword, in the arena, or by suffocation—are these not greater than the man Jesus Christ? [But for such questions to be valid, for such comparisons to be legitimate, the others] *would need to have been in hell for some time* in order to understand what it is that is tearing Jesus apart in the garden" (Klass Schilder, *Christ in His Sufferings,* 289).

involved "a horror of which the rest of the human race knows nothing" (Morris, *The Cross of Christ*, 193). A glimpse into it is found in 2 Corinthians 5.21, *wherein He who knew no sin was made to be sin for us*. Bearing the guilt of the world's sin and God's wrath against sin formed a special kind of hell that no one but Christ experienced. Matthew doesn't want us "to think that Jesus was troubled in the same way as we all are from time to time" (Morris, 667). His anguish wasn't due to the fact that He would die, but was due to the dying He experienced as the sacrifice that took away the sins of the world.

Stay here and watch with Me is a request for the disciples' sympathy, solidarity, and supplication in His hour of trial (v 41).

The First Prayer, 26.39–41

26.39 He went a little farther and fell on His face, and prayed, saying, "O My Father, if it is possible, let this cup pass from Me; nevertheless, not as I will, but as You *will*."

Walking on a few steps, Jesus gives way to His anguish. Falling face down, and with *strong crying and tears* (Heb. 5.7), He asks that God exempt Him from the very thing He knew He could not avoid. This is the only time when Christ ever asked the Father to change His mind. It's significant that He addresses God the way He taught His disciples, as *Father* (6.9); even during the most horrible hour man has known, Jesus still saw God as a loving Father. As we grow old in this valley of tears, nothing does more to stabilize our soul than the conviction that we are in the hands of a loving Father who causes all things to work together for good. Christ doesn't demand but pleads with the caveat *if it is possible*—if it is consistent with Your *will*—*let this cup pass*. *Cup* is again used metonymically (v 27), referring to the betrayal, condemnation, and crucifixion (vv 17–19) involved in exposing Himself to the divine wrath He experienced as man's vicarious substitute. But the hellishness and hopelessness of the reality is so extreme that He asks if there isn't some other way for securing human redemption.

Nevertheless, not as I will, but as You will—doing God's will was His highest desire.

26.40–41 Then He came to the disciples and found them sleeping, and said to Peter, "What! Could you not watch with Me one hour? Watch and

pray, lest you enter into temptation. The spirit indeed *is* willing, but the flesh *is* weak."

When Christ returns, He finds the Three asleep. The disciples were present *with* Jesus bodily, but emotionally and sympathetically absent. *I have trodden the winepress alone, and from the peoples no one was with Me* (Isa. 63.3). The interjectory *What!* probably awakened them. The question that follows was meant for all but is directed at Peter, probably because of his earlier bragging (v 35); *could you not watch with Me one hour?* recalls 24.12 and 25.13.

Jesus isn't the only one facing danger; a crisis loomed for the disciples (Lk. 22.40). Recalling 6.13, they needed to find strength through prayer for their own ordeal. The Three illustrate the human predicament: their intentions (spirit) were noble (vv 33,35) but their limitations (flesh) were a distraction. If ever there was a time when they needed to "force their heart, and nerve, and sinew to serve their turn long after they were gone" (Kipling), now was the time. "In the most central conflict of human existence Jesus exhibited the victory of the spirit over the flesh while the disciples displayed the victory of the flesh over the spirit" (Fenton, qtd. by Mounce, 244).

The Second Prayer, 26.42–43

26.42–43 Again, a second time, He went away and prayed, saying, "O My Father, if this cup cannot pass away from Me unless I drink it, Your will be done." And He came and found them asleep again, for their eyes were heavy.

Again Christ prays, but this prayer differs in two ways from the previous one (v 39). First, He acknowledges that the only way the cup will pass is by Him drinking it. Second, *not as I will, but as You will* becomes *Your will be done.* Christ's willingness to put himself absolutely and obediently into the hands of God, regardless of the consequences, is the highest act of moral courage of which man is capable.

The Third Prayer, 26.44–46

26.44–45a So He left them, went away again, and prayed the third time, saying the same words. Then He came to His disciples and said to them, "Are *you* still sleeping and resting?

The third prayer is the same as the second. That Christ prays a third time indicates the depth of His pain (2 Cor. 12.8).

One of the hardest tests of faith is unanswered prayer, and Jesus is tested by this test. *Why do my cries of anguish bring no help? I cry by day, but thou wilt not reply* (Ps. 22.1–2, MOFFATT). Note that had God granted the *form* of Christ's petition, He would have denied the *substance* of Christ's desire. Christ came *to save that which was lost* (18.11) and to do this, He had to drink the cup of God's wrath (v 39); if He didn't, He couldn't have lived up to His name (1.21). It's possible for us to pray for that which is at cross-purposes with our deepest desires and best interests. Thank God for those times when He has denied our requests because what we asked is incompatible with what we need.

Jesus again finds the disciples asleep. *Sleep on now and take your rest* is not a question (*Are you still sleeping and resting?* NIV) or imperative (NKJV); rather, as the second half of v 45 shows, the words are meant as irony.

26.45b–46 Behold, the hour is at hand, and the Son of Man is being betrayed into the hands of sinners. Rise, let us be going. See, My betrayer is at hand."

The hour has come. The betrayer and his armed band are in sight (*Behold ... See*). A final command is given, *Rise, let us be going*—not to escape danger, but to meet it. Jesus has placed Himself within the will of His Father, which means He is now within reach of His enemies. When He leaves Gethsemane, He leaves carrying a cup that He will drink to the dregs.

ARREST, 26.47–56

Notes
The arrest scene involves three episodes: the arrest (vv 47–50), an incident involving a servant of the high priest (vv 51–54), and Jesus' words to the armed band (v 55), all of which are followed by a concluding observation (v 56).

26.47 And while He was still speaking, behold, Judas, one of the twelve, with a great multitude with swords and clubs, came from the chief priests and elders of the people.

Events escalate rapidly. While Jesus is *still speaking* to the disciples, Judas—described as *one of the twelve*, underscoring the enormity of his treachery—arrives with an armed crowd. Mention of *the chief priests and elders of the people* recalls vv 3–5 and illustrates Christ's command of the situation; He forced the Jews to act on the very day they didn't want to act.

26.48 Now His betrayer had given them a sign, saying, "Whomever I kiss, He is the One; seize Him."

The Jerusalemites with Judas likely probably wouldn't have recognized Jesus by sight, especially in the middle of the night, so a sign had been arranged: *whomever I kiss, He is the One; seize Him.* The presence of *swords and clubs* indicates that resistance was expected. Another angle may have been that by sending out such a large, armed force, the Jewish leadership hoped to bolster its claim to the Romans that Jesus was dangerous.

26.49–50 Immediately he went up to Jesus and said, "Greetings, Rabbi!" and kissed Him. But Jesus said to him, "Friend, why have you come?" Then they came and laid hands on Jesus and took Him.

As at supper earlier in the evening, Judas again refers to Jesus as *Rabbi* (v 25). In Jewish society, kissing the cheek was done for a variety of reasons—as a greeting, to show respect, as a sign of reconciliation, etc. In NT churches, a *holy kiss* was a sign of fellowship, the equivalent of a Western hug or handshake (Rom. 16.16; 1 Cor. 16.20; 2 Cor. 13.12; 1 Thes. 5.26; 1 Pet. 5.14). The word for Judas's kiss (*kataphilein*) is an intensified form of *philein*, the usual word for *kiss*. Judas's kiss, however, has become *the* symbol for the worst sort of treachery. "With the pledge of love," asked Ambrose, "do you inflict a wound? With the act of love do you shed blood? With the instrument of peace do you create death?"

In response, Jesus calls Judas, *Friend*, a word that can mean anything from colleague to true friend. In 20.13, however, it indi-cates a less than friendly relationship, and in 22.12, it has a threatening undertone. Here, given Judas's treachery, it is used ironically.

Why have you come? has caused translators and interpreters some trouble, but I understand the question rhetorically and elliptically: "Why have you led this band out here to seize One you've followed for three years, whom you saw do things only God can do, and whom you confessed as the Son of God?" It is a final, merciful appeal to Judas.

Judas says nothing, and Christ is arrested: *they came and laid hands on Him* (Acts 4.3) *and took Him*, as predicted in v 45 and 17.22.

26.51 And suddenly, one of those *who were* with Jesus stretched out *his* hand and drew his sword, struck the servant of the high priest, and cut off his ear.

Despite being outnumbered and outgunned, Peter (Jn. 18.10) springs to Christ's defense. In a display of courage that was both "magnificent and pathetic" (Carson, 547), he attempts to prevent Christ's arrest by armed resistance. It's a bit surprising that one of Christ's disciples is armed, but swords were often a part of a Jew's dress.[17] Attempting to cut off the man's head, Peter manages only to cut off an ear. I wonder whether Christ's miraculous restoration of the ear (Lk. 22.51) caused any second thoughts among those who saw it?

26.52 But Jesus said to him, "Put your sword in its place, for all who take the sword will perish by the sword.

Christ responds in four ways. First, He orders Peter to sheath his sword. Second, He says that *all who take the sword will perish by the sword*, applying the well-known principle of *measure for measure* (7.2; Gal. 6.7; Rev. 13.10). Christ, as He taught in 5.39, offers no resistance and insists that His disciples do the same.

26.53 Or do you think that I cannot now pray to My Father, and He will provide Me with more than twelve legions of angels?

Third, a rhetorical question—*do you think that I cannot pray?*—emphasizes Christ's command of the situation. In the early Roman Empire, a *legion* "was a force of between 5,000 and 6,000 men" (Lawrence Keppie, *The Making of the Roman Army*, 173); the number of legions at the end of Augustus's reign were about twenty-five. If Christ didn't want to be taken, He wouldn't have been taken, for He could have instantly summoned *twelve legions of angels*—60,000 to 72,000, one for Him and each of His disciples—to His side. When it's remembered that a single angel killed 185,000 Assyrian soldiers in one night (2 Kgs. 19.35), Christ had access to overwhelming, irresistible force. But as with the second temptation (4.7–8), so here, He refused angelic help.

26.54 How then could the Scriptures be fulfilled, that it must happen thus?"

Fourth, declining angelic intervention is substantiated by prophecy. Even though the passion narrative has not yet included a single fulfillment quotation, *How then will the Scripture be fulfilled, that it must be thus?* (12.26,

---

[17] As they were for Englishmen until the early part of the nineteenth century, when they were replaced by umbrellas.

22.43) implies that events must play out as foretold if the redemption of the world is to happen.

26.55–56 In that hour Jesus said to the multitudes, "Have you come out, as against a robber, with swords and clubs to take Me? I sat daily with you, teaching in the temple, and you did not seize Me. But all this was done that the Scriptures of the prophets might be fulfilled." Then all the disciples forsook Him and fled.

Christ exposes the farce by calling attention to the large number (v 47) sent to arrest Him: "Why are you treating me like a criminal (*lēstēs*, robber, thief, brigand)? *I sat daily with you, teaching in the temple, and you did not seize Me.* If you wanted to arrest Me, there are easier ways to do it than by losing a night's sleep. I was in the temple daily; why didn't you grab Me there?" It's impossible to know how many in the crowd knew of the events that led up to this dead-of-night foray (v 5), but if any of them had seen Jesus in the temple, he might have wondered about the very issue Jesus raised.

All this refers to the events connected with Christ's arrest; every detail had been predicted. From beginning (1.22) to end, Christ's story was foreseen by God.[18]

Human nature, even at its best, is such poor stuff; the final sentence in v 56 recalls v 31—when the Shepherd is struck, the sheep will scatter.

26.57–27.61: Friday
JEWISH TRIAL, 26.57–27.10

Notes

The night of the Passover was filled with memorable events: the institution of the Lord's Supper, the prayer in Gethsemane, the arrest, and the trial, to which we now come. The remainder of this chapter is set in the palace of the high priest and involves two scenes: v 57 prepares the way for vv 59–66 and Christ's interrogation by the high priest; v 58 prepares the way for vv 69–75 and Peter's denial. A brief interlude between these two sections, vv 67–68, records Christ's first physical abuse.

"The trial of Jesus was, from beginning to end, a travesty of justice;

---

[18] The apologetic value of prophecy is that it doesn't depend on *regularity*. Predicting an eclipse is possible because of the regularity of nature, but prophecy is humanly impossible owing to the irregularity and unpredictability of human nature. That God foresaw and revealed, in detail, the events associated with Christ's death is stunning proof of Scripture's divine origin.

and although it may be granted that our Master was a heretic according to the Jewish creed, so far as law went His was a judicial assassination" (J. Watson, *The Life of the Master*, 266).

26.57 And those who had laid hold of Jesus led *Him* away to Caiaphas the high priest, where the scribes and the elders were assembled.

Caiaphas (v 3) appears as the major antagonist. *Led away* (*apagō*) is a technical term indicating a carrying off to trial, to prison, or to execution (Acts 12.19). Jesus is taken to Caiaphas's residence. The archaeological evidence suggests that this was the Hasmonean palace on the western slope of the Tyropoeon Valley (which separated Mt. Zion from Mt. Moriah). When the Bordeaux Pilgrim visited Jerusalem in AD 333, he was shown the ruins of a building on Mt. Zion "where the house of Caiaphas the priest was" (Finegan, 152). Also assembled were *the scribes and the elders.* This was a highly irregular gathering; based on Josephus and rabbinic sources, it was not the custom of the Sanhedrin to meet at the high priest's palace or to convene in the middle of the night.

26.58 But Peter followed Him at a distance to the high priest's courtyard. And he went in and sat with the servants to see the end.

The focus shifts from Jesus to Peter, setting the stage for vv 69–75. Peter *followed Him at a distance,* "midway between courage (v.51) and cowardice (v.70)" (Bengel, qtd. by Carson, 553). For all the opprobrium that has been heaped on Peter for denying Christ, let it be said that his devotion to Christ took him into the lion's den.

Courtyard (*aulē*) can refer to a residence or courtyard, as well as the complex of buildings around it. Once inside, Peter sat with the servants (*hupēretēs*, lit. under-rowers, attendants), awaiting the inevitable.

ARRAIGNMENT, 26.59–66

Notes

Verses 59–66 are bracketed by the word *death* (vv 59,66) and consist of four scenes: in vv 59–60a, the Jews attempt to find false witnesses against Christ; in vv 60b–63a,64, two witnesses testify; in vv 63b–64, Jesus speaks for the only time; and in vv 65–66, the high priest accuses Christ of blasphemy, which was punishable by death.

26.59 Now the chief priests, the elders, and all the council sought false testimony against Jesus to put Him to death,

Sin has deadening power; it can anaesthetize the conscience, disabling the protective action of fear and guilt, making an individual capable of monstrous evil. And nothing better illustrates sin's heinousness than the Jewish establishment's determination to rid themselves of the innocent Son of God.

The chief priests and *elders* (vv 3,47) constituted the supreme Jewish deliberative body known as *the council* (*sunedrion*)—the Sanhedrin.[19] It wasn't going to be easy to find valid grounds for condemning a man who healed the sick, fed multitudes, was kind to all, and taught the love of God and neighbor—but condemn Him the Jews were determined to do. "Sentence first, verdict later," decreed the Queen of Hearts; the last thing the Sanhedrin was after was justice. But cooperative and damaging witnesses were hard to find, and the council finally had to solicit *false testimony*—which, in the Psalms, is a type of injustice the righteous suffer at the hands of the unrighteous (27.12, 35.11, 109.2–3). The murderous intent of this kangaroo court had been predicted in Isaiah 53.8 and was confirmed by Christ in v 54. I think it particularly noteworthy that Judas was neither asked, nor did he volunteer, to testify against Jesus.

Excursus on Jewish Jurisprudence

Our information about Jewish jurisprudence at the time of Christ largely relies on the second-century Mishnah tractate *Sanhedrin*. Based on this document, John Watson could rightly say, "Whatever may have been the fanaticism of the Jewish character, the spirit of Jewish law was merciful in the extreme. Under no system has there been a more anxious desire to guard the rights of a prisoner" (*The Life of the Master*, 266). According to the tractate, "All criminal cases must be tried during the daytime and must be completed during the daytime. Criminal cases could not be transacted during the Passover season at all. Only if the verdict was "Not Guilty" could a case be finished on the day it was begun; otherwise a night must elapse before the pronouncement of the verdict, so that feelings of mercy might have time to arise. Further, no decision of the Sanhedrin was valid unless it met in its own meetingplace, the Hall of Hewn Stone in the Temple precincts. In regard to witnesses, all evidence had to be guaranteed by two witnesses separately examined, and having no contact with each other. And false witness

---

[19] It is thought that in Jesus' time the Sanhedrin was comprised of seventy-one members.

was punishable by death. Still further, in any trial the process began by the laying before the court of all the evidence for the *innocence* of the accused, before the evidence for his guilt was adduced" (Barclay II, 390–391).

The problem is that there is no certainty these second-century regulations were in place in the first century. In the Roman Empire, local authorities were given wide latitude to establish legal guidelines for civil and criminal matters, and Rome rarely intervened (Jn. 18.31). "The inquiry whether the trial of Jesus was 'legal', i.e., whether it conformed to the rules in the Mishnah, is futile because it assumes that those [Mishnah] rules represent the judicial procedure of the old Sanhedrin" (George Foot Moore, qtd. by Harrison, 204). To illustrate: it is often asserted that a night session of the council was illegal, but the noted scholar A. N. Sherwin-White found that Roman officials started work very early in the day and "there was every reason to hold the unusual night session if [the Jews] were to catch the Procurator at the right moment" (qtd. by Morris, 679).

"If the Sanhedrin had in mind from the start, as apparently it did, to take the case to Pilate, it is inconceivable that it would have transgressed its own rules so flagrantly as to invite rejection by the governor on grounds of unlawful procedure" (Harrison, 204). Although the apostles later accused the Jews of putting Jesus to death (Acts 2.23,36, 3.15, 4.10, 7.52; 1 Thes. 2.15), they never raised the issue of irregularities regarding the trial. That the trial of Jesus was a miscarriage of justice is unarguable—the search for false witnesses blatantly violated Deuteronomy 19.15–21—but we shouldn't overstate the case.

26.60–61 but found none. Even though many false witnesses came forward, they found none. But at last two false witnesses came forward and said, "This *fellow* said, 'I am able to destroy the temple of God and to build it in three days.'"

Matthew doesn't tell us how it was that *many false witnesses* were available at such an early hour; presumably, they were part of preplanning done by the council (v 4). The twice repeated *found* none, however, implies that even their hand-picked liars were so blatantly untruthful that not even a corrupt council could accept their testimony as valid.

Finally (*husteros* can be used as a superlative, 21.37, 22.27), *two* (the minimum number of witnesses required in a legal trial, Deut. 17.6, 19.15) *false witnesses came forward* to testify that Christ said *I am able to destroy the temple of God and to build it in three days*—a garbled recital of Christ's statement in John 2.19. Had there been cross-examination, the following might have emerged. First, Jesus didn't say *He* would destroy the temple but that the *Jews* would destroy it. Second, Christ might have been asked whether He was speaking literally or figuratively—and if figuratively, what did He mean by what He said. Third, the witnesses would have been scrutinized and probably exposed for the liars they were (v 60; see 27.63–64; the Jews knew Christ hadn't threatened the temple!).

26.62 And the high priest arose and said to Him, "Do You answer nothing? What *is it* these men testify against You?"
The temple had symbolic, religious, and economic significance for the Jews, and a threat against it was a serious matter.[20] The testimony of the two witnesses, however, was too weak—and Caiaphas knew it. *Do You answer nothing* indicates that Christ has been silent (12.19; Isa. 53.7, *as a sheep before its shearers is silent, so He opened not His mouth*)—there was no point in replying to blatant malice; these men were not going to be convinced otherwise. But unless Caiaphas could get Jesus to incriminate Himself, the council's plan would collapse. *What do you say to the evidence that they bring against you?* (wms).

26.63 But Jesus kept silent. And the high priest answered and said to Him, "I put You under oath by the living God: Tell us if You are the Christ, the Son of God!"
Christ's silence accomplished two things. First, it showed that He was an innocent man who was being railroaded; the case against Him was so weak that nothing needed to be said. Second, although He was innocent, Christ wasn't seeking acquittal. He stood before the council for the express purpose of being condemned (v 45). Neither Caiaphas, Pilate (Jn. 19.9–10), nor the disciples (prior to the cross) ever grasped this.[21]

Caiaphas is desperate and intensifies his efforts by placing Jesus under oath. *I adjure You by the living God that You tell us if You are the Christ, the Son of God.* To *adjure* (*exorkizō*, to exact an oath, only here in the NT; 1 Kgs. 2.42) can

[20] "When the Old Testament prophets predicted the downfall of the temple and the nation at the hands of their enemies, the Jews were so infuriated that they wanted to kill the prophets. They were considered traitors. Jeremiah was cast into the dungeon to die for predicting the fall of Jerusalem at the hands of the Chaldeans. The Jews of Christ's time doubtless resented His predictions in the same way" (Foster III, 217). Josephus reports that prior to the war against Rome, the leading citizens of Jerusalem arrested one Jesus ben Ananias for persistently pronouncing woes against the city and the sanctuary. In hopes of silencing him once and for all, they brought him before the Roman governor who had him flayed to the bone (Josephus, *Wars* 6.5.3).

[21] Note the irony in the fact that Caiaphas hoped Jesus would break His silence so that

mean "to make someone swear by someone"; Christ is being asked to swear by God. Matthew has already established that Jesus is the Son of God using testimony from God (3.17, 17.5), the devil (4.3,6), demons (8.29), the disciples (14.33), and Peter (16.16). To this point, however, Jesus has not explicitly declared Himself on the subject. He is now challenged to do so under oath (that He does so should be factored into any interpretation of 5.34).

26.64 Jesus said to him, "*It is as* you said. Nevertheless, I say to you, hereafter you will see the Son of Man sitting at the right hand of the Power, and coming on the clouds of heaven."

Christ gives a two-part reply. First, He says *It is as you say*, which is ambiguous. Is He saying "Yes"? Is He saying, "Those are your words, not mine"? Or is He refusing to answer altogether? A glance back to v 25 and a glance ahead to 27.11 indicates that He is saying, "Yes."

Second, Jesus expands on His answer by asserting His role as Judge: *You will see the Son of Man sitting at the right hand of the Power, and coming on the clouds of heaven*—some then alive would live to see Jesus vindicated in His judgment on the Jews. In 19.28, Christ spoke of when He would sit on His throne; in 22.44, He quoted Psalm 110 and its reference to the Messiah sitting at God's right hand; and in 25.31, He spoke of sitting on His throne to judge the world. At the moment, His Jewish judges saw Him as a hapless prisoner, but *hereafter* (23.39) the roles will be reversed, and they will see Him as their Judge. *Son of Man* is Jesus' customary description of Himself (8.20). *Coming on the clouds of heaven* recalls the judgment on the Jews (24.30) that was forty years in the future (ch 24). The year of Caiaphas's death isn't known, but most certainly there were men in the room who lived to see the devastation, and possibly died in it.[22] Even if Caiaphas didn't live to see Jerusalem's fall, he saw enough—the tearing of the temple veil and earthquake (27.51), the appearance of the dead (27.52–53), and the disappearance of Jesus' body (28.11–15)—to know better.

26.65 Then the high priest tore his clothes, saying, "He has spoken blasphemy! What further need do we have of witnesses? Look, now you have heard His blasphemy!

---

he could convict Him (v 62), whereas Pilate hoped that Jesus would break His silence so that he could release Him (Jn. 19.10).

[22] "The hereditary priestly families, and the traditional Jewish upper class as a whole, perished in the ruin of the city" (Johnson, 149).

Forgotten is any threat against the temple; Jesus gave Caiaphas what he wanted. *He has spoken blasphemy!* John 5.18: *Therefore the Jews sought all the more to kill Him, because [He said] that God was His Father, making Himself equal with God.* John 10.32–33: *Jesus answered them, "Many good works I have shown you from My Father. For which of those works do you stone Me?" The Jews answered Him, saying, "For a good work we do not stone You, but for blasphemy, and because You, being a Man, make Yourself God."* With Jesus, the Jews defined *blasphemy* as self-deification (9.3), and in a theatrical outburst, Caiaphas tears hi clothes[23,24] and declares further testimony unnecessary since the assembly heard what Jesus said.

26.66 What do you think?" They answered and said, "He is deserving of death."

What do you think? And the council answers as Caiaphas knew it would: *He is guilty of death,* which was a legal term (Heb. 2.15). The formal sentencing is delayed until daybreak (27.1,3).

The legal reason for Jesus' condemnation by the Jews was blasphemy; but a statement isn't blasphemous if true. The real blasphemers were Caiaphas and the council who denied Christ's deity (12.31–32).

ABUSED, 26.67–68

26.67–68 Then they spat in His face and beat Him; and others struck *Him* with the palms of their hands, saying, "Prophesy to us, Christ! Who is the one who struck You?"

For the first time, Jesus is physically mistreated. That this was done by the council underscores their depravity. To *spit* in another's face is the ultimate indignity. *Beat* translates *kolaphizō* and means to hit with the fist. *Struck (hrapizein) Him with the palms of their hands* means they slapped Him (5.39). *Prophesy to us, You Christ! Who is the one who struck You?* was mockery. Addressing Jesus as *Christ* recalls vv 63, and the council further humiliates Him by playing blind man's bluff, challenging Jesus to identify the one who struck Him.

"Such a text demands emotional involvement. It leaves us dumb and

---

[23] "He acts as if he is overwhelmed with grief, though he could have shouted for joy" (Hendriksen, 933).

[24] It is sometimes said that Caiaphas's action violated Lev. 21.10, but that passage says only that the high priest may not tear his official robe should his daughter be executed for immorality.

calls us to remain quiet. Saying that is for me the most important thing here" (Luz III, 452).

DENIAL, 26.69–75

Notes

Here the narrative picks up the thread of Peter's story where v 58 left off. It consists of three parts: an introduction (v 69a), a conclusion (vv 74b–75), and the main body describing Peter's three denials (vv 69b–74a). Judas was the first to abandon Him (v 14), then the other disciples (v 56), and now Peter, the first one called to be a disciple (4.18–20, 10.2) and the one nicknamed *Rock* (16.17–18).

26.69–70 Now Peter sat outside in the courtyard. And a servant girl came to him, saying, "You also were with Jesus of Galilee." But he denied it before *them* all, saying, "I do not know what you are saying."

During Christ's trial, Peter is outside in the courtyard (v 58). At some point, a *servant girl* (*paidiskē*, young woman or female slave) approaches and says, *you also were with Jesus of Galilee*. Matthew doesn't tell us how she knew this, but the reference to *Galilee* "is the kind of derogatory remark one might expect from a Jerusalemite convinced of her geographical and political superiority" (Carson, 558).

The girl's statement gets the attention of those nearby, which leads to Peter's denial (*ameomai*, contradict, v 34) *before them all*. Playing dumb, he says, *I do not know what you are saying.* His sense of self-preservation has kicked in. At the very time Christ is confessing the truth (v 64), Peter is denying it.

26.71–72 And when he had gone out to the gateway, another *girl* saw him and said to those *who were* there, "This *fellow* also was with Jesus of Nazareth." But again he denied with an oath, "I do not know the Man!"

Peter's fall can be traced by geographical indicators and by the intensification of his language. In v 69, he is *outside* Caiaphas's quarters; here, he has made his way *to the entrance* (*pulon*, the gateway to the street), where another *girl* recognizes him and says *this fellow was also with Jesus of Nazareth*. This time, Peter attaches an oath to his denial and disrespectfully refers to Jesus as *the Man*—analogous to Judas's disrespectful use of *Rabbi* (vv 25,49). To use an *oath* means that Peter either called God as a witness to his truthfulness or called on God to punish him if he was lying (v 74; Acts 23.12). When placed under oath, Christ confessed the truth (w 63–64); Peter placed himself under oath and committed perjury.

26.73–74a And a little later those who stood by came up and said to Peter, "Surely you also are *one* of them, for your speech betrays you." Then he began to curse and swear, *saying,* "I do not know the Man!"

After a while was about an hour later (Lk. 22.59). Peter hasn't left, and some bystanders approach and accuse him of being one of Christ's followers based on his Galilean dialect. Apparently, the Galileans slurred consonants, especially the gutturals (aleph, hey, chet, ayin, resh; Robertson, 220). Peter's conflicted thinking is apparent in that he wants to see the *end* (v 58), but staying only gets him into trouble (v 71).

In the strongest terms yet, he repudiates Jesus with cursing and swearing. In our vernacular, cursing and swearing means to use vulgar, filthy language, but here, it likely means to place a curse on someone. So far as is known, this is the first time the word for *curse* (*katanathematizein,* a cognate of *anathematize*) appears in ancient literature. The question is: who was the object of Peter's curse? As hard as it is to believe, the evidence points to Christ—Peter was calling down a curse on Christ. Two considerations suggest this. First, as Hare argues, "The verb translated 'curse' is regularly transitive and not reflexive, that is, in all other instances it takes a direct object other than the speaker. The rendering of the RSV, 'Then he began to invoke a curse *on himself* (*so* also NIV) cannot be defended linguistically. It represents an attempt to soften a statement. The object is euphemistically omitted but implicit because of the context; Peter cursed Jesus as a way of firmly disassociating himself" (311). Second, in the subsequent history of Christian persecution, "reviling the name of Christ" was one of the ways by which apostates exonerated themselves before Roman officials (see Pliny, xcvii).

Denying Christ to save our skin is a temptation that comes to all; we should be slow to criticize Peter for his failure. Let him who is without sin cast the first stone.

26.74b–75 Immediately a rooster crowed. And Peter remembered the word of Jesus who had said to him, "Before the rooster crows, you will deny Me three times." So he went out and wept bitterly.

The prediction of v 34 is fulfilled. A rooster's crow jogs Peter's memory, and he suddenly realizes that he has done the very thing he said he would never do,[25] and the realization shatters him. He goes out into the night and weeps as one who knows he has sinned against love.

This is Matthew's last mention of Peter. The other Gospels assure the reader concerning his restoration, but if all we had was Matthew's Gospel, we could still hope for Peter by remembering that *every sin and blasphemy against the Son of Man* can be forgiven (12.31–32).

> *The first time that Peter denied his Lord*
>   *He shrank from the cudgel, the scourge and the cord,*
> *But followed far off to see what they would do,*
>   *Till the cock crew — till the cock crew —*

Rudyard Kipling, *The Song at Cock-Crow*

---

[25] Cf. John 12.27 and Mk. 14.35 where Jesus prayed for the very thing that He said He would not pray for.

CHAPTER 27

27.1–61: Friday

FORMAL SENTENCE, 27.1–2

27.1 When morning came, all the chief priests and elders of the people plotted against Jesus to put Him to death.

The Jewish leadership has arrested, convicted, and sentenced Jesus; all that remains is to secure His execution (26.4).

At dawn, *all* the council formally ratifies the sentence reached in 26.66. *Plotted* translates the rare phrase *sumboulion lambanein*, which means to make a decision (v 7, 28.12).

27.2 And when they had bound Him, they led Him away and delivered Him to Pontius Pilate the governor.

With the examining, condemning, and abusing over, and true to His prediction that He would be turned over to the Gentiles (20.18–19), Christ is placed in some sort of restraint (*bound*[1]) and taken to *Pontius Pilate the governor*. *Pontius* presumably refers to the region of Pontus; *Pilate* (*pilum*, javelin) was the family surname; his given name is unknown. *Governor* (*hēgemōn*) was a general, nontechnical term meaning leader or chief person and was used in Roman provinces to designate imperial governors (Acts 23.24, 26.30; Josephus also describes Pilate by this term, *Ant.* xviii.3.1). Pilate administered Judea from AD 26 to AD 36. He was headquartered in Caesarea but relocated to Jerusalem during Jewish festivals. The historical records (Gospels, Josephus, Philo) indicate that he was a ruthless, insensitive administrator of the Jews. An inscription found in 1961 by Italian archaeologists in the theater at Caesarea identified him as a *prefect*, a military title (*procurator* was a civilian title). "Prefects were

---

[1] "As Isaac was bound before he was laid upon the altar, so was the great Anti-type bound before he was 'brought as a lamb to the slaughter'" (Spurgeon).

army officers 'placed in charge' (*praefecit*) of difficult or isolated districts. Such a governor was often a military man (as was Pilate) whose primary responsibility was that of maintaining order; he 'supervised rather than managed the government as an executive'" (Morris, 692).

Though a minor bureaucrat, Pilate, by coincidence of his contact with Christ, is better known today than almost any Roman of his time. In AD 36, he was ordered to Rome by his immediate superior, Vitellius, to answer charges of mismanagement. It's possible, though, that he lost his office because Tiberius had died and the new caesar (Caligula) wished to install his own people in the Roman bureauacracy. Eusebius (*EH* 2.7) preserves a report that Pilate was forced to commit suicide during the reign of Gaius (AD 37–41). Little did Pilate know that the trial he was about to conduct was the most important event of his life.

JUDAS'S DEATH, 27.3–10

Notes

Matthew alone records Judas's death. The account has three parts: vv 3–5 tell of Judas's reaction to Christ's sentence; vv 6–8 tell what the Jews did with the betrayal money; and vv 9–10 show how it all fulfilled prophecy.

27.3–5 Then Judas, His betrayer, seeing that He had been condemned, was remorseful and brought back the thirty pieces of silver to the chief priests and elders, saying, "I have sinned by betraying innocent blood." And they said, "What *is that* to us? You see *to it!*" Then he threw down the pieces of silver in the temple and departed, and went and hanged himself.

Some things that energize us in anticipation, leave us empty once accomplished; when Judas learns of Christ's condemnation, the enormity of his evil overwhelms him. *Remorse* translates *metamellomai* (to care afterward, 21.29,32), which is a synonym for *metanoeō* (3.2), the usual word for *repent*.[2] Three considerations show the depth of Judas's remorse: first, he tries to return the money he was paid; second, he admits his sin; third, he testifies to Jesus' *innocence* (*athōos*, not guilty; in NT, only here and v 24). *Innocent blood* is an OT expression that occurs a handful of times: *cursed be anyone who takes a bribe to shed innocent blood* (Deut. 27.25, NRSV). After three years spent with Christ, in his final utterance, Judas testifies to Jesus innocence.

---

[2] In the LXX, both verbs are used to translate the same Heb. word for repent.

The chief priests and elders are callously indifferent and probably despised Judas for the role he played in their plot. Having obtained from him what they wanted, they have no further use of him. *What is that to us? You see to that!*—"That's your problem, not ours." No interest is shown in his claim that they have condemned an innocent man (vv 19,24).

Unable to undo his deed, Judas *threw down* (*hriptō*, a strong verb) the money in *the temple* (*naos*, the sanctuary, consisting of the Holy Place and the Holy of Holies). Matthew doesn't say whether Judas went into the Court of Priests or threw the money over the wall; regardless, it was found (v 6). Leaving the temple, he went out *and hanged himself*; his was a repentance that needed to be repented of (2 Cor. 7.10). Throughout history, various cultures have viewed suicide as a noble death in certain situations, but in the Bible, every suicide is tragic, done by hopeless men (Ahimelech, Ahithophel, King Saul; some see Samson as an example of a noble suicide). Although historians admire the mass suicide at Masada at the end of the Jewish War, there's nothing admirable in Judas's death (26.24), its ignobility heightened by the method he chose. According to ancient sources, hanging seems to have been the most common form of suicide in the Mediterranean world, especially among the lower classes (upperclass suicides usually fell on their sword). Hanging, though, brought one under God's curse (Deut. 21.23).[3] Judas's death was tragic in every way. His stark eulogy as spoken by Peter was that *he has gone to his own place* (Acts 1.25).

The greatest tragedy about Judas was not his deed, but that he despaired of grace.

27.6–8 But the chief priests took the silver pieces and said, "It is not lawful to put them into the treasury, because they are the price of blood." And they consulted together and bought with them the potter's field, to bury strangers in. Therefore that field has been called the Field of Blood to this day.

This may be the ultimate example of Jewish gnat straining and camel swallowing (23.24). The very ones who had no scruples about convening a kangaroo court are now concerned over a bookkeeping matter. Because

---

[3] Acts 1.18 indicates that Judas hung until he, *falling headlong, burst open in the middle and all his entrails gushed out*. Whatever precipitated the fall (rope breaking? body rotting?), it was a gruesome end.

the thirty pieces of silver was *the price of blood*,[4] the Jews thought it wrong to return it to the temple *treasury* (*korbanas*, corban; see Mk. 7.11). How they concluded this isn't said, but it underscores their sick hypocrisy.

They decide to use the money to purchase *the potter's field* (a place where potters obtained clay) as a cemetery in which to bury *strangers*. Whether *strangers* (*xenos*) refers to Gentiles, Hellenistic Jews, or both isn't stated.[5] At the time Matthew wrote (this is the first of two references to the time of his writing, 28.15), the site was known as *the Field of Blood*, which may have reflected either the betrayal money or the gory nature of Judas's death (Acts 1.18–19).

27.9–10 Then was fulfilled what was spoken by Jeremiah the prophet, saying, "And they took the thirty pieces of silver, the value of Him who was priced, whom they of the children of Israel priced, and gave them for the potter's field, as the LORD directed me."

This is the final fulfillment quotation in Matthew, and in formula, it is identical to 2.17. The transaction involving the money had been foretold by God. A difficulty involves Matthew ascribing to Jeremiah a prophecy that seems to come from Zechariah 11.12–13. Numerous resolutions have been proposed, including: Matthew got it wrong; *Jeremiah* is a scribal error; Jeremiah was the first book of the prophetic section in the Hebrew Bible and served as a generic heading (though Jeremiah was sometimes placed first, Isaiah usu-ally occupied that position); the Jeremiah passage cited by Matthew has been lost; or Matthew was referencing an oral prophecy handed down from Jeremiah.

A better explanation is that the purchase of the field fulfilled a *nonverbal prophecy*, as suggested by Jeremiah 19.1–13 and 32.6–9. To complete the prediction, the Zechariah mention of the thirty pieces of silver is added with the entire reference being attributed to Jeremiah (cf. Mk. 1.2–3, where Mal. 3.1 is fused to Isa. 40.3, and both quotes are attributed to Isaiah; see Bales, *Prophecy and Premillennialism*, 140–142).

---

[4] This expression also occurs in rabbinic sources in reference to the price for which Joseph was sold.

[5] "At the time of the Passover, when hundreds of thousands were crowded in a confined space, the question of burying strangers was doubtless urgent" (Carr, 302).

ROMAN TRIAL, 27.11–31

Notes

As a rule, the Romans were disinclined to meddle in religious squabbles, but they were alert to any hint of resistance to their authority. Tiberius was not one to show leniency to treasonous activity, and it would have been fatal for any bureaucrat in his government to be unaware of or indifferent to such behavior.

Pilate would have been busy with many things during Passover and would not be expected to take more than a passing interest in any matter sent to him by the Sanhedrin. The Jews undoubtedly thought he would quickly rubber-stamp their request, and they were greatly annoyed when he asserted his authority over the proceedings. They were especially piqued when their charge against Jesus was shown to be legally vacuous.

This section has two scenes: the trial in vv 11–26 and the physical abuse in vv 27–31. The trial contains three subsections: Pilate's interrogation of Jesus (vv 11–14), his conversation with the Jews (vv 15–23), and his acquiescence to the Jews (vv 24–26). This section recalls ch 2—here, as there, the subject is the *King of the Jews* (v 11, 2.2), and it is Gentiles (the wise men, Pilate's wife) who understand the truth about Jesus, whereas Jerusalem and the Jewish leadership are hostile and want Him killed. But unlike ch 2, Jesus will not escape death this time.

27.11 Now Jesus stood before the governor. And the governor asked Him, saying, "Are You the King of the Jews?" Jesus said to him, *"It is as you say."*

Matthew picks up the story from v 2. Without any preliminaries, Pilate asks *Are You the King of the Jews?* We tend to see this title in messianic terms, but Pilate was asking a political question (vv 29,37,42). According to Luke, he asked this question because this was one of the charges the Jews brought against Jesus (Lk. 23.2–3). Pilate's job was to keep tabs on would-be revolutionaries; I think it a safe conclusion that he had prior knowledge of Jesus and knew that one who lacked soldiers, weapons, money, or position was no threat to Rome.

In answer, Jesus, surprisingly, says, *It is as you say*—Yes! (26.25,64).

27.12 And while He was being accused by the chief priests and elders, He answered nothing.

The *chief priests and elders* pile on with their accusations (Lk. 23.2), to which—recalling 26.62—Christ *answered nothing*.

27.13–14 Then Pilate said to Him, "Do You not hear how many things they testify against You?" But He answered him not one word, so that the governor marveled greatly.

Pilate doesn't respond to the Jews but asks Christ: *Do You not hear how many things they testify against You?* It's obvious to Pilate that Christ's silence isn't an admission of guilt, but the silence of one who isn't interested in living. And Pilate is *amazed* (*thaumazō,* wondered at) at this.

27.15–16 Now at the feast the governor was accustomed to releasing to the multitude one prisoner whom they wished. And at that time they had a notorious prisoner called Barabbas.

Matthew gives some background to explain an unusual turn the story takes at this point. Pilate had a Passover custom of allowing the Jews to select a prisoner for release.[6] Although there is no evidence that this was common practice among Roman governors, there are examples of governors freeing prisoners in response to requests of the people or during pagan festivals.[7]

At the time, the Romans held a *notorious prisoner* named *Barabbas. Notorious* translates *episēmos,* which means famous or infamous, depending on the context. *Barabbas* means *son of Abbas* (father); per Mark 15.7, he had been involved in some murders committed during an uprising.

27.17–18 Therefore, when they had gathered together, Pilate said to them, "Whom do you want me to release to you? Barabbas, or Jesus who is called Christ?" For he knew that they had handed Him over because of envy.

A crowd has assembled (v 20), apparently, for the prisoner release. Pilate will release a prisoner, but he limits the choice to either *Barabbas* or *Jesus who is called Christ*—the *so-called Messiah.* This seems a shrewd move, for Pilate knows that *envy*—not insurrection—was behind the Jews' accusations. The Jewish leadership was envious of Jesus' popularity with the masses (9.33–34, 12.23–24, 21.15–16), and Pilate hopes His popularity

---

[6] It's impossible to know whether Pilate's custom extended to other feasts besides Passover.

[7] For a list of ancient sources, see Luz III, 497.

will result in a call for His release. Snubbing the clergy, Pilate appeals directly to the crowd.

27.19 While he was sitting on the judgment seat, his wife sent to him, saying, "Have nothing to do with that just Man, for I have suffered many things today in a dream because of Him."

The Roman governors had appropriated the palaces of Herod the Great as their residences, both in Caesarea and Jerusalem. In Jerusalem, two Herodian buildings were used: Herod's palace on the west side of Mt. Zion, and Antonia, on the northwest corner of the temple. Both locations were fortresses, analogous to National Guard armories. Because Roman governors wanted to be present should unrest break out during Jewish festivals, it's probable that this scene occurred at Antonia (named after Herod's friend, Mark Antony).

Roman trials were held in public, and Pilate sat on his *judgment seat*, the judicial bench. *Judgment seat* translates *bēma,* which, strictly, was not a seat but rather a step or platform, a dais. At this point, there is a remarkable interruption, for Pilate's wife sends him a message urging him to *have nothing to do with that just Man, for I have suffered many things today in a dream because of Him.* This recalls chs 1 to 2, where God directed events through dreams (1.20; 2.12–13,19,22), but Matthew gives no indication this dream was heaven-sent. Romans, however, viewed dreams as omens, and this message would have been unsettling to Pilate, who already suspected he was being asked to condemn an innocent man. Pilate's wife is the second witness to Christ's innocence in this chapter, Judas being the first (v 10).[8]

.27.20 But the chief priests and elders persuaded the multitudes that they should ask for Barabbas and destroy Jesus.

The chief priests and elders work the crowd, persuading it to request the release of Barabbas and the execution of Jesus.

27.21–23 The governor answered and said to them, "Which of the two do you want me to release to you?" They said, "Barabbas!" Pilate said to them, "What then shall I do with Jesus who is called Christ?" *They all said to him, "Let Him be crucified!" Then the governor said, "Why,*

---

[8] In tradition, Pilate's wife (whose name was Procula or Claudia, depending on the source) became a Christian. Why she didn't get word to her husband earlier may be because noble Roman women liked to lounge in bed in the morning after their husbands got up and went to work.

what evil has He done?" But they cried out all the more, saying, "Let Him be crucified!"

Pilate repeats his question of v 17: *which of the two do you want me to release to you?* and the cry of *Barabbas* catches him off guard. *What then shall I do with Jesus who is called Christ?* The crowd answers, *Let Him be crucified!* Pilate protests, *Why, what evil has He done?* But the crowd—exhibiting the psychology of a mob—cries more loudly, *Let Him be crucified!*

Pilate's reason for asking the crowd what he should do with Jesus is difficult to understand—he, not the crowd, was in charge, and his disdain for the Jews was well known. Further, just because Barabbas was released didn't mean Jesus had to be crucified. Believing Christ innocent, Pilate could have used his imperium to free Jesus, and no one could have stopped him. Part of Pilate's acquiescence is explained by the threat of political blackmail (Jn. 19.12), but Matthew makes clear that Pilate wasn't forced to do as he did. He could have stopped a legal murder, but failed to do so.

It is frequently asked how a crowd that welcomed Jesus as Messiah in 21.8–11 could turn on Him so quickly. The probable answer is that they who acclaimed Christ at His entry into Jerusalem were Galilean, whereas this multitude was made up of native Jerusalemites who were disturbed by Christ's presence (21.10) and who "were accustomed to ask the yearly favor of the governor and who had learned to conform to the wishes of the chief priests and elders" (Harrison, 213). The explanation may be as simple as the fact that crowds are fickle and the Jewish leadership were skilled rabble-rousers.[9]

27.24 When Pilate saw that he could not prevail at all, but rather *that a tumult was rising,* he took water and washed *his* hands before the multitude, saying, "I am innocent of the blood of this just Person. You see *to it.*"

This is Pilate's last interaction with the crowd. Realizing that he is getting nowhere, and that pushing the issue could trigger a *tumult* (*thorubos,*

---

[9] "The cruelty of men is potentially so great that it can hardly be exaggerated. There are few scenes in which mankind demonstrates its unloveliness more than in a mob. The members of the mob are wonderfully safe, for the victim is wholly at their mercy. They know that they are invulnerable because the lone person is not in a position to defend himself. This is why mob action is essentially cowardly. It is cowardly because the many who bait the one run no personal risks. Mob action is, accordingly, among the most despicable of human actions" (Trueblood, *Confronting* Christ, 166–167).

uproar; v 5[10]), he bows to political expediency. Taking his wife's advice (v 19), he tries to distance himself from *the blood of this just Person* (for the third time in this chapter, Jesus is declared innocent, vv 4,19). Washing the hands as a claim of innocence was a Jewish ritual found in Deuteronomy 21.6–9. In the case of murder by an unknown assailant, the elders of a city were to sacrifice a cow, wash their hands, and absolve themselves from bloodguilt with a solemn declaration. What Pilate did differed from this in two significant ways: in Deuteronomy, the murder had already occurred, and the elders really were innocent; whereas here, the murder had not yet occurred, and Pilate could have stopped it. Refusing to decide doesn't mean you evade responsibility. Washing his hands didn't remove Pilate's culpability.

27.25 And all the people answered and said, "His blood *be* on us and on our children."

All the people refers to the crowd (v 20), but Matthew may use this phrase to designate the entire nation, for the nation as a whole had said *no* to Christ (11.16–19; Jn. 1.11; Rom. 9.1–3, 10.1–3, 11.7ff).

In response to Pilate's attempt at self-exoneration, the people shout, *His blood be on us and on our children*. The three occurrences of *blood* in this chapter offer some insight into the psychology of guilt. In v 4, Judas is swallowed up by overmuch sorrow due to his betrayal of *innocent blood*; in v 24, Pilate claims he is innocent of condemning *an innocent man*; and in this verse, the people accept for themselves and their children the *guilt* of killing Jesus. And in asking for the release of a criminal and the crucifixion of Christ, they were indeed guilty. Interestingly, in Acts 5.28, when the apostles take them up on their offer and accuse them of killing Christ, they become indignant and reject any responsibility. For their crime, God's wrath fell on them and their children (3.7, 24.2–36). The time would come when they who clamored for Christ's crucifixion were crucified by Titus at the rate of 500 per day, until, says Josephus, "room was wanting for the crosses, and crosses for the bodies" (*Wars* v,11.1).

---

[10] See Jn. 19.12. Pilate was appointed governor of Judea by the antisemitic Sejanus, who had been given administration of the empire by Tiberius. So long as Sejanus held power, Pilate's anti-Jewish policies raised no official eyebrows. But when Tiberius had Sejanus executed ca AD 31, his anti-Jewish policies were reversed, and his political appointees' loyalty to the emperor was critically evaluated. It was not a good time for any doubt to be cast on Pilate's allegiance to Tiberius.

27.26 Then he released Barabbas to them; and when he had scourged Jesus, he delivered *Him* to be crucified.

Pilate caves, releasing Barabbas and *delivering Jesus to be crucified*. In 20.19, Jesus predicted that He would be *scourged* (*phragelloō*, only here in Matt.), which was a horrible torture that often resulted in death. The victim was bound to a pillar and was beaten with a whip in which were fastened bones or pieces of lead. Not infrequently, the prisoner died during the scourging (Josephus, *Wars* ii.5.3). It "was so terrible that even Domitian was horrified by it. We know little about the details. The number of strokes was not prescribed. It continued until the flesh hung down in bloody shreds" (*Kittel's* IV, 517).

"For the Roman, this was all in the day's work, just part of the necessary task of keeping a troublesome society in order. The probability is that [Pilate] never thought of the affair again" (Trueblood, *Confronting* Christ, 161–162).

27.27 Then the soldiers of the governor took Jesus into the Praetorium and gathered the whole garrison around Him.

Just as Christ's Jewish trial ended with ridicule and abuse (26.67–68), so too does the Roman. *The soldiers of the governor* could have been auxiliary forces shipped to Jerusalem for Passover or members of the local garrison. To them, the matter about Jesus being a king was a joke, and they take Him into the *Praetorium* (*praitōrion*, originally, the headquarters in a Roman camp; in the provinces, it became the name for the governor's house), which probably refers to an inner courtyard in Antonia (v 19). There, the entire company (*band, speira*, anything rolled into a circle or ball; a military cohort) gathered round to engage in sadistic farce.

27.28–29 And they stripped Him and put a scarlet robe on Him. When they had twisted a crown of thorns, they put *it* on His head, and a reed in His right hand. And they bowed the knee before Him and mocked Him, saying, "Hail, King of the Jews!"

Ridicule is always deeply wounding. Because He claimed to be *King*, the soldiers give Christ the royal treatment. After stripping Him of His clothes, they place on Him three insignias of royalty: *a scarlet robe* (*chlamus*, a military cape or cloak; in the NT, only here and v 31; the scarlet color was produced by a dye made from the Kermes oak scale insect),[11] *a crown of*

---

[11] On the difference between Matthew's *scarlet* robe and Mark's *purple* robe (Mk. 15–17), Carson writes, "the ancients did not discriminate among colors as closely as we do" (573).

thorns (*akantha*, a general term for prickly, thorny weeds of which there are several varieties in Judea), and a *reed* for a scepter. The parody proceeds as the soldiers *bow the knee before Him and mock Him saying, "Hail, King of the Jews!"* The *mockery* was predicted in 20.19.

27.30 Then they spat on Him, and took the reed and struck Him on the head.

The verbal abuse turns physical when the soldiers, as did the Jews, *spit* on Jesus (26.67). They take the reed from His hand and use it as a stick to beat (*struck, tuptō,* pummel) the thorns into His scalp; the verb used (the only imperfect verb in the narrative) indicates they *kept hitting Him* (wms). How much pressure could be applied by a single reed prone to bruising (12.20) isn't stated, but not much would have been needed for the thorns to puncture Christ's scalp and cause profuse bleeding.

27.31 And when they had mocked Him, they took the robe off Him, put His *own* clothes on Him, and led Him away to be crucified.

After outfitting Him like a fool and treating Him shamefully, they return Christ's clothes. Noteworthy is that Matthew doesn't provide a single detail of the horrors of the scourging (v 26).

CRUCIFIXION, 27.32–56

Notes

"In all Athens' history," wrote Edith Hamilton, "Socrates was the only man put to death for his opinions. His executioners killed him by giving him a poison that made him die with no pain. They were Greeks. The Romans hung Christ upon a cross" (*The Echo of Greece*, 219). Cicero called crucifixion *crudelissimum deterrimumque supplicium* — a *most cruel and terrible punishment.* But by crucifixion the Son of God died, and in this, everything that most makes men *disbelieve* in God and everything that most makes men *believe* in God is found. There is no greater paradox than the cross.

"Long ago, outside Jerusalem, a man hung on a cross, so far as outward eye could see, a pitiable failure if ever there was one. ... I have thought about it for a lifetime, and I cannot yet see how what happened there could happen. For that so fragile appeal of the spirit to the spirit

---

Might the mention of *scarlet* be designed to make us recall Isa. 1.18, *though your sins are like scarlet?*

has turned out to be tremendous, incredibly transforming, obdurate as granite in its endurance and, in its conquest of mankind's noblest souls, powerful beyond belief. Since then many an empire has tumbled down, but the influence of that life and character and sacrifice goes on. Believe it or not, there in the realm of spirit, we find what lasts and triumphs in the end. The victories of physical force, however noisy and ostentatious, and however necessary we may think them, are temporary; only the spirit's victories that inwardly persuade and transform men, last" (Fosdick, "The Urgency of Ethical as Well as Economic Reconversion").

This section divides into three parts: to Golgotha (vv 32–38), the crucifixion (vv 39–50),[12] and the aftermath (vv 51–56).

To Golgotha, 27.32–38

27.32 Now as they came out, they found a man of Cyrene, Simon by name. Him they compelled to bear His cross.

As they came out of the Praetorium (v 27; but readers often understand this as the execution squad leaving Jerusalem, Heb. 13.11–13). Part of the ignominy of crucifixion was that the condemned was driven and beaten to the death site, while being forced to carry the instrument of death—a cross. According to some ancient sources, it was the *patibulum* or crossbeam (a Lat. word for which there is no Gr. equivalent) that was carried.

Along the way, *Simon, a man of Cyrene*, is *compelled* (5.41) to carry Christ's cross. Cyrene was a North African town located in Libya, over 800 miles from Jerusalem. Why Simon was present isn't stated (was he on his way for the day's first prayers at the temple?), nor are we told why he was pressed into service (after a sleepless night, scourging, etc., had Jesus fallen under the load?). To be pulled out of the crowd to carry a cross had to be a humiliating experience. Mark 15.21 identifies Simon as *the father of Alexander and Rufus*, whom Mark assumes his readers knew, and Paul in Romans 16.13 sends greetings to a Christian named *Rufus*. Many have speculated that Simon and his sons became well-known Christians, but the case for this is only circumstantial.

---

[12] The Roman Catholic tradition involving the so-called "stations of the cross" traces not to the NT but to the desire of medievals to visualize the suffering of Jesus in greater detail. Contributing to their recreation of Christ's passion was information about Jerusalem brought back by Crusaders. Mel Gibson's 2004 movie, *The Passion of Christ* utilized much of this Middle Age tradition.

27.33–34 And when they had come to a place called Golgotha, that is to say, Place of a Skull, they gave Him sour wine mingled with gall to drink. But when He had tasted *it*, He would not drink.

The Aramaic name for the execution site was Golgotha—skull place.[13] How it got this name is unknown. All we know about it from Scripture is that it was outside the city walls but near the city (Jn. 19.20), near a road (v 39), and near a garden that had a rock-hewn tomb belonging to Joseph of Arimathaea (Jn. 19.41).

Upon reaching Golgotha, Jesus is offered *sour wine mingled with gall to drink*. It is not known whether the *gall* (*cholē*, a vague word for drugs with a bitter taste) is offered because it "had a stupefying effect which made it easier for the executioners to handle condemned persons" (Vos, 181) or whether it was part of the soldiers' abuse. The ordeal has left Christ extremely thirsty (Jn. 19.28), but when He tastes the gall He refuses it. We live in an age when anesthetics are a normal part of life, and it is difficult to comprehend how terrible raw, undulled pain can be. But Christ met His death with His senses unimpaired by any drugs.[14] We do not know why God allows so much pain in this world, but we do know that His Son shared it (2.17–18).

Excursus on Golgotha

The traditional site of Golgotha has much to recommend it as the actual site of Christ's death. It is almost certain that Jerusalem Christians prior to AD 70 would have known its location. When these believers fled Jerusalem ahead of the Roman investment (24.15–18), many went to Pella, fifty miles away (Eusebius, *Ch. Hist.* iii, 5.3). Later, some returned to Jerusalem and Jewish Christians lived there until AD 135 when Hadrian banned all Jews from the city (Eusebius iv, 6.3). Gentile Christians, however, who would have also known the location of Golgotha, were not expelled. It would seem, then, that a solid line of tradition about the location of Golgotha and Christ's tomb can be traced from the time of Christ's death to the middle of the second century and beyond.

Epiphanius (*Weights and Measures*, 14) wrote that when Hadrian decided to rebuild Jerusalem, he launched a systematic profanation of Jewish and Christian

---

[13] The Lat. Vulgate translated *skull* as *calvariae*, which became *Calvary* in the KJV.

[14] Dr. Brockelsby, Samuel Johnson's doctor, was with the great Englishman to the last. Johnson asked if he had any chance of recovery. "Give me," he begged, "a faithful answer." Brockelsby told him the truth. "Then," said Johnson, "I will take no more physic, not even my opiates; for I desire to render up my soul to God unclouded."

shrines. Eusebius (*Life of Constantine* III, 26) says that included in this was an order that Christ's tomb be buried under dirt, paved over, and that a shrine to Venus be built atop it. Constantine later ordered the shrine removed, and while this was being done, a tomb was uncovered. As it was the only tomb found in the area, it was presumed to be the tomb of Christ. Over it, Constantine built a *basilica* (church). In the *Onomasticon* (a dictionary-type listing of proper names), Eusebius locates Golgotha as being "north of Mt. Zion."

The earliest extant account (333) of someone who journeyed to Jerusalem to see places associated with Christ is from an individual known as the *Bordeaux* [France] *Pilgrim*. In describing his sight-seeing near the Neapolis Gate on the north side of the city, he wrote, "On the left hand is the little hill of Golgotha where the Lord was crucified. About a stone's throw from thence is a crypt where his body was laid and the third day was raised. There by the command of the Emperor Constantine a basilica has been built, that is, a church" (*Itinerary of the Pilgrim of Bordeaux*). This building became known as the Church of the Holy Sepulcher.

Finegan's conclusion in *The Archaeology of the New Testament* seems reasonable: "The location of Golgotha and the tomb of Christ thus indicated by Eusebius and the Bordeaux Pilgrim, north of Mount Sion and on the left hand as one proceeds toward the Neapolis Gate in the north wall of Jerusalem, corresponds with the location of the present Church of the Holy Sepulcher.... outside the second wall, i.e., the wall of the time of Jesus, ... and in the area of an old quarry which had been utilized as a cemetery ... ; thus it may be accepted as the correct site in accordance with the earliest Christian tradition" (164).

Crucified, 27.35–38

Notes

"Crucifixion was the most degrading form of capital punishment, reserved for rebels, mutinous slaves and other unspeakable enemies of society; and it was also the most prolonged and painful" (Johnson, *A History of Christianity*, 29). In the sixteenth century, Reformation theologian Wolfgang Musculus spoke for many when he expressed surprise that the Gospels say so little about the details of crucifixion. "One wonders why not a single evangelist mentions how Jesus was crucified." But according to John C. Robison in his splendid essay "Crucifixion in the Roman World: The Use of Nails at the Time of Christ" (*Studia Antiqua*, Vol. 2, No. 1, June 2002), any study of crucifixion is limited due to "the general way that most crucifixions are described in antiquity. Of some 275 accounts researched, 223 use only general verbs or phrases such as *in crucem suffere* (to be raised on a cross), *in crucem tolli* (to be lifted up on a cross), *staurō* (to crucify, impale) and *skolopizō* (to crucify, to impale)." Matthew uses *stauroō* to describe Christ's execution and throughout the narrative is reserved in his description of it.

Crucifixion "was of Eastern origin, and had been in use among the Persians and Carthaginians long before its employment in Western countries. Alexander the Great adopted it in Palestine, from the Phenicians, after the defence of Tyre, which he punished by crucifying two thousand citizens, when the place surrendered. Crassus signalized its introduction into Roman use by lining the road from Capua to Rome with crucified slaves, captured in the revolt of Spartacus, and Augustus finally inaugurated its general use, by crucifying six thousand slaves at once, in Sicily, in his suppression of the war raised by Sextus Pompeius" (Geikie II, 525). To the Romans, crucifixion was a horror show, meant to deter crime and rebellion among subject peoples.

27.35 Then they crucified Him, and divided His garments, casting lots, that it might be fulfilled which was spoken by the prophet: "They divided My garments among them, And for My clothing they cast lots."
They crucified Him. Crucifixion originally consisted of a single sharpened stake (the *crux simplex*) on which victims were impaled.[15] Later modifications included the *crux commissa*, shaped like a capital T (with the crossbeam laid on top of the vertical beam), the *crux decussata*, shaped like the letter X, and the *crux immissa*, shaped like a lower-case t (the mention of the inscription in v 37 suggests this style).

The crucified would be tied or nailed to the beams[16]; John 20.25 says Jesus was nailed.[17] Whether He was put on the cross while it was upright or while it lay on the ground before being hoisted upright isn't stated.

---

[15] Seneca wrote of "the stake which they drive straight through a man until it protrudes from his throat" (*Ad Lucilium epistulae morales* 14.5, trans., Richard M. Gummere. https://archive.org/details/adluciliumepistu01seneuoft

[16] "The men ordered to lead the slave to his punishment, having stretched out both his arms and fastened them to a piece of wood which extended across his breast and shoulders as far as his wrists, followed him, tearing his naked body with whips" (Dionysius of Halicarnassus, *Ant. Rom.* 7.69.2).

[17] Nails of a victim crucified were considered among the most powerful medical amulets in antiquity. Lucian, in his story of Erithco the witch, writes that she "purloins the nails that pierced the hand" of crucifixion victims for magical use (Lucan, *De Bello Civili*).

Nor are we told whether there was a *sedile* on the vertical beam, a peg or seat on which the victim could rest some of his weight. In 1968, an ossuary discovered at Giv'at ha-Mivtar (Ammunition Hill) near Jerusalem held the remains of a crucified man by the name of Johanan. Based on pottery found at the site, his death is believed to have occurred between AD 7 and AD 66. His arms had been nailed to the crossbeam. The right foot had been placed on top of the left and an iron nail, still in place, had been driven through both heels. A fragment of wood on the nail was analyzed and found to be olive wood. And his legs had been broken, presumably by a blow like those described in John 19.32.

Terrible spasms, cramps, convulsions, and even tetanus would ravage the crucified. Victims could linger for days before dying of suffocation, hunger, exposure, loss of blood, or the predation of wild animals. Jewish revulsion at crucifixion was heightened because the Law of Moses placed a curse on anyone hanged on a tree (Deut. 21.23); to be crucified was to be repudiated by man and God.

Ancient sources indicate that crucified people were normally naked, thus increasing the victim's shame.[18] Christ's clothes were taken from Him, and it seems that the Roman detail (which usually included four members) each took an article of clothing—possibly a belt, sandals, head covering, and cloak (5.40)—and then cast lots for Christ's seamless tunic (shirt), which would have been ruined if torn. What *casting lots* involved isn't explained; what is most important for Matthew is that this is the first of three scenes that invoke Psalm 22, the psalm of suffering. The casting of lots fulfilled Psalm 22.18, and by this we know that Christ was in God's will and hands at Golgotha.

27.36–37 Sitting down, they kept watch over Him there. And they put up over His head the accusation written against Him: THIS IS JESUS THE KING OF THE JEWS.

After crucifying the victims, all that's left is for the soldiers to stand guard, presumably to discourage any rescue attempt.[19] Above Christ's head is placed *the accusation* (*aitia*, cause, reason) *against Him*: THIS IS JESUS THE

---

[18] In the apocryphal *Gospel of Nicodemus*, Jesus is pictured as wearing a loincloth, and the crown of thorns has been put back on His head, two features that have been in almost every portrayal of the crucifixion since.

[19] Josephus said he was able to obtain the release of three acquaintances who had been crucified by the Romans at Jerusalem, one of whom survived (*Life*, 75).

KING OF THE JEWS. Thomas Cooper's comments bear repeating: "You will remember how Pontius Pilate is described as being most unwilling to condemn Christ—how he strives to release him—and how he publicly washes his hands, according to Matthew, to shew his innocence of the blood of Jesus—and how, at last, Pilate was *stung* into action by the cry 'If thou let this man go thou art not Caesar's friend!' That cry warned Pilate that the Jewish priests and rulers meant to impeach him to the Roman emperor and senate, if he did not comply with their blood-thirsty demand. So he condemns Christ, and *stings* the priests and rulers in return, by placing an inscription over the head of Christ which describes the crucified Saviour as 'the King of the Jews.' See how they fume when they have read the inscription! They know that the transaction will be reported, in full, to the Roman emperor and senate, by Pilate; and their long-standing bad character for rebellion be thus increased. 'Write *not*, "The King of the Jews," say the chief priests to Pilate, "but—that *he said* 'I am the King of the Jews.'"—'What I have written I have written,' was the stern and scornful answer they had from Pilate. He discerned that they had been plotting his ruin; and this inscription above the cross was the beginning of his counterplot. He knew that when the report of the transaction was read at Rome, it would be said, immediately, either in the Senate, or by the imperial secretaries—'This Pilate is just the man to hold the reins tight among these rebellious Jews: he has crucified another of their pretended kings'" (*The Verity of Christ's Resurrection from the Dead*, 52–53).

Although it may have been a way for Pilate to thumb his nose at the Jews while covering his back, in the inscription, believers see the *wrath of man praising God* (Ps. 76.10), for it expressed the truth—Jesus was, indeed, the *King of the Jews* (2.2; Col.2.14).

27.38 Then two robbers were crucified with Him, one on the right and another on the left.

For the first time, Matthew mentions *two robbers* (*lēistai*, Josephus used this term to designate Jewish freedom fighters, who sometimes robbed to support their cause; possibly they were members of Barabbas's gang) who were executed alongside Christ, *one on the right and another on the left*, alluding to Isaiah 53.12's prediction that the suffering Servant would be *numbered with the transgressors*.

On The Cross, 27.39–50

Notes

Here is the last temptation of Christ. Early on, the devil challenged Him to do something extraordinary to demonstrate that He was the Son of God (4.6); Satan now proposes the same, this time through the Jews, who challenge Jesus to save Himself by coming down from the cross. But Christ doesn't take the bait. Having told His disciples *whosoever desires to save his life will lose it*, He stands by His teaching and stays on the cross. More than anything, it is Christ's obedience that proves Him to be the Son of God—an obedience motivated by love, for only love has the power to make a man endure horrific pain he could easily avoid.

27.39–40 And those who passed by blasphemed Him, wagging their heads and saying, "You who destroy the temple and build *it* in three days, save Yourself! If You are the Son of God, come down from the cross."

Christ's enemies will not allow Him to die in peace, and Matthew breaks from his terse reporting to give details about their verbal abuse.

The first to taunt are those *who passed by*, who just happen on the scene but take the opportunity to *blaspheme* and *wag their heads*. Blasphemy (claiming to be God) was the charge for which the Jews condemned Jesus (26.65), but here it means *to speak evil of*—they were critical of one falsely claiming to be their king. *Wagging the head* was a gesture of ridicule and recalls the scorn predicted in Psalm 22.7. They challenge Jesus to save Himself, again mangling His statement in John 2.19 (26.61); after all, anyone capable of building the temple in three days should be able to extricate himself from a cross.

27.41–43 Likewise the chief priests also, mocking with the scribes and elders, said, "He saved others; Himself He cannot save. If He is the King of Israel, let Him now come down from the cross, and we will believe Him. He trusted in God; let Him deliver Him now if He will have Him; for He said, 'I am the Son of God.'"

The next to join the taunting, as foretold in 16.21, are *the chief priests, scribes, and elders*. Long frustrated over their inability to destroy Jesus, they cannot hide their glee and come out to dance on His grave. *He saved others*, they said; *Himself he cannot save*, and they were right on both counts. Jesus was able to save men from sin, disease, despair, etc. precisely because He refused to save Himself (20.28, 26.28). Mockingly, they promise to believe Jesus if He would just come down from the cross. But they were lying, for after Christ performed the greater miracle of coming out of the grave, they still refused to believe (28.11–15). Their final insult implicated God: "Jesus claimed God as His Father so let's see if God will claim Jesus as His Son. If He doesn't, it proves we are right." In carrying out His sovereign will, God is willing to let good (1.19) and wicked men draw wrong conclusions.

But everything the Jews said out of malice was true: Jesus is the Son of God, He did save others, He didn't save Himself, He is the King of Israel, and He died trusting in God.

27.44 Even the robbers who were crucified with Him reviled Him with the same thing.

The third mockery comes from the thieves who repeat what they hear, expressing no sympathy with a fellow sufferer. In Matthew's Gospel, Jesus dies completely alone (Ps. 142.4).

27.45 Now from the sixth hour until the ninth hour there was darkness over all the land.

The central scene of the crucifixion is in vv 45–50, which is bracketed by references to Christ *crying out with a loud voice* (vv 46,50). Between these cries is the mocking crowd and their two references to Elijah (vv 47,49).

Whereas light (from a star) is associated with Christ's birth, darkness attends His death. From *the sixth* (noon) until *the ninth hour* (3 PM), *there was darkness over all the land* (*gē*, the earth). The absence of a geographical modifier (Ex. 10.21) may indicate that the entire earth was shrouded in darkness, which wouldn't be surprising seeing that the entire earth was involved in the drama being played out. What is certain is that this darkness wasn't due to natural phenomena (just as no natural cause accounts for the star of Bethlehem) but resulted from divine intervention.[20] Matthew doesn't explain its significance, and interpretations are varied—including the idea that it was a sign of heavenly sorrow, when "the sun covering its face from shame, not wanting to see what is about to happen." A better interpretation, I think, is that the darkness indicated divine judgment (Joel 2.2, 3.15; Amos 5.18,

---

[20] The darkness was not caused by an eclipse, for Passover occurred at full moon, when an eclipse of the sun is impossible.

8.9–10; Zeph. 1.15; Isa. 13.10–11; Jer. 15.9), analogous to the ninth plague and the three days of darkness that preceded the Passover (Ex. 10.21–23).

27.46 And about the ninth hour Jesus cried out with a loud voice, saying, "Eli, Eli, lama sabachthani?" that is, "My God, My God, why have You forsaken Me?"

Around 3 PM the darkness ends, and Jesus shouts, *Eli, Eli, lama sabachthani?* Out of His complete knowledge of sacred literature, Psalm 22.1 is the passage where He finds expression for "one of those horrible cries which cannot be written in any human language" (Hugo, *The Hunchback of Notre Dame*). *Eli, Eli, lama sabachthani* is Aramaic and translates as *My God, My God, why have You forsaken me?* This is the only time when Jesus used *God* rather than *Father* in prayer, and it's the only time He asks *Why?* Abandoned by His disciples, denied by Peter, surrounded by enemies, completely alone, and abandoned by God—these words signal the climax of His agony. It was "an exclamation wrung from his fainting nature by the extremity of anguish. But this was not bodily anguish; for then the malefactors must be considered as superior to Christ in their patience under torture. It was not repining language, that God had so forsaken him as to leave him the hands of his enemies. It was a deeper anguish which extorted this mournful cry, than that produced by corporal suffering. ... They are not the words of complaint as implying reluctance to suffer, but as expressive of deep internal agony, internal desertion of sensible support and consolation; in a word, the completion of what was begun in the garden, the drinking of the last dregs of bitterness out of the cup of wrath, when he having placed himself voluntarily in the room and stead of the guilty, was dealt with as though he were really such" (R. Watson, 427–428).[21]

There is deep significance in Christ's use of the possessive My—He still claims God as His God, even when He feels abandoned by God.

The job of a slave (20.28) is to obey; for this, he needs to know the "what," he doesn't need to know the "why."

---

[21] In a 1946 fictional short story, "Yosl Rakover Talks to God," written by Jewish author Zvi Kolitz, the protagonist, Yosl Rakover, writes his last testament before dying in the War-saw Ghetto: "My rabbi used to tell me, again and again, the story of a Jew who escaped the Spanish Inquisition with his wife and child and made his way in a small boat across the stormy sea to a stony island. A flash of lightning exploded and killed his wife. A whirlwind arose and hurled his child into the sea. Alone, wretched, discarded like a stone, naked and barefoot, lashed by the storm, terrified by thunder and lighting, his hair disheveled and his hands raised to God, the Jew made his way up onto the rocky desert island and turned thus to God.

27.47–49 Some of those who stood there, when they heard *that,* **said, "This Man is calling for Elijah!" Immediately one of them ran and took a sponge, filled** *it* **with sour wine and put** *it* **on a reed, and offered it to Him to drink. The rest said, "Let Him alone; let us see if Elijah will come to save Him."**

Christ is mocked for the last time. Matthew doesn't tell us who the *some* are who think He is calling for *Elijah.* In Jewish superstition of the time, Elijah was viewed "as a helper in time of need" (Kittel's II, 930). Christ hasn't saved Himself, and God hasn't saved Him, so some think He's down to His final straw by appealing to Elijah. The Heb. words for *God* and *Elijah* are similar, and this may have contributed to the misunderstanding.

One of the mockers fetches a *sponge and filled it with sour wine, put it on a reed, and gave it to Him to drink.* Most crosses were the height of an average man, but the height of Jesus' cross necessitated the use of a reed to lift the sponge to His mouth. *Sour wine (oxoi)* can refer to either a cheap, sour wine or to vinegar. Allusion is made to Psalm 69.22 and its prediction of this incident (v 34). It's hard to determine if this is an act of compassion or torture—a drink would refresh the victim, but it might thereby also prolong life and suffering.

Let Him alone (aphei) is ambiguous; it can mean *leave off/stop,* in which case it is addressed to the one giving Jesus the wine, or it can be a comment in the sense of *now then, let us see if Elijah comes.* I lean toward the second possibility.

27.50 And Jesus cried out again with a loud voice, and yielded up His spirit.

Crying out with a loud voice (v 46), Jesus *yielded up His spirit.*[22] "None of the Evangelists uses any of the usual ways of saying that Jesus died, and this may be part of the way they bring out the truth that there was something in his death that set it apart from all other deaths" (Morris, 723). In John

---

"'God of Israel,' he said, 'I have fled to this place so that I may serve You in peace, to follow Your commandments and glorify Your name. You, however, are doing everything to make me cease believing in You. But if You think that You will succeed with these trials in deflecting me from the true path, then I cry to You, my God and the God of my parents, that none of it will help You. You may insult me, You may chastise me, You may take from me the dearest and the best that I have in the world, You may torture me to death—I will always believe in You. I will love You always and forever—even despite You'"

[22] Matthew doesn't provide the specific contents of Christ's last prayer (26.44) in Gethsemane or His last word from the cross. Most likely, Christ's last words were those in Lk. 23.46: *Father, into Your hands I commend my spirit.*

10.17–18, Christ said that He would retain sovereignty over His death, and two factors in this text indicate that He did. First, that He cried with *a loud voice* implies that He still retained a measure of physical vigor and didn't die due to trauma or suffocation. Second, *yielded* (*aphiēmi,* to send away, expire) indicates an active rather than passive process. No man took Christ's life from Him; He died when He was ready to die, by an act of His will, after accomplishing all God intended for Him.

Aftermath, 27.51–56

27.51 Then, behold, the veil of the temple was torn in two from top to bottom; and the earth quaked, and the rocks were split,

The denouement has come. For the past three hours, there has been only darkness with no indication of God's interest or involvement. But with Christ's last breath, God asserts Himself with a vengeance. In vv 51–53 are three stupendous events that the ancients would have interpreted as divine demonstrations.

First, *the curtain of the temple was torn in two from the top to the bottom. The curtain* was the massive piece of cloth in the temple that separated the Holy Place from the Holy of Holies. This

tearing didn't signify the coming destruction of the temple (24.3) or God tearing His garments in grief over His Son's death (cf. 26.65) but that access to God was made possible by Christ's death (Heb. 6.19–20, 10.19–20). Edersheim wrote that "the Veils before the Most Holy Place were 40 cubits [60'] long, and 20 [30'] wide, of the thickness of the palm of the hand, and wrought in 72 squares, which were joined together; and these Veils were so heavy, that, in the exaggerated language of the time, it needed 300 priests to manipulate each" (II, 611). This tearing of the curtain from top to bottom was indisputably an act of God. Because Jesus died around 3 PM (v 45), the priests who were offering incense at the evening sacrifice would have had a front-row seat to this phenomenon, and their consternation would almost certainly have been communicated to the worshipers outside (whose numbers would be swollen at Passover).[23]

The tearing of the curtain signaled the end of Judaism (5.17–18), for the Mosaic covenant had found its completion in the great event it typified — the death of Jesus on the cross.

---

[23] Matthew doesn't tell us if the phenomena at Christ's death inclined any priest(s) toward the kingdom, but Luke's statement in Acts 6.7 that *a great many of the priests were obedient to the faith* should not be overlooked.

Second, *the earth quaked, and the rocks were split.* It's unusual during an earthquake for rocks to break; that they did so on this occasion indicates supernatural involvement (1 Kgs. 19.11–12). In Scripture, earthquakes were sometimes used by God to indicate His presence (e.g., at the initiating of a covenant [Ex. 19.18, Hag. 2.6] and judgment [Joel 2.10, 3.16; Nah. 1.5–6]).

27.52–53 and the graves were opened; and many bodies of the saints who had fallen asleep were raised; and coming out of the graves after His resurrection, they went into the holy city and appeared to many.

Third, and most extraordinary of all, resurrections occured — *many bodies of the saints who had fallen asleep were* raised. That Matthew writes from a Jewish perspective hints at why he is the only one to record this miracle, for Jewish eschatology believed that the era of the Messiah would be marked by the resurrection of the dead.

Determining the sequence of events depends on how these verses are punctuated. If a period is placed after *and the graves were opened*, this would be the third phenomenon mentioned, and *many bodies of the saints who had fallen asleep were raised* would be the next sentence, describing events that happened on Sunday. But if the punctuation in the NKJV is correct, the graves were opened and the dead were raised on Friday, but they didn't leave their tombs until after Christ left His. Almost all versions follow this punctuation, but I have to wonder why God would raise people, only to have them cool their heels for a couple of days in their tombs? *Fallen asleep* occurs twice in Matthew; here it means death, but in 28.13, it indicates normal sleep. We can only speculate on who these saints were, but common sense suggests individuals known to Jews then alive, rather than OT personages or people who died before the appearance of the generation then alive. If a man showed up claiming to be Louis IX, I'd think him an escapee from a dementia facility, but if my grandfather Louis, whom I knew well, showed up, my reaction would be much different. The word translated *resurrection* (*egersis*) occurs only here in the NT.

We don't know what impression this miracle made on Jerusalem but the subsequent conversion of priests (Acts 6.7) and Pharisees (Acts 15.5) may indicate a profound impression. A question often asked is why Jesus didn't appear to others in Jerusalem besides His followers, but it may be that the appearance of these resurrected dead left as strong an impact as if Christ Himself had openly appeared in the city. We don't know what subsequently happened to these individuals, but it doesn't seem a stretch to believe that at least some among the three thousand converts on Pentecost (Acts 2) were helped to faith by the appearance of these dead.[24]

27.54 So when the centurion and those with him, who were guarding Jesus, saw the earthquake and the things that had happened, they feared greatly, saying, "Truly this was the Son of God!"

The reaction of the Romans contrasts sharply with that of the Jews. The darkness, earthquake, and splitting of the rocks enabled the centurion and his squad to see the light, and they confess *Truly this was the Son of God!* It's possible this confession was made within the parameters of Gentile paganism and its view of heroes, but the words *the Son of* God argues for a deeper meaning.[25] *Son of God* is one of the singular titles for Christ in Matthew (2.15, 3.17, 14.33, 16.16, 17.5), and this confession rounds off the Gospel, corresponding to the faith of another centurion introduced earlier (8.11).

27.55–56 And many women who followed Jesus from Galilee, ministering to Him, were there looking on from afar, among whom were Mary Magdalene, Mary the mother of James and Joses, and the mother of Zebedee's sons.

Here's a postscript that serves as a bridge to v 61 and the resurrection account in 28.1–10. For the first time, Matthew reveals that *many women* witnessed the execution *from afar*. *Mary Magdalene*, who is mentioned in all four Gospels, is introduced for the first time in Matthew. Her surname indicates that she came from Magdala, a town on the northwestern shore of the Sea of Galilee (15.39). She was a former demoniac who had been healed by Christ (Lk. 8.2). There is no evidence to support the medieval legends that she was a prostitute or was the one who anointed Christ in Luke 7.36–50. Mary the mother of Jesus had two sons named James and Joseph (13.55), but *Mary the mother of James and Joses* mentioned here is the

---

[24] The Talmud contains some bizarre notions about the resurrection. Some rabbis believed that only those buried in the land of Israel would be resurrected—and that the Jews buried outside Israel would burrow underground until they had reached Israelite territory so that they could be included in the resurrection (Ketubot, 111).

[25] The fact that in the Gr. the definite article isn't used before *Son of God* doesn't mean that *the Son of God* is an incorrect translation. "It is not missing because for the soldiers Jesus was only *one* son of God among many but because the verb appears after the predicate noun. In such cases the definite article is usually missing in New Testament Greek" (Luz III, 570). The definite article is also missing in the disciples' confession in 14.33.

mother of *James the less* (Mk. 15.40), who was one of the Twelve. *Salome* may have been the name of *the mother of Zebedee's sons*, James and John (20.20; Mk. 15.40). Come resurrection morning, these women will be the first to hear the greatest news ever told.

"As far as anyone that day did see, or could see, Christianity was now dead—annihilated with the utter destruction of its founder and sole leader" (Culver, 262).

BURIAL, 27.57–61

27.57 Now when evening had come, there came a rich man from Arimathea, named Joseph, who himself had also become a disciple of Jesus.

Based on v 62, *when evening had come* should be understood as late afternoon on Friday, just before sunset. *Joseph of Arimathea*, a *rich disciple of Jesus* appears for the first time.[26] Arimathea was a city of Judea (Lk. 23.51); the mention of Joseph's wealth connects what transpires to God's foretold plan (Isa. 53.9).

The likelihood that Joseph's involvement was fabricated is highly improbable considering the bitterness Christians may have harbored against the Sanhedrin. If Matthew was making this up, why would he put a member of the Sanhedrin in such a favorable light? If Joseph wasn't involved in the burial, the Sanhedrin, to protect its reputation, would have exposed it as fake news. But this the Council never did.

27.58 This man went to Pilate and asked for the body of Jesus. Then Pilate commanded the body to be given to him.

In later times, Roman law allowed families to claim and bury the bodies of condemned family members so long as the crime didn't involve the emperor's authority and the burial was not a political statement. The bodies of the crucified were often left on crosses to rot, but Joseph, who had standing (Mk. 15.43) and courage, goes to Pilate and *asked for the body of Jesus*. Pilate may have been weak and irresolute, but he was not unfavorably disposed toward Jesus, and he commands that the corpse be turned over to Joseph.

---

[26] Mk. 15.43 and Lk. 23.51 tell us that Joseph was a member of the Sanhedrin who had not consented to Christ's death.

27.59 When Joseph had taken the body, he wrapped it in a clean linen cloth,

Joseph wrapped (*entulissō*, to roll up, twist) Christ's body *in a clean linen cloth*, a fitting shroud for He who was without spot or blemish (1 Pet. 1.19). Two important customs in Jewish burial practices are not mentioned: Christ's body was neither washed nor anointed (26.12).

27.60 and laid it in his new tomb which he had hewn out of the rock; and he rolled a large stone against the door of the tomb, and departed.

Jesus is buried in a tomb owned by Joseph. It was a *new tomb which had been hewn out of the rock* — born of a virgin womb, buried in a virgin tomb. By *new* is meant that no corpse had previously been placed in it (Lk. 23.53). The evidence suggests that the tomb was a normal Jewish tomb. Examples of tombs from the Herodian period "consisted of an antechamber which was cut out of the rock and entered perhaps by some steps, then a low doorway closed by a stone door or by a rolling stone, and a passageway leading into a generally rectangular tomb chamber. In the tomb chamber the graves were usually of either the kokim or the arcosolia type. The kok was a horizontal shaft driven back into the vertical rock face, into which the body was placed lengthwise. The arcosolium provided a ledge cut laterally into the rock with a vaulted arch over it. In either case the body, wrapped in a winding-sheet, was usually laid on the bare rock" (Finegan, 167). The information in ch 28 suggests that Joseph's tomb involved a ledge rather than shaft (Roman catacombs usually included examples of both).

To seal a tomb, the entrance was barricaded with a closing stone, either a rough boulder or a circular stone that rolled in a groove cut in the rock. This groove "was on an incline, making the grave easy to seal but difficult to open: several men might be needed to roll the stone back up the incline" (Carson, 584; Mk. 16.3–4). Extant closing stones weigh between 500 and 600 pounds.

27.61 And Mary Magdalene was there, and the other Mary, sitting opposite the tomb.

Two of the women — *Mary Magdalene and the other Mary* (*the mother of James and Joses*, v 56) — remain behind after Joseph finishes his work. This detail assures us that they returned to the correct tomb on the third day (28.1).

27.62–66: Saturday

27.62–64 On the next day, which followed the Day of Preparation, the chief priests and Pharisees gathered together to Pilate, saying, "Sir, we remember, while He was still alive, how that deceiver said, 'After three days I will rise.' Therefore command that the tomb be made secure until the third day, lest His disciples come by night and steal Him *away*, and say to the people, 'He has risen from the dead.' So the last deception will be worse than the first."

On the next day, which followed the Day of Preparation would be the Sabbath which began after sundown. *The Day of Preparation*, then, would have been Friday, the day on which Sabbath preparations were made (Mk. 15.42). The chief priests and Pharisees go to Pilate, concerned about something Jesus had said (see Jn. 18.28).

In 12.38 and 16.1, some Pharisees (reappearing for the first time since 22.41) and scribes demand a sign of Jesus. In His answer, Christ spoke of *the sign of the prophet Jonah* and the prediction that *the Son of Man would be three days and three nights in the heart of the earth* (12.39–40, 16.4). Incredibly, the disciples had forgotten this, but the chief priests and Pharisees hadn't, which shows that they understood the figurative nature of the words they tried to twist into a threat against the temple (26.61). The Jews had become pathological, having no conscience.

Sir translates *kurios* (Lord), and *deceiver* (*pianos*, imposter, pretender, only here in Matt.) reveals their undiminished contempt. Despite the apparent support of the people (vv 20–25), the Jewish leadership is concerned about any residual influence Christ might have, and they ask Pilate to order that His tomb be guarded to prevent the disciples from stealing the body and explaining the empty tomb by claiming *He has risen from the dead*. Such, they said, would be a *worse deception than the first* (i.e., the lie of a resurrection would be worse than the prediction of a resurrection). Perception can be as influential as reality, and any rumor of Christ's resurrection could cause unnecessary problems for the Jewish establishment (for the irony of this, see 28.15).[27]

On *after three days* and *until the third day*, see 12.40.

27.65 Pilate said to them, "You have a guard; go your way, make *it* as secure as you know how."

---

[27] "The Pharisees, who believed in resurrection from the dead were especially afraid the populace might accept such a report if it were circulated" (Vos, 184).

You have a guard is ambiguous, for it can be understood either as an imperative or indicative. If an imperative, it would seem that Pilate is being accommodating and makes Roman guards available to the Jews—as may be implied by the Latin loanword for *guard* (*koustōdia*, custodian) and the statement in 28.14.

I think it more likely, though, that Pilate reverted to his normal surliness and told the Jews that if they wanted the tomb guarded, they could do it themselves. *You have a guard* would refer to the temple police; *go your way, make it as secure as you know how* would give the Jews permission to deploy their force outside the temple precincts, with the assurance that their actions would not be interpreted as hostile.[28] Matthew isn't concerned with the nationality of the guard but with making it clear that Christ's tomb was guarded.

27.66 So they went and made the tomb secure, sealing the stone and setting the guard.

So they went and made the tomb secure, sealing the stone, and setting the guard. That the Jews took every measure to keep Christ's body in the tomb only strengthens the certainty of what occurs the third day. "Because of your preventive measures the proof of his resurrection is incontrovertible" (John Chrysostom). The tomb in the rock could be entered only by the door opening into it, and this is where security was focused. *Sealed the stone* most likely meant that a cord or rope was stretched across the stone covering the entrance and embedded on either side in wax or clay. A signet, possibly of the high priest or Sanhedrin, was then stamped into the wax or clay. Any movement of the cord would break the wax and indicate tampering (cf. the sealing of the lion's den, Dan. 6.17). *Setting the guard* means armed men were posted (v 65). Carr doesn't cite his source, but says that "The full complement of a *koustodia* appears to have been 60 men" (Carr, 318).

Christ's tomb was placed under maximum security, which, by itself, is enough to refute the lie told by the Jews in 28.13–15.

---

[28] "It is so often assumed that 'the watch' consisted of Roman soldiers, yet the whole inference of the passage is otherwise. There is not the slightest doubt that Pilate's attitude to the chief priests precludes any kind of cooperation from him, and if their request was for a military guard, then clearly his reply was in the negative! The priests had a Jewish Temple guard—a kind of civil police force—granted to keep order in and around the Temple area (John 7, 32 and 45). Pilate referred them to the forces at their own disposal, and one can sense a note of sarcasm in his parting words, 'Go your way, make it as sure as ye can' (Matt. 27,65). The following words add to the impression, 'So they went, and made the sepulchre sure, sealing the stone and setting a watch' (Matt. 27,66)" (Cornfeld, 178).

CHAPTER 28

28.1–20: Epilogue—Sunday

28.1–10: Conquest

Notes

Death could not keep its prey.

The resurrection of Jesus from the dead is the most important fact in history; next to it, all else pales in comparison. On the resurrection rests everything; it is the bedrock of our belief and the hope of humanity.

The opening section (vv 1–10) is easily outlined: it is bracketed by references to two of the women mentioned in 27.55,56,61, between which is a scene involving an angel announcing the resurrection.

28.1 Now after the Sabbath, as the first *day* of the week began to dawn, Mary Magdalene and the other Mary came to see the tomb.

Now after the Sabbath is an unusual way to speak of Sunday, the first day of the week. *Opse* is usually an adverb meaning *late*: *in the end of the Sabbath* (KJV; *late on the Sabbath*); only rarely is it a preposition meaning *after*. Two considerations, however, indicate its prepositional use here. First, *as the first day of the week began to dawn* indicates that this is the day *after* the Sabbath, and second, Mark 16.2, Luke 24.1, and John 20.1 explicitly say that it is the first day of the week. *The first day of the week* translates *mia sabbatōn, one of the Sabbaths,* "which is a common Jewish designation for the first day of the week" (Luz III, 594).

Mary Magdalene and the other Mary, the mother of James and Joses (27.56)—are mentioned for a third time. So far as the Gospel records are concerned, no woman was ever an enemy of Jesus; women are consistently pictures as sympathetic and supportive of Christ. And here, again (e.g., 26.6–13), it is women, rather than the disciples, who show special devotion. Cornfeld says that "The beginning of the 8th chapter of *Semahot* deals with the verification of the dead for three days after burial. This chapter of Mishna *Semahot* states that 'one should go to the cemetery to check the dead within three days and not fear that such smacks of pagan practices; it once happened that a (buried) man was visited and went on to live another twenty-five years.' This regulation shows that it was customary to go and verify that the buried person was really dead; for as burial followed death so quickly, errors might sometimes occur" (176). Matthew doesn't tell us why the women were at the tomb so early on Sunday morning (but see Mk. 16.1; Lk. 24.1).

28.2 And behold, there was a great earthquake; for an angel of the Lord descended from heaven, and came and rolled back the stone from the door, and sat on it.

In the prologue of this Gospel, an angel appeared in a dream to direct action (1.20, 2.13,19); now, in the epilogue, an angel appears in person to direct action.

For the second time in three days, the area around Golgotha is hit by an earthquake (27.51) that was likely interpreted by residents as an aftershock. An angel *descends from heaven* (if the Jews wanted a *sign from heaven*, 12.38, 16.1, here it is!), *rolls back the stone from the door, and sat on it.* Matthew doesn't say whether this was done to let Christ out or the women in, but since Jesus isn't seen leaving, I think it was done for the benefit of the women who had *come to see the tomb* (v 1). In v 6, the open tomb facilitates their seeing for themselves that Christ's body was gone.

No human being witnessed the actual resurrection of Jesus—the moment when His spirit returned to His body and His eyes awakened to a new existence—but Christ will soon demonstrate the reality of His resurrection by His appearances. The earthquake, the descent of the angel, and the rolling back of the stone constitute the curtain going up on God's greatest performance.

28.3–4 His countenance was like lightning, and his clothing as white as snow. And the guards shook for fear of him, and became like dead *men*.

The angel's appearance is described in language similar to other angelic epiphanies. *His countenance* (*idea*, external appearance, face; only here in NT) *was like lightning* recalls Daniel 10.6, (17.2); *clothing as white as* snow reflects the color of glory (Dan. 7.9).

The shaking of the ground led to a shaking (*seiō*, to shake, agitate, cause to tremble, 21.10) of the guards, who *became like dead men.* It's not said that they saw the risen Lord; but they felt the earthquake and, presumably, saw the angel's activity.

28.5–6 But the angel answered and said to the women, "Do not be afraid, for I know that you seek Jesus who was crucified. He is not here; for He is risen, as He said. Come, see the place where the Lord lay.

Fear is the normal reaction when men encounter the supernatural (17.6, 27.54), so the angel reassures the women. He knows they are there on account of *Jesus who was crucified. Crucified* translates a perfect participle—*was crucified and continues to be crucified*—a theme Paul will later expound (1 Cor. 1.23, 2.2; Gal. 3.1).

The angel's message is short but stupendous: *Christ is risen from the dead!* The women are invited to see for themselves that His body is gone, but Matthew doesn't indicate whether they do so. *As he said* is a mild rebuke (Lk. 24.5); everything happened just as Christ predicted (16.21. 18.22–23, 20.18–19), but His followers were still caught unprepared

28.7 And go quickly and tell His disciples that He is risen from the dead, and indeed He is going before you into Galilee; there you will see Him. Behold, I have told you."

The women are told to *go quickly and tell His disciples that He is risen from the dead* and will keep the scheduled meeting with them in Galilee (26.32). "The emphasis on *Galilee* in vv. 7, 10, 16, making it the place where the whole story ends, is the culmination of Matthew's tendency throughout to emphasize Galilee as the place where light dawns (4.12–16)" (France, 407). Angels are messengers, and *Behold, I have told you* signals the fulfilment of this angel's mission.

Just as women are conspicuous on the first page of the Gospel (1.3,5,6,16), so they occupy a major role on its last page. Their presence here is a subtle testimony to the facticity of these events. If the Gospel accounts of the resurrection were fiction, women would never have been the first to see the empty tomb or the risen Christ (v 9), for in first-century Judea, women had virtually no legal status and were not accepted as witnesses (cf. Paul's all-male list of witnesses in 1 Cor. 15.5–8).

28.8 So they went out quickly from the tomb with fear and great joy, and ran to bring His disciples word.

The women ask no further questions and *depart quickly*. The angel had not completely allayed their fear, for they leave with a mixture of *fear* and *joy*—but it is *great* joy. They run to tell the disciples everything.

28.9 And as they went to tell His disciples, behold, Jesus met them, saying, "Rejoice!" So they came and held Him by the feet and worshiped Him.

Before they find the disciples, Jesus finds them and greets them with *Joy to you!* (*chairete*, rejoice). Matthew says nothing about Christ's appearance but tells us that the women *held Him by His feet and worshipped Him.* The wise men (2.11), many sick (8.2, 9.18, 15.25), and the disciples (14.33) had worshiped Jesus previously—worship here is the proper response to the risen Lord. That they held Him by the feet indicates Christ's physical corporeality.

"However important the empty tomb may be as evidence for the resurrection, the fact remains that it was not convincing to the original followers of Jesus" (Harrison, 233; Lk. 24.22–24). What ultimately convinced the Twelve was seeing the risen Christ (1 Cor. 5.5).[1]

28.10 Then Jesus said to them, "Do not be afraid. Go *and* tell My brethren to go to Galilee, and there they will see Me."

Christ repeats almost word for word what the angel said (vv 5,7), but instead of using the angel's word *disciples*, He uses *brethren* (12.49–50, 25.40). What a word of love this was to they who had abandoned Him when He needed them most! Despite their failure, Christ's love would not allow His brotherliness with them to be disrupted.

That Christ appeared first to women was an act of honor to women. Woman was involved in the unleashing of the curse (Gen. 3), and now, by the news they carry to the disciples, women are involved in the undoing of the curse. From two sources—the angel and Christ—we know that something significant will happen in Galilee. The women's commission prepares the way for a greater commission (vv 18–20).

---

[1] The NT lists twelve post-resurrection appearances of Jesus: first, to the women (v 9); second, to Mary Magdalene (Mk. 16.9–11; Jn. 20.11–18); third, to Cleopas and companion (Mk. 16.12–13; Lk. 24.13–35); fourth, to Peter (Lk. 24.34; 1 Cor. 15.5); fifth, to the apostles, with Thomas absent (Mk. 16.14–18; Lk. 24.36–40; Jn. 20.19–23); sixth, to the apostles with Thomas present (Jn. 20.26–28); seventh, to several disciples at the Sea of Galilee (Jn. 21.1–23); eighth, to the apostles in Galilee vv 16–20); ninth, to 500 brethren (1 Cor. 15.16); tenth, to James (1 Cor. 15.7); and eleventh, to the apostles at the time of the Ascension (Mk. 16.19; Lk. 24.50–52; Acts 1.3–8; some of these appearances may have occurred simultaneously). The final appearance was to Saul of Tarsus, Acts 9.3–8; 1 Cor. 15.8.

28.11–15: Conspiracy

Notes

The pinnacle of priestly depravity is reached in this paragraph. In the history of its interpretation, almost all commentators have made an effort to point out how stupid the disciples would have been to try to steal Jesus' corpse—and, correspondingly, how stupid was the explanation for the empty tomb given by the priests and elders. Nothing better illustrates the deadening power of sin than the attempt to cover-up the resurrection.

The narrative picks up the thread of v 4 and 27.62–66, and for a final time, Jesus' opponents take center stage.

28.11 Now while they were going, behold, some of the guard came into the city and reported to the chief priests all the things that had happened.
Two actions occur simultaneously. While the women are on their way to deliver their message to the disciples, *some* members of the *guard* return to Jerusalem and report to the chief priests *all things that had happened*.[2] Matthew doesn't tell us why only *some* of the guards returned to Jerusalem; throughout his recounting, he only concerns himself with the major elements of the story. *All things* would include everything that happened before they lost consciousness and *became like dead men* (v 4)—the earthquake, the appearance of the angel, the rolling back of the stone, and the angel sitting on it. There is no indication that they saw Jesus, but based on the lie of v 13, the guards apparently knew His body was missing.

28.12–13 When they had assembled with the elders and consulted together, they gave a large sum of money to the soldiers, saying, "Tell them, 'His disciples came at night and stole Him *away* while we slept.'
The hardness of the Jews' hearts is astonishing. *When they had assembled with the elders* recalls 26.3,57. The priests believed the guards without either cross-examining them or sending others out to confirm their report. The priests' concern is with damage control.[3]

Taken counsel involved formulating a counter-explanation for the empty tomb. The weak link in their lie would be the soldiers (*stratiōtēs*, a common soldier), so to ensure their cooperation, the priests pay them a large bribe (*arguria hikana*, ample silver; recalling 26.15) to say that Jesus' *disciples came*

---

[2] If these are Roman guards, they would report to the chief priests because Pilate had put them under their authority (but see ch 27, fn 26).

[3] Gamaliel's advice in Acts 5.38–39 might presuppose the fact of the resurrection.

at night and stole Him away while we slept. The absurdity of this is apparent on several counts. First, it has the guards asleep at their posts, which, in the first century, was a capital offense. Second, it testifies to the utter failure of the extensive measures meant to keep Christ's corpse in the tomb (26.66). Third, it is patently ridiculous for men who are asleep to claim to know what happened while they slept. In their haste, the Jews didn't see the many holes in their talking points and became guilty of the very type of collusion of which the Gospel writers are sometimes accused.[4]

28.14 And if this comes to the governor's ears, we will appease him and make you secure."

For a guard to admit he slept at his post was to sign his death warrant (Acts 12.19, 16.27). So, in addition to the bribes paid them, the chief priest and elders promise that if Pilate hears of the matter, they would *appease him and make them secure. Comes to the governor's ears* probably refers to a legal proceeding rather than to rumor or gossip. Luz says that the Gr. phrase indicates "before someone," as in standing before a judge (III, 611). Should the guards be hauled into court and accused of dereliction of duty, the chief priests would get them off the hook. They had already demonstrated their sway with the crowd (27.20) and with Pilate and were confident they could control events. The Jews don't explain to the guards how they will do as they promise, but the word *appease* (*peithō*) was sometimes associated with bribery.[5]

28.15 So they took the money and did as they were instructed; and this saying is commonly reported among the Jews until this day.

From one standpoint, the explanation the Jews crafted was plausible, for grave robbing was not uncommon in the first century; in fact, it was such a problem that it was made a capital crime (this information comes from a decree thought to date from the time of Claudius, which was discovered in a text known as the "Nazareth Inscription").

Matthew ends this account with another reference to the time when he wrote (27.8): *this saying is commonly reported among the Jews until this day.*

---

[4] "They had used treachery to lay hold on Him. They had used illegality to try Him. They had used slander to charge Him to Pilate. And now they were using bribery to silence the truth about Him" (Barclay II, 416).

[5] "At Rome, in Cicero's time, judicial bribery was so organized that contracts were taken to secure acquittal by this means" (Carr, 318). History shows that Pilate was not above taking bribes; see Philo, *Legatio ad Gaium*, 302.

Maybe, in an instance of psychological projection, the ones so concerned about a lie being circulated (27.64) were the ones circulating a lie. The last deception was indeed worse than the first (27.64).

Excursus on the Stolen-Body Theory

"The stolen-body theory founders on two insurmountable obstacles: the problem of motive and the problem of execution. To plan a tricky grave robbery of a closely guarded tomb would have required an incredibly strong incentive by a daring and extremely skillful group of men. But who had this incentive? Who had the motive and then the courage necessary to bring it off? Certainly not the dispirited disciples, huddling and hiding in their despair over Jesus' evident failure and in fear of the Temple authorities—hardly a pack of calculating schemers enthusiastically planning to dupe their countrymen. But even if the disciples did have the overpowering motive and the incredible courage to steal a body and then—with total cynicism—to announce a resurrection, how could they hope to achieve it? The grave area was crawling with guards specifically instructed to forestall any such attempt. Guards in ancient times always slept in shifts, so it would have been virtually impossible for a raiding party to have stepped over all their sleeping faces. The commotion caused by breaking the seal, rolling the stone open, entering the tomb, and lifting out the body was bound to awaken the guards even if they had all been sleeping" (Cornfeld, 180–181).

Regarding motive, why would the disciples do something (steal Christ's body, then spread the lie that He was resurrected) that brought them nothing but torture and death (1 Cor. 4.9–13)? It's totally against human nature to embark on a conspiracy that is utterly without benefit to the conspirators, but this is what the disciples did if the stolen-body theory is true.

Regarding ability, the stolen-body theory raises a number of questions for which no Jewish answer was forthcoming. How did the disciples get past the guards unnoticed? How did sleeping guards know what happened while they were asleep? Why would grave robbers have taken the time to unwrap a body before stealing it (Jn. 20.6–7)? Why would the guards ever agree to admitting they committed a capital crime by sleeping at their post? And on top of all this, why did the champion Pharisee, Saul of Tarsus, take up the Christian lie?

Even though all the evidence is against the stolen-body theory, it was still in vogue when Matthew wrote. "What is narrated here was prompted by the need to answer an actual accusation current in the time of the evangelist" (Hill, 360). "Well into the second century A.D. and long after Matthew recorded its first instance, the Jerusalem authorities continued to admit an empty tomb by ascribing it to the disciples' stealing the body. For, in his Dialogue with Trypho, Justin Martyr, who came from neighboring Samaria, reported c. AD 150 that the Jewish authorities even sent specially commissioned men across the Mediterranean to counter Christian claims with this explanation of the resurrection" (Cornfeld, 184).

All who deny the bodily resurrection of Jesus face an insoluble problem: how to account for the complete and lasting change that came over the disciples. "What event, apart from the actual and literal resurrection, could be stupendous enough to change these humble persons from defeated men to men who were bold as lions, not temporarily, but for all the rest of their days" (Trueblood, *Confronting Christ*, 177). Whatever changed the disciples, the explanation was not that they stole the body of Christ. Only the resurrection of Christ explains.

28.16–20: Commission

Notes

If a man is to be blessed when his master comes (24.46), and be among the wise who are admitted to the wedding feast (25.1–12), and be found watching and ready (25.13), and hear the words, *Well done, good and faithful servant, enter into the joy of your master* (25.21), the closing of the Gospel is of utmost importance, for it summarizes how a man prepares himself for eternity.

The end of the Gospel consists of two parts: an introduction focused on the disciples (vv 16–17) and a conclusion focused on Christ (vv 18–20). Jesus' last words include a claim of authority (v 18a), a commissioning (vv 18b–20a), and a promise (v 20b). The attributive *all* ties everything together: *all authority, all nations, all things, always.*

A great variety of threads are pulled together in the closing. *To the mountain* recalls the third temptation (4.8), the Sermon on the Mount (chs 5–7), and the mount of transfiguration (17.1,9). *Galilee* takes us back to 2.23 and 4.23–25. The disciples' *worship* reminds of v 9, 2.11, and 14.31–33. The disciples' doubt recalls 14.26. Christ's statement of authority looks back to 7.28 and 11.25–27. The mention of *heaven and on earth* recalls 6.10 and the Lord's prayer.

Thus in Matthew are two great directives—*the great commandment* (22.36–39) and *the great commission* (v 19). Taken together, they encompass all of a man's obligations to God, his fellows, and himself.

28.16 Then the eleven disciples went away into Galilee, to the mountain which Jesus had appointed for them.

For a second time in Matthew, it is noted that Jesus leaves Judea for Galilee (2.22). The disciples follow, just as they were told to do (vv 7,10).

We aren't told which mountain was designated for the rendezvous (26.32), but associations with other mountains in Matthew are suggestive. On the Mount of Temptation, the devil offered Jesus mastery over all the kingdoms of the world (4.8–9), but God has now given His Son all authority in heaven and earth (Rev. 11.15). And the mountain of the Sermon (chs 5–7) is an obvious possibility, for what Christ taught there His disciples were to teach everywhere (v 20a; 5.2, 7.28–29).

28.17 When they saw Him, they worshiped Him; but some doubted.

The disciples see Jesus, but Matthew doesn't describe His appearance (v 9); more important to Matthew is the reaction of the disciples. That *they worshipped Him* isn't surprising (v 9). What is surprising is the statement that *some doubted*—who was it that doubted, and what was it they doubted?

The only other instance of *distazō* (*doubt*) in Matthew is in 14.31, where Peter, after walking on water, is chided by Christ for doubting. It's hard to believe that after the infallible proof (Acts 1.3) the Eleven have seen that any of them were in doubt about the resurrection. Possibly, the statement means that some of the disciples simply didn't recognize Jesus when they first saw Him in Galilee (cf. Jn. 21.4). Some commentators believe the doubters were some of the 500 mentioned by Paul (1 Cor. 15.6), but since Matthew only mentions the Eleven, the likelihood is that the doubters were among the Eleven. If the phrase isn't referring to a lack of recognition, it likely refers to self-doubt—some of the disciples doubted their own fitness to be used by Christ after their sorry behavior during His arrest and trial.

28.18 And Jesus came and spoke to them, saying, "All authority has been given to Me in heaven and on earth.

The One who a short time before had died on a cross, excoriated, mistreated by the people, and abandoned by God, has now been raised by God to the highest place of honor (Rom. 1.4, Eph. 1.20–22, Phil. 2.9–11, Col. 1.18–20, Heb. 1.3–4, 1 Pet. 3.22). Throughout Matthew, Christ's authority (*exousia,* power) has been displayed in His teaching (7.29), forgiving (9.6,8), healing (chs 8–9), exorcisms (12.28–30), delegating

(10.1), knowledge (11.27), and righteous actions (21.23). Now, He claims *all authority in heaven and on earth*.

Some commentators ask how can someone who always had all power, because He is God, be given all power? The answer goes back to the first verse of the book: the authority given Christ refers not to His *inherent* authority as God, but to His inherited authority as David's Son (Ps. 110.1; Acts 2.29–36).

28.19–20 Go therefore and make disciples of all the nations, baptizing them in the name of the Father and of the Son and of the Holy Spirit, teaching them to observe all things that I have commanded you; and lo, I am with you always, *even* to the end of the age." Amen.

Therefore tells us that the following command flows from the authority Christ posseses. *Go* means the disciples were to move, scatter, travel (2.8, 11.4, 17.27) for the purpose of *making disciples of all nations*. *Make disciples*, a phrase used almost exclusively in Matthew, means that non-Christians are to be made into Christians. It was to his end that Matthew wrote his Gospel.

Following the order of 1.1, v 18 alludes to the Davidic promise, and v 19a to the Abrahamic promise. *All the nations* translates *panta ta ethnē*, the exact phrase used in Genesis 22.8 (LXX) to speak of the universal blessing God promised through Abraham's seed. In every place where Matthew speaks of *all nations* (24.9,14, 25.32), the reference is inclusive, transcending every racial and ethnic wall of partition.

A question long debated is whether this *great commission* was meant only for the apostles or for the church as well. Despite the legend that the apostles divided the world among themselves in order to carry out the commission,[6] we have no information on how they handled the logistics. It's likely that each was guided to his field of labor by the Spirit, as was Paul in Acts 16.6–10. Furthermore, no details are given about what it meant to preach the gospel *to every creature* (Mk. 16.15). Regardless, it is certain that believers always have an obligation to the world (5.16), and it's because believers have taken this obligation seriously that there are followers of Christ two millennia after the gospel was first preached.

---

[6] "At that season all we the apostles were at Jerusalem, Simon which is called Peter and Andrew his brother, James the son of Zebedee and John his brother, Philip and Bartholomew, Thomas and Matthew the publican, James the son of Alphaeus and Simon the Canaanite, and Judas the brother of James: and we divided the regions of the world, that every one of us should go unto the region that fell to him and unto the nation whereunto the Lord sent him" (*Acts of Thomas*, 1).

Making disciples involves two steps: *baptizing* and *teaching.*[7] On *baptizing*, see 3.6. The reference to *the Father, the Son, and the Holy Spirit* is not a baptismal formula (if it is, why wasn't it used in Acts 2.38, 8.36–38, etc.?)[8] but recalls 3.17, when the Father spoke from heaven and the Spirit descended from heaven at Jesus' baptism. Baptism is not just *in* (by the authority of; cf. "Stop in the name of the Law!"), but *into* (*eis*) *the name* of the Father, Son, and Holy Spirit, into a relationship that didn't exist prior to baptism (Acts 8.16, 19.5; 1 Cor. 1.13, 10.2; Gal. 3.27). To be baptized *into the name* doesn't mean baptism *by the authority* of the Father, Son, and Spirit (though such is true), but baptism into *fellowship* with the Father, Son, and Spirit. Note that *name* is singular and encompasses the unity of the Godhead. Every member of every nation needs to be baptized, for all have sinned and all are in need of God's saving grace (Jn. 3.3,5).

The second part of discipleship is *teaching*: the lost are to be taught to be baptized, and the baptized are to be taught to *observe all things Christ commanded His followers to observe,* for only in this way can God's will be done on earth as it is in heaven (6.10). Discipleship involves continuing education. The church is Christ's school (11.29), He is the *Teacher* (23.8), the curriculum includes *all things* He taught—with love being the greatest subject (5.20, 22.37–39; 1 Cor. 13.13). As disciples observe Christ's teachings, their soul grows (2 Pet. 3.18), they let their light shine, and they influence the unforgiven to glorify God (5.16).

The Gospel of Matthew closes with a promise traceable on every page of the book: *Behold, I am with you always, even to the end of the age. Always* (*passas tas hēmera*, only here in the NT) means *all the time, the whole of every day.* Jesus is *Immanuel*, the *God-with-us* God, whose presence makes possible a true, personal relationship between Himself and His people. The promise here given the apostles has been given the church (Heb. 13.5–6)—Christ is still with us, curing our blindness (9.27–31, 20.29–34), raising us up (9.18–26, 11.5), casting out our demons (9.18–26), calming us amidst the storm (8.23–27), saving us when we sink (14.22–23).

The risen Christ is the earthly Jesus presented in Matthew. His church

---

[7] "*The active participle in connection with an imperative either declares the manner in which the imperative shall be obeyed, or explains the meaning of the command.* For example:—'Cleanse the house, sweeping it;' 'Cleanse the garment, washing it,' shows the manner in which the command is to be obeyed, or explains the meaning of it. Thus, 'Convert (or disciple) the nations, immersing them, and teaching them to observe,' &c., expresses the manner in which the command is to be obeyed" (Campbell, *The Christian System*, 211).

[8] For an extensive discussion of baptismal formulas, see Whiteside, *Reflections*, 244–248.

is His family (12.49–50), comprised of those who have been baptized into a relationship with Him and who have given themselves to learn of Him (Eph. 4.20) and obey what they learn. Such are the *great multitude out of all nations, tribes, peoples, and tongues who have washed their robes and made them white in the blood of the Lamb.*

There is an old story that when Jesus returned to heaven the angels asked, "What happens now?" Jesus replied, "I left twelve men with a command to go throughout the world proclaiming the gospel." "What if they fail?" the angels want to know. To which the Lord said, "I have no other plan."

May the followers of Christ be true to the will of the One to whom belongs the kingdom, the power, and the glory forever.

Amen.

Walk Worthily
Jeff Smelser

The Epistle of Ephesians was both an assurance to Gentile Christians of their place in God's scheme and an exhortation walk worthily of their calling such that the unity of the body of Christ might be practical and not merely theoretical. In *Walk Worthily*, Bible students accustomed to working with the Greek text will find both textual and grammatical issues pertaining to the original language thoroughly addressed. Greek words and phrases are almost always translated into English in an effort to make the point under consideration accessible to all readers. But those who choose to skip over the discussions of the Greek text will nonetheless find this commentary to be helpful, always analyzing what is said in light of the overall message. 273 pages. $24.99.

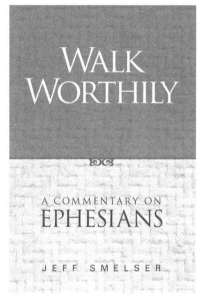

More Bible Commentaries by DeWard Publishing

Exposition of Genesis (volumes 1 and 2), H.C. Leupold

The Growth of the Seed: Notes on the Book of Genesis, Nathan Ward

Thinking Through Job, L.A. Mott

Thinking Through Jeremiah, L.A. Mott

Let Us Search Our Ways: A Commentary on Lamentations,
Evan and Marie Blackmore

Original Commentary on Acts, J.W. McGarvey

Uncommon Sense: The Wisdom of James for Dispossessed Believers,
James T. South

The Lamb, The Woman, and the Dragon: Studies in the Revelation of St. John,
Albertus Pieters